Contemporary Ethnic Geographies in America

Contemporary Ethnic Geographies in America

EDITED BY
INES M. MIYARES AND CHRISTOPHER A. AIRRIESS

ROWMAN & LITTLEFIELD PUBLISHERS, INC.
Lanham • Boulder • New York • Toronto • Plymouth, UK

ROWMAN & LITTLEFIELD PUBLISHERS, INC.

Published in the United States of America
by Rowman & Littlefield Publishers, Inc.
A wholly owned subsidary of The Rowman & Littlefield Publishing Group, Inc.
4501 Forbes Boulevard, Suite 200, Lanham, Maryland 20706
www.rowmanlittlefield.com

Estover Road
Plymouth PL6 7PY
United Kingdom

The editors gratefully acknowledge Michael Hradesky, Cartographer, Ball State University, for map and table design.

British Library Cataloguing in Publication Information Available

Library of Congress Cataloging-in-Publication Data

Contemporary ethnic geographies in America / edited by Ines M. Miyares and
Christopher A. Airriess.
    p. cm.
  Includes bibliographical references and index.
  ISBN-13: 978-0-7425-3772-9 (cloth : alk. paper)
  ISBN-10: 0-7425-3772-2 (cloth : alk. paper)
 1. United States—Ethnic relations. 2. United States—Race relations. 3. Minorities—United
States. 4. Multiculturalism—United States. 5. Pluralism (Social sciences)—United States.
6. Human geography—United States. I. Miyares, Ines M. II. Airriess, Christopher A.
  E184.A1C5975 2007
  305.800973—dc22

2006020403

Printed in the United States of America

♾™The paper used in this publication meets the minimum requirements of American National Standard for Information Sciences—Permanence of Paper for Printed Library Materials, ANSI/NISO Z39.48-1992.

Contents

Figures, Maps, and Tables

Figures

Maps

Tables

CHAPTER 1

Exploring Contemporary Ethnic Geographies

Christopher A. Airriess and Ines M. Miyares

Ethnic diversity and ethnic geographies have marked America's history and historical geographies throughout her entire history. From the arrival of the first residents, the ancestors of the many Native American nations, to the increasingly diverse immigrant populations, it is impossible to separate the ideas, concepts, processes, and spatial manifestations of ethnicity from an understanding of the United States as a country and "Americans" as a people. This book explores the contemporary ethnic geographies of the United States by studying the experiences of a selected number of ethnic groups in both a historical and contemporary context.

Often the ethnic portrait of the colonial era and early independence years is of a primarily British population, often presumed to be culturally homogeneous with the exception of the Catholics in Maryland, and their African-descent slaves, displacing a Native American population also presumed to be culturally very similar. However, the Native American population was ethnically and culturally quite diverse, as were the initial European settlers. By the early 1800s, this diversity included British, Germans, Dutch, French speakers in southern Louisiana and New England, multiple Native American nations, African Americans, and Spaniards in the Southwest. Complementing this diversity were large influxes of Irish, German, and French immigrants during the 1820–1880 period.

Between 1880 and 1930, a substantial immigrant flow from eastern and southern Europe arrived in part to provide inexpensive industrial labor and diversified the source regions that had been dominated by northwestern Europe. Between the 1930s and 1950s, immigration slowed substantially because of the Great Depression, World War II, and immigration quotas on immigrants from non-Western regions. The majority of immigrants during this period were from Europe, but also included a new and significant slice from Latin America, primarily Mexico.

Entering a New Era

Since World War II, and particularly beginning in the late 1960s, many of the industrialized countries of the world, and especially the English-speaking "settler countries" of the United States, Canada, and Australia, have become far more ethnically diverse in a new *age of migration*.[1] While long-distance migration has always been characteristic of human societies, this new age of migration possesses fundamentally different circumstances and dimensions when compared to earlier periods.[2] First, international migration during the past thirty years is characterized by the *globalization of migration* because immigrants originate from a more culturally diverse constellation of countries. Second, the collapse of Communist governments has engendered a resurgence of ethnic nationalism during the post–Cold War era that has often created political instability resulting in long-distance migration. Third, less democratic government regimes have relaxed constraints on the movement of people as part of the larger response to structural changes in national economies associated with globalization.

Fourth, revolutions in communications and transportation have dramatically transformed the propensity and ability of individuals and families to migrate from poorer developing countries to more affluent developed countries. Advances in global communications have exposed potential developing-country migrants to images, whether real or not, of life and economic opportunities elsewhere. Long-distance air transport has also become less expensive and more frequent because of the deregulation of transport associated with globalization. In part as a consequence of advances in communication and transport, the fifth characteristic of this new age of migration is the ability of immigrants to exhibit identities that span the cultural, social, economic, and political worlds of both origin and destination countries. In part as a result of the civil rights culture of the 1960s, immigrants are arriving in a country that values the inherent differences in culture or *multiculturalism*, rather than subscribing to the linear and single-direction process of *assimilation* whereby newcomers must conform to the dominant and majority population culture that is essentially White. Last, this new age of migration is characterized by immigrants arriving as families rather than individuals as well as the proportion of females in the immigrant streams being greater than males.

These new circumstances and dimensions that characterize the new age of migration have led to Europe being replaced by Latin America and Asia as the primary source regions of immigrants, both legal and illegal, over the past forty years. Of the 27.6 million foreign-born residents in 2000, approximately 52 percent were from Latin America and 26 percent from Asia (Fig. 1.1). While Mexicans (54%) continue to comprise the majority of Latin American foreign-born, those from the Caribbean (19%) and South America (13%) make for a far more diverse Latin American population. The same is true for Asian foreign-born as well. Long dominated by ethnic Chinese (19%), Filipino (17%), and Japanese (4%), the Asian American foreign-born now include Asian Indians (13%) and Vietnamese (12%). As a result, the proportion of the non-European descent population of the United States is projected to increase from 27 percent in 1996 to a near majority of 47 percent by 2050.

Based on population projections, immigrants in 2050 will account for approximately 60 percent of national population growth. A statistical observation that highlights this dramatic and short-term swing associated with this new age of migration is the percentage change of foreign-born population during the 1900–2002 period (Fig. 1.2). The highest percentage of foreign-born in the twentieth century was in the 1910s

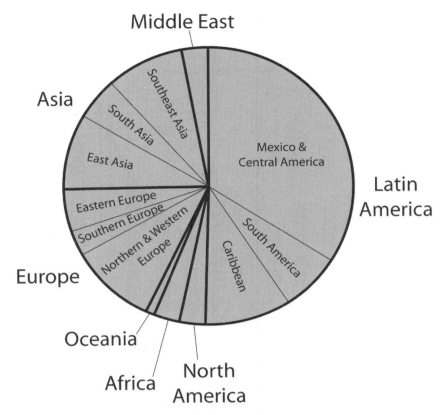

Figure 1.1.   Source Regions of Foreign-Born Population in the United States in 2000. Source: <www.census.gov/population/socdemo/foreign/ ppl-145/tab.pdf> (March 15, 2004).

with almost 15 percent not being U.S. citizens at birth. The percentage of foreign-born declined until bottoming out at almost 5 percent in 1970. After some sixty years of decreased immigration, however, the percentage of foreign-born dramatically increased throughout the 1970s, 1980s, and 1990s. By 2002, the percentage of foreign-born reached its post–World War II high of 11.5 percent of the total population. In 2002, the percentage of foreign-born was highly concentrated in the West (38.1) and the South (28.2) with lower concentrations in the Northeast (23.1) and the Midwest (10.6). The foreign-born are also more likely to live in metropolitan regions (43.3%) when compared to the native-born population (27%). This has transformed places and landscapes and what it means to "be American" (Fig. 1.3).

The purpose of this book is to explore these transformed places and landscapes in order to understand the evolution of America's contemporary ethnic geographies. We open with a discussion of concepts and processes that will reappear as the book progresses.

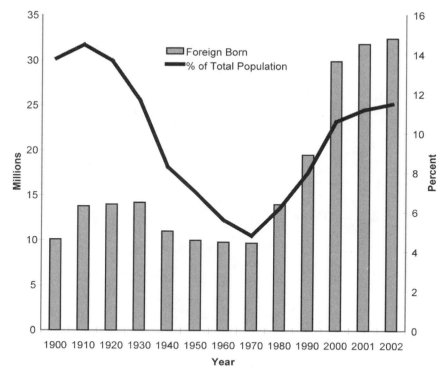

Figure 1.2.   U.S. Foreign-Born Population, 1900–2002.
Source: Adding Diversity from Abroad: The Foreign-Born Population, 2000,
<www.census.gov/population/pop-profile/2000/chap.17.pdf> (March 15,
2004), and U.S. Census Bureau, Foreign-Born Population of the United States
Current Population Survey—March 2002 Detailed Tables (PPL-162),
<www.census.census.gov/population/www/socdemo/foreign/ppl-161.html>
(March 15, 2004).

This is followed by a presentation of the role immigration law has played in defining and controlling who could enter and who could become "American." We then present case studies of both old and new groups who fall into the category of "minority populations," but who as a whole are progressing into majority status, and who are the majority in a number of regions of the country. The final chapters discuss some of the implications of this ethnic diversity and contemporary immigration in terms of urban landscapes, ethnic economies, and ethnic festivals.

Ethnic Geography

The subfield of ethnic geography possesses a long and proud tradition within the larger discipline of geography. Much like the contributions to ethnic studies from anthropol-

Figure 1.3.   Advertisement in Los Angeles for the PBS miniseries American Family: Journey of Dreams *based on the experiences of a Mexican American extended family.*
Source: Christopher Airriess.

ogy, sociology, and history, the majority of the past work in ethnic geography has focused on ethnic Europeans and thus in a sense reflected a Eurocentric bias. This research is labeled as Eurocentric despite the existence of Black, Native American, Hispanic, and Arab minorities that were in effect "invisible" by virtue of their relative absence in the academic literature. As with these cognate disciplines, however, geographical research has engaged the new post-1960s ethnic experiences, and this book is an expression of this new, but continuing interest. Indeed, the theoretical and conceptual cross-fertilization and borrowing among these allied disciplines as well as the emergence of ethnic studies programs at many universities have engendered a healthier multidisciplinary approach to ethnicity that increasingly intersects with issues of race, class, and gender.

Studying ethnicity is critically important for the basic reason that periodic surveys inform us of American ignorance relative to the rest of the world. Because the growing diversity of immigrants coming to America over the past forty years, it is incumbent upon the majority population to acquire a greater sensitivity and appreciation of these new Americans. In disposing of the melting pot and assimilationist models that have guided the national perspective on ethnicity, we need to understand, embrace, and celebrate ethnic and cultural difference.

Studying ethnicity from a geographical perspective is highly rewarding for a number of reasons. Most obvious is geography's basic and traditional conceptual focus on human movement, settlement, and distributions that helps us specifically understand the spatial patterns of the complex coast-to-coast kaleidoscope of ethnic geographies in the United States. The geographical concept of landscape has also assisted in the greater appreciation of ethnicity as ethnic communities produce a distinctive visual material culture to satisfy their particular needs, wants, and desires. Building upon these basic geographical foundations are the more complex behaviorally-centered geographical concepts of place and space.[3] All human groups are collectively and emotionally attached to place and thus experience a "sense of place" that is often ethnic specific, but is also influenced by generation, gender, and class. In addition, there exist specific spaces in which individuals and groups operate socially, economically, and politically that influence the way ethnic identities are expressed and experienced.

Ethnicity: Fluid Definitions and Imagined Identities

The word origin or etymology of the term *ethnicity* is derived from the ancient Greek *ethnos*, which means a "distinct people." In this sense, an ethnic group is comprised of individuals who believe themselves to be different from other culture groups. There is a religious dimension to *ethnos*, as it is derived from the Greek word *ethnikos*, which meant "heathen" or "pagan," or those that were not Christian or Jewish. This idea of cultural difference arose in Europe only in the eighteenth century as national states engaged in colonialism and imperialism over non-Europeans, which in turn engendered the invention of a homogeneous national culture based on perceived racial superiority.[4] The notion of cultural difference as expressed by "Us" and the "Other" was common in the United States by World War II as the Irish, Jews, southern Europeans, and others were politely, but pejoratively referred to as "ethnics" by the dominant Anglo-Saxon ancestry population.[5] The term *ethnicity*, or the condition of belonging to an ethnic group, in fact did not appear until the first third of the twentieth century, and thus is a relatively new term associated with modernity.[6]

Although no concise and modern definition of the term *ethnic* satisfies all those interested in studying ethnicity, a working definition of *ethnic group* is a group of persons who perceive themselves as sharing a common ancestry and a set of shared characteristics such as language, religion, territory, and sometimes race. There is no single ethnic characteristic, however, that defines an ethnic group in that a characteristic important in defining one group may be less important or irrelevant for another group. Qualifying this simple definition includes observations that ethnic groups can be real or imagined, originate with reference to relationships to other groups, and that awareness of being a member of an ethnic group changes through time and space.[7] Let us first examine these qualified observations with reference to the assumed characteristics or markers of ethnic groups.

We are able to better understand the terms *ethnicity* or *ethnic identity* by considering the observation that ethnic groups are not naturally occurring human groupings. Borrowing from the term *imagined communities*[8] to describe cultures at the national scale, not all members of an ethnic community are given the opportunity to interact with one another to determine the form and nature of the cluster of ethnic markers that separate their ethnic group from others. It is of course this cluster of intertwining ethnic markers such as language, religion, territory, and race that provides a sense of belonging and authenticity to members of an ethnic community.[9] The reason why we claim that ethnicity or ethnic belonging is imagined, invented, or socially constructed is that the cultural markers that delimit ethnic boundaries are ever changing or fluid through both space and time, and are dependent upon the age, gender, educational status, class, or political orientation of an individual member of an ethnic group. The fact that ethnic identity is imagined and constantly being reformulated disposes of the myth that ethnic groups are static and possess prehistorical roots. It is this problem of the many social and economic contexts or situations that makes a single definition or theory describing ethnicity inadequate.

We are able to explain such a seemingly illogical statement that ethnic groups are socially constructed by harnessing two observations. Earlier immigrants from Europe did not perceive themselves as being Polish Americans, Italian Americans, or German Americans upon arriving in the United States, but culturally identified with the particular villages, counties, or provinces from which they originated. After all, the modern political states of Poland, Italy, and Germany did not exist or were only newly created when they emigrated.[10] The process in which peoples become aware of their ethnic identity only after settling in the destination country is referred to as *ethnogenesis*.[11]

A similar phenomenon exists among both the historical immigration of Filipinos and more modern Asian Indian immigrants. Among Filipinos, their communal identification during the late 1800s was strongest among others with similar district and regional origins, rather than possessing identities solely based on nationalistic loyalties.[12] The numerous Asian Indian social and cultural organizations found throughout the United States are based on members sharing a similar state of origin such as Gujarat, Kerala, or Tamil Nadu rather than India as a whole. As a settler country then, the United States has witnessed the constant genesis of ethnic groups in many regions over the past three hundred years.

Self-identification with a particular ethnic group is often a matter of choice, but ethnic identification is simultaneously and externally imposed by other ethnic groups or the majority population. National governments, for example, classify races and ethnic groups in the decadal national census based upon political or ideological rationalities that sustain their power.[13] In doing so, governments as dominant societal institutions are able to define ethnic identities and boundaries by classifying individuals, for example, as African American, Asian American, or Hispanic American. In response to political pressure of the 1960s and 1970s civil rights era, the U.S. government introduced in the 1980 census the category of "ancestry" that changed the self-image of an ethnic group because of that group's "official" status. In the 2000 Census, the number of racial/ethnic categories increased from five to fifteen and allowed those being enumerated to choose multiple racial categories. An officially designated status based on a name strengthens collective identity, but possesses little bearing on the dynamics of self-identity change because in a sense they are static categorical predictors of values, behavior, and habits.[14] Another externally imposed source of identity that may designate difference is the name given, such as Hungarian Americans *amerikai magyarság* or Overseas Vietnamese *Viet Kieu*, by those in the origin country. This formal naming of distant co-ethnics who no longer live in the homeland is a way of geographically extending home country space beyond national borders.

Ethnicity: Markers of Difference

Having defined the term *ethnic* and highlighted the socially constructed and thus fluid nature of ethnicity, we must question some often assumed characteristics or markers of ethnic group identity. Ethnic groups possess distinguishing markers of difference, and these markers maintain the boundaries between "Us" and the "Other." While language, religion, territory, and race are often perceived as the most important markers that anchor ethnic identity and difference, we need to recognize that individual markers are unstable anchors and unable to sustain ethnic identity over time. As a result, ethnic boundaries are fluid based on the mix or package of markers as well as the changing nature of markers through time.

LANGUAGE

Language is often cited as that single marker critical to maintaining ethnic identity for several reasons. Language is one of the most basic bodily expressions of self[15] and is identified as being critical to the maintenance of culture across generations. In a sense, speaking a language of an origin region in a destination country can be a substitute for that "lost" place.[16] From the majority population perspective, language is indeed an externally imposed ethnic marker because the inability of new immigrants to adequately speak English is a frequent complaint among those with anti-immigrant sentiments and has prompted eighteen state legislatures since 1980 to adopt some form of English-only law. Much the same could be said concerning Ebonics or the Black dialect of English backlash in the mid-1990s.

Despite language functioning as a critical ethnic marker, it is simultaneously one of the first markers to disappear in the process of acculturation; usually by the third generation, English has become the primary language in both public and private space. While the disappearance of ethnic languages among older Euro-American groups is an accepted fact, it is also true that although the communicative and public function of language has receded because of acculturation, the symbolic function or private use of language remains important to ethnic identity in part because it does not evoke majority population penalties.[17] The persistent use of selected Yiddish words by Jewish Americans provides an example of the symbolic function of language in maintaining ethnic identity. Unlike older ethnic groups, however, the opportunity for the persistence of ethnic languages among more recent immigrants is greater because of the emergence of Spanish-language television and radio or the proliferation of videos or DVD movies produced in Hong Kong for the Overseas Chinese population or *Bollywood* in Mumbai for Overseas Indians. Despite these observations, however, language in and of itself is not a sufficient marker to maintain ethnic identity into the third generation.

For example, if a third-generation Mexican American possesses only a rudimentary knowledge of Spanish, does that disqualify that individual as Latino or Hispanic?

RELIGION

Coupled with language, the marker of religion is also perceived as a significant marker in the maintenance of ethnic identity and is often manifested as a central landscape feature of an ethnic community[18] in part because religious persecution provided the impetus for immigrant movement to the United States during both the historical and modern periods. Indeed religion and language are ethnic markers that are mutually reinforcing because ethnic churches often use the ethnic language in churches, synagogues, temples, and mosques. Religious institutions have long been recognized as providing a mediating or balancing function between past origin region and present and future destination region in the process of acculturation.[19] This mediating function of religious institutions is not only in the spiritual realm, but the practical realm as well by providing a wide range of social services during the early years of immigrant settlement and acculturation.

Nevertheless, religious affiliation does not authenticate an adherent as an ethnic group member. For example, it is not uncommon for immigrants to switch forms of Christianity after settling in the destination country. Does a Brazilian, for example, become less of an ethnic Brazilian if an individual converts from being a Roman Catholic to an evangelical Protestant?

TERRITORY

Another perceived quality of ethnic belonging, one that is explicitly geographical in nature, is the notion that identity requires attachment to a piece of territory. The concept of territory as an abstract emotional connection to ethnic identity should be viewed at two different geographical scales. The first is an attachment to a homeland as a place from which immigrants originated or to which they possess a bond based on ancestry. Palestinian American attachment to the West Bank in Israel, Jewish American attachment to the state of Israel, the connections between Cajuns and the lowlands of south Louisiana or between some Mexican Americans and their home states in Mexico provide appropriate examples of ethnic group attachment to place. While such attachment to a place of origin, whether it is symbolic or mythical, is an important component of group identity, it is not a necessary precondition to maintaining that identity. One appropriate example is that of Native Americans. The quasi-autonomous reservations that dot the American West are constructed as space to preserve Native American heritage, but would a Native American individual residing in a large city distant from a reservation homeland be considered less of a Native American when compared to a reservation resident?[20]

The second geographical scale for examining the role of territory in sustaining ethnic identity is that of the neighborhood. In the past, particular older sections of a city evolved as ethnic residential and business enclaves replete with ethnic churches, and ethnic businesses such as grocery stores, restaurants, movie theaters, and ethnic professionals serving co-ethnics. Enclaves functioned as a place to sustain ethnic identity because of relative isolation from the majority population. Ethnic persistence is fostered over time, particularly if this "port of entry" part of the city is continually refreshed through time by co-ethnic immigrants. Good examples would be the Italian Old North End in Boston, the Jewish Lower East Side of Manhattan or, based on domestic migration, South Central in Los Angeles as a particularly dense concentration of African Americans.

While these more traditional settlement enclaves remain common today, in post-industrial America immigrants are settling the suburbs. One pattern is an *ethnoburb* that single or multiple ethnic groups inhabit, but no one ethnic group comprises the majority of the population.[21] Another is a *heterolocal* settlement pattern that is characterized by a more scattered residential population and ethnic business location in which spatial concentration is less of a factor in maintaining ethnic identity.[22] Territory, then, whether identification with a past homeland or a present neighborhood, is a common feature of ethnic identity tied to place, but is not a necessary condition of ethnicity.

RACE

Ethnicity has sometimes been conflated or combined with the idea of race to create "ethno-racial" groups, particularly in plural or multi-ethnic countries such as the United States. While race may have bearing on ethnic identity, the distinction between the two concepts is that ethnicity is about group self-identification as "Us" while race is oriented to categorizing the "Other" and is almost always externally imposed.[23] The connection of race to ethnicity is problematic because geneticists question whether racial boundaries are fixed as a result of substantial mixing between the so-called races. In addition, there exists greater genetic variation between members of the same race than between individuals of different races. Thus, race as a surrogate for ethnicity in the census, for example, is a "fictive" or fabricated cultural category and is not a naturally or biologically determined community.[24] Indeed, it was common in this country until the early twentieth century to refer to the Irish, southern Europeans, and Jews as separate races.

Some examples provide evidence of the dubious connections between race and ethnicity in that some people sharing the same ethnicity possess different skin color and those of the same skin color are not considered co-ethnics. Although first-generation Haitian Americans and other Afro-Caribbean immigrants may not self-identify themselves as Black in part because of the historical stigma of being labeled as being African American, the second generation as well as the majority culture may do so.[25] Much the same is true for Puerto Ricans with a strong African component not being categorized as being Black, or Native Hawaiians being labeled as Asian and Pacific Islander rather than Native American. The combination of race and ethnicity is especially problematic for the category of Arab American. Classified by the government as Caucasian, Arab Americans are not perceived as such because of the historical legacy of defining "White" as European. This ambiguous space is captured by the observation that "Arab Americans are not quite 'white' enough, not quite 'American' enough."[26]

Equally problematic with regard to ethnicity and race is the increasing number of mixed-race partnerships and their offspring. While fewer than 3 percent of the U.S. population chose the multiracial category on the 2000 Census, many did not do so primarily because of political choices about racial identity. If Hispanics are counted as a racialized group, approximately 5 percent of total marriages were cross-racial in 2000. In 1990, the two groups most likely to "out-partner" were Native Americans (60%) and Hispanics (19%), followed by Asians (15%) and Blacks (5.8%). Between 1980 and 1990, only the Asian rate of out-marriage declined in part because of the high proportion of foreign-born who are less likely to out-marry than native-born, and because Asian immigrants tend to arrive already married. Regionally, the percentage of out-marrying Hispanics is greatest in the West (40.1), and the South (32.9), and lowest in the Midwest (13.6) and the Northeast (13.4). In 1990, mixed marriages in general were three times more likely in California than the nation as a whole, and they ranked number three behind all-Hispanic and all-White couples.[27] The racial and ethnic identities of mixed-race offspring are complex and varied. They occupy "paradoxical spaces" in which they are able to contest the inflexible and socially constructed categories of race and ethnicity by building multiple, open, and flexible identities in different social spaces. It is exactly their position on the margin, or "third space," that allows mixed-raced offspring to become emancipated by undermining externally imposed categories.[28]

Before leaving the issue of race as an ethnic marker behind, questioning the nexus of race and ethnicity with reference to Whites deserves attention. While Whites of different national origins before World War II were self-defined as being different from each other, upward mobility coupled with large-scale non-European immigration beginning in the 1960s engendered a homogenized category of Whiteness and simultaneously "othered" the newcomers. While it is true today that ethnic attachment is important to some Euro-Americans, those of northern European ancestry often perceive themselves as not possessing ethnic qualities or ethnic status for various reasons. First, Whites presently occupy a majority privileged position in the national culture and, unlike other racial identities, are perceived as invisible or "normal."

Second, although European Americans might identify with a particular ethnicity, they are not persuaded to do so because Whites are not targets of government programs fashioned specifically for particular ethnic or racial groups.[29] Indeed, while Americans of northern European ancestry do not view themselves as possessing ethnic qualities, they are "no less 'ethnic' than minorities."[30] Like other ethnic groups, identity changes are based on situation or context and can take on different geographical scales in that an individual is "Welsh in England, British in Germany, European in Thailand, [and] White in Africa."[31] While ethnic groups are commonly numerical minorities within the larger national state, the existence of White ethnicity informs us that minority status is not necessary for ethnic status.

Ethnic Re-Identification

The idea that ethnicity possesses fluid meanings is appropriately expressed in the process of *ethnic re-identification*, which is defined as the "adoption of an ethnic identity after a period of non-identification."[32] The re-identification process involves varying degrees of participation in ethnic activities. The "new tradition" of celebrating Kwanzaa among African Americans during the Christmas season is a good example of ethnic re-identification. Some re-identification activities require strong commitment such as joining ethnic organizations, ethnic protests, and periodic tourist visits to an ethnic homeland as *ethnic pilgrims*. These pilgrims are in search of the "authentic" experiences and place of the ancestors.

A return to strict adherence to traditional religious practices is another example of this "retraditionalization" process. There also are those who engage in less demanding and nostalgic ethnic re-identification in the form of the greater consumption of specific ethnic foods and consumer goods, attending ethnic festivals, or learning ethnic dances. This less serious form of ethnic re-identification is what is referred to as *symbolic ethnicity* whereby ethnic pride can be felt without a substantial impact on an individual's everyday lifestyle.[33] Obviously, these forms of ethnic identity expression are far more common among the second and third generations. Quantitative evidence of this resurgence of ethnic identity among Native Americans is apparent in the U.S. Census in that the number of Native Americans who identified their race as American Indian increased from 523,591 in 1960 to 1,878,285 in 1990, a rate of growth that cannot be explained by normal demographic growth, but reflects ethnic re-identification.

The origins of ethnic re-identification are complex. One common source is explained as a response to social and political events and processes associated with time periods that engender a renewal of ethnic pride. The civil rights movement, for example, contested the "melting pot" rhetoric associated with a linear and determinist assimilationist model and afforded opportunities for heightened ethnic awareness and pride among Native Americans, Blacks, Hispanics, and Asian Americans. One expression in this civil rights–induced ethnic awareness, for example, was the proliferation of ethnic studies programs at universities between the 1970s and 1990s. Native American ethnic re-identification was inspired by the 1968–1970 occupation of Alcatraz Island in San Francisco Bay by many Indian tribes as well as the 1973 Wounded Knee, South Dakota, siege.

Political events in the source region also provide contexts for the emergence of ethnic re-identification. When both Lithuania and Hungary gained political independence with the collapse of the Soviet Union, ethnic Lithuanians and Hungarians in the United States experienced a renewed interest in their homeland culture which in turn promoted ethnic consciousness.[34] Interestingly, this period of social change also initiated greater ethnic awareness among older European groups, that block of the population that has experienced the greatest degree of ethnic erosion because inter-ethnic marriage is so common. Re-identification among the second or third generation is attractive because unlike the immigrant generation that was preoccupied with "fitting in," later generations are surer of their position in the national culture and thus possess the luxury to retrieve their ethnicity.[35]

Pan-Ethnicity

The social construction of ethnic identity in terms of markers and boundaries and the way in which ethnic groups in a multi-ethnic country assert their identity where none previously existed is expressed in the formation of multi-ethnic pan-ethnic groups such as Hispanic American or Asian American. A pan-ethnic group is a "politico-cultural collectivity made up of people of several, hitherto distinct, tribal or national origins."[36] The formation of pan-ethnic groups in a multi-ethnic country such as the United States is linked to access to the political process. Race and ethnicity are viewed as resources to gain access to scarce government programs such as housing, education, and employment that have been generally withheld because of discrimination and inequality. The formation of pan-ethnic groups through the alliance of several ethnic groups under a single pan-ethnic bloc increases the strategic advantage for access to such programs.[37] Simultaneously, pressure placed on the government for this political recognition prompted the U.S. government to establish Hispanic as a census category in 1980.

While pan-ethnic groups promote a new sense of identity among once separate ethnic groups, this larger-scale identity construction is fraught with divisions. For example, the second generation is far more likely to identify with a wider and inclusive pan-ethnic group while their immigrant parents remain tied to ethnicity based on the country of origin.[38] While ethnic Puerto Ricans, Mexicans, and Cubans possess a common language and religious roots to justify inclusion into a larger Hispanic American pan-ethnic group, each possess quite different historical and cultural traditions. Indeed, Cubans do not necessarily identify with the Hispanic label. Unlike Hispanics, Asian Americans possess a diverse array of cultural traditions, thus making for a more problematic pan-Asian collective identity. Asian Indians, for example, are marginalized in a larger pan-Asian identity that is East Asian (Chinese, Korean, and Japanese)-centered.

As the largest-scale level of ethnic identification, a pan-ethnic identification informs us of the fluid nature of ethnic boundaries based upon particular social, economic, and political situations at differing geographical scales and social spaces. For example, Native Americans can choose to identify at the levels of subtribal (clan and lineage), tribal (linguistic, reservation, official), regional (Oklahoma, Alaska), and supra-tribal or pan-Indian (Native American, Indian American). As a pan-Indian group, characteristics from each group in a single urban region, for example, are used to construct a pan-ethnic identity expressed in the form of pow-wows, Indian bowling leagues, and popular music groups.[39]

Transnational Identities

Perhaps the concept that most challenges the unilinear and Euro-American–centered assimilationist model is that of *transnational identities*. It is also a concept that thoroughly engages geography because of its implicit demand that we rethink the notion of space in all its intertwining facets. Transnationalism has been defined as the "process by which immigrants forge and sustain multi-stranded social relations that link together their societies of origin and settlement . . . [and] whose social fields . . . cross geographic, cultural and political borders." Furthermore, these particular immigrants make decisions, develop identities, and experience life in a "network of relationships that connect them simultaneously to two or more nation-states."[40] This results in a cultural identity of "in-betweenness" or "syncretization" in relation to both the origin and destination state culture. The networks that comprise these social fields across space are very much gendered in the sense that males and females, even in the same family, may establish and utilize different transnational networks as resources.[41]

Intimately linked to the concept of transnationalism and thus transnational identities is the term *diaspora*, which refers to a community of persons dispersed from a homeland, but possessing a sustained and conscious social or economic relationship with that homeland.[42] Originally applied to the expulsion of Jews from historic Palestine during the Roman occupation, and later to the forced displacement of African Blacks, Armenians, Irish, and Palestinians, the term has taken on new meaning when applied to various modern and globalized immigrant groups.

This continued social and economic connection of immigrants to their country or region of origin in this new age of migration challenges traditional notions of migration as being a permanent movement between one fixed space and another, or from origin to destination country. Likewise, it upsets our conception of a linear assimilation theory that immigrants should be tied to one territorial state and national culture as well as questions the linkages between the territorial state and citizenship in that immigrants may possess U.S. citizenship, but their identity is in part tied to home or origin region and culture rather than exclusively to the national culture of their country of residence.[43] A transnational identity is of course heightened in cases of dual citizenship, which introduces perceived problems of exclusive "national belonging" to a single state. Whether transnational identities are based on social, economic, or political connections to a specific homeland, they can be conceived as a "deterritorialization" or "respatialization" of relationships that were once confined to localized regions in the origin country. Based on the formation of both local and global identities, such a condition or process only strengthens the case that ethnic identity is not necessarily dependent on a distinct piece of territory.

For some immigrant groups, the conditions that promote maintaining cultural ties to the home country are a result of majority culture suppression of immigrant identity, creating, in a sense, a *reactive minority identity*.[44] This reactive identity is afforded expression by the rise of communications media at the global scale. Inexpensive international phone connections available through the use of phone cards as well as e-mail allow immigrants to keep in contact with distant friends and relatives. Movies and television programs accessed through videos, DVDs, and satellite TV comprise the *mediascapes*[45] that provide opportunities for diasporic populations to maintain contact with the popular culture, although a somewhat selective sample of that culture, of the origin country. The reverse is also true in that popular culture produced in multiple destination countries have impacts in the origin country. Websites catering to particular diasporic populations promote the "stretching out" of informal and formal social relations across space to create and maintain transnational identities through "virtual spaces," particularly among more affluent and educated immigrants and their offspring.[46] This nexus between technology and diasporic populations is in effect "labor's analog to the multinational corporation"[47] because these economic entities harness similar technologies to create and maintain their global space. The immigrant-based phenomenon is characterized as "transnationalism from below" while corporations are perceived as "transnationalism from above."[48]

Intertwined with the emergence of transnational cultural identities is the engagement of immigrants with the political process of their origin country. In Haiti in the early 1990s, for example, President Aristide successfully lobbied ethnic Haitians in Miami and New York to contribute to his re-election campaign. To further create a uniform transnational political space, Aristide added a tenth "department" or overseas political administrative unit to this "deterritorialized" Haitian political interest group.[49] Guatemalan Mayans in Los Angeles have become active participants in the pan-Mayan Movement at home, calling on the Guatemalan government to eliminate centuries-long discriminatory and anti-Indian policies in employment and education.[50] Ethnic Vietnamese and ethnic Chinese, particularly from Taiwan, have active quasi-political groups that lobby the U.S. government to place pressure on their origin country governments to observe basic human rights conventions.

In the economic sphere, immigrant "transnational entrepreneurs" often invest in their origin country in the form of small and medium-scale industries. A good example is Asian Indian software entrepreneurs in the United States reinvesting in the software industries of Bangalore and Hyderabad, or ethnic Chinese in manufacturing facilities in South China; also included is less high-profile transnational investment such as in the Dominican Republic. On the basis of existing transnational social networks, origin country governments favor such investment by their overseas co-ethnics because of a greater level of shared cultural trust and understanding when compared to foreign multinational corporations.

An additional and important socioeconomic avenue for maintaining transnational identities is the sending of remittances or money earned by immigrants to relatives and friends in the origin country (Fig. 1.4). The quantity of remittances sent from the United States often exceeds foreign direct investment and U.S. foreign aid to a specific country. In 2003, for example, the average Latin American immigrant sent between $100 and $200 home per month, and in the same year remittances totaled approximately $30 billion. In Mexico, the largest recipient country, remittances are the third largest foreign income earner. Remittances coupled with return visits to the origin communities for festivals, marriage proposals, and weddings possess social meaning and increase the social status of those initiating and maintaining these transnational ties and spaces.[51] These financial transfers are also a response to perceived social obligations related to the guilt felt by those immigrants who were fortunate not to be "left behind."[52] Remittances are so important to origin country economies that many sending governments promote emigration as an economic development tool because these international financial transfers help reduce the cost of providing basic social services.

Migration Theory

There are several theoretical explanations for people to engage in international migration, none of which are exclusively confined to one single academic discipline. Nor have these stand-alone theories been explicitly constructed through the cross-fertilization or sharing of ideas. These theories are categorized into two distinct approaches. The Neo-Classical Theory and the New Economics of Migration approaches are based upon the

Figure 1.4.   A Western Union advertisement in Chicago promoting the convenient electronic transfer of remittances between Asian Indian Americans and India. Source: Christopher Airriess.

micro-level, cost-benefit, and human agency decision-making models of potential immigrants who engage in migration voluntarily for self-betterment. In contrast, labor migrants within Dual Labor Market Theory and World Systems Theory are conceived as involuntary casualties of larger-scale structural forces operating at the national and global levels.[53] In a sense, these theories move from particular or specific explanations to those that are more general in nature. With few exceptions, the international migration experiences of a hypothetical immigrant cannot be adequately explained by a single theory, but only by a host of not necessarily incompatible theories operating simultaneously at different geographical scales. For example, larger structural forces may directly impact individual decisions to migrate.

NEO-CLASSICAL THEORY

The oldest of theories explaining international migration is the Neo-Classical Theory, which adopts a perspective that is based on the rational and individual decision-making process of a potential immigrant and conditions of labor markets.[54] Based largely on the discipline of economics, Neo-Classical Theory states that the migration of workers across international boundaries is determined by differential employment opportunities and wage rates between the origin and destination countries. The greater the differences in employment opportunities and income-earning potential, the higher the likelihood that an individual migrant will choose international movement. Without these spatial differences in income-earning potential, international migration would not occur. Neo-Classical Theory recognizes that governments in both the origin and destination countries are able to control migration through regulating labor markets, income taxes, or minimum wages.

THE NEW ECONOMICS OF MIGRATION

While still based on exclusively economic assumptions, this perspective explaining international migration differs from the more simplistic Neo-Classical Theory in a number of respects.[55] First, the decision to engage in international migration is not based on individual actors, but upon larger social units such as families or households that are conceptually a single economic production unit. Migrating as a family or household might afford opportunities to enhance income generation even if wage differentials do not exist between origin and destination countries. Differential access to employment opportunities in the destination country often introduces restructured and unpredictable gender relationships within an immigrant household as husband or wife might possess greater employment chances.[56] Single production units may in fact continue to possess economic assets in the origin country controlled by some family members that remain behind as a strategy to reduce the financial risk of migration.

In addition, government policies in destination countries that promote immigrant movement are not restricted only to labor markets. The availability of unemployment insurance in its various forms or better access to credit reduces the financial risk of immigration. In turn, economic policies that discriminate against a particular slice of the population in the origin country, whether rich or poor, promote emigration.

DUAL MARKET THEORY

This theory argues that international migration originates from the labor needs of modern industrial societies, rather than poor economic conditions in the developing origin countries. More precisely, international migration is highly influenced by the structural labor needs of a particular national economy, rather than wage differences across space. Because advanced economies are characterized by segmented labor markets (divided into capital-intensive and high-paying versus labor-intensive and low-paying), and native populations often find such low-wage and -status work unattractive, immigrants meet this labor demand.[57] While an agricultural worker, domestic worker, taxi driver, non-union construction worker, and food server are viewed as low status by immigrants, these sources of employment are perceived as providing the opportunity for upward economic mobility.

The role of national governments and/or corporations in attracting immigrants to fill employment gaps in particular industries must also be recognized with a handful of examples. In 1942, for example, the U.S. and Mexican governments signed an agreement called the *bracero* program that managed the flow of Mexican agricultural labor north of the border to temporarily fill labor deficits caused by military recruitment during World War II. Approximately 4.6 million individuals participated in this cross-border labor flow until the program was terminated in 1964. Since the late 1960s, low-skilled clothing apparel and microelectronic industries have recruited primarily female immigrants from Latin America and Asia based on the false "gender logic" that females are more physiologically and psychologically suited to this more regimented work environment.[58] Part of this segmented labor market includes skilled and educated immigrants that are recruited by corporations through labor recruitment agencies to fill particular occupations not being filled by natives.[59] For example, India and the Philippines supply a substantial number of information technology and health care professionals, respectively. There exists a nexus between corporate labor needs and government policy because U.S. immigration policy favors skilled workers through an occupational preference status. Indeed, the 1965 Immigration Act was in part enacted to allow greater flows of skilled immigrants to enter the labor force.[60]

WORLD SYSTEMS THEORY

Explicitly disposing of wage differences as a cause of international migration as well as immigrants as "active agents" in the decision to migrate, this complex theory asserts that as capitalism spatially spread across the globe beginning in the sixteenth century, international migration as a byproduct of this economic and political process followed.[61] While the flow of capital and goods spread from the global core to the periphery, the international flow of labor moved in the opposite direction, that is, from the periphery to the core. The causes of this return labor flow were the spatial penetration of capitalist investments that upset traditional economies and in turn displaced labor, which then engaged in international migration. For example, offshore foreign investments which manufacture goods that compete with domestically produced goods displace domestic workers, some of whom migrate overseas. In a slightly different situation, experience earned by local workers in these foreign-owned factories preconditions them to labor markets in the core and sets in motion their movements overseas.[62]

Linked to colonialism and the historical process, political and cultural linkages that persist during the post-colonial period also promote international migration between the former colonial possession and colonial power. Such a relationship for the United States is less developed when compared to the great colonial empires of Europe, but does apply to immigrant origin regions such as the Philippines, certain Pacific Islands, and Puerto Rico. Nevertheless, indirect and direct U.S. military intervention in numerous non-Western countries acts as a surrogate in the absence of direct colonial connections to explain immigrant flows. The creation of refugee streams through indirect military intervention in the Central American countries of Guatemala and El Salvador, for example, was in part a result of President Reagan's support of brutal and dictatorial regimes in those countries during the late 1980s. Examples of substantial refugee streams as a result of direct military intervention include South Korea, Vietnam, and Cuba.

Sustaining Immigration Flows

The various theories above describe the "push" and "pull" conditions that initiate the process of international migration of individuals, families, and households across space. There exist, however, additional theories that explain and describe the perpetuation of the flow of immigrants once that movement is under way from a specific origin region or country. These conditions in the form of networks and institutions provide a migration environment that makes further movement more likely through time. This self-sustaining movement of immigrants through time and space is referred to as "chain migration." These conditions help explain, for example, the high spatial concentrations of single ethnic groups in particular locations in the United States such as Poles in Chicago, Iranians in Los Angeles, Asian Indians in Northern New Jersey, Hmong in St. Paul, and Dominicans in New York City.

NETWORK THEORY

Once immigration is under way and a particular numerical threshold of immigrants is established in the destination region, interpersonal social ties between immigrants, non-immigrants, and those remaining in origin regions are forged into a network of individuals possessing knowledge of the migration and settlement experience. In a sense, these networks of countries and individuals that connect origin and destinations comprise a "unified space" of migration flows or a migration region[63] that is a form of transnational field. Most often this network is based on kinship ties anchored in mutual obligations that become a form of "social capital" that is used to reduce the risk of migration, settlement, and employment. The flow of information from an ethnic enclave in the destination country functions as "feedback" and increases the probability of continued migration in a chain or "cumulative causation" fashion.[64] A network theory approach possesses implication for theories explaining the causes of migration. First, because immigrant networks reduce the risks and costs of movement, the volume of migration is more affected by these networks than by wage or employment opportunity difference. Second, once these networks are established, the economic circumstances that originally promoted migration weaken in significance. Third, immigration policies that favor the reunification of families only enhance these immigrant networks by granting family members overseas distinctly favorable conditions for entry.

INSTITUTIONAL THEORY

Like network theory, this particular theory helps explain the growth of immigration flows and chain migration based on reducing the financial risks of long-distance movement and is unattached to the original causes of migration. Non-profit institutions such as churches and humanitarian organizations, as well as for-profit institutions that together are referred to as the "migration regime,"[65] emerge to assist potential immigrants to obtain visas before departure, and once they are settled in the destination country, provide social services, legal advice, housing searches, and employment opportunities. Access to these institutions by immigrants is also another form of social capital which new arrivals are able to use to improve their socioeconomic condition whether these institutions are internal or external to the immigrant community. Much like immigrant networks, these institutional networks work against government policies to control the volume of immigrant flows. In addition, it must also be recognized that these institutions are part of the larger "rights revolution" movement lobbying the U.S. government to enact policies promoting the fair treatment of immigrants, which in turn promotes continued international movement.[66]

Voluntary versus Involuntary Immigrants

The theories of migration just described generally apply to voluntary immigrants who comprise the vast majority of international migrants to industrialized countries, including the United States. The reasons for migrating, however, are primarily of an economic and voluntary nature. Whether classified as being labor immigrants, professional immigrants, or entrepreneurial immigrants, voluntary immigrants are "pulled" to permanently move for economic reasons.[67] Voluntary immigrants often possess knowledge of their destination location and are able to plan their long-distance movement years in advance. They also possess opportunities to return to their origin countries for short visits. If voluntary immigrants enter the destination country legally, their volume is constrained by entry quotas set by the destination country government.

There is an important category of migrants whose decisions are not volitional, but forced. Historically, two pan-ethnic groups were involuntary immigrants—African Americans and Native Americans. While Native Americans are rarely seen as immigrants, the expansion of the American territories into their historic homelands forced them to make boundary treaties that were ultimately broken. As Kate Berry et al. discuss in chapter 3, most lost access to their historic homelands and were forced to migrate to new territories within the ever-expanding United States. In the 1920s, they were granted U.S. citizenship, further confirming their "otherness" and grouping them with the foreign-born. The second group of historical forced migrants is the African-descent population who entered as slaves, as property. Bobby Wilson discusses both the geographies of African slaves and the spatial constraints placed on African Americans even a century after emancipation in chapter 4.

More recently, particularly since World War II, the United States has become the resettlement destination of growing numbers of refugees and asylum seekers. The decision to migrate in these cases is not based on explicitly economic circumstances, but on the real experience or perceived threat of violence as a result of the process of decolonialization, globalization, and the rise of "new nationalisms" in the origin country.[68] The United Nations High Commission for Refugees defines a refugee as a person residing outside his or her country of nationality, who is unable or unwilling to return because of a "well-founded fear of persecution on account of race, religion, nationality, membership in a particular social group, or political persecution."[69] The United States

Table 1.1.   Refugee, Amerasian, and Entrant Arrivals by Top Ten Countries of Origin, 1983–2001

Former USSR	468,150
Vietnam	458,210
Cuba	189,210
Former Yugoslavia	160,394
Laos	113,485
Cambodia	71,428
Iran	56,374
Iraq	41,103
Somalia	40,067
Haiti	38,684
Others	188,958
Total	1,813,760

Source: U.S. Department of Health and Human Services, Office of Refugee Resettlement, <www.acf.hhs.gov/programs/orr/policy/01arc10appendixA.htm> (April 23, 2004).

has legally framed refugee status as those seeking refuge from a Communist political state. Although departing from the origin country for similar reasons as refugees, *asylum seekers* are an official category of refugee who request asylum upon arriving in the destination country. Asylum seekers entering the United States may fit the United Nations definition of refugee but are fleeing from a non-Communist state.

Unlike economic immigrants, these "conflict migrants"[70] are forced to move, are unable to engage in the long-term planning of their departure, are not knowledgeable of their exact destination, and are fearful of never being able to return to their origin region. Having been wrenched from their homelands, refugees tend to be far more psychologically attached to their "lost" place of origin than are economic immigrants. Indeed, refugees can be viewed as special populations by governments because of their "uprooted" and "liminal" nature.[71] The U.S. government, for example, enacted the Refugee Act of 1980 that offers refugees a short-term package of federal and local assistance monies upon arrival. Nonetheless, some scholars claim that the economic and social assimilation process of refugees and economic migrants in the destination country is much the same.[72]

While the volume of refugees is less significant when compared to economic immigrants, their volumes during the past thirty years are worth discussion (Table 1.1). The top ten of the thirty-one source countries with greater than three hundred refugee arrivals during the 1983–2001 period comprise almost 90 percent of the almost two million refugees who entered the United States during the same period. The U.S. government establishes ceilings for refugee admission, and with the exception of 1983, the percentage of refugees admitted equaled or exceeded 80 percent of ceiling limits. Following September 11, 2001, the United States admitted the lowest volume of refugees since 1980. Directly linked to U.S. foreign policy, refugee source countries are former Soviet bloc countries and/or countries that experienced U.S. military intervention. Refugee flows have fluctuated through both time and space depending upon the political conditions in source countries and the nature of U.S. foreign policy. Refugees from the Southeast Asian countries of Vietnam, Laos, and Cambodia that comprised 35 percent of the 1983–2001 total have dwindled since the mid-1990s. The same is true for the former USSR and the former Soviet bloc country of Romania. However, the 1990s witnessed a stable or increased flow of refugees from the former states comprising Yugoslavia as well as Cuba, Haiti, Iran, and Iraq.

About This Book

The opening chapter of this book has introduced a number of concepts and processes that work together to form the ethnic geographies of the United States. In the second chapter, Ines Miyares and Christopher Airriess examine the role that legislation has played in framing the American population throughout the country's history. This legislation has primarily focused on defining insider and outsider status, who is part of "Us" and who is the "Other." By the twenty-first century, it becomes apparent that the "Other" is "Us."

These opening chapters are followed by a set of thirteen chapters, each of which focuses on a particular ethnic group or pan-ethnic group. Kate Berry et al. present historical and contemporary geographies of the Native American pan-ethnic group, exploring their ethnic, cultural, and spatial diversity, and the spatial and social implications of Indian identity, whether for urbanized Indians, reservation Indians, or those living on the margins of reservations. Bobby Wilson follows with a chapter discussing the spatial and social experiences of the African American population as they have fought to move from externally defined and constrained spaces based on race to being equal members of American society.

We then move to an examination of Western Hemisphere immigrants. Daniel Arreola opens this section with a study of the Mexican and Mexican American community in the United States. As our immediate neighbor to the South, Mexico is the largest source country for both labor migrants and family reunification immigrants, and Mexicans/Mexican Americans can now be found in nearly every county in the country. This chapter looks at both the historic Mexican/Mexican American settlement geographies of the Southwest and West and the emerging Mexican communities in the Northeast and the South.

This chapter is followed by two that focus on Caribbean immigration. Thomas Boswell and Terry-Ann Jones discuss three communities from the Spanish-speaking Caribbean—Puerto Ricans, Cubans, and Dominicans. The entry context of each of these island communities differs as do their subsequent ethnic geographies and American experiences. Milton Vickerman complements this chapter through his study of entrants from the non-Hispanic Caribbean region. Immigrants from the British, French, and Dutch Caribbean contribute to the new ethnic diversity in two key ways. They are both new immigrants and they are, for the most part, a foreign-born African-descent community.

From here we move back to the Latin American mainland with Miyares's chapter on Central Americans and Marie Price's chapter on South Americans. Miyares addresses the spatial experiences and adaptations of conflict migrants who did not receive refugee status. Price focuses on the growing Andean communities with a particular focus on the Washington, D.C., metropolitan area as a key gateway city for these source countries.

Wei Li opens our section on Asian immigration with a study of Chinese immigration to the United States. As discussed in chapter 2, this was the first origin country to be specifically restricted from sending labor migrants. Post–World War II changes to immigration law, especially the 1965 Immigration Reform Act, have opened the doors for Chinese immigration, now one of the largest source groups. Dana Reimer follows with a study of the Korean community in the United States, with a focus on gender roles in economic and social adaptations.

We then move to the insular Asian source country of the Philippines. James Tyner also focuses on gender as women are the driving forces in the growth of the Filipino community in the United States. Emily Skop then writes about the growing Indian community in the United States and the role that globalization of technology industries has played in the establishment and maintenance of their transnational connections. Airriess follows with his chapter on Mainland Southeast Asians, conflict migrants who did receive refugee status and whose ethnic geographies have been strongly influenced by refugee policies and benefit programs. Elizabeth Chacko closes this section with a study of the growing and very diverse Muslim immigrant communities. She discusses the Lebanese and Iranian communities and landscapes as examples of this diversity.

This book then shifts its focus to examine selected spatial implications of this new immigration. Brian Godfrey explores changing urban landscapes resulting from new immigration. Michael Reibel details several significant impacts of new immigration on labor markets and the new labor markets and economies created by immigrants. Michael Hawkins closes this book by presenting the importance of ethnic festivals and cultural tourism as vehicles for communities to maintain their ethnic identities and ties and to build bridges to their host communities.

The real-life world of ethnic identity and the immigrant experience is far more complex than depicted or described in the popular media, or even than what can be included in one book. Ethnic identities are not exclusively dependent upon the markers of language, religion, race, and territory. Geographically, these factors are expressed differently based upon region, or public versus private space. This book seeks to expose slices of that real-life world of "old" and "new" ethnic groups in order to paint a portrait of the complexities of America's contemporary ethnic geographies.

Notes

1. Stephen Castles and Mark J. Miller, *The Age of Migration: International Population Movements in the Modern World*, 2nd ed. (New York: Guilford Press, 1998).

2. Castles and Miller, *The Age of Migration*, 2–3; Nicholas Van Hear, *New Diasporas: The Mass Exodus, Dispersal and Regrouping of Migrant Communities* (Seattle: University of Washington Press, 1998), 8–9.

3. Kate A. Berry and Martha L. Henderson, "Introduction: Envisioning the Nexus between

Geography and Ethnic and Racial Identity," in *Geographical Identities of Ethnic America: Race, Space, and Place* (Reno: University of Nevada Press, 2002).

4. Eric Hobsbawm, "Introduction: Inventing Traditions," in *The Invention of Tradition*, ed. Eric Hobsbawm and Terence Ranger (Cambridge: Cambridge University Press, 1983).

5. Thomas H. Eriksen, "Ethnicity, Race and Nation," in *The Ethnicity Reader: Nationalism, Multiculturalism and Migration*, ed. Monserrat Guibernau and John Rex (Cambridge: Polity Press, 1997), 33–42.

6. Nathan Glazer and Daniel P. Moynihan, *Ethnicity: Theory and Experience* (Cambridge, MA: Harvard University Press, 1988).

7. Wilbur Zelinsky, *The Enigma of Ethnicity: Another American Dilemma* (Iowa City: University of Iowa Press, 2001), 43–44.

8. Benedict R. Anderson, *Imagined Communities: Reflections on the Origins and Spread of Nationalism* (New York: Verso, 1991).

9. Cynthia Enloe, "Religion and Ethnicity," in *Ethnicity*, ed. John Hutchinson and Anthony D. Smith (New York: Oxford University Press, 1996), 197–202; Joshua Fishman, "Ethnicity as Being, Doing, and Knowing," in *Ethnicity*, ed. John Hutchinson and Anthony D. Smith (New York: Oxford University Press, 1996), 63–69.

10. Zelinsky, *Enigma of Ethnicity*, 30–32.

11. Zelinsky, *Enigma of Ethnicity*, 28.

12. Robert N. Anderson, *Filipinos in Rural Hawaii* (Honolulu: University of Hawaii Press, 1984).

13. Richard Jenkins, " Rethinking Ethnicity: Identity, Categorization and Power," *Ethnic and Racial Studies* 17, no. 2 (1994): 197–223; Sharon M. Lee, "Racial Classifications in the US Census: 1890–1990," *Ethnic and Racial Studies* 16 (1993): 75–94.

14. Zoltán Fejös, "Variants of Ethnicity," *Acta Ethnographica Hungaria* 47, nos. 3 and 4 (2002): 363–382.

15. Fishman, "Ethnicity," 63–69.

16. Esther Fuchs, "Exile, Memory, Subjectivity: A Yoredet Reflects on National Identity and Gender," in *Women and the Politics of Military Confrontation: Palestinian and Israel Gendered Narratives of Dislocation*, ed. Nahla Abdo and Ronit Lentin (New York: Berghahn Books, 2002), 279–294.

17. John Edwards, "Symbolic Ethnicity and Language," in *Ethnicity*, ed. John Hutchinson and Anthony D. Smith (New York: Oxford University Press, 1996), 227–229.

18. Paul D. Numrich, "Recent Immigrant Religions in a Restructuring Metropolis: New Religious Landscapes in Chicago," *Journal of Cultural Geography* 17, no. 1 (1997): 55–76; Barbara A. Weightman, "Changing Religious Landscapes in Los Angeles," *Journal of Cultural Geography* 14, no. 1 (1993): 1–20.

19. Christopher A. Airriess, "Creating Vietnamese Landscapes and Place in New Orleans," in *Geographical Identities of Ethnic America: Race, Space, and Place*, ed. Kate A. Berry and Martha L. Henderson (Reno: University of Nevada Press, 2002), 228–254; Stephen R. Warner, "Immigration and Religious Communities in the United States," in *Gatherings in Diaspora: Religious Communities and New Immigrants*, ed. Stephen R. Warner and Judith G. Wittner (Philadelphia: Temple University Press, 1998), 3–34.

20. Mary E. Kelly and Joane Nagel, "Ethnic-Reidentification: Lithuanian Americans and Native Americans," *Journal of Ethnic and Migration Studies* 28, no. 2 (2002): 275–289.

21. Wei Li, "Los Angeles' Chinese Ethnoburb: From Ethnic Service Center to Global Economy Outpost," *Urban Geography* 19, no. 6 (1998): 502–528.

22. Wilbur Zelinsky and Barrett A. Lee, "Heterolocalism: An Alternative Model of the Sociospatial Behavior of Immigrant Ethnic Communities," *International Journal of Population Geography* 4, no. 4 (1998): 281–298.

23. Erikson, "Ethnicity."

24. Étienne Balibar, "Fictive Ethnicity and Ideal Nation," in *Ethnicity*, ed. John Hutchinson and Anthony D. Smith (New York: Oxford University Press, 1996), 164–168.

25. Mary Waters, "Ethnic and Racial Identities of Second-Generation Black Immigrants in New York City," *International Migration Review* 28 (1994): 795–819.

26. Lisa Suhair Majaj, "Arab-American Ethnicity: Locations, Coalitions, and Cultural Negotiations," in *Arabs in America: Building a New Future*, ed. Michael W. Suleiman (Philadelphia: Temple University Press, 1999), 320–336.

27. Richard Wright, Serin Houston, Mark Ellis, Steve Holloway, and Margaret Hudson, "Crossing Racial Lines: Geographies of Mixed-Race Partnering and Multiraciality in the United States," *Progress in Human Geography* 24, no. 4 (2003): 457–474.

28. Wright et al., "Crossing Racial Lines," 457–474.

29. Joane Nagel, "Constructing Ethnicity: Creating and Recreating Ethnic Identity and Culture," *Social Problems* 41, no. 1 (1994): 152–176.

30. Erikson, "Ethnicity," 34.

31. Ceri Peach, "Discovering White Ethnicity and Parachuted Plurality," *Progress in Human Geography* 24, no. 4 (2000): 5.

32. Kelley and Nagel, "Ethnic Reidentification," 275.

33. Herbert Gans, "Symbolic Ethnicity: The Future of Ethnic Groups and Cultures in America," *Ethnic and Racial Studies* 2 (1979): 1–20.

34. Kelley and Nagel, "Ethnic Reidentification"; Fejös, "Variants of Ethnicity."

35. Richard D. Alba, *Ethnic Identity: The Transformation of White America* (New Haven, CT: Yale University Press, 1990).

36. Yen Le Espiritu, *Asian American Panethnicity* (Philadelphia: Temple University Press, 1992), 2.

37. Miri Song, *Choosing Ethnic Identity* (Malden, MA: Blackwell, 2003).

38. Song, *Choosing Ethnic Identity*, 104–105.

39. Stephen Cornell, *The Return of the Native: American Indian Political Resurgence* (New York: Oxford University Press, 1988).

40. Evelyn Hu-Dehart, "Introduction: Asian American Formations in the Age of Globalization," in *Across the Pacific: Asian Americans and Globalization*, ed. Evelyn Hu-Dehart (Philadelphia: Temple University Press, 1999), 9.

41. Yen Le Espiritu, *Asian-American Panethnicity*.

42. James Clifford, "Diasporas," in *The Ethnicity Reader: Nationalism, Multiculturalism and Migration*, ed. Montserrat Guibernau and John Rex (Cambridge: Polity Press, 1997), 283–290.

43. Katharyne Mitchell, "Cultural Geographies of Transnationality," in *Handbook of Cultural Geography*, ed. Kay Anderson, Mona Domash, Steve Pile, and Nigel Thrift (Thousand Oaks, CA: Sage, 2003), 74–87.

44. Eric Popkin, "Guatemalan Mayan Migration to Los Angeles: Constructing Transnational Linkages in the Context of the Settlement Process," *Ethnic and Racial Studies* 22, no. 2 (1999): 267–289.

45. Arjun Appadurai, *Modernity at Large: Cultural Dimensions of Globalization* (Minneapolis: University of Minnesota Press, 1996).

46. Paul C. Adams and Rina Ghose, "India.com: The Construction of a Space Between," *Progress in Human Geography* 27, no. 4 (2003): 414–437.

47. Alejandro Portes, "Global Villagers: The Rise of Transnational Communities," *The American Prospect* 25 (1996): 74–77.

48. Michael P. Smith and Luis E. Guarnizo, *Transnationalism from Below* (New London, CN: Transaction Publishers, 1998).

49. L. Basch, N. Glick, and C. S. Blanc, *Nations Unbound* (New York: Gordon and Breach, 1994).

50. Popkin, "Guatemalan Mayan Migration."

51. Luin Goldring, "The Power and Status in Transnational Fields," in *Transnationalism from Below*, ed. Michael P. Smith and Luis E. Guarnizo (London: Transaction Publishers, 1998).

52. Adrian J. Bailey, Richard A. Wright, Alison Mountz, and Ines M. Miyares, "(Re) Producing Salvadoran Transnational Geographies," *Annals of the Association of American Geographers* 92, no. 1 (2002): 125–144.

53. D. J. Massey, J. Arango, G. Hugo, A. Kouaouci, A. Pellagrino, and J. Taylor, "Theories of International Migration: A Review and Appraisal," *Population and Development Review* 19, no. 3 (1993): 431–466.

54. Michael Todaro, *Economic Development in the Third World* (New York: Longman, 1989).

55. O. Stark, *The Migration of Labour* (Oxford: Basil Blackwell, 1991).

56. Yen Le Espiritu, "Gender and Labor in Asian Immigrant Families," *American Behavioral Scientist* 42, no. 4 (1999): 628–647.

57. Michael J. Piore, *Birds of Passage: Migrant Labor and Industrial Societies* (Cambridge: Cambridge University Press, 1979).

58. Espiritu, "Gender and Labor."

59. James A. Tyner, "The Politics of Employment: Overseas Job Fairs and Philippine Labor Recruitment," *Applied Geographic Studies* 3, no. 2 (1998): 109–119.

60. David Reimers, *Still the Golden Door: The Third World Comes to America* (New York: Columbia University Press, 1985).

61. Saskia Sassen, *The Mobility of Labour and Capital: A Study in International Investment and Labour Flow* (Cambridge: Cambridge University Press, 1988); Immanuel Wallerstein, *The Modern World-System, Capitalist Agriculture and the Origins of the European World-Economy in the Sixteenth Century* (New York: Academic Press, 1974).

62. D. Conway, M. Ellis, and N. Shiwdhan, "Caribbean International Circulation: Are Puerto Rican Women Tied-Circulators?" *Geoforum* 21, no. 2 (1990): 51–66.

63. Van Hear, *New Diasporas*.

64. Massey et al., "Theories of International."

65. Van Hear, *New Diasporas*.

66. Van Hear, *New Diasporas*.

67. Alejandro Portes and Rubén Rumbaut, *Immigrant America: A Portrait* (Berkeley: University of California Press, 1990).

68. A. R. Zolberg, A. Suhrke, and S. Aguao, *Escape from Violence* (New York: Oxford University Press, 1989).

69. Castles and Miller, *The Age of Migration*, 87.

70. Nancie Gonzalez, "Conflict, Migration, and the Expression of Ethnicity: Introduction," in *Conflict, Migration, and Expressions of Ethnicity*, ed. Nancie Gonzalez and Carolyn S. McCommon (Boulder, CO: Westview Press, 1989), 1–9.

71. L. H. Malkki, "National Geographic: The Rooting of Peoples and the Territorialization of National Identity among Scholars and Refugees," in *Culture, Power, Place: Exploration in Critical Anthropology*, ed. Akhil Gupta and James Ferguson (Durham, NC: Duke University Press, 1997).

72. Caroline B. Brettell, "Theorizing Migration in Anthropology: The Social Construction of Networks, Identities, Communities, and Globalscapes," in *Migration Theory: Talking across Disciplines*, ed. Caroline Brettell and James F. Hollifield (New York: Routledge, 2000), 97–135.

CHAPTER 2

Creating Contemporary Ethnic Geographies—A Review of Immigration Law

Ines M. Miyares and Christopher A. Airriess

While the American population is at its most diverse point in its history today, the United States has been a culturally diverse country throughout its history, both prior to the arrival of Europeans in the early seventeenth century and since. This diversity is in part the result of the evolution of two federal processes over time—the spatial expansion of U.S. territory and the elaboration of immigration and naturalization policy. The majority of the following chapters focus on immigrant communities that have grown primarily since passage of the 1965 Immigration Reform Act, the law that finally eliminated systematic discrimination in terms of national origin. In order to understand the significance of this act, it is crucial to review the laws that preceded it and have followed it, examining "the good, the bad, and the ugly" of American immigration history and subsequent ethnic geography.

This chapter is divided into five sections, according to the eras of immigration history. The first era encompasses the colonial period and early independence, when the focus was on who could be a member of this nascent society. The second era, which encompasses most of the nineteenth century, was a period of territorial expansion and of the implementation of policies that were not actual immigration laws, but became such by default. This was also an era of progressively increasing negative reactions to those perceived as the "Other." The third era, which begins with the Chinese Exclusion Act of 1882, was a period of legislative responses to those perceived as the "Other," with increasingly restrictive immigration laws. The fourth era, the 1940s through the present, involves the incremental elimination of these national origin restrictions and the shift toward a focus on family reunification and on attracting highly skilled professionals. The fifth and also current era has been one of ad hoc responses to refugees and political asylees, and to those who have entered the United States with the intent to stay but have done so without proper authorization. We see that the reaction to the "Other" is a consistent theme throughout each era, as is the ad hoc nature of the evolution of current federal government policy. Additionally, we note the continuing role of Cold War concerns in post–World War II responses to refugees and those requesting political asylum.

The Colonial Era and Early Independence Years

Historical accounts of the settlement geographies of the United States often begin with the arrival of Europeans, subtly implying that what became the territorial United States was empty land waiting to be explored and inhabited. Native American geographies, when presented in discussions of the ethnic geographies of the colonial era, are often treated as homogeneous and as vulnerable to conquest by stronger, more sophisticated cultures of Europe. As Kate Berry et al. present in detail in the next chapter, the pre-European peoples of the United States were very diverse linguistically, socially, and culturally, and in the case of the Iroquois Confederation in what became parts of New York State, served as sociopolitical models for the foundation of the nascent country. However, as the population of the United States grew, territorial incursions led these first peoples to become the "Other" in their own lands. One could argue that, as the borders of the United States moved westward, Native Americans became a form of immigrants, an important underlying story to the discussion to follow.

In most historical treatises of European arrival to what is now the territorial United States, the focus is typically on the British. Although their area of settlement was not part of the United States until the era of territorial expansion, the Spanish and the French were the first to arrive, expanding their colonial holdings in the Caribbean and New Spain.[1] The Spanish established forts, missions, and civilian settlements in what are today Florida, the Gulf Coast, Texas, the Southwestern states, and California, creating a cultural region Richard Nostrand has called the Spanish Borderlands.[2] The French established fishing, farming, and fur trade settlements along the St. Lawrence River inland to the Great Lakes region and extended their sugar plantations from Haiti to the Louisiana Gulf Coast. By the end of the eighteenth century, France held much of the territory of the Mississippi River watershed.[3] Even the British arrivals were not homogeneous, varying in terms of religious practice, agriculture, economic status, and preferred settlement patterns.[4] The Dutch held parts of what became New York and New Jersey until they exchanged "New Amsterdam" for the British colonial holdings in Suriname in 1667.[5] Despite the transfer of territory, the Dutch remained a significant cultural presence. Additionally, there were Germans, Scandinavians, French Huguenots, colonists from Spain and Portugal, and Africans from a variety of cultural groups in the American colonies.[6]

At the time of independence a large proportion of the population was foreign-born, and the responsibility for determining immigration and naturalization was left to individual states. Article I, Section 8 of the U.S. Constitution granted Congress the authority to pass uniform laws concerning naturalization, and this resulted in a series of legislative acts that defined the qualifications for citizenship in terms of length of residency and moral character. The first such act, passed in 1790, stated that any free, white, adult alien, male or female, with two years of residence in the United States could apply for citizenship. Aliens were required to apply to a common law court of record, whether local, state, or federal, and had to prove that they were of good moral character and to take an oath of allegiance to the Constitution. The residency requirement was increased to five years in 1795, and aliens had to declare their intentions to seek citizenship at least three years before naturalization.

Growing concerns in 1798 about the possibility that new immigrants might commit seditious acts against the nascent government led Congress to increase the residency requirement to fourteen years in 1798, and to require the registry of all aliens residing in the United States. Additionally, Congress that year passed a series of alien acts that authorized the President to arrest and possibly deport aliens deemed dangerous to the United States.[7] In 1802, Congress returned to the five-year residency period, a requirement that still stands today.

Although citizenship was restricted to free-born whites, there was a significant non-white, non-free population in the United States. As Bobby Wilson discusses in chapter 4, by 1790 there were at least 660,000 African slaves working on plantations of the American South, in addition to small free black populations and smaller slave populations in northern states. These forced migrants grew in number into the millions until slavery's abolition during the Civil War, and although they were granted the rights of citizenship, many still fight for equal treatment with all who entered from other regions of the world.

The first formal attempt to keep a record of the numbers of new immigrants entering the United States came with the Steerage Act of 1819, which required the captain or master-at-arms of arriving cargo ships to deliver a manifest to the local Collector of Customs listing all passengers traveling in steerage, that is, in the cargo hold. Copies of the manifests were to be sent to the Secretary of State, who was responsible to report the information to Congress. However, not all passengers intent on immigrating traveled in steerage. Those with the financial means to travel in a first- or second-class cabin were not included in the manifest, making the record incomplete. There was also no record of immigrants who entered overland via the Canadian or Mexican borders. Approximately 90 percent of immigrants to the United States during this period were from northern and western European countries, building on patterns of settlement and culture established during the colonial era (Table 2.1).

Territorial Expansion

The nineteenth century saw the United States fulfill its "manifest destiny" by expanding from the Atlantic to the Pacific, incorporating territory as well as indigenous and European descent populations. The first significant expansion was the Louisiana Purchase of 1803. This was followed by the annexation of Texas in 1845, the cession of the northern half of Mexico as a result of the Mexican-American War (1846–1848), and the Gadsden Purchase of 1853. In a period of only five decades, the territory of the United States more than tripled, and both national rhetoric and policy invited westward migration and immigration.

Settlement of these territories was facilitated by a series of acts that were not specifically immigration acts, but resulted in significant entry by the foreign-born. As the strength of the U.S. government increased, more and more areas held by Native American nations were ceded to federal control. Advances in transportation technology, especially railroads, allowed for settlement anywhere there were rail lines. Consolidating the new national territory would require a transcontinental railroad.

Table 2.1. Immigration by Era and Region and Country of Last Residence

Region and Country of Last Residence[1]	1820–1870	1871–1920	1921–1950	1951–1970
All countries	7,377,238	26,277,565	5,670,679	5,837,156
Europe	6,717,328	22,940,688	3,431,907	2,449,219
Austria	7,124	1,644,986	61,291	87,727
Hungary	484	1,570,133	42,010	42,038
Belgium	16,596	120,946	32,852	27,767
Czechoslovakia[8]	—	3,426	124,934	4,191
Denmark	22,634	277,402	40,382	20,185
France	244,049	288,716	101,042	96,358
Germany	2,333,944	3,161,747	752,838	668,561
Greece	188	370,217	69,176	133,577
Ireland[2]	3,392,335	1,966,015	241,996	81,328
Italy	25,518	4,170,362	581,004	399,602
Netherlands	30,681	188,980	48,958	82,883
Norway-Sweden[3]	145,427	1,702,396	194,245	77,232
Norway	—	623,824	83,371	38,419
Sweden	—	1,078,572	111,874	38,813
Poland[4]	3,686	166,309	252,331	63,524
Portugal	5,272	217,449	40,746	95,653
Romania	—	85,428	72,593	3,570
Soviet Union[8]	3,886	3,276,363	63,683	3,136
Spain	22,945	114,962	35,114	52,553
Switzerland	61,019	199,473	45,735	36,128
United Kingdom[2, 5]	1,401,213	2,494,296	510,448	416,646
Yugoslavia[8]	—	1,888	56,475	28,606
Other Europe	135	73,310	63,054	27,954

Region and Country of Last Residence[1]	1971–1980	1981–1990	1991–2002	Total 183 years, 1820–2002
All countries	4,493,314	7,338,062	13,959,426	68,217,481
Europe	800,368	761,550	1,917,403	38,816,282
Austria	9,478	18,340	31,479	1,848,107
Hungary	6,550	6,545	15,768	1,679,815
Belgium	5,329	7,066	14,239	219,490
Czechoslovakia[8]	6,023	7,227	17,033	159,400
Denmark	4,439	5,370	11,205	377,887
France	25,069	32,353	67,449	833,434
Germany	74,414	91,961	209,526	7,219,222
Greece	92,369	38,377	134,228	734,145
Ireland[2]	11,490	31,969	46,428	4,785,052
Netherlands	10,492	12,238	26,930	391,740
Norway-Sweden[3]	10,472	15,182	30,312	2,168,505
Norway	3,941	4,164	9,157	759,949
Sweden	6,531	11,018	21,155	1,263,129
Poland[4]	37,234	83,252	146,145	795,742
Portugal	101,710	40,431	145,115	527,151
Romania	12,393	30,857	53,999	266,793
Soviet Union[8]	38,961	57,677	207,201	4,017,143
Spain	39,141	20,433	63,066	305,797
Switzerland	8,235	8,849	20,383	374,579
United Kingdom[2, 5]	137,374	159,173	334,862	5,309,331
Yugoslavia[8]	30,540	18,762	99,339	252,865
Other Europe	9,287	8,234	39,860	261,964

Table 2.1. *continued*

Region and Country of of Last Residence[1]	1820–1870	1871–1920	1921–1950	1951–1970
Asia	106,529	839,743	165,682	580,891
China[5]	105,744	241,594	51,544	44,421
Hong Kong	—	—	—	90,548
India	196	7,295	4,143	29,162
Iran	—	—	1,816	13,727
Israel	—	—	476	55,078
Japan	186	241,995	36,965	86,238
Korea	—	—	107	40,757
Philippines	—	—	5,219	117,683
Turkey	301	326,046	35,687	13,661
Vietnam	—	—	—	4,675
Other Asia	102	22,813	29,725	84,941
North America	349,171	2,375,542	2,031,557	2,713,318
Canada & Newfoundland[7]	271,020	1,701,666	1,204,760	791,262
Mexico[7]	19,957	276,692	542,195	753,748
Caribbean	49,533	307,037	140,126	593,304
Cuba	—	—	51,785	287,484
Dominican Republic	—	—	6,777	103,189
Haiti	—	—	1,102	38,941
Jamaica[9]	—	—	—	83,775
Other Caribbean	49,533	307,037	80,462	79,915
Central America	1,063	26,461	43,295	146,081
El Salvador	—	—	5,805	20,887
Other Central America	1,063	26,461	37,490	125,194
South America	7,598	63,686	71,849	349,568
Argentina	—	—	4,687	69,207
Colombia	—	—	5,081	90,076
Ecuador	—	—	2,754	46,621
Other South America	7,598	63,686	59,327	143,664
Other America	—	—	29,332	79,355
Africa	648	17,376	15,403	43,046
Oceania	413	53,904	25,760	38,098
Not specified[22]	203,149	50,312	370	12,584

Region and Country of Last Residence[1]	1971–1980	1981–1990	1991–2002	Total 183 years, 1820–2002
Asia	1,588,178	2,738,157	4,990,772	9,479,289
China[5]	125,326	346,747	577,868	1,440,285
Hong Kong	113,467	98,215	229,941	430,268
India	164,134	250,786	547,700	951,556
Iran	45,136	116,172	177,101	261,200
Israel	37,713	44,273	91,849	186,800
Japan	49,775	47,085	116,474	549,800
Korea	267,638	333,746	641,431	846,461
Philippines	354,987	548,764	1,003,295	1,630,142
Turkey	13,399	23,233	44,043	457,950
Vietnam	172,820	280,782	520,675	811,495
Other Asia	244,783	648,354	1,040,395	1,913,332
North America	1,982,735	3,615,225	6,550,088	18,506,482
Canada & Newfoundland[7]	169,939	156,938	384,379	4,545,074

Table 2.1. *continued*

Region and Country of Last Residence[1]	1971–1980	1981–1990	1991–2002	Total 183 years, 1820–2002
Mexico[7]	640,294	1,655,843	2,718,299	6,560,312
Caribbean	741,126	872,051	1,804,375	3,873,162
Cuba	264,863	144,578	463,034	971,625
Dominican Republic	148,135	252,035	443,900	889,117
Haiti	56,335	138,379	236,438	456,125
Jamaica[9]	137,577	208,148	375,391	628,393
Other Caribbean	135,216	128,911	285,612	927,902
Central America	134,640	468,088	742,311	1,486,126
El Salvador	34,438	213,539	309,568	552,058
Other Central America	100,204	254,549	432,743	934,068
South America	295,741	461,847	899,267	1,931,624
Argentina	29,897	27,327	64,494	165,032
Colombia	77,347	122,849	235,017	458,673
Ecuador	50,077	56,315	126,650	252,617
Other South America	138,420	255,356	473,106	1,055,302
Other America	995	458	1,460	110,184
Africa	80,779	176,893	364,016	795,428
Oceania	41,242	45,205	100,236	274,256
Not specified[22]	12	1,032	36,911	345,744

Source: 2002 Yearbook of Immigration Statistics, Table 2.
Notes:
1. Data for years prior to 1906 relate to source country; data for 1906–1979 and 1984–2002 are for country of last permanent residence; and data for 1980–1983 refer to birth country. Because of changes in boundaries, changes in lists of countries, and lack of data for specific countries for various periods, data for certain countries are not comparable throughout.
2. Data for Austria and Hungary not reported until 1861.
3. Data for Austria and Hungary not reported separately for all years during the period.
4. No data available for Czechoslovakia until 1920.
5. Prior to 1926, data for Northern Ireland included in Ireland.
6. Data for Norway and Sweden not separated until 1871.
7. No data for Romania until 1880.
8. Since 1925, data for the United Kingdom include England, Scotland, Wales, and Northern Ireland.
9. In 1920, a separate enumeration was made for the Kingdom of the Serbs, Croats, and Slovenes. Since 1920, these were recorded as Yugoslavia.
10. Beginning in 1957, "China" includes Taiwan.
11. Data not reported separately until 1952.
12. Data not reported separately until 1925.
13. Data not reported separately until 1949.
14. Data not available for Japan until 1861.
15. Data not reported separately until 1948.
16. Prior to 1934, Philippines reported as insular travel.
17. Prior to 1920, Canada and Newfoundland recorded as British North America. From 1820 to 2001, figures include all British North American possessions.
18. Land arrivals not enumerated until 1908.
19. No data available for Mexico from 1886 to 1894.
20. Data not reported separately until 1932.
21. Data for Jamaica not collected until 1953. In prior years, consolidated under British West Indies, which is included in "Other Caribbean."
22. Included in countries "Not Specified" until 1925.
23. From 1899 to 1919, data for Poland included in Austria-Hungary, Germany, and the Soviet Union.
24. From 1938 to 1945, data for Austria included in Germany.
25. Includes 32,897 persons returning in 1906 to their homes in the United States.
Additional notes: From 1820–1867, figures represent alien passengers arriving at seaports; from 1868–1891 and 1895–1897, immigrant alien arrivals; from 1892–1894 and 1898–2002, immigrant aliens admitted for permanent residence. From 1892–1903, aliens arriving by cabin class were not counted as immigrants. Land arrivals were not completely enumerated until 1908. Data for Czechoslovakia, the Soviet Union, and Yugoslavia include independent republics. For this table, fiscal year 1843 covers 9 months ending September 1843; fiscal years 1832 and 1850 cover 15 months ending December 31 of those respective years, and fiscal year 1868 covers 6 months ending June 30, 1868. "—" represents zero.

The expressed purpose of the Kansas-Nebraska Act of 1854 was to open a corridor for the forthcoming transcontinental railroad by organizing the remaining territory within the Louisiana Purchase for settlement in anticipation of its admission to the Union.[8] Although most of the historical treatment of this act focuses on the issue of free- versus slave-state status and its role as a prelude to the Civil War, this act also resulted in the westward migration of farmers seeking larger holdings that could be cultivated as commercial enterprises. The Preemption Act of 1841 had permitted squatters to stake a claim of 160 acres of federal land and after about fourteen months of residence, to purchase the claim from the government for as little as $1.25 an acre before it was offered for public sale.[9] The Homestead Act of 1862 made westward settlement even more inviting—any adult citizen or immigrant intending to become a citizen could apply for 160 acres at the cost of a nominal registration fee, and after proving five years of residence and cultivation, homesteaders would receive title to the land from the federal government. This coincided with growing land poverty and political oppression in various European countries, resulting in massive waves of immigration to the Midwest and Great Plains. Immigrants included Norwegians, Swedes, German-Russians, Czechs, and Hutterites (Table 2.1).[10]

While the population of the Midwest and Great Plains was increasingly foreign-born, some immigrant groups remained in East Coast urban centers. One such group was the Irish. At the time of independence, approximately 10 percent of the country's population was Irish. However, the largest concentrated waves of Irish immigration followed the potato famine of the 1840s. The blight on the potato crop resulted in approximately 750,000 deaths from starvation and related diseases and the emigration of more than two million Irish, a large proportion of whom migrated to the United States (Table 2.1). Unlike the aforementioned immigrants who took advantage of opportunities to remain in agriculture, the Irish tended to settle in urban centers such as New York and Boston, entering urban public-service professions and construction. During the building of the transcontinental railroad, many of the laborers on the westward portion were first-generation Irish immigrants.

A significant challenge faced by the Irish was that they were Roman Catholic, while the majority of the country's population was Protestant. The popular press used the medium of political cartoons to present negative stereotypes of the Irish, portraying them as rowdy and dangerous.[11] This was enough for anti-Irish political movements to emerge under the guise of immigration control. Among these were the Know Nothings, a secret society whose expressed purpose was to support anti-immigrant political candidates.

The Irish were not the only immigrant group to benefit from employment with the railroad or to experience anti-immigrant sentiments. The western portion of the railroad became an important labor niche for the Chinese, a very different immigrant group. Chinese laborers had begun to migrate northward from Mexico after the discovery of gold in California. Chinese miners had worked the silver mines for decades and saw the opportunity to ply their trade in the Sierra foothills. Within a short period of time, Chinese laborers were coming directly from China, entering California via San Francisco. Chinese laborers often came as either single men or as transnational laborers intending to return home to their families. Despite their relatively small numbers

(Table 2.1), the Chinese were the most culturally "different" immigrants who had entered the United States to this point. They were willing to accept more difficult jobs for lower pay, and their different dress, language, religion, and demeanor caused them to be seen as the "Other" and to be demonized in politics, the press, and the emerging labor movement.

While the Irish were victims of discrimination in employment and in their personal lives, the Chinese experienced discrimination on a much broader level. Most Chinese resided in California, and state and local governments passed ordinances restricting where the Chinese could live and segregating their children into Chinese-only schools. In 1862, in an effort to curb immigration and employment of Chinese laborers, the California state legislature passed the "anti-coolie" tax act, which charged a $2.50 monthly tax on "Mongolians" working in the mines or running a business, and defined penalties for failure to pay the tax.[12] The anti-Chinese fervor spread from the Sacramento Statehouse to Washington, D.C., moving the country into a new era of restrictive legislation targeting specific ethnic groups deemed undesirable.

The Legislative Reactions to the "Other"

In 1880, the United States negotiated a treaty with the Chinese government that would allow the United States to consider regulating the immigration of Chinese laborers, but assuring the protection of the civil rights of Chinese laborers already in the United States.[13] This treaty did little to curtail anti-Chinese sentiments and activities. Instead, it laid the foundation for restrictive legislation toward Chinese laborers. In 1882, Congress passed the Chinese Exclusion Act. The act's preamble justified the act as follows: "Whereas, in the opinion of the Government of the United States the coming of Chinese laborers to this country endangers the good order of certain localities within the territory thereof."[14] Although Chinese laborers represented a very small percentage of total immigrants, their entry was perceived to be a threat to existing laborers, particularly in California. The act barred entry of skilled and unskilled laborers and miners, and imposed punitive fines on ship captains who transported Chinese laborers to the United States. It did not bar entry of teachers, students, diplomats, or tourists. The latter three categories were seen as temporary entrants and not a threat to the labor movement, and allowing the entry of teachers facilitated the continued segregation of schools. The act specified a 10-year duration of the ban, but it was renewed and remained in place until it was finally repealed in 1943.

Unlike Chinese laborers, Japanese laborers and farmers were restricted from emigrating by their own government. During the Meiji Restoration of 1868, Japanese students were encouraged to travel to the United States to learn western technology, but it was not until 1885 that the Japanese government allowed its citizens to emigrate. Passage of the Chinese Exclusion Act did not curb the need for cheap labor, and soon Japanese laborers were migrating to the United States to fill the void.[15] The United States negotiated a treaty with Japan in 1894 that allowed free immigration of Japanese laborers, but as the majority were settling in California, the Japanese were soon victims of the same discriminatory attitudes and actions as the Chinese. By 1900, Japan agreed to deny passports to Japanese laborers intent on immigrating to the United States, but many continued to enter via Mexico, Canada, and Hawaii. By 1906, San Francisco extended its school segregation laws to include all Asians. While the Japanese government was willing to work with the United States to control emigration of its laborers, the actions taken by San Francisco inflamed simmering tensions between the two countries. President Roosevelt desired to keep Japan as an ally, especially in light of Russia's expansionist activities. Instead of a legislative act as had been passed against Chinese laborers, Roosevelt negotiated an agreement by which San Francisco would rescind its discriminatory policies toward the Japanese, and the government of Japan would deny passports to Japanese seeking to enter the United States and recognize the authority of the United States to deny entry to Japanese if they successfully reached the United States.[16] This "Gentlemen's Agreement," signed in 1907, was extended to Korea when Japan annexed that country in 1910.

The first comprehensive law for national control of immigration was the Immigration Act of 1891. This act established the Bureau of Immigration as part of the Treasury Department and gave it the authority to administer all immigration laws other than the Chinese Exclusion Act. Additionally, it expanded the list of inadmissible classes of immigrants to include those likely to become a public charge, those suffering from selected contagious diseases, felons, persons convicted of other crimes or misdemeanors, polygamists, and contract laborers, and it made it illegal to recruit or advertise for immigrants. It also authorized the Bureau of Immigration to deport immigrants who entered unlawfully.[17]

In 1903, Congress transferred the Bureau of Immigration to the Department of Commerce and Labor and expanded the list of inadmissible aliens to include anarchists in response to growing concerns about political instability in several European countries.[18] It also allowed for the deportation of immigrants who became public charges within two years of otherwise lawful entry. The Naturalization Act of 1906 transferred the process of naturalization to the Bureau of Immigration, creating the Bureau of Immigration and Naturalization, and made knowledge of English a prerequisite for naturalization. The Immigration Act of 1907 further codified these ad hoc revisions to immigration policy and added to the list of inadmissible aliens

> imbeciles, feeble-minded persons, persons with physical or mental defects which may affect their ability to earn a living, persons afflicted with tuberculosis, children unaccompanied by their parents, persons who admitted the commission of a crime involving moral turpitude, and women coming to the United States for immoral purposes.

It also created a Joint Congressional Commission on Immigration (the Dillingham Commission) to research the immigration system, whose findings were the basis for the Immigration Act of 1917 and the Quota Law of 1921.[19]

The most significant component of the Immigration Act of 1917 was the comprehensive exclusion of Asian immigrants. As Table 2.1 shows, there had been fewer than one million immigrants from Asia by 1920, but their entry was perceived as a threat to American labor and culture. To be certain that no new groups of laborers from Asia would assume the roles held by Chinese, Japanese, and Koreans, already excluded by that point, Congress created an "Asiatic barred zone," referred to as the Asia-Pacific Triangle, and listed specific nationalities that were excluded solely because of their region of birth.[20] The countries of the Asia-Pacific Triangle included China, India, Afghanistan, Arabia (Saudi Arabia), Burma (Myanmar), Siam (Thailand), the Malay States (Malaysia), the Dutch East Indies (Indonesia), Asiatic Russia (those from west of the Ural Mountains were permitted to immigrate), and most Polynesian islands.

The growing turmoil in eastern and southern Europe during the early twentieth century, the pogroms against Jews, and the growing number of land-poor farmers from this region seeking new opportunities in America resulted in a shift in origin countries of European immigrants. Italians and Russians became the two largest immigrant nationalities, with Austrians and Hungarians close behind. Greeks, Poles, and Romanians also arrived in significant numbers (Table 2.1). These represented a new wave of the "Other"—Roman Catholics, Eastern and Russian Orthodox, Jews, gypsies, speakers of Romance and Cyrillic languages, with darker hair, skin, and eyes than earlier European immigrants. They came seeking religious and political freedom and economic opportunities as had earlier waves of northern and western Europeans, but their arrivals in East Coast and Midwestern cities were seen as threats to the future of American culture. The Dillingham Commission had come to several significant conclusions concerning these new European immigrants. Among these were that they were "racially inferior," were inclined to violent crimes, resisted assimilation, and drove old-stock Europeans out of some lines of work. While the federal government did not specifically bar entry of eastern and southern Europeans, Congress did pass the first quantitative immigration law, the Quota Act of 1921. This law limited the number of immigrants from any one country to 3 percent of the foreign-born persons of that nationality who had been enumerated in the 1910 census. Approximately 350,000 persons were admitted annually under this law, and 60 percent of these were from northern and western European countries.

These progressively more restrictive immigration acts culminated in the Immigration Act of 1924, also referred to as the National Origins Act, which stood with the Immigration Act of 1917 as the foundations for immigration policy until 1952. This act had two quota provisions and defined ceilings for immigration. The first, which was in effect until June 30, 1927, set the annual quota of any quota nationality at 2 percent of the number of foreign-born persons of that nationality already residing in the continental United States in 1890, with a total quota of 164,667. After that date (actually implemented July 1, 1929), the total quota was reduced to 150,000, and admissible nationalities were granted quotas in relation to the 150,000 based on the ratio between a nationality's enumerated population in 1920 and the total U.S. population in 1920.[21] Approximately 82 percent of immigrant visas under this law were allotted to northern and western European countries, 16 percent to southern and eastern European countries, and 2 percent to all other Eastern Hemisphere admissible nationalities. There were no ceilings for Western Hemisphere nationalities. The Dillingham Commission had seen Mexico as an important source of low-wage laborers, and most of the other immigrants from the Americas were coming from Canada.

The National Origins Act included several other significant deterrents to immigration. First, it barred from entry any aliens ineligible for citizenship, a stipulation primarily targeted at the Japanese who were entering via Hawaii. Second, it established the consular control system, which required those who desired to immigrate to obtain a visa from an American consular office abroad, resulting in shared control of immigration by the State Department and the Immigration and Naturalization Service. Third, it authorized the establishment of the Border Patrol in order to regulate unauthorized overland immigration primarily from Mexico.

During the 1930s, immigration declined substantially. The Great Depression in the United States and economic and political crises in Europe combined with the new restrictions of the National Origins Act, reducing immigration to a total of 528,431 new entrants between 1931 and 1940, less than 10 percent of the total for 1911–1920. This number doubled to 1,035,039 between 1941 and 1950 as World War II brought about the seeds of change in immigration policy and attitudes toward Asian immigrants (Table 2.1).[22]

Immigration Reform

World War II transformed the way Americans viewed the rest of the world, and this worked its way into major reforms of what had become highly restrictive immigration policies. The American military served in Europe, Africa, Asia, and the Pacific, and in the latter two regions, they fought to liberate peoples who had been denied entry or the possibility of naturalization solely based on national origin. Soldiers desired to marry women they met while stationed on foreign soil, but if these women were Asian, they would be denied visas. The U.S. government sought out China as a military ally, and yet had continued to renew the Chinese Exclusion Act. It was this contradiction in perspective toward China that led to the beginning of immigration reform.

As stated earlier, immigration from Asia had been incrementally and systematically stopped, first from China, then from Japan and Korea, and eventually from the entire Asia-Pacific Triangle. During World War II, Japanese immigrants and Americans of Japanese descent were assumed to either be enemy combatants or assisting the enemy, and were forcibly detained in internment camps for much of the duration of the war, while the famed 442nd, a segregated Japanese American regimental combat company based out of Hawaii, became the most decorated combat unit for its size and duration of service in U.S. military history. After the war, reconstructing Japan became a major component of the Pacific front of the Cold War, despite Japanese ineligibility to immigrate or naturalize as citizens.

Attitudes toward China changed when the United States saw the need for a military alliance during the war. As a national security measure, Congress had passed an Alien Registration Act in 1940 that had required all foreign-born non-citizens over the age of fourteen who were eligible for naturalization to register and be fingerprinted. In 1943, the act was amended to add Chinese persons to those eligible for citizenship. A visa quota of 105 individuals per year was allotted to China. This essentially repealed the Chinese Exclusion Act and initiated change in immigration policy toward Asia. However, it took another two decades and more incremental acts to truly open the door to the Asia-Pacific Triangle.

A second significant step toward change came in response to the denial of visas to war brides from restricted source countries. The War Brides Act of 1945 waived visa requirements and national origin provisions for foreign nationals who had married members of the American military during World War II. The only requirements that were enforced were those pertaining to the immigrant's physical and mental health. In 1946, this was extended to fiancé(e)s of members of the American armed services. That same year, Congress amended the Immigration Act of 1917, removing India and the Philippines from the list of excluded nationalities and giving nonquota status to Chinese wives of American citizens. By 1950, foreign-born spouses and minor children of members of the armed forces were made eligible for immigration and nonquota status, regardless of race and national origin.[23]

World War II drew men and women from all social classes into the military at a time when the economy was recovering from the prolonged Great Depression. Despite the number of women who entered assembly-line jobs during the war, there were significant labor shortages. To meet the need for laborers, the federal government looked to neighboring countries for temporary workers. Mexicans and Central and South Americans were recruited as temporary agricultural laborers, laying the foundation for the Mexican *Bracero Program* that continued until 1964. Manufacturing and services workers were recruited from British Honduras (Belize), Jamaica, Barbados, and the British West Indies. This latter program was focused on the war effort and did not continue, but it laid the foundation for the growing Afro-Caribbean community that is an important component of contemporary immigration.[24]

The post-war era initiated a period of Cold War policies that extended to immigration laws and framed refugee resettlement policies. The Internal Security Act of 1950 declared membership in the Communist Party or other totalitarian political party grounds for inadmissibility. It also curtailed the Attorney General's authority to admit otherwise inadmissible aliens or to "parole" those requesting political asylum or suspension of deportation. However, even in the midst of the extremist concerns and "McCarthyism" of the 1950s, Congress passed the McCarran-Walter Immigration and Nationality Act of 1952, that, although heavily amended, still stands as immigration law today.

The most significant component of the 1952 Immigration and Nationality Act was that it made all nationalities eligible for citizenship and eliminated gender-based discrimination with respect to immigration. Although it retained the quota system, it gave a minimum quota of 100 visas, with an aggregate ceiling of 2,000 visas, to the previously excluded countries of the Asia-Pacific Triangle. It created a four-tiered preference system for the allotment of quota visas in order both to draw members of highly skilled professions needed in the Cold War race against the Soviet Union and to allow for reunification of extended family members who did not qualify for nonquota visas. The first 50 percent of all visas were awarded to highly skilled immigrants whose services were in great demand in the United States, and the spouses and children of these immigrants. Spouses and unmarried minor children could apply for nonquota visas, but additional extended family members of citizens and permanent residents had to apply for second, third, and fourth preference visas. While this was an imperfect revision to the quota system, it allowed members of previously excluded nationalities to gain an initial foothold. As noted in Table 2.1, this resulted in new directions for immigrant source countries, opening the doors for later entrants as provisions for family reunification expanded in subsequent legislation.

This policy change also created a significant shift in the socioeconomic character of new immigrant communities. In order to qualify for nonquota visas or for extended family visas, one had to be related to a U.S. citizen or permanent resident alien. This meant that the first immigrant waves from previously excluded countries had to qualify for first preference visas—those reserved for highly skilled and well-educated persons and their immediate families. No longer were new immigrant communities founded by the working class and the working poor as they had been in the nineteenth and early twentieth centuries. New immigrants, particularly those from Asia, had to be educated professionals in order to receive a quota visa.

Congress continued to make incremental changes in immigration law while maintaining the foundation of the McCarran-Walter Act of 1952. In 1961, with the growing number of European colonial possessions in Africa, Asia, and the Caribbean finally gaining their independence, a number of revisions to the 1952 act were made. The aggregate ceiling of 2,000 visas for the Asia-Pacific Triangle was eliminated, and newly independent countries were assured a minimum of 100 visas. Questions about race and ethnic origin were removed from visa applications, allowing for a fairer treatment of ethnic and racial minorities in other countries in the allotment of visas. This would affect, for example, Chinese populations who had migrated to Latin American or African countries in earlier generations and now desired to migrate to the United States as natives of their current countries and not as Chinese citizens. Additionally, with the growth of international adoptions, regulations for the admission of foreign-born adopted children were codified.[25]

The Civil Rights Era of the 1950s and 1960s was a turning point in American history in many ways. Congress and the federal courts finally began to address longstanding injustices against the African American community. In the midst of the much-needed reforms in the fair and equal treatment of African Americans in areas such as housing, education, employment, voting rights, and the court systems came a watershed act that restructured the visa system and has ultimately transformed the ethnic and social geography of the country. The Immigration Reform Act of 1965, also known as the Hart-Cellar Act, amended the 1952 act in a way that finally eliminated national origin, race, ethnicity, or ancestry as a basis for immigration. It also made family reunification a more important component of the visa system by reordering the preference system so that two extended family preference categories came before professional and highly skilled laborer preferences and by moving more extended family members to nonquota status. The third preference, that for "members of the professions and scientists and artists of exceptional ability," accounted for only 10 percent of the visas awarded. Skilled and even unskilled laborers could apply for a new sixth preference if the annual total number of visas had not yet been reached. A special preference was created for refugees from Communist countries and the Middle East, a category that was later eliminated with the passage of the Refugee Act of 1980.

Immigrant visas were now to be awarded on a first-come, first-served basis within the new preference system. It changed the numerical totals system by allotting 170,000 visas to the Eastern Hemisphere, with a 20,000-visa limit for each country. For the first time, a ceiling of 120,000 visas was set for the Western Hemisphere, but neither the preference system nor the 20,000-visa limit was applied. It also included protections for American workers by requiring certification that those applying for labor-based preferences were not going to negatively affect American workers either by wage depression or as replacements for available native workers. By 1970, there was a major shift in the ethnic composition of incoming migrants (Table 2.1). Asian communities that had begun to form under the 1952 preference system experienced explosive growth as first-wave immigrants who had entered as highly skilled professionals gained permanent residency and citizenship, and were able to sponsor extended family members. By the 1990s, nearly half of all new immigrants were from Asian countries.

The 1965 act coincided with economic and political crises in a number of Latin American countries. Until then, most immigrants were coming from neighboring Mexico, but South American middle-class entrepreneurs, particularly from Colombia and Ecuador, began to establish footholds in several U.S. cities. Additionally, special visa categories were created in response to selected crises. The Dominican Republic experienced a revolution in 1965 that resulted in a U.S. military invasion and the installation of a puppet government. Special immigrant visas to the United States were granted to would-be or actual revolutionaries, and Dominicans who received the initial post-revolution visas were able to obtain visas for networks of immediate family members under the 1965 preference system.[26] Cubans also began to enter in large numbers during this time, having been granted refugee status after the Communist revolution in their homeland.

Additional changes were made to the 1965 act in 1976 and 1978. In 1976, the 20,000-visa-per-country limit was applied to Western Hemisphere countries, as was a slightly revised preference system. In 1978, the hemispheric ceilings were replaced by a global ceiling of 290,000. However, to this day, two-thirds of all post-1965 immigrants enter on nonpreference family reunification visas.

The 1965 act also served as a catalyst in shifting the settlement geography of new immigrants away from only the traditional coastal and Midwest industrial port-of-entry cities. Cities and states in the Southeast and the Great Plains that had not received significant numbers of immigrants since the nineteenth century began to experience ethnic transformations due to a more open immigration system. The foreign-born populations of previously non-immigrant states also grew as a result of refugee resettlement policies that followed immigration reform. Map 2.1 shows the percent of the 2000 population of each state that was foreign-born. Of the foreign-born, the percent that entered after 1965 is shown in Map 2.2. While the historical port-of-entry states do have the highest percentages of foreign-born populations, nearly all immigrants in low immigration states arrived after 1965. Thus the 1965 Immigration Reform Act not only opened the door for a more diverse pool of immigrants; it had the indirect effect of diversifying the national ethnic geography as new immigrants settled in inland states.

As discussed in chapter 5, the largest source country for contemporary documented immigration is Mexico. It is also the largest source country for undocumented immigrants. As mentioned earlier, during World War II and the two decades that followed, a

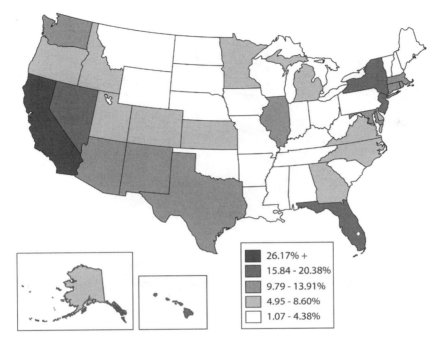

Map 2.1.   Percent of the 2000 Population of Each State That Was Foreign-born. Source: 2000 Census of Population and Housing SF3, <www.factfinder.census.gov> (September 15, 2005).

federal program entitled the Bracero Program was developed to recruit temporary agricultural laborers from Mexico to the United States. The 1952 act had exempted employers from sanctions otherwise meted out to persons who harbored undocumented immigrants and did not impose sanctions for employing them. Even after a century of incorporation into the United States, Mexican culture and the Spanish language continued to dominate much of the Southwest and Southern California, particularly as one approached the border. Thus, thousands of *braceros* remained in the United States after the expiration of their labor visas, often finding housing in Mexican-dominated areas and continuing to be employed in their agricultural jobs. Occasional major raids and repatriations, such as "Operation Wetback" in 1954, rounded up and repatriated thousands of undocumented Mexican laborers (and often documented laborers and Mexican Americans as well), but the cycle of both documented and undocumented entry and re-entry continued throughout the duration of the program.

The Bracero Program was terminated in 1964, but a generation of Mexican households had become dependent on migrant remittances for their economic well-being. Farmers had also become accustomed to this source of cheap labor. Raids and repatriations became commonplace in the West and Southwest, and the undocumented migrant, the "illegal alien," became the new demonized "Other" who could be blamed for many of the country's social and economic problems. A major problem was that

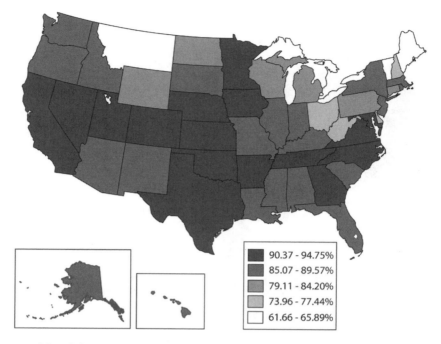

Map 2.2.   Of the Foreign-born Population in 2000, the Percent That
Entered after 1965. Source: 2000 Census of Population and Housing SF3,
<www.factfinder.census.gov> (September 15, 2005).

deportation did not serve as a sufficient disincentive since employers were continuing
to hire undocumented laborers. Although there were undocumented immigrants from
many countries, the undocumented Mexican migrant came to symbolize the problem.
Even efforts such as the *machiladora* program that worked to develop the Mexican border region's economy were inadequate to provide enough jobs for Mexicans, and the
lack of employer sanctions ensured that jobs would be available if one successfully
evaded the Border Patrol.

By the mid-1980s, the government realized that the problem of undocumented
immigration could not be resolved without revising the 1952 act to address the lack of
employer sanctions, and that there were too many undocumented migrants in the
country to effectively address the problem with raids and deportations. In 1986, Congress passed the Immigration Reform and Control Act (IRCA), which took the very
different direction of amnesty for the undocumented. Under the IRCA, undocumented immigrants who could prove they had continuously resided in the United
States since January 1, 1982 could regularize their status, first to temporary resident
and then permanent resident status without risking deportation. The IRCA also created sanctions prohibiting employers from knowingly hiring immigrants, whether documented or not, who did not have visas allowing general employment.[27] It also
authorized the adjustment to permanent resident status of Cubans and Haitians who

had entered without documentation or inspections and resided continuously since January 1, 1982. Although the IRCA did increase enforcement at the borders, it opened the door for over 3 million undocumented migrants to come forward and regularize their status.

The IRCA addressed three additional problems concerning immigration. First, it created a new visa category of seasonal agricultural worker and laid out provisions for the legalization of such workers. Second, it created a special immigrant category for retired employees of international organizations who had entered as H1 employment-based non-immigrants with their families. Third, it allocated 5,000 non-preference visas for each fiscal year 1987 and 1988 for immigrants from countries "adversely affected by the 1965 act."[28] The government had recognized that by removing the hemispheric limits and by preferencing family reunification, Europeans who desired immigrant visas but did not qualify for immediate family non-preference visas often had to wait years before a visa would become available. This set the stage for a subsequent reform—the visa lottery system.

The Immigration Act of 1990 ushered in the next major revision of the 1952 act. The global ceiling had been incrementally increased several times, but the 1990 act set it at 675,000 per year beginning in 1995, with ceilings of 700,000 for fiscal years 1992–1994. The visa composition of the 675,000 ceiling would be 480,000 family-sponsored, 140,000 employment-based, and 55,000 "diversity immigrants." A list of countries qualifying for diversity visas would be announced annually, and those desiring such visas could apply to the visa lottery, hoping for the best. This program was indirectly addressing the problem of European undocumented immigration by giving visa overstayers and other undocumented entrants an opportunity to regularize their status.

The 1990 act created a new category of entrant, a quasi-documented "temporary protected status" for undocumented immigrants from specific countries experiencing natural disasters or armed conflicts and for whom remaining in their countries would place their lives at risk. The principal recipients of temporary protected status (TPS) were Salvadorans escaping their civil war, but since its creation, TPS has been granted to those from Burundi, Honduras, Liberia, Nicaragua, Montserrat, Somalia, and Sudan. TPS is not an immigrant status because it allows the applicant to remain in the United States until his or her case for protection has been reviewed by an immigration judge. If the person can prove that he or she has a well-founded fear of persecution upon return or if it is impossible to return due to a natural disaster, then the applicant receives a permanent resident visa. Until then, applicants receive work permits and social security numbers, but are much more constrained in their activities than immigrants. It is a status that must be renewed annually until the case is adjudicated, and the delay can be as long as a decade or more. The nature of TPS is discussed in greater detail in chapter 8 on Central Americans since they continue to be the primary recipients.

Despite the reforms of 1986, undocumented immigrants or illegal aliens continued to be a major concern for the American public. Although they do receive some federal funding for public services, states are primarily responsible for public education, indigent health care, and general cash public assistance. Prior federal legislation had not specified whether states were responsible to provide education, care at publicly funded healthcare facilities, and other public services to undocumented immigrants. California hosts the largest number of both documented and undocumented immigrants, as well as refugees, and was experiencing a major anti-immigrant political movement. In 1994, California voters approved the controversial Proposition 187, which would have denied access to public services by undocumented immigrants on the grounds that the citizens of the state had suffered economic hardship as a result of illegal immigrants. It also obligated public servants, whether teachers, healthcare providers, social workers, police, or anyone else who might come in contact with undocumented immigrants, to verify an immigrant's status before provision of services and to report the undocumented to the INS for deportation.[29] This revision to the state's constitution was never implemented. A temporary restraining order was issued, arguing that the state was assuming the federal role of policing immigration and would be denying undocumented immigrants due process of law in violation of the Fourteenth Amendment if the procedures outlined in the proposition were implemented. Although the state argued that the proposition was not in conflict with federal law, the case was never resolved and the proposition became moot with the election of Gray Davis, an opponent of 187, as governor in 1996.

This episode in the country's most populous state served as an impetus for Congress to revisit the issue of undocumented immigration and of indigent services to immigrants who had in essence become a public charge. In 1996, Congress passed the Illegal Immigration Reform and Immigrant Responsibility Act (IIRIRA). This law increased the patrolling of the border and created more stringent penalties for those who entered unlawfully or who smuggled undocumented immigrants into the country. The IIRIRA reformed deportation procedures, expediting removal and making re-entry more difficult. It also addressed many of the concerns raised by Proposition 187 by requiring the foreign-born to provide proof of citizenship or lawful immigration status to receive public benefits and giving states the authority to limit the general public cash benefits given to immigrants. College students would need to show proof of lawful status and residency to receive public higher education benefits such as in-state tuition. Additionally, persons sponsoring extended family members for family-based preference visas would have to show proof of the financial ability to support the immigrant if necessary, and the affidavit of financial support would become a legally binding contract.[30] While this was portrayed as unjust treatment of Latino immigrants, the most common source region of working-class documented as well as undocumented immigrants, the law withstood legal challenges.

The attacks of September 11, 2001, on the World Trade Center in New York City, on the Pentagon in the nation's capital, and the aborted attack that crashed near Shanksville, Pennsylvania, raised unprecedented concerns about immigration and protection of the nation's borders. Several of those involved in the attacks had entered unlawfully via the Canadian border, which while patrolled, never received the attention that the border with Mexico had. Others had received student visas to attend the flight schools where they received the training necessary to carry out the attacks. Scrutiny of the Immigration and Naturalization Service (INS) revealed myriad problems, including visa and naturalization backlogs, TPS backlogs, improper processing of applications, and lost or destroyed records. While these problems had long been the concern of immigrants and immigrant advocacy groups, the revelations that the hijackers had used these methods to gain entry resulted in both public and political outcries for reform in the structure of the system. Within five weeks of the attack, Congress passed the USA Patriot Act, which, among its many counterterrorism components, called for increased patrolling of the northern border with Canada and more stringent scrutiny of immigrant visa applicants.[31]

The weaknesses in the immigration system were further magnified by continuing revelations of problems with the INS. It was finally determined that a complete restructuring of immigration and naturalization was necessary, again as a question of national security. By November of 2002, President Bush created a new cabinet-level department, the Department of Homeland Security (DHS), and the newly restructured Bureau of Citizenship and Immigration Services (BCIS) responsible for visa and naturalization applications was moved from the Department of Justice to this newly created department. Border enforcement was also moved to DHS, under the Directorate of Border and Transportation Services.

The process of immigrant entry continues to evolve. For example, in 2004, application for the diversity visa lottery moved entirely to the Internet. It has yet to be seen how the "digital divide" will affect those nationalities eligible for diversity visas, especially since this visa allotment process was created specifically for those adversely affected by the family-based preference system. Backlogs in adjudicating TPS applications and naturalization applications still exist, and several of the more extreme investigatory authorities granted by the USA Patriot Act are regularly being challenged. Another key area of immigration that is also evolving is refugee resettlement and the granting of political asylum.

Refugee Resettlement and Political Asylum

World War II brought about a significant change in immigration policy by reopening the door to Asian immigrants. It also brought about a change in response to those displaced by war and, particularly, those adversely affected by the Cold War.

Unlike immigration, which has proceeded continuously with intermittent policy changes, responses to refugees and displaced persons have been ad hoc and policies have not been consistent from crisis to crisis. The first crisis of displaced persons to which the United States responded with resettlement assistance was post–World War II Germany, Italy, and Austria. The war had left over one million displaced persons in its wake, and this was seen as a potential destabilizing force challenging the success of the Marshall Plan. In 1948, Congress passed the Displaced Persons Act, which permitted the admission of up to 205,000 displaced persons over a two-year period beginning July 1, 1948. These immigrants were to be charged against future quotas. However, no comparable plan was implemented for post-war Japan.

The post-war period saw the expansion of Soviet influence into Eastern Europe and the success of the Communist revolution in China. Selected religious and political groups in these countries were targeted as threats to the success of the new socialist or Communist governments, as were protesters against these governments. As Cold War tensions increased, these persecuted populations sought refuge in noncommunist states, and the nascent United Nations was called upon to respond. In 1951, the UN established a convention concerning refugees. This convention defined a refugee as a "person with a well-founded fear of being persecuted for reasons of race, religion, nationality, membership of a particular social group, or political opinion,"[32] and laid out what it believed to be appropriate responses in terms of treatment of refugees. Nineteen member countries were original signatories (the United States was not a signatory to the 1951 convention), and over the next four decades, 121 additional countries agreed to the convention, many adding their own caveats to the initial document.[33] This convention laid the foundation for the United Nations Protocol on Refugees, signed in 1967, to which the United States is a signatory, but as the Cold War escalated, the United States implemented a refugee policy targeted at "victims of Communism."

Refugee admissions were exempt from the quota and preference systems and received entry visas and, in some cases, humanitarian aid, something not given to regular immigrants. Under the Refugee Relief Act of 1953, the United States continued to admit displaced persons from Italy and Germany, and extended this category of admission to Greeks and Yugoslavs who were still limited by the 1952 quota system. A letter from President Eisenhower that accompanied the draft legislation set the stage for this and subsequent refugee policy by stating:

> These refugees, escapees, and distressed peoples now constitute an economic and political threat of constantly growing magnitude. They look to traditional American humanitarian concern for the oppressed. International political considerations are also factors which are involved. We should take reasonable steps to help these people to the extent that we share the obligation of the free world.[34]

The 1952 Immigration and Nationality Act had been implicitly influenced by Cold War events by making 50 percent of all quota visas available to highly skilled professionals that could prospectively help maintain a competitive edge over the Soviet Union. Among its provisions was authority given to the Attorney General to grant parole to immigrants who entered unlawfully but requested political asylum. Both implementation of the parole provision and subsequent refugee policy were explicitly geared toward Cold War foreign policy. The first application of this policy direction was toward refugees from the unsuccessful Hungarian revolution of 1956. Thirty-eight thousand Hungarian refugees were admitted to the United States, some 6,130 with Refugee Relief Act visas and the rest under the parole authority.[35]

A key weakness of the Refugee Relief Act was that it was essentially borrowing quota visas from future years to respond to immediate refugee crises. Congress addressed this problem in 1957 through the Refugee-Escapee Act, which removed the visa mortgaging requirement of the earlier act. This act also provided the policy definition of a refugee as a person fleeing persecution in Communist countries or in the Middle East, a definition that remained in effect until the passage of the Refugee Act of 1980. An additional 29,000 refugees were admitted under this act, primarily from Hungary, Korea, Yugoslavia, and China.[36]

During the 1950s, the Cold War appeared to be an Eastern Hemisphere phenomenon. Policies shifted drastically when Fidel Castro, leader of the Cuban Revolution of

1959, revealed that he was a Communist and that Cuba would now be strongly allied with the Soviet Union. Now both of the United States's closest non-contiguous neighbors were under Communist rule and seen as a security threat.[37] Cubans seeking to escape the new regime began to stream into Miami, and this new refugee crisis drew a country-specific policy response. The Refugee Resettlement Act of 1962 dispersed Cubans throughout the country in an unsuccessful attempt to prevent the development of a Cuban ghetto or a politically conscious Cuban enclave.[38] Cubans were admitted as refugees or were paroled and were given economic assistance to resettle outside of Miami. However, many secondarily migrated back to Miami or to pre-existing Cuban communities in New Jersey.

Thousands of Cubans continued to find ways of getting to the United States, assured that they would receive refugee status upon arrival, and subsequent to 1966, would receive permanent residency.[39] Fewer came during the 1970s as exiting Cuba became more difficult. A new wave of approximately 120,000 Cubans arrived in 1980 as a result of what became known as the Mariel Boatlift (Table 2.1). By then, though, a new refugee crisis had emerged—victims of the new Communist regimes in Vietnam, Cambodia, and Laos.

In 1975, the fall of Saigon to the Communist government of North Vietnam resulted in the mass exodus of South Vietnamese military families and civilians who had worked for U.S. or South Vietnamese government agencies. In the same year, Pol Pot began his reign of terror in Cambodia, and the Pathet Lao, the Lao communist party, took control of the government in Vientiane, both resulting in refugee migrations. The United Nations High Commissioner for Refugees (UNHCR) established refugee camps in nearby countries in order to process the hundreds of thousands of refugees who were streaming across the borders. UNHCR called upon UN-member countries, particularly signatories of the UN convention or the UN protocol on refugees, to receive these refugees for resettlement. Over the next fifteen years, the United States became the world's largest resettlement country, receiving approximately one million refugees from Southeast Asia. The needs of these refugees were much greater than those of the Cubans, and Congress responded with the Indochina Migration and Refugee Assistance Act to help meet the economic and cultural adjustment crisis that immediately resulted from this influx of migrants.

By 1980, it became apparent that there was a real need to codify refugee law and to establish an Office of Refugee Resettlement that would be distinct from the Immigration and Naturalization Service. The Refugee Act of 1980 removed the category of refugee from the 1965 preference system and established procedures for determining how many refugees would be resettled annually. It formalized the ad hoc responses to refugee needs by establishing a comprehensive refugee assistance program. It provided for the adjustment to permanent resident status of refugees and asylees within one year of resettlement or granting of asylum. It also defined refugees according to the UN Protocol on Refugees, but continued to preference "victims of Communism" in awarding refugee status. The act defined refugees as persons outside of their country of nationality, within their country of nationality, or having no nationality, who are unable or unwilling to either remain or return because of actual persecution or a well-founded fear of persecution on account of race, religion, nationality, membership in a particular social group, or political opinion.

The 1980 act differentiated between refugees and asylees in that refugee status would be granted prior to entry to the United States, whereas political asylum could be requested upon arrival in the United States. With this codification, refugee status and subsequent refugee assistance were also awarded to those exiting the former Soviet Union and other Eastern Bloc countries, particularly members of targeted religious groups such as Jews and Pentecostals. It was only preapproved refugees and not those whose asylum cases were pending who would receive the coveted refugee assistance.

The continuing role of the Cold War in the designation of refugee status became apparent during the 1980s when waves of Central Americans escaping their civil wars came to the United States hoping to be received in the same manner as the Cubans had been. However, it was the Nicaraguans escaping the short-lived Communist government of Daniel Ortega who received refugee status, while Guatemalans and Salvadorans petitioned for, and were typically denied political asylum. As was mentioned above, it was this pattern of systematic denial of asylum that resulted in the development of temporary protected status or TPS. The distinction among Central Americans seeking permanent residency in the United States was further solidified by the Nicaraguan Adjustment and Central American Relief Act (NACARA), passed in 1997. This law granted blanket amnesty to Nicaraguans and Cubans who had entered the United States without authorization since 1994, but further clarified the burden of proof Salvadorans and Guatemalans would need to provide to be granted political asylum and thus permanent residency.

Conclusion

Within two centuries, concerns over the presence of the foreign-born have come full circle. What began as a question of protecting the newly independent United States had by the 1800s become a concern for protecting native-born workers while remaining economically competitive. By World War I and World War II, certain immigrant groups were seen as threats to national security, but the selection of those groups was based more on cultural prejudice and perceived threat than on actual threats. The post–World War II era was the greatest period of economic expansion in the country's history to that point, and despite "McCarthyist" rhetoric and activities against the perceived threat of Communism, Congress radically restructured immigration, opening the doors to previously excluded regions of the world, and creating a globally representative population. By the late twentieth century, the question was whether the doors had been opened too widely, and the undocumented migrant became the perceived threat to economic security. Now in the early twenty-first century, in a period of unprecedented high and sustained immigration, entry into the United States with intent to stay is again seen as a national security concern. That said, though, post–World War II and Civil Rights Era immigration reform have redefined the ethnic geography of the United States, transforming its culture, reviving its cities, and establishing familial ties to every corner of the world.

Notes

1. New Spain incorporated what are now Mexico, the American Southwest, the Spanish Caribbean, and Central America.

2. Richard L. Nostrand, "The Spanish Borderlands," in *North America: The Historical Geography of a Changing Continent,* ed. Robert D. Mitchell and Paul A. Groves (Totowa, NJ: Rowman & Littlefield, 1987), 48–64.

3. Cole Harris, "France in North America," in *North America: The Historical Geography of a Changing Continent,* ed. Robert D. Mitchell and Paul A. Groves (Totowa, NJ: Rowman & Littlefield, 1987), 65–72.

4. Robert D. Mitchell, "The Colonial Origins of Anglo-America," in *North America: The Historical Geography of a Changing Continent,* ed. Robert D. Mitchell and Paul A. Groves (Totowa, NJ: Rowman & Littlefield, 1987), 93–120.

5. David L. Clawson, *Latin America and the Caribbean: Lands and Peoples* (Boston: McGraw-Hill, 2003).

6. Mitchell, "The Colonial Origins of Anglo-America."

7. U.S. Citizenship and Immigration Services, "Naturalization Act of June 18, 1798," "Aliens Act of June 25, 1798," "Aliens Enemy Act of July 6, 1798," <uscis.gov/graphics/shared/aboutus/statistics/legishist> (1 August 2004).

8. David J. Wishart, "Settling the Great Plains, 1850–1930: Prospects and Problems," in *North America: The Historical Geography of a Changing Continent*, ed. Robert D. Mitchell and Paul A. Groves (Totowa, NJ: Rowman & Littlefield, 1987), 255–278.

9. The Columbia Encyclopedia, "Preemption Act," <www.bartleby.com/65/pr/Preempti.html> (1 August 2004).

10. Wishart, "Settling the Great Plains, 1850–1930: Prospects and Problems."

11. Two web sites with excellent collections of anti-immigrant images are the Historical Society of Pennsylvania's Primary Sources: Anti-Immigrant Images (www.hsp.org/default.aspx?id=394#images) and the University of California, Davis History Project (historyproject.ucdavis.edu/imageapp.php?Major=IM&Minor=F), 10/27/04.

12. SanFranciscoChinatown.com, "California's Anti-Coolie Tax," <www.sanfranciscochinatown.com/history/1862anticoolietax.htm> (1 August 2004).

13. SanFranciscoChinatown.com, "Presidential Proclamation," <www.sanfranciscochinatown.com/history/1880proclaimation.html> (2 August 2004).

14. SanFranciscoChinatown.com, "1882 Chinese Exclusion Act," <www.sanfranciscochinatown.com/history/1882exclusionact.html> (2 August 2004).

15. Ines M. Miyares et al., "The Japanese in America," in *Ethnicity in Contemporary America*, ed. Jesse O. McKee (Lanham, MD: Rowman & Littlefield, 2000), 263–282.

16. A Reader's Companion to American History, "Gentlemen's Agreement," <college.hmco.com/history/readerscomp/rcah/html/ah_035600_gentlemensag.htm> (2 August 2004).

17. U.S. Citizenship and Immigration Services, "Immigration Act of March 3, 1891," <uscis.gov/graphics/shared/aboutus/statistics/legishist> (2 August 2004).

18. In 1913, at the separation of the Departments of Commerce and of Labor, the Bureau was transferred to the Department of Labor. In 1940, the Immigration and Nationalization Service was transferred to the Department of Justice as a World War II–era measure of national security. The concern for immigration as a national security issue was magnified by the attacks on September 11, 2001, and the reorganized Bureau of Citizenship and Immigration Services (BCIS) came under the umbrella of the new Department of Homeland Security in 2002.

19. U.S. Citizenship and Immigration Services, "Immigration Act of February 5, 1917," "Quota Law of May 19, 1921," <uscis.gov/graphics/shared/aboutus/statistics/legishist> (2 August 2004).

20. U.S. Citizenship and Immigration Services, "Immigration Act of February 5, 1917," <uscis.gov/graphics/shared/aboutus/statistics/legishist> (2 August 2004).

21. U.S. Citizenship and Immigration Services, "Immigration Act of May 26, 1924," <uscis.gov/graphics/shared/aboutus/statistics/legishist> (3 August 2004).

22. U.S. Citizenship and Immigration Services, "Fiscal Year 2002 Yearbook of Immigration Statistics, Table 2," <uscis.gov/graphics/shared/aboutus/statistics/ybpage.htm> (3 August 2004).

23. U.S. Citizenship and Immigration Services, Act of August 19, 1950, <uscis.gov/graphics/shared/aboutus/statistics/legishist> (4 August 2004).

24. U.S. Citizenship and Immigration Services, "Act of April 29, 1943," "Act of February 14, 1944," <uscis.gov/graphics/shared/aboutus/statistics/legishist> (4 August 2004).

25. U.S. Citizenship and Immigration Services, "Immigration and Nationality Act of June 27, 1952," <uscis.gov/graphics/shared/aboutus/statistics/legishist> (4 August 2004).

26. Ines M. Miyares, "Changing Latinization of New York City," in *Hispanic Spaces, Latino Places*, ed. Daniel D. Arreola (Austin: University of Texas Press, 2004), 145–166.

27. This would include those who enter with valid visas such as students, who are employable only by the college or university that accepted them, and tourists, who are not employable in the United States.

28. U.S. Citizenship and Immigration Services, "Immigration Reform and Control Act of November 6, 1986," <uscis.gov/graphics/shared/aboutus/statistics/legishist> (4 August 2004).

29. Proposition 187: Text of Proposed Law, <www.americanpatrol.com/REFERENCE/prop187text.html> (5 August 2004).

30. U.S. Citizenship and Immigration Services, "Illegal Immigration Reform and Immigrant Responsibility Act of September 30, 1996," <uscis.gov/graphics/shared/aboutus/statistics/legishist> (5 August 2004).

31. Electronic Privacy Information Center, "USA Patriot Act of October 24, 2001," <www.epic.org/privacy/terrorism/hr3162.html> (5 August 2004).

32. Convention relating to the Status of Refugees adopted on 28 July 1951 by the United Nations Conference of Plenipotentiaries on the Status of Refugees and Stateless Persons convened under General Assembly resolution 429 (V) of 14 December 1950.

33. United Nations Treaty Collection, "2. Convention Relating to the Status of Refugees, Geneva, 28 July 1951," <www.unhchr.ch/html/menu3/b/treaty2ref.htm> (5 August 2004).

34. FAIR U.S. Immigration History, "Refugee Admissions in the 1950s and 1960s," <209.25.133.193/html/03102603.htm> (6 August 2004).

35. FAIR U.S. Immigration History, "Refugee Admissions."

36. FAIR U.S. Immigration History, "Refugee Admissions."

37. The northeast coast of Siberia is 55 miles from the Alaskan border, making Russia the United States' nearest noncontiguous neighbor, followed by Cuba, whose northernmost point, Boca Camarioca, is 90 miles south of Key West, Florida.

38. Felix R. Masud-Piloto, *With Open Arms* (Totowa, NJ: Rowman & Littlefield, 1988).

39. U.S. Citizenship and Immigration Services, "Act of November 2, 1966," <uscis.gov/graphics/shared/aboutus/statistics/legishist> (6 August 2004).

CHAPTER 3

Native Americans

Kate A. Berry, Zoltán Grossman, and L. HoMana Pawiki

The indigenous peoples of the United States—Native Americans—include a variety of people who identify as American Indians or Alaska Natives, but most commonly identify by a tribal nation affiliation.[1] While the percentage of individuals in the United States identifying as Native American (or American Indian/Alaska Native) is not large, the ethnic geographies of non-immigrant indigenous people are distinctive in many respects and provide essential insights to understanding the construction of the American state and the plurality of ethnic and national identities in the United States.

In discussing Native American people in the early twenty-first century, there must be an understanding of times past. The experience of colonization deserves attention in understanding contemporary Native Americans and their geographies. As the indigenous people of North America, Native Americans were colonized on their own land, the places to which they trace their social, cultural, and religious origins. Russell Thornton describes America as a series of changing frontiers created through interactions between Europeans (and later Euro-Americans) and diverse Native peoples, through which all were changed.[2] Today many Native Americans seek to remain as sovereign nations distinct from American society while simultaneously participating in it. Native Americans are unique among ethnic and racial groups in their formal tribal affiliations and in their relationship with the larger United States.

This chapter underscores the diversity of tribes/bands, languages, governments, cultures, spiritual beliefs, resource use, and land control among Native Americans. At the same time, important commonalities have been highlighted: the importance of the past in shaping present indigenous identity, the significance of U.S.-tribal governmental relations, the resiliency of Native Americans, the character of Indian Country, and issues of tribal sovereignty and nationalism.

Historical Experience

At least 500 distinct indigenous peoples lived in the present-day territory of the United States at the time of the Conquest. Estimates of their precolonial population range from

51

1 million to 18 million to many millions more.[3] Theories of their origins include the theory of an Asian origin across the Bering Strait land bridge, as well as the many varied "creation stories" of individual tribes that trace their origin elsewhere. Whatever their origins or population numbers, the Native peoples of pre-colonial America were marked by incredible cultural diversity in terms of language, land use, material culture, spiritual systems, social customs and organization, and political and economic structures.

SPATIAL DIVERSITY

Native languages developed as part of different language families, ranging from the small Keresan or Penutian families to the spatially widespread Algonquian, Siouan, Iroquoian, and Athabascan families. The spatial extent of the larger families provides evidence of ancient migrations. The Algonquian family, for example, includes the Mi'kmaq (Micmac) and Ojibwe (Chippewa) in the east, and the Skisika (Blackfeet) and Yurok in the west. The Athabascan family includes the Dene in Alaska and the Northwest Territories, and the Hoopa and Diné (Navajo) in the south.

Although tribes may be related linguistically, they have adapted to the material culture of the area in which they settled. The Hoopa and Yurok, for example, are of different language families, but have a remarkably similar riverine culture and ceremonial life revolving around salmon, deer, plant reeds, and other natural resources of the northern California coast. Tribes can be defined as part of larger "culture areas" based on ecological similarities such as the Arctic tundra, Subarctic boreal forests, Northeast woodlands, the Southeast, and semiarid Southwest, as well as areas defined by the landscapes of the Pacific Northwest and inland Plateau region, the California coast, Great Basin, and the Great Plains.

Within each of these culture areas, different tribes or bands practiced different modes of subsistence, stressing hunting, fishing, gathering, or farming, usually in seasonal cycles. These cycles coincided with distinct migratory cycles of individual villages located within well-defined territories, in movements later mistaken by Europeans for nomadic roaming. In the Columbian Exchange, Native peoples of the Americas contributed many crops, such as corn, tomatoes, potatoes, chocolate, and many medicines, and traditional ecological knowledge to the rest of the world.[4]

The social organization, family structures, and customs of Native peoples also exhibited wide spatial variations. Native peoples lived in highly decentralized and democratic bands subsisting on roots and tubers in the Great Basin, or fish and wild rice in the northeastern woodlands. Mississippian-culture peoples built Cahokia (near present-day St. Louis), which at its height around 1200–1400 A.D. was a large city with 20,000 inhabitants organized in a highly centralized and religiously hierarchical society centered on huge ceremonial mounds. In addition to strict behavior codes, Native American family and kinship were heavily influenced by a deep sense of spiritual relationship.[5] Types of social organizations and lifeways could even vary within a cultural area. As some culture groups lived on fish or marine mammals, others actively shaped the landscape through fire to enhance prospects of hunting or growing crops.

The Conquest beginning in 1492 also affected different Native peoples in different ways. The European "Doctrine of Discovery" defined the Americas as *Terra Nullis* (Empty Land) that could be inhabited by Native peoples, but not under their sovereign control. European powers were interested in religiously converting Native peoples, and in controlling natural resources, such as land, gold, and furs. Some eastern tribes positioned themselves as valuable "middlemen" in the fur trade, and at first held a military and political advantage over European powers in their domains.[6] Some tribes (particularly on the coasts) were devastated by common European diseases that had not yet swept across American territories.[7] In response, some tribes or parts of tribes converted to Christianity or had children with Europeans, while other tribes strongly held onto their spiritual and cultural beliefs, even if they practiced them underground. Native peoples who adopted Christianity sometimes mixed it with indigenous beliefs and customs.

Euro-Americans emphasized not only religious conversion but transformed Indians into farmers who would practice the more "civilized" form of sedentary agriculture, settling them on reservations to make way for American settlement. Native resistance to American settler colonialism had some limited successes, such as unity around Tecumseh's rebellion in the 1810s, or Lakota defeats of the U.S. Army in the 1860s–1870s. Yet Americans prevailed by dividing and conquering tribes, carrying out massacres of Native rebels and civilians, and exterminating their natural resource base (such as trees and buffalo). By the 1890s, most Native Americans in the continental United States were confined to reservations, which were only a tiny fraction of their original homelands. Others were forced to move from their original homelands, and some were left completely landless. To most U.S. citizens at the turn of the twentieth century, Native Americans had become a tiny minority that had lost their cultures and lands, and were on their way to disappearing as distinct peoples.

CONTESTING GOVERNMENT CONTROL

Early formal treaty-making was a colonial policy to secure alliances with Native peoples before rival colonial powers did so. As a result, these policies generally treated the Native nations as sovereigns.[8] The U.S. government signed approximately 371 treaties with Native nations, whether as part of peace settlements, land cessions, material aid agreements, or a combination of different provisions before federal processes were changed in 1871. The treaties also played a major role in consolidating different Native bands into a single voice in relation to the settler society. Treaties also defined and set boundaries between Native "national" territories, where only mutual understandings and shifting land-use agreements between Native peoples had previously existed.[9] As a result, Native nations assumed some characteristics of European sovereign states—with more centralized authority and demarcated boundaries.

Federal Indian policy is commonly misinterpreted as having granted Native peoples new political or territorial rights, or as having "accorded special group rights."[10] Rather than serving as gifts to the tribes, many treaties instead served as the tribes' concessions of their preexisting rights over land and resources to the United States, with certain access and use rights retained by the tribes in order to end or prevent armed conflict between the two signatory nations.[11] Many of the treaties contained clauses for continued use of the treaty-ceded territories outside reservations for cultural or economic sustenance uses—such as religious ceremonies, hunting, gathering or fishing—in effect maintaining treaty lands as part of "Indian Country." This is why many recent Native rights battles have centered on treaty rights, since those rights contain or imply a larger recognition of nationhood. Article VI of the U.S. Constitution defined treaties as the "supreme law of the land."

Federal Indian policy in the nineteenth and twentieth centuries swung like a pendulum between unilateralist policies that sought to assimilate Indians, and bilateralist policies that recognized tribes as distinct peoples.[12] Policies that were intended to weaken Native territorial or cultural identity often backfired on government policymakers, and had the unintended effect of heightening Native nationalism.

During the *Removal Era* of the 1820s–1850s, federal troops marched many Native peoples westward to new reservations west of the Mississippi River. While some forced removals were largely successful from the federal government's perspective, such as the "Trail of Tears" from the Southeast to Oklahoma, other attempts, notably in the western Great Lakes region, were strongly resisted and stimulated a Native determination to stay in or return to their homelands. After the 1850s, a primary concern of federal Indian policy was to settle Native Americans on reservations and diminish their control over their homelands, while recognizing at least a modicum of Native territoriality. Ironically, the "trust responsibility" established by federal agencies toward their Indian "wards" was later used as a legal tool to defend tribes from control by state and local governments.[13]

Federal policies changed in the *Allotment Era* of the 1880s–1920s, as the federal government privatized many reservation lands and sold off large tracts of "excess" lands to non-Indians.[14] Allotment undermined tribal control over the reservation land base. At the same time, many Native youths were moved to boarding schools in a coordinated church-government effort to forcibly assimilate them into mainstream American culture. The schools brought Native youths into contact with each other, and inadvertently educated some of the youths in the skills they later used to fight for tribal rights. Under the 1924 Citizenship Act, all American Indians were made U.S. citizens, in addition to their Native national citizenship.

The resulting economic devastation of the *Allotment Era* led to calls by the late 1920s for increased Indian self-government, which were realized under the 1934 Indian Reorganization Act (IRA). The IRA, initiated as part of the "Indian New Deal," established federally approved tribal council governments on reservations that voted for the system. While most tribes approved the IRA system, some tribes or factions within tribes rejected the IRA as undermining their traditional chief system or self-organized tribal council. Other tribes that adopted this model for government structure, such as the *Apsaalooke*, or Crow, managed to use the reservation council system to reinforce their tribal identity.[15] In other cases, federally recognized tribal government and the traditional governance system functioned as parallel institutions for decades—sometimes in intense conflict (such as on South Dakota's Pine Ridge Reservation). While the IRA was partly intended to replace Native governance structures with U.S. models of governance, it did not replace all traditional forms of leadership.

In the *Termination Era* during the 1950s and early 1960s the federal government unilaterally sought to "terminate" the federal status of some economically successful tribes, such as the Menominee in Wisconsin and the Klamath in Oregon. The stated goal was to encourage tribal members to more fully assimilate into American society. Termination policies triggered a cultural and political counterreaction among both traditionalists and IRA tribal governments that brought an end to the policy. Concurrent with termination policies were federal policies that sought to assimilate Native Americans and improve their economic standing by relocating them to urban areas. Tribal members were provided with some minor financial incentives to move to urban areas and given the false promises of jobs and good housing, while at the same time termination policy foresaw a cutoff of federal aid to rural reservations, giving tribal members little choice but to leave for the cities. Federal Indian urban relocation policy resulted in members of different tribes being brought together in cities such as Chicago, Minneapolis, Denver, and Los Angeles, which led to increased mutual discussions and action, and the emergence of a loose "pan-Indian" social identity.[16] Urban-based Indians were also directly exposed to the civil rights and "Black Power" movements, showing them how a pan-Indian community could be politically mobilized.

Urbanization served as a "transmission belt for nationalism" by overcoming localism and increasing alienation.[17] The birth of the "urban Indian" built bridges between indigenous peoples that would not have been possible on reservations spatially isolated from one another. Native militancy and the formation of the American Indian Movement (AIM) in the late 1960s and 1970s furthered this process as dislocated Indians became a receptive audience, especially those who had been brought up by traditionalist families on the reservations. Diverse tribes externally became defined as a single Amerindian "race"—a status that many Native Americans resented, but also utilized in order to increase intertribal unity. The Indian rights movement pushed U.S. policy and legal decisions toward recognizing tribal governments' political "self-determination," that in some respects is similar to the bilateral policies of the Indian New Deal. As an example, in 1978 Native religions were legalized when Congress passed the American Indian Religious Freedom Act.

This trend toward greater federal recognition of Native sovereignty stimulated a counterreaction among some non-Indians both on and off of the reservations. Several anti-treaty organizations were founded in the 1970s to protest Indian treaty rights and tribal sovereignty. Such groups united non-Indian reservation residents who opposed tribal jurisdiction with sportsmen who opposed tribal hunting and fishing rights. Tribes were criticized both for their social and economic dependency on the federal government and for promoting tribal economic development and cultural revitalization on reservations. At the same time, non-Indians continued to romanticize Native Americans and often exploited Native cultures and religions for their own purposes.

The 1990s ushered in a new era in Indian Country that extended the idea of "self-determination" beyond the political realm to include economic, cultural, and environmental concerns. AIM activists diversified their organizing to form reservation-based environmental and women's groups. The rise of Indian casinos gave some tribes economic opportunities they had not had for centuries. The protection of burials, sacred objects, and cultural images became somewhat easier, and some tribes began to regulate environmental quality, in some cases even protecting the environment of rural non-Indians living outside the reservations. Despite these advances, there are continuing problems facing Indian Country with reference to diminishment of reservation land bases, rising rates of disease, crime, and youth alienation in many Native communities, and continued poverty for many Native Americans.[18]

Settlement Patterns

In 2000 nearly two-thirds of Native Americans (64%) lived off reservations or tribal lands (Fig. 3.1). Many lived in major urban areas as indicated by the largest absolute population of Native Americans being concentrated in urban counties. Table 3.1 shows that many of the counties with highest populations of Native Americans are large urban counties in the western United States, such as Los Angeles County, and Maricopa County centered in Phoenix and Tucson. In these urban counties the proportion of Native Americans to the total population is quite low.

The concentration of Native Americans in urban areas is partially the result of mid-twentieth-century federal policies on urban relocation. Economic and social reasons, such as more employment opportunities and greater educational options, also

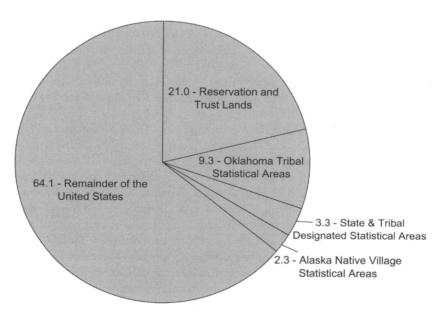

Figure 3.1.   *Percent Native American Population by Place of Residence, 2000.*
Source: Census 2000, Summary File 4.

Table 3.1. Counties with Highest Population Numbers of American Indians/Alaska Natives (AIAN) in 2000

County Rank	Name	State	Total County Population	Total AIAN Alone Population	Percent
1	Los Angeles	CA	9,519,338	76,988	0.8
2	Maricopa	AZ	3,072,149	56,706	1.8
3	McKinley	NM	74,798	55,892	74.7
4	Apache	AZ	69,423	53,375	76.9
5	Robeson	NC	123,339	46,896	38.0
6	Navajo	AZ	97,470	46,532	47.7
7	San Juan	NM	113,801	41,968	36.9
8	Coconino	AZ	116,320	33,161	28.5
9	Tulsa	OK	563,299	29,316	5.2
10	Pima	AZ	843,746	27,178	3.2

Source: Census 2000.

provide an explanation for the growing number of Native Americans residing in cities. Specific places within a city may be invested with meanings in ways that contribute to pan-Indian urban culture and community, such as a common reference for a particular coffee shop, art gallery, business, or roadside wall.[19] So-called urban Indians often spend part of their lives in a city and part on a reservation. Circular migration between city and reservation corresponds to individual options and family and community obligations.[20] Urban tribal members can vote in most tribal elections.

In addition to large metropolitan areas, many Native Americans live in towns and cities adjacent to their reservation (Map 3.1). These "border towns" may provide enhanced economic and educational options for tribal members and still allow for spatial proximity to family and opportunities on the reservation. On the other hand, these communities often are a major source of friction with reservation residents and exploit tribal members for financial gain. An example of an off-reservation border town is White Clay, Nebraska, a tiny community adjacent to the Pine Ridge Reservation. While there is a population of only 22 people, four million cans of beer are sold in White Clay annually to residents of the "dry" reservation, contributing to problems of alcoholism and social instability among the Oglala Lakota.

Native Americans in pre-contact periods lived in traditional settlement communities. Traditional homelands provided familiar sources of sustenance that met physical and spiritual needs. For those tribes relocated to far-removed sites in the nineteenth and twentieth centuries, their new reservation lands often seemed barren and harsh. Geographically based cultural and spiritual systems that were attached to particular environments were difficult to maintain. Destruction of these environments caused spiritual and psychological injury for many Native Americans, as in the case of the inability of Mohawks on the St. Regis (Akewesasne) Reservation to fish in the polluted

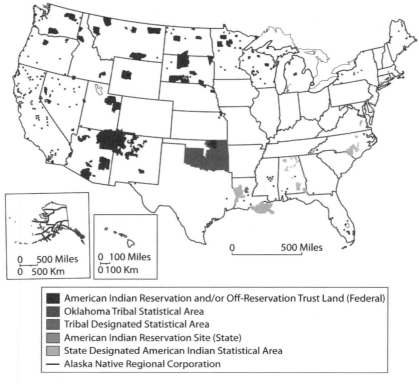

Map 3.1.   Indian Country, 2000.
Source: Census 2000, Summary File 2 (One Race).

St. Lawrence River. Nevertheless, decades of family living on reservations has invested reservation lands with a sense of place for many tribal members.[21]

Many Native Americans today still spend part of their lives residing on a reservation. Table 3.2 and Map 3.2 show that counties with the highest proportion of Native Americans are primarily rural counties with dispersed populations. Many of these counties are adjacent to or surround one or more reservations or Alaska Native communities.

Economic conditions on some reservations have changed with the advent of tribal gaming on reservation lands. Tribal gaming has enabled Native nations to fund social programs, add to the reservation land base, develop businesses, protect the environment, and lobby and litigate for their legal protection. In many counties with casinos, the tribes have become the largest employers, not only of tribal members but of non-Indians, and welfare rates have dropped dramatically. Yet gaming has also led to divisions and high debt within tribes, conflicts with tribes situated in areas with less population or tourist access, and increased conflicts with state and local governments wanting a stake in the economic gains.

Table 3.2. Counties with Highest Proportion of American Indian/Alaska Native (AIAN) Population in 2000

Rank	County Name	State	Total County Population	Total AIAN Alone Population	Percent
1	Shannon	SD	12,466	11,743	94.2
2	Wade Hampton Census Area	AK	7,028	6,503	92.5
3	Menominee	WI	4,562	3,981	87.3
4	Todd	SD	9,050	7,747	85.6
5	Sioux	ND	4,044	3,421	84.6
6	Northwest Arctic Borough	AK	7,208	5,944	82.5
7	Bethel Census Area	AK	16,006	13,114	81.9
8	Buffalo	SD	2,032	1,658	81.6
9	Apache	AZ	69,423	53,375	76.9
10	Nome Census Area	AK	9,196	6,915	75.2

Source: U.S. Census Bureau, Census 2000 Summary File 1; Internet release date: August 13, 2001.

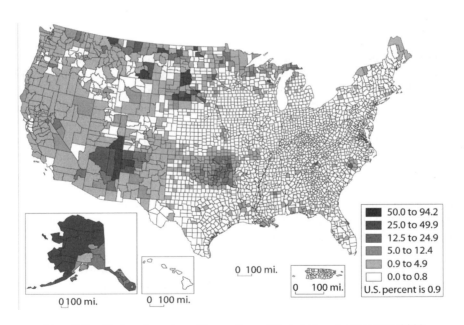

50.0 to 94.2
25.0 to 49.9
12.5 to 24.9
5.0 to 12.4
0.9 to 4.9
0.0 to 0.8
U.S. percent is 0.9

0 100 mi.

Map 3.2. Native American Proportion of Population by County, 2000.
Source: Synthia Brewer and Trudy Suchan, Mapping Census 2000:
The Geography of Diversity *(Redlands, CA: ESRI, 2001).*

Native American Identity and Population

Any discussion about settlement patterns of Native Americans in the United States raises significant issues about who is Native American. In other words, central to any geographic discussion of where Native Americans live are questions about how identity is distinguished. Two basic perspectives have developed with respect to Native American identity. The first is that each federally recognized tribal government defines its own members. The second is self-identification, and this is the basis of U.S. Census demographic profiles of Native Americans. The growth and decline of Native American population counts reflect both historical conditions and governmental policies.

Each tribal government determines its criteria for membership so that membership is not based on self-identification. Some tribes establish that a member must be of a specified blood quantum, and others define a member to be a descendant enrolled on a historic membership list. Other criteria that have been used to demarcate a population include community recognition, cultural association, residence within a geographic boundary, and common language usage.[22]

The enrollment process has origins in the historical practices of the federal government vis-à-vis American Indian and Alaska Native people and their rights as specified in treaties. "As the U.S. government dispossessed Native peoples, treaties established specific rights, privileges, goods, and money to which those party to a treaty—both tribes as entities and individual names of tribal members—were entitled. The practices of creating formal censuses and keeping lists of names of tribal members evolved to ensure an accurate and equitable distribution of benefits."[23]

Today 562 federally recognized tribal governments maintain databases of tribal member enrollees. Federal legislation as well as increasing tribal government needs require formal maintenance and regulation of tribal rolls by tribal governments. Tribal members have tribal membership cards and usually have a tribal enrollment number. Tribal membership is a hallmark—one in a succession—that depicts relationships between the federal government and Native Americans.

In contrast to formal identification as a tribal member, the U.S. Census does not require proof of membership from an individual who identifies as American Indian or Alaska Native. In 2000, the Census identifies American Indian/Alaska Native as one of five possible self-identified racial categories based upon Office of Management and Budget definitions and guidelines. Population estimates of Native Americans based on racial data in the U.S. Census represent a single moment in time that relies upon individuals' self-identification of ethnicity and race.[24]

Self-identification as Native American warrants examination. An individual (or group of individuals) may change responses to race and ethnic identity questions over time due to variations in question wording or changes in political, social, or economic conditions.[25] Some of the stigma of being identified as Native American was reduced by indigenous political mobilization in the 1960s and 1970s (through AIM and other groups) along with other ethnic pride movements. This change affected people of mixed racial and ethnic ancestry who previously might have refused to identify their Native American background because of a stigma as well as individuals with trace

Native American background who wanted to affirm their support for marginalized groups or a romanticized ethnic identity.[26]

Improving fertility and mortality rates in combination with increased numbers of people identifying as Native American who had only partial or distant indigenous ancestry produced a phenomenal growth rate in Native Americans from 1960 to 1990, which Jeffrey Passel described as "demographically impossible without immigration"[27] (Fig. 3.2). Gary Sandefur, Ronald Rindfuss, and Barney Cohen attribute a 4.2 percent increase of the Native American population during this time period to changes in self-identification from one census to the next.[28]

Between the 1990 Census and 2000 Census federal government definitions and public perceptions converged to produce an extraordinary range of population growth estimates from 26.4 percent to 110 percent (Table 3.3). The 26.4 percent increase, twice the U.S. general population growth, includes those people who indicated only *one* race—that of American Indian/Alaska Native. But because the 2000 Census allowed for single or multiple racial categories, a total of 2.2 million people (1.5% of the U.S. population) identified as American Indian/Alaska Native. This statistic includes those with only a single racial identity as American Indian/Alaska Native as

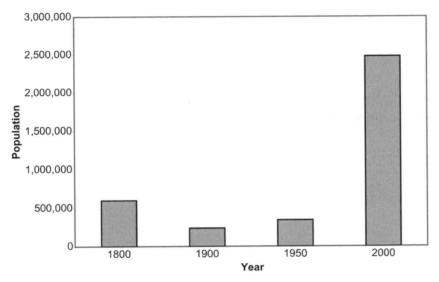

Figure 3.2.   American Indian Population, 1800–2000. Source: For 1800 data, Russell Thornton, American Indian Holocaust and Survival: A Population History since 1492 *(Norman: University of Oklahoma Press, 1987), 133. For 1900 and 1950 data, Campbell Gibson and Kay Jung, "Historical Census Statistics on Population Totals by Race, 1790 to 1990, and by Hispanic Origin, 1970 to 1990, for the United States, Regions, Divisions, and States," U.S. Census Bureau Population Division Working Paper Series no. 26, 2002. For 2000 data, U.S. Census 2000 for American Indian/Alaskan Natives alone. Figures are rounded to the nearest 1000.*

well as all those who identified as American Indian/Alaska Native in combination with one or more other racial identities. This results in a 110 percent increase from the 1990 Census when respondents could report only one race.

Scholars often portray ethnic movements as a throwback to preserve consciousness from a past era.[29] Native nationalists are often accused of seeking a return to premodern social and political forms. Yet Native traditional systems today are not simply backward-looking. The contemporary Native movement can instead be viewed as a resurgence, or even as a renaissance.[30] Much as the Italian Renaissance adapted Greco-Roman values to a new historical context, the Native Renaissance adapts traditional values to modern society, without necessarily re-creating old societies. Native scholars tend to reject both premodernist and modernist analysis, arguing that Native nationalists do not seek a strict reimplementation of previous forms, but a selective revitalization of elements of an existing culture, adapted to a global technological society.[31] The goal is not a simple regression to the tribal past, but for modern Native nations to move beyond the colonial "negation" of tribal societies, and progress on their own terms.

Native communities in the United States today are not monolithic, and contain their own diversity and schisms. Non-Indian outsiders attending a powwow may see a singular pan-Indian identity. But to the Native dancers and their families, differences between tribal identities are always in the foreground, as are band, clan, and family differences within tribes. Class differences affect Native communities, though they are profoundly shaped by Indian-white relations and tribal government structures. Gender, sexuality, and age differences also affect the Native social landscape, and interact with cultural and spiritual practices in ways that are often unfamiliar to non-Indians.

Table 3.3.   National Change in Native American Population, 1990–2000

	Population Size (U.S. totals)	Percent of Total U.S. Population	Percentage Increase, 1990 to 2000
1990 American Indian, Eskimo, or Aleut	1,959,234	0.8%	—
2000 American Indian and Alaska Native (AIAN) only	2,475,956	0.6%	26.4%
2000 American Indian and Alaska Native (AIAN) alone and in combination with one or more races	4,119,301	1.5%	110.0%

Source: American Indian and Alaska Native Population: 2000; Census 2000 Brief.

While Native Americans have their cultural and spiritual life strongly integrated with the rest of the natural world, their distinct spiritual identities cannot be simply defined as part of a vague indigenous animism. Cultures have identified specific sacred sites as important in their origin stories, clan structures, spiritual mythology, or ancestral burials. Protecting these sacred sites from modern abuse or development has become a priority of some tribes, rendered more difficult by the prohibition on revealing spiritual matters to nonadherents. The sites construct a sacred geography that equates spirituality with place, rather than only with religious dwellings.[32]

Different tribal factions may take diverse approaches to basic questions of Native rights and land use, particularly under strong economic or political pressure from the dominant society. Different factions within tribes may address land use with terms so vastly different that it is difficult to tell they are describing the same plot of land. Tribal officials often take a proprietary or economic approach to land use, tribal attorneys usually stress legal jurisdictional questions, and tribal traditionalists emphasize ethnohistorical and spiritual values attached to land.[33] This is an oversimplified picture, since tribal factions often overlap, and Native political survival skills seem to overcome most temporary factional schisms. But at any point in time, an overly generalized view of Native perspectives can gloss over the range of identities and opinions within Native nations.

Case Study: The Nez Perce Nation

> The life that we have is the life that we want to hold on to—our Indian ways. These ways were left here from our old people. Our ancestors done it that way—one heart to the other. It's still here.
>
> —Nez Perce elder Horace Axtell[34]

The homeland of the Nez Perce (*Nimiipu*) Nation once encompassed 13.2 million acres in Oregon, Idaho, and Washington. After the introduction of livestock by the Spanish in North America, the Nez Perce became known for their vast herds of Appaloosa horses and Spanish cattle, and became one of the most powerful tribes in the Plateau culture area (Map 3.3).

The Nez Perce welcomed the peaceful message of the Lewis and Clark expedition in 1805. It was not long, however, before their homeland was overrun by traders who introduced diseases and alcohol, American settlers who took tribal lands, and Christian missionaries who took issue with the *Nimiipu* Longhouse religion.

Like other tribes in the Columbia-Snake Basin, the Nez Perce signed the 1855 treaty with the federal government. The treaty recognized their control over a 7.5 million-acre reservation.[35] With the discovery of gold in the Wallowa Valley of northeastern Oregon, the tribe was forced to negotiate an 1863 treaty that further diminished their reservation to 750,000 acres.[36] The band led by Chief Joseph was offered a reservation in the Wallowa Valley, but local settlers vociferously opposed the offer.

In 1877, land conflicts in the valley led to all-out war between the U.S. Army and those Nez Perce who had refused to sign the treaty. Chief Joseph led the efforts of

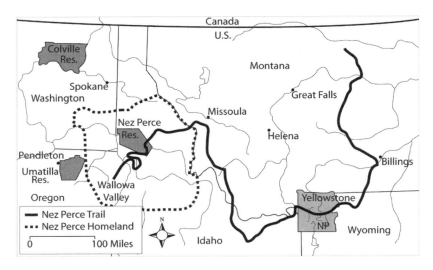

Map 3.3.   *The 1877 Nez Perce War was a turning point in the history of the Nez Perce nation. Chief Joseph and other chiefs who refused to sign a treaty giving up their Wallowa Valley homeland retreated, and successfully repelled U.S. military attacks until they almost reached Canada. After their defeat, most Nez Perce ended up on a reservation in Idaho, while Joseph's followers were sent to the Colville Reservation in Washington State and others settled on the Umatilla Reservation, closer to the Wallowa Valley.*

"nontreaty" Nez Perce who did not want to sign away their homeland. As spiritual leader Toolhulhulsote stated in talks with the U.S. Army, "The earth is part of my body and I never gave up the earth. . . . What person pretended to divide the land and put me on it?" Chief Joseph and other nontreaty chiefs led 800 refugees in a 1,600-mile, three-month retreat across four states.[37] Two hundred fifty Nez Perce warriors fought a running series of battles that held off U.S. soldiers in more than twenty engagements. The soldiers targeted not only Nez Perce civilians, but also killed many of their Appaloosa horses. Finally, in the Bear Paw Mountains of Montana, only forty miles from safety in British Canada, the Nez Perce were defeated. Chief Joseph delivered his famous "I will fight no more forever" speech, and surrendered to the U.S. Army.[38]

The remnants of Joseph's band were forcibly removed to unfamiliar and distant lands in Oklahoma and Kansas, where many died. After ten years they were allowed to return to the Northwest, but not to the Wallowa Valley. Joseph returned twice to Wallowa Valley to resecure land, but was rebuffed both times by white settlers. His band settled instead on the Colville Reservation, at Nespellem, Washington, where Joseph died in 1904. Other nontreaty Nez Perce moved to the Umatilla Reservation in Oregon.[39]

Bands that signed the treaty were allowed to form a federally recognized reservation around Lapwai, Idaho, where many Nez Perce were converted to Presbyterianism. Yet they lost most of their tribal landholdings during the Allotment Era, with 500,000 acres opened to white settlement, and only 250,000 acres remaining in the hands of the tribe or individual tribal members. The dispossession of much of their reservation land base, combined with the loss of their horse and cattle herds, rendered the Nez Perce economically dependent and poor. Access to the salmon runs that had been guaranteed in the treaties was also severely restricted, and the salmon themselves were threatened by the loss of habitat and dam construction.

Through the late twentieth century, the Nez Perce remained geographically divided between the Lapwai, Colville, and Umatilla reservations, but their divisions were not only physical in nature. The splits between treaty and nontreaty Nez Perce, and adherents of traditional and Christian religions also remained. The Nez Perce of Idaho set up an IRA government during the Indian New Deal, but Nez Perce on other reservations had to function as minorities within multitribal governments. Like other Native Americans, the Nez Perce were pressured to leave the reservations for boarding schools and urban employment (in cities such as Seattle), particularly during the mid- and later twentieth century.

Facing a potential loss of their culture and the natural resources upon which it depended, the Nez Perce began to again fight for their rights, this time in the courts. In a 1943 fishing case and a 1951 deer hunting case, tribal members reasserted their off-reservation treaty rights. Their court victories were part of the larger and mostly successful fight for tribal treaty rights in the Northwest during the mid-1960s and 1970s. The political and cultural resurgence of the tribe was marked by the 1977 centennial of the Nez Perce War, which initiated Lapwai's annual Chief Joseph and Warriors Pow-wow, honoring the descendants of the warriors who earlier fought the U.S. Army.

With three other reservations, the Nez Perce Tribe is part of the Columbia River Inter-Tribal Fish Commission (CRITFC), which advocates for tribal positions on salmon restoration.[40] The CRITFC tribes have called for the dismantling of four hydroelectric dams on the Snake River, which adversely affect salmon migration and spawning. In 2004, the tribe initiated a federal lawsuit accusing the state and federal governments of prioritizing hydroelectric production over implementing an agreement to restore salmon runs.[41] The Nez Perce have been critical of the Dworshak Dam on the North Fork Clearwater River within the reservation. The tribal government established an office of fisheries program, which cooperated with local, state, and federal agencies to repair salmon habitat and restore salmon runs.

In the 1990s, the tribe began to regain a foothold in the Wallowa Valley, and even limited control over land and natural resources.[42] In 1997 the tribe took title to 10,300 acres in the valley as mitigation for past tribal land losses, and these lands are currently held in escrow by a nonprofit group. The Nez Perce named the site the "Precious Lands," and negotiated a payment agreement that met the county's economic needs without compromising tribal sovereignty by paying taxes.[43] Furthermore, this return of the Nez Perce has been supported by some non-Indian Wallowa County residents mindful of the tribe's historical experiences.

In response to the tribal reassertion of its sovereignty and territorial rights, many non-Indian residents of the Lapwai reservation have joined with local and county governments around the reservation to form the North Central Idaho Jurisdictional Alliance (NCIJA). Fearful of losing their tax base, some non-Indian local governments have challenged Nez Perce tribal land acquisitions. These types of responses reflect larger regional and national initiatives to legally extinguish or politically modify tribal sovereignty. The tribe, however, offered a "payment in lieu of taxes" as compensation for a land parcel it took off the tax rolls in one case in Nez Perce County, Idaho. As a result, the Nez Perce County government has declined to join in the NCIJA challenges to Nez Perce sovereignty.

In 1997, a 320-acre powwow grounds was purchased in the Wallowa Valley by a partnership of Nez Perce and local non-Indian citizens to fulfill the longstanding dream of a tribal return to the valley. The annual *Tamakaliks* powwow draws Nez Perce from the Lapwai, Colville, and Umatilla reservations, educates non-Indian residents about *Nimiipu* culture, and brings money into the ailing logging community.[44] One organizer commented, "It's ironic that they boot us out of there in 1877 because they wanted the land and resources. Now they're asking us to come back and help them with their economic development because they're not surviving." The powwow grounds have become a designated site of the Nez Perce National Historic Park.[45]

The return to the Wallowa Valley is one part of a larger, ongoing project to rebuild a Nez Perce identity and begin to reunite dispersed tribespeople. Symbolic "homelands" represent both their past "golden age" and future resurgence. Defending their Idaho reservation, asserting tribal sovereignty, and restoring the salmon and horses as central icons of their culture, are other essential elements as the Nez Perce nation moves into the twenty-first century.

Conclusion

Studying Native American geography and history involves not only exposing the oppression and conditions of a racial group, but examining the conquest and colonization of diverse ethno-national groups. In questioning the role of the U.S. government, Native American geography raises issues about the territorial origins of the United States. Native geography critiques federal and state government policies and the clouded acquisition of the resource and land base on which those policies take place. It not only addresses political, economic, and demographic systems but the cultural underpinnings of European civilization. Native American geography therefore encompasses studying the indigenous peoples of North America, and in so doing it opens a Pandora's box about societies that colonized those peoples.

In the United States, many people tend to view Native Americans as the smallest and least significant minority group, who live on isolated reservations and do not affect national politics or the labor market to nearly the same degree as other minority groups. Treatment of American Indians as merely a demographic afterthought ignores the role that Native nations have played in American history, their complex geographies, and the continued existence of their cultures and land rights within the boundaries of the United States.

Different perspectives within U.S. society today view Native Americans as a single race, as a collection of ethno-linguistic groups, or as sovereign (or semi-sovereign) national entities. These views often correspond, respectively, to biological, cultural, and political explanations for differences between peoples. The very concept of Native Americans reflects a constructed racialized identity rooted in historical developments in

Figure 3.3.   Tribal members from the Mole Lake Ojibwe and Potawatomi Reservation join with non-Indian allies in celebrating the tribal purchase of the proposed Crandon mine site in October 2003, ending a 28-year battle to protect wild rice beds and the sacred Wolf River in Wisconsin. Source: Zoltán Grossman.

North American history. A collective pan-Indian image of Native Americans has been constructed in the United States, partially through the articulation of non-Indian perspectives, through Native reactions, and through federal Indian policies, such as those of the 1950s which terminated some reservations and relocated tribal members to urban areas. Yet most indigenous North Americans prefer their distinct national (tribal) identities, which have themselves been constructed by tribal self-definition and colonial relations (Fig. 3.3).

A nation can be generally defined as a people or ethnic group that has been territorialized (or attached to a specific land base), possesses an awareness of common social attributes (such as language), and claims a common past, present, and future. Before the arrival of Europeans in North America, most indigenous peoples possessed a band-based or clan-based identity. Some bands unified as tribes, and some tribes even unified as confederacies, such as the Haudenosaunee (Iroquois Six Nations Confederacy), whose political unity served as a model for the emerging United States.[46] Through their interactions with the colonial and settler societies, localized identities coalesced into ethno-linguistic groups, which became recognized and territorialized as tribal nations.

Until recently, debates over nations and nationalism often focused on the development of European nations.[47] Yet European notions of nations and nationalism are notoriously difficult to apply to Native Americans. Without a peasantry, bourgeoisie, intelligentsia, industrialization, or strong class stratification, Native peoples obviously developed different paths to nationhood and nationalism than did European peoples. A Native-centered analysis cannot center on what made "peasants into Frenchmen," but rather can examine what made "Oglalas into Lakotas"—the processes that coalesced diverse peoples into tribal "nations."[48] Native American nationalism cannot be explained by labor market roles or a goal of equal political representation, but rather by centuries of resistance to cultural assimilation, economic marginalization, and the diminishment of Native national territories.

Nations are constructed not only territorially, but by claiming a people's common past, present, and future in a place. Claims upon the past encompass Native American treaty rights and preexisting aboriginal rights in ways that reinvigorate forms of indigenous sovereignty originating in the past. In the present, tribal governments extend their powers through control over reservation lands. As for the future, Native sovereignty may lie in creative combinations of tribal territorial powers on and off the reservations, drawing on the cultural past to create new economic and political realities on the land.

Notes

1. Although indigenous to the lands of the United States, Native Hawaiians have not been covered in this chapter.

2. Russell Thornton, "Introduction and Overview," in *Studying Native America: Problems and Prospects*, ed. Russell Thornton (Madison: University of Wisconsin Press, 1998), 17–39.

3. Charles C. Mann, "1491," *Atlantic Monthly* 289, no. 3 (March 2002): 41.

4. Jack Weatherford, *Indian Givers: How the Indians of the Americas Transformed the World* (New York: Crown Publishers, 1988), 59–78.

5. Bonnie Duran, Eduardo Duran, and Maria Yellow Horse Brave Heart, "Native Americans and the Trauma of History," in *Studying Native America: Problems and Prospects*, ed. Russell Thornton (Madison: University of Wisconsin Press, 1998), 60–76.

6. Richard White, *The Middle Ground: Indians, Empires and Republics in the Great Lakes Region, 1650–1815* (New York: Cambridge University Press, 1991).

7. Alfred Crosby, *Ecological Imperialism: The Biological Expansion of Europe, 900–1900*, 2nd ed. (New York: Cambridge University Press, 2004).

8. Rodolfo Stavenhagen, "Indigenous Peoples: Emerging International Actors," in *Ethnic Diversity and Public Policy: A Comparative Inquiry*, ed. C. Young (Basingstoke, U.K.: Macmillan and UNRISD, 1998), 145.

9. Patricia Albers and Jeanne Kay, "Sharing the Land: A Study in American Indian Territoriality," in *American Indians: A Cultural Geography*, ed. Thomas E. Ross and Tyrel G. Moore (Boulder, CO: Westview Press, 1987), 47–92.

10. Allen Buchanan, *Secession: The Morality of Political Divorce from Fort Sumter to Lithuania and Quebec* (Boulder, CO: Westview Press, 1991), 39.

11. Stavenhagen, "Indigenous Peoples," 138.

12. Steven E. Silvern, "Scales of Justice: American Indian Treaty Rights and the Political Construction of Scale," *Political Geography* 18, no. 6 (1999): 645.

13. Brad A. Bays and Erin Hogan Fouberg, eds., *The Tribes and the States: Geographies of Intergovernmental Interaction* (Lanham, MD: Rowman & Littlefield, 2002).

14. Roxanne Dunbar Ortiz, *The Great Sioux Nation* (Berkeley, CA: American Indian Treaty Council Information and Moon Books, 1977), 100.

15. Frederick E. Hoxie, *Parading through History: The Making of the Crow Nation in America, 1805–1935* (Cambridge: Cambridge University Press, 1995).

16. Donald L. Fixico, *Termination and Relocation: Federal Indian Policy, 1945–1960* (Albuquerque: University of New Mexico Press, 1986).

17. Ernest Gellner, *Nations and Nationalism* (Oxford: Basil Blackwell, 1983).

18. Zoltán Grossman, "Unlikely Alliances: Treaty Conflicts and Environmental Cooperation between Native American and Rural White Communities," PhD dissertation, University of Wisconsin, 2002.

19. Julian Lang, "The Cid," in *American Indians and the Urban Experience*, ed. Susan Lobo and Kurt Peters (Walnut Creek, CA: AltaMira Press, 2001), 149–151.

20. Donald L. Fixico, "Foreword," in *American Indians and the Urban Experience*, ed. Susan Lobo and Kurt Peters (Walnut Creek, CA: AltaMira Press, 2001), ix–x.

21. Duran, Duran, and Brave Heart, "Native Americans and the Trauma of History," 60–76.

22. Russell Thornton, "The Demography of Colonialism and 'Old' and 'New' Native Americans," in *Studying Native America: Problems and Prospects*, ed. Russell Thornton (Madison: University of Wisconsin Press, 1998), 17–39.

23. Russell Thornton, "Tribal Membership Requirements and the Demography of 'Old' and 'New' Native Americans," in *Changing Numbers, Changing Needs: American Indian Demography and Public Health*, ed. Gary D. Sandefur, Ronald R. Rindfuss, and Barney Cohen (Washington: National Academy Press, 1996), 103–129.

24. Jeffrey S. Passel, "The Growing American Indian Population, 1960–1990: Beyond Demography," in *Changing Numbers, Changing Needs: American Indian Demography and Public Health*, ed. Gary D. Sandefur, Ronald R. Rindfuss, and Barney Cohen (Washington: National Academy Press, 1996), 79–102.

25. Passell, "The Growing American Indian Population," 79–102.

26. Thornton, "The Demography of Colonialism," 17–39.

27. Passell, "The Growing American Indian Population," 79.

28. Gary D. Sandefur, Ronald R. Rindfuss, and Barney Cohen, "Introduction," in *Changing Numbers, Changing Needs: American Indian Demography and Public Health*, ed. Gary D. Sandefur, Ronald R. Rindfuss, and Barney Cohen (Washington: National Academy Press, 1996), 1–13.

29. David Harvey, *Spaces of Hope* (Edinburgh: Edinburgh University Press, 2000), 85.

30. Stephen Cornell, *The Return of the Native: American Indian Political Resurgence* (New York: Oxford University Press, 1988).

31. Gerald R. Alfred, *Heeding the Voices of Our Ancestors: Kahnawake Mohawk Politics and the Rise of Native Nationalism* (Toronto: Oxford University Press, 1995).

32. Keith H. Basso, *Wisdom Sits in Places: Landscape and Language among the Western Apache* (Albuquerque: University of New Mexico Press, 1996).

33. Imre Sutton, "Preface to Indian Country: Geography and Law," *American Indian Culture and Research Journal* 15, no. 2 (1991): 3–35.

34. Horace P. Axtell and Margo Aragon, *A Little Bit of Wisdom: Conversations with a Nez Perce Elder* (Lewiston, ID: Confluence Press, 1997), 206.

35. Nez Perce Tribe Environmental Restoration and Waste Management Program, *Treaties: Nez Perce Perspectives* (Lewiston, ID: Confluence Press, 2003).

36. Dennis W. Baird, Diane Mallickan, W. R. Swagerty, eds., *The Nez Perce Divided: Firsthand Accounts of Events Leading to the 1863 Treaty* (Moscow, ID: University of Idaho Press, 2002).

37. Lucullus McWhorter, *Hear Me, My Chiefs* (Caldwell, ID: Caxton Printers, 1952).

38. Merrill D. Beal, *I Will Fight No More Forever: Chief Joseph and the Nez Perce War* (Seattle: University of Washington Press, 1963).

39. Alvin M. Josephy, Jr., *The Nez Perce Indians and the Opening of the Northwest* (Lincoln: University of Nebraska Press, 1965).

40. Dan Landeen and Allen Pinkham, *Salmon and His People: Fish and Fishing in Nez Perce Culture* (Lewiston, ID: Confluence Press, 1999).

41. Associated Press, "Nez Perce File Lawsuit over Salmon Policies," *Spokane Spokesman-Review*, 15 June 2004.

42. Sissell A. Waage, "(Re)claiming Space and Place through Collaborative Planning in Rural Oregon," *Political Geography* 20, no. 7 (2001): 839–858.

43. Kim Murphy, "A Healing Closure to Nez Perce's Sad Voyage," *Los Angeles Times* (14 June 1997).

44. Lyris Wallwork Winik, "We're Doing It Because We Think It's Right," *Parade* (15 June 1997).

45. Alex Tizon, "Nez Perce Invited Back to Land of Winding Rivers," *Seattle Times* (25 May 1997).

46. Bruce E. Johansen, *Forgotten Founders: Benjamin Franklin, the Iroquois, and the Rationale for the American Revolution* (Ipswich: Gambit, 1982).

47. Benedict Anderson, *Imagined Communities: Reflections on the Origin and Spread of Nationalism* (London/New York: Verso, 1991).

48. Eugèn Weber, *Peasants into Frenchmen: The Modernization of Rural France, 1870–1914* (London: Chatto & Windus, 1977).

CHAPTER 4

The Historical Spaces of African Americans

Bobby M. Wilson

The transatlantic slave trade was the western world's first multinational enterprise and responsible for exporting almost 12 million Africans to the so-called New World. It was without doubt the largest forced spatial transfer of human beings in world history. With the geographical shift in commerce from the Mediterranean to the Atlantic seaboard in the fifteenth century, the feudal system of Western Europe, especially in England, disintegrated. The period from about 1500 to 1715 was one in which the accumulation of surplus wealth arose from the expansion of trade and commerce, laying the foundation for industrial capitalism. Commercial capitalism stimulated demands for new goods, which led to land alienation and exploitation of raw materials in the Americas. It initially exploited the labor of Native Americans and indentured whites, but black slavery eventually took precedence over all others, becoming an almost inexhaustible, cheap, and tractable labor supply.

The transatlantic slave trade commenced in 1444 with the shipment of 235 Africans from the Guinea Coast of Africa to Portugal, where they were sold as slaves. And in 1501 Africans were taken to the Americas, mainly to the Spanish and Portuguese colonies in Latin America. By 1750 there were at least 236,000 slaves in the English colonies of the Americas. The first settlement in the English colonies, Jamestown, Virginia, established tobacco as the commodity on which the Virginia plantation would be based. By 1700 the tobacco industry spread into colonies in North Carolina, Maryland, and throughout Virginia. The growth of the tobacco industry assured that the Virginia Colony, and the South itself, would survive.

Large-scale production of tobacco required a more "spatially fixed" laboring class. The first significant spatial concentration of black slaves developed in the tobacco-growing region of Virginia, Maryland, and North Carolina. A second concentration of black slavery was the coastal region of South Carolina and Georgia—the core area of rice cultivation that produced approximately 90 percent of the nation's crop during the antebellum period. However, much of the popular conception of the plantation South came from the cotton-producing region of the South in the black belt (Map 4.1). Since cotton production was also labor intensive, African slaves were imported to labor on cotton plantations. By 1790 there were 660,000 African slaves in the American South.

And by 1850, the proportion of blacks in the "black belt" was frequently above 50, 60, and 75 percent of the total population. At the time of the Civil War there were four million slaves in the South, and over half were owned by planters who had 20 or more slaves (Map 4.2). However, more than three-quarters of the southern white population owned no slaves at all. The plantation system sustained slavery and created a permanent imprint on the cultural landscape of the South, where it became a powerful icon of the region that lasted into the twentieth century.[1]

Slavery was one of many ways in which economic surplus was appropriated from blacks in America. The U.S. Constitution helped to sustain the plantation regime as a national power. Although they were considered nonhuman, Article One, Section Two, of the Constitution counted each slave as three-fifths of a human being for purpose of congressional representation. Article Four, Section Two, of the U.S. Constitution required that fugitive slaves be returned to their owners. As slaves, blacks were not proprietors of their labor power and did not participate in commodity exchange and consumption. The slaveholder purchased the labor power of the slave in a lump sum, once and for all. The only position the slave had in the marketplace was as a commodity to be bought and sold. The fugitive slave was property that must be returned to its rightful owner.

One force countering the hegemony of the slave plantation was the "Underground Railroad," which consisted of a network of mostly northern abolitionists who assisted as many as 100,000 blacks to escape from the plantation. Harriet Tubman (1820–1913),

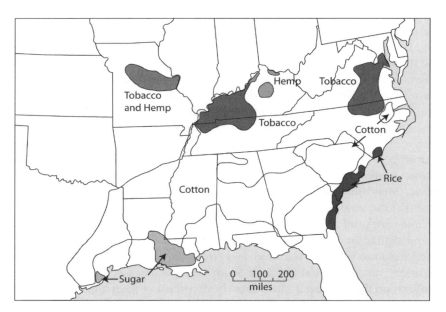

Map 4.1.   Southern Mosaic of Agriculture Specialization prior to the Civil War. Source: Sam B. Hilliard, "Plantation and the Molding of the Southern Landscape," in The Making of the American Landscape, *ed. Michael P. Conzen (New York: Routledge, 1994), 106.*

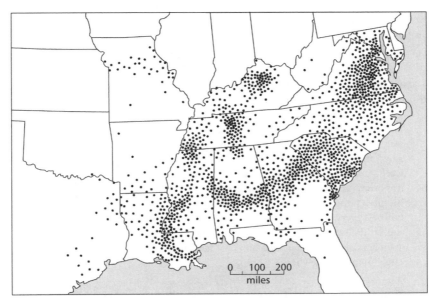

Map 4.2.   Slave Distribution, 1850. Source: Sam B. Hilliard, Atlas of Antebellum Southern Agriculture (Baton Rouge: Louisiana State University Press, 1984), 33.

herself an escaped slave, was a prime force in this network. Described as "the Moses of her people," she personally made nineteen trips into the South, helping more than 300 slaves to freedom. Aside from the Underground Railroad, many blacks escaped slavery by residing among Indian tribes such as the Creeks, Cherokees, and Seminoles and in "maroon colonies"—isolated mountainous or swampy areas that provided a haven for fugitive slaves.

Free Blacks

Early in its development America lent significant support to the idea of colonizing free blacks. In case of emancipation, Thomas Jefferson in his *Notes on the State of Virginia* proposed to exclude blacks from society to prevent integration.[2] By 1822 the American Colonization Society established the black slave settlement of Liberia in Africa that ironically used almost word for word the American Constitution as its founding charter. But in 1828 the U.S. Senate Foreign Relations Committee rejected the idea of black colonization, fearing it would create a labor vacuum.[3] Abraham Lincoln raised the issue of black colonization once again at the time of the Civil War. His solution to the "Negro problem" also was colonization, stating that blacks and whites are of a different race, having "a broader difference than exists between almost any other two races. . . . It is better for us both, therefore to be separated."[4] In 1862 the House introduced a bill appropriating $20,000,000 to colonized blacks. But in 1864 all laws relating to colonization were repealed due to the fear that forcible deportation would create a labor shortage.[5]

Emancipation decommodified the black body. Having ownership of their labor, former slaves met the owner of money in the market. Places of consumption in growing towns and cities of the postbellum South became places of racial mixing. The country store was one of the very few spaces where blacks and whites mixed. This newly created social space generated more contacts between blacks and whites than the workplace, courthouse or polling place, schools, and churches.[6] According to Edgar Thompson,

> Local churches were divided racially as well as denominationally, and they were used, ordinarily, only one day in the week. Schools were racially segregated and used only seasonally and for limited times during the day and the week. Courthouses were few and far between, and none of these played an important community wide integrating role. So the full force of the community's population could and did focus on the store, which was opened for business every day, except Sunday, throughout the year. Blacks and whites in the postbellum South more nearly approached equality in the store than anywhere else. . . . There was an air of familiarity and tolerance at the store rarely matched elsewhere.[7]

This growing availability, and inherent democracy, of exchange and consumption deracialized the space of commerce, undermining the racial status quo. A postbellum regime attempted to preserve as much as possible the old antebellum way of life, including many of the working practices of the old slave regime.[8]

The Spaces of Separate but Equal

One of the rights associated with property was the right to exclude. The power to exclude was one of the most valued strands in an owner's bundle of property rights.[9] After the Civil War, this common-law rule of exclusion was adopted and extended to all businesses. The South immediately reestablished black codes to retain the antebellum policy of racial exclusion. The common law of exclusion enabled businesses to serve white customers while *choosing* to exclude black customers who could not compel whites to serve them. Lawmakers could have affirmed the right of businesses to choose their customers by abolishing the right of access for everyone, whites and blacks. Businesses could choose which race they would serve and then serve everyone of that race without discrimination. Lawmakers also could have limited rights of spatial access to businesses responsible for the public allocation of use values, i.e., collective consumption, or the government could require all businesses to serve all without discrimination.

The court selected to affirm rights of access but with an option of providing service in a segregated manner—adopted as the ruling theory in *Plessy v. Ferguson* (1896).[10] While the Plessy decision targeted collective consumption, it also applied to the private allocation of commodities. John W. Cell argued that segregation in its early phase was closely associated with progressive forces—"cities, factories, modern politics"—allowing white supremacy to remain "at least superficially compatible" with the need of capitalism to expand the sphere of commodity exchange and consumption.[11] In the 1880s one of the South's principal spokespersons behind these progressive forces and an advance agent of the "separate but equal" doctrine was the editor of the *Atlanta Constitution*, Henry Grady. As leader of the "New South" movement, Grady rejected the exclusionary race policies of the more radical racists. A moderate on the race question, he supported the idea "that there should be equal accommodation for the two races, but separate. . . . In every theater there should be a space set apart for the colored people with precisely the same accommodations that are given to white people for the same price, and the same should apply elsewhere."[12] Joel Williamson suggests that such a policy would also provide blacks protection from radical racist whites who resented blacks' assertiveness in the sphere of reproduction.[13]

Following Emancipation and for most of the twentieth century, the geographical and social solution to the race problem in America was the doctrine of "separate but equal," not black colonization or separate development. The doctrine of "separate but equal" allowed blacks to engage the sphere of commodity exchange and consumption while also providing the spatial fix—black spaces of various kinds and scales—needed to remind blacks of their marginal status.[14] Cell contends that it was "one of the most successful political ideologies of the past century. It was, indeed, the highest stage of 'white supremacy,' providing for the right amount of racial inclusion and exclusion."[15] Right of access to engage in individual and collective consumption could be granted to blacks but segregation was required—Jim Crow statutes in railroads and streetcars.[16] Many white businesses, especially those concerned with losing white customers—fearful of contamination—exercised the right to exclude blacks from their establishments. But in an increasing market-oriented society, many more took advantage of the Plessy ruling and allowed blacks access to their establishment, but without the spatial "commingling of the two races." The court held,

> Laws permitting, and even requiring, [the separation of the races] in places where they are liable to be brought into contact, do not necessarily imply the inferiority of either race to the other, and have been generally, if not universally, recognized as within the competency of the state legislatures in the exercise of their police power.[17]

Blacks could patronize a restaurant, department store, cinema, or park, as long as they waited until white patrons had been served. In the South, blacks and whites attended the same county fairs, but on separate days. Blacks could ride the city bus as long as they sat in the back of the bus, but if the bus was crowded, they were expected, like good servants, to give up their seats to a waiting white person. On the other hand, if seats were available in the white section but not the "color" section, blacks were expected to stand in the aisle. Blacks drank water as long as it was at the "colored only" fountains, saw the same doctor as whites but as long as they waited in the back room, waited for the bus or train as long as they waited in spatially segregated sitting rooms at the terminals. Throughout America blacks entered through the back doors and basements of department stores, sat in the balconies of cinemas, backrooms of restaurants. These spaces were

> vigilantly undemocratic and potentially dangerous. Jim Crow signs, filthy and inoperable public toilets, white police officers, dark bodies standing in

the aisles of half-empty buses, black pedestrians stepping off the sidewalk or walking with their eyes turned down or away, and other acts of interracial social "etiquette"—all reminded black people every day of their second-class citizenship.[18]

"Separate but equal" stamped blacks with a badge of inferiority. It allowed for a clear spatial distinction to be made between blacks and whites without working against the logic of the marketplace. Instead of total exclusion, race-connected spatial practices effected a balance between colonization (exclusion) and assimilation (inclusion).[19]

Blacks could not escape the persistent stereotypes that reinforced them as biologically inferior to whites. The 1893 World's Columbian Exposition in Chicago, designed to advance the causes of American nationalism, imperialism, and consumerism, produced exhibits that ridiculed and denigrated blacks, portraying images of blacks as happy in servitude to whites. A prominent Midwestern flour-milling firm, R. T. Davis Milling Company, persuaded Nancy Green, a fifty-seven-year-old former slave, to become a living advertisement at the fair for the company's Aunt Jemima Pancake Mix. Green played the role of a stereotypical plantation mammy, which won the milling firm an award at the fair and became a corporate trademark that gained national acceptance as an early icon of America's emerging culture of mass consumption. And the stereotypes of Africans put on display in the Dahomeyan Village at the Chicago Exhibition as exemplars of "savagery" were used routinely by corporate America.[20] There is nothing natural about race; the doctrine of spatially separate but equal race constructed social relations that dialectically acted to construct relations in ways that reproduce those in the economy.[21]

Spaces of the Black Economy

Low wages and postbellum proscriptions kept most blacks on the economic margin. Power relations within production made possible a rigid racial division of labor that restricted the vast majority of southern blacks to a few manufacturing occupations, and these were primarily unskilled positions (Table 4.1). The white working class remained structurally distinct from the black working class. In agriculture, landlords made every effort to purchase black labor in a lump sum, spatially tying once again blacks to the land. Through indebtedness the landlord was able to purchase the cropper's labor power for an extensive period, making the cropper less the owner of its labor power and more an outright commodity—a slave—possessed by the landlord. Both the "standing wage" and convict lease labor systems were common labor practices used to exert maximum control over black labor. In the former, employers paid workers only every six months as opposed to a weekly basis, and the state leased black convicts to private enterprises for an extensive period.[22] These labor practices left blacks with little cash to purchase discretionary consumer goods. They had to spend a greater percentage of their scarce cash on food because landowners allowed them few opportunities to grow their food.[23]

Although power relations in the sphere of production relegated blacks to the lowest wages and occupations, collectively their earning power was significant and

Table 4.1.   Percent of Black Males in Unskilled Positions, 1910

State	Total Blacks Employed in Manufacturing, 1910	% Unskilled
Alabama	32,604	64
Arkansas	15,718	77
Florida	25,492	70
Georgia	39,345	48
Kentucky	17,715	61
Louisiana	38,138	72
Mississippi	25,702	74
North Carolina	31,891	67
South Carolina	34,952	46
Tennessee	21,939	63
Texas	27,027	81
Virginia	39,737	68
West Virginia	4,207	68
Total	360,700	65

Source: Carole Marks, *Farewell—We're Good and Gone: The Great Black Migration* (Bloomington: Indiana University Press, 1991), 40–41.

increased over time. In 1869 and 1876 the annual income of black farm laborers in South Carolina was only $60, but the southern black population with more than five million people had a purchasing power of at least $300 million.[24] The combined wealth of the 1886 black population in Nashville, Tennessee, was estimated at $1,000,000. By 1929 the purchasing power of blacks in the South's seventeen largest cities was estimated to be $308,000,000.[25] Nationally, the spending power of blacks was estimated at $3,055,000,000 in 1920, increasing to $10,290,000,000 by 1943 when the per capita income of blacks in certain cities compared favorably with white per capita earnings nationwide.[26] For W. E. B. DuBois, blacks needed to develop a "nation within the nation" based on this spending power.[27]

Blacks never developed a wholly and spatially separate economy—a nation within a nation. Economically, they were never fully isolated from whites.[28] Race-connected practices did not take the form of separate developments. The "separate but equal" race doctrine allowed white businesses to capture

> most of the black consumer dollars that came primarily from wages paid by whites. Ironically, the surplus value of the labor of twentieth century black wage earners was returned to whites in much the same way that the surplus value of the slaves' labor was absorbed by their master. The black purchasing dollar in black business districts, then, circulated back into the white community.[29]

Black businesses that successfully competed against white businesses for the black dollar were deemed disrespectful and threatened. In 1892 a white merchant in Memphis,

Tennessee, charged three black merchants who opened a store across the street with the crime of competition and sought to have the store closed. The incident precipitated a riot in which the black merchants were subsequently murdered.[30] Gunnar Myrdal observed,

> Since the [black entrepreneurs] are excluded from the white market, it becomes important for them to hold the Negro market as a monopoly. The monopoly over the Negro market of teachers, preachers, undertakers, beauticians and others is generally respected. . . . [But] these are the only Negro businesses in which Negroes are protected from white competition. In all other businesses of any consequence Negro businessmen are able to keep only a small portion of the Negro market. . . . The Negro storekeeper, on the other hand, is in severe competition with the white storekeeper, and only a fraction of the purchasing power of Negro patrons passes his counter. . . . Seldom have Negroes succeeded in keeping a substantial white market.[31]

In the predominantly black town of Clarksdale, Mississippi, blacks owned none of the town's clothing, dry goods, or general merchandise stores.[32] And in 1910 nearly all the white-owned stores on Atlanta's Decatur Street traded exclusively with blacks.[33] In a series of six articles on "race patronage," *The New York Age* (1916) reported a similar pattern for Harlem where nearly all of the consumers were black, but 75 percent of the businesses were white, and black merchants received only about 20 to 25 percent of the retail trade.[34] When blacks were denied land ownership in the postbellum South, the frontier became an escape valve for some who purchased land and developed the spaces of all-black towns in Kansas, Oklahoma, and Iowa.[35] They migrated directly from the plantation fields to the more productive agricultural lands of Louisiana, Texas, and Oklahoma in the late 1860s and early 1870s, and later to the plains of Kansas and to Indian Territory in 1879. Others migrated to the mining camps of Appalachia in the late 1880s and 1890s.

The New Deal's agriculture policy effectively made for an "enclosure" movement that forced blacks off the land to work as wage laborers in urban areas. Government programs reduced crop acreage and discriminated against tenant farmers.[36] Landownership and tenant farming declined significantly. Just after the turn of the twentieth century black farmers numbered approximately 900,000 and landownership was at its peak. In 1910 blacks owned some 16 million acres of land in the South, but since then there has been a steady and sharp decline in the amount of black-owned land. By 1970 less than 5.5 million acres of land in the South was black-owned. Due to both legal and extralegal means, it is estimated that at one time blacks lost land at a rate of 6,000 acres per week, resulting in an insignificant amount of black-owned land by the 1990s.[37] In 2002 the census counted fewer than 30,000 black farmers in America, and less than 1 percent of blacks in America worked in agriculture or related occupations. However, The National Black Farmers Association estimates the number of black farmers at 94,000 who continue to be affected by the long legacy of discrimination in receiving government subsidies and loans from banks.[38] Government policy then has been directly responsible for the "spatial draining" of African Americans from many rural areas of the American South.

Blacks' hope of gaining access to the fruits of capital was couched more emphatically in urbanization than in agriculture. With little hope of owning land, blacks left the South for new—albeit unsteady—employment in towns and cities outside the South, spatially distancing themselves from the plantation tradition of the rural South.[39] The vast majority of blacks that left the land migrated to the factories of the industrial North. Blacks engaged in gainful occupations in manufacturing and mechanical industries increased 56.1 percent during the 1890s. Deskilling of labor allowed northern industrialists to "tap the hitherto practically untouched labor reserve of the plantation South."[40] It made black labor in the South compatible with the labor needs of northern capitalists. New technologies, combined with "scientific management," simplified many industrial work tasks. In 1902 a Carnegie steel official estimated that the company could train an agricultural worker of average intelligence to be a "melter" in six to eight weeks, whereas it would have taken two years to master the art of puddling.[41]

Black newspapers, some subsidized by northern capitalists, published editorials encouraging the exodus of blacks from the South to work in northern industries.[42] Robert Abbott, editor of the *Chicago Defender*, was relentless in encouraging this exodus.

> The *Defender* invites all to come north. Plenty of room for the good, sober industrious man. Plenty of work. . . . Anywhere in God's country is far better than the Southland. . . . Come join the ranks of the free. Cast the yoke from around your neck. See the light. When you have crossed the Ohio river, breathe the fresh air and say, "Why didn't I come before?"[43]

One of the most significant periods of black migration occurred around World War I—the Great Migration. Between 1916 and 1918 some half-million blacks migrated from the South to the North. From 1870 to 1940, there was a net out-migration from the South of two million blacks, and in the 1940s the South experienced a net out-migration of 1.6 million. This trend continued during the 1950s when the South lost 1.5 million blacks and 1.4 million in the 1960s. Between 1940 and 1960, the South Atlantic and East South Central regions became the two largest source regions for the out-migration to the North (Map 4.3). The West South Central source region produced two migration streams, a larger one to the West and a smaller one to the North. From 1940 to 1942 approximately one million blacks moved to the nation's urban areas, most to centers of defense industries in the West. Due to the volume of these migration streams, the proportion of the black population residing in the South decreased from 90 percent in 1890 to 50 percent in 2000. This substantial migration stream dramatically changed the ethnic face of northern cities and is primarily explained by Neo-Classical Migration theory based on geographical differences in employment and wages between sending and receiving regions.

The proportion of the black population residing in urban areas increased from 20 percent in 1890 to almost 50 percent in 1940. At the end of the 1920s seven cities had a black population of more than 100,000. The number of blacks residing in urban areas increased more than 800 percent between 1900 and 1970. And by 2000 almost 90 percent of the black population resided in urban areas compared to only 20 percent in

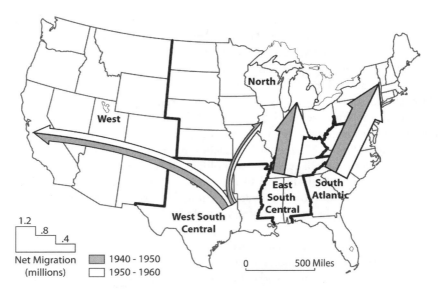

Map 4.3.   Volume and Direction of Net Black Migration from the South, 1940–1960. Source: Harold M. Rose, "Social Processes in the City: Race and Urban Residential Choice," Resource Paper Number 6, Commission on College Geography (Washington: Association of American Geographers, 1969), 6.

1890. Over one-half of the black population now resides inside the central cities of metropolitan regions.

Spaces of Housing Segregation

The right to buy and sell property was usually granted to free blacks during the antebellum period. This right was sometime limited when it came to land, however. In Mississippi,

> all freedmen, free Negroes and mulattoes may . . . acquire personal property and choses [sic] in action by descent or purchase, and may dispose of the same in the same manner and to the same extent that white persons may: *Provided*, that the provisions of this section shall not be so construed as to allow any freedman, free Negro or mulatto to rent or lease any lands or tenements, except in incorporated towns or cities, in which places the corporate authorities shall control the same.[44]

Provisions like this contributed early on to housing segregation. The entry of large numbers of black migrants into urban areas following emancipation intensified housing segregation, which differed between the North and South only in the form of its spatial character. In the South, de jure segregation produced a form more rigid on a block-by-block, street-by-street basis. In the North, de facto segregation produced a spatial form that was greater in geographical scale, i.e., the contiguous ghetto.[45]

In an attempt not to violate property rights, most segregation laws restricted access to housing but not ownership. But in *Buchanan v. Warley* (1917), the court ruled that access cannot be separated from ownership, stating that "Property is more than the mere thing which a person owns. It is elementary that it includes the right to acquire, use, and dispose of it."[46] Although the court ruled that laws restricting access to residential properties were unconstitutional, the proliferation of "restrictive covenants"— private agreements among signatories not to sell to blacks—effectively negated the court decision. According to David Delaney, "property owners had only to agree among themselves to effect the same end [as the residential segregation laws]: exclusion of black people from 'white communities.'"[47] But in *Shelley v. Kraemer* (1948), the U.S. Supreme Court held that judicial enforcement of restrictive covenants constituted government action that is unconstitutional under the equal protection clause of the Fourteenth Amendment.[48]

Following the court ruling against restrictive covenants, financial institutions played an important role in maintaining housing segregation. In housing, consumption rights for a relatively long period of time are purchased with a large outlay of money at one point in time. Consequently, financial institutions played a very important role in the housing commodity circuit. With the full support of federal law, intentional racial discrimination was an explicit requirement of housing finance and related housing practices for most of the twentieth century.

Motivated by exchange value, realtors found ways to profit from discriminatory practices within the housing circuit. In financial circles the term *arbitrage* refers to the simultaneous buying of securities in one market at a low price and selling them at a higher price in another market. A parallel situation, known as "block busting," exists in housing where discrimination has produced a segregated housing market. Black demand for housing creates a fear of racial change that depresses the price of housing in adjacent white neighborhoods. In their rush to avoid what they see as potential losses, realtors encourage whites to sell in a depressed market, increasing circulation within the housing sector. Realtors were able to increase circulation within the housing sector, while maintaining segregation. The racial marking of space became decisive in housing patterns. The 1960 census produced evidence of the absolute loss of white population and gain of black population in many large central cities.[49] Karl E. Taeuber predicted "that the racial problem of the U.S., still festering in the rural South, will become equally, perhaps most acutely, a problem of the urban North" as a result of housing segregation.[50]

With the confinement of black residents to certain sections of the city came also the spatial confinement of black entrepreneurs, which produced the black business districts like 125th Street in Harlem, Auburn Avenue in Atlanta, Beale Street in Memphis, and South Parkway in Chicago.[51] Much of the black retail business was carried out "in small stores with small stocks of goods, where the owner works side by side with one or two helpers, and makes a personal profit less than a normal American wage. Black businesses, shielded from the larger economy by fixed boundaries, also were destined 'to end up a ghetto.'"[52] Antebellum and postbellum proscriptions continue to play a major role in maintaining these fixed spatial boundaries, preventing black entrepreneurs "from developing the business acumen and accumulating the capital necessary for large-scale economic enterprises."[53] Black commercial districts lack the range of businesses necessary for interdependency or interlinking economic structures associated with spatial agglomeration. They never develop localization economies necessary to attract additional businesses and compete in the larger marketplace. A survey by *Black Enterprise* found that almost half of their readers (mostly middle-class blacks) spent less than 10 percent of their income at black-owned businesses.[54] And it is estimated that for every eight or ten dollars spent in the black community, only one dollar remains there.

Geographical Scale and the Pan-African and Black Struggle for Liberation

Working outside old constraints of planter domination, urban blacks had more opportunities to participate and assert themselves socially. For Alain Locke, the city made a difference because it forced the "Negro" from the simple life of the rural community to the complex life of the city.[55] The urban "Negro" saw himself in broad and sophisticated terms. The "New Negro" did not abide by the old standard of passive behavior, but created new social geographies by moving and crossing the rigid boundary drawn by the race doctrine of "separate but equal." During the 1920s, the black northern ghetto produced a vibrant culture symbolized by the "Harlem Renaissance," which popularized the culture of southern blacks who migrated north. The Harlem Renaissance symbolized this "New Negro" identity that rejected the old racial stereotypes and clichés exhibited at the 1893 Chicago World Fair. The "New Negro" insisted on integrity of race and personality.[56] It provided for more choices of cultural identity, somewhat countering the cultural form that marginalized blacks. Marcus Garvey, the black nationalist, and his Universal Negro Improvement Association (UNIA) contributed to this new identity by linking the condition of blacks in America and the Caribbean to the European colonization of Africa.

The political struggle that decolonized much of Africa and Asia after World War II led to a further re-evaluation of black identity in the United States, causing a new generation of blacks to explore their cultural heritage in Africa and adopt a pan-African perspective on the race problem. Malcolm X and the black power movement especially contributed to this perspective. Malcolm X broadened further the geographical scale of the black freedom struggle in America by placing it at the level of human rights: "The Afro-American Problem is not a Negro problem, or an American problem, but a human problem, a problem for humanity."[57] For Malcolm X, the difference between "civil" and "human" rights was one of geographical scale.

> Civil rights means you're asking Uncle Sam to treat you right. Human rights are something you were born with. Human rights are your God-given rights. Human rights are the rights that are recognized by all nations of this earth. Any time any one violates your human rights, you can take them to the world court.[58]

By identifyng the issues of American racial oppression with global oppression, Malcolm X sought to bridge political oppression in Africa and Asia with lynching and other racial atrocities in the American South.[59]

Like Malcolm X, Martin Luther King Jr. also saw civil rights as part of a larger movement.

> Whether we want to be or not, we are caught in a great moment in history. . . . The vast majority of people of the world are colored. . . . Up until four or five years ago most of the one and one-quarter billion colored peoples were exploited by empires of the West. . . . Today many are free. . . . And the rest are on the road. . . . We [civil rights movement] are part of that great movement.[60]

He saw the need for "jumping scale"—a geographical rescaling of the civil rights struggle.

> Our loyalties must become ecumenical rather than sectional. Every nation must now develop an overriding loyalty to mankind as a whole in order to preserve the best in their individual societies. This call for world-wide fellowship that lifts neighborly concern beyond one's tribe, race, class and nation is in reality a call for an all-embracing and unconditional love for all men.[61]

Speaking in more specific terms about the need to jump scale, King explained,

> We must honestly face the fact that the [civil rights] Movement must address itself to the question of restructuring the whole of American society. There are forty million poor people here. And one day we must ask the question, "Why are there forty million poor people in America?" And when you begin to ask that question, you are raising questions about the economic system, about broader distribution of wealth. When you ask that question, you begin to question the capitalist economy . . . we've got to begin to ask questions about the whole society.[62]

The state attempted to prevent any kind of coalition building across space. The "Anti-Riot" Act of 1968, which was attached to the Civil Rights Act of 1968, was designed to limit the geographical scale of dissent. The act made it a felony to "travel in interstate commerce . . . with the intent to incite, promote, encourage, participate in and carry on a riot." The act was crafted to address the public expression of dissent by blacks. In fact, the act was named after H. Rap Brown, who as a member of the Black Panther Party was arrested and charged with inciting people to riot. It was a legal tool to contain black dissent within a confined space.[63]

The civil rights struggle was confined mainly to the South where through legal and extralegal means blacks historically were situated on the margin. The store, the restaurant, and the bus were spaces where segregation was experienced most acutely and would be contested most bitterly in the struggle for civil rights. Boycotting was one of the most forceful statements blacks could make about their place in the consumer society.[64] The Montgomery bus boycott, which was inspired by the 1953 Baton Rouge bus boycott, lasted for more than a year and is probably the most notable example of this resistance.[65] With the growth of television, both civil rights and anti-apartheid activists increasingly relied on exposing the inhumanity of the system through the media to change public opinion and policy. The images of police dogs and fire hoses abusing black children in the South became a spectacle that galvanized thousands into action. And the equally horrific images of the Sharpeville and Soweto massacres in South Africa produced a generation of African Americans who linked the inhumanity in America with that in Africa.

For Malcolm X, however, landownership and community control were the basis of independence, not desegregation of lunch counters, theaters, parks, and public toilets.[66] In 1966 Willie Ricks, a staff member of the Student Non-Violence Coordinating Committee (SNCC) in Mississippi, used the phrase "black power" in delivering a speech against racism to symbolize such control and independence. A young Stokely Carmichael (Kwame Ture) working in an election campaign in rural Alabama popularized the phrase and countered the white rooster used to symbolize white supremacy in the state with the symbol of the "black panther" to represent the strength and dignity of blacks. Huey Newton and Bobby Seale, inspired by the revolutionary theories of Frantz Fanon's *Wretched of the Earth* (1963), organized the Black Panther Party, which produced a new understanding of black identity and the place of identity in politics. Carmichael also saw the "black power" movement as a part of the pan-African struggle for liberation.[67] The constant exchange and mutual influences between the American black movements and the various African and Caribbean ones were continuous and incalculable.[68]

Black power rejected values that politically and culturally subjugated blacks. A counter-consciousness emerged that asserted a positive group cultural identity to counter the racial stereotypes of the past. This counter-consciousness emerged as early as the 1940s when a group of black jazz artists challenged the modernist artistic form by excluding white artists. John Coltrane, Miles Davis, and others produced a music style that informed a new self-consciousness. These artists rebelled against attempts to "whiten" jazz—"to bleach away its African-American roots."[69] This counter-consciousness was epitomized also in the music of black artisans like James Brown's "Say It Loud, I'm Black and I'm Proud," and Curtis Mayfield's "People, Get Ready." Influenced by the European existentialist movement, the black novelist Richard Wright predicted this new cultural direction, writing such works as *Native Son* (1944), *Black Boy* (1945), and *The Outsider* (1953).

As the French philosopher Jean-Paul Sartre saw it, this counter-consciousness appeared as a dialectical progression from the theoretical and practical affirmation of racial stereotypes as the thesis to counter-consciousness as the antithetical value and the moment of the negativity.[70] Eager to accentuate and promote what they considered to be a positive cultural identity, the black power generation took their name from the African past. The wearing of the dashikis became popular attire for many blacks. And the "Afro" and "cornrowing" were the "natural" look in hair styling.[71]

Politics of Neoliberalism

In terms of domestic politics, the black power movement took the form of the "interest group" or "ethnic group" model of U.S. politics and led to the election of hundreds of black city, state, and national representatives.[72] This radicalization of black politics was fueled in part by the politics of "neoliberalism," a right turn in domestic politics that is firmly rooted in the states' rights rhetoric of the Old South. This right turn has continued unabated, electing Richard Nixon in 1968 and Ronald Reagan in 1980.[73] Affirmative action programs, minority voting districts, and the Keynesian welfare state, which expanded rapidly in the post–World War II period, were attacked by enacting neoliberal policies that vastly cut back social programs. Right-wing reactionary politics adopted what some call "authoritarian populist character," which sharply contrasts with traditional conservatism.

This populism allowed many white workers to blame blacks for the poor economic situations associated with the global economy. Whites felt aggrieved and began to attack civil rights legislation and affirmative action as "reverse discrimination." George Wallace took advantage of such feelings among the white working class, winning the Michigan Democratic primary and capturing a significant part of the labor vote in the 1972 presidential election. Such blaming also was evidenced at the 1992 Republican National Convention, where Pat Buchanan blamed immigrants and affirmative action for a poor economy, displacing rage onto the "Other" who are socially and economically weak. Neoliberalism spearheaded an anti-democratic offensive, centered on negative liberty, property, and the individual, which attempts to recover an early-modern vision of rights.[74] This offensive looks to the Fourteenth Amendment to attack affirmative action and other state remedies to combat discrimination. Neoliberalism claimed not only the "end of history" but also the "end of racism."[75]

Home-Place Migration

In the late 1960s the black population continued to flow out of the South, mainly due to racism and the struggle over civil rights. But in the early 1970s the South experienced a net migration gain of blacks for the first time in the twentieth century. Between 1970 and 1975, the South experienced a net gain of 14,000 blacks, increasing to a gain of 195,000 between 1975 and 1980 (Table 4.2). By the late 1990s, the number of blacks moving to the South from other parts of the United States totaled 680,000, whereas those leaving the region numbered 334,000, generating a net migration gain

Table 4.2. Black Migration to and from the South: Age 5 and Over (Thousands)

	1965–1970			1975–1980			1995–2000		
	To	From	Net	To	From	Net	To	From	Net
Northeast	69	120	–51	192	50	+142	313	98	+215
Midwest	57	164	–107	121	94	+27	211	137	+74
West	38	94	–56	102	76	+26	157	98	+59
Total	162	378	–216	415	220	+195	681	333	+348

Source: U.S. Census Bureau, 1970, 1980, and 2000 Censuses.

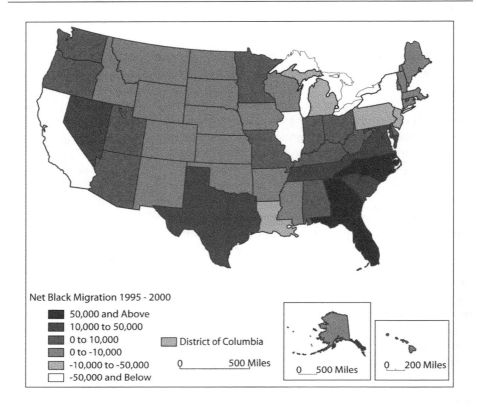

Map 4.4.   Net Black Migration, 1995–2000.
Source: U.S. Census Bureau, Census 2000.

of 346,000. For every black who left the South, two moved in. Georgia had a net migration gain of 130,000 blacks, the highest among all states, followed by North Carolina (53,000), Florida (51,000), Maryland (44,000), and Texas (42,000) (Map 4.4). Due to these gains, the proportion of the black population residing in the South increased from 52 percent in 1990 to 55 percent in 2000.

Blacks migrating to the South tend to be older than those who are leaving the South, which suggests some degree of return or home migration. They left the South at a young age and returned at an older age.[76] This return migration reflects not only the South's economic growth and improved race relations, but also longstanding cultural and kinship ties to the region.[77] The massive out-migration from the South never broke these strong ties. As the old home place, the South remains a significant place in the minds of many black migrants. Sometimes, all that was needed to "think of home," according to Albert Murray, writer and native Alabamian, was to listen to the sounds of a

> downhome church organ secularized to the Kansas City four-four or sounds
> from storefront churches, whether somewhat sedate or downright sanctified

> . . . and you are all the way back even before you have time to realize how far
> you are supposed to have gone . . . the sounds, smells and tastes encountered
> in Harlem . . . evoke church meetings, revivals, picnic and camp meetings
> with white potato salad and sweet potato pies, dasher-turned ice cream after
> a sermon on Sunday—and also road side beer-joints, Alabama pine-needles
> breezes, and blue steel locomotive on northbound tracks.[78]

And for Dwayne Walls, the South was still

> home even when home is a shack owned by the man up the road. It is a nail
> beside the kitchen door where the hat has been hung for 30 years. It is the
> old cane-bottom chair under the shade trees, where ice water tastes so good
> at the end of a summer day. It is the smell of manure and old harness leather,
> and the memory of young love carved on the barn door. . . . It is the church
> and the graveyard, where parents and brothers, sisters and babies are buried.
> It is the debt still owed to the bank or the store or the landlord—a debt that
> never seems to go away no matter how good the crop.[79]

Many blacks migrated northward not because they wanted to move but because
they had to move. They reluctantly headed for northern ghettos that were no promised
land, streets that were not so smooth. Some were able to act on those thoughts and
memories of the South as a "very old place" and return to the region, although to a different place. Blacks may have fond memories of the "old home place," but they are not
returning to the "old home place," for most are no longer in possession of it. Only 7
percent of blacks migrating to the South from the Northeast and Midwest between
1990 and 1995 returned to rural areas from where most migrated. Over half of the
black migrants to the South resided in suburban areas.

Conclusion: Fifty Years after Brown

Fifty years have passed since the court in *Brown v. Board of Education of Topeka, Kansas*
(1954) overturned the "separate but equal" race doctrine of *Plessy v. Ferguson* (1896).
Should we celebrate the Brown decision or should we mourn its failure? The ghetto riots
in the aftermath of the civil rights struggle are testimonies that the Brown decision may
not have produced all that blacks needed and wanted. Central cities of large metropolitan
areas have become the epicenter of spatial segregation. In 1988, approximately 55 percent
of black students in the South attended schools that were 50 to 100 percent minorities.
By 2000, almost 70 percent attended such schools. Only 15 percent of intensely segregated white schools are schools of concentrated poverty, whereas 88 percent of the
intensely segregated racial minority schools are schools of concentrated poverty.[80]

The most fundamental difference between today's spatially segregated black communities and those of the past is the much higher level of joblessness.[81] The unemployment and poverty levels consistently remain at twice the level of the total
population (Table 4.3). Access to jobs, already disproportionately tenuous for black
workers, has become even more constricted in the current era of globalization. Without

Table 4.3.   Socioeconomic Status of Blacks, 2000

	Population	
	Black	Total
% Unemployed	11.6	5.8
Male	12.3	5.7
25–29	12.2	5.5
Female	10.9	5.8
25–29	11.5	6.0
% Below Poverty Level	24.9	12.4
% Less than High School Diploma	27.7	19.6
% Occupation		
Management/Professional	25.2	33.6
Service	22.0	14.9
Sales/Office	27.3	26.7
Agriculture	0.4	0.7
Construction	6.5	9.4
Production/Transportation	18.6	14.6
Median Family Income	33,255	50,046

Source: U.S. 2000 Census, STF3 and STF4 Data Files.

meaningful work, the impact of racially segregated communities is much more perva-sive and devastating. The vast majority of intensely racial and ethnically segregated minority places face a growing surplus of labor determined to survive by any means necessary. Two-thirds of the people in prison are now racial and ethnic minorities. The proportion of young black males who are incarcerated, on parole, or on probation nationwide continues to reach record levels. Blacks represent 12.3 percent of the total population but make up 43.7 percent of the incarcerated population. The number of black men in prisons increased from 508,800 in 1990 to 899,000 in 2004, which is nine times the number incarcerated in 1954, the year of the Brown decision. There are 25 percent more black men in prison than are enrolled in institutions of higher educa-tion. One out of every eight black males in the 25–29 age cohort, which has an unem-ployment rate more than twice that of the total population (Table 4.3), is incarcerated on any given day. The incarceration rate for black women is also increasing.

Many black communities are left with little social capital to enhance community development. Black median family income is only 66 percent of that for the total pop-ulation. Nearly 28 percent of the black population has less than a high school diploma compared to 19.6 percent for the total population. And almost half are employed in low-paying service and sales occupations (Table 4.3).

While there are no longer social structures designating "for colored" and "for white" spaces, Mike Davis found one of the most postmodernist and hyperrealist cities in America, Los Angeles, still structured along race and class lines.[82] In this postmod-ern environment, we use techniques of visual observation—electronic monitors with their central surveillance—to protect an urban spatial order segregated around race and class lines. The "panopticon prison" of the postmodern era is the "panopticon mall," which dramatically captures the continuities between modern and postmodern techniques of visual observation.[83] Although all are watched in the "panopticon mall," blacks are deemed suspicious and given close scrutiny. Like those in Michel Foucault's "panopticon," it is common for blacks to be closely watched, or ignored outright, to receive low-quality service, or to encounter unfriendly, disrespectful treatment in the sphere of commodity exchange and consumption.[84] One does not have to cite the difficulties many blacks have in obtaining taxicabs in certain parts of the city and such nationally infamous cases as Denny's, Shoney's restaurants, and Dillard's department store and Adam Marks hotels to illustrate the continual importance of race fifty years following the Brown decision. Blacks continue to experience real differences whereas neoliberal policies find it difficult to accept differences of any kind. What appears as indifference for neoliberalism, however, is progressive segregation for many blacks.

Notes

1. Sam B. Hilliard, "Plantation and the Molding of the Southern Landscape," in *The Making of the American Landscape*, ed. Michael P. Conzen (New York: Routledge, 1994), 104–126.

2. Thomas Jefferson, *Notes on the State of Virginia*, ed. William Peder (Chapel Hill: University of North Carolina Press, 1955).

3. Leon Litwack, *North of Slavery: The Negro in the Free States, 1790–1860* (Chicago: University of Chicago Press, 1961), 158.

4. Roy P. Baler, *The Collected Works of Abraham Lincoln*, vol. 5 (New Brunswick, NJ: Rutgers University Press, 1953), 371–375.

5. W. E. B. DuBois, *Black Reconstruction in America* (Cleveland: World Publishing Company, 1964), 149.

6. Grace Elizabeth Hale, *Making Whiteness: The Culture of Segregation in the South, 1890–1940* (New York: Vintage Books, 1999); Ann Satterthwaite, *Going Shopping: Consumer Choices and Community Consequences* (New Haven: Yale University Press, 2001), 78–82.

7. Edgar T. Thompson, "Country Store," in *Encyclopedia of Southern Culture*, ed. Charles Wilson and William Ferris (Chapel Hill: University of North Carolina Press, 1989), 16.

8. Bobby M. Wilson, "Race in Commodity Exchange and Consumption," *Annals of the Association of American Geographers*, 95, no. 3 (2005): 587–606.

9. Joseph William Singer, "No Right to Exclude: Public Accommodations and Private Property," *Northwestern University Law Review* 90 (Summer 1996): 1301.

10. *Plessy v. Ferguson*, 163 U.S. 537 (1896).

11. John W. Cell, *The Highest Stage of White Supremacy: The Origins of Segregation in South Africa and the American South* (Cambridge: Cambridge University Press, 1982), 18.

12. Quoted in Paul M. Gaston, *The New South Creed: A Study in Southern Mythmaking* (New York: Knopf, 1970), 148–149.

13. Joel Williamson, *The Crucible of Race: Black-White Relations in the American South since Emancipation* (New York: Oxford University Press, 1984), 254.

14. Wilson, "Race in Commodity Exchange and Consumption."

15. Cell, *White Supremacy*, 19.

16. Singer, "No Right to Exclude."

17. *Plessy*, 537.

18. Robin G. Kelley, "We Are Not What We Seem: Rethinking Black Working Class Opposition in the Jim Crow South," *Journal of American History* 80 (1993): 102.

19. Wilson, "Race in Commodity Exchange and Consumption."

20. Robert W. Rydell, "Editor's Introduction: Contend, Contend!" in *The Reason Why the Colored American Is Not in the World's Columbian Exposition*, ed. Ida. B. Well, Frederick Douglas, Irvine Garland Penn, and Ferdinand L. Barnett (Urbana: University of Illinois Press, 1999), xix–xx, xxxii–xxxiii; see also Maurice M. Manring, *Slave in a Box: The Strange Career of Aunt Jemima* (Charlottesville: University of Virginia, 1998); and Carl Pedersen, "Black Responses to Consumption: From Frederick Douglass to Booker T. Washington," in *Consumption and American Culture*, ed. David E. Nye and Carl Pedersen (Amsterdam: VU University Press, 1991), 194–203.

21. Wilson, "Race in Commodity Exchange and Consumption."

22. Bobby M. Wilson, *America's Johannesburg: Industrialization and Racial Transformation in Birmingham* (Lanham, MD: Rowman & Littlefield, 2000).

23. Ted Ownby, *American Dreams in Mississippi: Consumers, Poverty, and Culture, 1830–1998* (Chapel Hill: University of North Carolina Press, 1999), 106.

24. Juliet E. K. Walker, *The History of Black Business in America: Capitalism, Race, Entrepreneurship* (New York: Twayne, 1998), 160.

25. P. K. Edwards, *The Southern Urban Negro as a Consumer* (New York: Prentice-Hall, 1932), 39.

26. Robert E. Weems, *Desegregating the Dollar: African American Consumerism in the Twentieth Century* (New York: New York University Press, 1998).

27. W. E. B. DuBois, "A Nation within the Nation," *Current History* 42 (June 1935): 265–270.

28. Wilson, "Race in Commodity Exchange and Consumption."

29. Walker, *Black Business in America*, 215.

30. Loren Schweninger, *Black Property Owners in the South, 1790–1915* (Urbana: University of Illinois Press, 1990), 228.

31. Gunnar Myrdal, *An American Dilemma: Negro Problem and Modern Democracy* (New York: Harper and Row, 1962 [1944]), 304–305, 310.

32. Ownby, *American Dreams in Mississippi*.

33. Howard Rabinowitz, *Race Relations in the Urban South, 1865–1890* (New York: Oxford University Press, 1978), 90.

34. "Negro Dealers and Race Trade: A Study in Race Patronage," *New York Age*, 9 March 1916, 1.

35. W. Sherman Savage, *Blacks in the West* (Westport, CT: Greenwood Press, 1976); Nell Irvin Painter, *Exodusters: Black Migration to Kansas after Reconstruction* (New York: Alfred A. Knopf, 1977); Robert G. Athearn, *In Search of Canaan: Black Migration to Kansas, 1879–80* (Lawrence: The Regents Press of Kansas, 1978).

36. Clyde Woods, *Development Arrested: Race, Power, and the Blues in the Mississippi Delta* (London: Verso, 1998); Wilson, *America's Johannesburg*.

37. Earl Caldwell, "Gaining Ground on Black Property," *Black Enterprise* (May 1978): 21–24, 48.

38. "USDA Stonewalls African American Farmers in Landmark Civil Rights Settlement," <www.ewg.org/reports/blackfarmers/execsumm.phy.html> (15 November 2005).

39. Madhu Dubey, *Signs and Cities: Black Literary Postmodernism* (Chicago: University of Chicago Press, 2003), 145.

40. James Allen, *The Negro Question in the United States* (New York: International Publishers, 1936), 138.

41. Henry McKiven, *Iron and Steel: Class, Race, and Community in Birmingham, Alabama, 1875–1920* (Chapel Hill: University of North Carolina Press, 1995), 94.

42. Cedric Robinson, *Black Marxism: The Making of the Black Radical Tradition* (London: Zed Press, 1983), 285.

43. "Invites All North," *Chicago Defender* (10 February 1917), 3.

44. Quoted in DuBois, *Black Reconstruction*, 173.

45. Herbert Hill, "Demographic Change and Racial Ghettos: The Crisis of American Cities," *Journal of Urban Law* 44 (Winter 1966): 245–277.

46. *Buchanan v. Warley*, 245 U.S. 60 (1917).

47. David Delaney, *Race, Place, and the Law, 1836–1948* (Austin: University of Texas Press, 1998), 151.

48. *Shelley v. Kraemer*, 334 U.S. 1 (1948).

49. Reynolds Farley and Karl E. Taeuber, "Population Trends and Residential Segregation since 1960," *Science* 159 (March 1968): 953–956.

50. Karl E. Taeuber, "Residential Segregation," *Scientific American* 213 (August 1965): 12.

51. John H. Johnson, *Succeeding against the Odds* (New York: Warner Books, 1989), 89.

52. Michael Hardt and Antonio Negri, *Empire* (Cambridge, MA: Harvard University Press, 2000), 206.

53. John W. Blassingame, *Black New Orleans 1860–1880* (Chicago: University of Chicago Press, 1973), 215; see also Walker, *Black Business in America*.

54. Robert A. Bennett, "Having Your Say," *Black Enterprise* 26, no. 1 (1995): 65.

55. Alain Locke, *The New Negro: An Interpretation* (New York: Albert and Charles Boni, 1925).

56. Locke, *The New Negro*, 3–16.

57. Quoted in Francis Njubi Nesbitt, *Race for Sanctions: African Americans against Apartheid, 1946–1994* (Bloomington: Indiana University Press, 2004), 58. See also James A. Tyner and Robert J. Kruse II, "The Geopolitics of Malcolm X," *Antipode* 36 (January 2004): 24–42.

58. Malcolm X, *Malcolm X Speaks: Selected Speeches and Statements*, ed. G. Breitman (New York: Grove Weidenfeld, 1965), 35.

59. Tyner and Kruse, "The Geopolitics of Malcolm X."

60. Peter Camejo, *Who Killed Jim Crow? The Story of the Civil Rights Movement and Its Lessons for Today* (New York: Pathfinder Press, 1975), 5.

61. Martin Luther King Jr., *Where Do We Go from Here: Chaos or Community?* (New York: Harper and Row, 1967), 190.

62. Martin Luther King Jr., "The President's Address to the Southern Leadership Conference, 16 August 1967," in *The Rhetoric of Black Power*, ed. Robert Scott and Wayne Brockriede (New York: Harper and Row, 1969), 161–162.

63. Bruce D'Arcus,. "Protest, Scale, and Publicity: The FBI and the H. Rap Brown Act," *Antipode* 35 (September 2003): 718–741.

64. Ownby, *American Dreams in Mississippi*.

65. Regina Austin, "A Nation of Thieves: Consumption, Commerce, and the Black Public Sphere," *Public Culture* 7 (1994): 230–231.

66. Malcolm X, *Malcolm X Speaks*, 9.

67. Nesbitt, *Race for Sanctions*.

68. Fredric Jameson, "Periodizing the 60s," in *The 60s without Apology*, ed. Sohnya Sayres, Anders Stephanson, Stanley Aronowitz, and Fredric Jameson (Minneapolis: University of Minnesota Press, 1984), 178–209.

69. Frank Kofsky, *John Coltrane and the Jazz Revolution of the 1960s* (New York: Pathfinder Press, 1998), 57.

70. Jean-Paul Sartre, *Black Orpheus*, translated by S. W. Allen (Paris: Présence Africaine, 1976).

71. William L. Van Deburg, *New Day in Babylon: The Black Power Movement and American Culture, 1965–1975* (Chicago: University of Chicago Press, 1993), 192–247.

72. Nesbitt, *Race for Sanctions*, 64.

73. Nesbitt, *Race for Sanctions*, 71.

74. Nicholas K. Blomey, "Mobility, Empowerment and the Rights Revolution," *Political Geography* 13 (September 1994): 407–422.

75. Francis Fukuyama, *The End of History and the Last Man* (New York: Free Press, 1992); Dinesh D'Souza, *The End of Racism: Principles for a Multiracial Society* (New York: Free Press, 1995).

76. Jason P. Schachter, "Migration by Race and Hispanic Origin: 1995 to 2000," Census 2000 Special Reports, Censr-13 (October 2003).

77. William H. Frey, *The New Great Migration: Black America's Return to the South, 1965–2000,* Center on Urban and Metropolitan Policy, Living Cities Census Series (Washington: Brookings Institution, 2004).

78. Albert Murray, *South to a Very Old Place* (New York: McGraw-Hill, 1971), 4–5.

79. Dwayne Walls, *The Chickenbone Special* (New York: Harvest Book, 1971), 59.

80. Gary Orfield and Chungmei Lee, *Brown at 50: King's Dream or Plessy's Nightmare?* (Cambridge, MA: Harvard University Press, 2004).

81. William J. Wilson, *When Work Disappears: The World of the New Urban Poor* (New York: Alfred A. Knopf, 1997).

82. Mike Davis, *Ecology of Fear: Los Angeles and the Imagination of Disaster* (New York: Metropolitan Books, Henry Holt and Company, 1998); see also Mike Davis, *City of Quartz: Excavating the Future in Los Angeles* (London: Verso, 1990).

83. Davis, *Ecology of Fear*; Dubey, *Signs and Cities*.

84. Michel Foucault, *Discipline and Punishment: The Birth of the Prison* (New York: Vintage Books, 1995).

CHAPTER 5

Settlement Geographies of Mexican Americans

Daniel D. Arreola

The ancestors of Mexican Americans were the first Europeans to settle what is now the southwestern United States. A majority of their descendants still reside in the borderlands that stretch from Texas to California. Today, Mexican Americans are found in nearly every county in the United States, and they represent the largest subgroup of all Hispanic/Latino Americans. The Mexican American minority is the second largest in the United States, and its numbers are growing more rapidly than the national population as a whole. This minority today is more urban than the general population. In 2000, approximately nine of every ten Mexican Americans lived in cities, with Los Angeles being the largest single home of Mexican Americans in the United States. Cities like San Antonio and El Paso are predominantly Mexican American, and Phoenix, the sixth largest city in the country, will soon be chiefly Mexican American.

Origins in the Borderlands

The Mexican American population had their origins in the borderlands that stretch from California in the west to Texas in the east. Between 1598 and 1821, Spanish-speaking peoples from New Spain or present-day Mexico settled parts of the states of California, Arizona, New Mexico, Colorado, and Texas. After 1821, portions of this region became part of the Republic of Mexico, and each of the settled areas developed its own regional identity. Since 1848, the major settled areas have come under Anglo (non-Hispanic) political and cultural influence. Today, these five states remain the principal concentrations of Mexican American people. The transformation of these areas from Spanish outposts to Mexican provinces to Mexican American subregions represents the planting, germination, and rooting of Mexican American culture in the United States. The origins of many of the features associated with Mexican American culture from place names to architecture and numerous social customs can be traced to this early period of settlement in the borderlands.

EARLY SETTLEMENT

The initial settlement of the borderlands was in New Mexico (Map 5.1). This colonization followed the successful sixteenth-century settlement of the mining and livestock frontier of northern Mexico. In 1598, colonists ventured to the upper drainage of the Rio Grande Valley to settle among the Pueblo Indians. In 1610, Santa Fe was founded as the provincial capital and principal center of the region. Missions and presidios were established between Taos and Socorro and down river at Paso del Norte near present El Paso. Albuquerque was founded in 1706 following a Pueblo Indian revolt that temporarily forced the Spanish out of the northern settlements. At the close of the Spanish period in 1821, most of the borderlands population resided in New Mexico. A road connecting New Mexico with Chihuahua in northern Mexico was the principal link between the frontier and Mexico City farther south.[1]

Southern Arizona was a second region of Spanish settlement in the borderlands (Map 5.1). Like New Mexico, the Spanish presence in Arizona was an extension of a settlement effort that originated in Mexico. During the 1600s, Jesuit missions were founded in Mexico's northwest, and the few settlements established in Arizona were the northernmost reach of this frontier. Southern Arizona became known as Pimería Alta, or the upper Pima Indian area. The most successful settlements—the mission at San Xavier del Bac (1700), and the presidios at Tubac (1752) and Tucson (1776)—were

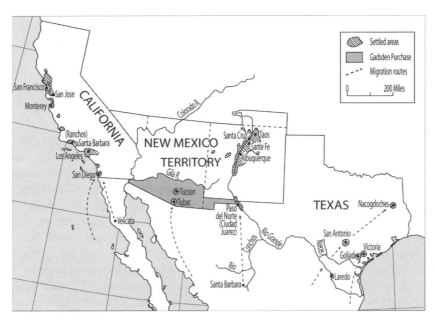

Map 5.1.   Spanish and Mexican Settlement in the Borderlands.
Source: After Richard L. Nostrand, Annals of the Association of American *Geographers 60 (December 1970): 645.*

situated along the Santa Cruz River. Settlements were extended to the San Pedro Valley to the east and for a short time on the Colorado River near present Yuma. In both areas, native hostilities prohibited successful colonization. In the Santa Cruz Valley, Apache raiding continued to be a threat to populations well into the nineteenth century. These conditions made difficult any firm footing in Pimería Alta, where populations never exceeded 2,000 during the Spanish and Mexican periods.[2]

Texas became a third area of Spanish settlement in the borderlands (Map 5.1). Colonization was prompted by the desire to confront French influence in the lower Mississippi River valley. Settlements in Texas were also an extension of the northern Mexico mining and livestock frontier. Three major mission-presidio complexes were founded in the Texas area: (1) Nacogdoches, west of the Sabine River in 1716; (2) San Antonio, situated between the central plateau and the gulf coastal plain in 1718; and (3) La Bahía, near present-day Victoria in 1722. This last settlement was relocated to the lower San Antonio River near present Goliad in 1749. Another community, Laredo, was founded in 1755 on the north bank of the Rio Grande in the province of Nuevo Santander. By the late 1700s, San Antonio had become the major provincial settlement of Spanish *Tejas* (Texas). Road connections with northern Mexico and few native hostilities allowed for permanence in the Texas borderlands. By 1850, some 14,000 *Tejanos* (Mexican Texans) populated the region.[3]

California was the last of the borderland outposts to witness Spanish and Mexican settlement (Map 5.1). Although explorations and coastal reconnoitering had taken place along the Pacific coast as early as 1542, permanent settlement did not commence for over two centuries. The threat of Russian and British intrusion into California finally led to its settlement in 1769. In that year, land and sea parties converged on San Diego, where a mission-presidio complex was built. Within twenty years, additional settlements were established at the provincial capital of Monterey (1770), and in San Francisco (1776) and Santa Barbara (1782 and 1786). By the early 1800s, a chain of twenty missions connected the settlements of coastal California, including two civil communities founded at San Jose (1777) and Los Angeles (1781), the latter via overland colonization from Sonora, Mexico, by way of southern Arizona. Sea and land connections between the California settlements and an ocean link to Mexico ensured this region's viability. By 1850, over 9,000 *Californios* (Mexican Californians) inhabited this part of the borderlands frontier.[4]

SETTLEMENT INSTITUTIONS

Settlement in the borderlands was shaped in part by the Laws of the Indies. These legal codes set forth in theory how new lands should be settled. As a result of practical problems encountered in each settlement area, not all regions of Spanish-Mexican settlement complied precisely with these laws. The institutions that developed, however, were remarkably similar from one end of the borderlands to another.

The mission and presidio were the initial frontier institutions. The mission was, in essence, an extension of the religious agreement made by Spain with the Catholic church to convert native populations. Missions were usually established where aboriginal populations were concentrated. In the borderlands, both Jesuit and Franciscan religious orders were involved in mission founding, although at different times and in different regions. The priests converted natives to the Catholic faith, with varying degrees of success. In addition, native inhabitants were trained to the ways of the Spaniard and employed as laborers to make the missions viable. They erected buildings, dug irrigation ditches, planted and harvested crops, cared for livestock, and performed work essential to the success of a mission.

The presidio was a military settlement or garrison. Presidios were sometimes founded in conjunction with missions. Often, they were located at strategic points along a line of transport or situated to defend a mission from native or foreign attack. Many missions and presidios were abandoned as the settlement frontier fluctuated. Some persisted and became centers of population concentration. The presidio in Tucson, Arizona, for example, survived as a settlement through the Mexican period to become a modern and vibrant American city.[5]

The pueblo or town was a third Spanish settlement institution brought to the borderlands. While the functions of the mission and presidio were religious and military respectively, the pueblo was a civil community. According to the Laws of the Indies, the civil settlement was the climax institution whereas missions and presidios were, conceptually, only temporary frontier settlements. Pueblos were to be situated on grants of land measuring four leagues or approximately forty-two square miles. The center of the pueblo included a plaza, surrounded by government offices and a parish church. A rectangular grid of streets emanating from the plaza accommodated houses. Surrounding these were lands for cultivation, pasture, and woodland. The pueblos became major nuclei of population and attracted merchants, artisans, and farmers. Los Angeles, California, and San Antonio, Texas, for example, were founded as pueblos.[6]

A final means of settlement introduced by the Spaniards to the borderlands was the land grant. This form of settlement persisted in the border region during the Mexican period after 1821. Parcels of land were granted to private individuals. Land grants were allocated as an economic incentive to settle areas and make them productive. These lands were transformed into livestock *ranchos* where cattle and sheep became the economic mainstay of the settlement unit as in California and Texas. In other areas, where sufficient water could be controlled for irrigation, land grants became farmsteads where wheat and corn were cultivated as in New Mexico. Today, many land grants remain as legal definitions of property in the borderlands. They persist also as place names, and stand as examples of the legacy of Spanish and Mexican imprints in the border region.[7]

After the United States–Mexico War, much of the borderland became United States territory. By the Treaty of Guadalupe Hidalgo, signed in 1848, many resident Mexicans of these borderlands became Mexican Americans. After the Gadsden Purchase in 1853, Arizona south of the Gila River became United States territory as well (Map 5.1). In 1850, there were perhaps 80,000 Mexican Americans.[8] In a short time, the rapid influx of Anglos began to transform the borderlands into an American province, culturally as well as politically. The proportion of Mexican Americans to Anglos continued to decrease during the latter nineteenth century as the Anglo American population increased.

IMMIGRANT EXPERIENCE

Immigration has been and continues to be an important contributor to the Mexican American population. From the middle of the nineteenth century to the present, Mexican immigrants have been an important source of labor north of the border. Their availability helped make possible the economic development of agriculture and industry in the southwestern United States, and their continued immigration, both legal and illegal, provides a labor pool to agriculture, manufacturing, and the service sector of urban economies throughout the Hispanic American borderland and beyond. Conceptually, this movement of labor is explained by both Neo-Classical and Dual Market Theories.

Mexican labor migration to the United States dates to the middle of the nineteenth century. The early Mexican migrants foreshadowed the coming of *mojados* ("wetbacks"), *braceros* (people who work with their *brazos*, arms), and others in the twentieth century. Together these streams have been part of a larger historical process of labor scarcity in the United States and a surplus of underemployed labor in Mexico. Scholars have argued that there has been a long tradition of a migrant subculture in Mexico, marginal populations that moved seasonally with economic opportunity.[9] When opportunity emerged in the United States, migrant Mexicans moved to satisfy the labor demand. This occurred slowly at first as specific economic circumstances pulled migrants to regional nodes during the nineteenth century, then en masse during the twentieth century with the swelling of population in Mexico, civil war in Mexico, changes in transport technology on both sides of the border, and the economic development of the southwestern United States.

Mexican immigration in this century has occurred in two distinct waves. The first took place from approximately 1900 to 1930, after which the Great Depression reduced the flow. The second was initiated by the Second World War economy of the 1940s, and continues largely undiminished to this day. Between 1910 and 1930, Mexican immigrants to the United States averaged 30,462 per year with the greatest number (87,648) coming in 1924 and the lowest number (10,954) entering in 1913. Between 1961 and 1984, Mexico was the major sender of immigrants to the United States with nearly 1.4 million.[10]

The mining frontiers of the western United States were the first major attraction for Mexican migrant labor. Mexican laborers from the northern states of Sonora, Chihuahua, Durango, and Zacatecas responded to the demand for workers in California, Nevada, and Arizona.[11] Practically every mining community in the West had a Mexican district. Jerome and Bisbee, Arizona, for example, were copper mining towns where Mexican labor contributed from the late nineteenth century to the peak of the production years just before the Depression. The towns became major destinations for Mexican immigrants and redistribution points for migration to other parts of the West. Clifton-Morenci, also in Arizona, is a copper mining town still and it is chiefly populated by Mexican Americans.

Railroads became the primary means for dispersing Mexican migrants in the United States. The rails bridged the expanses of the West and effectively shortened distances between population centers. In 1884, El Paso became connected by rail to Los Angeles and Chicago, and to Chihuahua and Mexico City. In the following decades, Nogales, Arizona, was linked by rail to Hermosillo, Sonora; and San Antonio and Corpus Christi, Texas, were joined to Monterrey, Nuevo León, by way of Laredo, Texas. Spur lines, like capillaries, grew from these main arteries and brought Mexican migrants everywhere the railroad went. By 1930, colonies of Mexican migrants could be found in nearly every town and city along the rail routes. The railroads also transported Mexicans to the inner cities of the region where they were hired and redistributed by labor contractors.[12]

The development of the Southwest was made possible, in part, by the northward migration of Mexicans who labored in many places. Railroads integrated the Southwest into the nation's industrial economy, and Mexican labor became a major source for factory and mining employment as well as railroad construction and maintenance. When federal legislation encouraging western irrigation projects was passed in 1902, Mexican labor again proved important to the success of citrus and cotton cultivation in California, Arizona, and the lower Rio Grande Valley in Texas. The mobility of Mexican labor likewise became vital to the beet sugar industry in Colorado, Kansas, and Nebraska and to the expansion of truck farming in Southern California, Arizona, and Texas.[13]

The depression of the 1930s slowed the flow of Mexican migrants to the United States. High unemployment north of the border initiated a reverse movement of Mexican migrants back to Mexico that included forced repatriations. From 1931 to 1943, an average of 2,013 Mexicans per year migrated to the United States, representing a considerable ebbing of the previous twenty-year flow. In 1942, the American government instituted a contract farm labor agreement with Mexico known as the Bracero Program. Under this agreement, Mexican laborers were transported to agricultural areas in this country to help alleviate the labor shortage brought on by the Second World War. The program served agricultural interests well since farmers were supplied with a steady and inexpensive source of labor. The Bracero Program also benefited Mexican migration. It pointed the way to *el norte* (the north, or United States) and provided a view of the economic opportunities that awaited legal and illegal migrants to this country.[14]

BORDERLAND SUBREGIONS

Today, the preponderance of the Mexican American minority resides in the five southwestern states that have been called the Hispanic American borderland.[15] Parts of California, Arizona, New Mexico, and Texas are the major cores of this province, but a portion of southern Colorado is also part of the region. These areas represent the early nuclei of Spanish and Mexican settlement and expanded areas of the earliest settlements. Many of the Mexican immigrants who have entered the United States since the early twentieth century also inhabit parts of this region.

Although Mexican Americans are considered the dominant Hispanic group in this province, there are distinct regional identities. This differentiation originated with the varied periods of Spanish-Mexican settlement in the borderlands, and the development of separate self-referents. In Texas and California during the Mexican period, the appellations *Tejano* and *Californio* were used respectively. In New Mexico and parts of southern Colorado, many of the Hispanic people refer to themselves as *Hispano* or Spanish American, not Mexican American. This subgroup claims ancestry from the earliest Spanish colonists of the region and considers itself culturally distinct from the Mexican groups that constitute the majority of the Mexican American population like the *Tejanos* in Texas.[16]

A Geographic Portrait

The 2000 census designated Mexican Americans part of the Hispanic/Latino/Spanish Origin population. This population numbered 35.3 million and also included Puerto Rican, Cuban, Central and South American, Dominican, and Other Hispanics. Mexican Americans numbered 20.6 million or 58 percent of the Hispanic/Latino/Spanish Origin group. In 1990, the census counted 13.5 million people of Mexican origin or descent. The difference suggests that the Mexican American population increased 7.1 million or 53 percent between 1990 and 2000. While these figures may reflect an undercount of Mexican Americans in 1990, they reveal the phenomenal growth of the Mexican American population, now the second largest minority group behind African Americans.[17] The Mexican American population is largely concentrated in the borderlands, yet areas outside of this hearth region count significant numbers.

POPULATION DISTRIBUTION

The Mexican American population in the borderlands totaled 15.3 million in 2000 (Table 5.1). California ranked highest in the nation with 8.4 million Mexican Americans, followed by Texas with 5.0 million and Arizona with 1.0 million. New Mexico and Colorado each counted less than one-half million Mexican Americans. Mexican Americans are located in four regional concentrations outside of the borderlands: the Midwest, especially Illinois and Michigan; the West, particularly Washington; the South focused on Florida; and the Northeast, chiefly New York (Table 5.1).

The map of Mexican American population distribution makes immediate how this pattern is spatially tilted to the Southwest (Map 5.2). The borderland states accounted for 74 percent of all Mexican Americans in 2000. This percent distribution declined significantly from 1990, although the absolute number of Mexican Americans who reside in borderland states increased by some four million (Table 5.1). The changed distribution in the borderlands is counterbalanced by a greater dispersion of Mexican Americans across the country. In the Midwest and South, Mexican Americans have increased their presence, especially in the South where the percentage of Mexican Americans has more than doubled. In the Northeast and West both absolute numbers and percentages of the distribution increased from 1990 to 2000 (Table 5.1).

The absolute and percentage gains by regions notwithstanding, the concentration of Mexican Americans remains skewed to the southwest and west of the nation. The density of Mexican Americans by county reinforces the dominance of this population

Table 5.1.   Mexican Americans by Region and Leading States, 1990 and 2000

Region	1990	% Distribution	2000	% Distribution
Borderlands	11,237,325	83.3	15,374,276	74.4
CA	6,118,996		8,455,926	
TX	3,890,820		5,071,963	
AZ	616,195		1,065,578	
NM	328,836		330,049	
CO	282,478		450,760	
Midwest	1,153,296	8.5	2,200,196	10.6
IL	623,688		1,144,390	
MI	138,312		220,760	
West[1]	477,618	3.5	1,110,952	5.3
WA	155,864		329,934	
South[2]	452,703	3.4	1,476,113	7.1
FL	161,499		363,925	
Northeast	174,996	1.3	479,169	2.3
NY	93,244		260,889	
Total U.S.	13,495,938	100.0	20,640,711	100.0

[1] Excludes California, Arizona, New Mexico, Colorado.
[2] Excludes Texas.
Sources: U.S. Bureau of the Census, *1990 Census of Population and Housing*, Summary Tape File 1A
   (Washington: U.S. Bureau of the Census, 1991); U.S. Bureau of the Census, *Census of the Population:
   2000*, Summary Tape 1 (Washington: U.S. Bureau of the Census, 2001).

in the borderlands, especially Texas, despite the percentage decline for the borderland states seen in Table 5.1. Only a handful of counties outside Texas had greater than half of their population Mexican American, including for example, Imperial County (CA), Santa Cruz County (AZ), and Doña Ana County (NM). Along the Texas border, no fewer than thirty-two counties were greater than half Mexican American population, and twenty of these were more than 70 percent Mexican ancestry.[18]

Economic opportunity first brought Mexicans to the upper Midwest during the First World War. Railroads, steel mills, and meatpacking houses provided employment opportunities. The industries continued to draw immigrants during the Second World War as migrants established large permanent populations in the industrial cities of the Midwest.[19]

Unlike the Mexican migrants who moved to the cities of the upper Midwest, Mexican American populations in the West region had their origins in rural and small town settlements. As miners, livestock herders, and agriculturalists, Mexicans and Mexican Americans migrated to these areas when economic activities created a demand for their labor in the second half of the nineteenth century. Agricultural labor, again, was in high demand during the twentieth century and Mexican migrant laborers largely filled this need. Over time, temporary rural centers developed services that catered to Mexicans and permanent populations became established. The Yakima Valley and parts of southeastern Washington, as well as the fertile Willamette Valley of Oregon and the Snake River Valley in Idaho have been major agricultural districts that have accommodated Mexican migrant labor, creating satellite communities far from the borderland.[20]

Map 5.2.   Mexican-origin Population in the United States, 2000.
Source: Betsy Guzmán, The Hispanic Population (Washington: U.S. Bureau
of the Census, 2001), Table 2.

The South grew rapidly in the decade from 1990 to 2000, and the Mexican American population expanded considerably in this region. The arc of states from Virginia to Florida, west to Louisiana, and including the states of Arkansas, Tennessee, and Kentucky, counted 452,703 Mexican Americans in 1990 and 1,476,113 by 2000 (Table 5.1). Florida is the primary center among this group of states, having counted 160,000 Mexican Americans in 1990 and greater than two times that number ten years later (Table 5.1). The dramatic change in Mexican Americans in the South suggests a demand for labor in extractive economies such as agriculture, as well as industrialization, especially chicken-processing plants that have exploded in this region.[21]

In the Northeast, New York has become the focus of 260,000 people of Mexican ancestry (Table 5.1). During the early 1990s, Mexicans in New York were dubbed *La Gran Manhatitlán* because mostly they are an urban immigrant community on the island of Manhattan. Today, however, Mexicans are found in all boroughs, with Brooklyn and Queens counting the greatest concentration. The population includes migrants from other U.S. states as well as a significant number of immigrants, especially from the Mexican state of Puebla.[22] Mexican immigrants are also found in selected smaller towns in the Empire State like the Oaxacan migrants in Poughkeepsie.[23]

AN URBAN PEOPLE

Despite the sometimes stereotyped rural origins of their past, Mexican Americans like all Hispanics/Latinos in 2000 were overwhelmingly an urban people. In 2000, the census calculated that 89.4 percent of persons of Mexican origin lived in metropolitan areas. This percentage was higher than the corresponding proportion, 81 percent, for the U.S. population.[24] Moreover, about one of every two persons of Mexican origin resided in the central cities of their metropolitan areas. In recent decades, however, there has been a dispersion of population to suburban locations in some cities. In 2000, 44 percent of all Mexicans resided in suburbs.[25]

The cities with the greatest numbers of Mexican Americans are almost exclusively in borderland states; only Chicago is outside this realm (Table 5.2). Most top-ranked places are spread across the borderlands in Texas and California. New Mexico is conspicuous in the absence of places in this hierarchy, emphasizing its chiefly rural/small-town settlement geography. Although New Mexico counted some 330,000 people of Mexican ancestry in 2000, mostly in southern counties, the majority of the state's Hispanics self-identified as "Other Hispanic" in the census because most of New Mexico's Hispanic population considers itself *Hispano* or Spanish American, not Mexican American.[26]

Los Angeles had the greatest number of Mexican Americans, some one million in the city and 4.9 million in the consolidated metropolitan statistical area.[27] The Mexican heritage of the city dates to the colonial era, and, recently, Central American immigrants, particularly Salvadorans and Guatemalans, have occupied distinctive quarters in parts of the central city.[28] San Antonio, although smaller than Los Angeles, is also a recognized center of Mexican American population.[29] This city's population is almost half Mexican American and, unlike Los Angeles, Mexican Americans are not challenged by other Hispanic ethnic groups. Chicago and Houston are yet other strongholds. El Paso, like San Antonio and unlike Chicago, Houston, or Los Angeles, is predominantly Mexican American (Table 5.2). Being situated on the international border and across the Rio Grande from Ciudad Juárez reinforces the "Mexicanness" of the place. Other cities

Table 5.2.   Largest Urban Places for Total Mexican Population, 2000

Place	Total Population	Hispanic/ Latino	Mexican	% Mexican
Los Angeles	3,694,820	1,719,073	1,091,611	30.0
Chicago	2,896,016	753,644	530,565	18.0
Houston	1,953,631	730,865	527,684	27.0
San Antonio	1,144,646	671,394	473,332	41.0
Phoenix	1,321,045	449,972	375,276	28.0
El Paso	563,662	431,875	359,751	64.0
Dallas	1,188,580	422,587	350,032	29.0
San Diego	1,223,400	310,752	259,167	21.1

Source: Betsy Guzmán, *The Hispanic Population*, Census Brief 2000 (Washington: U.S. Bureau of the Census, 2001) <www.census.gov/prod/2001pubs/c2kbr01-3.pdf>.

with intermediate-size Mexican American populations in 2000 are Phoenix, Dallas, and San Diego (Table 5.2).

Yet another measure of urban hierarchy is places where Mexican Americans are a large percentage of a city's population. Places with the highest Mexican percentage include, for example, East Los Angeles, California (96.8), Laredo, Texas (94.1), and Santa Ana, California (76.1). The majority of these cities are also in the borderlands, but they are not the same places as those with the largest Mexican American populations. Most are places with populations of less than 200,000, yet they are typically places that are greater than 70 percent Mexican American. More than half of these places are in south and west Texas, the remainder in southern California, emphasizing the states with the largest Mexican populations. The proximity to the international border is a striking characteristic of nearly all these communities.

Social and Economic Characteristics

The social and economic character of the Mexican American population differed from the total U.S. population in 2000. Family income and educational attainment were lower, on the average, than for the majority of Americans. Further, other social and economic indices also vary when Mexican Americans are compared to other Hispanic/Latino subgroups across the country. Finally, Mexican Americans' social and economic indices were higher in some regions of the country than in other regions. The measurements signal the social and economic variation among Mexican Americans compared to other Hispanics/Latinos as well as within the subgroup. These patterns suggest a regional social and economic geography for the Mexican American population.

AGE AND FAMILY STRUCTURE

The Mexican-origin population in 2000 was younger, on the average, than the entire United States' population, and it was the youngest subgroup population among all Hispanics/Latinos (Table 5.3). About 32.7 percent were under fifteen years old, whereas only 21.8 percent were in this age bracket for the general population. Compared to other Hispanic/Latino subgroups, Mexicans were significantly younger than Puerto Ricans, Cubans, and Central and South Americans. Furthermore, in 2000 Mexicans had the lowest percent of population 65 years and over, just 3.8 percent compared to 4.2 percent for Central and South Americans, 5.4 percent for Puerto Ricans, and 19.6 percent for Cubans. The general fertility rate, the number of births per 1,000 women in the 15–44 age group, has been higher for Mexican American women than Anglo women since the nineteenth century; in 1995 this rate was 117 for Mexican American and 66 for all American women.[30] Also, since 1920, the growth of the Mexican stock population—native-born and foreign-born Mexican Americans—largely has been a function of natural increase.[31] High fertility rates in a population usually mean large families. According to the 2000 census, 35.5 percent of Mexican households

Table 5.3. Social and Economic Indicators by Percent for Hispanic Population by Subgroup, 2000

Category	Total U.S.	Mexican	Puerto Rican	Cuban	Central/ South American	Other Hispanic	Non- Hispanic
Under 15 years	21.8	32.7	28.2	15.1	24.7	29.3	20.6
65 years and over	12.1	3.8	5.4	19.6	4.2	6.1	13.3
Married-couple families	76.9	69.8	56.4	77.3	65.0	64.3	78.0
Female householder	17.5	21.1	36.1	18.1	24.4	27.6	16.8
Unemployed	4.4	7.1	8.5	6.0	5.2	8.2	4.0
Below poverty level	11.9	24.1	25.7	17.0	16.6	21.7	10.3
Managerial & professional	30.1	11.6	16.7	23.2	14.5	21.5	32.2
Technical, sales, administrative	29.4	22.2	35.2	34.4	23.2	29.8	30.0
Service	13.9	18.9	18.3	13.3	22.8	19.2	13.2
Production, craft, & repair	10.7	16.0	10.0	11.0	14.2	8.5	10.2
Operators, fabricators, & laborers	13.4	23.1	19.0	17.5	23.0	19.0	12.3
Farming, forestry, & fishing	2.4	8.1	0.8	0.6	2.3	2.0	2.0
High school graduate	33.1	26.6	29.8	33.3	29.5	32.0	33.7
Bachelor's degree	17.0	5.2	8.5	13.9	11.7	9.1	18.7
Homeowner	67.3	49.6	34.9	58.5	37.1	47.1	69.5

Source: U.S. Bureau of the Census, *Current Population Survey, Hispanic Population in the United States: March 2000* (Washington: U.S. Bureau of the Census, 2003).

included five or more people; the comparables for Central and South Americans were 27.9, for Puerto Ricans 18.1, and for Cubans 14.0.[32]

The character of the Mexican American family is also revealed in census data about type of household. Of all Mexican households, nearly 70 percent were married-couple families in 2000 (Table 5.3). Only Cuban households ranked higher. Whereas Puerto Ricans had the highest percent of female heads of household, Mexicans ranked second lowest by this measure after Cubans, suggesting the cultural predilection for couple-family households (Table 5.3).

ECONOMIC AND EDUCATION PATTERNS

Hispanic/Latino economic measures contrast significantly with those for non-Hispanics and all Americans. Whereas unemployment in 2000 was 4.0 percent for non-Hispanics and 4.4 percent for all Americans, Mexican unemployment was 7.1 percent, less than Puerto Rican but higher than that for Cuban and Central and South American (Table 5.3). By the federal government measure, 24.1 percent of Mexicans were below poverty level compared to 25.7 percent of Puerto Ricans, 17.0 percent of Cubans, and 16.6 percent of Central and South Americans (Table 5.3). Mexican Americans like all Hispanic/Latino subgroups were significantly below the poverty level compared to non-Hispanics and to all Americans.

Compared to the occupational status of all Americans, Mexican Americans like all Hispanic/Latino subgroups were underrepresented in managerial and professional occupations, and Mexican Americans, like Central and South Americans, but unlike Puerto Ricans and Cubans, ranked low in technical and administrative jobs in 2000 (Table 5.3). On the other hand, Mexican Americans were overrepresented in farming, forestry, and fishing as well as operator, fabricator, and laborer occupations and in precision production, craft, and repair as well as service work. These associations mirror many decades of labor sector imbalance for the minority.[33]

Mexican American occupational status suggests a pattern of low educational attainment. In 2000, only 26.6 percent of Mexican Americans 25 years or older graduated from high school and just 5.2 percent from college (Table 5.3). The comparable figures for all Americans were 33.1 and 17.0 percent, respectively. While the average years of schooling completed have risen for Mexican Americans since 1960, they still have the lowest educational attainment of all Hispanic/Latino subgroups, below Cuban, Central and South American, and Puerto Rican.[34]

Ethnic Identity in Space and Place

Ethnic identity is one dimension used by scholars to interpret and to distinguish among American ethnic groups.[35] Geographers especially have contributed to this larger project through their studies of ethnic identity in place. In spatial terms, geographers ask questions about ethnic identity in space, typically in regional patterns, but they also investigate ethnic identity at the scale of local landscapes.[36]

RESIDENTIAL SPACE

In most cities, Mexican Americans are a minority and live in distinct districts within urban regions.[37] Before the second half of the nineteenth century, borderland cities were predominantly Mexican and populations were concentrated around the plazas that were established with a town's founding.[38] When railroads reached these cities and the Anglo population increased, Mexican American districts became isolated as the city expanded around or away from the old nucleus. This pattern is evident in the 1893 town plan of

Tucson, Arizona. The irregular streets in the city that are west of the railroad track date from the early Spanish-Mexican period while the standard grid of streets to the north and south resulted largely from Anglo subdivision after 1880. The Mexican American district became known as a *barrio,* by literal translation, a neighborhood.

Barrios, sometimes referred to as *colonias* (suburbs) because they were once located far from the center of town, also formed in the borderlands as urban expansion engulfed agricultural settlements housing Mexican American workers. In Southern California, Pacoima was one such *colonia.* The town became enveloped by the urbanization of the San Fernando Valley, a once fertile agricultural district northwest of the Los Angeles city center.[39] Still other rural communities like railroad worker settlements or labor camps followed a similar pattern, evolving into urban *barrios.* In his study of a Mexican American neighborhood in Weslaco, Texas, a lower Rio Grande Valley town, Arthur Rubel described the *barrio* of "Mexiquito" (Little Mexico) and its perception by residents and outsiders. The author suggests that the north and south sides of the railroad tracks are more than spatial districts in the city; they are also societies with separate characteristics and traditions.

> New Lots (Weslaco) is a city bisected by the railway of the Missouri Pacific. In 1921, the town's first year, the north side of the tracks was allocated by municipal ordinance to the residences and business establishments of Mexican Americans, and to industrial complexes. Mexican Americans refer to the north side of the tracks as Mexiquito, *el pueblo mexicano, nuestro lado;* even the traffic light north of the tracks is referred to as *la luz mexicana.* The other side of the tracks is spoken of as *el lado americano, el pueblo americano,* and other similar terms. Those who live south of the tracks also distinguish the two sides: "this side" and "the other side," "our side" and "their side," and "Mexican town" are all descriptive terms heard in the City of New Lots.[40]

Geographical isolation, housing restriction, and voluntary congregation have perpetuated residential segregation in the cities of the borderlands.[41] Mexican Americans are often segregated in the central cities of their metropolitan areas. There are two general explanations for this pattern. First, *barrios* became engulfed as the city expanded, as described above. A second process that helps explain the central city concentration is the filtering down of housing from one group to another. When a central city district becomes vacated as Anglos or other groups move out, lower-income populations, including some Mexican Americans, move into the inner-city neighborhood.[42] Many of the east side districts of Los Angeles such as Boyle Heights, City Terrace, and Lincoln Heights became populated by Mexican Americans in this manner as Jewish residents moved out of the east side to west side neighborhoods.[43] Similarly, in Chicago, the Mexican American population grew by 84 percent between 1960 and 1970, expanding mostly into older ethnic neighborhoods that once housed Czechs and Poles.[44] A survey of thirty-five cities in 1960 and ten in 1980 indicated that the mean index of residential dissimilarity, a measure of the degree of segregation between Anglo and Mexican American populations, was moderate.[45] Nevertheless, Los Angeles with the nation's largest Mexican American population is beginning to develop a "megabarrio" of nearly two hundred square miles that includes most of the county's Hispanic population, chiefly Mexican origin but with significant Central American subgroups.[46]

Since the Second World War, many urban Mexican Americans have dispersed into suburban areas. In Los Angeles County, for example, there were twenty-three municipalities in 1970 in which Mexican Americans accounted for 10 to 20 percent of the population, and twenty-five cities or unincorporated areas in the county in which they made up 5 to 9 percent of the total. Ten suburbs in the county showed that Mexican Americans increased significantly between 1960 and 1970.[47] Similar studies in Texas and Arizona have found that dispersal from traditional *barrios* into the suburbs escalated after the Second World War and the Korean conflict as veterans took advantage of federal legislation that allowed low-interest loans and participation in the new housing market.[48] This movement to the suburbs was also an indication of the upward economic mobility achieved by Mexican Americans.

URBAN CULTURAL LANDSCAPES

An axiom of human geography holds that landscape is a clue to culture.[49] Analyzing patterns of the built environment allows us to understand the social construction of a landscape and how cultures imprint and shape place. The cultural landscapes of Mexican American *barrios* are distinct, and differ from the landscapes of Anglo communities or those of other minority communities. *Barrios* surveyed in Texas, Arizona, and California include particular landscape elements; for example, brightly colored houses, fences enclosing house properties, colorful murals in residential and commercial areas, and ethnic shopping streets.

Houses are important elements of the material landscape, and they offer clues to the social groups that build and occupy them. In most *barrios*, Mexican Americans did not build the homes they now occupy. In fact, in many urban *barrios*, the housing stock is older than in other parts of the city, passed down to numerous and different populations. Old houses, however, have not kept Mexican Americans from embellishing their residences. Houses in urban *barrios* are sometimes painted in bright shades of blue, pink, yellow, or green. The use of these colors, an ancient Mexican tradition, has persisted and is evident in the vernacular or everyday landscapes of *barrios* in the borderlands.[50]

Yard fencing is another trait found in *barrios*. The persistent use of fences in residential landscapes has been studied in Tucson's Mexican American neighborhoods.[51] In these areas, fences and fence types were found to be keys to the identification of Mexican American households. The pattern of fence use indicates a traditional attitude about enclosed space in the urban landscape. Houses in urban Mexico in the present as well as the past have been built tight to the street with open space in the interior or back. The preference for fences as property markers in Mexican-American *barrios* illustrates the persistence of this vernacular landscape design.

Street murals have become popular elements of the vernacular landscapes of *barrios* (Fig. 5.1). The street art movement in Mexican American districts started in the late 1960s—coincident with the U.S. civil rights movement—and spread quickly to cities with large Mexican American populations.[52] Today, highly stylized wall paintings that reflect the mural traditions of Mexico can be seen in many *barrios* in the borderlands. Murals are painted by artists in communities who often employ *barrio* youth to

Figure 5.1.   *Mexican American murals decorate* barrio *urban landscapes, and bring social messages to community residents. This mural spotlights the importance of education as an alternative to drugs and street culture in the Guadalupe neighborhood of San Antonio, Texas. Source: Author.*

assist in the construction of the mural. The street art movement has heightened neighborhood identity by decorating *barrio* landscapes. In San Diego, murals "personalize" otherwise sterile institutional landmarks like freeway pillars and thus mark these landscapes as symbolic places for *barrio* residents.[53]

In many cities with large Mexican American populations, distinct immigrant quarters have become part of the cultural landscape. These smaller *barrios* are distinguishable from the larger Mexican American communities in that they house principally Mexican nationals or immigrants. In Los Angeles, these quarters, often a single apartment complex, have multiplied with the growth of immigrants from Mexico, and a Mexican immigrant colony in the San Francisco Bay area revealed a similar village atmosphere.[54] Immigrant families were found to reside on the same street or on several nearby streets. Residents maintained village social-behavioral patterns that reinforced their identity as immigrants from a particular province of Mexico, and they distinguished themselves from Mexican Americans and other Mexican immigrants. In the early morning hours, the sidewalks and street corners near these little *barrios* are filled with Mexican men who wait to be picked up by temporary employers. These day-labor pick-up spots are common in many cities of the borderlands.

Another landscape that has become common in cities and suburbs where Mexican nationals including Mexican Americans concentrate is the Mexican-Latin shopping street. Typically, this street is one that has been abandoned by Anglo or non-Hispanic merchants who relocate to suburban shopping centers. Mexican and Latino tenants rent-lease the retail spaces and what emerges is a kind of Mexican downtown. Broadway in downtown Los Angeles is, perhaps, the most celebrated of this type of ethnic shopping street.[55] However, many other downtowns in communities from McAllen, Texas, to Huntington Park, California, have been witness to a similar transformation. In McAllen, regarded as the retail center of the lower Rio Grande Valley, the traditional Anglo main street shopping district was converted to a Mexican downtown when upscale retail stores fled to suburban malls. In 1997, some 149 commercial properties existed in a six-block-long area. Nearly half of the establishments were clothing and jewelry retailers. Another 22 percent were discount variety stores that market inexpensive goods, and electronics stores. These retail types have been identified as diagnostic of Mexican American shopping districts in south Texas.[56]

Community Case Study

Mexican communities are exploding across the United States, not only in familiar borderland locations but also in regions like New England and the South that have no history of Mexican influence.[57] In 1998, geographer Terrence Haverluk advanced a model to describe the types of Hispanic/Latino communities found in the American West.[58] Communities were labeled continuous, discontinuous, and new. Continuous communities are places founded as Hispanic/Latino settlements and they have remained predominantly Hispanic/Latino to the present day. Places like Laredo, Texas; Las Vegas, New Mexico; Nogales, Arizona; and Calexico, California, are some examples of continuous communities. Discontinuous communities are places that were founded as Hispanic/Latino communities, but changed to become non-Hispanic/Latino places as Anglos settled the communities, and changed again to predominantly Hispanic/Latino places when migration and Hispanic/Latino population growth transformed the places in recent times. San Antonio, Texas; Albuquerque, New Mexico; Tucson, Arizona; and Los Angeles, California, are examples of discontinuous communities. New communities were originally settled as Anglo communities and have only recently experienced Hispanic/Latino populations. Lubbock, Texas; Garden City, Kansas; Reno, Nevada; and Pasco, Washington, are new communities. While continuous and discontinuous communities are in borderland states, new communities are scattered across the West, and especially in non-borderland locations. Further, Haverluk identified some 25 continuous communities, 22 discontinuous communities, but 60 new communities in the American West. These new communities are in frontier locations where Hispanic/Latino immigrants, chiefly of Mexican ancestry, are reshaping the social and cultural geography of the region.

TREASURE VALLEY: A NEW COMMUNITY

Treasure Valley is a fictitious community, yet one representative of many small towns in the Intermountain West that have emerged as new Hispanic communities. Like most of these places, Treasure Valley's Hispanic/Latino population is predominantly Mexican. In

2000, Treasure Valley counted some 26,000 residents and approximately 7,300 were of Mexican ancestry. The population of Treasure Valley was thus 28 percent of Mexican ancestry and therefore similar to Los Angeles (29.5) and Phoenix (28.4).

Mexicans migrated to parts of the Intermountain West during the mid to late nineteenth century to labor in mining, ranching, and railroad economies. By the early twentieth century as irrigated agriculture emerged in river environments of the West, Mexicans became increasingly common in settlements because they labored both to create the irrigation systems and to work and harvest crops. During this era, Treasure Valley sugar beet farmers who were chiefly Anglo sought Mexican labor from Texas and Mexico.[59] Mexicans in Treasure Valley trace their roots to Texas border towns like Eagle Pass, Pharr, and McAllen. These early connections created the cultural links that would shape the Mexican population of Treasure Valley and other Intermountain West new communities. Treasure Valley's agricultural economy continued to draw Mexicans to the town, both seasonal migrants as well as permanent settlers. A 2000 U.S. Census report revealed that two states—California and Texas—were places of residence for the greatest number of Hispanics who moved to Treasure Valley's state.

The family histories of permanent Mexicans who reside in Treasure Valley suggest that most families first came to the area as migrant workers. Many will tell you that the key to establishing permanence in the community is to secure full-time employment. Permanent employment often comes as a result of family and relatives who have already settled in the community. Thus social and familial linkages in the form of social capital that anchors chain migration are critical to the creation of a new community because they provide temporary shelter and the potential for employment contacts.

Some Mexicans in Treasure Valley travel a migrant circuit through Arizona, California, Oregon, and Washington.[60] In Treasure Valley, some farm workers labor for a single Anglo farmer year around, repairing equipment, driving tractors, and irrigating land. Many others work seasonally, during harvest or when their labor is in greatest demand, but they typically face some seasonal unemployment. Wages for seasonal labor are generally just above minimum wage so the poverty level as defined by the federal government is a near constant for these workers. Some Mexicans in Treasure Valley work in food processing industries, and these positions pay better than most field labor. Some Mexicans from Treasure Valley have achieved management status, but typically not in proportion to Anglos in the same positions. A small number of Mexicans operate businesses in Treasure Valley, especially restaurants, but even here it is not uncommon for family members to work both the business and another job like food processing (Fig. 5.2).

In Treasure Valley, unlike what Haverluk found in the new community of Hereford, Texas, Mexicans in significant percentages have not yet elevated themselves from farm and industrial labor to skilled crafts and professional occupations.[61] Haverluk found that the key to this transformation was education and the ability to speak English. Mexicans born and raised in Treasure Valley are unlikely to be fluent in Spanish because parents emphasize the importance of English to their children as a critical factor in their adjustment process. Nevertheless, educational attainment measured by high school and college graduation for Mexicans in the community is still far below that achieved by the non-Hispanic population.

Figure 5.2.   Mexican residents in "new communities" outside of the borderland like Treasure Valley often open restaurants and eateries to cater to local tastes. Entrepreneurship is an important employment goal for some immigrants who typically hire family to help run the eatery. Source: Author.

In other ways, Mexicans in Treasure Valley live lives not unlike Mexicans in segregated communities all across the Southwest. They spatially concentrate in "Little Mexico" as it is called, a residential and small business district set apart from the dominant Anglo community. In this *colonia*, Treasure Valley Mexicans find comfort and support through a host of familiar cultural institutions including Catholic and Protestant churches, entertainment venues, and annual celebrations like the Cinco de Mayo and the Diez y Seis de Septiembre, the latter being Mexican Independence Day. The most significant characteristic of Treasure Valley Mexicans, however, is the importance of family. This is evident in the primacy attached to extended family households where relatives might reside in the same house with a nuclear family, where social institutions of *comadre* and *compadre* (female and male godparentage), *padriños* (co-parents), and *quinceañera* (female debutant celebration at fifteen years) all reinforce the network of familial association.

Transnational Dynamics

Mexican immigration continues as a major social and economic engine transforming America. As discussed above, this geographical process is more than a century old yet it continues to evolve to meet the demands especially for low skilled and service sector labor in the American economy. The process has both a demographic social-political dimension, often inflamed by political rhetoric, and a human side rarely appreciated by the American public. To be sure, Mexicans come north from villages, towns, and cities in their homeland, seeking employment and, for some, permanent residence in the United States. But that is only part of the story. Rarely glimpsed or understood is the reciprocal or transnational flow of resources, typically in the form of remittances through electronic wire transfers of cash sent to homeland communities. Thus, the dynamic is not a one-sided affair but involves financial capital as well as human capital in a slow dance that helps sustain both immigrant in the new home and family back home.

THE "MEXICAN PROBLEM"

In recent times, the migration of Mexicans to the United States has become a headline issue that is especially acute during election years when politicians and others stump the "Mexican problem." Beyond the numbers of legal entrants, undocumented immigrants continue to migrate to the United States, and their numbers especially inflate the estimates of Mexican American residents. The termination of the Bracero Program in 1964, and the quotas set for legal immigration changed the circumstances of Mexican immigration. Illegal immigration grew as a consequence of the restrictions of legal entrance. The apprehensions of undocumented Mexicans rose from 55,000 in 1965 to 90,000 the next year and to 200,000 by 1969. These numbers climbed to 710,000 in 1974 and 978,000 in 1979.[62]

In 1986, the Immigration and Reform and Control Act (IRCA) granted amnesty to a large number of illegal or undocumented immigrants. Some 1.8 million people applied for legalization under the regular IRCA program, and an additional 1.3 million applied under the special agricultural workers program. The majority of IRCA applicants were Mexican, approximately 70 percent of the regular applicants and almost 82 percent of the special agricultural applicants. In 1991 alone, some 893,000 Mexican applicants were granted permanent resident status.[63]

The illegal Mexican immigrant situation has received much publicity in the borderlands and across the country. Newspapers, magazines, and television have reported countless times on the immigrant dilemma, and words like *mojado* (wetback or illegal immigrant), *coyote* (illegal immigrant smuggler), and *la migra* (the former Immigration and Naturalization Service or INS) have become part of media language. The situation has also become heavily politicized. A frequently heard argument against Mexican immigration is its alleged tendency to depress wages and increase unemployment. Undocumented or illegal Mexicans are often found performing low-skilled tasks shunned by American workers. The fact that Mexicans have little difficulty finding these jobs in the United States might suggest that they do not displace American labor to any great extent. Also, it must be remembered that undocumented Mexicans do not, by themselves, depress wages. Rather, employers offer pay scales well below what United States citizens might accept if they were willing to work these low-skilled jobs, and undocumented Mexicans and others fill the labor demand. As in other periods of American immigrant history, public pressure is usually directed against the migrant who is merely seeking to better his or her livelihood. Rarely is attention focused on the employer who hires the migrant. If illegal Mexican migration to the United States were stopped completely, one result might be higher prices for goods and services now produced by undocumented workers.

Since 1996, the militarization of the U.S. border with Mexico has not deterred the numbers of immigrants who venture north. A recent analysis of the economic and social consequences of this policy demonstrates that immigration has transformed from a largely regional phenomenon into a broad social movement that reaches to almost every part of the United States and that has lowered wages and working conditions of undocumented migrants.[64]

A second charge against Mexican immigrants is that they "freeload" on community services. This has not been well documented; in fact, the evidence suggests the contrary. Undocumented Mexican workers pay state and local taxes, and must have federal income and social security taxes deducted from their earnings if they are paid a salary. Field studies suggest that undocumented Mexicans make very little use of social services beyond public schools for their children who, if born here, are entitled as citizens to public education. In California and Texas, for example, undocumented Mexicans are estimated to have used public assistance services, yet contributed many times the amount annually to the support of such services.[65] Also, researchers have indicated that some undocumented immigrants are only here temporarily and ultimately return to Mexico. Their use of local services in those cases is occasional, whereas they contribute greatly to a fund that benefits the total population.

The total number of undocumented Mexicans in the United States is unknown. Mexico was estimated in 1992 to be the country of origin for 1.3 million undocumented immigrants, nearly 40 percent of all estimated illegal aliens.[66] Presently, estimates of the total number of undocumented immigrants in the United States run as high as 10 million, and Latin Americans including Mexicans are likely the largest segments of these estimates. These estimates may be misleading, and the basis for them varies widely among sources. Undocumented Mexican immigrants in the United States are usually located in the same areas where Mexican American populations are highest. Although undocumented aliens are just as likely to be in rural and suburban areas, they tend to concentrate in cities because Mexican American districts provide cultural familiarity and familial or friendship ties, and because jobs are more plentiful in cities. Beyond the agricultural sector, industries that often employ undocumented Mexicans include apparel, furniture, manufacturing, food processing, and commercial and residential construction. Service sector occupations include restaurants-eateries and commercial-residential cleaning. Immigration officials are known to occasionally raid these industries, round up the undocumented, and return them to Mexico. Studies have shown, however, that apprehended aliens often find their way back to similar types of employment.[67]

A HOME IN TWO PLACES

In Chinantla, a small town in the eastern Mexican state of Puebla, Monica Cruz, a native-born New Yorker, sits in her parents' grand brick and marble house, paid for by thousands of floors mopped, orders cooked, and garments sewn in the Big Apple. "Sometimes I think we all have too much love for this tiny town."[68] For tens of thousands of Mexican immigrants, this verbal refrain reflecting territorial and cultural inbetweenness is all too common. These immigrants are transnationals, literally migrants with feet in two nations, a homeland in Mexico and a new home in America.

Mexican transnationalism is a growing phenomenon and the latest wrinkle in the generations-old Mexican immigrant saga. In the past, Mexican migrants might have come north, established themselves and their families in America, become nationalized citizens, and set roots in a new land. On special occasions, these Mexican Americans might return to Mexico to their natal villages, but for others there was no return. Today, however, increasing numbers of Mexican immigrants use air travel to shuttle between their new homes in the United States and their ancestral hometowns in Mexico. Others cross long distances by car and bus to cement the connections between two homes; an immigrant community in *el norte* (the north) and a home village south of the border in their *patria chica* (little country).[69]

Transnationals are found among Mexican communities all across Mexico and in this country. In his chronicle of a Mexican family on the migrant trail, Rubén Martínez lived with an extended family from the Mexican village of Cherán in the highlands of Michoacán in southwest Mexico, an emigrant region that has been sending its citizens to *el norte* for more than a century. The Chavez clan from Cherán has extended family members in Watsonville, California; Norwalk, Wisconsin; St. Louis, Missouri; and Warren, Arkansas.[70] While the Chavezes are rooted in these places, working in the fields, in factories, and in slaughter houses, they remain linked to their spiritual home of Cherán, to which they return regularly for visits with family and friends and to transport goods and resources to the home community.

A recent documentary film, *The Sixth Section* by Alex Rivera, tells the story of two communities and the Mexican transnationals that connect the two places, of Boqueron, Puebla, and Newburgh, New York.[71] The Boqueronos (people of Boqueron) in Newburgh, some 300 residents, formed a social club known as a *club de oriundo*, a hometown association. This association collects monies from Boqueronos working in Newburgh and returns it in lump sums to the hometown in Puebla to fund public works and social projects. Monies raised by the *club de oriundo* in Newburgh paid for a baseball stadium, a clinic, a well, and an ambulance in Boqueron. Boqueronos in Newburgh are so important to the livelihood of the hometown in Mexico that they are called The Sixth Section, a reference to the five neighborhoods of Boqueron.

In 2003, it was estimated that $23 billion in migrant remittance—wired money, called *envío y remesa* in Spanish—was sent from Hispanic/Latino workers in the United States to their home communities in Latin America; some $9.3 billion of that total was sent to places in Mexico.[72] In Mexico, remittances are now considered the third largest source of income after oil exports and tourism. In Mexican states like Zacatecas and Michoacán, hardscrabble migrant homelands, remittances exceed local and state budgets.

Immigration and migration, thus, are more than simple to and fro movements, they are social and economic processes, constructed and maintained by human networks. Too often, perhaps, the media privileges a particular view of the process like the tragedy of undocumented crossers who sometimes die when they fail to negotiate the border pathways into Arizona and the scorching Sonoran desert summer, or those who are smuggled across the border through subterranean channels.[73] Most Americans hear these stories because they capture media attention and are promoted via our continual appetite for that which is alarming. Less well reported are those stories where transnationals succeed, both crossing into America and establishing themselves in communities through hard work and entrepreneurship.[74]

Mexican transnationals, like their brethren Latin American transnationals, are reshaping twenty-first-century America. And as Richard Rodríguez has so aptly surmised, "What Hispanic immigrants learn within the United States is to view themselves in a new way, as belonging to Latin America entire—precisely at the moment they no longer do."[75]

Conclusion: Toward the Future

Mexican Americans emerged in the borderlands where Spanish and later Mexican settlement made the first European imprints on the landscapes of the region. The legacy of this early colonization remains evident in the states of California, Texas, Arizona, New Mexico, and Colorado. These borderland states count 74 percent of the total Mexican American population. Outside of the borderland states, Mexican Americans are concentrated in parts of the Midwest, the West, the South, and the Northeast. The Mexican American population as a whole is younger, characterized by larger families, and is growing more rapidly than the U.S. population.

During the twentieth century, the two major social processes of immigration and urbanization have been important in the spatial evolution of the Mexican American people. Immigration has occurred in two separate phases from 1900 to 1930 and since the 1940s to the present. In both eras, Mexican immigrants have responded to the economic opportunities available in the United States. Their labor contributions to the economic development of the United States have been substantial. They continue today to provide steady and inexpensive labor in many of the cities of the West and Midwest, and elsewhere across the country. Largely because of changes in legal immigration to the United States and as a result of continued underemployment in Mexico, the majority of Mexican migrants to the United States enter illegally. This situation will not likely change in the near future, unless by political agreement between the United States and Mexico. As long as Mexico's population remains chronically underemployed and American industries and service sector economies demand lower-wage labor, the push-pull factors of migration will continue to operate.

What this continued migration portends for the United States is a greater plurality within the Mexican American minority. If large numbers of undocumented Mexicans remain in this country, they will certainly change the ratio of foreign-born Mexicans to native-born Mexican Americans. In 1996, some 32 percent of the Mexican-origin residents were not U.S. citizens.[76] Over time, the children of foreign-born migrants born in the United States will themselves become Mexican Americans and fuel the already rapidly growing native-born population of resident Mexican Americans. It is conceivable that the nation's second largest minority could become the nation's largest minority, surging past the African American population, if population growth rates in the Mexican American group remain high and immigrants continue to contribute to this population.

Urbanization has also been an important dimension of the Mexican American experience. The Mexican American population was predominantly urban in 2000, and as that base grows they will continue to transform the ethnic character of cities. Not only will the major Mexican American cities of Los Angeles, Chicago, Houston, San Antonio, and Phoenix become more populated with Mexican Americans, this process will affect intermediate and small urban areas as well.

In many metropolitan regions with a large Mexican American population, the central cities showed the greatest settlement concentrations. In these areas, preliminary studies suggest that a Mexican American landscape can be distinguished from other urban cultural landscapes. In some cities, Mexican Americans are dispersing out of traditional barrios and into suburbs. Historian and sociologist Ernesto Galarza sees this as an inevitable development in the process of cultural evolution for the Mexican American population.[77] As economic prosperity improves, and the process of acculturation to the dominant Anglo society tends to accelerate, Mexican Americans will become more like Anglo Americans in traditions and values. Further study will be necessary, however, to evaluate the relationship between changing economic status and traditional social values and landscapes in Mexican American communities before any conclusions can be reached about urbanization and the Mexican American minority.

While the majority of Mexican Americans still reside in the borderlands, the populations inside and outside of this hearth show variation in 2000, especially by measures of education, employment, and income. This variation has its roots in the early plurality of the borderlands where different settlement cores developed separate regional identities. As these regions developed differentially, the populations in some cases preserved particular folk traditions and in others more quickly adapted to changing circumstances. Thus, Mexican Americans have evolved independently in these regions. This regional variation is likely to persist into the future because Mexican Americans are not a single, homogeneous group socially, economically, or politically.[78]

Despite internal variations within the Mexican American minority, a distinct regional pattern may be evolving in the borderlands. Some scholars and writers have speculated about the regional dimensions of the future Mexican American population. It has been suggested, for example, that the 2,000-mile-long boundary between Mexico and the United States is emerging as the main axis of a new cultural province called "MexAmerica."[79] This hybrid region represents what geographer Richard Nostrand has called the major zone of Anglo-Latin "cultural convergence" in the hemisphere.[80] It is a region where Mexican and American cultural influences are intermingled, where Anglo traditions are spiced with Mexican cultural characteristics as immigrants move into and across the borderlands. It is also a process that has been evolving over many generations. In some respects it is a kind of *mestizaje*, a blending and overlapping of races, cultures, and lifestyles.[81] The ongoing changes in the borderlands are likely to prove our best clue to the future population characteristics and landscape influences of the nation's soon-to-be largest ethnic minority.

Notes

1. Richard L. Nostrand, "Spanish Roots in the Borderlands," *Geographical Magazine* 51 (December 1979): 203–209; Arthur L. Campa, *Hispanic Culture in the Southwest* (Norman: University of Oklahoma Press, 1979); and Carl O. Sauer, *Sixteenth Century North America: The Land and the People as Seen by the Europeans* (Berkeley: University of California Press, 1971).

2. D. W. Meinig, *Southwest: Three Peoples in Geographical Change, 1600–1970* (New York: Oxford University Press, 1971); James E. Officer, *Hispanic Arizona, 1536–1856* (Tucson: University of Arizona Press, 1987); Henry F. Dobyns, *Spanish Colonial Tucson: A Demographic History* (Tucson: University of Arizona Press, 1976).

3. D. W. Meinig, *Imperial Texas: An Interpretive Essay in Cultural Geography* (Austin: University of Texas Press, 1969); Daniel D. Arreola, *Tejano South Texas: A Mexican American Cultural Province* (Austin: University of Texas Press, 2002); and Arnoldo De León, *The Tejano Community, 1836–1900* (Albuquerque: University of New Mexico Press, 1982).

4. Leonard Pitt, *The Decline of the Californios: A Social History of the Spanish-Speaking Californians, 1846–1890* (Berkeley: University of California Press, 1971); and David J. Weber, *The Mexican Frontier, 1821–1846: The American Southwest under Mexico* (Albuquerque: University of New Mexico Press, 1982).

5. Max L. Moorehead, *The Presidio: Bastion of the Spanish Borderlands* (Norman: University of Oklahoma Press, 1975).

6. Gilbert R. Cruz, *Let There Be Towns: Spanish Municipal Origins in the American Southwest, 1610–1810* (College Station: Texas A&M University Press, 1988).

7. David Hornbeck, "Land Tenure and Rancho Expansion in Alta California, 1784–1846," *Journal of Historical Geography* 4 (October 1978): 371–390; David Hornbeck, "Mexican-American Land Tenure Conflict in California," *Journal of Geography* 75 (April 1976): 209–221; Terry G. Jordan, *North American Cattle-Ranching Frontiers: Origins, Diffusion, and Differentiation* (Albuquerque: University of New Mexico Press, 1993); Jack Jackson, *Los Mesteños: Spanish Ranching in Texas, 1721–1821* (College Station: Texas A&M University Press, 1986); Joe S. Graham, *El Rancho in South Texas: Continuity and Change from 1750* (Denton: University of North Texas Press, 1994).

8. Richard L. Nostrand, "Mexican Americans circa 1850," *Annals of the Association of American Geographers* 65 (September 1975): 378–390; Oscar J. Martínez, "On the Size of the Chicano Population: New Estimates, 1850–1900," *Aztlán* 6 (Spring 1975): 43–67.

9. Arthur F. Corwin, ed., *Immigrants—and Immigrants: Perspectives on Mexican Labor Migration to the United States* (Westport, CT: Greenwood Press, 1978); Harry E. Cross and James A. Sandos, *Across the Border: Rural Development in Mexico and Recent Migration to the United States* (Berkeley: Institute of Governmental Studies, 1981); Alejandro Portes and Robert L. Bach, *Latin Journey: Cuban and Mexican Immigrants in the United States* (Berkeley: University of California Press, 1985); Douglas S. Massey, Rafael Alarcon, Jorge Durand, and Humberto Gonzalez, *Return to Aztlán: The Social Process of International Migration from Western Mexico* (Berkeley: University of California Press, 1987); Abraham F. Lowenthal and Katrina Burgess, eds., *The California-Mexico Connection* (Stanford: Stanford University Press, 1993); Richard C. Jones, *Ambivalent Journey: U.S. Migration and Economic Mobility in North-Central Mexico* (Tucson: University of Arizona Press, 1995).

10. Rogelio Saenz and Clyde S. Greenless, "The Demography of Chicanos," in *Chicanas and Chicanos in Contemporary Society*, ed. Roberto M. De Anda (Boston: Allyn and Bacon, 1996), 9–23.

11. Carey McWilliams, *North from Mexico: The Spanish-Speaking People of the United States* (New York: Greenwood Press, 1968).

12. Mario T. García, *Desert Immigrants: The Mexicans of El Paso, 1880–1920* (New Haven: Yale University Press, 1981); Lawrence A. Cardoso, *Mexican Emigration to the United States, 1897–1931* (Tucson: University of Arizona Press, 1980).

13. Mark Reisler, *By the Sweat of Their Brow: Mexican Immigrant Labor in the United States, 1900–1940* (Westport, CT: Greenwood Press, 1976).

14. Abraham Hoffman, *Unwanted Mexican Americans in the Great Depression: Repatriation Pressures, 1929–1939* (Tucson: University of Arizona Press, 1974); Robert R. McKay, "Mexican Americans and Repatriation," in *The New Handbook of Texas* 4, ed. Ron Tyler (Austin: Texas State Historical Association, 1996), 676–679.

15. Richard L. Nostrand, "The Hispanic-American Borderland: Delimitation of an American Culture Region," *Annals of the Association of American Geographers* 60 (December 1970): 638–661.

16. Alvar W. Carlson, *The Spanish-American Homeland: Four Centuries in New Mexico's Rio Arriba* (Baltimore: Johns Hopkins University Press, 1990); Richard L. Nostrand, *The Hispano Homeland* (Norman: University of Oklahoma Press, 1992); Arreola, *Tejano South Texas*, 2002.

17. Leo Grebler, Joan W. Moore, and Ralph Guzman, *The Mexican-American People: The Nation's Second Largest Minority* (New York: The Free Press, 1970); Daniel D. Arreola, ed., *Hispanic Spaces, Latino Places: Community and Cultural Diversity in Hispanic America* (Austin: University of Texas Press, 2004).

18. Daniel D. Arreola, "Mexican Texas: A Distinctive Borderland," in *A Geographic Glimpse of Central Texas and the Borderlands: Images and Encounters*, ed. James F. Peterson and Julie A. Tuason (Indiana, PA: National Council for Geographic Education, 1995); Daniel D. Arreola, "The Texas-Mexican Homeland," *Journal of Cultural Geography* 13 (Spring/Summer 1993): 61–74.

19. Dionicio Nodín Valdés, *Barrios Norteños: St. Paul and Midwestern Mexican Communities in the Twentieth Century* (Austin: University of Texas Press, 2000).

20. Terrence W. Haverluk, "The Changing Geography of U.S. Hispanics, 1850–1990," *Journal of Geography* 96 (May/June1997): 134–145.

21. William Kandel and Emilio A. Parrado, "Hispanics in the American South and the Transformation of the Poultry Industry," in *Hispanic Spaces, Latino Places: Community and Cultural Diversity in Hispanic America*, ed. Daniel D. Arreola (Austin: University of Texas Press, 2004), 255–276.

22. Inés Miyares, "Changing Latinization of New York City," in *Hispanic Spaces, Latino Places: Community and Cultural Diversity in Hispanic America*, ed. Daniel D. Arreola (Austin: University of Texas Press, 2004), 145–166.

23. Alison Mountz and Richard A. Wright, "Daily Life in the Transnational Migrant Community of San Agustín, Oaxaca, and Poughkeepsie, New York," *Diaspora* 5 (1996): 403–428.

24. U.S. Census of Population: 2000, *Hispanic Population in the United States: March 2000*, Current Population Survey (Washington: U.S. Bureau of the Census, 2003).

25. Roberto Suro and Audrey Singer, "Latino Growth in Metropolitan America: Changing Patterns, New Locations," *The Brookings Institution Survey Series* (July 2002): 1–17.

26. Nostrand, *The Hispano Homeland*; Carlson, *The Spanish-American Homeland*; Betsy Guzmán, *The Hispanic Population*, Census Brief 2000 (Washington: U.S. Bureau of the Census, 2001). <www.census.gov/prod/2001pubs/c2kbr01-3.pdf>

27. James P. Allen and Eugene Turner, *Changing Faces, Changing Places: Mapping Southern Californians* (Northridge: Center for Geographical Studies, 2002); Guzmán, *The Hispanic Population*.

28. Nora Hamilton and Norma Stoltz Chinchilla, *Seeking Community in a Global City: Guatemalans and Salvadorans in Los Angeles* (Philadelphia: Temple University Press, 2001).

29. Daniel D. Arreola, "Mexican American Cultural Capital," *Geographical Review* 77 (January 1987): 17–34; Daniel D. Arreola, "Hispanic American Capital," in *Regional Geography of the United States and Canada*, 2nd ed., ed. Tom L. McKnight (Upper Saddle River, NJ: Prentice Hall, 1997), 44–46.

30. Frank D. Bean and Gray Swicegood, *Mexican American Fertility Patterns* (Austin: University of Texas Press, 1985); Jorge del Pinal and Audrey Singer, "Generations of Diversity: Latinos in the United States," *Population Bulletin* 52 (October 1997).

31. Thomas D. Boswell, "The Growth and Proportional Redistribution of the Mexican Stock Population in the United States: 1900–1970," *Mississippi Geographer* 6 (Spring 1979): 57–76.

32. Melissa Therrien and Roberto R. Ramirez, *The Hispanic Population in the United States: March 2000*, Current Population Reports (Washington: U.S. Bureau of the Census, 2001). <www.census.gov/prod/2001pubs/p20-535.pdf>

33. Frank D. Bean and Marta Tienda, *The Hispanic Population of the United States* (New York: Russell Sage Foundation, 1987).

34. Del Pinal and Singer, "Generations of Diversity"; Bean and Tienda, *The Hispanic Population of the United States.*

35. Wilbur Zelinsky, *The Enigma of Ethnicity: Another American Dilemma* (Iowa City: University of Iowa Press, 2001).

36. Daniel D. Arreola, "Introduction," in *Hispanic Spaces, Latino Places: Community and Cultural Diversity in Hispanic America*, ed. Daniel D. Arreola (Austin: University of Texas Press, 2004), 1–12.

37. Shirley Achor, *Mexican Americans in a Dallas Barrio* (Tucson: University of Arizona Press, 1978); Richard Griswold del Castillo, *The Los Angeles Barrio, 1850–1890: A Social History* (Berkeley: University of California Press, 1979); Thomas E. Sheridan, *Los Tucsonenses: The Mexican Community in Tucson, 1854–1941* (Tucson: University of Arizona Press, 1986); Richard A. García, *Rise of the Mexican-American Middle Class: San Antonio, 1929–1941* (College Station: Texas A&M University Press, 1991); Arnoldo De León, *Ethnicity in the Sunbelt: A History of Mexican Americans in Houston* (Houston: Mexican American Studies Program, University of Houston, 1989); Robert Lee Maril, *Poorest of Americans: The Mexican-Americans of the Lower Rio Grande Valley of Texas* (Notre Dame: University of Notre Dame Press, 1989); George J. Sánchez, *Becoming Mexican American: Ethnicity, Culture and Identity in Chicano Los Angeles, 1900–1945* (New York: Oxford University Press, 1993).

38. Nina Veregge, "Transformations of Spanish Urban Landscapes in the American Southwest, 1821–1900," *Journal of the Southwest* 35 (Winter 1993): 371–460; Daniel D. Arreola, "Plaza Towns of South Texas," *Geographical Review* 82 (January 1992): 56–73.

39. Joan W. Moore and Frank G. Mittelbach, *Residential Segregation in the Urban Southwest: A Comparison Study*, Advance Report 4, Mexican-American Study Project, U.C.L.A., Division of Research, Graduate School of Business Administration (Los Angeles: University of California, 1966).

40. Arthur J. Rubel, *Across the Tracks: Mexican-Americans in a Texas City* (Austin: University of Texas Press, 1966), 3.

41. W. Tim Dagodag, "Spatial Control and Public Policies: The Example of Mexican-American Housing," *Professional Geographer* 26 (August 1974): 262–269; Ellwyn R. Stoddard, "The Adjustment of Mexican American Barrio Families to Forced Housing Relocation," *Social Science Quarterly* 53 (March 1973): 749–759.

42. James R. Curtis, "Barrio Space and Place in Southeast Los Angeles," in *Hispanic Spaces,*

Latino Places: Community and Cultural Diversity in Hispanic America, ed. Daniel D. Arreola (Austin: University of Texas Press, 2004), 125–142.

43. Moore and Mittelbach, *Residential Segregation in the Urban Southwest.*

44. Alvar W. Carlson, "A Cartographic Analysis of Latin American Inmigrant Groups in the Chicago Metropolitan Area, 1965–76," *Revista Geografica* 96 (July–December 1982): 91–106.

45. Douglas S. Massey and Nancy A. Denton, "Residential Segregation of Mexicans, Puerto Ricans, and Cubans in Selected U.S. Metropolitan Areas," *Sociology and Social Research* 73 (January 1989): 73–83.

46. William A. V. Clark, "Residential Patterns: Avoidance, Assimilation and Succession," in *Ethnic Los Angeles*, ed. Roger Waldinger and Mehdi Bozorgmehr (New York: Russell Sage Foundation, 1996), 109–138.

47. Francine F. Rabinovitz and William J. Siembieda, *Minorities in Suburbs: The Los Angeles Experience* (Lexington, MA: D. C. Heath, 1977).

48. Carl Allsup, *The American G.I. Forum: Origins and Evolution* (Austin: Center for Mexican American Studies, University of Texas Press, 1982); James E. Officer, "Sodalities and Systemic Linkage: The Joining Habits of Urban Mexican-Americans," Ph.D. dissertation, University of Arizona, 1964.

49. Peirce F. Lewis, "Axioms for Reading the Landscape: Some Guides to the American Scene," in *The Interpretation of Ordinary Landscapes: Geographical Essays*, ed. D. W. Meinig (New York: Oxford University Press, 1979), 11–32.

50. Daniel D. Arreola, "Mexican American Housescapes," *Geographical Review* 78 (July 1988): 299–315.

51. Daniel D. Arreola, "Fences as Landscape Taste: Tucson's *Barrios,*" *Journal of Cultural Geography* 2 (Fall/Winter 1981): 96–105.

52. Daniel D. Arreola, "Mexican American Exterior Murals," *Geographical Review* 74 (October 1984): 409–424.

53. Larry R. Ford and Ernst Griffin, "Chicano Park: Personalizing an Institutional Landscape," *Landscape* 25, no. 2 (1981): 42–48.

54. Michele Markel-Cohen, "Port of Entry: Sawtelle Area Carries on Long Tradition as Migrant Labor Colony in Heart of Middle-Class West L.A.," *Los Angeles Times* (9 January 1983), X: 1, 10; Laura Zarrugh, "Home Away from Home: The Jacalan Community in the San Francisco Bay Area," in *The Chicano Experience*, ed. Stanley A. West and June Macklin (Boulder: Westview Press, 1979), 145–163.

55. Curtis C. Roseman and J. Diego Vigil, "From Broadway to 'Latino Way': The Reoccupation of a Gringo Retail Landscape," *Places: A Quarterly Journal of Environmental Design* 8 (Spring 1993): 20–29.

56. Arreola, *Tejano South Texas*, 2002.

57. Arreola, ed., *Hispanic Spaces, Latino Places*; James H. Johnson Jr., Karen D. Johnson-Webb, and Walter C. Farrell Jr., "Newly Emerging Hispanic Communities in the United States: A Spatial Analysis of Settlement Patterns," in *Immigration and Opportunity: Race, Ethnicity, and Employment in the United States*, ed. Frank D. Bean and Stephanie Bell-Rose (New York: Russell Sage Foundation, 1999), 263–310.

58. Terrence W. Haverluk, "Hispanic Community Types and Assimilation in Mex-America," *Professional Geographer* 50 (November 1998): 465–480.

59. Richard Baker, *Los Dos Mundos: Rural Mexican Americans, Another America* (Logan: Utah University Press, 1995).

60. Ted Conover, *Coyotes: A Journey through the Secret World of America's Illegal Aliens* (New York: Vintage Books, 1987); Jo Chilango, "The Palm Springs of Washington," *Landscape* 32, no. 2 (1994): 35–41.

61. Terrence W. Haverluk, "Hispanization of Hereford, Texas," in *Hispanic Spaces, Latino Places: Community and Cultural Diversity in Hispanic America*, ed. Daniel D. Arreola (Austin: University of Texas Press, 2004), 277–291.

62. U.S. Bureau of the Census, *Statistical Abstract of the United States: 1981* (Washington: U.S. Bureau of the Census, 1981); Walter Fogel, *Mexican Illegal Alien Workers in the United States*, Institute of Industrial Relations Monograph Series 20 (Los Angeles: University of California, 1979); Paul R. Ehrlich, Loy Bilderback, and Anne H. Ehrlich, *The Golden Door: International Migration, Mexico, and the United States* (New York: Ballantine Books, 1979).

63. U.S. Bureau of the Census, *Statistical Abstract of the United States: 1996* (Washington: U.S. Bureau of the Census, 1996); Saenz and Greenless, "The Demography of Chicanos," 1996.

64. Douglas S. Massey, Jorge Durand, and Nolan J. Malone, *Beyond Smoke and Mirrors: Mexican Immigration in an Era of Economic Integration* (New York: Russell Sage Foundation, 2002).

65. Manuel Vic Villalpando et al., *A Study of the Socioeconomic Impact of Illegal Aliens on the County of San Diego* (San Diego: County of San Diego Human Resources Agency, 1977); Sidney Weintraub and Gilberto Cardenas, *The Use of Public Services by Undocumented Aliens in Texas: A Survey of State Costs and Revenues* (Austin: Lyndon B. Johnson School of Public Affairs, University of Texas, 1984).

66. Saenz and Greenless, "The Demography of Chicanos," 1996.

67. George Vernez and David Ronfeldt, "The Current Situation in Mexican Immigration," *Science* 251 (8 March 1991): 1189–1193.

68. Deborah Sontag, "A Mexican Town That Transcends All Borders," *New York Times*, 21 July 1998, A1, A10.

69. Mountz and Wright, "Daily Life in the Transnational Migrant Community of San Agustín, Oaxaca, and Poughkeepsie, New York"; Carlos G. Vélez-Ibañez and Anna Sampaio, *Transnational Latina/o Communities: Politics, Processes, and Cultures* (Lanham, MD: Rowman & Littlefield, 2002).

70. Rubén Martínez, *Crossing Over: A Mexican Family on the Migrant Trail* (New York: Picador, 2001).

71. P.O.V.—*The Sixth Section*, PBS television documentary, 2003, <www.pbs.org/pov2003/thesixthsection> (12 August 2004).

72. Xochitl Bada, "Mexican Hometown Associations," P.O.V.—*The Sixth Section*, PBS website, 2003, <www.pbs.org/pov/pov2003/thesixthsection/special_mexican.html> (12 August 2004).

73. John Annerino, *Dead in Their Tracks: Crossing America's Desert Borderlands* (New York: Four Wall Eight Windows, 1999); Lawrence J. Taylor and Maeve Hickey, *Tunnel Kids* (Tucson: University of Arizona Press, 2001).

74. Leo R. Chavez, *Shadowed Lives: Undocumented Immigrants in American Society* (Orlando: Harcourt Brace Jovanovich College Publishers, 1992); Alex Oberle, "*Se Venden Aquí*: Latino Commercial Landscapes in Phoenix, Arizona," in *Hispanic Spaces, Latino Places: Community and Cultural Diversity in Hispanic America*, ed. Daniel D. Arreola (Austin: University of Texas Press, 2004), 239–254.

75. Richard Rodríguez, *Brown: The Last Discovery of America* (New York: Penguin Books, 2002), 117.

76. Del Pinal and Singer, "Generations of Diversity."

77. Ernesto Galarza, "Mexicans in the Southwest: A Culture in Process," in *Plural Society in the Southwest*, ed. Edward M. Spicer and Raymond H. Thompson (Albuquerque: University of New Mexico Press, 1972), 261–297.

78. Walker Conner, ed., *Mexican-Americans in Comparative Perspective* (Washington: Urban Institute Press, 1985).

79. Joel Garreau, *The Nine Nations of North America* (Boston: Houghton Mifflin, 1981); Lester D. Langley, *MexAmerica: Two Countries, One Future* (New York: Crown Publishers, 1988).

80. Richard L. Nostrand, "A Changing Culture Region," in *Borderlands Sourcebook: A Guide to the Literature on Northern Mexico and the American Southwest*, ed. Ellwyn R. Stoddard, Richard L. Nostrand, and Jonathan P. West (Norman: University of Oklahoma Press, 1983).

81. Matt S. Meier and Feliciano Rivera, *Dictionary of Mexican American History* (Westport, CT: Greenwood Press, 1981).

CHAPTER 6

Caribbean Hispanics: Puerto Ricans, Cubans, and Dominicans

Thomas D. Boswell and Terry-Ann Jones

The year 2001 was a bellwether year for ethnicity in the U.S. population. It was sometime during that year that Hispanics surpassed African Americans as this country's largest minority population. This chapter tells the story of three of the four largest components of the Hispanic population, the ones whose origins derive from the Caribbean. These include Puerto Ricans, Cubans, and Dominicans, the nation's second, third, and fourth largest Latin national groups, respectively. It is true that Puerto Ricans, Cubans, and Dominicans possess much in common, such as a Spanish colonial history, use of the Spanish language, practicing Catholicism, and coming from islands in the Caribbean with tropical climates. Their experience in the United States, however, is directly related to the historical time period of entry and the status with which they entered. This has affected both their entry experience and their ability to establish and maintain a transnational community. This chapter will examine the differences and similarities among these groups and the impacts that entry status has had in maintaining a distinction between them.

Puerto Ricans are U.S. citizens by virtue of their birth in an American possession. As such, they have complete freedom to move back and forth between Puerto Rico and the U.S. mainland. Cubans, on the other hand, fled an economic and social revolution when they left their island homeland. Most arrive with virtually no financial resources. However, Cubans are usually able to benefit by being classified as refugees because they are viewed by the U.S. government as fleeing from a Communist regime. The importance of this is that it entitles them to special types of financial assistance from the U.S. government that most other immigrants are not able to utilize. However, most do not have the option of returning to Cuba, should they decide that they are not able to comfortably adjust to life in the United States.[1] Dominicans arrive in the United States with neither refugee status nor U.S. citizenship, benefiting instead from family reunification policies instituted by the 1952 and 1965 immigration acts. Dominicans are motivated primarily by economic considerations, and they come from one of the poorer developing countries in the Caribbean. When they arrive in the United States, they tend to keep strong ties to their homeland through financial remittances and social ties to family members still living in the Dominican Republic.

Histories of Immigration

Because the immigration histories are so different for Puerto Ricans, Cubans, and Dominicans, they are discussed separately in this section. While ethnic Mexicans numerically dominate, Puerto Ricans comprised almost 10 percent (3,406,178) of the Hispanic population in 2000. Cubans (1,241,685) and Dominicans (764,945) accounted for about 3.5 percent and 2.2 percent of the Hispanics, respectively.[2] Because of Puerto Rico's political status, those migrating to the mainland are classified as internal or domestic migrants. Thus the data in Fig. 6.1 are for the number of Puerto Ricans residing on the mainland who were born in Puerto Rico. While not ideal, these data function as a surrogate in the absence of immigration data. For comparison purposes, the data for Cubans and Dominicans are also for those born in the Caribbean who reside in the United States.

PUERTO RICANS

Some Puerto Ricans like to say that Ponce de Leon, who founded the initial European settlement in Puerto Rico in 1508 and then searched for "The Fountain of Youth" in Florida, was the first Puerto Rican to migrate to the United States. Puerto Ricans have been living in New York City since the 1830s. During the latter half of the nineteenth century, a few students from wealthy Puerto Rican families attended universities on the mainland. In addition, there were handfuls of Puerto Rican revolutionaries periodically living in New York City and plotting, often with Cuban exiles, against the Spanish government that then controlled Puerto Rico.[3] Shortly after the beginning of the American occupation of the island in 1898, Puerto Ricans were recruited to work in the sugar cane fields of Hawaii. By 1901, there were six thousand of these labor migrants, some of whom subsequently resettled in California and New York.[4]

The first year in which the U.S. Bureau of the Census listed Puerto Ricans as a separate group in its publications was 1910. At that time just over fifteen hundred people who were born in Puerto Rico lived in the United States, with 37 percent of them residing in New York City. Migration to the U.S. mainland picked up during the 1920s when about 41,000 new Puerto Rican residents were added to the U.S. population (Fig. 6.1). The economic boom that followed the end of World War I and the strong curtailment of European immigration through enforcement of the United States Immigration Act of 1924 were factors prompting this surge. The 1930s, however, witnessed a significant decline in the flow of Puerto Ricans. This was caused by the decrease in the number of job opportunities associated with the Great Depression. There was actually a significant net return migration to Puerto Rico during the early 1930s as a result of these troubled economic times. As a former colonial possession and with its continuing status as a commonwealth associated with the United States, sustained immigration beginning during this early period is generally explained within the context of World Systems Theory.

By 1940, New York City had established its maximum degree of dominance as the primary residence for Puerto Ricans living on the mainland. At that time, 88 percent of all people born in Puerto Rico but living on the mainland were residing in the state of New York, with almost all of them living in New York City. Migration from the island increased somewhat during the Second World War because of the need for more workers in American factories to support the war effort. When compared to the heavy European immigration that influenced United States history from the 1800s to the early 1920s, Puerto Rican movements were insignificant until 1946. Immediately after World War II, however, the flow of Puerto Ricans rapidly increased for various reasons (Fig. 6.1). There was a backlog of people who might have moved from the island during the early 1940s but did not because of the war. Second, many Puerto Rican men who had fought in the war had been trained in the United States and, as a result, had developed an awareness of the opportunities on the mainland. By 1946, there were

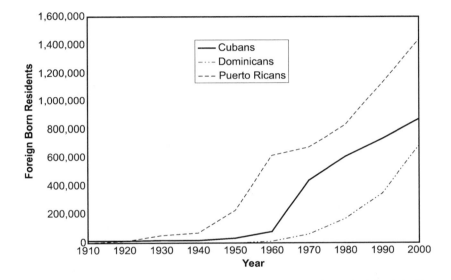

Figure 6.1. Puerto Rican-, Cuban-, and Dominican-Born Residents in the United States, 1910–2000. Source: For Puerto Rican data, Thomas D. Boswell and Angel D. Cruz-Báez, "Puerto Ricans Living in the United States," in Ethnicity in Contemporary America: A Geographical Appraisal, ed. Jesse O. McKee, 2nd ed. (Lanham, MD: Rowman & Littlefield, 2000), 184; and 2000 American FactFinder, SF3, Table P21, <www.census.gov>. For Cuban data, Campbell Gibson and Emily Lennon, "Historical Census Statistics on the Foreign-Born Population of the United States: 1850–1990," Working Paper no. 29, Population Division, U.S. Bureau of the Census, Washington, D.C., February 1999, Tables 3 and 4; and Thomas Boswell and James R. Curtis, The Cuban-American Experience: Culture, Images and Perspectives (New York: Rowman and Allanhead, 1984), 40. For Dominican data, Campbell Gibson and Emily Lennon, "Historical Census Statistics on the Foreign-Born Population of the United States: 1850–1990," Working Paper no. 29, Population Division, U.S. Bureau of the Census, Washington, D.C., February 1999, Table 3; and 2000 American FactFinder, SF3, Table P19, <www.census.gov>.

already over one hundred thousand Puerto Rican–born residents on the mainland. They served as a "family intelligence service," that is, a form of social capital for friends and neighbors who would soon follow them in a classic example of chain migration.

In addition, the Puerto Rican government created a Migration Division within its Department of Labor that facilitated movement to the mainland and assisted the new arrivals in making the necessary adjustments. The cost and effort of traveling to New York City were drastically reduced. By ship the trip had formerly taken a minimum of four days and cost close to a month's pay. After the war, surplus aircraft were available and air fares were lowered to as little as $35 for a six-hour, one-way trip, closer to a week's salary. Furthermore, financing was frequently available, so passengers could make a $5 down payment, and the rest could be paid through installments after their arrival in New York City. Rapid population growth in Puerto Rico was creating population pressure and heavy strains on the island's labor force capacity that further motivated moves. The 1950s and 1960s were characterized by a shift in the island's occupational structure. Agricultural employment was about to experience a precipitous decline. Both the intensity of increasing population pressure and declining agricultural employment provided strong incentives to leave the island, especially from rural areas.

The decade of the 1950s represents one of the two periods of heaviest flow of Puerto Ricans toward the United States. The total net movement to the U.S. mainland between 1950 and 1960 was 457,275 people.[5] In 1953 alone, 76,252 Puerto Ricans moved to the mainland, representing the most for any year. The migration flow during the 1960s was moderate in nature, but increased more dramatically during the 1970–1980 period.

However, the 1980s saw an increase once again in the out-migration of Puerto Ricans to the U.S. mainland that led to the second period of heavy flow as the number of Puerto Ricans residing on the mainland increased from 832, 920 to 1,134,009 (Fig. 6.1). Some of the people involved in this migration may have included migrants from the Dominican Republic and other Caribbean neighbors of Puerto Rico who illegally immigrated to the island first and then traveled to the mainland. Research covering this period has clearly shown that both wage differentials between the island and mainland as explained by Neo-Classical Theory and differing employment opportunities explained by Dual Market Theory have played a role in this renewal of heavy emigration to the United States.[6] As the economic gap between the island and the mainland widened, certain groups of Puerto Rican workers such as nurses and engineers particularly benefited from this divergence when they moved to the United States.[7] Changes in the U.S. minimum wage, when extended to Puerto Rico, had considerable impact on the Puerto Rican labor market. The higher wages slowed employment growth, which had the effect of keeping unemployment rates high on the island and dampening labor force participation rates, all of which further encouraged out-migration during the 1980s. Overall, the 1980s constituted a period of significant economic growth on the mainland, a pace that was not matched on the island. Although the Puerto Rican economy expanded during the second half of the decade, this growth was not as strong as that experienced in the United States.

The 1990s again witnessed moderate rates of emigration to the U.S. mainland (Fig. 6.1). What happened during this period was very similar to what happened during the 1970s. It is also possible that this moderate growth can be attributed to Puerto Rican officials and the U.S. Coast Guard who worked hard to curtail the illegal immigration of Dominicans to Puerto Rico, many of whom would then move again to the United States.[8]

By the time the 2000 Census was taken, there were almost as many Puerto Ricans living on the U.S. mainland as there were living on the island. The population of Puerto Rico that year was 3.8 million, but only about 3.6 million were Puerto Ricans because some were immigrants from other countries living in Puerto Rico. For example, there were 19,973 Cubans and 56,146 Dominicans enumerated in Puerto Rico that year, accounting for 55 percent of non–Puerto Rican population living on the island. Almost 49 percent of all Puerto Ricans lived on the mainland in 2000.

CUBANS

The history of Cuban emigration to the United States is simpler than that of Puerto Ricans because since 1959 it has been controlled by the dictates of the Cuban government, rather than responding to variable economic conditions in a series of ebbs and flows. The vast majority of Cuban immigrants then are classified as conflict migrants. The first wave was represented by a "Trickle Movement" that, for all intents, began in the middle 1800s and continued until Fidel Castro's revolution in 1959. During this earlier period, New York City, Key West, and Tampa became particularly notable as places of refuge for Cuban political exiles who were plotting the overthrow of their Spanish rulers.[9] In addition, during the 1860s and 1870s, several cigar manufacturers moved their operations from Havana to these three cities, thereby providing additional employment opportunities for Cuban immigrants.[10]

Miami did not emerge as a center of Cuban influence until the 1930s, when exiles fled the effects of the revolution against Gerardo Machado. Another spurt in the stream to Miami occurred from 1953 to 1959 as would-be revolutionaries fled the regime of Fulgencio Batista[11] (Fig. 6.1). The early experience of Cubans living in New York and Florida proved crucial for the ability of future generations of Cuban immigrants to adjust to life in the United States. The exiles who emigrated after the introduction of Communism in Cuba were at least partially aware of the Hispanic cultural concentrations in New York and Miami, and they were familiar with the geographic and climatic similarities between Cuba and southern Florida.

The second phase of Cuban immigration to the United States occurred between 1959 and 1962, as the Communist revolution was being consolidated. More than 215,000 Cubans emigrated during this four-year period. In the beginning, this emigration was dominated by members of the former economic and political elite openly affiliated with the government of Fulgencio Batista who had just been overthrown by the Castro revolution. However, by the middle of 1959, members of the landholding aristocracy began to leave as an agrarian reform law was instituted in June of that year, with the stated purpose of breaking up large land holdings. In July 1960 a law was passed authorizing the expropriation of all American-owned property. In the same year, an urban reform law was enacted in October that was designed to confiscate private rental properties in the cities.[12] By this time the revolution was also being felt by middle-class entrepreneurs, thus widening its impact. Because it was disproportionately comprised of people from the upper and middle classes, this emigration phase is often referred to as being the wave of "Golden Exiles."

Relations between the United States and Cuba began to cool rapidly in early 1961. On January 3, the American government broke diplomatic relations with Cuba. The ill-fated Bay of Pigs invasion was launched in April, with disastrous consequences for the Cuban Americans involved. President Castro announced in December of that year that he was a Marxist-Leninist and that Cuba was destined to become a socialist state. He then proceeded to place severe restrictions on the amount of property and money that could be taken out of the country. Finally, in October 1962, the Cuban Missile Crisis resulted in the termination of air traffic to the United States. Legal emigration to America remained suspended for about three years, until September 1965.[13]

On September 28, 1965, President Castro announced he would permit Cubans with relatives living in the United States to emigrate. The departures would take place by boat through the small port of Camarioca on the northern coast of Matanzas Province, about sixty miles east of Havana. Immediately, hundreds of boats departed southern Florida for Cuba to pick up friends and relatives. Unfortunately, not all the craft were seaworthy, and a number of tragedies occurred. The chaos that ensued, as a result of the panicky rush and accompanying accidents, created a source of embarrassment for the Cuban government. As a consequence, United States and Cuban authorities signed a "Memorandum of Understanding" that established arrangements for an airlift between Miami and a Cuban airport located east of Havana, in the seaside town of Varadero. The agreement was organized through the Swiss Embassy in Havana, and the flights became known as the "Freedom Flights," "Aerial Bridge," or "Family Reunification Flights." On April 6, 1973, these flights were discontinued by the Cuban government. About 302,000 Cubans had immigrated to the United States during the eight years of the Freedom Flights. As a result of this politically contentious period stretching from 1960 to 1980, the number of Cuban-born residing in the United States increased dramatically from 79,150 to 607,814 (Fig. 6.1).

Unexpectedly, in April 1980 a new phase of Cuban emigration to the United States was initiated that lasted about five months, until September, during which about 125,000 Cubans would emigrate to the United States by sea through the port city of Mariel, located about forty miles west of Havana. It became known as the "Mariel Exodus." It had been precipitated by more than 10,000 Cubans storming the grounds of the Peruvian Embassy in Havana to demand political asylum. After a tense stand-off, the Cuban government decided to let all who wanted to leave the island to do so. But the emigration stream was much larger than had been anticipated by the Cuban government.

Once it became apparent that the number of people who wanted to leave Cuba was much greater than the Cuban authorities had originally predicted, Castro tried to turn an embarrassing situation into an advantage for his government. He decided to force many of the captains of the boats that had been sent from Florida to pick up family members also to take back to the United States many of Cuba's social undesirables. Included in this were a number of people with criminal records, gays, patients from mental institutions, and even deaf-mutes. Approximately 26,000 of the Mariel refugees had prison records, but many had been jailed for political reasons or for minor crimes, such as stealing food or trading on the black market for a pair of blue-jeans.[14]

In addition to the perception that the Mariel sea-lift was being used by Castro to empty his jails and mental institutions, the "Marielitos" were not welcomed upon their arrival in Florida. The suddenness and massive size of the influx intensified problems in helping them become settled. Many who did not have relatives or friends to help them adjust were temporarily housed in military camps in Florida, Arkansas, Pennsylvania, and Wisconsin. Additionally, the U.S. economy in 1980 experienced a recession, accompanied by inflation. In Miami-Dade County it was estimated that the unemployment rate jumped from about 5 percent to 13 percent, primarily due to the Mariel influx. Also, the apartment vacancy rate was reduced to less than 1 percent, creating an acute housing shortage and high rents.[15] By 1980 public opinion was in favor of reducing immigration, as a result of attention given by the news media to the problems encountered during the immigrations of Vietnamese, Mexicans, and Haitians to the United States, thus compounding the challenges faced by Marielitos. Finally, between 70 and 75 percent of all the Mariel emigres settled in South Florida, especially in Miami-Dade County. This degree of concentration was greater than for earlier Cuban waves and thus made adjustment problems more visible and newsworthy.[16]

Unfortunately, the unwelcome attitude toward the Marielitos diffused among many of the Cuban Americans who arrived prior to 1980. It became common to hear members of the Cuban community in Miami speak in terms of "new" and "old" Cubans. The "old" Cubans were sometimes among the harshest critics of the "new" ones. The tendency for immigrants who arrived earlier to criticize newer arrivals has been noted historically among other ethnic groups living in the United States, but it was aggravated by the special set of circumstances that accompanied the Mariel wave, particularly the forced inclusion by Castro of the criminal element. Many of the "old" Cubans feared that the "new" ones would tarnish their hard-earned reputations, just as Fidel Castro had hoped they would.[17]

As economic and social conditions deteriorated in Cuba in the late 1980s, people became increasingly desperate to leave the island for the United States. About the only way to escape was to take to the sea in homemade boats or rafts. The people who did so are called *balseros*.[18] The term derives from the Spanish word "balsa," which means "raft." Sometimes these rafts were little more than large truck tire inner tubes. The number of *balseros* started becoming noticeable in 1991, when about 2,203 were counted by U.S. immigration officials. Among the numerous dangers the *balseros* encountered were an inability to hold a small boat or raft on course in rough seas, food and fresh water being washed overboard, hot days with intense sunlight, dehydration, hypothermia at night, shark attacks, seasickness that intensified dehydration, food shortages, and rough seas that damaged and frequently swamped the poorly constructed rafts.

Gradually, the numbers of Cuban *balseros* increased between 1991 and 1994. The latter was the banner year as about 37,000 were interdicted at sea by U.S. authorities. The Cuban government tried to repeat the history of the Mariel emigration phase when President Castro announced on August 12, 1994, that anybody who wanted to leave the island could. No longer, he said, would officials try to stop Cubans from leaving the island. However, shortly after Castro's announcement, on August 19, U.S.

Attorney General Janet Reno stated that Cuban rafters would not be allowed into the United States. The next day President Clinton confirmed that rafters would be interdicted at sea by the U.S. Coast Guard and taken to the U.S. Navy Base at Guantanamo Bay, Cuba, where they would eventually be returned to Cuba. Also, the president said monetary remittances to Cuba would be stopped, as would family visits, gift parcels, and most charter flights to the island from the United States.

With its major source of foreign income slashed, the pressure was on Cuba to resolve the situation. Unlike Mariel, the flood of refugees had been deflected to Guantanamo without causing a rift between the Cuban American community and the U.S. government. As a consequence, the Cuban and U.S. governments agreed to talks during early September. On September 9, 1994, an agreement was announced. The United States agreed to allow 20,000 yearly visas for eligible Cubans, to reduce the motivation for future rafters from making the risky journey to the United States. They also established a policy to refuse parole to those who entered illegally. In turn, the Cuban government agreed to take measures to prevent future illegal departures. By December 1994, the number of rafters being picked up by the Coast Guard was reduced to zero. In May, 1995, President Clinton agreed to let all but a few criminals in the Guantanamo refugee camp immigrate to the United States. However, he also noted that all future *balseros* would be immediately returned to Cuba upon their apprehension at sea. The 1994 agreement between the United States and Cuba allows 20,000 to come to the United States yearly. From 1995 to 2003, almost 196,000 Cubans immigrated to the United States, which is an average of slightly under 22,000 per year.[19] This is a little more than 20,000 because some additional Cubans are allowed to enter the United States through other programs as well.[20] The twenty-year period of *marielitos* and *balsero* refugees coupled with those who immigrated after 1994 increased the numbers of Cuban-born residents in the United States from 607,814 in 1980 to 872,716 in 2000 (Fig. 6.1).

DOMINICANS

Immigration from the Dominican Republic to the United States did not become significant until about 1962 (Fig. 6.1). From 1930 to 1961 the island republic was ruled by the iron-fisted dictator Rafael Leonidas Trujillo. Among other things, President Trujillo severely restricted emigration. Some suggested this policy was implemented to prevent disgruntled Dominicans from denouncing his government abroad, especially in the United States and Europe. This was probably true, but he also believed that population growth was good for the economy of the Dominican Republic. He reasoned that people were both producers and consumers, and he associated slow population growth with a shortage of workers which in turn inhibited economic vitality. In 1920, the population of the Dominican Republic was about 900,000, but by the end of Trujillo's regime it increased to about three million.[21] The flow of Dominicans to the United States was so low that U.S. immigration officials did not provide separate statistics for them until 1932. During the decade of the 1930s only 1,150 Dominicans were registered as having immigrated to the United States. During the decades of the 1940s and

1950s it increased to 5,627 and 9,897, respectively. Still, by 1960 emigration to the United States was averaging less than 1,000 per year.

In 1961 President Trujillo was assassinated, resulting in a period of political and economic turmoil in the Dominican Republic. When it appeared that the left-leaning political forces might gain control, the United States military intervened in 1965, ostensibly to establish order and to prevent the Dominican Republic from turning into another Cuba in the United States' backyard. In 1966, Joaquin Balaguer, a former supporter and confidant of Trujillo, who had himself resided in exile in New York City between 1962 and 1965, became president.[22]

In the late 1970s it appeared the Dominican Republic might be making economic progress as a number of free trade zones were established on the island with the hope of attracting foreign investment capital. But rising oil prices of the 1980s, a decline in exports, and a rapidly increasing foreign debt broke the back of the efforts to promote industrial growth. In an attempt to solve its foreign debt problem, the Dominican government radically restructured its economy, under the advice of the International Monetary Fund. The combination of economic restructuring, a brutal persecution unleashed by conservative governments against revolutionaries, and the 1965 change in U.S. immigration policy all played major roles in creating an environment whereby immigration from the Dominican Republic to the United States would play a major role in Dominican society.[23] Indeed, between 1960 and 1980, the number of Dominican-born immigrants increased from 11,883 to 169,147 (Fig. 6.1). By the beginning of the 1980s, the Dominican Republic was sending more emigrants to the United States than any other country in the Western Hemisphere, except for Mexico. The immigrant flow from this Caribbean island has not slowed; between 1980 and 2000, the Dominican-born population in the United States increased from 169,147 to 687,677 (Fig. 6.1).

Concentrated Settlement Patterns

The tendency toward channelized migration and resulting settlement concentrations clearly characterizes these three Caribbean groups. We describe these concentrations first at a geographical scale of the state and then at the scale of major metropolitan areas. Finally, we pick the single metropolitan area of greatest concentration for each of the three groups and examine their distributions by census tracts.

STATE DISTRIBUTIONS

Table 6.1 shows the geographical distributions of the three Caribbean Hispanic groups for the eight states where the largest numbers of these groups are found. Almost six out of every ten Latinos live in these states. Approximately 83 percent of Puerto Ricans are found in these states, with the heaviest concentrations in the states of New York, Florida, and New Jersey, respectively. Collectively, 56 percent of all Puerto Ricans on the mainland live in these three states. As discussed later in this chapter, the vast majority of Puerto Ricans reside in the greater New York metropolitan area that also includes

Table 6.1.   Distribution of Caribbean Hispanics by State, 2000

	Number of Hispanics	% of Hispanics	Number of Puerto Ricans	% of Puerto Ricans
United States	35,305,818	100.0	3,406,178	100.0
California	10,966,556	31.1	140,570	4.1
Connecticut	320,323	0.9	194,443	5.7
Florida	2,682,715	7.6	482,027	14.2
Illinois	1,530,262	4.3	157,851	4.6
Massachusetts	428,729	1.2	199,207	5.8
New Jersey	1,117,191	3.2	366,788	10.8
New York	2,867,593	8.1	1,050,293	30.8
Pennsylvania	394,088	1.1	228,557	6.7
TOTALS	20,307,447	57.5	2,819,736	82.7
Puerto Rico	3,762,746	—	3,623,392	—

	Number of Cubans	% of Cubans	Number of Dominicans	% of Dominicans
United States	1,241,685	100.0	764,945	100.0
California	72,286	5.8	5,047	0.7
Connecticut	7,101	0.6	9,546	1.2
Florida	833,120	67.1	70,968	9.3
Illinois	18,438	1.5	2,934	0.4
Massachusetts	8,867	0.7	49,913	6.5
New Jersey	77,337	6.2	102,630	13.4
New York	62,590	5.0	455,061	59.5
Pennsylvania	10,363	0.8	12,186	1.6
TOTALS	1,090,102	87.7	708,285	92.6
Puerto Rico	19,973	—	56,146	—

Source: U.S. Bureau of the Census, American FactFinder, 2000, Summary File 1, PCT11.

northern New Jersey. Florida's Puerto Rican population is primarily found in two met-ropolitan areas, one in Orlando and a second smaller one in Miami–Fort Lauderdale. Two-thirds of all Cuban Americans live in the state of Florida, with significant (but much smaller) numbers also in New Jersey, California, and New York, respectively. Dominicans are most heavily concentrated in New York, New Jersey, and Florida. Slightly more than 82 percent of all Dominican Americans live in these three states, with the largest concentration being in New York.

MAJOR METROPOLITAN AREA DISTRIBUTIONS

Puerto Ricans, Cubans, and Dominicans are primarily urban dwellers. Furthermore, they tend to live primarily in large metropolitan areas.[24] About 62 percent of all main-land Puerto Ricans live in six metropolitan areas, specifically New York City, Philadel-phia, Chicago, Orlando, Boston, and Miami (Table 6.2). In fact, the New York metropolitan area possesses the world's second largest concentration of Puerto Ricans. Only San Juan has more, with 2.3 million, compared to 1.3 million in New York.

Almost 57 percent of all Cuban Americans are found in the Miami–Fort Lauderdale metropolitan area. Secondary concentrations are found in the New York metropolitan region (especially the counties in northeastern New Jersey), Los Angeles, and Tampa–St. Petersburg. Three-quarters of all Cuban Americans live in these four metropolitan areas. Miami possesses the second largest Cuban population in the world; only Havana, Cuba, has more (about 2.1 million versus 702,000).

Almost three-quarters of all Dominican Americans live in the New York metropolitan region that includes northern New Jersey and Long Island. Secondary concentrations are found in the Boston and Miami–Fort Lauderdale metropolitan areas. It is relevant to note that the New York metropolitan region is characterized by the second largest Dominican population in the world. Only the capital of the Dominican Republic, Santo Domingo, has more (2.1 million versus 551,538).

Puerto Ricans are the least concentrated of the three Hispanic Caribbean populations in part because they have been migrating to the United States in large numbers for the longest period of time. In 2000 almost 39 percent lived in the New York metropolitan area. However, in 1940, about 88 percent lived in New York State. Gradually, they have dispersed to other parts of the United States, especially to other metropolitan areas in the northeastern United States.

Cubans, who started immigrating to the United States in large numbers only in 1959, increasingly concentrated in Miami-Dade County until 1990. In that year slightly more than 54 percent lived in this one county.[25] There are signs now that Cuban Americans are beginning to disperse outside of metropolitan Miami because in 2000 the percentage of Cubans living in Miami-Dade County declined slightly to 52 percent.[26] Still, Cubans are more concentrated in metropolitan Miami than Puerto Ricans in metropolitan New York. It is Dominicans who are most concentrated among the three Caribbean Hispanic groups, with 72 percent living in the metropolitan area of New York in 2000. They are also the most recently arriving Caribbean Hispanics.

DISTRIBUTIONS IN MAJOR METROPOLITAN AREAS

The Puerto Rican population is scattered through nine readily identifiable neighborhoods in New York City (Map 6.1). The largest single concentration by far is found throughout the Bronx. There are also several notable concentrations in the boroughs of Brooklyn and Queens (Middle Village, Williamsburg, Borough Park, Ozone Park, and Far Rockaway). Two notable Puerto Rican neighborhoods are found in Manhattan in East Harlem and the Lower East Side (Fig. 6.2). Staten Island historically had few Hispanics, but that began to change during the 1980s and 1990s. By 2000, a Puerto Rican enclave had been established at Rose Bank at the eastern end of Staten Island.

Dominicans are somewhat more concentrated in New York City when compared to Puerto Ricans (Map 6.2). Still, there is clearly some spatial overlap in the neighborhoods where these two Caribbean Hispanic groups reside. The largest single concentration, and the most visible Dominican neighborhood, is found in Washington Heights in northwestern Manhattan. A second concentration of almost equal size is found in western Bronx. Secondary concentrations are found in several locations in Queens, such as

Table 6.2. Distribution of Caribbean Hispanics by Major Metropolitan Areas, 2000

Metropolitan Areas	Number of Hispanics	% of Hispanics	Number of Puerto Ricans	% of Puerto Ricans
Boston-Worcester-Lawrence CMSA	358,231	1.0	137,373	4.0
Chicago-Gary-Kenosha CMSA	1,498,507	4.2	164,509	4.8
Los Angeles–Riverside–Orange County CMSA	6,598,488	18.7	66,340	1.9
Miami–Fort Lauderdale CMSA	1,563,389	4.4	135,265	4.0
New York–Northern N.J.–Long Island CMSA	3,852,138	10.9	1,325,778	38.9
Orlando MSA	271,627	0.8	139,898	4.1
Philadelphia-Wilmington-Atlantic City CMSA	348,135	1.0	206,802	6.1
Tampa–St. Petersburg–Clearwater CMSA	248,642	0.7	75,621	2.2
Totals	14,739,157	41.7	2,251,586	66.0
San Juan–Caugas–Arecibo CMSA	2,416,024	—	2,297,244	—

Metropolitan Areas	Number of Cubans	% of Cubans	Number of Dominicans	% of Dominicans
Boston-Worcester-Lawrence CMSA	8,404	0.7	49,874	6.5
Chicago-Gary-Kenosha CMSA	17,251	1.4	2,802	0.4
Los Angeles–Riverside–Orange County CMSA	53,839	4.3	2,756	0.4
Miami–Fort Lauderdale CMSA	701,512	56.5	46,952	6.1
New York–Northern N.J.–Long Island CMSA	134,973	10.9	551,538	72.1
Orlando MSA	18,797	1.5	9,966	1.3
Philadelphia-Wilmington-Atlantic City CMSA	8,641	0.7	10,890	1.4
Tampa–St. Petersburg–Clearwater CMSA	41,602	3.4	4,992	0.7
Totals	985,019	79.4	679,770	88.9
San Juan-Caugas-Arecibo CMSA	17,833	—	52,720	—

Source: U.S. Bureau of the Census, American FactFinder, 2000, Summary File 1, PCT 11.

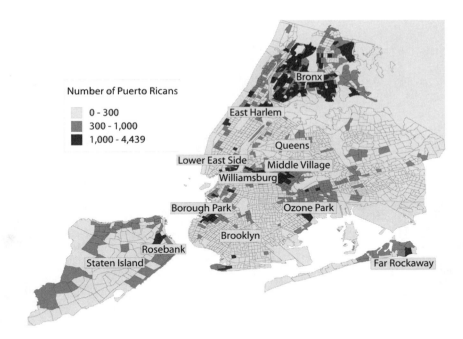

Map 6.1.   Puerto Ricans by Census Tract, New York City, 2000.
Source: U.S. Bureau of the Census, American FactFinder, 2000,
Summary File 1, PCT11.

Corona, Middle Village, Williamsburg, and Woodhaven. There are smaller concentrations in the Lower East Side of Manhattan and in Borough Park in Brooklyn.

Although the earliest concentrations of Cuban Americans were found in New York City, Key West, and Tampa, by the early 1960s it became apparent that Miami had risen to prominence as the preeminent Cuban city. Cubans chose Miami for a variety of reasons. First, Miami was nearby, being located only about 250 miles from Havana.[27] Many Cubans who moved during the 1959 to 1962 "Golden Exile" phase thought living in Miami would be only a temporary move; thus it would be relatively easy to return from nearby Miami. Many middle-class and upper-class Cubans had visited Miami on shopping and vacation trips before the fall of the infamous Batista regime, and they felt comfortable based on past experience. Additionally, there was a modest Cuban population of about 20,000 already living in Miami at the time of the Castro Revolution in 1959. These were the people who would lay the foundation for establishing a social and economic network for future waves of Cuban immigrants. Inexpensive housing was available in Miami, and there were buildings in an area southwest of the Central Business District along Southwest 8th Street (Tamiami Trail) that could be easily renovated for new businesses. This area would soon become known as Little Havana.

Cubans are widely scattered throughout Miami-Dade County, but they are especially concentrated in places like Little Havana, Hialeah, Westchester, Miami Beach,

Figure 6.2. A Spanish Harlem mural in northeastern Manhattan that represents many aspects of Puerto Rican culture. Source: I. Miyares.

and Kendall (Map 6.3). Hispanics now comprise about 60 percent of Miami-Dade County's population, and Cubans represent about half of the county's Hispanics. From these areas of settlement concentration, the growth in the Cuban population has been both toward the south and toward the north in Miami-Dade County. In the north-western corner of the county there is some spillover into the municipality of Miramar in Broward County. This area is experiencing a housing construction boom that is explained by Cuban suburban settlement. Little Havana remains primarily Cuban, but has experienced a modest residential succession process involving other Hispanic groups, primarily Nicaraguans. However, Little Havana's commercial district remains in Cuban hands especially along Southwest 8th Street, or *Calle Ocho* (Fig. 6.3).

Demographic and Socioeconomic Characteristics

In analyzing the basic demographic characteristics of Puerto Ricans, Cubans, and Dominicans we specifically examine gender composition, age structure, racial composition, and citizenship status. Socioeconomic characteristics include English language ability, educational attainment, and employment and income variables. While the three

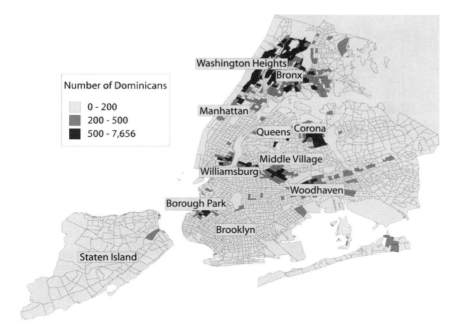

Map 6.2.   Dominicans by Census Tract, New York City, 2000.
Source: U.S. Bureau of the Census, American FactFinder, 2000,
Summary File 1, PCT11.

groups exhibit similarities in some demographic and socioeconomic characteristics, there exists divergence with reference to others (Table 6.3). Cubans possess the highest socioeconomic status and Dominicans the lowest.

DEMOGRAPHIC CHARACTERISTICS

The almost equal percentages of males and females tell us that there was little gender selectivity to the immigration process in the sense that males and females were equally likely to emigrate and the proportions for each of the three groups mirror the non-Hispanic population (Table 6.3). Many Caribbean Hispanics left for the United States with their families, or if they left alone their families soon joined them. The gender compositions of the Puerto Rican and Dominican populations are particularly similar to the non-Hispanics, with slight female majorities of between 51 and 52 percent. There is a slight male majority among Cuban and other Hispanic populations. The slight male majority among the Cubans reflects the Mariel wave of immigration in the 1980s that was predominantly male.

Puerto Ricans, Dominicans, and other Hispanics all have more youthful age structures than do Cubans and non-Hispanics (Table 6.3). This reflects the higher fertility rates of the former three groups of Latinos. The older age structure (median age of 40

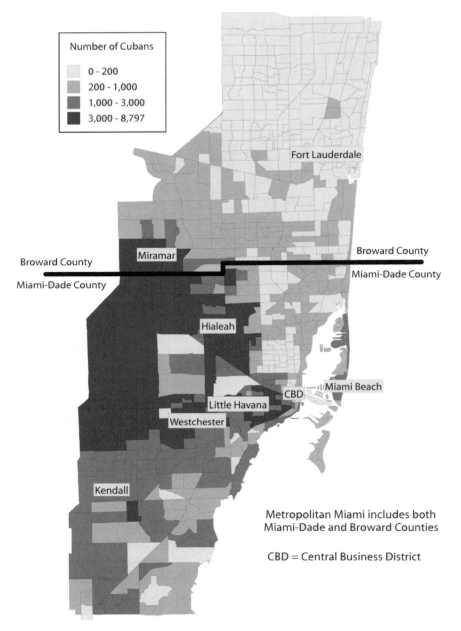

*Figure 6.3.   With a corporately sponsored billboard and a formal welcome sign,
Calle Ocho has become a commercially promoted ethnic-tourism district.
Source: Tom Boswell.*

years) of Cubans is explained by their lower fertility and the fact that the Cuban government was more willing to allow older people to leave the island. Younger males were required to provide military service for Cuba before leaving. In addition, the Castro government was more willing to allow elderly or near elderly people to emigrate because they were more likely to be out of the labor force and be dependent upon the Cuban government for a variety of social services.[28]

Unlike gender structure, racial composition among Caribbean Hispanics varies considerably (Table 6.3). Among Hispanic Americans, Dominicans and Puerto Ricans have the highest percentage being self-classified[29] as Black (12.7 percent and 8.3 percent, respectively). Still, their percentages of being Black are somewhat less than for the non-Hispanics[30] living in the United States (14 percent). This might suggest that the majority of migrants from these two places are of European descent. However, among Puerto Ricans and Dominicans in New York City, ethnic identity and Latino identity supersede racial identity. The majority of Dominicans in New York are of either African or mixed race descent, yet as they are the majority race in their home country, racial identity differs from that of African Americans. Many identify as either "White" or "Other" when responding to the census' race question. Puerto Rico has a long tradition of mixed race families, dating to the early colonial era. As a result, it is not unusual for family members to represent a range of European to African skin tones and facial features. As with Dominicans, Puerto Ricans commonly identify as "White" or "Other" to distinguish themselves from African Americans.

Table 6.3. Demographic and Socioeconomic Characteristics of Caribbean Hispanics, 2000

Variables	Puerto Ricans	Cubans	Dominicans	Other Hispanics	Non-Hispanics
Gender Composition					
Percent Males	48.6	50.3	47.8	51.7	48.7
Percent Females	51.4	49.7	52.2	48.3	51.3
Age Composition					
% 0–19 Years	37.3	20.0	34.3	39.6	27.1
% 20–39 Years	33.6	28.9	36.3	36.8	28.0
% 40–64 Years	23.6	32.1	25.0	19.4	31.5
% 65 Years & Older	5.4	19.0	4.4	4.2	13.5
Mean Age	29.1	41.4	29.4	26.8	37.0
Racial Composition					
Percent Black	8.3	4.9	12.7	1.7	14.3
Citizenship Status (Percentages)					
U.S. Citizen—born in U.S.	59.9	29.8	29.5	56.5	92.4
U.S. Citizen —born in P.R.	38.1	0.6	0.5	0.2	0.1
U.S. Citizen—born abroad to U.S. parent or parents	0.6	0.7	0.8	0.8	0.7
U.S. Citizen by naturalization	0.5	41.7	24.2	10.7	3.5
Not a U.S. Citizen	0.9	27.1	44.9	31.8	3.4
Ability to Speak English (Percentages)					
Very Well and Well	88.7	69.4	67.4	75.4	98.5
Highest Grade Completed for Persons 25 Years & Older (Percentages)					
Not High School Graduate	36.8	36.9	48.4	49.4	16.4
High School Graduate but no B.A. Degree	51.0	42.0	41.3	40.9	57.6
B.A. Degree or Higher	12.2	21.1	10.3	9.6	26.0
Unemployment Rates for Persons 25 Years & Older and Who Are in the Labor Force					
Percent Unemployed	8.3	5.7	9.6	7.4	3.9

Variables	Puerto Ricans	Cubans	Dominicans	Other Hispanics	Non-Hispanics
Occupations for Persons 25 Years & Older and Who Are in the Labor Force					
Management, Professional, & Related Occupations	42.8	48.7	33.9	33.0	51.1
Services	15.5	11.0	19.8	17.9	10.2
Sales & Office Occupations	19.5	19.7	18.3	15.7	19.9
Farming, Forestry, & Fishing	0.4	0.4	0.3	2.9	0.4
Construction, Extraction, & Maintenance	6.6	7.8	6.6	11.5	7.1
Production, Transportation, & Material Moving	15.0	12.4	20.9	18.9	11.1
Income Levels for Persons 25 Years & Older (U.S.)—1999					
Mean Income ($)	18,926	23,523	15,150	16,502	28,805
Percent Living below the Poverty Level	25.3	14.7	25.9	22.6	10.8

Source: U.S. Bureau of the Census, 2000 Census of Population, 1 percent Public Use Microdata Sample.

A much larger proportion of Puerto Ricans are U.S. citizens and a larger number were born and raised on the U.S. mainland than is the case for both Cuban and Dominican Americans (Table 6.3). Among both of the latter two groups, almost 70 percent were not born in the United States. Almost 28 percent of the Cubans are not citizens and close to 45 percent of the Dominicans are not U.S. citizens. The high rate of non-citizen status for Dominicans is in part because some 46 percent have only arrived since 1990. Citizenship status is also important because it means that there are certain types of government financial and medical assistance available to citizens, but not to non-citizen immigrants.

SOCIOECONOMIC CHARACTERISTICS

When compared to Cubans and Dominicans, Puerto Ricans possess the best English-speaking abilities (Table 6.3). Almost nine out of ten (89%) Puerto Ricans living on the U.S. mainland claim to speak English either very well or well. This is at least partly a reflection of the fact that a much larger proportion of Puerto Ricans were born in the United States when compared to Cuban Americans and Dominican Americans. It is interesting to note, however, that English ability is not necessarily indicative of other socioeconomic characteristics.

Among the three Caribbean Hispanic groups, Cubans have the highest socioeconomic status (Table 6.3). They have the highest percentage of people who have received a B.A. degree or higher[31] and are characterized by the lowest unemployment rates and the highest mean incomes.[32] Cubans also have the highest percentage of persons employed in high-paying management and professional jobs and the lowest proportion employed in the blue-collar occupations of production, transportation, and material moving. Conversely, Dominicans possess the lowest status measured by these same socioeconomic dimensions. Puerto Ricans are intermediate between Cubans and Dominicans in terms of their socioeconomic status.

Cuban Americans have the highest socioeconomic status because of the selection process that operated when they emigrated. Most Cubans who immigrated to the United States have come from the upper and middle classes; they were the ones who economically lost the most during the 1959 Communist Revolution.[33] Many were business owners and owners of property that was confiscated by the new Cuban government. Some also were political refugees, having supported the Batista government that ruled the country before Fidel Castro took power. Many of the Cuban immigrants were settled under the Cuban Refugee Act which provided special economic assistance because of their refugee status. They were given financial assistance, courses in English, and participated in special job-training programs, all of which provided them with advantages denied most immigrants.

Dominican Americans have the lowest status for at least three reasons. First, their origin country is economically poorer than either Cuba or Puerto Rico. Second, as noted earlier in this chapter, they are the most recently arrived of the three Caribbean Hispanic immigrant groups and thus have had less time to acculturate to American society and its economy. Finally, related to their recency of arrival, a high proportion of the Dominicans are not U.S. citizens, and thus do not have the opportunity to receive most of the types of economic assistance usually afforded to Puerto Ricans.

Puerto Ricans have intermediate socioeconomic status between that of Cubans and Dominicans (Table 6.3). They are economically better off than Dominicans because a larger proportion of the Puerto Rican population were born and raised in the United States and have had the advantages of participating in the American educational system. They are more comfortable speaking English, and thus are able to take advantage of opportunities provided by the American economy. They possess lower economic status when compared to Cuban Americans because Cubans were drawn more from the middle and upper classes. Conversely, Puerto Ricans were more frequently drawn from the lower and lower-middle classes of Puerto Rico.

Caribbean Hispanic Cultural Contours

Culture is expressed in a multitude of ways, but the cultural expressions of family, language, and religion are three of the most important, particularly with reference to the acculturation process. Indeed, culture change associated with the move from source to destination country can be quite dramatic, particularly with reference to gender and intergenerational conflict.

THE CARIBBEAN HISPANIC FAMILY

The traditional family structure in Puerto Rico, Cuba, and the Dominican Republic is typical of that for most of Latin America. In the traditional Latin American family there is a sharp distinction between the role of men and women, with a double standard being applied in work, play, and sex. The wife is expected to stay at home and attend to the running of the household and care of children. A pattern of male dominance prevails, and the husband makes most of the major family decisions. The tradition of *machismo* dictates that males demonstrate virility through physical strength, courage, and business success. It is not unusual for males to have extramarital affairs. Whether or not a husband has a regular mistress is frequently more affected by economics than conscience. Daughters and wives, on the other hand, are protected against temptation. A strict tradition of chaperoning is the norm for respectable unmarried women who date.[34]

Sociologists have developed a concept known as *resource theory* for explaining the position of decision-making power that members of any particular family have relative to each other. An individual gains power if the resources that he or she contributes to the family increases. These resources may be economic, intellectual, or emotional in nature.[35] Economic difficulties that many Hispanics faced upon their arrival in the United States affected their adjustment. Often the husband was unable to find work or found work at a lower-status job than he had experienced in Puerto Rico, Cuba, or the Dominican Republic. As a result, it became necessary for many wives to enter the labor force to help contribute to the support of the family. Most of these wives had not previously worked outside the home in their sending countries. Thus, as the wife's resource contribution to the family became greater through employment, usually her power to help make decisions also increased, whereas that of her husband declined. For example, a study of Cuban women in Washington, D.C., concluded that their entrance into the labor force was the single most important change in their lives as immigrants.[36] As a result, the traditional patriarchal family structure for Caribbean Hispanics began to change toward greater equality in decision-making abilities for husbands and wives. Also, a lessening of the former double standard began to take place. As a result, the typical Caribbean Hispanic family living in the United States today is less male-dominated, and the roles of husbands and wives are less segregated than the traditional Latin American family norm.

Despite the fact that the Caribbean Hispanic family structure has changed in the United States, it is still different enough from the American norm to cause some conflict between the first and second generations. Studies of acculturation stresses among Hispanics living in the United States have found that the second generation generally has adopted Anglo attitudes and behavior patterns more quickly than their first-generation immigrant parents. Sometimes a crisis in authority emerges, as the parents find themselves being led and instructed in new ways by their children. Many of the traditional norms become labeled "old-fashioned." Chaperoning for dating, as an example, has become a focal point of tension in many families. Many second-generation Caribbean Hispanics feel they are caught between two cultures, by being neither completely Hispanic nor American. They want to maintain selected aspects of both cultures and as a result feel that they do not belong to, or are not completely accepted by either.[37]

SPEAKING SPANISH AND ENGLISH

Virtually all first-generation Puerto Ricans, Cubans, and Dominicans living in the United States speak Spanish as their mother tongue.[38] Like most other immigrant groups coming from non-English-speaking countries, the first-generation immigrant Caribbean Hispanics teach Spanish to their second-generation children. However, the Spanish that is learned in the home by the second generation is usually very basic or elementary. More often than not, the second-generation children converse with neighborhood friends in a mixture of Spanish and English, called *Spanglish*. In short, they learn a different quality of Spanish that sometimes serves as a source of embarrassment for their parents because of the perceived close connection between language and ethnic identity. Furthermore, their ability to speak English may also be impaired, especially if they live in a predominantly Hispanic neighborhood where little English is spoken. Mixed marriages that involve an immigrant Hispanic spouse and a native Anglo seldom produce children who are truly fluent in "good" Spanish. One exception to this generalization is encountered when the mother works and the children are raised by a Spanish-speaking relative.

Where Puerto Ricans, Cubans, and Dominicans are heavily concentrated, as in the metropolitan areas of New York and Miami, speaking Spanish can become an emotionally charged issue. For example, language is often listed as the main obstacle to harmony between Anglos and Hispanics living in Miami. Some Anglos in Miami feel it is becoming necessary to be bilingual in Spanish and English in order to compete for local jobs. They are afraid that Spanish is being forced upon them by the large number of Hispanic immigrants who, they perceive, are not making a serious effort to learn English. When asked what the most important problem posed by living in the United States is, Caribbean Hispanic immigrants most frequently cite the language barrier. Their lack of facility with English hinders their employment opportunities and affects their abilities to obtain government services.

RELIGIOUS PREFERENCES[39]

Most Caribbean Hispanic immigrants are at least nominally Roman Catholic. Their arrival in the New York and Miami metropolitan areas has had a major impact on the membership of many local parishes. Many, but not all Catholic churches in both metro areas have priests who can give mass, hear confessions, and offer counsel in Spanish. In Hispanic neighborhoods, the Catholic Church has become one of the key ethnic institutions of self-identity and a center of community life.

In addition to those professing the Catholic faith, a sizable number of Caribbean Hispanics are members of various Protestant sects and a lesser number are Jews. Also, an increasingly significant number have joined Pentecostal churches; as length of residence in the United States passes, the likelihood of joining a Pentecostal church significantly increases. The latter are popular because they are small-scale operations and they have no trouble accommodating to small clusters of Puerto Rican, Cuban, and Dominican families. There may be several in a given neighborhood operating out of small storefront structures. In addition, they are almost always directed by a minister who was born in Puerto Rico, Cuba, or the Dominican Republic. Often families coming from the same town or neighborhood in the home country will attend the same church in New York City or in Miami. Thus, the Pentecostal churches have been successful in being able to satisfy some of the needs for security and cultural maintenance that the Catholic Church has been unable to provide.

Community Case Study: Miami as a Cuban American Homeland in Absentia

Although in the eyes of many Cuban Americans it is recognized that the island of Cuba is the first homeland, it can be argued that Miami has become a second homeland in absentia. Miami is a city with a relatively short history since it was incorporated only in 1896. As a consequence, the more than forty-five years that Cubans have been living here in large numbers is a comparatively long time, especially in a city where most people have in-migrated from someplace else. In 2000, more than 70 percent of Miami-Dade County's population was born outside the state of Florida, with about 51 percent being foreign-born. Simply stated, Cubans are one of Miami's most established groups, despite the fact they are newcomers. Many Cubans now have a sense of rootedness in Miami.[40] Miami has been described as "the capital and Mecca for U.S. Cubans."[41]

The word *absentia* is used to describe an essential characteristic of Miami as a new homeland for Cubans. Whereas between one-third and one-fourth of most immigrants to the United States eventually return to reside in their countries of origins, probably less than one-tenth of one percent of the Cuban Americans have returned to live in Cuba since the 1959 revolution.[42] Indeed, Miami Cubans find it impractical, difficult, and sometimes dangerous to return. It is impractical to return because the standard of living and the economic opportunities are much less than in the United States. It is difficult because the Cuban government carefully screens the documents of anybody entering Cuba, and they are especially suspicious of Cuban Americans returning home. Also, it can be dangerous for those Cuban émigrés who left Cuba illegally to move to the United States. For instance, if an emigrant is suspected of stealing a boat or hijacking a plane, he or she is subject to the Cuban justice system upon return to the island.

It is significant that few Cuban Americans return to live in Cuba. Because only a few return to their island origin, more return instead from elsewhere in the United States to the next best thing, Miami. Thus, Miami has become a type of surrogate homeland for many Cuban Americans. For example, between 1995 and 2000, 19,462 Cuban Americans moved to Miami-Dade County from other places in the United States. This was equal to 22 percent of all Cubans moving to this county during this five-year period.[43]

In Miami, speaking Spanish has become an emotionally charged issue and is often listed as the main obstacle to harmony between Anglos and Hispanics. In 1973, Miami-Dade County commissioners passed an ordinance that officially declared the county to be bilingual. Seven years later, in November 1980, just after the Mariel Cuban exodus, the electorate of Miami-Dade repealed the ordinance in a referendum by a voting ratio of three to two. The new ordinance stipulated that public funds were not to be used to teach languages other than English or to promote a culture other than the culture of the United States. Many Miami businesspeople feared that this action might have a damaging effect on South Florida's lucrative trade with Latin America. Then, in 1992, Florida voters passed a referendum that made English the official language of the state. However, in 1994, Dade County commissioners voted to make both English and Spanish the official languages of Miami-Dade County.

Two studies conducted during the 1990s in Miami suggest that even though Miami-Dade County has a large Hispanic population, the greatest concern is not that Spanish will become the dominant language in the county, but rather that the second-generation Hispanic children are not becoming sufficiently proficient in Spanish to be able to use it to conduct business with Latin American countries.[44] Many business leaders in Miami express the strong fear that the city will lose its lead as the gateway city to Latin America if there are not enough people sufficiently proficient in Spanish to be able to talk intelligently with business leaders from these countries. Interestingly, a survey undertaken in South Florida determined that 85 percent of the second-generation Hispanic children questioned said they preferred to speak in English instead of the Spanish their parents speak.[45] Given this evidence, it does not appear that English is a language threatened with extinction in South Florida.

Transnational Connections

The lack of diplomatic relations between the United States and Cuba and the anti-Castro fervor maintained among Cubans in Miami constrain the ability of the Cuban community to physically circulate between their home country and the United States. Many in the first generation still see themselves as exiles waiting to return and reclaim what was lost, despite being naturalized U.S. citizens. Despite their political rhetoric and passionate desire to see the downfall of the Castro government, many Cubans send remittances in the forms of money, household goods, medicines, and nonperishable foodstuffs when U.S. policies allow, knowing that to do so indirectly supports the Castro regime.

In some ways it is Miami's status as homeland in absentia or what can be perceived as a deterritorialized Cuba that creates a form of transnational network for Cuban Americans who do not reside in Miami.[46] Cubans circulate to and from Miami to maintain cultural and social links that were lost during the Revolution, but that have been re-created by the exile community. For example, many of Havana's elite social clubs and restaurants were reestablished in Miami with the same names, and often the same owners and members. In many ways, Miami provides a continued connection to a Cuba that no longer exists except in the minds and hearts of the exiles.

Puerto Ricans, by nature of their citizen status regardless of residence on the island or mainland, also maintain unique forms of transnational identity. This political status allows people greater spatial mobility between their island of origin and the mainland diaspora, and as a result, the people of *la nación en vaivén* or "the nation on the move" possess more fluid and hybrid identities[47] when compared to the "in-betweenness" of more common forms of transnational identities. Indeed, because of this unique political status and high mobility, the term *translocal* rather than *transnational* might be more appropriate. It is difficult to assess how much of the island's economy is comprised of monies and material goods sent from the mainland as they do not differ from packages and money transfers that would be sent to relatives across state lines. The island's continued status as a commonwealth of the United States grants its residents most of the rights and privileges of citizenship, including the freedom to circulate as opportunity or need arises. The primary differences lie in the costs and standards of living and in political power through this franchise. It is only on the mainland that Puerto Ricans can vote for president, and the congressperson from the island is a nonvoting member of the House of Representatives.

Among these three groups, it is Dominicans who maintain a true transnational community. In Washington Heights, the economic and residential center of the Dominican community, transnational connections are evident everywhere on the economic landscape. Every block along major streets has at least one if not several transnational businesses. These include travel agencies, international telephone calling centers, and businesses that facilitate the shipping of *envios* and *cargas*, that is, money and packages. American Airlines billboards and travel agents are ubiquitous, as the airline flies daily between New York and both Santo Domingo, the capital, and Puerta Plata on the north coast.[48]

The Dominican Republic is so strongly integrated with the Dominican community in the United States that even its current president is a transnational. Leonel Fernández Reyna was born in the Dominican Republic, but lived much of his life in Washington Heights and was residing there when elected to his first term in 1996. While he served as president, his family remained in New York, making him the first U.S.-based transnational president. He subsequently returned to New York in 2000, from which he was elected to a second term as president (2004–2008).

Conclusion

Although it is true that Puerto Ricans, Cubans, and Dominicans possess much in common, there are many differences between them as well. These differences are framed by their entry and settlement experience in the United States and by their ability to maintain ties with their homeland.

By virtue of their status as native-born American citizens, Puerto Ricans do not face many of the challenges and obstacles experienced by most immigrants. They do not need visas to enter the U.S. mainland or to travel back and forth to the island. The community on the mainland is also mature enough to have a growing number of social, economic, and political leaders, entrepreneurs, educators, and other professionals. Although there is a significant proportion of the Puerto Rican community that continues to be trapped in poverty, there is a growing Puerto Rican middle class in multiple regions of the country.

Cubans established a homeland in absentia in Miami as a launching point for a return to Cuba when Castro fell. After more than four decades, Miami continues to serve as the capital of this exile community. While many still await the long-expected return to their homeland, Cubans in Miami and elsewhere have used the human capital with which they entered the United States to regain the social and economic status they possessed before leaving Cuba. This was facilitated by the many forms of financial assistance reserved for refugees fleeing Communist states and by the successful transformation of several sectors of Miami's economy into a trade bridge to Latin America. This combination of positive human capital and refugee assistance programs makes the Cuban success story unique for both Caribbean Hispanics and recent immigrants in general.

Dominicans are more representative of the post-1965 immigration experience. Although present in small numbers prior to 1965, Dominicans benefited from changes in immigration law that coincided with stressful political and economic conditions in the country. They are the most spatially concentrated of these three groups, with a social, economic, and political center in the Washington Heights neighborhood of Upper Manhattan in New York City. This community continues to grow through family reunification, and in recent years has begun to settle in new regions and states such as South Florida, Maryland, Georgia, and North Carolina.

As the most recent arrivals among these three groups, Dominicans maintain the strongest transnational ties, even to the point of electing a transnational president of their homeland. The strength and importance of the U.S.–Dominican Republic political and economic ties are reflected in the choices that Dominicans have in maintaining their original citizenship when naturalizing as U.S. citizens and in the ability to register and vote in Dominican elections from the United States if they can claim to have resided in the Dominican Republic for at least six months during the election year. This is a new model of immigrant experience that other groups such as Mexicans are seeking to replicate, and may become a more prevalent model of immigration and integration into American culture in the future.

Notes

1. Technically, they can return to Cuba, but few do because they and their children would almost certainly be discriminated against or possibly be arrested by the Cuban government depending on their circumstances of departure. Less than one percent of Cuban Americans return to live in Cuba. Historically, between one-fourth and one-third of most immigrant streams to the United States have returned to their country of origin, for a variety of reasons.

2. It has been reported that the 2000 U.S. Census of Population badly underestimated the number of Dominicans living in the United States because of the way the question on Hispanic ethnicity was asked. John Logan, former director of the Luis Mumford Center for Urban Studies at the State University of New York at Albany, estimates that the correct number of Dominicans in the United States in 2000 was slightly more than 1.1 million. This error had less of an impact on Mexicans, Puerto Ricans, and Cubans. John Logan, *The New Latinos: Who They Are, Where They Are* (Albany, NY: Luis Mumford Center for Comparative Urban and Regional Research, University of Albany, 2001).

3. Adalberto Lopez, "The Puerto Rican Diaspora: A Survey," in Adalberto Lopez and James Petras, eds., *Puerto Rico and Puerto Ricans* (New York: John Wiley, 1974), 316.

4. Clarence Senior, *Our Citizens from the Caribbean* (New York: McGraw-Hill, 1965), 77.

5. The information we are using on net passenger flows comes from Gerardo E. Sanchez-Duvarge, Bureau of Economic Analysis, Puerto Rico Planning Board, San Juan, Puerto Rico, 21 March 2005.

6. Francisco L. Rivera-Batiz and Carlos E. Santiago, *Island Paradox: Puerto Rico in the 1990s* (New York: Russell Sage Foundation, 1996), 47.

7. Francisco L. Rivera-Batiz, "The Characteristics of Recent Puerto Rican Migrants: Some Further Evidence," *Migration World* (October 1989): 10.

8. Thomas D. Boswell and Angel David Cruz-Baez, "Puerto Ricans Living in the United States," in Jesse O. McKee, ed., *Ethnicity in Contemporary America: A Geographical Appraisal* (New York: Rowman & Littlefield, 2000), 182–226.

9. Patrick Lee Gallagher, *The Cuban Exile: A Socio-Political Analysis* (New York: Arno, 1980), 23–36.

10. J. Jaffe, Ruth M. Cullen, and Thomas D. Boswell, *The Changing Demography of Spanish Americans* (New York: Academic Press, 1980), 246–248.

11. Gallagher, *The Cuban Exile*, 34–35.

12. Gallagher, *The Cuban Exile*, 37–39.

13. University of Miami, "The Cuban Immigration, 1959–1966, and Its Impact on Miami-Dade County, Florida" (Coral Gables: Research Institute for Cuba and the Caribbean, Center for Advanced International Studies, University of Miami, 10 July 1967), 1 and Appendix A.

14. Juan M. Clark, José L. Lasaga, and Rose S. Reque, *The 1980 Mariel Exodus: An Assessment and Prospect* (Washington: Council for Inter-American Security, 1981), 15–57.

15. Clark et al., *The 1980 Mariel Exodus*, 12.

16. Frederick Tasker, "Refugees Have Revised Census Data," *The Miami Herald*, 31 January 1981, p. 1B.

17. Guillermo Martinez, "Cuban Miamians Prone to Highlight How They Contrast with Marielitos," *The Miami Herald*, 26 May 1981, p. 7A; and Zita Arocha, "Mariel's Scorned Youths Feel Sting of Rejection," *The Miami Herald*, 23 March 1981, p. 2B.

18. This section draws heavily on the following source: Holly Ackerman and Juan M. Clark, *The Cuban Balseros: Voyage of Uncertainty* (Miami: Cuban American National Council, 1995), 22.

19. U.S. Department of Homeland Security, *2003 Yearbook of Immigration Statistics*, 19.

20. We think that the best discussion of how Miami has adjusted to the heavy immigration of Cubans and Haitians is found Alex Stepick, Guillermo Grenier, Max Castro, and Marvin Dunn, *This Land Is Our Land: Immigrants and Power in Miami* (Berkeley: University of California Press, 2003).

21. Silvio Torres-Saillant and Ramona Hernandez, *The Dominican Americans* (Westport, CT: Greenwood Press, 1998), 33–34.

22. Patricia R. Pessar and Pamela M. Graham, "Dominicans: Transnational Identities and Local Politics," in Nancy Foner, ed., *New Immigrants in New York* (New York: Columbia University Press, 2001), 229–249.

23. Torres-Saillant and Hernandez, *The Dominican Americans*, 29–31.

24. In this chapter we use Metropolitan Statistical Areas (MSAs) and Consolidated Metropolitan Statistical Areas (CMSAs) as approximations of the largest metropolitan areas in which our three Caribbean Hispanic groups are concentrated.

25. Boswell and Cruz-Baez, "Puerto Ricans Living in the United States," 156.

26. U.S. Bureau of the Census, *2000 Census of Population*, "Hispanic or Latino by Specific Origin," Table PCT11, States, Summary File 1, American FactFinder. Available at: <www.census.gov>.

27. Havana is located about 90 miles from Key West, Florida.

28. Thomas D. Boswell and Angel David Cruz-Baez, "Cuban Americans," in Jesse O. McKee, ed., *Ethnicity in Contemporary America: A Geographical Appraisal* (New York: Rowman & Littlefield Publishers, 2000), 139–180.

29. The U.S. Bureau of the Census asks people being enumerated to classify themselves according to what they consider their race to be.

30. The "Not Hispanics" include Blacks, Whites, Asians, and Pacific Islanders, with all the people who consider themselves to be Hispanics taken out.

31. We limit our analysis of educational achievement to persons who are 25 years of age or older because these people have mostly completed their education.

32. The *2000 Census of Population* includes incomes only for persons 15 years and older. We limit our analysis of unemployment and occupation to persons 25 years and older for the same reason we limit the education analysis to people of this age. In the United States, many people under 25 years of age are still in school or otherwise not working full-time.

33. Guillermo J. Grenier and Lisandro Pérez, *The Legacy of Exile: Cubans in the United States* (New York: Allyn and Bacon, The New Immigrant Series, 2003), 15–28.

34. Marie LaLiberte Richmond, *Immigrant Adaptation and Family Structure among Cubans in Miami, Florida* (New York: Arno, 1980), 33–39.

35. R. O. Blood and R. L. Hamblin, "The Effect of Wife's Employment on the Family Power Structure," *Social Forces* 36 (May 1957): 347–352; and S. J. Bahr, "Comment on the Study of Family Power Structure: A Review 1960–1969," *Journal of Marriage and the Family* 34 (May 1972): 239–243.

36. Margaret Stanley Boone, "Cubans in City Context: The Washington Case," Ph.D. dissertation, Ohio State University, 1977, 18.

37. John Dorschner, "Growing Up Spanglish in Miami," *Miami Herald*, Tropic Magazine, 11 September 1977, p. G13.

38. For the purposes of this discussion, first-generation Caribbean Hispanics are all those persons of Hispanic origin living in the United States who were born in either Puerto Rico, Cuba, or the Dominican Republic, regardless of their age upon arrival in America. Their American-born children are regarded as the second generation . Their grandchildren, who were also born in the United States, are the third generation. Some researchers also refer to a hypothetical "1.5 generation." These are persons who were born abroad but moved to the United States before they were ten years old.

39. This section draws heavily on the following two sources: (1) Thomas D. Boswell and Angel David Cruz-Baez, "Puerto Ricans Living in the United States," in Jesse O. McKee, ed., *Ethnicity in Contemporary America: A Geographical Appraisal* (New York: Rowman & Littlefield, 2000), 213–216; and (2) Thomas D. Boswell and Angel David Cruz-Baez, "Cuban Americans," in *Ethnicity in Contemporary America*, 170–171.

40. Kevin E. McHugh, Emily H. Skop, and Ines M. Miyares, "The Magnetism of Miami: Segmented Paths in Cuban Migration," *The Geographical Review* 87, no. 4 (1997): 504–519.

41. Lisandro Perez, "The 1990s: Cuban Miami at the Crossroads," *Cuban Studies* 20 (1990): 3.

42. Telephone conversation with Lisandro Perez, Department of Sociology and Anthropology, Florida International University, 6 April 1992.

43. U.S. Bureau of the Census, *2000 Census of Population*, "Residence in 1995 for the Population 5 Years and Over—State, County, and Place Level," Table PCT49, Cuban, Summary File 4, American FactFinder. Available at: <www.census.gov>.

44. Sandra H. Fradd, *The Economic Impact of Spanish-Language Proficiency in Metropolitan Miami* (Miami: Cuban American National Council, 1996), and Sandra H. Fradd and Thomas D. Boswell, "Spanish as an Economic Resource in Metropolitan Miami," *Bilingual Research Journal* 20, no. 2 (Spring 1996): 283–337.

45. Fabiola Santiago, "Children of Immigrants Embrace Ethnicity," *The Miami Herald*, 14 June 1997, p. 1A.

46. McHugh et al., "The Magnetism of Miami."

47. Jorge Duany, *The Puerto Rican Nation on the Move: Identities on the Island and the United States* (Chapel Hill: University of North Carolina Press, 2002).

48. Miyares, "Changing Latinization."

CHAPTER 7

Non-Hispanic West Indians in New York City

Milton Vickerman

In the minds of many Americans, immigrants from Caribbean countries are primarily Spanish-speakers from Cuba, Puerto Rico, and the Dominican Republic. While Cubans and Puerto Ricans numerically dominate the Caribbean-origin migration stream, there are many other non-Spanish-speaking immigrant groups from the "islands" that have greatly diversified the Caribbean ethnic mosaic in the United States. Except for French Creole–speaking Haitians, the balance of non-Hispanic West Indians speak English or originate from countries where English is widely spoken. These origin countries include Jamaica, Trinidad, Barbados, the many islands that comprise the Lesser Antilles, the Bahamas, as well as the mainland countries of Belize in Central America and Guyana and Suriname in northeastern South America (Map 7.1). While immigrants from Jamaica, Trinidad, and Barbados have been on the American scene for over one hundred years, drawn by proximity and economic and historical ties to the United States, other immigrant groups from Belize, Suriname, and Guyana with strong historical, political, or racial ties to these earlier West Indian groups have emigrated to the United States during the post-1965 period. In America, these ties may or may not lead to greater social cohesiveness but they separate these non-Latino immigrants from their Latino neighbors.

In discussing Caribbean-origin, non-Latino immigrants, definitions become important because from an American point of view the nature of the relationship between these people is often obscured. European colonization of the Caribbean Sea and adjacent mainland areas bequeathed four distinct culture zones based on Spanish, Dutch, French, or English rule. The logic of colonialism produced similar economic outcomes in the four zones: plantation-based sugar monoculture powered by African slaves. Wars between the European powers sometimes blurred the lines between the culture zones, as territories shifted hands back and forth between the powers. Suriname, a former Dutch colony, is a notable example of this. However, other territories such as British-owned Barbados remained firmly within the grasp of particular European powers for centuries. Moreover, these powers encouraged their particular colonies to cultivate vertical relationships with the "mother" country, rather than horizontal relationships with colonies in neighboring, but different, culture zones.

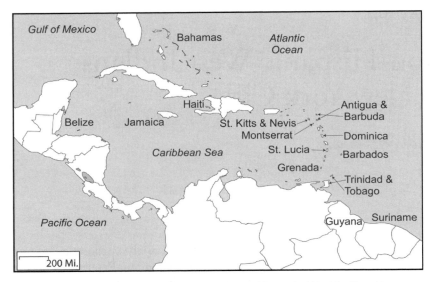

Map 7.1.   Source Countries of Non-Hispanic West Indians.

This vertical integration of colonizer and colonized territories not only achieved the primary goal of intensifying political domination of colonies, it also sharpened the cultural barriers between Spanish, Dutch, French, and English colonies. Consequently, despite short distances between them, people in the four culture zones tend to conceptualize "their" Caribbean as existing only within the confines of their particular culture zone. For instance, to the typical Barbadian, the West Indies consists of such places as Trinidad, Antigua, Grenada, and Jamaica—that is, countries in which the English language is spoken and where British institutions prevail. Jamaicans, to take another instance, do not usually view either Cuba or Haiti—both within 150 miles of the island—as part of "their" world. However, as outlined below, the large influx of Haitians into predominantly English-speaking West Indian American neighborhoods is breaking down these barriers and creating a sense of unity between the groups.

Considering all this, Guyana, Suriname, and Belize seem like anomalies. The three territories lie on mainland South and Central America and are surrounded by Spanish-speaking countries. Yet, historical and cultural ties bind them closely to two of the other culture zones mentioned above. Both Guyana and Belize are part of the British West Indies, while former Dutch Suriname is often discussed in the same breath with the British West Indies because of its historical ties to that region. Individuals from Guyana and Belize move easily among, say, Trinidadians, Barbadians, and Jamaicans because all speak the same language and have had similar historical experiences. A good example of the latter is that Asians were introduced into all British West Indian territories at the same time because of planters' region-wide fear of black withdrawal from plantation life following Britain's abolition of slavery and subsequent serfdom in 1838. Planters viewed Asians as ideally suited to fill the projected labor gap and facilitated their entry by the thousands across the region, from Jamaica to Suriname.[1]

In the United States, settlement patterns provide a good indicator of immigrant West Indians' affinity for each other. Aside from the powerful fact of racial discrimination, which tends to push non-white immigrants together, groups often agglomerate on the basis of culture. Consequently, in cities with high concentrations of non-Hispanic West Indians such as New York, Guyanese immigrants and Belizeans are to be found living where there are large numbers of other English-speaking Caribbean immigrants. In contrast, these immigrants as a whole tend not to live among Spanish-speaking immigrants. However, as early as the 1930s it was noted that French- and Dutch-speaking West Indian immigrants often lived alongside their numerically preponderant co-regionalists.[2] If anything, this trend has accelerated since the 1960s such that today, though Anglophone Caribbean immigrants continue to outnumber all others, French speakers—notably Haitians—are an increasingly visible presence in America's West Indian neighborhoods.

Migration

Although English speakers—especially Jamaicans—have long dominated non-Hispanic Caribbean population movements (Table 7.1), many nationalities in the region exhibit similar migration characteristics. Most important, West Indians (including the Surinamese) view migration positively and expect to travel as a matter of course at some point in their lives. Evidence for this exists in the high proportion of foreign-resident West Indians relative to the population size of these countries. For instance, Belize's population is only 226,000 but 44,000 Belizeans live in the United States. The Guyanese population in the United States amounts to 30 percent of the 762,000 people living in Guyana and the same is true of Grenadian immigrants.

The emigration rate, which computes the propensity of people to leave particular countries relative to the size of those countries, gives another indication of the importance of migration to West Indians. In 2002, Mexico, the country sending the most people to the United States, experienced an emigration rate of 31.35, but Jamaica, with its much smaller population, experienced a rate of 73.75.[3] This indicates that, relative to their population in 2002, Jamaicans were more than twice as likely to leave their country as were Mexicans. The Surinamese and Guyanese were even more likely to migrate, as these immigrants exhibited rates of 95.9 and 105.1 respectively. The Haitian pattern is similar and different because Haitians also demonstrate a high propensity to migrate, but unique among Caribbean nations, large numbers of Haitians enter the United States as refugees.

This migratory impulse originated early on in West Indian history and has always been rooted in the region's economic underdevelopment expressed in relatively low per capita GDP and high unemployment rates. In some cases, overpopulation has only exacerbated depressed economic opportunities. With greater income earning potential elsewhere, most West Indians are classified as voluntary immigrants. The lone exception would be Haitians; although economic opportunity is low in this poorest of Western Hemisphere countries, most Haitians have primarily entered the United States as refugees. In responding to this economic reality, many West Indian governments, as a

Table 7.1.   West Indian Immigrants to the United States, 1956–2002

Country of Birth	1956–1960	1961–1965	1966–1970	1971–1975	1976–1980
Antigua	298	866	1729	1969	4014
Bahamas	1646	1203	1132	1609	2498
Barbados	1514	1992	7312	7878	12603
Belize	677	1213	2945	2591	4646
Dominica	219	432	1767	1182	3294
Grenada	216	602	1907	2388	5182
Haiti	3265	9889	27648	27130	30294
Jamaica	6518	8335	62676	61445	78476
Montserrat	253	531	877	932	959
St. Kitts	283	870	3132	1960	4220
St. Lucia	116	481	884	1305	3560
St. Vincent	199	559	1384	1613	3040
Trinidad	1497	2149	2236	33278	27297
Guyana	896	1239	5760	14320	32040
Suriname	278	392	369	387	379

Country of Birth	1981–1985	1986–1990	1991–1995	1996–2002	Total
Antigua	8081	1762	2828	18719	
Bahamas	2660	4648	3563	4922	23881
Barbados	9406	8076	5366	5828	59975
Belize	13204	10320	5848	5191	46635
Dominica	2818	3626	3572	2204	19114
Grenada	5254	5325	3832	362	25068
Haiti	43890	96273	95977	133176	467542
Jamaica	100560	136222	90731	113099	658062
Montserrat	700	651		517	5420
St. Kitts	7096	3513		2915	23989
St. Lucia	2964	3146	2906	4016	19378
St. Vincent	3673	3880		3589	17937
Trinidad	17018	22515	33708	41984	181682
Guyana	37271	52649	34134	40020	218329
Suriname	463	801	1030	1436	5535

Source: U.S. Department of Justice,
Statistical Yearbook of the Immigration and Naturalization Service, 1991; 1995; 2002.

matter of policy, have encouraged the migration of their nationals, in part because of the perceived positive role of remittances in bolstering the sending country's economy. Just as important for modern-day West Indian immigration is the myriad of transnational family networks as a form of social capital that facilitates the movement of people and West Indian culture between countries. In short, West Indians are not only psychologically oriented toward migration, many factors encourage them to do so.

The beginnings of this movement lie in the abolition of slavery in 1834, and subsequent serfdom in 1838, which saw blacks withdrawing from plantation labor in large numbers. In colonies with available land (e.g., Jamaica and Guyana) they adopted peasant farming, but lack of such land caused former slaves in smaller eastern Caribbean colonies to migrate. Trinidad early on became a target of such migration. However, migrants soon spread throughout the entire Caribbean. By the 1850s, Jamaicans and other West Indians were migrating to Central America as construction and plantation workers. The construction of the Panama Canal was the most significant factor pulling these workers in the last decades of the nineteenth century. Jamaica alone sent 84,000 laborers between 1891 and 1889 and the second (American-led) project pulled in as many as 200,000.[4] Intra-Caribbean movement, as well as migration out of the region, continued unabated in the first few decades of the twentieth century. Typically, as work in certain locations dried up, or as obstacles were placed before West Indians, they would divert to new ventures and locations. Work in foreign countries tended to dry up because it revolved around the completion of specific projects or the work was seasonal. The Panama Canal is a good example of the former, and Bonham Richardson's analysis of Caribbean migrations gives a systematic account of how the need for labor drew thousands of eastern Caribbean men to the Dominican Republic season after season.[5] In the first two decades of the twentieth century, the volume became so large that a number of Latin American countries such as Venezuela (1918), Honduras (1923), and Panama (1928) introduced racist legislation to restrict or exclude black West Indians.[6]

As a region, however, mainland Latin America was only one of the destinations favored by West Indians. After 1900, West Indians migrated to the United States in three waves. The first ended in the late 1920s, the second lasted from the mid-1940s to the early 1960s, and the third began in the late 1960s after the passage of the 1965 Immigration Act and has continued into the present. First-wave West Indian immigrants established the community in the United States. Females were as numerous as males, and being restricted by racial segregation, these pioneer West Indians lived in Harlem in New York City. Skilled workers and laborers predominated, but near the end point of the first wave of migration, halted by the restrictive National Origins System and the Great Depression, professionals began to increase in number. Approximately 107,000 individuals migrated to the United States from the West Indies between 1899 and 1930.[7] Typically, English speakers, especially Jamaicans, predominated. For instance, the Immigration and Naturalization Service records 5,195 British West Indians as having migrated to the United States between 1925 and 1930. During the same period, only 614 Guyanese, 404 Haitians, 164 non-Haitian French West Indians (Martinique and Guadeloupe), 161 Dutch West Indians, and 38 Surinamese individuals migrated to the United States.

Generally speaking, with the exception of Guyana and Haiti, these proportions have endured in subsequent periods of West Indian migration. After the economic downturn in the 1930s a second wave of migration occurred in the 1940s, as Jamaicans and some Barbadians came to the United States for farm and factory work. Smaller numbers came to enroll in American colleges and to join relatives already in the United States. In 1952, in a move that many Jamaicans viewed as being specifically anti-Jamaican, the McCarran-Walter Act limited the number of West Indian immigrants to 100 per year.[8] In any case, following World War II, British West Indians (including the

Guyanese) were far less interested in migrating to the United States than to the United Kingdom. Starting in 1948, the volume of West Indian migration to that country swelled. By 1961 an estimated 280,000 West Indians had moved to the United Kingdom.[9] The anti-black 1961 Commonwealth Immigration Act sought to bring this movement to a halt, but by that time the British West Indies was on the verge of independence and American immigration policy was about to take a very liberal turn. The 1965 Immigration Act abolished the National Origins System, thereby basing immigration on the principle of family reunification rather than on nationality. As independent countries (starting in August 1962 with Jamaica), the former British West Indian colonies fell under the 120,000-visa ceiling for Western Hemisphere countries. These factors sharply boosted emigration from all West Indian territories, ushering in the third and present wave of American-oriented West Indian migration.[10]

Table 7.1 illustrates that Jamaicans continue to outnumber all other West Indian immigrants, accounting for 46 percent of post-1956 America-bound settlers from the region. While their numbers have grown 16-fold over the period 1965–2002, Haitian growth at 40-fold has been even more impressive. Haitians now comprise the second largest West Indian group in the United States. The Guyanese are third, at 15 percent of West Indians, but their 43-fold growth rate has outstripped even that of Haitians. However, Surinamese immigration remains small in both absolute and proportional terms. Though their numbers have grown over 400 percent in the period between 1965 and 2000, at present, they constitute less than one percent of immigrants from the West Indies and affiliated regions. The dynamics of colonialism and World Systems Theory explain this since colonial peoples migrate most heavily to their "mother" countries. As Puerto Ricans have looked to the United States and British West Indians to Britain in the post–World War II period, so the Surinamese have looked toward Holland as a migration destination.[11]

Settlement Patterns

Most West Indians reside along the East Coast, with New York and Florida proving to be the most attractive locations. Actually, the population is more concentrated than this because just a few neighborhoods in New York City and in South Florida cities such as Miami account for the bulk of West Indian immigrants. Forty-three percent of West Indians reside in New York and 26 percent in Florida.[12] Only a few other states evince noticeable, though much smaller, concentrations: New Jersey (7%), Massachusetts (4%), Connecticut (3%), and Maryland (3%). California (3%) is the only non–East Coast state characterized by a noticeable concentration of West Indians. Surinamese immigrants evince a broadly similar pattern, except that they are more equally distributed between Florida (32%) and New York (29%). Also, unlike other non-Hispanic West Indians, more Surinamese live outside East Coast states. Eight percent reside in California, 4 percent in Illinois, and 3 percent in Texas.

A focus on New York City, the historic center of the non-Latino population in the United States, reveals that West Indians primarily live in Brooklyn, the Bronx, and Queens (Map 7.2). The first two boroughs are representative of older sections of the city that have functioned as "ports of entry" for earlier arriving immigrant groups. Few live on Staten Island or in Manhattan, a fact, which in the case of the latter, represents a sea change from the early decades of the twentieth century when Harlem functioned as the neighborhood of first settlement (Map 7.2). However, the major West Indian groups (Jamaicans, Haitians, the Guyanese, and Trinidadians) vary in their settlement patterns in the three boroughs of highest concentration. New York City Department of City Planning data on intended West Indian settlement patterns for the first half of the 1990s provide some indication of this distribution. Jamaicans predominate in the Bronx, while Haitians are highly concentrated in Brooklyn. Seventy percent of Haitians indicated central Brooklyn as their intended residence, as did 61 percent of Trinidadians, 43 percent of Jamaicans, and 41 percent of Guyanese immigrants. Forty-two percent of Guyanese, 26 percent of Trinidadians, and 24 percent of Jamaicans indicated Queens as their intended residence.

Within these boroughs, West Indians are concentrated in specific neighborhoods (Map 7.2). Jamaicans locate in Williamsbridge, Baychester, and Wakefield in the Bronx;

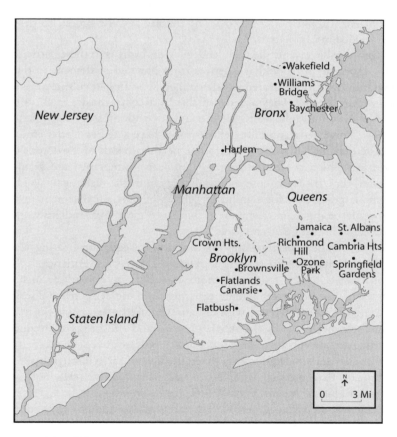

Map 7.2. Location of West Indian Neighborhoods in the
New York City Region.

Flatlands, Flatbush, Brownville, and Crown Heights in central Brooklyn; and Cambria Heights, St. Albans, and Springfield in eastern Queens. Haitians strongly overlap with Jamaicans and other West Indians in Brooklyn, as virtually all Haitians (90%) in that borough indicated the previously mentioned Brooklyn neighborhoods as their destination in the City Department of Planning survey. The same was true of 30 percent of Trinidadians. In contrast to Brooklyn, Queens resident West Indians exhibit greater population dispersal. For instance, eastern Queens neighborhoods such as Cambria Heights and St. Albans tend to be Jamaican strongholds, while the Guyanese concentrate in Richmond Hill, Ozone Park, and Jamaica; 38 percent of Guyanese immigrants indicated these areas as their intended destination in the early 1990s.

Many Trinidadians reside in these neighborhoods as well. Race plays a role in this settlement pattern, since Indian Guyanese and Trinidadians concentrate in Richmond Hill, a neighborhood with a large Indian immigrant community, in disproportionate numbers. However, as shown, it is also true that the settlement patterns of many Guyanese and Trinidadians of all races spatially overlap with other West Indians. Very few Surinamese live in New York City. For instance, the Department of City Planning recorded their total 1996 population at 281 individuals with 39 percent of this total living in Queens. Brooklyn accounted for 31 percent and the Bronx, 23 percent. The remainder resided in Manhattan.[13]

To a considerable extent, the prevalence of West Indians in these particular neighborhoods—especially in Brooklyn—derives from previous settlement in the form of chain migration which has created clearly defined West Indian culture areas or neighborhoods within the city. They are identifiable by accents, music, small stores selling products typical of multiple West Indian countries, and, most tellingly, national flags and symbols. These geographically defined zones have acted as nuclei around which ever larger settlement has materialized. Some neighborhoods of New York City (and other cities with high concentrations of Caribbean immigrants) are so identifiably "West Indian" that, if they choose to, immigrants from the region can avoid interacting with the larger society for significant periods of time. Involvement in the larger economy would be the main exception to this, since most West Indians work at regular jobs, rather than being self-employed.[14]

The other, and perhaps more important, side of the equation creating West Indian neighborhoods is that their existence is not benign. Like African Americans, West Indians are constrained in their residential choice by racial discrimination. Such discrimination confined first-wave immigrants to living in Harlem. As overt discrimination declined somewhat over the years, West Indians were able to leave Harlem and colonize the various neighborhoods in Brooklyn, Queens, and the Bronx mentioned above. However, the decline in racial discrimination is only relative, since much evidence shows that it continues to significantly shape the lives of these immigrants.[15] Residentially, this means that so-called West Indian neighborhoods are really only segregated black zones with high concentrations of West Indian immigrants.

John Logan and Glenn Deane[16] have shown that West Indian–white segregation is extraordinarily high, reaching 82.7, 78.0, and 73.2 percent in New York City, Newark, and Boston respectively.[17] Like African Americans, West Indians' entry into European American–dominated neighborhoods has often been met by violence and white flight.

Indeed, West Indians may experience more such violence because, being less attuned to American racial conditions, they may be more likely to pioneer settlement in previously all-white areas.[18] The outcome of such efforts can be observed in the south-central Brooklyn neighborhood of Canarsie. Previously Jewish and Italian, and the scene of much racial tension decades ago as blacks started moving in, the area is now heavily West Indian. Whites have fled the neighborhood for such still-white-dominated areas as Staten Island and Long Island.

Socioeconomic Characteristics

In general, West Indians' socioeconomic characteristics place them midway between European Americans and African Americans (Table 7.2), though sometimes closer to the former than to the latter. For instance, their median household income approximates that of non-Hispanic whites. This is also true of the labor force participation rate, a statistic that has drawn much attention to West Indians because of their elevated levels of economic activity. This high rate of participation occurs because, like other immigrants, West Indians are "strivers." Research on West Indians over the past century has consistently noted that these immigrants view themselves as hard-working, goal-oriented people.[19] Hard work, in this case, means not only high labor force participation, but also multiple family members holding jobs and many individual West Indians performing multiple jobs. The 2000 census notes, for example, that while only 16 percent of European American families in New York State have three or more working individuals, 27 percent of West Indian families fall into this category.[20]

The goal of this hard work is the attainment of a better life, as reflected in prestigious high-paying jobs, higher education, and material attainment. The well-known West Indian penchant for home ownership is a classic example of the latter. In practice, the actual attainment of West Indians' goals is determined by the interaction of cultural expectations, human, social, and monetary capital, gender, and race. Colonialism conditioned West Indians to devalue manual labor because of its association with slavery and to measure success, instead, by the attainment of such high-credentialed professions as medicine, law, and teaching. In so doing, it elevated education as the means for achieving success.[21] The high literacy rate in the source region is one indicator of this "striver" mentality. Although most West Indians possess only a high school education, the cultural orientation toward higher education endures in America and affects how they adapt to society. For instance, their rate of self-employment lags behind the American average, in part because of a preference for employment in professional occupations. Surinamese are a major exception.

Linguistically, the Surinamese also stand apart because 70 percent of these immigrants speak Dutch and, of course, Haitians are mainly speakers of Creole. Most non-Hispanic people from the Caribbean, including Guyana, speak English, and this fluency helps them penetrate the labor market. Indeed, the lack of English fluency could help explain the Surinamese's high rate of self-employment. But if West Indians penetrate the American labor market at high rates, they do so unequally as men and women. In general, males display higher labor force participation rates and their

Table 7.2. Socioeconomic Characteristics of West Indian Immigrants, 2000

	Income Median Household Income	Labor Force Participation Rate		Families in Poverty (%)	Percent Self-Employed	Education up to High School	College Graduates[b]	Home Ownership Rate
		Male	Female					
Total U.S.	$50,000	72.0	59.0	12.1	9.4	46.8	24.4	67
Non-Hispanic Whites	$54,000	73.0	58.0	8.0	10.6	44.0	27.0	75
Blacks	$36,000	61.0	60.0	23.0	4.4	56.5	13.5	53
West Indians								
Guyana	$54,100	75.0	63.0	13.0	5.7	57.0	17.3	62
Barbados	$51,600	72.0	66.0	13.0	4.9	56.0	18.0	54
Jamaica	$49,300	74.0	69.0	14.0	6.5	53.0	18.0	58
Antigua-Barbuda	$48,500	80.0	70.0	15.0	5.9	49.0	21.0	45
Dominica	$48,170	73.0	63.0	23.0	5.2	59.0	15.0	39
Grenada	$48,000	72.0	67.0	15.0	8.2	57.0	18.0	46
Trinidad & Tobago	$47,300	74.0	65.0	16.0	7.2	52.0	18.0	50
St. Vincent	$47,000	74.0	65.0	16.0	5.2	57.0	16.0	47
St. Kitts-Nevis	$47,000	79.0	70.0	17.0	4.1	50.0	23.0	47
Belize	$47,000	73.0	62.0	18.0	7.4	55.0	13.0	41
Haiti	$42,000	70.0	61.0	21.0	4.8	56.0	14.0	47
St. Lucia	$40,500	74.0	68.0	19.0	5.9	59.0	15.0	45
Suriname	$50,628			17.0	28.0	53.0	19.0	53

Source: 2000 PUMS 5% Sample.
[a]2000 1% sample
[b]25 years or older

occupational distribution differs markedly from females. Most saliently, West Indian women concentrate disproportionately in health care, with up to 29 percent of all females working in that industry at various levels. In this, West Indian women have transferred a home-grown cultural and economic orientation to an American context. In this case, Dual Market Theory partially explains their concentration in health care because of the high demand for such work in the destination country. Though lower, at 20 percent, women also concentrate in administrative-support occupations (e.g., clerks). Almost an equal proportion of women find employment in the management and professional category. West Indian males exhibit less occupational concentration, with approximately 19 percent working in the former category, 13 percent in the transportation and moving industry, 10 percent in construction, and 10 percent in office administration and support.

Aspects of West Indian Migration

Numerical data on West Indian migrants reveal important aspects of their place in American society but do not fully capture the more subjective or qualitative aspects of the migratory experience. Pivotal here is that migration is a process that the people undertaking the journey imbue with subjective meaning. The presence of settled communities of West Indians in the United States acts as a magnet on co-ethnics still living in the Caribbean, pulling them in to better their lives. Leaving aside the special case of Haiti, with its extreme poverty and turbulent politics, a typical pattern emerges. West Indians will form long lines outside American embassies and consulates, typically in capital cities, to apply for visas to migrate to the United States. Most can count on the social capital of family connections to help aid the process, although the degree of facilitation this provides depends on the closeness of the relatives. Having American relatives does not necessarily mean that the wait to enter the United States will be a short one. Most seek a "green card," which enables West Indians to travel to and from the United States at will and, in America, to almost live as full citizens. Though green-card holders cannot vote, holding a green card confers permanent residency and a raft of quasi-citizenship benefits. Consequently, West Indians are slow to naturalize, taking on average more than ten years to do so.

Although obtaining a green card is an eventual goal, the immediate objective of many waiting in the West Indies is to gain access to the United States and its economic opportunities. Most do so legally but illegal migration also occurs, taking the form of slipping across the Canadian-American border or overstaying short-term visas. Among legal immigrants, West Indian women generally lead the way, a fact that reflects their relative autonomy in still patriarchal societies and their difficulties accessing local job markets. Jamaican women, for instance, are twice as likely as their male counterparts to experience unemployment in their sending country.[22] Because of American demand for such "female" jobs as domestic work, nursing, and low-level clerical work, West Indian women have much incentive to migrate to the United States. Relevant data show that they respond to this incentive, constituting 55 percent of all West Indians migrating to the United States between 1967 and 1998. That women are pioneers in this respect is cost-effective, since many West Indian families do not possess the means to send whole families to America.

Furthermore, female migration has implications for families, since it usually means leaving children behind. In this instance, fathers, aunts, or grandparents become surrogate parents for a time because, in migrating, women do not abrogate their family responsibilities. In fact, the opposite is true: migration is part of a deliberate strategy whereby the pioneering parent intends to establish herself, first, economically. Once that is achieved, papers will be filed to reunite with children and/or spouses in the United States. Putting it another way, "serial" migration, which is synonymous with long-term chain migration, carries with it an implied promise of eventual benefits for relatives who have been left behind in the West Indies. Discussing this, Ransford Palmer has argued that serial migration differs significantly from older conceptions which posited a short-duration, completed migration sequence consisting of departing the sending country and arriving in the receiving country.[23] In contrast, serial migration is drawn out over months or even years and ends only when the portion of the family that has been left behind in the source country is reunited with the pioneering immigrant in the destination country.

The Community and Family

In America, West Indian immigrants find themselves in communities that are at once familiar and different. A good example is Crown Heights in Brooklyn, the archetypal West Indian neighborhood in New York City (Map 7.2). A mixed middle- and working-class neighborhood, approximately one square mile in area, Crown Heights is surrounded by adjacent West Indian and African American communities. Geographically, it is bounded on the north by Eastern Parkway, an eight-lane east-west highway that separates it from Bedford Stuyvesant. In the east, north-south-running Buffalo Avenue separates it from East New York; east-west Empire Boulevard separates it from Flatbush to the south; and its western edge is bounded by north-south Washington Avenue. Utica Avenue, which bisects the neighborhood in a north-south direction, is the business district of Crown Heights. Here, immigrants are surrounded by West Indian symbols and people with island accents. Many small shops and restaurants advertise the selling of such food items as Jamaican patties, hard-dough bread, and Trinidadian Rotis. Record stores and car radios blare dancehall and soca music. Churches—large edifices as well as store-front structures—promise to feed the spirituality that is an integral aspect of West Indian life. Travel agencies advertise trips back to the islands and many also offer shipping services. West Indians habitually send large cylindrical containers—"barrels"—filled with commodities ranging from food to electronics back to their relatives in the Caribbean.

Over the years, an entire industry catering to this impulse has grown up. Neighborhood businesses, intent on catering to every nationality, display flags of various West Indian nations, indicating the multinational nature of their endeavors. This symbolism is significant because it demonstrates how neighborhoods such as Crown Heights serve as seedbeds for the germination of a pan–West Indian identity in America. In so doing, they help overcome the nationalistic insularity that centuries of colonialism have bred into West Indians. Ironically, it is in these foreign settings that West Indians truly come to realize that their similarities outweigh their differences. Everything in West Indian neighborhoods is geared to reminding these immigrants that they constitute a unique people. Even the Korean-owned grocery stores, ubiquitous in such areas, specialize in the selling of merchandise that is peculiarly West Indian and that can be found nowhere outside of these neighborhoods.[24]

However, West Indian neighborhoods exist within the context of a larger American culture, and new immigrants become immediately aware of this. For one thing, whites are much more evident than in the West Indies. In Crown Heights, many are Hasidic Jews, whose presence gives race relations in that neighborhood a unique tinge. Also, housing differs in form and pattern. In a West Indian society such as Jamaica, urban houses typically have yards separated from adjoining houses by metal, chain link, or concrete fences. House and yard size vary with social class, such that wealthier neighborhoods display larger—even elaborate—houses and are associated with larger yards. The opposite is true in poorer neighborhoods. However, in the American neighborhoods where the typical West Indian immigrant first settles, housing is usually denser. Private houses have little yard space and, indeed, as in Crown Heights, may only be of the semi-detached variety.

The epitome of dense housing is the high-rise apartment block. Though not entirely alien to West Indians, this form of housing is not typical of the origin region, and getting used to apartment life is one of the greatest challenges West Indians face in adjusting to America. This can be particularly hard on middle-class West Indians for the reasons outlined above. On the other hand, it should be noted, the apartment building functions as space for the creation of a pan–West Indian ethnic identity. Such buildings constitute a sort of United Nations of West Indian nationalities, and by compressing so many different peoples together, they help dissolve national differences. Perhaps most important here is the incorporation of Haitians, who in the West Indies have often been stigmatized, but in apartment buildings such as those found in Crown Heights, Flatbush, and East Flatbush are recognized as constituting just another West Indian group.

As with other immigrant groups, the family is central to West Indians, not least because it helps facilitate the new immigrant's adjustment to American society. As noted previously, many West Indian American families are reconstituted in that they represent the rejoining of children or spouses with pioneering West Indian immigrants. This rejoining process can be bumpy if the pioneering parent has spent a long time away from either child or spouse. Though serial migration makes good economic sense, it often leaves children scarred with emotional and psychological problems, as they experience something akin to abandonment.[25] These resentments often carry over when the child is reunited with parents in America.

Serial migration can also strain marriages because of the time spouses spend apart and, also, because West Indian men often practice visiting relationships wherein they will have children with multiple women. However, census data show that most marriages remain intact since over time the percentage of married couples with both spouses present increases, while the percentage of single female–headed families declines. Because West Indian women participate in the American labor force at high levels they may not be able to devote as much time to their immigrant children as they want. This is particularly true if they work multiple jobs, or jobs taking them far distances, as live-in domestics are prone to do. Such jobs may see West Indian women being away from home for days or even weeks at a stretch. As noted below, a possible outcome of such situations is that peers gain relatively greater influence over children than parents, resulting in a loss of the West Indian ideal of achievement.

Work, Race, and Identity

Finding work is a priority for newly arrived West Indians and their families because economic advancement is their primary goal in America. So important is this to them that it becomes a pivotal part of their identity, but ironically it also thrusts them deeper into America's racial politics. The type of work sought will depend on level of education, and actually getting jobs depends on social networks and newspapers. West Indians believe that white employers favor them over African Americans and there is evidence to support this view. For instance, such favoritism enables West Indian service workers to recommend unemployed co-ethnics because employers may already be satisfied with West Indians who are working for them. For newly arrived immigrants or those whose credentials may be shaky because of expired visas, such support is invaluable. However, the quality and extensiveness of West Indian networks are limited, so most West Indians rely on classified advertisements to find jobs. And, as mentioned previously, gaining higher education is usually mixed with these aspirations of upward mobility.

In pursuing their economic goals West Indians often encounter racism. Indeed, in America race becomes centrally important, to the extent that it significantly shapes their life chances and that of their American-reared children. American racism surprises and troubles West Indians. Some even assert that they discovered their "blackness" only after migrating to America.[26] This is ironic because race and racism are central to the slave-driven colonialism that dominated the West Indies for over three centuries. Furthermore, some West Indian societies—notably Trinidad, Guyana, and Suriname—have experienced tensions between blacks and Asian Indians over the past few decades. Moreover, West Indians know of America's history of discrimination against blacks and other minorities through their relatives and the media.

The answer to this seeming paradox lies in the relativity of racism, political expediencies, the population dynamics of West Indian societies, and historical views of race. Although both West Indian and American societies were constructed on racist principles throughout their respective histories, American racism has been more intense and persistent. Even in the nineteenth century, when West Indian societies were undoubtedly racist, colonial officials argued that their societies were more tolerant than was the United States.[27] This dissembling of race evolved into post-colonial (i.e., post-1962) policies officially downplaying race. The national mottoes of several West Indian countries reflect this officially sanctioned view of multiracial harmony. For instance, Trinidad's motto reads: "Together we Aspire, Together we Achieve"; Guyana's states: "One People, One Nation, One Destiny"; and Jamaica's proclaims: "Out of Many, One People." On the surface, such policies seem like mere ideology but, in fact, they are quite convincing to the average West Indian. This has come about because West Indian societies have changed more quickly than has the United States. The withdrawal of overt white political power, combined with black upward mobility in societies that are mostly monoracial (that is, black), has removed race as a daily consideration for West Indians. Moreover, in many societies race is rarely part of the political agenda, and newspapers hardly ever discuss it. Consequently, despite the racially tinged social inequality marking many West Indian societies, race is not a public or pressing issue for ordinary West Indians. Racism is still reflected in these societies' Eurocentric notions of beauty. However, this too has been powerfully countered by Rastafarianism, with its pro-Africa orientation. Instead of race, a strong conviction exists that education and self-effort are what matter.[28] A key fact here is that since black role models fill every social niche in these societies—from prime ministers to homeless people—the average West Indian does not associate race with achievement.

Added to all this is West Indians' complex conceptualization of race, which eschews simple American-style black/white distinctions, and in calculating race, factors in such criteria as skin shade, ancestry, social class, and education. It is in fact true that on a day-to-day basis the typical West Indian person in countries such as Jamaica does not ordinarily encounter blatant racial discrimination. Trinidad, Guyana, and Suriname are different because those societies are multiracial in the true sense of the word and the sites of undoubted racial tension. This tension spills over into New York City, where Trinidadian and Guyanese immigrants of Asian Indian descent often prefer the company of Indians from the subcontinent who do not necessarily reciprocate the feeling.[29] Yet black Trinidadians also downplay the extent of the racial problems in their societies and express surprise at American racism. One possible reason for this is that Asian Indians and black West Indians may experience race differently in the United States, with blacks being more likely to encounter discrimination. Hanan Orna,[30] for instance, notes that black (Creole) Surinamese immigrants have more such experiences than do their Asian Indian counterparts.[31]

Racism strongly impacts West Indian immigrants because, being mostly of African origin, the majority population identifies them as black and discriminates against them accordingly. Such discrimination poses major obstacles to their adjustment to American society since it effectively relegates them to second-class status. As is the case with African Americans, anti–West Indian racism is systematic. The reality of residential segregation, which determines quality of life in many other areas such as the cleanliness of streets or the quality of schools, has already been mentioned. In encounters with the law, West Indians are as likely as African Americans to experience mistreatment at the hands of the police. The 1997 case in which New York City police officers were convicted of sodomizing Haitian immigrant Abner Louima with a wooden object is the most graphic example of this. In public spaces, Americans do not distinguish between African Americans and West Indians. Males, especially, are automatically suspect and constantly experience slights ranging from women avoiding them on the street (e.g., by crossing over to the other side) to being followed in stores. Though less common, verbal and physical abuse also occurs, and in the extreme case of Crown Heights, in 1991, actual rioting might happen. It should be noted, however, that the Crown Heights situation was atypical, inasmuch as it represented the outcome of years of friction between two quite different cultures that share the same neighborhood space. Many blocks in Crown Heights are integrated, with West Indian–owned homes alternating with Jewish-owned homes. Indeed, it is common to find situations in which Jews and West Indians live in the same physical structure, separated only by a wall. Also, some Jews live in West Indian–owned buildings and vice versa. Despite this, little socio-spatial interaction exists between Hasidic Jews and West Indians, and for the most part, the two communities live quiet, parallel lives.[32]

West Indians, even those from multiracial societies such as Suriname, experience persistent difficulty coping with racial discrimination.[33] This difficulty is particularly acute where such discrimination targets their jobs because the notion that they are hard-working achievers lies at the heart of the West Indian self-identity in the United States. Although some employers favor West Indians in hiring, many others discriminate against them at this stage and also on the job.[34] Employment-related discrimination especially, and discrimination in general, makes West Indians' relationship with African Americans more tense because in coping with these problems West Indians have often sought to distance themselves from black Americans. Making matters worse is the claim of some writers that West Indians achieve and African Americans do not because of a purported "cultural superiority."[35] In reality, no such superiority exists, and West Indians and African Americans commonly form strong bonds of friendship because of everyday interaction in the neighborhoods where both groups live and because of shared experiences of discrimination. Indeed, it is noteworthy that West Indian distancing from African Americans derives not from a rejection of "blackness" per se, but from the specifically negative American conception of it. Reaching back to their own socialization in largely black-dominated societies, West Indians desire to broadcast the message that being black, and achieving, are correlated. That is, they carry a more positive view of what it means to be black. Generally speaking, newly arrived West Indians are most likely to practice distancing, whereas long-term residents of the United States, seasoned by discrimination, are most likely to express kinship with African Americans. In Crown Heights and other West Indian neighborhoods in New York City, this sense of kinship expressed itself strongly in 1989 when African American David Dinkins campaigned to be the city's first black mayor. Ninety-two percent of Crown Heights residents voted for him.[36] However, separatist sentiments among West Indians continue to exist and even grow because immigration is ever increasing the size of the West Indian population, nourishing the view that they are an ethnic group distinct from African Americans.[37]

Politically, this expresses itself in candidates who campaign as ethnics rather than as African Americans, and in non–West Indian politicians who seek to tap the ethnic vote. If burgeoning population growth is the medium facilitating this ethnic upsurge, the underlying cause is West Indians' desire to gain the respect of the larger society and achieve upward mobility.

Public festivals are a particularly typical New York City means of asserting ethnic identity and West Indians are no exception to this rule. Crown Heights is home to the prototypical and largest West Indian festival in the country. Centered on Eastern Parkway, the annual Labor Day carnival draws Caribbean people of every nationality and consists of miles of colorful floats on flatbed trucks, accompanied by a host of gaudily costumed performers who mix and mingle with thousands of local, national, and international onlookers. Loud Caribbean music, mixed with food, drinking, and revelry, is at the heart of this festival, but as a site of ethnic identity construction it has also become increasingly politicized over the years. Now an institution, the carnival is planned by a permanent organizing committee, and local and national politicians seeking the West Indian and black vote view the carnival as a necessary stop. The carnival is a dynamic manifestation of the process whereby West Indians are adjusting to America by the temporary appropriation of public space.

The Future of West Indians

West Indians' future in America will be shaped by a number of distinct, but contradictory, trends. Race is fundamentally important because it guides Americans' social expectations of West Indians. If the issue of immigration is ultimately about assimilation, then American society expects West Indians to assimilate into the larger black community and become African American. The first two waves of immigrants (1900s to 1950s) conformed to these expectations, but there are signs that the post-1960s third-wave immigrants are intent on establishing a separate identity. Transnationalism fuels this tendency by creating social spaces in which interaction between West Indian Americans and the Caribbean becomes routine. This interaction reinforces West Indian culture in the United States, thereby strengthening immigrants' already strong connections with their homelands. West Indians routinely remit money and goods back to their countries of birth, and such remittances sometimes constitute a substantial portion of these nations' foreign exchange. This is especially true of Jamaicans, who remitted seven times as much money (approximately $6 billion) between 1992 and 1999 as Haitians, the next highest remitters (at $838 million). In contrast, the Guyanese and Surinamese remitted very little money, sending home only $3 million each during this time period. Immigrants from other English-speaking countries averaged $500 million over the seven-year period.[38]

Frequent visits between the Caribbean and West Indian American enclaves are possible because the regions lie in such close geographical proximity to each other. Many West Indians with green cards live part-year in the Caribbean and part-year in the United States. Moreover, West Indians typically express a desire to live out their retirement years in the Caribbean. Many never actually do so, moving instead to South Florida, which they view as a good compromise between living in the United States and enjoying the climate and lifestyle of the Caribbean. The 2000 census data show that Florida is by far the largest receiver of West Indians who migrate from other states. Atlanta, Georgia, is second.[39] All of these movers are not retirees, however, because West Indians usually migrate out of central city locations such as Crown Heights as they become upwardly mobile. Some move to more affluent suburbs, while others move to other states. Overall, future West Indian American population growth and accelerating cultural exchange between West Indian Americans and the Caribbean will likely enlarge the transnational social spaces linking the two regions. Ironically, however, growing population size could also impede aspects of transnationalism in the United States because as West Indian communities become larger, the impetus to actually travel to the region might decline. Increasing numbers of West Indian immigrants may come to see the West Indian culture embodied in neighborhoods such as Crown Heights, Flatbush, or St. Albans as being an acceptable substitute for the "real" thing. This implies that transnational processes have limits.

For obvious reasons, the second generation represents the real future of West Indian Americans. Research has increasingly turned to this group, trying to decipher their likely course in American society. The key question is whether they will assimilate as blacks and suffer discrimination or as "West Indians" and possibly avoid that fate. The answer is not simple because in a society in which African Americans have experienced significant upward mobility over the past forty years, the question becomes: "Which blacks?" Also, it is unclear whether identifying as "West Indian" will be a net plus for the second generation because while American society has long harbored positive stereotypes of West Indians, it has also cultivated negative ones. Moreover, as shown, in many instances Americans do not distinguish between African Americans and West Indians.

The answer to these questions revolves partly around perceptions and partly around objective realities. West Indian immigrants believe, and transmit to their American-born children, the idea that education is key to upward mobility. In West Indian terms, education refers not just to book learning, but to conventional behaviors as well. Thus, an "educated" person is not only learned, but speaks Standard English, is polite, and dresses neatly. In America, parents conceive of this view as being "West Indian," and transmitted to their children, it becomes translated into the notion that ethnic identity should be cultivated. The implication here is that these parents view some inner-city African American youth as embodying different tendencies. Mary Waters has theorized that the fate of second-generation West Indian youth depends on the identity options and lifestyle they choose.[40] This, in turn, is conditioned by their settlement geography of inner city versus more affluent neighborhoods, parents' social class, and the degree of discrimination to which they are subject. She sees three possibilities: an "American" identification for inner-city West Indian youth from poor families; greater possibilities for upward mobility for more affluent youth who do not reside in such areas and who cultivate an "ethnic" (i.e., West Indian) identity; and an "island identification" for youth who are so West Indies–oriented that possessing an American or ethnic identity is not even an issue. Waters argues that this third option is unsustainable. Consequently, identity options will resolve to the first two choices. She expects American-identified youth to become so traumatized by the combination of poverty and persistent racial discrimination that they will develop an aversion to competing for success, while ethnic-identified youth will embrace the possibility of upward mobility because of their more positive social circumstances.

Census data and research lend support to Waters' theory and West Indian parents' perceptions. Second-generation West Indian youth who live in suburban areas are noticeably more affluent than those who do not and are somewhat more likely to attend private schools. For instance, comparing New York City with suburban Nassau County shows that second-generation youth in the city are more likely than those in the suburbs to live in families headed by single women. Moreover, their median household income is noticeably lower, standing at $38,980, compared to $71,160 in Nassau. Also, 14 percent of New York students (compared to 17 percent of suburban students) attend private school. These data imply that suburban youth enjoy more favorable conditions for success than do their urban counterparts. Along the same lines, Ruben Rumbaut's study of second-generation youth from a variety of nationalities in California and South Florida showed that though they were more likely to fear racial discrimination than other groups, Jamaican youth were very nationalistic and expressed the highest level of self-confidence in their abilities.[41] Concomitantly, they exhibited the highest GPA of any non-Asian group. These findings tend to support the argument that youth who identify with their ethnicity leverage their qualitative sense of ethnic difference in an attempt to overcome racial barriers. Vickerman in his studies of West Indian immigrants and of second-generation West Indians found this to be exactly the case.[42] Concordant with Waters's theory, West Indian parents were found to encourage their children to maintain a West Indian identity, believing this to correlate with eventual socioeconomic success. Moreover, middle-class children tended to accept and cultivate such notions.

The conclusion is that the future path of second-generation West Indian youth remains uncertain. They are less imbued with a transnational "consciousness" than are their parents, being more likely to embrace the West Indian culture of neighborhoods such as Crown Heights as a viable substitute for travel to the Caribbean. Moreover, many also embrace their American birth, recognizing that it makes them different from people who were born in the West Indies.[43] However, their upbringing is steeped in West Indian culture. The likelihood is that they will slowly assimilate into the African American community but this will take time, and if musical trends are any indication, the second generation will influence African American culture as much as they are influenced by it.[44]

Conclusion

Non-Hispanic West Indians have migrated to the United States for over one hundred years in part because of close geographical proximity and historical ties between the Caribbean and the United States. However, this migration increased sharply at the beginning of the twentieth century as West Indians, steeped in a culture of migration, and motivated by their region's economic underdevelopment, sought out new economic opportunities in America. Most of these immigrants were Jamaicans, though large numbers of other British West Indies immigrants also arrived in New York City. This first large-scale wave of migrants from the West Indies (from the early 1900s to the late 1920s) settled in Harlem. From the beginning, their settlement patterns reflected the linguistic and cultural divisions in the Caribbean where, historically, colonial subjects cultivated closer relationships with their respective colonial powers than with neighboring islands. Most saliently, in the United States, this has meant that English- and Spanish-speaking West Indians live in different neighborhoods. Linguistic and cultural divisions also exist among non-Hispanic West Indians even though they tend to live in the same residential areas. Traditionally, English speakers predominated in this group since it consisted mostly of people from the Anglophone West Indies (which includes Guyana on the South American mainland). Surinamese Dutch speakers, for example, have comprised a narrow slice of the total flow. The same has been true of French speakers, but in the present third wave of West Indian migration to the United States that began in the late 1960s, Haitians have become a major presence in the total flow of immigrants. Currently, these immigrants constitute the second largest segment (after Jamaicans) of the non-Hispanic West Indian population.

Although the various non-Hispanic nationalities maintain their cultural distinctiveness to some degree, they are also merging with each other because of their similarities. These include a universally high propensity to migrate, similar racial background (most are of African ancestry), and a tendency to cluster in the same neighborhoods in cities along the East Coast. The West Indian neighborhoods of New York City are a good example of this since these hold the highest concentration of West Indians in the United States. This clustering is influenced by historical settlement patterns but is largely determined by residential discrimination. More generally, race melds West Indians together as a distinct ethnic group by subjecting them, as blacks, to new blatant forms of discrimination. This racism interferes with the economic advancement that is their primary motive for migrating and complicates their relationship with African Americans with whom they are usually compared. By this is meant that West Indians both distance themselves from and form strong bonds with African Americans, the latter being particularly true of second-generation West Indians. Overall, non-Hispanic West Indians exist in a transnational social field which continually orients them back to the West Indies, strengthens their culture in the United States, and renders the question of their eventual assimilation into American society problematic.

Notes

1. The inclusion of Suriname illustrates the interconnectedness of West Indian nations. Although not English-speaking, historically, Suriname has been closely associated with these countries. If anything, its nineteenth-century influx of Asians was more diverse than in the British West Indies, including not only Indians and Chinese but also Javanese. For a discussion of this issue see, for example, Eric Williams, *From Columbus to Castro: The History of the Caribbean* (New York: Vintage Books, 1984).

2. Ira D. A. Reid, *The Negro Immigrant* (New York: Columbia University Press, 1939).

3. The emigration rate, expressed per 10,000 of population, is the ratio of legal immigrants to a country's population size. These calculations are based on United Nations (Population Division) data for 2002.

4. Gisela Eisner, *Jamaica: 1830–1930* (Manchester: Manchester University Press, 1961); Michael Conniff, *Black Labor on a White Canal: Panama, 1904–1981* (Pittsburgh: University of Pittsburgh Press, 1985); Bonham Richardson, "Caribbean Migrations," in *The Modern Caribbean*, ed. Franklin W. Knight and Colin Palmer (Chapel Hill: University of North Carolina Press, 1989).

5. Bonham Richardson, *Caribbean Migrants* (Knoxville: University of Tennessee Press, 1993).

6. Malcolm J. Proudfoot, *Population Movements in the Caribbean* (Port-of-Spain: Kent House, 1950); Reid, *The Negro Immigrant*; Richardson, "Caribbean Migrations."

7. Reid, *The Negro Immigrant*; Walter Wilcox, *International Migrations*, vol. 1 (New York: Gordon and Breach Science Publishers, 1969).

8. T. E. Smith, *Commonwealth Migration* (London: Macmillan, 1981).

9. Richardson, "Caribbean Migrations."

10. Philip Kasinitz, *Caribbean New York: Black Immigrants and the Politics of Race* (New York: Cornell University Press, 1992).

11. In his comparison of emigration from the Netherlands Antilles and Suriname, Koot emphasizes the very marked orientation of the latter toward the Netherlands. See Wim Koot, "Socio-Economic Development and Emigration in the Netherlands Antilles," in *Contemporary Caribbean: A Sociological Reader*, ed. Susan Craig, vol. 1 (Maracas: The College Press, 1981).

12. The census utilizes both the foreign-born and ancestry data in counting West Indians. Each method possesses strengths and weaknesses. Reliance on foreign-born data gives an accurate indicator of the actual origin of West Indians but misses individuals who, though born elsewhere, may also claim that identity. For instance, many children of West Indians born in the United States also identify themselves as West Indian but this would not be picked up by an analysis using foreign-born data. Ancestry data solves this problem because it focuses on these second-generation individuals, thereby giving a broader estimate of the number of West Indians in the country. However, this indicator also misses individuals who may qualify as "West Indian." For instance, many black immigrants from the United Kingdom and some Central American countries such as Panama could rightly claim West Indian ancestry. It is well known that the majority of blacks in Britain are of West Indian, especially Jamaican heritage. In addition the nineteenth-century movements of West Indians have left descendants in many Central American nations. However, immigrants from those countries likely identify themselves by nationality, rather than ancestry. Unless otherwise noted, this essay uses the place-of-birth estimate.

13. New York City Department of City Planning, *The Newest New Yorkers: 1995–1996* (New York: New York City Department of City Planning, 1999); Hanan Orna, "East Indian Surinamese Women in the United States: Acculturation, Group Relations, and the Managing Strategies in Perspective," in *Sojourners to Settlers: The Indian Migrants in the Caribbean and the Americas*, eds. Mahin Gosine and Dhanpaul Narine, <http://saxakali.com/indocarib/sojourner1.htm> (11 November 2004).

14. Milton Vickerman, *Crosscurrents: West Indian Immigrants and Race* (New York: Oxford University Press, 1999); Milton Vickerman, "Second Generation West Indian Transnationalism," in *The Changing Face of Home: The Transnational Lives of the Second Generation*, ed. Peggy Levitt and Mary Waters (New York: Russell Sage, 2002).

15. Vickerman, *Crosscurrents*; Mary Waters, *Black Identities: West Indian Dreams and American Realities* (Cambridge: Harvard University Press, 2000).

16. John Logan and Glenn Deane, "Black Diversity in Metropolitan America," Lewis Mumford Center for Comparative Urban and Regional Research, University of Albany, 2003, <mumford.albany.edu/census/BlackWhite/BlackDiversityReport/black-diversity01.htm> (11 November 2004).

17. On this scale, 100 represents complete segregation.

18. William Douglas and Merle English, "Bitter Memories for Hate Victims," *New York Newsday*, 14 February 1990, A.8; Sara Rimer, "Block's First Blacks: Ashes to an Open House," *New York Times*, 17 February 1991, A.1; Somini Sengupta and Vivian S. Toy, "United Ethnically, and by Assault," *New York Times*, 7 October 1998, A.21.

19. See, for example, Reid, *The Negro Immigrant*; Raphael Lennox, "West Indians and Afro-Americans," *Freedomways* (Summer, 1964): 438–445; Gilbert Osofsky, *Harlem: The Making of a Ghetto* (New York: Harper and Row, 1966); Roy S. Bryce-Laporte, "Black Immigrants, the Experience of Invisibility and Inequality," *Journal of Black Studies* 3, no. 1 (1972): 29–56; Vickerman, *Crosscurrents*; Waters, *Black Identities*.

20. The notion of the obsessively hard working West Indian is one stereotype held by American society of this group. See, for example, the lampooning of West Indians on the 1990s television program, *In Living Color.*

21. M. G. Smith, *The Plural Society in the British West Indies* (Berkeley: University of California Press, 1965); Adam Kuper, *Changing Jamaica* (London: Routledge and Kegan Paul, 1976); Diane J. Austin, *Urban Life in Kingston, Jamaica: The Culture and Class Ideology of Two Neighborhoods* (New York: Gordon and Breach, 1987); Nancy Foner, *Status and Power in Rural Jamaica: A Study of Educational and Political Change* (New York: Teachers College Press, 1973).

22. Statistical Institute of Jamaica, "Jamaican Statistics," <www.statinja.com/stats.html#2> (11 November 2004).

23. Ransford Palmer, "Caribbean Development and the Migration Imperative," in *In Search of a Better Life: Perspectives on Migration from the Caribbean*, ed. Ransford Palmer (New York: Praeger, 1990).

24. This is not to deny the importance of language, culture, educational institutions (such as the University of the West Indies), and trade groups such as CARICOM in helping to bridge the gap between the various West Indian cultures. However, migration to foreign countries amplifies and completes the process.

25. Knolly Moses, "The 'Barrel Children,'" *Newsweek* (19 February 1996): 45.

26. Nancy Foner, "The Jamaicans: Race and Ethnicity among Migrants in New York City," in *New Immigrants in New York*, ed. Nancy Foner (New York: Columbia University Press, 1987); Vivienne Walt, "Caught between Two Worlds: Immigrants Discover Success, Racism in the U.S.," New York *Newsday*, 15 April 1988, 9–27; Vickerman, *Crosscurrents.*

27. Philip Curtin, *Two Jamaicas: The Role of Ideas in a Tropical Colony, 1830–1865* (New York: Atheneum, 1970).

28. Kuper, *Changing Jamaica.*

29. Sengupta and Toy, "United Ethnically, and by Assault."

30. Orna, "East Indian Surinamese Women in the United States."

31. For a description of hate crimes directed at Guyanese and Trinidadian Asians moving into a white neighborhood in New York City, see Somini Sengupta and Vivian S. Toy, "United Ethnically, and by Assault."

32. The writer lived in Crown Heights for many years and has conducted research in that neighborhood.

33. Reid, *The Negro Immigrant;* Bryce-Laporte, "Black Immigrants, the Experience of Invisibility and Inequality"; Vickerman, *Crosscurrents*; Orna, "East Indian Surinamese Women in the United States."

34. See, for example, Vickerman, *Crosscurrents* and Roger Waldinger, *Still the Promised City? African-Americans and New Immigrants in Postindustrial New York* (Cambridge, MA: Harvard University Press, 1996).

35. See, for example, Thomas Sowell, *Ethnic America: A History* (New York: Basic Books, 1981).

36. "The Vote for New York City Mayor," *New York Times*, 8 November 1989, B.8.

37. For a discussion of the applicability of the term African American versus Black to recent immigrants of African ancestry see Rachel Swarns, "African-American Becomes a Term for Debate," *New York Times*, 29 August 2004, A.1.

38. These calculations derive from International Monetary Fund Balance of Payments Statistical Yearbooks. See Migration News, "Remittances," <migration.ucdavis.edu/mn/data/remittances/remittances.html> (11 November 2004).

39. Karen DeWitt, "Immigrants Look Outside New York for Better Life," *New York Times*,

4 September 1990; Garry Pierre-Pierre, "Heading to Florida, Nearer the Homeland," *New York Times*, 13 July 1993.

40. Mary Waters, "Second-Generation Black Immigrants in New York City," in *The New Second Generation*, ed. Alejandro Portes (New York: Russell Sage, 1996).

41. Ruben Rumbaut, "The Crucible Within: Ethnic Identity, Self-Esteem, and Segmented Assimilation among Children of Immigrants," in *The New Second Generation*, ed. Alejandro Portes (New York: Russell Sage, 1996).

42. Vickerman, *Crosscurrents*; "Second Generation West Indian Transnationalism."

43. Vickerman, "Second Generation West Indian Transnationalism."

44. Strong cross-influences exist between 1980s and 1990s reggae and hip hop. The version of reggae known as "toasting"—where 1970s Jamaican DJs talked over musical tracks—is credited with influencing the birth of hip hop. However, reggae itself owes its origin to ska, a fast 1960s Jamaicanized version of American rhythm and blues. Post-1980s reggae—"dancehall"—and hip hop increasingly converged in the 1990s. In fact, a number of popular hip hop artists—e.g., Biggie Smalls, Busta Rhymes, and Shinehead—were of Jamaican and/or West Indian ancestry. See, for example, Vivien Goldman, "How Jamaica Changed the World's Music," *CommonQuest* 4, no. 3 (2000): 20–31.

CHAPTER 8

Central Americans: Legal Status and Settledness

Ines M. Miyares

Central Americans are fairly recent arrivals to the United States. Although they entered in small numbers as agricultural laborers during World War II, the largest waves of Central Americans began arriving in the late 1970s and 1980s, seeking asylum as conflict migrants from the devastating civil wars in which their countries were embroiled. This source region truly exemplifies the differential treatment given to those seeking asylum relative to Cold War–influenced immigration, refugee, and asylum policies.

The 2000 Census enumerated 1,686,937 Central Americans, with Salvadorans (655,165 or 38.8%) and Guatemalans (372,487 or 22.1%) comprising the majority. Hondurans follow with 217,569 or 12.9 percent and Nicaraguans comprise 10.5 percent of the population with 177,684. It is quite probable that the total number of Central Americans is much higher since thousands have entered as undocumented migrants seeking relief from the continued economic crises that followed the civil wars and from the natural disasters that have struck the region over the past decade. This is a population whose struggle for legal status has created and defined how community is established and maintained. For twenty years, these people have struggled to be recognized as legitimately meeting the standard for political asylum as broadly defined by both the United Nations and the Immigration Act of 1990, but have met with limited success. As a result, they have created communities with a sense of "permanent temporariness."[1]

Civil Wars and the Battle for Legal Status

One of the ironies of the Cold War is that it remained overtly "cold" between the superpowers but was covertly fought through proxy civil wars in a number of developing countries. Central America, like Southeast Asia, was one of the regions hotly contested by militaries and paramilitaries that were directly or indirectly assisted by competing superpowers. Unlike Southeast Asia where Eastern and Western bloc alliances seemed to be more clearly defined, the political and military/paramilitary waters in Central America were much more muddied. Thus, unlike Southeast Asians who were granted refugee status, and thus refugee assistance, whether from Vietnam, Cambodia, or Laos,

Central Americans were treated differently according to national origin. One could argue that granting refugee status and thus assistance would obligate the U.S. government to publicly admit questionable policies toward right-wing repressive governments with which it was allied.

Nicaragua has long experienced U.S. intervention in politics and internal military conflict. Its most recent civil war has its roots in a 1909 revolution against then-president José Santos Zelaya in which two Americans were killed. As was typical of foreign policies of the day, the United States sent naval forces to Nicaragua to patrol the Caribbean coastal region and subsequently stationed marines in the capital city of Managua on a "peacekeeping" mission. The marines remained there until 1933, when they were withdrawn as part of Franklin Roosevelt's "good neighbor" policy. Resistance forces led by General Augusto César Sandino opposed the military occupation. Sandino was assassinated in 1934 by the U.S.-trained National Guard led by Anastacio Somoza García. Somoza became president of Nicaragua in 1937 and led a corrupt and oppressive "dynasty." His son, Anastasio Somoza Debayle, the last of the Somoza regime, governed the country as dictator in the 1970s. By then, the Somoza clan controlled at least half of the country's wealth.[2]

A coalition of opposition paramilitaries drove Somoza into exile in 1979, and a leftist group, the Sandinistas, named for Sandino, assumed power in the vacuum of the Somoza regime's wake. The Sandanista government, led by Daniel Ortega, allied itself with the Soviet Union, establishing a military state with a centrally controlled economy. The United States intervened again, this time covertly supporting a counterrevolutionary force, the Contras, and the country became embroiled in a decade-long proxy civil war.[3] Nicaraguans who entered the United States during that time period were perceived to be "victims of Communism," and their applications for political asylum or refugee status were approved at an approximate rate of 50 percent. Nicaraguans were not quite as well received as Cubans had been, but they were arriving at the same time as large waves of Southeast Asian refugees, and recent memories of the Vietnam War led to public outcries concerning U.S. involvements in Central America.

As in Vietnam, this was not the only place where the United States was involved, but it was the only place where it was a self-identified leftist regime that was being overtly and covertly opposed. In Guatemala, the United States intervened on the basis of a distorted interpretation of decisions made by a democratically elected administration. In 1944, a group of junior military officers had led a revolt, overthrowing the last of a long line of liberal dictators. This opened the door for a progressive movement known as the October Revolution, leading to the election of Juan José Arévalo, a school teacher, to the presidency. His administration focused on reforming land tenure, education, labor practices, and the electoral system. He was succeeded by another democratically elected president, Jacobo Arbenz Guzmán. Arbenz developed a plan to address profound disparities in land tenure and the social and economic inequities that accompanied it. In 1950, 70 percent of Guatemala's land was in the hands of only 2.2 percent of the country's landholders, including a number of U.S. corporations, and less than 25 percent of this land was actually under cultivation.[4]

Arbenz expropriated these unused lands to redistribute to landless peasants, using landholders' tax records to determine remuneration. The United Fruit Company, the

U.S. corporation with the largest landholdings, took advantage of the fear of Communism that was dominating American policy and convinced the CIA that Arbenz's act was Marxist. The CIA coordinated an overthrow of Arbenz, bringing into power a repressive military junta and initiating a civil war that lasted over thirty years.[5] During that time, especially during the 1980s, hundreds of thousands of Guatemalans sought refuge in neighboring countries and struggled to enter the United States, hoping to receive asylum as had the Nicaraguans and Cubans who preceded them.

In El Salvador lines between right wing and left wing were even more blurred. Chronic poverty, government corruption, and repression led to a 12-year civil war fought overtly by the Salvadoran National Guard and the Farabundo Marti National Liberation Front (FMLN) rebels, with neither group having clearly defined purposes or support. Salvadoran citizens, including children, could be conscripted into either military force, regardless of whether they supported the side for which they were fighting. As in Guatemala, death squads fought a covert or "dirty war," assassinating or causing the disappearances of key leaders and other civilians accused or suspected of anti-government activities. Families hid their children to protect them from conscription and gave food and shelter to both sides. Their focus became surviving until the next day. And as among Guatemalans, hundreds of thousands of Salvadorans crossed the border to Honduran or Mexican refugee camps or sought asylum in the United States or Canada.[6] One key problem, though, was that the Salvadoran government claimed to be anti-Communist despite its repressive tactics and human rights abuses, and thus the United States supported the government in power.

Upon entering the United States, both Salvadorans and Guatemalans seeking asylum were considered undocumented immigrants with 98 percent being denied asylum, while Nicaraguans, considered "victims of Communism," experienced only a 50 percent denial rate.[7] This apparent systematic discrimination based on national origin led a group of Central American advocates and churches to file a lawsuit against the U.S. government. This case, *American Baptist Churches v. Thornburgh* (760 F. Supp. 796, N.D. Cal. 1991), was settled out of court. According to the settlement, the immigration courts would give second hearings to those who had been denied asylum, and those who had not yet applied for asylum would be given the opportunity to do so. The government created a temporary program, called ABC as an abbreviation of the court case, for those whose new asylum applications were pending.

Under ABC, Salvadorans and Guatemalans were granted temporary and annually renewable work permits and social security numbers while they awaited the adjudication of their cases. The ABC backlog meant it could be years before cases were processed, and eventually anyone who applied for asylum under ABC received temporary permission to work. Thus, ABC became a means for Salvadorans and Guatemalans to become quasi-documented and remain in the country, whether or not they had experienced persecution during the civil wars.[8]

The Immigration Act of 1990 was passed in the same year as the settlement of ABC. One of the components of this act was the creation of a new quasi-documented status, Temporary Protected Status (TPS), that is, protection from deportation for eighteen months. Salvadorans were the first to be eligible to apply for TPS, which like ABC gave recipients a social security number and enabled them to apply each year for a work permit. The INS encouraged Salvadorans awarded TPS to apply for ABC, each of which was extended beyond multiple deadlines. Receiving political asylum and thus qualifying for permanent residency required sufficient proof of a well-founded fear of persecution upon returning to their homeland. However, since they were typically escaping death squads or illegal conscription, experiences that would be difficult to document, meeting the burden of proof of persecution became a challenge. Additionally, INS backlogs extended to beyond the official cessation of hostilities in each of the civil wars. This made it difficult to argue that a threat of persecution from the early 1980s would still be grounds for asylum in the mid-1990s.

The 1997 Nicaraguan Adjustment and Central American Relief Act (NACARA) further delineated the continued role of the Cold War in asylum policy, even though the Cold War was seen as "over." This law, originally entitled "The Victims of Communism Act," granted blanket amnesty to undocumented Nicaraguans and Cubans, extending the presumption of persecution, and thus qualifying them for asylum and residency. It only postponed resolution of the Salvadoran and Guatemalan situation since it merely outlined how they could prevent deportation orders.

Honduras was geographically caught in the middle of the civil wars. Refugees from neighboring countries were housed in camps within its territory. Overt and covert American troops were based there and Honduran military bases were used as training camps for U.S.-backed combatants. Hondurans were also victims of natural disasters that struck the region. They were extended TPS in 1998. Most recently, those who entered as undocumented migrants, but who could not be repatriated as a result of the devastation caused by Hurricane Mitch, could also apply for TPS. The end date for their TPS has also been extended numerous times.

Under the temporary statuses of ABC and TPS, Salvadorans and Guatemalans must prove that they have a well-founded fear of persecution upon returning home, and they must show evidence of a settled life here in the United States such as owning a home or a business, lawful employment, involvement in the community, and bank accounts. This status restricts their geographic mobility in that if those on ABC or TPS move out of the BCIS area[9] in which their applications were initiated, they have to begin the process over again. Work permits issued under TPS and ABC are temporary and must be renewed annually. There are no guarantees that a case will be positively adjudicated, making home ownership or other major financial investments very risky. Many left spouses and children behind, assuming that they would receive asylum and would be able to reunite their families, but delays in adjudication can stretch over a decade, and returning to their home countries to visit families typically negates the claim that they have a well-founded fear of persecution if repatriated.

Central Americans who entered on immigrant or refugee visas, who have received asylum, or who received amnesty and thus permanent residency after the Immigration Reform and Control Act (IRCA) are able to circulate between the United States and their homelands. Undocumented Central Americans who have not applied for ABC or TPS also circulate between homeland and the United States, but at the risk of being caught and deported. Those on TPS or ABC are caught in a form of "permanent temporariness"[10] and have created transnational communities in which corporal circulation is often impossible.[11] Since approximately half of the Central American community in the United States holds a form of temporary status, this affects the types of ethnic communities and ethnic economies they have formed.

Settlement Patterns and Socioeconomic Characteristics

Central Americans have established a settlement pattern that is similar in many ways to that of Hispanic communities who preceded them, with a few striking exceptions. Map 8.1 shows the settlement patterns by county of Salvadorans and Guatemalans in 2000, and Map 8.2 shows the settlement patterns by county of Nicaraguans and Hondurans. These national origin groups have been paired on the maps because their settlement patterns are very highly correlated.[12]

The largest Central American population is predictably in Los Angeles County. Nearly a quarter of the country's total Central American enumerated population (372,777 or 22.1%) resides in L.A. County, with half of these (187,193) being from El Salvador. Guatemalans comprise 27 percent of L.A.'s Central Americans with a population of 100,341 (Map 8.1). As Map 8.2 shows, Miami-Dade County hosts the second largest total population (128,903), but in this case, Nicaraguans are the dominant group (69,257). Third-ranked is Harris County, centered in Houston, Texas. As with Los Angeles, Salvadorans comprise the largest proportion at 47,282 or 60 percent. However, Hondurans are the second largest at 12,942 (Maps 8.1 and 8.2).

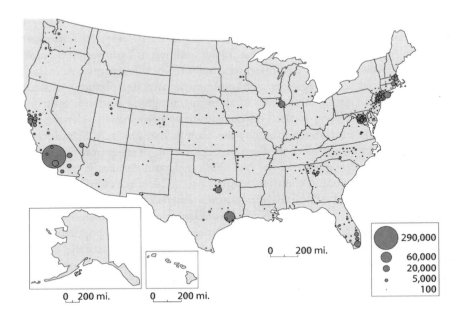

Map 8.1.   Salvadoran and Guatemalan Populations by County, 2000.
Source: 2000 Census of Population and Housing, SF1.

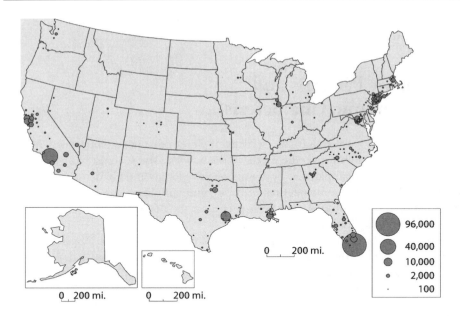

Map 8.2.   Nicaraguan and Honduran Populations by County, 2000.
Source: 2000 Census of Population and Housing, SF1.

Settlement patterns within these counties also differ. As one would expect, Central Americans in Los Angeles and Houston are concentrated within the inner-city areas previously settled by recent Mexican arrivals. For example, Pico Union, the settlement hub for Central Americans in Los Angeles, has a long tradition of Latin American immigration and has developed formal and informal economies for this community. It also hosts a number of social service agencies and community-based organizations dedicated to meeting the unique immigration needs of an immigrant group predominantly on temporary protected status and focused on the pursuit of permanent residency status for those on TPS. There are also community associations that link L.A. Salvadorans with home villages and towns in all of the fourteen departments or states in El Salvador.[13]

The settlement geography in the New York metropolitan area is quite different. New York's four Long Island counties, whether part of New York City or the suburbs, host significant Central American communities, whereas Manhattan's community is much smaller. Queens, Nassau, and Kings (Brooklyn) counties respectively are home to the next three largest Central American populations, with Suffolk's population ranking thirteenth nationally. Hudson County in nearby New Jersey hosts the eighteenth-ranked community, but despite its proximity, it exists as a distinct community from the one on Long Island. With fewer than 9,500 Central Americans, Manhattan serves as a perceived barrier between the Queens–Brooklyn–Long Island communities and those in New Jersey. The Bronx hosts a substantial Honduran population, dominated by Garifuna from the Caribbean coastal region. Additionally, as will be discussed in more detail later in this chapter, the economic and social hub is not within New York City, but is in the Nassau County village of Hempstead.[14] Within these counties, there is no visible Central American neighborhood. Instead, settlement is dispersed or heterolocal in areas where affordable housing coincides with public transportation and employment opportunities.

Two other significant settlement areas are the suburban ring of Washington, D.C., and the San Francisco Bay area. Fairfax County in Virginia (seventh with a population of 31,894) and Montgomery County (ninth with 29,611) and Prince George's County (twentieth with 18,462) in Maryland host predominantly Salvadoran communities. San Francisco County and San Mateo County, ranked fourteenth and fifteenth nationally, host communities of 23,367 and 21,830 respectively, half of whom are from El Salvador. As is reflected in Table 8.1, San Francisco's Central American population followed earlier waves of immigrants since over 30 percent of the city's and county's Salvadoran population arrived in the United States prior to 1980. As in the New York area, the more recent arrivals are concentrated in the suburbs. Again, this does not necessarily mean that they have formed ethnoburbs. Instead, they tend to enter service professions, whether domestic or commercial/retail, for which there is significant demand in the suburbs.

Socioeconomic conditions vary both geographically and by country of origin. Since Salvadorans and Guatemalans are the largest communities, this discussion will focus on their socioeconomic characteristics in selected urban regions. Table 8.1 lists socioeconomic characteristics of Salvadorans and Guatemalans in five selected counties; three are urban and two are suburban.

An unusual and telling set of statistics are the percents of males and females in these places. The sex ratios suggest different types of communities. San Francisco's Salvadoran community is the "oldest" among these, with more than 30 percent arriving prior to the civil war, and the percents of male and female are just about equal. However, among San Francisco's Guatemalans, there are more females than males. This is in contrast to Nassau, Harris, and Fairfax counties, where the percents of Guatemalan males are substantially higher than for females. This suggests these communities include many Guatemalan and Salvadoran households in Nassau and Fairfax counties that are more traditional transnational families, with males working in the United States supporting the family back in the home country. This differs from families divided by TPS travel restrictions. The TPS families are also transnational, but household members in the United States are as likely to be male as female depending on whose life was at risk during the war. Combatants conscripting new "recruits" did not discriminate by gender, and the civil wars made mothers and female college students politically active and thus at risk of persecution and disappearances.

The more male-dominated the community, the younger and the more recently the population arrived. This again suggests that a significant proportion of the population are either single men or fathers working in the United States to support a family in the home country. The largest households with the highest median incomes are in the suburban counties, again implying that typical households include several working adults pooling their incomes. Levels of education do not correspond to income levels since approximately three-fourths of the Central Americans in these suburban counties have less than a high school education. The cost of living in these

Table 8.1. Selected Socioeconomic Characteristics of Salvadorans and Guatemalans in High-concentration Counties, 2000

	Los Angeles, CA	San Francisco, CA	Nassau, NY	Harris, TX	Fairfax, VA
Total Population: Salvadoran	187,193	10,655	23,987	47,282	20,084
Total Population: Guatemalans	100,341	3,196	2,991	9,077	3,906
Gender					
Percent Male: Salvadorans	47.79	49.05	54.09	51.15	57.13
Percent Female: Salvadorans	52.21	50.95	45.91	48.85	42.87
Percent Male: Guatemalans	51.21	46.86	54.37	59.78	54.32
Percent Female: Guatemalans	48.79	53.14	45.63	40.22	45.68
Percent Entering U.S. post-1980					
Salvadorans	80.45	68.93	89.37	91.9	94.03
Guatemalans	83.3	77.58	83.49	93.58	90.35
Median Age					
Salvadorans	30.5	32.5	27.7	27.8	27.1
Guatemalans	29.9	29.3	29.2	27.6	27.6
Average Household Size					
Salvadorans	4.05	3.93	5.27	3.99	4.86
Guatemalans	4.09	4.47	4.47	3.69	4.72
Median Household Income					
Salvadorans	29,097	43,866	47,232	28,991	48,845
Guatemalans	28,572	47,723	48,333	29,825	45,139
Percent Speaking English "Well"					
Salvadorans	39.24	45.47	36.49	34.68	31.36
Guatemalans	35.1	37.89	40.86	30.77	34.48
Percent Speaking English "Not at all"					
Salvadorans	12.04	8.55	15.21	15.56	15.57
Guatemalans	13.9	9.45	11.12	17.73	18.6
Percent over 25 with Less than High School					
Salvadorans	65.3	46.58	66.75	75.86	71.49
Guatemalans	66.32	55.19	49.78	63.15	57.21
Percent over 25 with Four or More Years of College					
Salvadorans	4.48	8.89	4.03	3.09	4.91
Guatemalans	4.86	8.31	11.7	5.97	8.96

Source: 2000 Census of Population and Housing, SF4.

suburbs is high, demanding multiple incomes in any one household to both pay housing costs and be able to remit monies to one's homeland. An impressive statistic, considering the recency of their arrival, is the percent of the population that speaks English "well," and how relatively low the percentage is of those who do not speak English at all.

The Long Island Central American Community

While Queens and Brooklyn have centuries-long traditions of immigration, new immigration of semiskilled and unskilled laborers to Nassau and Suffolk counties is a new and uncomfortable phenomenon. Until recent years, Latinos on Long Island were suburbanizing middle-class Cubans, Puerto Ricans, Dominicans, and South Americans. Direct immigration to the suburbs has been dominated by Asian professionals holding H1-B or skilled professional immigrant visas. One does not expect the development of a large undocumented and quasi-documented immigrant community in the suburbs.

The initial Salvadoran migrants to Long Island entered on immigrant visas prior to the civil war. On return trips to their homeland they communicated the employment opportunities available to unskilled and semiskilled laborers, but by the beginning of the civil war, obtaining an immigrant visa or a tourist visa had become much more difficult. Most Salvadorans who came to Nassau and Suffolk entered as undocumented migrants, many of whom later applied for ABC or TPS. The passage of IRCA in 1986 made obtaining a job much more difficult since applicants now needed to provide legal evidence of their right to work in the United States. This gave birth to a "documents industry" as charlatans sought to take advantage of desperate migrants needing some form of documentation, whether legitimate or not, to obtain a job. Those with TPS or ABC status are considered lucky because they are able to obtain work authorizations legally, despite needing to renew them annually.

Unlike the Los Angeles community that hosts Salvadorans from all fourteen departments, or states, most Salvadorans on Long Island are from the two easternmost departments of Morazan and La Union.[15] Migration chains have formed as village-based networks send waves of workers northward seeking employment opportunities perceived as lucrative. Community associations and soccer leagues develop along these same village-based lines, sometimes even organizing remittance-based development projects in their origin villages or regions.

Employment opportunities take various forms. Those with work authorizations are able to find employment in factories or in retail or food service. Many are employed in domestic services such as nannies, housekeepers, and landscapers. *Esquiñeros*, or day laborers who line up on street corners hoping to be hired for the day, are common sights in Southern California, but they have now emerged on New York's and Long Island's landscapes.

Within New York City, Central Americans are an invisible minority. Although Queens and Brooklyn rank high nationally in terms of community size, there is no Salvadoran or Guatemalan neighborhood. Settlement tends to be in neighborhoods with long histories of immigration and with Latino ethnic economies, allowing Central Americans to shop and obtain necessary social services in Spanish. Stores owned and operated by Latinos from the Caribbean, South America, and Mexico now carry Central American products and advertise the availability of services to that community.

Esquiñeros have become a common sight, but Salvadorans and Guatemalans have also entered particular labor niches within the city. While the city's ubiquitous green grocers (fresh fruit and vegetable vendors) are almost exclusively Korean, their employees tend to be Central American (or Mexican). Additionally, the waitstaff, busboys, and counter persons in a growing number of the city's eat-in and take-out restaurants are from Central America. However, very few Central American entrepreneurs have opened businesses within New York City's boroughs. The one key exception is Pollo Campero, a fast-food chicken restaurant chain that has recently opened in the Corona neighborhood of Queens and in Sunset Park in Brooklyn.

Pollo Campero, or "country chicken," was founded in Guatemala in 1971 and spread rapidly throughout El Salvador and the rest of Central America and Mexico. Although the globalization of fast-food chains led to McDonalds and KFC becoming common in Central America, Pollo Campero became part of the region's cultural identity. In 2002, Pollo Campero opened its first U.S. location in Los Angeles and it met with immediate success. By 2003, Pollo Campero had opened in Herndon and Falls Church in Fairfax County, Virginia, and the outlets in Queens (Fig. 8.1) and in Brooklyn opened in 2004. As in its other U.S. locations, the Corona store met with immediate success. The restaurant offers more than just affordable and familiar meals. Pollo Campero is a part of Central America's cultural identity, and its presence in Queens is an unquestionable landscape marker of the Central American presence in the city despite the lack of either a residential or economic enclave.

There is one place where Central Americans, particularly Salvadorans, have established an ethnic economy for both goods and professional services—the village of Hempstead in Nassau County. Central Hempstead has become a focal point for the region's Central American community, again linked to the availability of public transportation. Although there is limited public transportation on Long Island when compared to New York City, buses connect Nassau County with the last stops of several eastern Queens subways and buses and accept Metrocards, electronic fare cards used for the city's subways and buses. One can travel by subway or bus from within the city to central Hempstead without paying an additional fare. As one walks out of the Hempstead bus terminal, the Salvadoran economic landscape becomes immediately apparent. Within a few blocks of the bus terminal are numerous transnational shipping and remittance businesses, often two or three on any one block. Because ABC and TPS status prohibit actual transnational migrant circulation, and post-9/11 border and airport vigilance has made undocumented migrant circulation much more difficult, enterprising Salvadorans with either permanent resident status or who have naturalized have established courier services in partnership with the various Central American national airlines to transport goods and monies to and from home areas (Fig. 8.2). *Viajeros*, or travelers, are employed to ensure the safety and delivery of precious cargo that can range from food (including Pollo Campero flying north!) to clothes, toiletries, money, and video and audio recordings with personal messages for family and friends.

Stores and restaurants carrying Salvadoran products are named for the hometowns or home departments of the owners. Salvadoran and Guatemalan flags are visible on

Figure 8.1.   Pollo Campero chicken franchise in Corona, Queens. An emerging Central American cultural landscape signature. Source: Author.

most storefronts. Signage is in Spanish, and signs, storefronts, and buildings are painted in the blue and white of most of the Central American national flags. Transnational professional services have also developed near the bus station. El Salvador's largest banks have opened branches in Hempstead, facilitating the safe deposition of remittances (Fig. 8.3). There are even transnational real estate and law offices, allowing those who cannot travel home to resolve legal issues from a distance.

The Salvadoran and Guatemalan communities of this urban region and across the country have developed a unique form of transnationalism—truncated in that their legal status inhibits actual transmigrant circulation but nevertheless real. The economies of El Salvador and Guatemala have become dependent on remittances, and their importance as part of each country's GNP has led the Salvadoran and Guatemalan governments to join the battle for legal status. This battle for permanent residency underlies the ethnic and social identity of immigrants from this region.

Figure 8.2. One of the many Central American courier services located in Hempstead. Source: Author.

Figure 8.3. Salvadoran banks now have branches in central Hempstead. Source: Author.

Legal Status, Identity, and Transnational Dynamics

There are various multiple identities that characterize the Central American community beyond those of national origin. These identities are related to one's legal status. Additionally, forms of transnational circulation are governed by one's legal status. These statuses include naturalized or native-born citizen, permanent resident, ABC or TPS, and undocumented migrant.

Because the Central American population is so recent in its arrival, only 24.2 percent is native-born. Among Salvadorans, this increases to 24.4 percent, while only 22 percent of Guatemalans are native-born. Although the smallest of the Central American populations in the United States, Panamanians have the largest proportion of native-born at 37.9 percent. This number must be interpreted with care since many of those born in the Canal Zone prior to the transfer of sovereignty to Panama would be considered U.S. citizens. Panamanians are also the most likely to have naturalized as U.S. citizens (33.3%). Guatemalans have the lowest naturalization rate at 16.7 percent, followed by Hondurans at 18 percent and Salvadorans at 18.3 percent. Of those without the unique relationship with the United States that Panama held, Costa Ricans have both the highest percentages of native-born (29.4%) and of naturalization (24.8%). Between 1991 and 2002, the most recent year for which data are available, 382,765 Central Americans naturalized as citizens, with 43.3 percent of those being Salvadoran, the largest national origin group.[16] Additionally, some 278,000 Salvadorans have been granted legal permanent residency, with 178,000 of those eligible for citizenship.[17]

Citizenship and legal permanent residency (LPR) are precious commodities for a transnational community. With either one of these two legal statuses, one can travel freely back to a homeland without concern about re-entry. It is those with citizenship or LPR who establish transnational businesses such as the shipping companies mentioned earlier on which the rest of the community relies. Central Americans on TPS or ABC are much more constrained in their travel. Physically returning home would imply to an immigration judge that they no longer have a well-founded fear of persecution, rendering their asylum petition null and void. Moving out of the BCIS administrative district in which they originally apply for TPS or ABC requires reapplying in the new district. Family reunification, even within the United States, is very difficult, if not impossible, with ABC/TPS. On the one hand, applicants gain the legal right to work until their cases are adjudicated and, if necessary, appeals are exhausted. On the other, only those who gain LPR are able to apply for family reunification visas for their children, spouses, or parents. Thus, hundreds of thousands of Central Americans on ABC/TPS live in a transnational limbo, tied to their families at home by remittances, gifts, letters, and phone calls, but legally unable to physically circulate.

A similar challenge is faced by undocumented migrants, particularly since September 11, 2001. BCIS estimated that of the top five sending countries of undocumented migrants, three are in Central America—El Salvador is second with approximately 189,000, Guatemala third with 144,000, and Honduras is fifth with 138,000.[18] Central Americans must cross multiple national borders, often at significant costs, to enter the

United States without proper documentation. In a post-9/11 security climate, border inspections and airport security increase the likelihood of interception and deportation. If one enters the United States successfully as an undocumented migrant, he or she typically travels to a pre-existing Central American community, using social networks to find work and a place to live. The goal then becomes to work for as long as possible to support the family in the origin country until either the migrant chooses to return home or is obligated to return.

The battle for LPR and citizenship has become a unifying factor for the Central American community and significantly affects their identity and daily behavior in the United States. To qualify to have a deportation order deferred, applicants must prove a certain degree of "settledness" in their community of residence. However, their tenuous legal status makes becoming settled very difficult. Evidence of a settled life includes knowledge of English, home ownership, business ownership, and bank accounts, as well as commitments to the local community through church involvement or activism in local community organizations. If one is unsure if his or her application for asylum will be positively adjudicated, purchasing a home or starting a business is a risk rarely taken. Most Salvadorans and Guatemalans work full-time, sometimes at more than one job, making the time it takes to learn English a challenge. This is a deeply religious community and a very high proportion of Central Americans are active in their churches, whether Catholic or Protestant.

Community organizations tend to fall into two categories—remittance-based projects linked to particular towns in the home country and politically active groups that lobby for LPR and amnesty legislation. The first set of groups have been integral in constructing roads, schools, hospitals, and other infrastructural needs in home towns and villages. While they are an essential part of maintaining transnational links, they are counterproductive in the battle for residency as they do not show settledness in the United States. The second set has been critical in the battle to make the public aware of the plight of Central Americans in the United States who were victims of the "wrong" civil wars. These also provide services such as information and application assistance for the various programs such as TPS for which Central Americans qualify.

Among Central Americans, legal status affects social status and identity. At the top of the social hierarchy are those who are citizens or have LPR. Below them are those possessing TPS/ABC status. The undocumented occupy the lowest rung on the social ladder. Despite its limitations, ABC/TPS status makes one at least quasi-documented with a social security number and a legal right to work. In Latin America, social class matters, and among Central Americans in the United States one's social class position is now based on legal status.

Conclusion

The principal impetus for Central American emigration was the civil wars in the region over the past several decades. These conflicts were actually proxy wars of the Cold War era, subjecting those who fled to the United States in search of sanctuary to a prolonged battle for legal status. Unfortunately, even though the Cold War is essentially over, U.S.

immigration and refugee policies continue to preference "victims of Communism." This is evidenced among Central Americans through the continued preferential treatment of Nicaraguans who received amnesty and LPR through NACARA in 1997, while the same act reiterated the criteria for deferral of deportation, but not amnesty and LPR for Salvadorans and Guatemalans.

The battle for legal status has defined the geography of settlement and the dynamics of transnational circulation. Only those who have been granted legal permanent residency are free to physically circulate, creating a community that travels vicariously through remittances, letters, phone calls, gifts, and other similar substitutes. At least half the Central American population in the United States is either quasi-documented, holding ABC or TPS status, or is undocumented. Lack of legal status unites this community in the battle for new legislation but divides households who have already endured prolonged civil wars. This paradox is unlikely to be resolved soon as recent environmental disasters such as hurricanes and earthquakes have only served to extend temporary protected status in terms of both who qualifies and dates of termination. It is as if the U.S. government has created a status through which it can put off resolution until a future date that can be continually delayed. In the meantime, Central Americans create community, circulate vicariously through remittances, and lobby for change while negotiating this state of "permanent temporariness."

Notes

1. Adrian Bailey et al., "(Re)producing Salvadoran Transnational Geographies," *Annals of the Association of American Geographers* 92, no. 1 (2002): 125–144.

2. David L. Clawson, *Latin America and the Caribbean: Lands and Peoples* (New York: McGraw-Hill, 2004).

3. Clawson, *Latin America*.

4. W. George Lovell, *A Beauty That Hurts: Life and Death in Guatemala* (Austin: University of Texas Press, 2000), 139–142.

5. Lovell, *A Beauty*, 140.

6. Ines M. Miyares et al., "The Interrupted Circle: Truncated Transnationalism and the Salvadoran Experience," *Journal of Latin Americanist Geography* 2, no. 1 (2003): 73–85.

7. Sarah J. Mahler, *American Dreaming: Immigrant Life on the Margins* (Princeton, NJ: Princeton University Press, 1995), 159.

8. Miyares et al., "The Interrupted Circle," 78.

9. The Bureau of Citizenship and Immigration Services, formerly the INS, has regional offices that process applications for a designated area. Once an asylum case has been filed in one area's regional office, its adjudication is completed within that office. If the applicant moves to a new BCIS region, the asylum case must be refiled.

10. Bailey et al., "(Re)producing Salvadoran Transnational Geographies."

11. Miyares et al., "The Interrupted Circle."

12. In 2000, Salvadoran and Guatemalan populations by county had a correlation of r=0.956, sig.=.0001; and Nicaraguan and Honduran populations by county had a correlation of r=0.811, sig.=.0001. Nicaraguan populations by county have much lower correlations with Salvadoran and Guatemalan populations, r=0.343 and r=0.384 respectively, and thus are mapped separately. Honduran populations by county have correlations with Salvadoran and Guatemalan populations of

r=0.641 and r=0.633 respectively. They have been mapped with Nicaraguans because of the slightly higher correlations.

13. Sarah J. Mahler, *Salvadorans in Suburbia: Symbiosis and Conflict* (Boston: Allyn and Bacon, 1995), 5.

14. Although Hempstead has the character of a large town or small city, it is legally a village.

15. Mahler, *Salvadorans in Suburbia*, 47.

16. Bureau of Citizenship and Immigration Services, *Fiscal Year 2002 Yearbook of Immigration Statistics*, Table 35, <uscis.gov/graphics/shared/aboutus/statistics/NATZ2002yrbk/NATZ2002list. htm> (20 September 2004).

17. Bureau of Citizenship and Immigration Services, *Estimates of the Legal Permanent Resident Population and Population Eligible to Naturalize in 2002*, <uscis.gov/graphics/shared/aboutus/ statistics/lprest2002.pdf> (20 September 2004).

18. Office of Policy and Planning, U.S. Immigration and Naturalization Service, "Estimates of Unauthorized Immigrant Population Residing in the United States: 1990 and 2000," <uscis.gov/graphics/shared/aboutus/statistics/Ill_Report_1211.pdf> (21 September 2004).

CHAPTER 9

Andean South Americans and Cultural Networks

Marie Price

Throughout the twentieth century, South Americans migrated to the United States in limited numbers. It was only in the 1980s that a significant increase in immigrants from South America began to merit greater scholarly attention. According to the 1990 census nearly one million South Americans resided in the United States. By 2000 the number of South Americans almost doubled to 1.9 million, representing 6 percent of the 31 million foreign-born individuals enumerated.

It is easy to view South Americans as new additions to the nation's established Hispanic population that includes Mexicans, Central Americans, Cubans, Puerto Ricans, and Dominicans. Indeed, the majority of South Americans share a common history of Spanish colonialism that resulted in the adoption of the Spanish language and the Catholic faith. The diversity of South American immigrants is substantial (Table 9.1). The largest sending country is Colombia. With 509,872 individuals, Colombian immigrants account for one in four of all foreign-born South Americans in the United States. Ecuador and Peru are next, each with nearly 300,000 immigrants. Together, these three countries account for over half of all South American immigrants. If one adds immigrants from Bolivia, Venezuela, and Chile, immigrants from the Andes account for two-thirds of the South American flow.

Brazil also contributes substantially to the flow of South Americans to the United States. As the largest state in South America and populated by Portuguese speakers, Brazilians do not consider themselves Hispanic and would not identify themselves as such on a census form. As an ethnically diverse country, it is difficult to generalize about the ethnic makeup of Brazilians; most who settle in the United States, however, are of European ancestry.[1] Because Brazil does not fit neatly into U.S. census categories, the experience of over 200,000 Brazilians in the United States is not well known.[2] Similarly, Guyana was a former colony of the United Kingdom, not of Spain. Guyanese are usually of African or South Asian ancestry and speak English and are more likely to be classified as a Caribbean group.

Brazil and Guyana aside, this chapter focuses primarily upon the Andean sending countries and explores the reasons for emigration as well as the relative concentration of Andeans in a few select U.S. cities, most notably the New York metropolitan area. It

**Table 9.1.   Place of Birth of U.S. Foreign-Born
Population from South America, 2000**

	United States
Total Foreign	31,107,889
South America	1,930,271
Argentina	125,218
Bolivia	53,278
Brazil	212,428
Chile	80,804
Colombia	509,872
Ecuador	298,626
Guyana	211,189
Peru	278,186
Venezuela	107,031
Other	53,639

Source: Census Bureau 2000, SF 3.

also demonstrates that Hispanic South Americans are a relatively privileged group, with social and economic characteristics similar to or exceeding U.S. averages. In addition, Andean groups possess strong ties to their home countries evidenced by culturally based celebrations as well as transnational identities.

Andean Migration to the United States

The combination of immigration reforms in the United States in the 1980s and 1990s, coupled with economic and political turmoil in the Andean countries themselves, helps to explain the rapid growth in South American immigrants, especially from Colombia, Ecuador, and Peru. South Americans have been settling in the United States since the 1960s, mostly as economic migrants seeking employment opportunities. As the Andean economic situation worsened in the 1980s, and political violence increased, immigrants took advantage of changes made by the Immigration Act of 1990 that increased the number of legal immigrants admitted annually and introduced diversity visas given out by lottery.[3] Those legally here as green-card holders or citizens could sponsor the immigration of family members, which also explains how many South Americans arrived in the 1990s.

CONTEXT OF DEPARTURE

For Latin America, the decade of the 1980s has been called the "lost decade" due to the economic downturn experienced throughout the region. The Andean states were especially hard hit by a combination of structural adjustment measures that included debt restructuring, currency devaluation, and declines in export revenue. Many states, especially Ecuador, Peru, and Bolivia, also experienced hyperinflation that further shook economic confidence. Ecuador in particular neared economic collapse by the late 1990s, which culminated in the country's defaulting on its Brady Bonds in 1999. In order to restore confidence in the financial system, the government took the radical step of making the U.S. dollar the country's official currency. The ensuing economic crisis in Ecuador resulted in a spike in emigration.[4]

As Andean households struggled to secure their economic livelihood, many considered the option of temporary or permanent migration to better their economic and social opportunities. Labor migration flows within South America were well established by the 1960s. Immigration to a neighboring country was viewed as part of a livelihood system in which certain members of the household would leave in order to send money and resources back to those who remained. Venezuela became an important destination for Colombian agricultural and domestic laborers, including both seasonal and long-term migrants. Argentina attracted skilled and unskilled labor from Bolivia, Paraguay, and to a lesser extent, from Peru. But by the 1990s, however, Argentina and Venezuela were also experiencing financial crises so foreign-labor flows into these countries steadily declined.

As economic opportunities within South America waned, the incidence of migration to the United States increased. The first economic migrants destined to the United States tended to be highly skilled professionals (professors, engineers, doctors, and other skilled workers). As early as the 1980s, scholars in the region began describing this exodus as a brain drain. Yet as the economic situation worsened in the Andes, both skilled and unskilled migrants used their social networks as a form of social capital to relocate household members to cities in the United States in a chain migration fashion.

Political violence in the past two decades also became an important reason for Andean emigration, especially from Colombia and Peru. The combination of left-wing insurgents, narcotraffickers, and paramilitary groups has made Colombia an extremely violent country. Politically motivated killings are common. Targets include politicians, public servants, teachers, trade unionists, human rights workers, and members of the clergy. In 2002 alone 3,000 people were kidnapped, including a presidential candidate and a senator. Violence, or the threat of violence, has led to massive population displacement, especially in rural areas. Recent estimates by the U.S. Committee for Refugees show that 2.5 million Colombians have been internally displaced and live in refugee-like conditions within the country.[5] Not surprisingly, violence and declining economic conditions also trigger emigration. One study in the late 1990s estimated that at least 3 million Colombians lived outside the national territory (almost 7 percent of the country's 43 million people).[6] One of the leading destinations for Colombians is the United States.

Peru's story, while not as extreme as Colombia's, also illustrates the impact of political and economic turmoil on the propensity to emigrate. In Peru's case the rise of a leftist insurgency, the Shining Path, in the 1980s caused tens of thousands to flee the rural highlands for shantytowns outside the national capital of Lima. Peruvian emigration is not as widespread as the Colombian case, but the number of Peruvians seeking economic opportunities outside the country is growing. In 1990, some 175,035 Peruvians were counted in the U.S. Census, but by 2000 the number of Peruvians in the United States had increased by 60 percent. It should be noted that very few Colombians or Peruvians receive asylum as political refugees. Most enter as economic migrants or are sponsored by family members.

CONTEXT OF RECEPTION

In a number of respects, South Americans have some familiarity with American culture before they arrive. They grew up, for example, with dubbed American movies and television shows. For most Andean countries, the United States is their largest trading partner, so attention is paid to U.S. foreign policy. Well-off South Americans have vacationed at Disney World and shopped in the United States for decades. Most South Americans even consider Miami the informal capital of Latin America. With its major Latin banks, port facilities, and airline connections, it is nearly impossible to conduct international business in South America without traveling to Miami. While the United States was never a colonial power in Andean South America, these cultural and economic ties that have evolved since World War II possess an almost dependent nature and thus qualify as a variant of World Systems Theory.

In contrast, the image of South Americans in the United States is sketchy. Mexican culture tends to be the lens through which all things "Hispanic" are viewed in the United States. The cultural differences that would easily distinguish Mexicans from Colombians or Peruvians, for example, are not readily appreciated by the average American. This changed somewhat in the mid-1980s as South Americans, especially Colombians, were stigmatized by the image of ruthless drug traffickers. In movies and television shows (think *Miami Vice* or the recent film *Maria Full of Grace*), South Americans were portrayed as cocaine dealers. True, there were South Americans residing in the United States who profited from the illegal trafficking of drugs, but they were a tiny fraction of the thousands of immigrants who settled in the United States. Andean immigrants, many of whom are of Amerindian or mixed-race ancestry, also faced racial discrimination and prejudice in the United States because of their darker skin color. Despite the negative stereotypes found in popular media and prevailing racism that confront South Americans, census data suggest that many are well integrated into the U.S. economy and society.

Since the late 1990s, and especially after the September 11, 2001, terrorist attacks, South American immigrants have had greater difficulty acquiring immigrant or tourist visas to legally enter the United States. Consequently, South American economic migrants have sought new countries of settlement. Colombians and Ecuadorians are going in large numbers to Spain where they have access to the massive EU labor market.[7] Argentines now emigrate to Italy, as many have ancestral ties to that country. Brazilians are settling in Portugal and Japan. The flow to Japan is due to the large Japanese-Brazilian population taking advantage of changes in Japanese immigration policy that permit people of Japanese ancestry to work in Japan.[8] There were 200,000 Brazilians and 40,000 Peruvians living and working in Japan in the late 1990s. Educated South Americans have responded to their declining economic position in the world economy by emigrating. The United States has been an important destination, but it may not remain so in the decades ahead.

Settlement and Distribution Patterns

While it is possible to meet someone from South America in nearly any U.S. state, this immigrant flow is decidedly directed to cities (Map 9.1). Although every major city possesses a substantial number of South Americans, there exists very strong spatial clustering in the urbanized counties of Florida, the Northeast corridor from Boston to Washington, California, and the Texas cities of Houston and Dallas as well as Chicago. The five metropolitan regions of New York (773,797), Miami (287,004), Los Angeles (132,032), Washington (90,744), and Boston (66,323) account for nearly 70 percent of all South Americans. Of these five major metropolitan regions, New York and Miami account for a remarkable 78 percent of all South American immigrants. This preference for urban living is connected to two factors. First, South America is considered the most urbanized region of the developing world so preference for urban living is grounded in prior experience in the sending countries. Second, South Americans who arrive in the United States tend to be well educated and are often from professional backgrounds. This distinguishes them from other Latinos from Mexico and Central America who, on average, have lower levels of education.

Map 9.1.   Population Distribution by Counties with 500 or More South Americans, 2000. Source: U.S. Census, American Fact Finder, File 1 (SF1).

Aside from the spatial clustering of South Americans in these major metropolitan regions, there are additional observations about their settlement and distribution patterns. First, there is no urban region where South Americans are the dominant immigrant group. Second, particular South American groups tend to be more common in some metropolitan regions than others. For example, Peruvians (25%) and Colombians (19%) make up 44 percent of all South Americans in the tri-county Los Angeles metropolitan region. In the Miami–Ft. Lauderdale urban region, Colombians account for 40 percent of all groups, and it is the only U.S. metropolitan region where Venezuelans (12%) comprise a substantial slice of the South American population. In the greater Washington, D.C., metropolitan region Peruvians (24%) and Bolivians (22%) comprise 46 percent of all South American groups. In the Boston-Worcester-Lawrence, Massachusetts urban region, which also includes small portions of Connecticut, New Hampshire, and Maine, Brazilians (51%) and Colombians (23%) make up 75 percent of all South American groups.

Although Miami might be the informal capital for Latin America, the New York metropolitan area is the primary destination for most country groups from South America. In other words, this largest of U.S. cities has attracted the greatest diversity of South American immigrants. Of the 773,797 South American immigrants, Ecuadorians account for 26 percent, Colombians 24 percent, and Guyanese 20 percent. The New York populations of Ecuadorians and Guyanese account for 67.3 and 73.2 of their respective U.S. totals. New York Colombians account for 36.4 percent of Colombians in the United States. The city has been an important destination since the late 1960s when the first Colombian immigrants settled there seeking a respite from political violence and to engage in entrepreneurial opportunities. By the early 1970s, Colombians were joined by other Andeans, primarily from Ecuador and Peru.[9]

Today Colombians are found throughout the metropolitan area, in the suburbs and the five boroughs (Map 9.2) in a heterolocal settlement pattern. In Northern New Jersey Colombians are clustered in North Bergen/Union City, Englewood, Hackensack, Paterson/Clifton/Passaic, Dover, Morristown, and Elizabeth. In Connecticut there are groups in Stamford and Norwalk. In the northern half of the New York City borough of Queens, neighborhoods such as Elmhurst, Jackson Heights, Corona, Sunnyside, and Woodside are major areas of Colombian settlement. This borough is a very diverse one where no one country-group dominates because there are Hispanic immigrants from the Dominican Republic, Ecuador, Central America, and Mexico. As far as Colombians are concerned, the hub of Colombian residential and commercial life in New York continues to be Jackson Heights.

Although far removed from tropical Colombia, the streets of Jackson Heights pulse with the sound of *cumbia* (a Colombian musical form) while the smell of *arepas* (a round fat corn muffin) fills the air. The area has a concentration of immigrant-related services such as travel agencies and money-transfer shops. In the small stores that line the streets one can find food products and beverages produced in Colombia. Local newspapers report Colombian news, and many discussions on the street are about political and sporting events in Colombia. A major Colombian media network, RCN, has a radio station and cable TV-channel in Jackson Heights.[10] For many Colombians, Jackson Heights is the first place of settlement or "port of entry" before relocating to

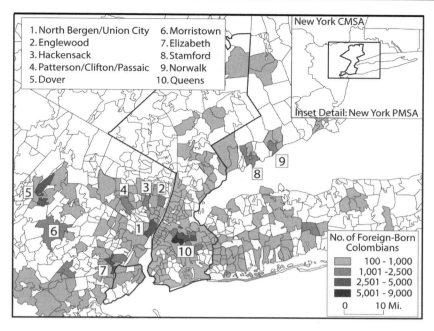

Map 9.2.   Population Distribution of Foreign-Born Colombians by Zip Code in the New York CMSA. Source: Census Bureau, SF 4.

other parts of the city or the country. It is a place that is well connected with communities back home.

Social and Economic Attainment

Both the native and foreign-born Hispanic population in the United States totaled 35 million in 2000. Of this total, Mexicans and people of Mexican ancestry account for nearly 60 percent of all Hispanics.[11] Andean immigrants, most of whom are Hispanic, are clearly fewer in number, but they also possess a different socioeconomic profile than Mexicans. The considerable distance traveled and the expense of travel from South America tend to screen out poorer and less educated potential immigrants. In general those who come to the United States have levels of education comparable to U.S. averages and in some cases higher. This higher social capital that Andeans possess tends to place them in a more privileged position compared to other Latino immigrants. One major study by anthropologist Sarah Mahler compared Salvadorans with South American immigrants in Nassau County, New York. She found that most South Americans came from, at a minimum, skilled urban-working-class backgrounds. There were virtually no peasants or poor among the South Americans studied by Mahler whereas many of the Salvadorans came from rural backgrounds and were quite poor.[12]

In many social and economic measures the Andean groups are very similar to U.S. averages, but in a few categories they are strikingly different (Table 9.2).[13] The relative newness of this ethnic group is reflected in how few were born in the United States. Only one-quarter of the people who claim South American ancestry were born in the United States while the majority were born in their native countries. The prominence of recent immigrants in this population is also reflected in the relatively low rates of exclusive English use in the home relative to the U.S. total. Between 8 and 12 percent of the Andeans spoke only English in the home, and roughly half of those surveyed in the census spoke English "less than very well."

Educational attainment is considered a good proxy measure for a group's overall social capital and potential for economic achievement. The Andean group, with the exception of Ecuadorians, have levels of educational attainment similar to or greater than the U.S. average (Table 9.2). In the United States 80 percent of the adult population have a high school degree or higher, whereas the percentage for Peruvians and Bolivians in the United States with high school degrees is greater still (83% and 96% respectively). Colombians, with 75 percent of the adults with a high school degree or higher, are below the U.S. national average by only 5 percent. Ecuadorians, with only 64 percent of the adults with high school degrees, are lower still. When one compares both bachelor's and master's college degrees all the Andean groups are at the U.S. average or higher with the exception of Ecuadorians. Despite the differences in educational attainment among the four Andean ancestry groups, these groups fare better when compared to the overall Hispanic population. Only 10 percent of all Hispanic adults 25 years and over have a bachelor's degree or higher, whereas each of the Andean groups has a greater percentage of their populations with college degrees (ranging from 14 to 36%).

Many educated South Americans who settle in the United States do not have their professional credentials fully recognized and are thus forced to obtain employment for which they are overqualified. It is not uncommon for medical doctors from Peru or Colombia to work as lab technicians or for engineers and architects trained in Bolivia to accept jobs in construction. Many women from South America with college degrees find jobs in childcare or eldercare. In short, migration to the United States often results in earning more money than one would in South America, but also experiencing a loss in professional status either temporarily or permanently.

Despite experiencing a decline in occupational status, Andean groups in the United States possess a median household income of almost $42,000, which is slightly greater than the U.S. average (Table 9.2). The ancestry group with the lowest median household income is Colombians, and the group with the highest is Bolivians. Likewise, in terms of percentage of families below the poverty line, Bolivians and Peruvians are near the national average of 12 percent whereas Colombians (17%) and Ecuadorians (16%) are higher. Adult participation in the labor force is above the national average of 64 percent for all groups. What the national ancestry data suggest with regards to economic status is that Andean employment as a whole reflects the occupational structure of U.S. households. They are, however, better represented in higher-income management and professional occupations. The lower economic status of Ecuadorian

Table 9.2. Comparative Social and Economic Variables for Andean Ancestry Population, 2000

	Colombians	Ecuadorians	Peruvians	Bolivians	U.S.
Total Population (2000)	496,748	273,013	247,601	45,188	281,421,906
Born in the U.S.	24%	24%	22%	24%	89%
Median Age	33.6 years	31.3 years	33.6 years	31.3 years	35.4 years
Average Family Size	3.52	3.83	3.66	3.74	3.14
Educational Attainment (Population 25 Years & Older)					
High School Diploma or higher	75%	64%	83%	96%	80%
Bachelor's Degree or higher	24%	14%	25%	36%	24%
Master's Degree or higher	10%	6%	10%	11%	9%
Economic Status					
Median Household Income	$38,514	$40,924	$42,333	$47,245	$41,994
% Families below Poverty Level	17%	16%	12%	13%	12%
% in Labor Force (16 years +)	65%	66%	68%	69%	64%
Occupational Structure (16 Yr. +)					
Management, Professional	26%	18%	26%	29%	34%
Service Occupations	23%	23%	22%	23%	15%
Sales & Office Occupations	24%	22%	25%	24%	27%
Construction, Extraction, etc.	8%	11%	8%	12%	9%
Production, Transportation, etc.	18%	25%	18%	12%	15%
Language Spoken at Home (5 Yr. +)					
Speak Only English	10%	8%	10%	12%	82%
Speak English Less Than "Very Well"	51%	55%	48%	43%	8%
Housing					
Own Home	45%	37%	50%	56%	67%
Median Value of Home	$142,400	$155,900	$151,100	$169,900	$119,600

Source: Census Bureau 2000, SF 4.

households is consistent with their lower levels of educational attainment when compared to other Andean groups.

Lastly, home ownership is often used as a measure to suggest a population's economic integration into the U.S. economy. Home ownership is high in the United States with 67 percent of households owning the home they inhabit (Table 9.2). The level of home ownership for the Andean groups, however, is far below the national average. At the low end, 37 percent of Ecuadorian households own their own home whereas 56 percent of Bolivian households do. Relatively lower rates of home ownership may be indicative of the newness of this ethnic group combined with the fact that Andeans are concentrated in some of the country's high-cost-of-living metropolitan regions. This is expressed in the median home values of Andean groups which are substantially higher than the national average. When compared to all native-born and foreign-born Hispanics, however, Andean groups fare much better. The median household income for all Hispanics (regardless of race) was less than $34,000. Although many Andeans left their countries as a result of economic and political turmoil, they have achieved levels of social and economic attainment on par with that of average U.S. households. This is not an ethnic group being left behind but seemingly navigating its way into the U.S. economic mainstream.

Community Case Study: Bolivians in Washington

The growth of the Bolivian colony in metropolitan Washington mirrors that of the overall growth in South Americans in the United States. The Bolivian population tripled in size from 1980 to 1990, then it doubled in size from 1990 to 2000, representing some 20,000 foreign-born Bolivians. Almost 40 percent of all Bolivians in the United States are found in the Washington metro region, which has become a center for Bolivian culture in the United States. South Arlington in Northern Virginia as well as Springfield, Virginia, and Wheaton, Maryland, are important areas of concentration for Bolivian immigrants, as well as many other immigrant groups who settle in Washington.

The case of Bolivians in Washington is interesting because it shows how a small community can grow via chain migration and government-based family unification policies. With the exception of a few self-identified pioneers, very few Bolivians lived in Metropolitan Washington until the 1980s. They came to Washington because at that time there were plenty of jobs and relatively little direct competition from other Latino immigrants. Like other Andeans, Bolivians maintain important social and economic ties with their co-ethnics in Washington as well as with communities in Bolivia. Although they live in a dispersed or heterolocal pattern throughout the metro region, Bolivian culture and identity are maintained through a variety of organizations, activities, and commercial centers.

Northern Virginia is one of the few places in the United States where one can eat at several Bolivian restaurants. Don Arturo's is a budget restaurant that caters to an immigrant clientele serving typical Bolivian dishes such as peanut soup or *salteñas* (Fig. 9.1). On Friday afternoons and weekends the restaurant is packed with recent arrivals eager to see friends and catch up on news. Bolivians also love their soccer; the Arlington Bolivian Soccer League was founded in 1988 and includes 16 co-ethnic teams. Three other Bolivian leagues were added in the 1990s. One of these leagues, INCO-PEA, actively raises money for development projects in rural Cochabamba, Bolivia.[14]

Several cultural spaces have been produced to promote Bolivian culture in greater Washington. The most significant is the Bolivian School established in 1998 in an Arlington elementary school. Each Saturday morning children may attend classes in Spanish based on Bolivian social science curriculum. Sponsored by the Bolivian Embassy, Arlington Public Schools, and the local Bolivian community, the school costs only $50 per semester. The teachers volunteer their time and most of the materials are purchased in Bolivia by returning immigrants. While anyone can attend, most of the students are the children of immigrants.

Bolivians in Washington have been actively celebrating their Independence Day on August 6 for over a decade. The outdoor festival attracts over 10,000 people, most of them ethnic Bolivians. There are two dozen Bolivian folk groups in the area, many of whom perform at the Independence Day celebration and other events (Fig. 9.2). Other attendees include professional soccer players from Major League Soccer, the locally elected Miss Bolivia, various musical groups from the United States and Bolivia, and plenty of food vendors.

Figure 9.1.   A Bolivian restaurant in Arlington, Virginia. Source: Author.

Figure 9.2.   A folk dance group holding Bolivian and U.S. flags at a Bolivian
Independence Day celebration in Northern Virginia. Source: Author.

Because the immigrant community is relatively new, ties to Bolivia are still strong. This "inbetweenness" is expressed in a mural at a busy Arlington intersection where many Bolivians reside in nearby apartments (Fig. 9.3). The painting is a manifestation of the dual lives that Bolivians lead. It is centered on Lake Titicaca, the highland lake that Bolivia and Peru share, where a native is fishing from a traditional reed boat. The lake gradually blends into an Arlington apartment complex with young girls on bicy-

Figure 9.3.   As a reflection of transnationalism, this mural in Arlington, Virginia, features Lake Titicaca in Bolivia blending into the nearby Arlington apartment complex. Source: Author.

cles and scooters. This street art neatly captures the transnational lives that many Bolivians experience as they make their way in the nation's capital.

Life in Metropolitan America

The Andean imprint on U.S. culture has been rather limited save for the recognition of a handful of Andean writers (Gabriel García Marquez, Isabel Allende, or Mario Vargas Llosa) and performers (Shakira from Colombia) as well as the acceptance of musical forms such as Andean folk music which focuses on winds and percussion or the rhythmic pulse of *cumbia* from Colombia. In sports, South Americans have had more of an impact, especially in soccer. There have been several Andean soccer stars who have played on Major League Soccer teams in the United States.

Andean life in America is not neatly outlined on a map. Most Andeans live in major metropolitan areas surrounded by other immigrant groups, many of them Hispanic, others not. Because the pattern of residential settlement in cities is rather dispersed, Andeans are not likely to see large numbers of Andeans on a day-to-day basis. Thus

Andean life is generally tied to special events or visiting certain commercial centers that sell Andean goods. Of note are the ways in which Andeans affirm their identity within the U.S. cultural milieu through numerous national celebrations, professional and hometown associations, and sports clubs. These gatherings, in either informal or formal settings, are generally not of a pan-Andean nature, but are based on town or country of origin. There are, however, larger Latino-based organizations that include Andean members.

NATIONAL CELEBRATIONS

One of the first major events that Andean immigrants organize is Independence Day celebrations. These are mostly day-long festivals in blocked-off streets or in parks. The point is to gather and celebrate the food, music, and dance of one's identity and country of origin. And gather they do for it is not unusual that Independence Day celebrations draw tens of thousands of participants in major cities of Andean settlement. Most of those who come are either from the celebrated country or have ancestral ties to it. Such gatherings require permits and careful planning throughout the year that helps solidify a sense of community.

The sheer size of the crowds also tends to attract politicians. When Colombians gather in Flushing Meadows Corona Park in Queens, nearly a quarter million people attend. At one celebration in 1997, then-Mayor Rudolph Guiliani spoke to the crowd, as well as several local politicians, a U.S. congresswoman, and Miss Colombia.[15] Such gatherings are truly transnational events, where Andeans celebrate their culture and share it with the broader community. Yet such gatherings are politically important events, with recent settlers being actively courted by both U.S. and Andean politicians. Local U.S. politicians are drawn by the sheer size of the crowd and the potential to recruit new votes. Andean politicians know that many of these migrants are economically successful and have maintained their right to vote in national elections in their country of birth. Recognizing this emigrant community and its potential economic and political power is increasingly seen as an important election strategy. It is not unusual for politicians (from the United States and the Andes) to attend such events.

Fortunately Andean Independence Days fall in the northern latitude summer, making it easier to organize massive outdoor gatherings. Colombians celebrate their independence on July 20, Peruvians on July 28. Ecuadorians and Bolivians have their independence day celebrations in August; Ecuador's is the tenth and Bolivia's is the sixth. Such events garner interest from the surrounding community. The parades and musical groups are a joyous spectacle. Moreover, the food is a huge draw, and also an excellent opportunity for food preparers to show off their national cuisines.

In addition to Independence Day celebrations, Andeans often have smaller gatherings to honor patron saints. In Catholic South America, most villages, cities, and even regions have patron saints or celebrations that honor religious icons that are believed to bestow special blessings. Marking these religious events in the United States is a way to maintain one's affiliation to home. In Ecuador the Lord of Giron is a venerated crucifix from the town of Giron. It is believed to bring rain in times of drought and prosperity overall. In southern Ecuador processions honoring Giron coincide with a festival of the bulls that lasts up to eight weeks in October and November. Since 2000, Ecuadorians in the city of Ossining, New York, in the lower Hudson River valley have been organizing their own annual procession to the Lord of Giron. In suburban New York such festivities include a mass, folk dancing, music, and feasting. As one Ecuadorian from Ossining explained, "We tried to bring our tradition from Ecuador. We have good health; we have good jobs. This is the time to give thanks."[16] Likewise, the Virgin of Urkupiña is a venerated icon for Bolivians from the department (state) of Cochabamba who have processions and dances every August in the streets of Cochabamba in her honor.[17] Not surprisingly, Bolivians in Northern Virginia—many of whom are from Cochabamba— annually give thanks to the Virgin of Urkupiña in more modest gatherings in area parks and churches.

PROFESSIONAL AND HOMETOWN ASSOCIATIONS

Less visible than street festivals, but an important backbone of Andean social life, are the various professional and hometown groups that form in cities where Andeans settle. Such organizations exist among many immigrant groups as a way to maintain contact with people from home and also to assist family and friends left behind. Andean groups organize clubs for social gatherings among similarly trained professionals to engage in cultural events such as folk dance groups and beauty pageants, or to provide services to other immigrant co-ethnics such as language training or legal assistance.

Colombians, Peruvians, Ecuadorians, and Bolivians have created numerous professional organizations in major destination cities. In these cities one finds associations of doctors and lawyers, such as the Peruvian-American Medical Society or the Colombian American Bar Association that meet socially and organize fund-raising events and charitable work. Such organizations are very class-conscious with membership closely tied to elite families from the countries of origin.

Scores of cultural organizations also exist to perpetuate aspects of Andean culture among co-ethnics and their children. Immigrants often enroll a son or daughter in a folk dance group or language classes to assure they maintain connections with their ancestral home. Dance groups perform in the Independence Day celebrations but also in various area festivals and parades to showcase Andean culture and music. For example, Peruvian and Bolivian dance groups march in the annual Cherry Blossom Festival parade held each spring in Washington, D.C. Local beauty pageants also exist in U.S. cities that celebrate national identity. Thus Colombians in New York will hold a Miss Colombia pageant and Bolivians in Washington will do the same. Such groups provide vital social networks for native-born and newly arrived Andeans to share cultural values and maintain friendships. The degree to which the activities of these groups reach out to a broader community is, however, somewhat limited.

Hometown associations represent a smaller geographical scale of identity maintenance and one that can have a profound impact on the lives of people living in the Andes. As is often the case, migration creates chains, with certain communities forming much larger migrant streams than others. In some cases, large numbers of migrants from particular towns or villages settle in cities in the United States and create associations dedicated to supporting their communities of birth. These groups are often informal and may exist for years or a few months.

Hometown associations form because of economic and social needs, often of a transnational nature. If an Andean town experiences a major landslide, earthquake, or drought, the sons and daughters of the community living abroad may pool together resources in the form of money, clothes, tools, and toys to send to the community in need. Over time a group may formalize and sponsor fund-raising events to improve community infrastructure. Thus these hometown groups will build schools, community centers, churches, renovate town landmarks or plazas, build basketball courts and soccer fields, and finance a health-care center. While there is very little data on hometown associations from the Andes, my own fieldwork in Bolivia has allowed me to see firsthand the power of these immigrant-led development efforts. Tens of thousands of dollars are poured into select rural communities in Bolivia where immigrants in the United States send back resources to improve the lives of those left behind. Such work is not part of the American ethnic landscape, but it does have a profound impact on distant communities that are increasingly linked together by a complex global web of migrants and money.

SOCCER LEAGUES

Many South Americans consider soccer a cultural necessity, and South American players, especially from Brazil and Argentina, have left their mark on this most international sport. Today soccer is widely played in the United States and a professional soccer league has existed since the mid-1990s. The head of Major League Soccer (MLS), Don Garber, has asserted that the success of the league in the United States is due largely to the "ethnic fan," especially recent immigrants from Latin America.[18] Over the years most MLS teams have had players from Latin America on their rosters, including Andeans. Yet the place where Andean identity is best expressed through sport is in the formation of immigrant recreational leagues.

Visit any playing field on a Sunday and one is likely to see adult recreational soccer leagues in action. The leagues create a cultural space that is familiar, inexpensive, and ephemeral where immigrants gather to reaffirm their sense of identity and have fun. For many male newcomers, this is the first organization that they join upon arriving in the United States.[19] Hundreds of Latino teams exist, often organized by country or even town of origin. In the Washington Metro area in the late 1990s it was estimated that there were over 30 Latino leagues that included over 450 teams.[20] Some leagues are international but many are organized by country; thus there are Bolivian and Peruvian leagues. Being far from home allows players to indulge in some soccer fantasy; uniforms from famous club teams at home are purchased, and players arrive on game day in the same attire that the stars at home wear.

While soccer leagues are almost exclusively for male Andean players, women and children attend the games. A Sunday game is often the highlight of a week filled with long hours of work and commutes. News from home is shared as is information about jobs, housing, and education. For a few hours, the soccer leagues allow Andeans to gather with people from their origin towns and villages and to share their common identity. When the game is over, the teams pack up and return to the less ethnic spaces of the wider world.

The celebration of Andean national and religious holidays, the formation of Andean associations, and the creation of soccer leagues are all examples of how Andeans work to maintain their cultural identity in the United States. Such events are for the ethnic groups themselves rather than a mechanism for intercultural exchange. Active participation in these organizations also means that one can live an Andean social life in the United States, celebrating festivals, playing soccer with fellow country-men, and organizing community-development projects in one's country of birth. This transnational space that many Andeans create in the United States is indicative of the close ties that are maintained with South America.

Transnational Networks

Many of the Andean populations in the United States exhibit a tendency toward transnationalism, or the maintenance of complex linkages between sending and receiv-ing communities across national borders. Transnational lives are those lived somewhere in-between, with immigrants not fully part of their country of birth or their country of settlement, but active in both. Many scholars see the increase in transnationalism as a result of globalization. In the case of the Andes, like other Latin American and Caribbean countries, the economies of the region are gradually shifting away from agro-exporting economies to labor-exporting ones through migration.[21] It is through the creation of migratory circuits that particular sending and receiving communities are linked through the movement of people, goods, capital, and ideas. Not all Andean migrants construct transnational lives, but many do.

Migration as a transnational experience, rather than simply an international move-ment, is partially explained by changes in technology. International travel is cheaper, communication is easier, and the transfer of capital is relatively unproblematic. Thus it is possible for labor to respond to global labor markets and not simply local ones. The increase in remittance income throughout the world, and especially in the Andes, is a compelling indicator of the power of international labor flows to redirect capital. Yet transnational migration is also concerned with dual identity, and how identity may be oddly uncoupled from territory. Can one be "Colombian" and yet spend one's entire life outside of Colombia? Andean immigrants themselves are challenging concepts of national identity by petitioning their governments for dual citizenship so they are able to cast ballots overseas for national elections in their countries of birth. Two significant examples of Andean transnational networks are found in exploring remittance patterns and political policies to accommodate Andean emigrants in their countries of birth.

REMITTANCES

Monies sent to families and communities back in the Andes from workers in the United States and other countries form a vital economic safety net for many households. Remittances are used for daily subsistence, medical expenses, buying cars, building larger houses, or for investment in land or businesses. Having someone working abroad who regularly remits money is able to vastly improve the economic well-being of a

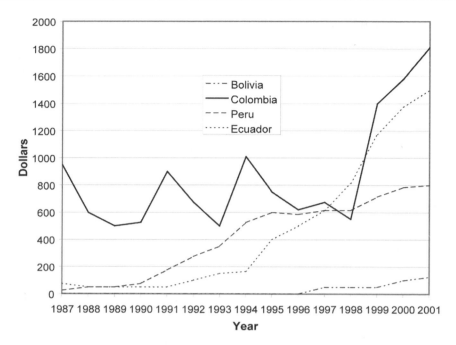

Figure 9.4.   *Growth in Remittances to Andean Countries, 1987–2002.*
Source: Solimano, "Workers' Remittances."

household. A typical emigrant who remits money generally makes less than $30,000 per year in the United States and sends roughly 10 percent back. The average range of remittances per month to the Andes is $200 to $300.[22] This money can come from men or women, but typically it requires that a member of a household leave for several months to several years in order to obtain a job and cover the cost of travel.

The rise of remittances in the last decade has been an important cushion against the negative impacts of the economic crises experienced in the Andean states. Economist Andrés Solimano estimates that between 1998 and 2002 net remittances increased by 150 percent in Bolivia, 510 percent in Colombia, 72 percent in Ecuador, and 73 percent in Peru (Fig. 9.4).[23] In the case of Ecuador, remittances represent between 7 and 8 percent of the country's gross domestic product. These are substantial sums of money; Peru receives over $1 billion in remittances annually while Colombia and Ecuador receive substantially higher amounts.

In bad economic times remittances can be seen as a privately funded safety net. When the economic situation improves, remittances can be viewed as a grassroots development effort. But in either case, dependence on remittances places enormous strains on both senders and receivers. For individuals working in the United States to send 10 percent of their income home requires sacrifice and austere living. For those who await the money, there is always the anxiety of it not arriving. Probably the most difficult aspect is the fact that many family members are split up for years. Mothers or fathers send money back to their children but don't see them grow up. Marriages are often irreparably strained through years of separation. Most agree that the intensity of remittance flows corresponds to a relatively new migrant stream. If fewer Andeans are admitted to the United States, would the intensity of remittances also decline?

TRANSNATIONAL POLITICS

Dual citizenship is an important political issue for South Americans living in the United States, especially with reference to the right to vote in presidential elections in their country of origin. Many Andeans stay well informed about political events at home through radio, television, newspapers, and the Internet. Major Andean newspapers have even created special U.S. editions filled with news from home along with ads that serve the needs of the immigrant community in the United States.[24] It can be argued that Andeans in the United States have placed more energy on maintaining their political voice in their countries of birth than building a political voice in the United States. Again, this may be a reflection of their uncertainty as to whether they are here permanently as citizens or temporarily as workers.

In 1991, after a long grassroots effort by migrants in New York and Miami, the Colombian government approved the right to dual citizenship. In 1997, electoral reform in Colombia allowed citizens living abroad to vote and run for the national Congress. The following year, five candidates ran for Colombian congressional offices from the New York metropolitan area, and Dr. José López won the election. Dr. López, a Colombian physician living in New Jersey, was elected to represent the department of Tolima in the Colombian Congress and began his term in 1998.

The participation of emigrants in Andean politics has changed the national discourse through the idea of creating a special electoral district that represents the interests of Colombians living abroad.[25] Peru now allows citizens to vote in national elections at designated polling places set up in U.S. cities where substantial numbers of Peruvians reside. The Bolivian government also recently recognized dual citizenship.

Transnationalism is a two-way street, and returning emigrants are not always warmly received. Bolivian President Sánchez de Lozada (1993–1997 and 2002–2003) was commonly referred to as the *falso gringo* (fake American) because of his thick American accent. Born in Bolivia, President Sánchez de Lozada was raised in the United States and did not return to Bolivia until after college. He resigned from office in his second term due to violent protests about his plans to privatize gas production. He has since returned to live in the United States.

Conclusion

Some 365 million people live in South America, yet the United States was home to just 2 million foreign-born South Americans in 2000. Like the United States, many South American countries received large numbers of immigrants at the turn of the twentieth century, especially Argentina and Brazil. As we move into the twenty-first century it appears that the region is sending labor rather than attracting it. Consequently, the presence of South Americans is growing in a few select U.S. cities. It is also growing in other countries such as Japan, Spain, and Italy.

As a group, most South Americans are able to blend into the larger Hispanic population in U.S. cities and suburbs because of the absence of Andean settlement enclaves. Many arrive as well-educated professionals seeking the economic opportunities that their native countries are unable to provide. As a result, their economic status generally mirrors that of the larger U.S. population. In part because of their being recent immigrants, various Andean groups have formed social and economic organizations that assist in the persistence of the sending-country culture. Although of short duration, Independence Day celebrations and soccer leagues provide the venues for cultural persistence. At the same time, this is a group that has developed an impressive web of transnational linkages to their countries of birth, particularly through the sending of remittances and participation in sending-country political activities. Many freely travel back and forth while others remain in legal limbo waiting for their residency papers or living as undocumented workers. In short, this is an ethnic group that so far has left a faint mark on the American ethnic landscape. Yet, they have also managed to position themselves in the socioeconomic mainstream. Just how their cultural and political identity unfolds in the United States in the years ahead depends upon whether their numbers continue to grow and how much of their attention and resources are turned to their continent of birth.

Notes

1. Nancy Foner, *From Ellis Island to JFK: New York's Two Great Waves of Immigration* (New Haven, CT: Yale University Press, 2000), 157.

2. Maxine Margolies, *Little Brazil: An Ethnography of Brazilian Immigrants in New York City* (Princeton, NJ: Princeton University Press, 1994).

3. Philip Martin and Elizabeth Midgley, "Immigration: Shaping and Reshaping America," *Population Bulletin* 58, no. 3 (2003): 17–19.

4. Brad Jokisch and Jason Pribilsky, "The Panic to Leave: Economic Crisis and the New Immigration from Ecuador," *International Migration* 40, no. 4 (2002): 75–101.

5. U.S. Committee for Refugees, *World Refugee Survey, 2004*, 241–245.

6. Luis E. Guarnizo, Arturo I. Sánchez, and Elizabeth Roach, "Mistrust, Fragmented Solidarity, and Transnational Migration: Colombians in New York City and Los Angeles," *Ethnic and Racial Studies* 22, no. 2 (1999): 367–396.

7. Brad Jokisch, "From Circulation to International Migration: The Case of South-Central Ecuador," *Conference of Latin Americanist Geographers Yearbook* 23 (1997): 63–67.

8. Joshua Hotaka Roth, *Brokered Homeland: Japanese Brazilian Migrants in Japan* (Ithaca, NY: Cornell University Press, 2002).

9. Inés M. Miyares, "Changing Latinization of New York City," in *Hispanic Spaces, Latino Places: Community and Cultural Diversity in Contemporary America*, ed. Daniel Arreola (Austin: University of Texas Press, 2004).

10. Guarnizo, Sánchez, and Roach, "Mistrust, Fragmented Solidarity."

11. Daniel Arreola, *Hispanic Spaces, Latino Places: Community and Cultural Diversity* in *Contemporary America* (Austin: University of Texas Press, 2004).

12. Sarah J. Mahler, *American Dreaming: Immigrants' Life on the Margins* (Princeton, NJ: Princeton University Press, 1995), 14–26.

13. Ancestry data is from the U.S. Census and includes anyone who claims an ancestral tie to an Andean country, in this case Colombia, Ecuador, Peru, and Bolivia. Ancestry includes both foreign-born and native-born populations.

14. Marie Price and Courtney Whitworth, "Soccer and Latino Cultural Space: Metropolitan Washington Fútbol Leagues," in *Hispanic Spaces, Latino Places: Community and Cultural Diversity in Contemporary America*, ed. Daniel Arreola (Austin: University of Texas Press, 2004), 172–173.

15. Guarnizo, Sánchez, and Roach, "Mistrust, Fragmented Solidarity."

16. Leah Rae, "Immigrants in Suburbia, Culture and Religion March On," *The Journal News*, Westchester County, New York, 15 February 2004, A15.

17. Robert Albro, "The Populist Chola: Cultural Mediation and the Political Imagination in Quillacollo, Bolivia," *Journal of Latin American Anthropology* 5, no. 2 (2000): 30–88.

18. Michael Wilbon, "In Crowded Field, MLS Adjusts Goals," *Washington Post*, 25 March 2000, D1.

19. Price and Whitworth, "Soccer and Latino Cultural Space," 167–186.

20. Gabriel Escobar, "The Other Pro Soccer: In Area's Latino Leagues, Part of the Game Is Profit, and the Best Players Are Paid," *Washington Post*, 29 November 1998, D1.

21. Manuel Orozco, "Globalization and Migration: The Impact of Family Remittances in Latin America," *Latin American Politics and Society* 44, no. 2 (2002): 41–66.

22. Andrés Solimano, "Workers' Remittances to the Andean Region: Mechanisms, Costs and Development Impact," unpublished paper prepared for the Multilateral Investment Fund–IDB's Conference on Remittances and Development, May 2003, Quito, Ecuador, p. 3, <www.iadb.org> (7 March 2005).

23. Solimano, "Workers Remittances."

24. In 2004, the Cochabamba daily, *Los Tiempos*, began publishing a weekly U.S. edition for its readers in the Washington area.

25. Luis Eduardo Guarnizo and Luz Marina Díaz, "Transnational Migration: A View from Colombia," *Ethnic and Racial Studies* 22, no. 2 (1999): 410–412.

CHAPTER 10

Chinese Americans: Community Formation in Time and Space

Wei Li

Numbering some 35 million individuals, it would be difficult to identify an ethnic diaspora as geographically large and developed as that of the Chinese diaspora. The lion's share of diasporic Chinese live in Southeast Asia countries (86%), but Europe (2.6%), Canada (3.4%), and the United States (6.8%) possess significant numbers of ethnic Chinese as well. The Chinese American population reached more than 2.4 million in 2000,[1] and is the largest ethnic-Asian group in the United States. This group merits close examination not only because they are the earliest and largest Asian group in the nation, but also their experiences reflect our nation's immigration history and population diversity. The 1882 Chinese Exclusion Act, which was aimed at curbing Chinese labor immigration, was the first and only federal immigration legislation that prohibited a single group from immigration to the United States solely based on race and class. The enforcement of such exclusionary legislation led to gate-keeping strategies as part of immigration law implementation, having profound historical and contemporary impacts.[2]

The 61-year-long exclusion era resulted in declining Chinese immigration and population, an extreme sex-ratio imbalance, limited occupation choices, and forced segregation of Chinese Americans. Contemporarily, the Chinese are one of the largest beneficiaries of the 1965 Immigration Act. Chain migration has brought a large influx of Chinese immigrants seeking both family reunification and economic opportunity. Chinese professionals and capitalists have joined immigration flows, which has contributed to the heterogeneity of the contemporary Chinese American population. In addition, the perception of Chinese Americans by the majority population can be seen as a mirror of changing global, national, and local circumstances. When the United States and China are political allies, Chinese Americans become a symbol of friendship between the two countries. When the two countries become more antagonistic, the Chinese face hostility as the "Other," despite the fact that many are American citizens. Such perceptions are manifested today in the era of accelerated economic globalization and competition, and transnational flows of population, goods, information, and financial resources. The Chinese American experiences are part of the American story and reveal how our nation's racial and ethnic dynamics have oscillated over the past 150 years.

Immigration History

The history of Chinese immigration and community development in the United States is roughly divided into four stages. Prior to 1882, Chinese laborers experienced open immigration, but as was discussed in chapter 2, by 1882 anti-Chinese sentiments resulted in the passage of the Chinese Exclusion Act. This act was effective until 1943 and limit the entry of new Chinese labor immigrants. During World War II, the door to Chinese labor immigrants was opened slightly in response to military alliances between the United States and China. This transitioned into a return of more open immigration resulting from the Immigration Reform Act of 1965.

FROM OPEN IMMIGRATION TO EXCLUSION

Early Chinese immigrants to the United States in the nineteenth century primarily originated from a seven-county area of the Pearl River Delta of Guangdong Province in China known as *Sam yap* and *Sze yap*, meaning three and four counties respectively in Cantonese. These first-stage immigrants were largely farmers who possessed little capital or formal education, and were seen as cheap laborers who were willing to accept low wages and work under harsh conditions. Heavy taxation, corruption, and oppression by the Qing Dynasty in China during the second half of the nineteenth century, in addition to population pressures and natural disasters, food shortages, and social unrest and rebellion prompted many to emigrate. They began arriving in the United States in large numbers after 1850; by 1860 the number of Chinese residents[3] increased to 41,397 (Fig. 10.1). Most of these early immigrants were young males who settled on the West Coast, particularly California, and were recruited to meet the demand for labor for economic growth. Most of them worked as manual laborers in mines, railway construction sites, or in farming and fishing. The Chinese population of the United States reached 105,000 by 1880, and accounted for 10 percent of the total population and one-quarter of the labor force in California. This first stage of immigration is explained by Neo-Classical Theory in that the differences in income-earning opportunities between origin and destination countries were substantial.

The Chinese brought with them a culture that was significantly different from the white European American norm. But racial ideology in addition to economic competition triggered animosity against the Chinese. Initially, employers welcomed the Chinese, since they provided cheap and industrious labor. They were often hired as strikebreakers, and this caused intense job competition between Chinese and white workers. Not surprisingly, white mobs who engaged in anti-Chinese violence during the late nineteenth century were mostly from the working class and this coupled with stock market speculations in 1872 and a severe drought in 1876 caused severe job losses. As a result, "The Chinese Must Go" became the leading slogan of the Workingman's Party, a vigilante-like pro-labor group that eventually evolved into a formal, but short-lived political party that possessed an explicit anti-Asian political platform. Cultural difference was only later deployed to unite whites against the Chinese, accusing them of remaining unassimilated. Thus, the Chinese became scapegoats during periods of economic recession, and a racialized group under continuous socioeconomic pressure in American society.

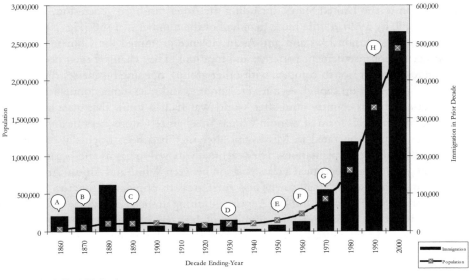

Law in Effect in Prior Decade

A: Open Immigration
B: Burlingame Treaty in 1868 encouraging Chinese immigration
C: Burlingame Treaty until 1882, then Chinese Exclusion Act
D: Chinese Exclusion Act and 1924 Act
E: Chinese Exclusion Act, then Repeal Act in 1943
F: Repeal Act, then Asia-Pacific triangle in 1952
G: Asia-Pacific triangle, then 1965 amendments
H: 1965 amendments and separate Taiwan quota, then 1990 Immigration Act

Figure 10.1.   Chinese Immigration and Population in the United States, 1850–2000. Data Sources: U.S. Census of Population, 1860; 1890; 1910–2000; U.S. Immigration and Naturalization Services.

There was also a deep-rooted racist attitude towards nonwhites, which stressed white superiority over "yellow inferiority." The Page Act of 1875 was the first federal legislation to restrict female immigration, attempting to prevent the importation of Chinese women on the explicit assumption that many of them were prostitutes. Then, in a report issued on February 25, 1878, the House Committee on Education and Labor singled out the Chinese male as "an undesirable citizen" for three reasons—his effect on labor, his debilitating effect on society, and his inability to assimilate.[4] They reflected the interrelations between race and gender ideologies. The Chinese were labeled "unassimilable," supporting a growing movement that argued that the ability to assimilate should be the measure of whether a group should be allowed to immigrate.

Anti-Chinese sentiment in the West prompted the Congress to pass the Chinese Exclusion Act of 1882, which marked the second stage of Chinese immigration. It was the first, and the only federal law to exclude a group of people solely based on their race and class. The Chinese Exclusion Act barred Chinese laborers from coming to the United States for a period of ten years, and was renewed several times and did not get repealed until 1943. All Chinese women were classified as the same labor class as their husbands regardless of their own status. Chinese exclusion became known as "the Chinese Question" in American politics during this period, and Congress enacted a total of fifteen anti-Chinese laws between 1882 and 1913. As a result, the total Chinese population in the United States, including the American-born generation, fell to less than 62,000 by 1920, a little more than half of the number in 1880 (Fig. 10.1).

Chinese exclusion laws and anti-Asian violence prompted the Chinese to change their occupations, settlement patterns, and locations. They changed their occupational structures in order not to compete with other groups, opening businesses that did not require much start-up capital. As a result, laundries and restaurants dominated Chinese occupations in this country until after World War II. It is ironic that male immigrants rarely performed this form of work in China. Small grocery stores became another business that Chinese operated in Mississippi after they had been originally recruited to replace Black labor on plantations. They eventually moved to towns and became owners of small groceries and occupied a class position between White and African Americans.[5]

Many Chinese left small towns and rural areas to populate Chinatowns in large cities such as San Francisco and Los Angeles, resulting in social cohesion and ethnic solidarity. However, even the small number of later-generation native-born Chinese Americans had tremendous difficulty finding jobs or living outside of Chinatowns, despite the fact that many had earned college degrees.[6] Chinatowns were usually in economically depressed downtown areas, where immigrants lived, worked, and sought to protect themselves from discrimination by the host society. Many Chinese lived and worked in restaurants and related service industries inside Chinatown. The exceptions were those who opened ethnic businesses such as mainly hand laundries or grocery stores, and located their businesses and residences in other urban districts. In the 1870s western frontier town of Phoenix, Arizona, with its small Chinatown, many Chinese families operated groceries in other parts of the city where the majority of residents were Mexican American. Chinese children in those areas grew up learning Spanish before English.[7] Moreover, many Chinese moved out of the hostile West and settled in other parts of the country, including large East Coast cities such as New York, where the number of Chinese increased and Chinatowns formed.

The impact of the Chinese Exclusion Act on the Chinese community was severe. U.S. laws made it illegal for Chinese male laborers to bring in their wives and all Chinese men to marry white women, adding to a sense that their only avenue was to earn enough money to return to China. Generations of Chinese men traveled back and forth between the Americas[8] and China, where they could visit their families and father children, and sojourning became their imposed way of life. The restrictions against Chinese female immigrants and the establishment of family ties for the majority of Chinese men in the United States resulted in an extremely unbalanced sex ratio. Chinatowns were communities of fathers and sons, uncles and nephews, male relatives and friends. The sex ratio in 1890 was 27 males to 1 female. This situation further fueled the social problems in Chinatowns, such as gambling and prostitution. Chinatowns became isolated communities and sanctuaries for Chinese immigrants as they faced prejudice and violence, along with exclusion from the mainstream society and deportation.[9]

WORLD WAR II TO THE PRESENT

During the 61-year long exclusion era, the exclusion laws successfully curbed Chinese immigration and family formation. The third stage of Chinese immigration commenced with the repeal of the Chinese Exclusion Act in 1943 in response to China becoming a World War II U.S. ally. The one-page Repeal Act repealed all previous exclusion laws against the Chinese and granted Chinese immigrants the rights to become naturalized citizens. However, the act also gave an annual immigration quota of 105, and limited the number of annual Chinese immigrants coming directly from China or born in China to less than 80. During a five-year period (1944–1949), 383 Chinese were admitted into the United States under this immigration quota. In addition, the end of World War II brought in large numbers of Chinese females as wives or fiancées of American GIs, whose entry revived not only Chinese American families but also communities, especially Chinatowns in large metropolitan areas. As a result, a total of 5,687 Chinese immigrants entered on a non-quota basis which changed the male to female ratio of the Chinese in the continental U.S. from 2.85 in 1940 to 1.89 by 1950.

After World War II though, the situation changed again for the Chinese due to the government's changing hands in mainland China and the Korean War. Chinese Americans were once again regarded as targets of suspicion and animosity, and they were prohibited from sending money back home as China again became an enemy of the United States. The U.S. government instituted a "Confession Program" in 1956 during the McCarthy era. It permitted the Chinese who had entered the country under fraudulent identities during exclusion era to confess then obtain legal status, but they had to implicate others in the community, including their own families and friends who helped them during their immigration process. This program was also used to uncover any communist agents among Chinese American community. During the ten-year period, there were 13,897 such confessions.

Fueled by this anti-Communist fervor, programs were enacted to assist Chinese students and scholars enrolling in U.S. colleges and universities[10] to establish residency after their graduations, and to assist Chinese immigrants who were political refugees, merchants, professionals, and former diplomats to find refuge in the United States. These elite immigrants changed the profile of Chinese Americans in the United States. Unlike the nineteenth-century Chinese entrants, who were mainly laborers and sojourners, these new immigrants brought financial resources to the United States, instead of seeking to earn money here to send back to China. Many did not live in Chinatowns, but they became the predecessors of contemporary suburban-bound immigrants. This twenty-year period comprising stage three was characterized by immigrant flows in response to both friendly political relations with China during World War II and hostility toward Communism that resulted in refugee admissions. This immigrant flow, however, was relatively low in volume (Fig. 10.1).

The beginning of stage four in Chinese immigration commenced with the 1965 Immigration and Naturalization Act, which removed immediate family reunification from the visa totals and allotted 80 percent of preference visas to extended family members; this was a landmark for Chinese Americans. For the first time in history, the Chinese were eligible for the same preference categories as immigrants from other countries. In addition, large numbers of family members immigrated on a non-quota basis. As a result, Chinese immigrant flows increased at rates like no other Asian-origin group. Between 1960 and 1970 there were approximately 100,000 arrivals, but between 1990 and 2000, some 520,000 immigrants of Chinese ancestry entered the United States (Fig. 10.1).

Unlike past waves of Chinese immigrants, this fourth-stage cohort is characterized by great heterogeneity in terms of country of origin, educational attainment, language ability, occupational status, income, and housing tenure, as well as political and ethnic identity. For example, many ethnic Chinese refugees who used to live in Southeast Asia arrived as the result of the Vietnam War after the mid-1970s. Forced to leave their homelands, they lost everything in the war and/or the dangerous sea voyage and were not prepared for such an international journey. On the other hand, Congress passed the Immigration and Nationality Act of 1990, tripling the worldwide ceiling on employment-based visas and creating a new investor visa category (EB-5) which has then resulted in an influx of highly-skilled or affluent Chinese immigrants from Hong Kong, Taiwan, mainland China, Malaysia, and Indonesia. Responding to the Chinese government crackdown on peaceful Tian An Men student demonstrators in 1989, the U.S. Congress passed the 1992 Chinese Student Protection Act (CSPA) granting permanent residency to Chinese nationals who resided in the United States at the time. As a result, some 100,000 Chinese reportedly adjusted their legal status, many of whom were Chinese students and scholars enrolling in or visiting American universities on F-1 or J-1 non-immigrant visas. Additionally, more highly-skilled Chinese immigrants arrived since the 1990s. As illustrated in Table 10.1, Chinese immigrants (including those from Taiwan and Hong Kong) accounted for a large proportion of worldwide employment-based visas[11] and an increasing percentage among worldwide H-1B visa[12] holders in the past decade.

Another unconventional but increasing source of Chinese immigrants are adoptees, typically baby girls, who are adopted by American families, thus becoming naturalized citizens. China has become the largest source country for international adoptions; of the 124,282 international adoptees during the 2000–2005 period, Chinese adoptees accounted for 29 percent of this total. In addition, the number of undocumented Chi-

Table 10.1. Employment-based Immigrant and H-1B Non-immigrant Visas, 1992–2002

	Employment-based Visas		H-1B Visas	
Year	World	China	World	China
2002	174,968	14.3%	197,537	10.2%
2001	179,195	2.5%	331,206	10.7%
2000	107,024	16.0%	257,640	11.7%
1999	56,817	12.8%	302,326	4.3%
1998	77,517	15.5%	240,947	10.4%
1997	90,607	18.9%	—	—
1996	117,499	18.8%	144,458	3.6%
1995	85,336	21.0%	117,574	3.6%
1994	123,291	31.6%	105,899	3.1%
1993	147,012	32.6%	93,069	3.5%
1992	116,198	19.1%	110,193	3.1%

Source: (1992–1997) INS Statistical Yearbook, Tables 8 and 38; (1998–2002) INS website
<www.immigration.gov/graphics/shared/aboutus/statistics/ybpage.htm> (last accessed 7/23/03).

nese immigrants who pay large sums of money to organized-crime "snakehead" smugglers also increased and commonly became breaking storylines in the media.[13]

Since 1965, the numbers of Chinese immigrants have been consistently higher compared to native-born Chinese Americans in the last three decades. From 1960 to 1990, the ethnic Chinese population in the United States almost doubled every decade, increased another 48 percent during the 1990s, and maintained a relatively balanced sex ratio. Although the native-born population exceeded the immigrant population with a ratio of 0.89 immigrants per native-born Chinese American in 1970, the trend has reversed in recent decades. By 1990, the Chinese population reached 1,645,472, and became the fourth largest ethnic minority group (excluding Blacks) in the United States according to origin after Mexicans, Puerto Ricans, and American Indians. The Chinese American population reached 2,432,585 in 2000,[14] many of whom are relatively new immigrants. Three-quarters of the 1,825,285 foreign-born Chinese in 2000 arrived during the last two decades, 42 percent in the 1990s alone. By 2000, China, including Hong Kong and Taiwan, became the second largest immigrant source country behind only Mexico.

Settlement Patterns

Chinese Americans tend to be highly concentrated in several states. The combined numbers in California, New York, Texas, New Jersey, and Massachusetts alone accounted for 70 percent of the national total in 2000 (Map 10.1).[15] They are also an urban-centered population, with almost 98 percent living in non-rural areas, compared to 79 percent of the total U.S. population. The three consolidated metropolitan areas of New York, San Francisco, and Los Angeles alone represent 48 percent of the total national ethnic Chinese population. However, the last decade has witnessed an increase of Chinese Americans in non-traditional "gateway" regions, such as Northern New Jersey, San Diego, San Jose, and Seattle, some of which is explained by the geographical distribution of high-tech employment opportunities (Map 10.1). For instance, the counties of Middlesex (New Jersey), San Diego and Santa Clara (California), King (Washington), and Travis and Hays (Texas) ranked among the highest in percent increase of Chinese in the past decade. In the meantime, most rural counties in the Midwest and South have fewer than 100 Chinese.[16]

Small and crowded Chinatowns were unable to absorb the tremendous influx of Chinese immigrants who arrived after 1965. Today, the proportion of Chinese who still live in Chinatowns is small, and these Chinatown residents often are older or newer immigrants who lack English skills, transferable human capital, and/or financial resources. As residential districts, most Chinatowns had, and continue to have, poor housing and overcrowded conditions. In many cases, residents stay not because Chinatown is their ideal place of residence, but because of their lack of choice, which is constrained by social, economic, and linguistic disadvantages relative to dominant American society. Chinatowns today function primarily as tourist attractions as well as small-scale ethnic business districts with relatively modest housing costs. However, some are attracting international investments, often due to ethnic affinity and local gentrification efforts.

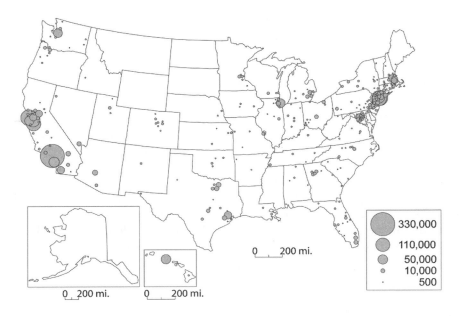

Map 10.1.   Distribution of Chinese in 2000 by County.
Source: U.S. Census of Population, 2000, SF2.

One of the important changes in Chinese American settlement patterns and community formation in recent decades, however, has been increasing suburbanization. Many ethnic Chinese move to the suburbs for better housing and neighborhoods; some settle in a heterolocal pattern and are socioeconomically joining mainstream society. Others form relatively concentrated communities in the suburbs, especially large metropolitan areas such as Los Angeles, Chicago, Houston, New York, San Francisco, and Washington, D.C. Living in the suburbs can no longer be equated with spatial dispersion because in some cases immigrants spatially cluster in new ethnic concentrations. This diverse mix of suburban-bound immigrants, as well as native-born Chinese Americans, includes wealthy people as well as the poor, unskilled, or undocumented workers employed in domestic and other services. As a result, ethnoburbs have materialized in some large metropolitan regions, especially in those globally connected cities that have pre-existing ethnic concentrations.

Chinese settlement patterns today represent a spectrum, from inner-city enclaves to ethnic suburbs, to dispersed ones without geographic propinquity. Traditional community organizations still play important roles although their influence becomes insignificant once beyond their neighborhood boundaries. Some new origin-based organizations among recent immigrants, however, have emerged in many large metropolitan regions. Simultaneously, various professional, trade, or service organizations have become more influential in community affairs.

Globalization and Contemporary Chinese American Communities

Given the complexities of global and national political and economic conditions, contemporary Chinese American urban settlement patterns and communities exhibit diverse material expressions. The differences between community types lie in their formation dynamics, level of spatial concentration, and a variety of socioeconomic characteristics.

DOWNTOWN CHINATOWNS AND NEWER SATELLITE COMMUNITIES

Almost exclusively characterizing Chinese settlement until the 1960s, Chinatowns historically stimulated ethnic solidarity. For mainstream society, however, Chinatowns symbolized racialized minority ghettos inhabited by marginalized, inassimilable, and perpetual foreigners. Chinatowns were perceived by mainstream society as unsanitary and filthy neighborhoods filled with social vices such as gambling, prostitution, gang warfare, and organized crime—some also became scapegoats as the source of diseases and ill health. Chinese people would even face violence should they dare to step outside Chinatown's perimeters. Thus, historical Chinatowns in the United States were stigmatized by a full range of negative connotations by the majority society.[17]

The historic 1965 Immigration Act made it possible for record numbers of Chinese to join their families already living in the United States for generations. Chinatowns were thus revived with an infusion of newly arrived immigrants. This demographic transformation is associated with a resurgence of the garment industry relying on inexpensive immigrant labor. Immigrant labor also benefited the Chinese restaurant industry for similar reasons. President Nixon's historic visit to China contributed to resurging interests in Chinese dining.[18] Continuously serving as a "port of entry" for many new immigrants, Chinatowns in large urban places are now considered as geographical sites for contests between capitalists and laborers, including the undocumented laborer. The nation's oldest Chinatown in San Francisco, for example, is dubbed the "informal capital city" of Chinese America, and is an example of a global *ethnopolis*.[19] Chinese account for more than 61 percent of the total population within Chinatown's boundaries. In 2000, 84 percent of the ethnic Chinese population was foreign-born, 72 percent had not completed a high school education, and 94 percent were renters.

Since the 1950s, waves of Chinese foreign students obtaining jobs in the mainstream economy after graduation coupled with native-born Chinese Americans largely moved to older suburbs in a heterolocal pattern and thus, by virtue of their place of residence, were considered a *model minority*. This started the initial small-scale residential and business clustering outside of Chinatowns. It marked the beginning of shifting Chinese settlement patterns, as demonstrated by emerging satellite communities and investments made in declining neighborhoods, such as Flushing, Queens in New York City, or the Richmond District in San Francisco. Chinese settlement has contributed to a resurgence of these urban districts, creating new and more middle-class Chinatowns.

MULTI-ETHNIC SUBURBS: ETHNOBURBS

Increasing immigrant quotas coupled with a vibrant Pacific Rim economy is indirectly expressed in the landscape by multiethnic suburbs or "ethnoburbs"[20] where new Chinese immigrants have a significant presence. Chinese settlement in these multiethnic ethnoburbs is economically fueled by businesses and their transnational financial and commodity ties with Asia, such as in the San Gabriel Valley in east suburban Los Angeles, or by economic restructuring that favors high-tech and service economies, such as in Silicon Valley. Rowland Heights (Los Angeles) and Fremont (Oakland) in California are good examples of two such Chinese American communities. Both exhibit suburban characteristics such as single family housing, higher home-ownership rates and household income, as well as high educational attainment levels, yet have high percentages of immigrants among their populations. The economic orientation of Chinese immigrants differs, however; in Rowland Heights it is based on international trade, while in Fremont it is high-technology industries. In major metropolitan regions, these ethnoburbs have emerged as ports of entry for new immigrants instead of, or in addition to, traditional Chinatowns. As will be discussed later in this chapter, transnational settlement patterns are also a prominent feature of ethnoburbs.

HETEROLOCAL COMMUNITIES

Some Chinese American communities exhibit heterolocal characteristics whereby spatial propinquity is absent, but cultural and social connections and institutions bind co-ethnics together. They are considered "invisible" cultural communities because of the absence of Chinese material landscapes. For example, Chandler, which is an eastern suburb of Phoenix, is a rapidly developing and relatively new municipality economically linked to the high-tech boom of the 1990s. Chandler is home to a small number of Chinese Americans, whose percentage of the total population and number of households is only 1.22 percent. Unlike in both Chinatowns and ethnoburbs, most Chinese Americans residing in these heterolocal communities have high incomes connected to both professional employment and high-tech industry.

In summary, the last fifteen years marked a continuation of, as well as distinction from, the trend in immigration flows beginning in 1965. Global economic integration entered a newer and deeper stage in the 1990s, and developed country economies were reducing labor costs to attract investors and recruiting a highly skilled labor force, both of which resulted in diverse immigrant flows. The outcome of these new immigration flows, coupled with a long-established Chinese American population, created contemporary ethnic Chinese settlement patterns as a manifestation of globalization.

Socioeconomic Characteristics

American-born Chinese populations have largely enjoyed higher socioeconomic attainment than both foreign-born Chinese and the U.S. population in general. The socioeconomic profiles of Chinese immigrants have changed dramatically since 1965. Traditional historic immigrants or *Lao Qiao*[21] originated primarily from Guangdong Province and spoke Cantonese. In contrast, new immigrants or *Xin Qiao* originated from a variety of provinces in mainland China, as well as Hong Kong, Taiwan, Southeast Asia, and other parts of the diaspora. These new immigrants vary in level of education, English-language ability, and job skills. Therefore there is a substantial difference socioeconomically among Chinese Americans regardless of place of birth (Table 10.2). For example, limited English ability often translates to limited job opportunity for many immigrants. Even though 68 percent of all Chinese immigrants five years or older whose native language is not English reported a good command of spoken English in 2000, about one-third of all 907,380 Chinese American households considered themselves "linguistically isolated."[22] A total of 46.7 percent of all Chinese Americans 25 years or older possessed a bachelor's degree or higher, with women being less likely to gain an advanced degree compared to men, on the other hand, another 22.2 percent did not graduate from high school.

Chinese Americans possess higher income levels compared to the U.S. population as a whole. Their overall high-income level is explained by a number of factors. These include high-salary occupations as more than half of all civilian Chinese American employees 16 years or older occupy management or professional positions, multiple workers per household, and many living in high cost of living areas, which upwardly skews their income. For example, the top ten PMSAs,[23] which are home to 62 percent of Chinese Americans in the nation, are among the highest cost of living metropolitan regions. However, 13.2 percent of Chinese Americans live below the federal poverty

Table 10.2.   Socioeconomic Characteristics of Chinese Americans, 2000

	Male	Female	Total for Chinese	U.S. Total
Percent with Bachelor's Degree or Higher	50.9%	42.9%	46.7%	24.4%
Percent Professional, Managerial, or Related Occupation	53.1%	47.5%	50.4%	33.7%
Median Household Income—1999	—	—	$51,119	$41,994
Per Capita Income—1999	$30,327	$17,640	$23,756	$21,587
Homeownership	—	—	57.8%	66.2%
Foreign-Born Population				
Percent Who Speak English Only, Speak Well, or Very Well	—	—	68.8%	70.8%
Percent Naturalized Citizen	52.5%	54.1%	53.3%	43.0%

Source: U.S. Census 2000, SF4.

line, two-thirds are immigrants, with 3.5 percent receiving some public assistance income. While 57.8 percent of Chinese American households have achieved their "American dream" by owning their homes, those who rent often struggle economically. Not only renters cannot enjoy mortgage tax relief, but 21 percent of them have to spend more than 50 percent of their monthly household income on rent, whereas only 12 percent of owners spend a similar percentage for housing. Some suffer crowded living conditions as more than 60 percent of renter households occupy studio apartments or one-bedroom apartments.

A Thriving Ethnic Economy

Chinese Americans are known for their burgeoning ethnic economic activities, both historically and contemporarily. During the historical exclusion era, the stereotypical Chinese laundries and restaurants that served non-Chinese clientele are perfect examples of the two primary Chinese-owned businesses. In Chinatowns across the nation, there were also grocery stores for ethnic Chinese and gift shops for tourists. This was the case until World War II, when legal job discrimination was outlawed. For the first time in history, public-sectors jobs—such as federal, state, and local government positions—were open to Chinese Americans, and this helped to diversify economic opportunity and mobility.

Chinese Americans continue to have a higher rate of self-employment or entrepreneurship today when compared to the working population as a whole. They own businesses ranging from restaurants or retail stores to professional services and large international corporations. Some Chinese workers, however, are trapped in the low-paying ethnic economy due to a lack of job skills or transferable human capital. Undocumented immigrants in particular are at the bottom of the socioeconomic ladder, and this subordinate position is linked to the lack of legal documentations and protection. While small retail businesses still dominate, it is trans-Pacific economic activities involving international trade and transnational capital that have flourished in recent years. The resulting landscapes often make distinct ethnic Chinese imprints in urban regions, in both the inner cities and suburbs. Their locations vary from small grocery stores in Chinatowns and other urban neighborhoods, to small strip malls, to large-scale suburban Asian theme malls, many with Chinese language signs and some with distinct Chinese-style architecture.

Chinese economic activities vary from place to place. Table 10.3 compares Chinese-owned businesses between 1987 and 1997 in the top twenty metropolitan regions with the largest Chinese population. Those regions with the longest tenure of Chinese settlements, such as Southern and Northern California, New York, and Honolulu continue to have high rates of entrepreneurship. What is somewhat surprising, however, are some non-traditional Chinese settlement concentrations, including Atlanta, Las Vegas, and Phoenix, which rank quite high. Their growth rate between 1987 and 1997 was phenomenal, with Las Vegas and Atlanta topping the list at 472 percent and 431 percent respectively. Sales and revenue also reflect the differential economic structure among Chinese American businesses. For example,

Table 10.3. Chinese Business in Top Twenty Metropolitan Areas

Top Twenty Chinese MSAs, 2000	Entrepreneurship Rate		No. of Chinese Firms		Business Change	Avg. Sale Receipts
	1987	1997	1987	1997	87–97	1997 ($,000)
New York CMSA	4.4%	11.7%	14,197	55,690	292.3%	307.5%
San Jose–San Francisco–Oakland CMSA	5.3%	9.0%	17,215	41,852	143.1%	549.0%
Los Angeles CMSA	6.6%	13.3%	20,233	53,623	165.0%	519.5%
Boston, MA-NH PMSA	2.3%	5.1%	1,124	3,655	225.2%	373.8%
Chicago, IL PMSA	4.5%	7.7%	1,955	5,305	171.4%	938.8%
Washington, DC-MD-VA-WV PMSA	4.6%	10.6%	1,808	6,663	268.5%	230.6%
Honolulu, HI MSA	7.1%	14.9%	4,477	8,006	78.8%	245.8%
Seattle-Bellevue-Everett WA PMSA	4.7%	8.6%	1,365	4,440	225.3%	409.9%
Houston, TX PMSA	7.4%	12.4%	2,226	5,643	153.5%	537.4%
Philadelphia, PA-NJ PMSA	4.0%	8.9%	1,101	3,503	218.2%	144.6%
San Diego, CA MSA	6.2%	6.1%	1,225	1,915	56.3%	349.3%
Sacramento, CA PMSA	4.4%	11.8%	1,296	3,654	181.9%	122.9%
Dallas, TX PMSA	5.7%	9.2%	1,026	2,603	153.7%	745.2%
Atlanta, GA MSA	5.2%	12.3%	494	2,625	431.4%	418.0%
Detroit, MI PMSA	3.1%	6.2%	426	1,091	156.1%	212.8%
Portland-Vancouver, OR-WA PMSA	5.7%	7.7%	559	1,256	124.7%	327.9%
Phoenix-Mesa, AZ MSA	5.8%	9.3%	555	1,510	172.1%	213.2%
Baltimore, MD PMSA	4.8%	11.2%	378	1,510	299.5%	377.6%
Austin-San Marcos, TX MSA	2.9%	4.9%	155	564	263.9%	310.6%
Las Vegas, NV MSA	4.2%	9.0%	177	1,012	471.8%	232.3%

Source: U.S. Census 1990: SF1; U.S. Census 2000, SF4; U.S. Economic Census, "Survey of Minority Owned Businesses." 1997; U.S. Economic Census, "Survey of Minority Owned Businesses," 1987.

those entrepreneurs in the nation's high-tech regions such as San Jose, California, and Northern New Jersey tend to have higher overall sales and receipts figures.

Transnational Connections

Chinese American communities have been transnational in nature since their inception. From earlier *Gam Saan Haak*[24] who left their families in China by choice to seek fortune in the "Gold Mountain" in the mid-nineteenth century to Chinese men forced to live in split households across the Pacific Ocean as stipulated by the Chinese exclusion laws in the late nineteenth and first half of the twentieth centuries, the only way for most Chinese immigrants to reunite with their families was to take cross-Pacific trips between the United States and China.

Although the word *transnational* has been widely used since the 1960s, the reinterpretation of immigration as a transnational process can be seen as reflections of the broader and accelerated trend of globalization since the late twentieth century. It can be seen as "an important transnational process that reflects and contributes to the current political configurations of the emerging global economy, . . . by which immigrants forge and sustain simultaneous multistranded social relations that link together their societies of origin and settlement."[25] The linkages to globalized financial flows and economies as the factors determining capital flow are seen to structure the global mobility of these transmigrants. This involves the continuous flows, circulation, and networks of population, capital, and information that fuel the emergence, sustainability, and growth of Chinese American communities. Transnational financial capital and financial institutions have played key roles in transforming traditional Chinatowns and developing suburban Chinese American communities in many metropolitan regions such as Los Angeles, New York, and San Francisco. Such transnational connections and patterns can be seen in residential patterns, business landscapes, and economic transactions.

TRANSNATIONAL FAMILIES: "ASTRONAUTS" AND "PARACHUTE KIDS"

As the result of immigration policies in the last two decades that have courted affluent and professional immigrants, many new Chinese immigrants are investors running businesses not just in the United States, but also across the Pacific Rim. Often overrepresented in affluent suburbs, many of these immigrants are highly motivated entrepreneurs or well-qualified professionals who participate in new forms of split families that have been described as "astronaut families" and "parachute kids."

The "astronaut" family phenomenon means a family lives on both Asian and U.S. sides of the Pacific Rim. Often the husband travels across the Pacific to conduct business, a practice that is common among Chinese business immigrants. These truly unconventional migrants are known as "astronauts" or "flying trapeze" (*kongzhong feiren*), because they shuttle between the United States and various Asian countries. Unlike their nineteenth-century sojourning predecessors, who sailed across the Pacific to visit their families in China, these transmigrants jet across the Pacific to visit families in the United States. They are also known among Chinese-speaking people as "wife in America" (*neizaimei*). Family instability and even divorce are problems associated with this form of transnational economic arrangement.

Another related form of nontraditional, transmigrant families is the phenomenon of "parachute kids," one special form of the astronaut/split households. In this case, both parents live primarily in Asia and their teenage children live alone or under the guardianship of relatives in houses purchased by their parents in the United States, often in affluent suburban areas. Youngsters are left alone to cope with their U.S. education and bicultural identity without daily parental guidance. Social problems associated with this phenomenon, such as kidnapping or gang activities, are also hot topics among Chinese and mainstream communities alike.

TRANSNATIONAL BUSINESSES AND FINANCIAL FLOW

Chinese American business landscapes often capture immigrants' fond memories of thriving businesses from their home countries. For instance, among the first Chinese businesses started in the San Gabriel Valley in the 1970s were the Chinese grocery store, DiHo Market, and *Pung Yan* Chinese restaurant, two very recognizable names representing the largest supermarket chain and a famous restaurant in Taiwan, respectively.

Concerning immigrant finance, the dominant image is immigrants sending remittances to their origin-country families and relatives. This is no exception among Chinese Americans who historically and continuously send remittance to countries of origin to support extended families, to build local infrastructure, and to finance philanthropic activities. However, what is often ignored in the era of globalization is that financial flows go both ways across the Pacific Ocean. For instance, San Gabriel Square in the San Gabriel Valley, considered the "crown jewel" of Chinese retail success, is financed by First Commercial Bank, one of the major commercial banks in Taiwan. The deal was negotiated by a Chinese banker who was the CEO of a local Chinese American bank. Indeed, transnational capital from Asia facilitated suburban transformation of residential and business landscapes in the San Gabriel Valley.[26] Similarly, the Chinese Cultural Center in Phoenix, Arizona (Fig. 10.2) is financed by COFCO, a mainland Chinese food and oil import and export company headquartered in Beijing, China.

With increasing economic globalization and China's ascendance in the world economy, increasing numbers of Chinese Americans forge business ties with China, or move back to China to conduct businesses. U.S. and other Western-educated returnees in China are called "sea turtles" (more recently "seaweeds," characterizing the increasing difficulty for them to land high-paid positions).[27] They often take their U.S. educational experiences and business practices with them, and engage in trans-Pacific business ventures. One interesting example is Ms. Zhou Zhu, a returnee from New York and hostess of a Chinese TV program showcasing an American middle-class lifestyle; she has become known as "China's Martha Stewart," while her husband remains in New York most of the time.[28] Another example is the proliferation of luxury American-style single family housing complexes in major Chinese metropolitan regions with names such as "Orange County" or "Newport Beach." There is no doubt

Figure 10.2.   Chinese Cultural Center, Phoenix, Arizona. Source: Author.

the economic connections between the two countries and beyond will further the transnational connections of Chinese Americans.

Ethnic Identity and Racialized Challenges

While Chinese Americans are an integral part of the American cultural fabric, they could not become naturalized citizens and were therefore denied legal rights, Chinese immigrants nevertheless fought against the discriminatory laws and won battles in court during the exclusion era. The 1960s civil rights movement energized Chinese Americans and as a result they sought justice through various legal means along with other racial minority groups. Chinese Americans occupy various prominent employment fields. In politics among the most notable is Elaine Chao, Secretary of Labor for the George W. Bush administration and the first Chinese American to be appointed to a cabinet-level position. Other prominent politicians include Gary Locke, a two-term governor of Washington, and David Wu, a two-term congressman from Oregon. Other leading Chinese American figures include I. M. Pei and Maya Lin (architects); T. C. Lee, C. N. Yang, Steve Chu, and Yuen T. Lee (nobel laureates); Ang Lee, Bruce Lee, Yo Yo Ma, and Anna May Wong (performing arts); Maxine Hong Kingston, Ha Jin, Amy Tan, and Iris Chang (literature); and Michelle Kwan and Michael Chang (sports).

Such accomplishments and contributions have not guaranteed the full acceptance of Chinese Americans, regardless of their citizenship status, nativity, or birth place in American society today.[29] Chinese Americans are often questioned about their loyalty to the United States, even facing hostility when the United States and Peoples' Republic of China are at odds in international geopolitics or trade. The 1982 beating death of Vincent Chin in Detroit as an ugly response to increased Japanese car imports and the 1999 wrongful charge of espionage against Taiwan-born Los Alamos nuclear scientist Wen Ho Lee are just two examples. For many first-generation Chinese and Taiwanese American scientists and entrepreneurs in the Silicon Valley area, it was not until the 1999 Wen Ho Lee case that they first realized that they too could easily become targeted as potential suspects without substantial evidence or due process. To this day, the fate of Chinese Americans varies from being perceived as a model minority or academic overachievers, to the image of perpetual foreigners or forever being the "Other." These majority-population perceptions make Chinese Americans, first and later generations alike, increasingly aware of their racial "place" in society.

As in the case of some other ethnic groups, many Chinese Americans actively seek to pass on their cultural traditions to later generations and promote their cultural heritage in American society by operating Chinese-language schools and cultural lessons, Chinese newspapers, radio and television stations, and celebrating Chinese festivals. Many first-generation adult immigrants feel nostalgia toward their countries of origin and passionately care about events there. Such endeavors, however, do not undermine their contributions and commitments to the United States, although there is room for further mutual understanding made possible with educational efforts. With the globalizing economy and society, increasing international flows of population, goods, financial resources, and information, and the rise of China's stature in the global economy and world affairs, transnational connections and identities have become a way of life for many people.

Conclusion

The Chinese were the first Asians in substantial numbers to emigrate to the United States. They were initially welcomed to fill labor shortages in the American western frontier in the mid-nineteenth century and experienced racial discrimination and scapegoating during periods of economic hardship. Cultural prejudice and racial discrimination prompted Congress to pass the 1882 Chinese Exclusion Act which lasted until 1943. This 61-year lull in Chinese labor immigration was substantially reversed only with the 1965 Immigration Act, which resulted in significant immigrant flows across the Pacific. Indeed, Chinese Americans now are the largest ethnic Asian population in the United States. Chinese immigrants are now far more economically and culturally heterogeneous than in the past in part because of their varied origins within the Chinese diaspora and the skilled labor needs of the U.S. economy during the age of globalization.

Changes in the volume and socioeconomic character of Chinese immigrants through time have expressed themselves in changing settlement patterns at both the regional and individual urban scales. While they are still highly concentrated in the greater San Francisco and New York metropolitan regions, other economically dynamic and globalized urban regions such as Los Angeles, San Diego, and Seattle have attracted large numbers of immigrants as well. Although not as substantial, growth has also taken place in the fast-growing sunbelt cities of Miami, Atlanta, Houston, and Dallas, where economic opportunities are also numerous. At the individual urban scale, settlement patterns have been transformed through time as well. Once spatially restricted to near-downtown Chinatowns, Chinese Americans have through time settled in suburban ethnoburbs where they comprise a significant minority, and also in more heterolocal suburban communities. Both of these more contemporary suburban settlement forms are linked to the increased human capital of newer immigrants, the heterogeneity of their diasporic origins, and increased family incomes based on high-tech employment or transnational investment flows associated with globalization.

The newest and largest wave of Chinese immigrants have developed complex webs of transnational activities. These include not only traditional remittances, but substantial investments in the United States that have transformed urban and suburban districts in a handful of major metropolitan regions where the Chinese American presence is strong. In the meantime Chinese Americans actively engage in investment opportunities in China. Whether in China or the United States, these transnational financial flows are often centered on property and real estate investments. The feeling of "in-betweenness" so inherent in transnational networks is heightened by frequent trans-Pacific travel and dual residences.

Despite an early immigrant presence in the United States and substantial immigrant flows during the past forty years of globalization, Chinese Americans are still sometimes viewed as the "Other," particularly in places and regions where their presence is not large. In part this distrust is tempered by the nature of political relationships between the United States and China, and despite the popular majority-population perception of Chinese Americans as the model majority. The Chinese presence in the United States will only increase as the U.S. economy becomes more spatially intertwined with Pacific Rim economic growth.

Notes

Some portions of this chapter are partially based on the following entry: Wei Li, "Chinese Americans," in *Encyclopedia of the World's Minorities*, ed. Carl Skutsch (New York: Routledge, 2004), 296–301.

I am grateful to the two editors of this volume, Chris Airriess and Ines Miyares, for their work, and to Alex Oberle and Kedi Wang of Arizona State University, and Melinda de Jesús of The California College of Arts for their invaluable assistance. Any possible remaining errors are entirely mine.

1. 2,432,585 if one-race data is used, and 2,865,232 if multi-race data is used.

2. Erika Lee, *At America's Gates: Chinese Immigration during the Exclusion Era, 1882–1943* (Chapel Hill: University of North Carolina Press, 2003).

3. The definition of "Chinese" used by the Bureau of the Census has been changed several times. During 1920–1950, the category of Chinese meant all the persons born in China, that is, Chinese immigrants. In 1960 and 1970, "Chinese" meant China-born Chinese and their offspring. From 1980 to 2000, it meant all those who identified themselves as of Chinese ancestry.

4. Chinese Historical Society of America (1994), *The Repeal and Its Legacy*, Proceedings of the Conference on the 50th Anniversary of the Repeal of the Exclusion Acts, San Francisco, CA.

5. James W. Loewen, *The Mississippi Chinese: Between Black and White*, Harvard East Asian series (Cambridge, MA: Harvard University Press, 1971).

6. Xiaojian Zhao, *Remaking Chinese America: Immigration, Family, and Community, 1940–1965* (New Brunswick, NJ: Rutgers University Press, 2002).

7. Author interview with Chinese American residents in the Phoenix area.

8. Chinese labor immigrants had very similar experiences in Latin American countries to which they immigrated.

9. Zhao, *Remaking Chinese America*.

10. There were 3,610 Chinese students and scholars enrolled in 454 colleges and universities in the United States in 1949. Many of these were supported by Nationalist government scholarships and were supposedly to return to China upon graduation. Many of them were stranded after 1949. The United States offered scholarships to these students to finish their study under the "China Area Aid Act" and provided employment and residence after their graduation. Many among this group were prominent scholars in various fields, including Nobel Physics Prize winners T. C. Lee (*Li, Zhengdao*) and C. N. Yang (*Yang, Zhenning*).

11. Note the surge of Chinese employment-based visa holders in fiscal years 1993 and 1994 after the passage of the CSPA, accounting for almost one-third of the world total.

12. H-1B is a non-immigrant visa designed for those temporary workers employed in "specialty occupations" that require highly specialized knowledge and at least a bachelor's degree or its equivalent. H-1B visa holders are allowed to bring families and are eligible to adjust their legal status to permanent residents during their six-year-maximum visa period.

13. Cindy Fan, "Chinese Americans: Immigration, Settlement, and Social Geography," in *The Chinese Diaspora: Space, Place, Mobility, and Identity,* ed. Laurence J. C. Ma and Carolyn Cartier (Lanham, MD: Rowman & Littlefield Publishers, 2003).

14. This number represents those who considered themselves as "Chinese alone" in responding to the 2000 Census.

15. If data for mixed-race Chinese are used, Hawaii ranks number three among all fifty states.

16. Data suppression prevents full disclosure of the numbers of Chinese in 2,525 out of the total 3,127 counties in the nation.

17. See, for example, Kay Anderson, *Vancouver's Chinatown Racial Discourse in Canada, 1875–1980* (Montreal: McGill-Queen's University Press, 1991); S. Craddock, "Embodying Place: Pathologizing Chinese and Chinatown in Nineteenth-century San Francisco," *Antipode* 31, no. 4 (1999): 351–371; Michael S. Laguerre, *The Global Ethnopolis Chinatown, Japantown, and Manilatown in American Society* (New York: St. Martin's Press, 2000).

18. Peter Kwong, *The New Chinatown,* rev. ed. (New York: Hill and Wang, 1996).

19. Kwong, *The New Chinatown*; Laguerre, *Global Ethnopolis*; Jan Lin, *Reconstructing Chinatown Ethnic Enclave: Global Change* (Minneapolis: University of Minnesota Press, 1998); and Min Zhou, *Chinatown: The Socioeconomic Potential of an Urban Enclave* (Philadelphia: Temple University Press, 1992).

20. Wei Li, "Anatomy of a New Ethnic Settlement: The Chinese *Ethnoburb* in Los Angeles," *Urban Studies* 35, no. 3 (1998).

21. The two terms *Lao Qiao* and *Xin Qiao* are customarily used among Chinese to refer to different waves of Chinese immigrants. In this chapter, the term *Chinese Americans* will be used most, as it encompasses both foreign-born Chinese immigrants as well as U.S.-born later generations of Chinese descendants.

22. With no one 14 years or older in the household speaking English only or fluently.

23. PMSA means Primary Metropolitan Statistical Areas.

24. Literally means "guests at Golden Mountain," representing the sojourner nature of earlier Chinese immigrants.

25. Glick, Schiller, Basch, and Blanc-Szanton, "From Immigrant to Transmigrant: Theorizing Transnational Migration," *Anthropological Quarterly* 68, no. 1 (1995): 48.

26. Wei Li, Gary Dymski, Yu Zhou, Maria Chee, and Carolyn Aldana, "Chinese American Banking and Community Development in Los Angeles County," *Annals of Association of American Geographers* 92, no. 4 (December 2002): 777–796.

27. "Sea turtles" and "seaweeds" represent "returning from overseas" and "returned from overseas but still waiting for jobs" respectively.

28. Howard W. French, "China's Martha Stewart, with Reasons to Smile," *New York Times,*

10 April 2004, 4(A), <www.nytimes.com/2004/04/10/international/asia/10profile.html?
ex=1082571265&ei=1&en=cc107cacbc66d99a>.

29. By 2000, for instance, 92 percent of all Chinese immigrants arriving before 1980, 69
percent of those arriving in the 1980s, and 18 percent of those arriving in the 1990s, were U.S.
citizens.

CHAPTER 11

Korean Culture and Entrepreneurship

Dana G. Reimer

Koreans are one of many new immigrant groups who have entered the United States in large numbers since the late 1960s.[1] Some groups, especially Asian Indians, Filipinos, and those from the Caribbean arrived in the United States with English-language skills and were able to find employment in both the public and private sectors of the mainstream economy. Other groups, however, become self-employed and operate small businesses. Indeed, there is a tradition in the United States of the association of certain retail and employment niches with specific ethnic groups—Jews with delicatessens, Italians with wholesale fruit and vegetable distribution, Germans with butcher shops, Native American Mohawks with high-rise construction, French as dry cleaners, the Irish as police officers, Indo-Pakistanis with newsstands and candy stores, Chinese with hand laundries, Greeks with coffee shops, and Eastern Europeans in the construction trades.

Today, Koreans have replaced Italians in the greengrocery business and French in the dry cleaning business; Korean women dominate the nail salon business. There is nothing surprising about the kinds of businesses that Koreans operate. They are the businesses that immigrants in America have operated for almost two hundred years—labor-intensive produce stands, convenience stores, dry cleaners, and garment factories. Koreans are relative newcomers to the United States as they did not begin to make their mark until the middle of the twentieth century. To understand Koreans in America, who they are and why they came, a brief history of Korean immigration to the United States is necessary.

Koreans as Immigrants

During the late 1800s, a small number of Korean students, political exiles, ginseng merchants, and migrant laborers began to arrive on American shores,[2] but the total number of Koreans in the United States before the twentieth century was estimated at fewer than fifty individuals. The first important period of immigration was between 1903 and 1905, when approximately 7,200 Korean laborers were contracted to work on the vast sugarcane plantations of Hawaii.[3] Most were brought in as strikebreakers to replace Japanese workers who demanded wage increases after they had served their time as contract laborers and subsequently initiated strikes in the sugarcane fields.[4]

Although the Hawaiian growers needed more Korean workers, the Japanese government in 1905 prohibited the Korean government from sending more workers to the islands. Korea had become a Japanese protectorate in 1905, the result of Japan's victory in the Sino-Japanese War and Japan's annulment of its guarantee of Korea's independence. This gave Japan the power to influence Korean emigration policy. The Japanese government wanted to stop what it perceived as anti-Japanese colonial resistance activities among the migrant Korean population and at the same time protect Japanese immigrants in the Hawaiian Islands from Korean labor competition.[5] However, approximately 2,000 additional Koreans immigrated to Hawaii and the western United States prior to legislation passed in the early 1910s that barred Korean immigration completely.

In 1922 the United States Supreme Court ruled that Japanese aliens were not eligible for citizenship. The court cited naturalization statutes dating back to 1790 that held that only free white persons and aliens of African nativity, but not Asians, were eligible for naturalization. Congress simply used the "aliens ineligible for citizenship" formula and excluded all Asians including, of course, Koreans.[6] However, between 1906 and 1924 the great majority of Koreans entering either Hawaii or the United States were "picture brides" of the first immigrants or political refugees engaged in the anti-Japanese movement in Korea.[7] After the Gentlemen's Agreement of 1907,[8] "picture brides" could immigrate but laborers were barred. Prospective bridegrooms enticed their brides, in part, with glowing accounts of the plentiful and pleasant life in Hawaii and the western United States.[9] A few students and refugees still entered, including Syngman Rhee, the future and first president of South Korea.

The United States' entry into World War II as an ally of China against Japan marked the first modification of national origin–based immigration policies. Racial and ethnic bigotry, which had led to the exclusion of Asians, began to decline in 1943 when Congress repealed the Chinese Exclusion Act. Increasing labor shortages in the United States as a result of national mobilization for World War II resulted in more and better jobs for minorities. For the first time, shipyards, aircraft plants, and other defense industries employed Asians and the foreign-born.

Beginning in late 1945, Congress made it possible for foreign-born spouses and minor children of American citizens serving in the military to enter the United States and be naturalized. Many American servicemen stationed overseas had married foreigners and now wanted to bring their new families back to the United States with them. However, some of these spouses were not able to enter the United States because they could not comply with various provisions of existing immigration laws. While what has come to be known as the War Brides Act of 1945, legislation designed to allow legal immigration to the United States of many of the foreign-born spouses,[10] was passed by Congress, servicemen marrying Asian women prior to 1947 still could not bring their wives to the United States. These women belonged to races still ineligible for immigration or naturalization. Finally, in 1952 Congress agreed to end this discriminatory legislation and changed the law. Eventually, between 1947 and 1975 over 165,839 Asian women entered the United States under the War Brides Act as amended (U.S. House 1947); among them were 28,205 Koreans.

With the outbreak of the Korean War in 1950, the United States and Korea developed close military, political, and economic ties. The relationship between the two countries helped promote the resumption of Korean immigration to the United States. The dislocations of the war and the growing ties with the United States encouraged Koreans to study abroad or emigrate. With a Korean quota of only 100 individuals, however, few could enter the United States as immigrants. As a result, most Koreans entered as non-quota spouses and children of American citizens until the passage of the 1965 Immigration Act.[11]

Over 17,000 Koreans immigrated to the United States between 1950 and 1964. Korean orphans adopted by American citizens[12] and Korean women married to U.S. servicemen stationed in South Korea comprised the vast majority of Korean immigrants during this period. The immigration of Korean children adopted by American citizens and married Korean women was expanded in the 1970s and 1980s, but has moderated since the late 1980s.[13] Although the War Brides Act expired by 1952, the elimination of racial barriers to citizenship and immigration permitted additional Asians married to American servicemen to immigrate.

The Korean population in the United States before 1970 was quite small, with fewer than 20,000 Koreans in the country. However, Korean immigration accelerated with the enactment of the 1965 Immigration Act. Korean immigrants numbered a few thousand in the 1960s, but the numbers rapidly increased by the end of the 1970s to almost 200,000 (Table 11.1). During the 1980s, the number dramatically increased again to 286,606 immigrants, making Koreans the third largest immigrant group in the decade following Mexicans and Filipinos. In the early 1990s the rate of Korean immigration dropped to less than 20,000 annually as a result of improvements in economic and political conditions in South Korea and better information about the difficulties Korean immigrants to the United States were experiencing.[14] Overall, however, the 1990s saw a slight increase in total Korean immigration to a decadal total of 311,733. This represented an increase from the 1980s in the actual numbers of Korean immigrants but a decrease in Koreans as a percentage of foreign-born immigrants (Table 11.1).

The influx of Korean immigrants over the last quarter of the twentieth century led to a marked growth in the Korean American population in the United States. The 1990 census enumerated approximately 800,000 Koreans in the United States, with those

Table 11.1.   Korean Immigration as a Percent of Total Post-1965 Immigration

Years	Total U.S. Immigrants	Total Korean Immigrants	Koreans as a Percentage of Total U.S. Immigrants
Prior to 1969		17,869	
1970 to 1979	4,235,328	233,090	5.5
1980 to 1989	6,332,218	337,981	5.2
1990 to 2000	13,178,276	311,733	2.4

Source: U.S. Census Bureau, "Sex by Year of Entry for the Foreign-Born Population," published April 21, 2002, <factfinder.census.gov/servlet/DTCharIterationServlet?_ts=157317927192>.

born in the United States making up 28 percent of the total. In contrast, the 2000 census counted 1,072,682 Koreans, an increase of almost 25 percent over 1990, of which 22.3 percent were native-born. While the immigration flow from other Asian countries increased in the 1990s, Korean immigration substantially declined during the same period. The Korean population, like the Japanese, will make up a smaller and smaller fraction of the future Asian American population. Indeed, Korea was ranked the seventh most important immigrant source country between 1980 and 1989, but slipped to fifteenth during the 1990–2000 period.

Dynamics of Immigration

The Immigration Reform Act of 1965 admitted aliens as legal immigrants using the three criteria of immigration based on family unification (having a relative in the United States), occupational immigration (possession of an occupational skill needed in the United States), and refugee immigration (vulnerability to political persecution). Few Koreans have immigrated to the United States as political refugees, because refugee status has usually been awarded to aliens in Communist and formerly Communist countries. As a result, almost all Korean immigrants have come to the United States as relatives of those already settled here or on the basis of the Dual Market Theory in that their occupational skills were in demand in the U.S. labor market.[15] With regard to the first motive, the U.S. Congress believed family reunification would be a conservative change in immigration law. There were no long lines for travel visas to the United States at Asian embassies and consulates because of the historically restrictive immigration policies. The second motive of economic and occupational opportunity is equally as important. The educated middle class in Korea realized that despite their education and skills, employment opportunities were not substantial in their own country. To many Koreans, wages and working conditions appeared better in America. Moreover, the unstable political and social conditions of Korea in the middle of the twentieth century and worries about the future prompted many to leave.[16]

The momentum to emigrate is based, however, on more than simple economics or political instability. Knowledge, too, is an equally important factor. In the period after World War II information about America became more readily available than ever before and penetrated deeply into the psyches of people in some developing nations.[17] But the question of why any specific individual emigrates remains unclear. Koreans do not emigrate because they are unable to physically or economically survive in their home country, but primarily because they dream of America. This dream was especially true of the early wave of immigrants between 1965 and 1976. While the later wave, from 1976 to the present, has additional reasons for emigrating to the United States, the vast majority of immigrants are both charmed and enchanted by the picture of an America they learned from both the Korean and American media. In Korea, this is described as "American fever."[18]

Individual motives alone, economic or noneconomic, cannot fully explain the substantial migration of Koreans to the United States before 1990. Korea sent the second largest immigrant group (following the Philippines) among Asian countries to the

United States in the 1980s. This migration can be explained, in part, by the military, political, and economic connections between the United States and Korea that were firmly established during the Korean War. While never a colonial possession of the United States, World Systems Theory partially explains this migration flow across the Pacific. But it was also American Christian missionaries who first established western-style schools and hospitals in Korea at the end of the nineteenth and beginning of the twentieth centuries that promoted migration. These cumulative connections have had a profound cultural influence in Korea. The long-term presence of U.S. military forces with their television station has also had a strong cultural influence, encouraging middle-class Koreans in the last two decades to choose the United States as their emigrant destination country.[19]

Post-1965 Korean immigrants to the United States are primarily economic immigrants who cross the Pacific to improve their economic status and opportunities. Although economic immigrants are largely motivated to come to the United States by a higher standard of living than that available in their home country, their motives for immigration are still complex. Many Koreans chose to immigrate to the United States to give their children a better opportunity for education, particularly a college education.[20] This motive may be more important than the purely economic motive for many Korean immigrants in the last two decades of the twentieth century because South Korea had already achieved economic prosperity.

Settlement Patterns

The United States census classified Koreans as a distinct group for the first time in 1970. Earlier, Koreans were included in the "other Asian" category. According to the 1970 census, there were 70,598 Koreans in the United States. By 1980, that number increased to 357,393 and Korean Americans accounted for 10.3 percent of all Asian Americans.[21] The 1990 census counted 798,849, and the 2000 census counted 1,072,682 or 10.7 percent of Asian Americans. Koreans were the fifth most numerous Asian American group in 2000.

Like many other ethnic groups, the settlement pattern and distribution of Koreans is spatially uneven (Map 11.1). At the geographical level of the state in 2000, the states of California (32.5%), New York (11.2%), and New Jersey (6.1%) account for 49.9 percent of Koreans in the United States. Primarily a large urban-place population, the distribution of Koreans is very much bicoastal in that the coalesced greater New York–Philadelphia–Washington, D.C., urban region accounts for 28 percent of the national total, and the spatially discontiguous West Coast cities of San Diego–greater Los Angeles–San Francisco–Portland and Seattle account for 38 percent of the national total. With 34,536 Koreans in 2000, Chicago is the only interior city with a substantial Korean population.

In California and New York, Koreans are highly concentrated in Los Angeles and New York City respectively. Koreans in Los Angeles County account for 53.8 percent of the state's total. More suburban Orange County just to the south accounts for 16 percent, and Santa Clara County at the southern end of San Francisco Bay is a distant

Map 11.1.   Distribution of Koreans by County, 2000.
Source: 2000 Census of Population and Housing.

third at 6.2 percent of the state total. In New York, the five counties (boroughs) comprising New York City account for 71.4 percent of the state's total Korean population.

The growth of the Korean population during 1990–2000 reveals some discernable spatial patterns, particularly with reference to the relative decline of population growth in older urban residential areas in favor of less dense inner and outer suburban areas. At the national scale, the Korean population increased by 34.2 percent between 1990 and 2000. California's growth kept pace during the decadal period with 33 percent growth. Los Angeles County, however, did not match this decadal growth rate with only 28 percent growth, while more suburban Orange County increased dramatically by 54 percent. At 28 percent, New York's growth rate also slipped relative to the national growth rate of the Korean population. Closer inspection of the five counties (boroughs) of New York City as well as the two spatially contiguous Long Island suburban counties of Nassau and Suffolk reveals a discernable changing settlement pattern between 1990 and 2000. In the densely populated counties of New York (Manhattan), Bronx, and Kings (Brooklyn), growth rates were 13 percent, but in the inner and outer suburban counties of Queens, Richmond (Staten Island), Nassau, and Suffolk, growth was more than double at 28 percent. Indeed, the inner suburban county of Queens accounts for 63 percent of the Korean population of these seven counties. Koreans also account for 25 percent of all Asian groups in Queens. This increasing suburbanization of Koreans is evidenced in adjacent New Jersey which experienced a 1990–2000 growth of 69 percent with much of that growth in Northern New Jersey.

Pennsylvania's Korean population, particularly in Philadelphia, declined by 16 percent between 1990 and 2000. Virginia's Korean population increased by 50 percent, primarily in the burgeoning suburbs of Northern Virginia, adjacent to Washington, D.C. In contrast, Cook County anchored by Chicago experienced only a 16 percent increase. The growth of the Korean population between 1990 and 2000 in the large urban regions of the "sunbelt" or economically dynamic states illustrates the attractiveness of economic opportunities. Georgia's Korean population experienced an amazing 88 percent growth rate between 1990 and 2000, Texas's 36.5 percent, and Washington's 57 percent.

Socioeconomic Contours

Recent Korean immigrants are generally drawn from the middle class, and this is reflected by educational attainment (Table 11.2). Almost 44 percent of Korean immigrants 25 years of age or older completed four years of college, and 86 percent had completed high school. By contrast, 24 percent of the native-born American population received a college education, and 80 percent completed high school. Moreover, recent Korean immigrants far surpass the educational level of the general population of Korea; in 1990, for example, only 14 percent of Korean adults had completed four years of college education.[22] Considering these high levels of educational attainment. the use of English is relatively low as some 50 percent of Koreans in the United States do not speak English very well and slightly greater than 80 percent speak Korean at home (Table 11.2).

Despite high levels of educational attainment, Koreans are less well represented in higher-income employment comprising management, professional, and related occupations (Table 11.2). While only 27.5 percent of Koreans 16 years and older are classified as being employed in management, professional, and related occupations when compared to the U.S. total of 33.6 percent, there do exist strong gender differences: while 43.4 percent of Korean males are employed in these occupations, Korean female participation is only 12.1 percent (Table 11.2). This stands in stark contrast to the total Asian American population where male participation in management, professional, and related occupations stands at 47 percent, but female participation is substantially higher at 41.7 percent. Perhaps reflecting the relative absence of females in these higher-income employment opportunities is median family income. For Koreans in 1999, median family income stood at $47,624, which is slightly lower when compared to the United States as a whole ($50,046) (Table 11.2), but significantly lower when compared to Asian American families in general ($59,324). It is interesting to note, however, that most recent Korean immigrants held professional white-collar jobs before they emigrated from Korea. Surveys in Chicago[23] and in Los Angeles[24] indicated that more than half their pre-immigration occupations had been professional, administrative, managerial, or technical in nature. Medical professionals are an excellent example. In the 1965 to 1974 period, 75,000 foreign physicians entered the United States either to work temporarily or to practice medicine on a permanent basis. In New York City in the mid-1970s, Asian immigrant doctors made up more than half of the interns in

Table 11.2.   Selected Socioeconomic Characteristics of Korean Americans, 2000

Characteristics	U.S.	Koreans in America
Total Persons	281,421,906	1,072,682
Language Persons 5 years & older, % Speak a language other than English at home	17.9	81.9
Do not speak English very well	8.1	50.1
Educational Attainment (Persons 25 years old & over, %) High school graduate or higher	80.4	86.3
Bachelor's degree or higher	24.4	43.8
Income ($) Per capita	21,587	18,805
Median household	41,994	40,037
Median family	50,046	47,624
Occupation (%) Management, professional, and related occupations	33.6	27.5
Male	—	43.4
Female	—	12.1

Source: 2000 Census of Population and Housing.

municipal hospitals, and 80 percent at voluntary hospitals such as Brooklyn Hospital. A large number of these doctors were Korean.[25]

The historical context is important to explain the employment niche in health services. Presbyterian missionaries introduced Western medicine to Korea in the late nineteenth century. Medical colleges were soon established and the Korean War further stimulated the practice of Western-style medicine. After the Korean War, American cultural and philanthropic organizations and educational and scientific exchange programs helped diffuse Western medical practices in Korea. Some pre-1965 medical college graduates entered the United States to work temporarily in American hospitals. The Immigration Reform Act of 1965 opened the door for this large trans-Pacific movement of Korean medical professionals to the United States; Koreans were second only to Filipinos in terms of the number of health care professionals.[26] In addition, a large number of Korean nurses also immigrated to the United States coupled with a small number of dentists, pharmacists, and other medical professionals. Conforming to Dual Market Theory, inner-city hospitals were experiencing shortages of nurses, and they turned to Korea as a source of professional labor. Nurses were eager to emigrate because of the oversupply of nurses in Korea or because of the better working conditions and higher wages in American hospitals. It was relatively easy for nurses to get licenses, and like Filipinos, many quickly answered the recruitment advertisements of American hospitals.[27]

The Korean American Dream

Before emigrating, Koreans, like many economic immigrants, have preconceived ideas about America. They come with dreams and ideas about how American society works. Kyeyoung Park found that until recently, Koreans had a rosy picture of America as a free and equal society with a clean, safe environment where everybody is publicly civil.[28] The Korean American dream includes several themes, the most powerful of which is that the individual will be rewarded in proportion to how hard he or she works (*norŏkŭi taekka*). This theme, of course, is not particular to Korean immigrant culture. The myth embodies the American ideal of success—wealth and power—and suggests that hard work is a simple way of achieving this goal. Koreans, however, understand the American dream from a purely Korean perspective. For them, success following hard work represents the natural order of things. Koreans interpret reward according to cultural ideas of cause and effect and worthiness. This conception of U.S. society is closely related to the Korean position in the U.S. labor market as part of the *petite bourgeoisie*. Because many Koreans in the United States own small businesses, they feel that their earnings correspond to how hard they work. For instance, they can make more money if they work sixteen-hour days instead of eight-hour days. Their perspective is also related to the ideology of individualism in American society.[29]

The idea of freedom and equality is another theme foremost in the minds of Korean immigrants to the United States. In research by both Park[30] and Tom Bottomore,[31] the Korean conception of freedom is the result of liberal political and Marxist theories—freedom as the absence of interference, oppression, or coercion. Undoubtedly not all Koreans think alike because class, background, gender, and personal experience in the United States influence the ideals and aspirations of immigrants.

Culture, Religion, and Ethnicity

Because few societies are as culturally and historically homogeneous as Korea, this condition provides a strong basis for identity and solidarity in the United States. Unlike other Asian immigrants such as the Chinese, Asian Indians, and Filipinos that have more than one national language, Koreans' single language helps to cement a more homogeneous ethnic identity in the United States. Korean literacy is almost one hundred percent, and in the United States many Korean immigrants depend primarily on Korean-language daily newspapers and Korean-language television and radio programs for news and information. In turn, this dependency on ethnic media strengthens ties within the ethnic community as well as with Korea. The result is that many first-generation Koreans experience relatively low rates of adaptation to mainstream American society.[32]

Recent Korean immigrants are characterized by both their urban[33] and Christian backgrounds. Although only 25 percent of Koreans are affiliated with Christian churches in South Korea,[34] most Korean immigrants practiced Christianity in Korea, a country dominated by Buddhism and Confucianism. There is thus a disproportionate representation of Christians among Korean immigrants in the United States.[35] The vast majority of Korean immigrants are affiliated with Korean Christian churches. Involvement in ethnic churches provides immigrants the religious basis for Korean ethnic ties, and thus functions as a source of ethnic identity. Not all who are associated with Christian churches, however, are actually Christian. Many are "pragmatic" Christians, who attend church to meet other Koreans and to speak their native language. Korean Christian church congregations thus serve as important social institutions for immigrants.[36] Korean immigrants typically do not live in concentrated ethnic enclaves, but they are able to make friends and business contacts through participation in Korean church services and other church-sponsored activities. Today there are close to 2,500 Korean ethnic churches in the United States providing spiritual, emotional, and social support, but also networking opportunities for both the pragmatic and committed Christian alike.[37] This is an ideal example of a heterolocally dispersed ethnic population being able to retain a sense of community and identity.

Korean churches offer an intense experience for churchgoers with almost the entirety of Sunday given over to a combination of worship and social activities. Korean small-business success is, in part, promoted by church-sponsored activities. Often church members organize rotating credit clubs or *kye* through their churches. Members network to help secure employment or information on business opportunities.[38] Church members also exchange information concerning housing, educational, and recreational opportunities. Korean churches also help in the persistence of many Korean cultural traditions. Churches provide language instruction and other cultural programs for children, teach traditional Korean values, and celebrate important Korean holidays. In their effort to sustain Korean ethnicity and identity through Christian churches, Korean immigrants have significantly "Koreanized" Christianity.[39]

The rise of Korean American Christianity has thus contributed to the decline of Confucian family rituals and values. While the majority of Koreans in the United States are Christian, the Chinese Confucian cultural tradition has had a deep influence on Korean society. An understanding of the influence of Confucianism is important to understanding traditional Korean culture and family dynamics. Confucius formulated several important principles for followers to adhere to for harmonious social relations. The foundations of his teachings are five categories of interpersonal relations centered on teaching the duties and obligations of each individual and their relationships with everyone else, from friends and siblings to children and parents.

Confucius taught that parents and children should maintain a mutual attitude of benevolence. Confucianism, as applied to the Korean family system and social life, demands adherence to the Confucian ethic of filial piety. Korean children are expected to take care of their parents and show great concern and devotion to their elders. The eldest son is expected to make his home with his parents after marriage, ensuring financial support and care as they age. This devotion to parents extends after death in the form of ancestor worship, and filial piety is still considered one of the central tenets of contemporary Korean culture, both in Korea and the United States. Confucianism emphasizes a clear role differentiation between husband and wife that has survived immigration almost intact. In traditional Korean society the husband is considered the primary breadwinner and decision-maker in the family and exercises authority over his wife and children. It is not surprising, then, that a Korean wife is expected to obey her husband, serving him and his family members, and to perpetuate her husband's family line by producing children. She is excluded from decision-making in important family affairs, including her children's education.[40]

Under the influence of this Confucian cultural tradition, education is highly valued in Korean families. This emphasis on education may stem from traditional Confucian respect for learning as a path to economic security, a better life, and a higher social status. In South Korea, colleges and universities accept only a small fraction of high school graduates each year, so competition for college admission is fierce. Similar to the experience of middle- and upper-class families in the United States, Korean families will often undergo extreme financial hardship to provide their children with additional academic tutoring and extracurricular activities after school. Parental expectations and aspirations, coupled with a test-oriented high school curriculum and a very limited number of places in colleges and universities, are seen as the root causes of many social problems in Korea. This cultural baggage of Korean daily life has accompanied Korean immigrants to the United States.[41]

Koreans as Small-Scale Entrepreneurs

When compared to Korean immigrant entrepreneurs, most new immigrant proprietors operate businesses within their own ethnic communities.[42] Korean entrepreneurs, however, do not necessarily serve a co-ethnic customer base. Explanations of immigrants' incentives for entrepreneurship, particularly in the case of Koreans, have emphasized labor market disadvantage theory, which sees Asian immigrants as pushed into self-employment because of limited English-language skills and/or the refusal of private employers or public agencies to recognize the educational and occupational credentials earned in their home countries.[43] Unlike some other immigrants, especially Asian Indians, Filipinos, and those from the Caribbean, Koreans arrive with very limited English-language skills. Some researchers claim that other disadvantages such as poverty, unemployment, underemployment, and discrimination in general push some immigrants to turn to self-employment.[44] Those immigrants with cultural capital successfully enter small business. Others, unable to obtain well-paying, secure jobs in the primary labor market, are faced with choices between self-employment in petty trade (street peddling) or illegal enterprises, unstable, low-paying menial jobs in the secondary labor market, or entrepreneurship.

Today, studies show that nearly half of all Korean immigrant workers are self-employed, with 30 percent working for Korean-owned businesses.[45] This has led not only to the persistence of language, culture, and tradition, but also to a high level of self-segregation that has delayed substantial adaptation to mainstream culture. For Korean immigrants, the introduction to self-employment in the United States first came with entry into the wig business in minority neighborhoods. Existing American businesses were unable to meet the demand for wigs with domestic production. Korean hair, once derided for its very dark color and thick texture, began to be imported by Koreans as a cheaper substitute for European hair. However, the wig business went into decline in the mid-1970s in large part because of the recession of 1971 and a change in

American fashion. This decline is also explained by severe intra-ethnic competition among Korean wig retailers.[46] With their accumulated capital and business experience, Korean immigrants shifted into more-capital-intensive businesses, such as service stations, garment manufacturing, dry cleaning, and grocery stores.

Racial conflict has unfortunately accompanied the rise of Korean-owned small business. In the borough of Queens in New York City in the mid-1980s several Korean businessmen were assaulted by police officers.[47] These incidents were preceded in 1982 in Harlem, Brooklyn, and Queens with conflicts between Korean shopowners and African Americans, usually over charges of shoplifting. The Harlem incident resulted in a boycott of Korean greengrocers for six months. Spike Lee's film *Do the Right Thing* forcefully depicts the deep mistrust between the two communities. The climax of Korean–African American conflict came during the Los Angeles riots of 1992. Approximately 2,300 Korean-owned businesses in South Central Los Angeles and Koreatown were damaged or destroyed, primarily by arson and/or looting, totaling more than $350 million in damage. Many of these businesses never recovered. The failure of the police to protect them and of the government to financially help them rebuild has bred long-lasting resentment. Pyong Gap Min[48] believes that while Korean merchants in New York City and Los Angeles felt victimized because of their race, the experience strengthened Korean immigrant solidarity and awakened a new political consciousness.[49] Many Koreans realized that it was not enough to be hardworking small-business owners, but they must work harder to participate in the political and social structures of their new country.

The literature on ethnic and gendered economies, entrepreneurship, and labor markets has focused primarily on the male Korean immigrant experience— who he is, his language skills, his level of education, how he votes, how he makes his living and supports his family, why he came to the United States—as the male-centered terms that are employed clearly indicate. The very term *middleman minority*,[50] the primary theoretical perspective applied to Korean entrepreneurs in the United States, presupposes a gender bias. Middleman minorities occupy an intermediate position not only in their social status, but also in their economic roles. They concentrate in trade, commerce, and other middleman occupations which connect producer and consumer, employer and employee, owner and renter, elite and the masses. Alejandro Portes and R. D. Manning coined the term *labor paternalism* to refer to a system of obligations based on kinship and friendship networks.[51] Kang suggests that researchers might expand these concepts to middle*women* minorities and labor *maternalism* to illuminate the experiences of women entrepreneurs.[52]

Many Korean immigrant women become self-employed entrepreneurs, yet their contributions are often hidden under the label of "unpaid family labor" instead of being counted as independent entrepreneurs. This gender invisibility is because women are usually not the legal owners of their establishments or because they have been categorized as dependents of their spouses. All immigrant women in the United States, however, make a significant contribution to the family economy. Indeed, it is very difficult for a Korean man to remain single and save enough to start his own business without the extra income from a working wife. In fact, wives are considered an economically valuable asset. This is a transformation of origin-country gender roles where women generally work before marriage but leave the work force once they marry.

In the United States, Korean women most often begin as wage workers outside the home and then join the family businesses established by spouses. As a result, Korean women find themselves holding down not one, but two full-time jobs—work in the family business in partnership with their spouses and work at home. While working in a family business can maximize income for the family, it removes Korean women from the outside labor market and increases their dependence on their husbands and isolation from mainstream society. In the traditional home, even Christian Koreans live by the Confucian ideal of *namŏn, yŏbi*—"men are honored, women are abased." In Korea, this has traditionally restricted the participation of Korean women in the work force, but changing gender roles in the United States coupled with the growth of female-intensive work in the service, health care, microelectronics, and apparel industries has created greater employment opportunities for Asian immigrant women relative to men.

In general, immigrant women employed in the United States as wage workers outside their homes or as business owners gain greater personal freedom and independence. This frequently leads to greater female control over household budgeting and domestic decision-making. This advantage makes women co-providers or in some cases even primary providers. In contrast, some researchers have found that most immigrant working-class families continue to exhibit some forms of traditional family structure emphasizing male authority and female subjugation.

Community Case Study—Female-Owned Nail Salons in New York City

While it is true that Korean immigrant women are wives and mothers, they are also workers and businesswomen responsible for the support of themselves and their families. Out of economic necessity many Korean women have become entrepreneurs and thus have responded to the disadvantages inherent in being Asian in a predominantly non-Asian country, to limited English-language skills, and to educational credentials that are dismissed. The significance here is that they have created an avenue for economic mobility not only for themselves but also for co-ethnic later arrivals. In other words, Korean women hire and promote other Korean women.

Korean immigrant women have created an innovative entrepreneurial niche in New York City that provides a significant source of small business ownership and employment that contributes to the increasing economic prosperity of the Korean American community. There are more than 500 Korean-owned manicure salons in the five boroughs of New York City. These establishments provide a secure source of employment and income for new immigrants while providing what was once a luxury item, the manicure and pedicure, to a highly diverse population. A manicure is no longer something a woman gives herself in the privacy of her own home. Rather, it is something she increasingly purchases in a nail salon. In the purchase of these services women expand the boundaries of the service economy to include formerly private regimes of personal hygiene.

Figure 11.1.   Two examples of Korean nail salons in Manhattan. Source: Author.

The late 1970s saw the establishment of the first Korean-owned and -operated nail salons (Fig. 11.1). The women who opened these salons did not find a pre-existing economic niche into which they could enter so they created their own. In doing so, they made a unique place for themselves in their new New York City home. They found it easy to enter this business because there were no pre-existing businesses like theirs to exert competitive resistance. The first Korean woman to open a nail salon remains unknown, but the early pioneers were most likely wives of Korean students or professionals or students themselves with professional aspirations. But this innovator, or perhaps innovators, took considerable initiative and risk and paved the way for other Korean women to enter the workforce. However, this unique enterprise could not be successful without a steady supply of women who are dedicated nailcare customers with the disposable income necessary to purchase the services offered by nail salons.

Disadvantage theory only in part explains entrance into the nail salon business. While it is true that virtually all the owners and workers were far from fluent in English, and that many of them had been professionals in their homeland prior to emigration to the United States, disadvantage theory cannot be relied upon as the sole explanation for their entrepreneurship or their decision to work as manicurists. Other factors, such as the desire to be free of spousal domination, more-flexible childcare opportunities, the attraction of working with other Korean women, and a desire to realize their own American dream of small business ownership, were contributing factors. As a result, Korean women have gained increased personal power within their families and communities as well as provided earnings for workers through wages and tips and even income and social status for owners.

Conclusion

Today there are over one million Koreans in the United States, and those who emigrated are primarily drawn from the educated middle class with white-collar employment experience in their home country. More than 43 percent of Korean immigrants over the age of 25 have at least a bachelor's degree and 86 percent are high school graduates, a greater proportion than the native-born American population. The vast majority of Korean immigrants are Christian although a Chinese Confucian tradition permeates their everyday lives.

Many Koreans in the United States own and operate the same kinds of labor-intensive businesses that have characterized immigrant self-employment in the past. And like every immigrant group before them, Koreans have arrived with their own version of the American dream. In the United States, Korean women waited, watched, and then emulated their self-employed fathers, brothers, and husbands. One example of female entrepreneurship is nail salons in New York City that have allowed them to gain substantial economic power. Some have gained personal freedom, in effect emancipating themselves from the patriarchal Confucian culture of their homeland. However, the majority appear to have compromised, and thus combine entrepreneurship with the somewhat modified traditional role of worker, wife, and mother. Ultimately, both Korean men and women find themselves becoming more and more like their native-born neighbors, working hard to find a balance in their lives between work and family and realizing the American dream.

Transnational dynamics among Koreans in the United States seem to be limited to Korean multinational corporations,[53] with attempts to mobilize the Korean community nationally as "overseas Koreans,"[54] and sending children ahead of parents as "parachute kids" to take advantage of educational opportunities in the United States.[55] Among the second generation, "transnational" activities may include learning to speak Korean or learning aspects of Korean culture that may have been abandoned by their parents in pursuit of being accepted as American.[56] Even U.S.-based Korean American political movements and Korean-language media are focused on facilitating incorporation and empowerment as a Korean American community.[57] Unlike many new immigrant groups to the United States that maintain strong ties to their home countries, Koreans seem to be traditional unidirectional immigrants. The greater focus seems to be on success in realizing the American dream, a goal that has attracted immigrants for two and a half centuries.

Notes

1. Unless otherwise explicitly stated, "Korean" and "Korea" in the context of this chapter refer to residents and former residents of the Republic of Korea, also known as South Korea.

2. Won Moo Hurh and Kwang Chung Kim, *Korean Immigrants in America: A Structural Analysis of Ethnic Confinement and Adhesive Adaptation* (Madison, NJ: Fairleigh Dickinson University Press, 1984).

3. Norris Hundley, ed., *The Asian American: The Historical Experience* (Santa Barbara, CA: American Bibliography Center, CLIO Press, 1976); Wayne Patterson, *The Korean Frontier in America: Immigration to Hawaii, 1886–1910* (Honolulu: University of Hawaii Press, 1998).

4. Patterson, *The Korean Frontier in America*.

5. Kyeyoung Park, *The Korean-American Dream: Immigrants and Small Business in New York City* (Ithaca, NY: Cornell University Press, 1997).

6. Ronald Takaki, *Strangers from a Different Shore: A History of Asian Americans* (Boston: Little, Brown, 1989).

7. Pyong Gap Min, *Changes and Conflicts: Korean Immigrant Families in New York* (New York: Allyn and Bacon, 1998).

8. The Gentlemen's Agreement was an agreement between the United States and Japan in 1907 that Japan should stop the emigration of its laborers to the United States and that the United States should stop discrimination against the Japanese. The "gentlemanly" part of the agreement involved the willingness of the Japanese to keep citizens from immigrating to the United States if the United States would abstain from making anti-Japanese immigration laws. The agreement was ended in 1924 by the act of Congress excluding immigration from Japan, just as immigration from China had been previously excluded.

9. B. B. H. Kim, "The Koreans in Hawaii," *Social Science* 9, no. 4 (October 1934): 409–413; David M. Reimers, *Still the Golden Door: The Third World Comes to America*, 2nd ed. (New York: Columbia University Press, 1992).

10. Marion Tinsley Bennett, *American Immigration Policies: A History* (Washington: Public Affairs Press, 1963).

11. Reimers, *Still the Golden Door*.

12. Congress has periodically enacted legislation to permit Americans to adopt foreign orphans. In 1983, for example, the legislators made it possible for Americans to adopt Amerasian children in Korea and Indochina. These were the children left behind by American soldiers who had fathered them. See J. Bauermeiser, "Amerasians in America," *America* 147 (17 November 1982): 331–333.

13. Howard Brett Melendy, *The Oriental Americans* (Boston: Twayne Publishing, 1972); Pyong Gap Min, "The Korean-American Family," in *Ethnic Families in America,* ed. Charles H. Mindel, Robert W. Habenstein, and Roosevelt Wright Jr., 4th ed. (Upper Saddle River, NJ: Prentice Hall, 1998).

14. Min, "The Korean-American Family."

15. Pyong Gap Min and Young I. Song, "Demographic Characteristics and Trends of Post-1965 Korean Immigrant Women and Men," in *Korean American Women: From Tradition to Modern Feminism,* ed. Ailee Moon (Westport, CT: Praeger, 1998).

16. Reimers, *Still the Golden Door*.

17. Charles H. Mindel, Robert W. Habenstein, and Roosevelt Wright Jr., "Diversity among America's Ethnic Minorities," in *Ethnic Families in America*, ed. Charles H. Mindel, Robert W. Habenstein, and Roosevelt Wright Jr., 4th ed. (Upper Saddle River, NJ: Prentice Hall, 1988).

18. Park, *The Korean-American Dream*.

19. Ivan Light and Edna Bonacich, *Immigrant Entrepreneurs: Koreans in Los Angeles, 1965–1982* (Berkeley: University of California Press, 1988); Pyong Gap Min, "Korean Americans," in *Asian Americans: Contemporary Trends and Issues,* ed. Pyong Gap Min (Newbury Park, CA: Sage Publications, 1995), 199–231. World Systems Theory is a sociological perspective that seeks to explain the dynamics of the capitalist world economy as a total social system. It was first

introduced by Immanuel Wallerstein in his seminal 1974 paper entitled *The Rise and Future Demise of the World Capitalist System: Concepts for Comparative Analysis* (New York: Academic Press) and subsequently in 1976's *The Modern World System I: Capitalist Agriculture and the Origins of the European World-Economy in the Sixteenth Century* (New York: Academic Press).

20. Pyong Gap Min, "Korean Americans"; In-Jin Yoon, *The Social Origin of Korean Immigration to the United States from 1965 to the Present* (Honolulu: East-West Population Institute, 1993).

21. Robert Waterman Gardner, Bryant Robey, and Peter C. Smith, *Asian Americans: Growth, Change and Diversity* (Washington: Population Reference Bureau, 1985).

22. Pyong Gap Min, *Changes and Conflicts: Korean Immigrant Families in New York* (New York: Allyn and Bacon, 1998).

23. Won Moo Hurh and Kwang Chang Kim, "Uprooting and Adjustment: A Sociological Study of Korean Immigrants' Mental Health," final report submitted to the National Institute of Mental Health, U.S. Department of Health and Human Services.

24. Min, "Korean Americans."

25. Rosemary Stevens, Louis Wolf Goodman, and Stephen S. Mick, *The Alien Doctors: Foreign Medical Graduates in American Hospitals* (New York: Wiley & Sons, 1978).

26. Illsoo Kim, *New Urban Immigrants: The Korean Community in New York City* (Princeton: Princeton University Press, 1981).

27. U.S. Department of Education, Office of Educational Research and Improvement, *Conference on the Education and Occupational Needs of Asian-Pacific Women* (Washington: General Publishing Office, 1980).

28. Park, *The Korean-American Dream.*

29. Park, *The Korean-American Dream.*

30. Park, *The Korean-American Dream.*

31. Tom Bottomore, ed., *A Dictionary of Marxist Thought* (Cambridge, MA: Harvard University Press, 1983).

32. Min, *Changes and Conflicts.*

33. Insook Han Park, J. Fawcett, F. Arnold, and Rosemary Gardner, "Korean Immigrants and U.S. Immigration Policy: A Pre-Departure Perspective," in *Papers of the East-West Population Institute,* no. 114 (Honolulu: East-West Center, 1990).

34. Insook Han Park and Lee-Jay Cho, "Confucianism and the Korean Family," *Journal of Comparative Family Studies* 24(1995):117–134.

35. Min, *Changes and Conflicts.*

36. Park, *The Korean-American Dream.*

37. L. I. Kim, "The Mental Health of Korean American Women," in *Korean American Women: From Tradition to Modern Feminism,* ed. Young I. Song and Ailee Moon (Westport, CT: Praeger, 1998).

38. Park, *The Korean-American Dream.*

39. Park, *The Korean-American Dream.*

40. Reimers, *Still the Golden Door;* K. C. Kim, Won Moo Hurh, and M. Fernandez, "Beyond Assimilation and Pluralism: Syncretic Sociocultural Adaption of Korean Immigrants in the U.S.," *Ethnic and Racial Studies* 16, no. 4(1993): 666–713.

41. Min, *Changes and Conflicts.*

42. Park, *The Korean-American Dream.*

43. Ivan Light, *Ethnic Enterprise in America: Business and Welfare among Chinese, Japanese and Blacks* (Berkeley: University of California Press, 1972); Jimmy Sanders and Victor Nee, "Limits of Ethnic Solidarity in the Ethnic Enclave Economy," *American Sociological Review* 54 (1987): 809–820; K. C. Kim, Won Moo Hurh, and M. Fernandez, "Intra-group Differences in Business

Participation: Three Asian Immigrant Groups," *International Migration Review* 23 (1989): 73–94.

44. Edna Bonacich, "A Theory of Middleman Minorities," *American Sociological Review* 38 (October 1973): 583–594.

45. Min, "The Korean-American Family"; Hurh and Kim, "Adhesive Sociocultural Adaptation," *International Migration Review* 18, no. 2 (1984): 188–216.

46. Yoon, *The Social Origin of Korean Immigration*.

47. Park, *The Korean-American Dream*.

48. Min, *Changes and Conflicts*.

49. Paul K. Ong, Kyeyoung Park, and Yasmin Tong, "The Korean-Black Conflict and the State," in *The New Asian Immigration in Los Angeles and Global Restructuring*, ed. Paul Ong, Edna Bonacich, and L. Cheng (Philadelphia: Temple University Press, 1994), 264–294.

50. Edna Bonacich, "A Theory of Middleman Minorities," *American Sociological Review* (October 1973): 583–594.

51. Alejandro Portes and R. D. Manning, "The Immigrant Enclave: Theory and Empirical Examples," in *Majority and Minority*, ed. Norman R. Yetman (Needham Heights, MA: Allyn and Bacon, 1986).

52. Millie Kang, "Manicuring Interactions: Race, Gender and Class in New York City Korean-Owned Nail Salons," Ph.D. diss., Columbia University, 2001.

53. Steven Vertovec, "Migrant Transnationalism and Modes of Transformation," Center for Migration and Development Working Paper #03–09m (May 2003).

54. Steven Vertovec, "Conceiving and Researching Transnationalism," *Ethnic and Racial Studies* 22, no. 2 (1999): 447–462.

55. Vertovec, "Migrant Transnationalism."

56. Jonathan D. Hill and Thomas M. Wilson, "New Identities," *Identities: Global Studies in Culture and Power* 9 (2002): 1–6.

57. Edward J. W. Park, "Friends or Enemies? Generational Politics in the Korean American Community in Los Angeles," *Qualitative Sociology* 22, no. 2 (1999): 161–175.

CHAPTER 12

Filipinos: The Invisible Ethnic Community

James A. Tyner

With a population of over 1.8 million in 2000, Filipinos and Filipino Americans constitute the second largest Asian group in the United States. And yet, historically, their presence is not as immediately felt or acknowledged when compared to other ethnic groups. In part, this "invisibility" is attributable to the lack of well-defined ethnic landscapes in that there are generally no distinguishing "Little Manilas" comparable to San Francisco's "Chinatown" or Los Angeles's "Little Tokyo." Filipinos in the United States, moreover, increasingly identify themselves in more global terms, as part of a larger Philippine diaspora that spans the world. The "spaces" of ethnic Filipinos, therefore, are more deterritorialized; their spaces are fluid and pan-national.

Context of Entry

The immigration of Filipinos to the United States is a story of labor migration, a story that covers a four-phase history and geography broader than that of the United States itself. The Philippines became a colony of Spain beginning in the sixteenth century, and for much of the "colonial" period the principal domestic and international economic activity of this Southeast Asian archipelago was based on the galleon trade. The galleon trade depended on the import of goods—silk, porcelain, linen, spices, and ivory—into the Philippines from China, Japan, India, Malaysia, and Indonesia. From there, the galleons would travel east across the Pacific toward Acapulco in New Spain (present-day Mexico) and ultimately to Spain. On the return voyage, silver, wine, wheat, and flour were imported back through the Philippines to other Asian markets.

Spain's dependence on the galleon trade relied greatly on the existence and maintenance of its ships. Filipino men, aged 16 to 60, were required to perform service in a *polo* system of forced labor. Under this system, Filipinos were assigned to work, often as carpenters, in various shipyards throughout the Philippines. Filipinos, however, also served as crew members aboard the galleons. Many Filipino seamen would subsequently "desert" ship and seek out a new existence in the various ports-of-call associated with the galleon trade. Other Filipinos accompanied the early Spanish explorations along the coastline of California. As missions, such as San Diego, were established during the 1700s—sites that also served as way stations for the Manila galleons—many Filipinos would remain.[1]

It is not known exactly how many Filipinos used the galleon trade as a pathway to migration during this "first" wave. Many of the "Indians" in the Spanish California missions, however, were in actuality Filipinos. One of the forty-six original founders of Pueblo de Nuestra Señora Reina de los Angeles (now the City of Los Angeles) in 1781 was probably a Filipino by the name of Antonio Miranda.[2] Also, Filipino settlements were established outside New Orleans as early as 1763. These early immigrants made their livelihood in the fishing and shrimping industries; their descendants are currently in their ninth generation as Americans.[3]

When the Philippines became a colony of the United States following the Spanish-American War (1898) and, later, the Philippine-American War (1899–1902), the creation of certain institutions and the implementation of various economic and social policies by the United States had a direct impact on the movement of Filipinos across the Pacific. Initially, educational policies contributed to this first wave of immigration of Filipinos to the United States in two fundamental ways. First, the U.S. government initiated the Philippines' first public schools—albeit to effectively assimilate the Filipinos under American control. Through novels, songs, and American teachers in public schools, education provided many young Filipinos with an awareness of opportunities outside the Philippines. Second, educational institutions offered Filipinos a chance to migrate to the United States to further their education. In 1903 the Pensionado Act, passed by the U.S. Congress, provided support to send young Filipinos to the United States for education on American life. The *pensionados*, as they were called, earned degrees throughout the United States, in institutions of higher learning such as Harvard, Stanford, Cornell, and the University of California, Berkeley. From an initial cohort of approximately 100 *pensionados* in 1903, the number increased to 14,000 individuals by 1938. Many founded student organizations, some of which remain in existence today. Upon completing their education, most *pensionados* returned to the Philippines where they assumed positions as political, social, and economic leaders. These early migrants also established social networks that facilitated later migrations.

Other Filipinos migrated to the United States seeking educational opportunities. Many were self-supporting. This migration was a decided risk, but given the conditions in the Philippines, many young men availed themselves of this opportunity. As one Filipino explained:

> In 1928 I came to the United States, "land of opportunity," where I planned to work my way through college. I graduated from high school. My desire to pursue higher education was during a poor time because of the depression.[4]

A "second" wave of Filipinos to the United States was related more directly to changing employment opportunities and the exclusion of other Asian immigrant groups. Beginning in the early 1850s powerful American landowners in the Hawaiian Islands had conducted recruitment campaigns in search of cheap labor. First, Chinese laborers were imported and, beginning in 1869, Japanese workers were also recruited. However, the racially motivated Chinese Exclusion Act of 1882 severely limited Chinese immigration, and the Gentlemen's Agreement of 1907–1908 impeded Japanese immigration. In response to continued labor shortages, sugar growers and other planters in Hawaii began to search for alternative sources. Classified as U.S. nationals, Filipinos were excluded from U.S. immigration policies and international agreements; from a capitalist standpoint, Filipinos were ideal.[5]

The recruitment of Filipino labor to Hawaii began in 1906 although the large-scale migration of Filipinos to the plantations did not materialize until 1909. Between 1907 and 1929 more than 102,000 Filipinos would ultimately be recruited to work in the islands. Geographically, most Filipino migrants originated from just a few provinces in the Philippines (Map 12.1). The majority were recruited in the northern and central regions of the main island of Luzon, and other islands in the Visayas central region. Over 68 percent of these early migrants, for example, came from the provinces of Abra, Ilocos Norte, Ilocos Sur, La Union, Pangasinan, and Tarlac; 27 percent originated from the Visayan provinces of Bohol, Cebu, Leyte, and Negros Oriental. Many of these provinces were principal sugar-producing regions.[6]

Over time, a secondary migration system developed as Hawaiian-employed Filipinos would seek better opportunities throughout the western continental United

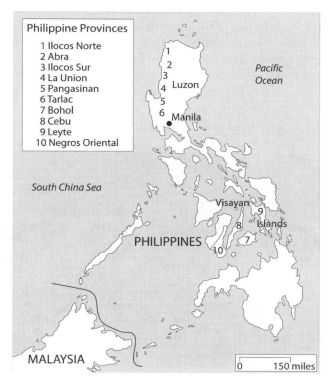

Map 12.1.   Provinces in the Philippines.

States. As social networks were reinforced, and as U.S. labor recruiters became more active, direct immigration from the Philippines to the United States was established.[7] During the 1920s, for example, about 45,000 Filipinos migrated to the United States. Most found employment in the agricultural regions of California and other western states. They would travel from season to season, from one farming community to another, following the harvest season.[8] Filipinos would also find employment in the fish canneries throughout the Pacific Northwest and Alaska. Gradually, a permanent Philippine population was established throughout Hawaii and (mostly) the Pacific Coast of the United States. The 1930 census reported approximately 45,000 Filipinos residing on the mainland, with over 63,000 Filipinos in Hawaii.[9]

The United States Navy served as another important linkage for Filipino immigration. After American military forces "pacified" the Philippines following the Philippine-American War, many Filipinos were hired by the U.S. Navy. Most were employed as stewards, performing menial tasks as cooks, waiters, pantrymen, dishwashers, or bedmakers. By 1930 there were an estimated 25,000 Filipinos serving in the U.S. Navy (Fig. 12.1). Because of this military connection many of these Filipinos would acquire U.S. citizenship and eventually settle in the United States.[10]

Philippine immigrants, similar to other groups newly arrived in the United States, encountered racial discrimination and prejudice, especially during the depression years of the 1930s. In part, the public outcry for Philippine exclusion found expression within the historical context of anti-Chinese and anti-Japanese discrimination. In 1934 the passage of the Tydings-McDuffie Act re-classified the Philippines as a U.S. commonwealth. As a result, Filipinos no longer held the status of U.S. nationals and were thus subject to immigration quota restrictions. Philippine immigration to the United States was reduced to just 50 migrants per year; it was only following the wartime per-

Figure 12.1.   Filipino World War II Veterans Gathering for a Reunion in San Francisco. Source: Christopher A. Airriess.

formance of Filipinos—in the conflicts of Corregidor and Bataan—that "whites" were forced to view and treat Filipinos in the United States more favorably.[11]

During, and in the years immediately following World War II, a "third" wave of Philippine immigration to the United States steadily increased. Between 1946 and 1965, for example, nearly 40,000 Filipinos entered the United States (Fig. 12.2).[12] These trends were facilitated by the passage of more liberal immigration policies (such as the War Brides Act and the Fiancées Act). Furthermore, in 1946 citizenship was made available through the Filipino Naturalization Act.[13] Combined, these acts facilitated the entry of predominantly women from countries that supported U.S. military installations, including not only the Philippines but also Japan and South Korea. Throughout the 1950s, an average of 1,200 Filipinas would immigrate to the United States as the wives of U.S. military personnel.

The U.S. Immigration and National Act of 1965 represents the most significant and unexpected change in immigration legislation. The chief thrust of the act was to eliminate the racist national-origins quotas and replace these with an emphasis on family reunification. To many scholars, an emphasis on family reunification signified that labor market aspects were not of primary importance. Yet the 1965 act did precipitate the large-scale recruitment of technicians and professionals, many of them from the Philippines.

Changes in U.S. immigration legislation occurred during a period of profound social, economic, and political changes within the Philippines. Philippine President Ferdinand Marcos had declared martial law in 1972 to counteract the political and economic instability caused in part by demonstrations by landless peasants, students, and

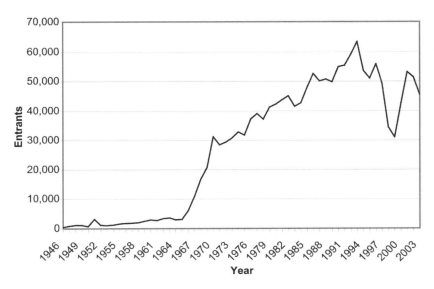

Figure 12.2.   *Filipino Entrants into the United States, 1946–2003.*
Source: *Statistical Yearbook of the Immigration and Naturalization Service,*
U.S. Immigration and Naturalization Service, various years.

workers. Repeated bombings and other acts of violence rocked the country. Economically, the Philippines could not absorb the increasing number of students in many professional sectors, including engineering and nursing. The educational system eventually came to be seen as a stepping-stone for overseas employment. The number of Philippine entrants to the United States rose tenfold between 1964 and the 1970s, increasing from 3,000 immigrants per year to more than 30,000 (Fig. 12.2).[14]

After the passage of the 1965 act, Philippine immigrants to the United States were concentrated in particular occupational categories. Between 1970 and 1974, for example, slightly more than half of the 100,700 Philippine immigrants who were subject to numerical limitations entered under the third and sixth preference categories that are occupationally based. The percentage of immigrant professionals in relation to total immigration from the Philippines, furthermore, more than doubled in the ten years following the 1965 act—from about 12 percent between 1961 and 1965 to 28 percent for the 1966–1970 period.[15]

The high-volume flow of Filipinos to the United States from the 1970s to the present has continued unabated (Fig. 12.2). Unlike the first three "waves" of Philippine immigration, however, the fourth "wave" has been female-dominated. During the 1960s, for example, two-thirds of all Filipino immigrants to the United States were women. This reflected changing structural conditions in both the United States and the Philippines. Women in the Philippines had obtained educational and occupational credentials in "preferred" sectors (e.g., health-related fields) and were able to take advantage of the third and sixth preference categories. These immigrants were likewise assisted by private recruitment agencies, both in the United States and in the Philippines.[16] Direct recruitment also selectively channeled Filipinas into hospitals, health organizations, and nursing homes. This unusual situation of high educational and occupational attainment for Filipino Americans and specifically females is reflected in socioeconomic data. The percentage of females in professional occupations is greater than for males (Table 12.1). In addition, the percentage of females earning their bachelor's and master's degrees is greater than males (Table 12.2).

The incorporation of Philippine women into the U.S. labor market was a response to structural changes in the overall provision of health management. Native-born U.S. workers were either ill prepared or less willing to satisfy labor demands. Government

Table 12.1.   Occupational Characteristics of Filipino Americans, 16 Years or Older, 2000

Occupation	Male	Female
Agricultural	0.9	0.5
Sales	13.9	12.5
Production & Manufacturing	28.3	13.4
Professional	47.5	65.8
Administration	4.9	3.9
Other	4.5	3.9

Source: *2000 Census of Population and Housing: Summary Tape File 4* (Washington: U.S. Government Printing Office, 2002).

Table 12.2.   Educational Attainment of Filipino Americans, 25 Years and Older, 2000

	% with High School Degrees	% with BA	% with MA	% with PhD
Male	15.7	32.0	3.4	0.6
Female	14.3	38.8	3.9	0.5

Source: *2000 Census of Population and Housing: Summary Tape File 4* (Washington: U.S. Government Printing Office, 2002).

reductions in educational spending created a shortage of trained personnel, and the lack of decent wages and long working hours in many of these sectors—including nursing—induced many qualified U.S. women and men to shun these occupations. Additionally, native-born American workers were less motivated to work in the increasing number of part-time, low-paying jobs available. The continued use of foreign workers in the health-related sectors of the U.S. economy also offered more flexible control over the supply of physicians rather than the continued expansion of medical schools.[17] At no or minimal cost to the United States, Philippine-based medical schools were able to provide a plethora of highly skilled workers.

Settlement Patterns

Although Filipinos are highly concentrated in many states, such as California and Washington, they have not established many easily recognized ethnic enclaves comparable to Chinatowns, Little Tokyos, or Little Saigons. The so-called Little Manilas in San Francisco and Los Angeles were, in fact, nothing more than "service centers" similar to the historic "porter towns" along the major rail lines, where Filipinos congregated between jobs or when they were in town.[18] Studies have also found spatial variation with respect to residential concentration. Filipino immigrants in Los Angeles, for example, tend to cluster in ethnic neighborhoods, whereas those in Chicago do not have a concentrated business or neighborhood community.[19] In Hawaii, many Filipinos continue to reside in plantation towns, although a fair number of these early communities have long since disappeared.[20] Honolulu remains a major location of Filipino settlement, as do the island of Molokai (Maui County) and various towns on the island of Lanai.

The relative "invisibility" of Filipino business and residential concentrations has been explained, in part, by the historical lack of development of a territorial community by the early immigrants. A "sojourner" mentality and the transient nature of early immigrants have both been identified as contributing factors. As one immigrant explained:

> I went to California with five dollars and I reached as far as Arizona with five dollars. After the cannery season because there's no job here [in Seattle], we went to California. We make our tent, no tent . . . just build shelter . . . some grass for a roof and the bed is grass. . . that thick, and we sleep on that in the Imperial Valley [in California].[21]

Filipinos largely settled in the United States after earlier Chinese and Japanese immigrant groups and thus were able to shop and perhaps gain employment in previously established Chinatowns and Little Tokyos. Some scholars suggest also that since recent Filipino immigrants are characterized by high education and professional backgrounds with a good command of the English language, there is less need to establish Filipino ethnic enclaves.[22]

Historically, however, there were some significant sites of Filipino settlement. Although many Filipinos were transitory, shifting employment sites with the changing agricultural seasons, important communities did emerge in the early decades. The central California cities of Delano, Fresno, and Stockton, for example, were home to many Filipino laborers. During the 1920s and 1930s, in the face of discrimination and violence, many Filipinos were also forced to retreat to urban shelters in the few "Little Manilas" or in Chinatowns of the large cities.[23]

The activities of the Filipino Navy-men also contributed to the dispersion of communities. Many of these seamen, having completed their service, would settle in those cities associated with Navy ports and other facilities. This accounts for some of the early Filipino communities in the Los Angeles region, especially around west Long Beach and Wilmington. On the Atlantic coast Filipino communities exist because of Navy operations around Norfolk in Virginia, and Pensacola and Jacksonville in Florida.

The 2000 U.S. Census recorded 1,864,120 Filipinos living in the United States. Much like other immigrants, their spatial distribution is geographically uneven (Map 12.2). With a total of 920,052 California accounts for the lion's share of all Filipinos (49.4%). The highest concentrations in California are found in Los Angeles and San Diego counties, with 28 percent and 13 percent of the state's Filipino population, respectively. Other significant counties include Alameda and Santa Clara counties (each with 8%), San Mateo (7%), and Orange County (5%).

Proportionately, Hawaii is significant in the distribution of Filipinos. With 171,678 Filipinos, Hawaii accounts for 9 percent of the national population. Moreover, over 73 percent of Hawaiian-based Filipinos are concentrated in Honolulu County. Other significant regional concentrations include Illinois, New York, and New Jersey, with each state accounting for approximately 5 percent of the national total. These states reflect well the concentration of Filipinos in university and medical-center settings. In New Jersey, for example, 14 percent of the state's Filipino population is located in Middlesex County, home of Rutgers University and the Robert Wood Johnson Medical Center.

Post-1965 immigrant trends have worked against earlier settlement patterns. Recent immigration, characterized by high proportions of professionals, tends to be more urban-oriented. Throughout California, as indicated, substantial Filipino communities have been established in and around Los Angeles and San Diego to the south, and San Francisco and San Jose to the north. In the Los Angeles metropolitan region, for example, Filipinos tend to concentrate in outlying areas and suburbs such as Glendale, Eagle Rock, Silver Lake, Carson, Long Beach, Cerritos, West Covina, and Diamond Bar.[24] Many of these communities reflect vastly different histories. Some, such as those in west Long Beach and the Wilmington-Carson area, tend to be related to the location of U.S. naval facilities; others, particularly those in West Covina and Eagle Rock, are related more to post-1965 professional immigrants. San Diego County has

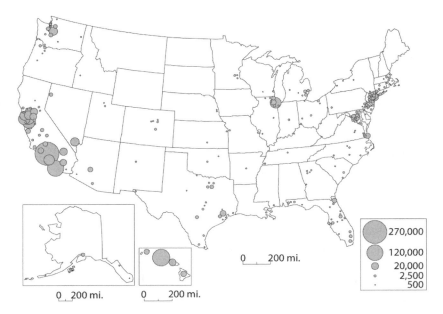

Map 12.2.   Geographic Distribution of Filipinos by County, 2000.
Source: 2000 Census of Population and Housing: Summary Tape File 4
(Washington: U.S. Government Printing Office, 2002).

also experienced substantial growth and expansion of Filipino communities. Some of this growth is associated with earlier naval-based communities around National City and Mira Mesa, but others such as Rancho Peñasquitos and Poway are of recent origin.[25] These suburban communities are the result of more Filipino entrepreneurs.

The Filipino populations of other metropolitan areas such as Chicago and New York City have also grown rapidly. As indicated above, most cities do not have identifiable ethnic enclaves, but substantial residential concentrations are found. Given the fluency in English, as well as the preponderance of relatively higher-educated immigrants, many Filipinos tend to locate in the suburbs. Apart from major urban areas, such as Los Angeles, San Francisco, and Chicago, Filipinos also are found throughout most of the United States, usually within regional urban centers and university towns. This patterning is a reflection of the myriad forms of immigration to the United States. As a sizeable number of Philippine immigrants are employed in health-related occupations, Filipino communities emerge in connection with hospitals and other medical establishments. Filipinos also enter the country as either students or faculty, and thus tend to concentrate in college towns. And lastly, many Filipinas immigrate to the United States as mail-order brides. It is not uncommon for these women to find themselves as the only Filipina, or perhaps one of just a handful of Filipinas, in their place of residence. As discussed later, this pathway of migration imparts a radical, but different migrant experience.

Immigrant Experiences

Reflective of the many different paths of migration, "settlement" patterns impart vastly different "migrant experiences" for Filipinos, ranging from the live-in maids of Singapore, to the construction worker housed in an isolated work-camp in Saudi Arabia, to the nurse working in the United States. But even within a country such as the United States there is tremendous variation in the "migrant experience." As Rick Bonus writes, "Filipino American settlements today are multiple, scattered, diverse, and heterogeneous. To refer to a Filipino American community, one must include men and women who came to the United States at different times; those who were born in the United States and who were born in the Philippines; those who are unskilled, semiskilled, and professional; those who are and are not educated; those who came from and live in urban and rural areas; those who entered as parents and as children; and those who are offspring of both early and recent arrivals. In other words, the breadth and variety of Filipino immigration to the United States necessitates the signification of a Filipino American community in the plural."[26] There is no typical experience.

As discussed above, settlement patterns of Filipino immigrants have undergone profound changes in recent years. One salient trend has been the emergence of Filipinos in small towns and rural areas. The "migrant experience" is fundamentally different in ethnically homogeneous places than it is in ethnically heterogeneous places.[27] In 1990, for example, approximately 225,000 Filipinos lived in Los Angeles County; by way of comparison, only 460 Filipinos lived in the counties of Portage and Summit in Northeast Ohio. Moreover, these two Ohio counties, as a whole, were over 90 percent white. In this section I present narratives of two Filipinas, Maria and Sabrine. Maria migrated to the United States as a mail-order bride; she has for the most part lived in isolated college towns throughout the Midwest. Conversely, Sabrine immigrated as a young girl with two of her sisters, and ended up residing in Los Angeles County. Through these narratives I provide insight into the varied lived experiences of Filipinas in vastly different geographic contexts.

Maria grew up in a small village in the southern Philippines. She recalls that her family was relatively impoverished, but she was able to obtain a solid education as well as vocational training. Maria, in fact, studied to be both an elementary school teacher and a beautician. As a teenager, Maria had no plans to migrate to the United States. However, her sister did consider the possibility and, in pursuit of this, she wrote a letter to a pen-pal organization. The sister, however, used Maria's name. Consequently, and partly out of curiosity, Maria, who was twenty at the time, began answering the letters that came to her. Gradually she began to concentrate on the letters of one man in particular. His name was Tom, and he was a university professor living in Illinois. During their correspondence Maria began to weigh the options of remaining in the Philippines, or of migrating to the United States. Maria was relatively well educated; she had earned her teaching credential, though at the time she worked as a hair dresser. And although Tom was considerably older than Maria (he was in his forties), and she knew him only through the exchange of letters, the thought of moving to the United States and of earning more money solidified her decision. Having made up her mind, and being supported in her decision by her parents, Maria asked Tom to journey to the Philippines for marriage.

After their wedding, Maria joined Tom in Illinois and, shortly afterwards, gave birth to their first and only child, Scott. Life for Maria revolved around the raising of their son, and the difficulties of adjusting to a new environment. There were few Filipinos in the small midwestern town in which Maria now lived. Maria's bouts of loneliness, however, were tempered somewhat by the fact that her husband served as faculty advisor for a Philippine student association. Those Filipinos she encountered, therefore, were mostly university students. However, although she was able to relate to these students age-wise, she was unable to relate to either their life experiences (many were born in the United States) or their daily experiences. As a young mother raising her son, Maria was not able to participate in the extracurricular activities of other Filipinos. She was, though, able to overcome her initial feelings of displacement and isolation.

After seven years Maria's husband obtained another position at a university in northeast Ohio. Following this move, Maria found herself considerably more isolated than she was previously. In her new place of residence there was no established Philippine organization. Nor did either Maria or Tom know any Filipinos in the area. Indeed, neither Maria nor Tom had any friends, relatives, or acquaintances in their new home. Gradually, through her participation at faculty wives' clubs, parent-teacher associations, and other civic events, Maria sought out Filipino friends. She explains that with other Filipinas, they could share common experiences, and reminisce about their homeland.

Sabrine's route to the United States was very different from that of Maria. Sabrine grew up in a small town in the northern Philippines. She was the fourth child of six—two older and two younger sisters, and an older brother. Sabrine's family was relatively well off; her father was in the U.S. Navy and, although he was often not present as Sabrine grew up, he regularly sent money to the family.

Similar to Maria, Sabrine had no intention of migrating to the United States. Rather, she wanted eventually to move to Manila and obtain a college degree. However, when she was eighteen, her parents decided that she should move to the United States. At the time, Sabrine's eldest sister (Jolene) was living in Los Angeles. She had moved to the United States while she was still a teenager, initially living with her father and an uncle. Over the years she worked at various jobs in San Diego and Los Angeles before marrying her husband, himself an immigrant from Iran.

Since her father was in the navy and had long since obtained U.S. citizenship, Sabrine and her siblings were able to easily migrate to the United States. However, to take advantage of this opportunity, they had to do so before they turned twenty-one years of age. It was decided, therefore, that Sabrine and the other two middle sisters would join Jolene.

Sabrine was not happy after her arrival in the United States. In the Philippines she had planned on attending college; in the United States those plans were put on hold. Sabrine and her two sisters (Gloria and Wilma) moved in with Jolene who, by this time, had three children. All three of the sisters were expected to work—they ultimately found jobs at a fast-food restaurant. Gloria, the next oldest sister, continued her education to be a medical technologist, and Wilma, the next youngest, was still in high school. Sabrine, by default, was responsible for babysitting Jolene's children.

Life was difficult for Sabrine. She was constantly juggling work, child-care, and attending college part-time. A major benefit was the presence of family members. Aside from her sisters, Sabrine was later reunited with her mother and youngest sister (both of whom migrated a year later). Sabrine also had a network of many aunts and uncles living throughout California, stretching from Sacramento in the north to San Diego in the south. Moreover, Sabrine could take advantage of the well-established and bustling Filipino communities throughout Southern California.

The modes of entry of Maria and Sabrine were vastly different. So too was the setting of their arrival. Consequently, their experiences have been profoundly different. Maria, for example, is often the only Filipino—indeed the only "Asian"—when she goes to the bank or the store. She explains that when she performs her daily activities, members of the mainstream society often view her simply as "Oriental." As testimony to this homogenizing process, Maria tells of an incident that took place when she attended an open house at her son's school. In the classroom, Maria recalls, the teacher had displayed flags representing the children's ancestry or nationality. Disappointedly, Maria looked around but could not find a flag of the Philippines. Wanting this part of her son's heritage to be recognized, she asked the teacher about the "missing" flag. With a puzzled look, the teacher pointed to the Korean flag that was on display. Maria laments that she had to explain the difference between Korea and the Philippines. Though seemingly a minor incident, to Maria this was reflective of a larger confusion and ambiguity of living in an isolated, predominantly white neighborhood. Moreover, this reaffirmed her attempt to retain her identity as a Filipina living in a foreign country.

Maria also talks of dealing with stereotypes that she must negotiate in her day-to-day interactions. It is not uncommon, for example, for people living in rural, non-ethnically diverse locations to have never encountered a person from the Philippines. Accordingly, their only source of information is obtained via television, print media, or academia. This, however, imparts an additional dimension to the "migrant" experience of Maria. In 1997, for example, *60 Minutes* aired a report on mail-order brides. During the broadcast the anchor, Lesley Stahl, reported:

> The reason [for mail-order marriage] is not only the irresistible charm of American men, it's that marriage is an escape route from poverty. Mired in the Third World, the Philippines relies heavily on exports to the First World, and one of its most valuable exports is its women. Each year close to half a million Filipinas go to foreign countries, many as nurses and maids, some as prostitutes and others as brides. And they send millions of dollars back home. There's an unwritten law that daughters sacrifice for the rest of the family.

Television shows reaffirm these representations. In a 1994 episode of the situation comedy *Frasier*, the father of the title character remarked, "For an extra five grand, you could have bought a whole new wife from the Philippines."[28]

Stories of poverty and prostitution, mail-order marriages and victimization, permeate the encounters between Filipinas and non-Filipinos. As it happens, of course, Maria is a mail-order bride. However, she laments the stereotypical representation of her life, which is the target of jokes. Maria relates the experience of playing in the park with her son. Another mother, who was not Filipina, approached her. As they sat watching their children, the woman asked Maria where she was from, to which Maria replied, "The Philippines." Without hesitation the woman followed with: "Oh, are you poor?" As this incident reveals, Maria cannot escape her multiple identities as being "different," a perceived outsider, and the signifying association between the Philippines and poverty. Maria explains,

> When Americans see me, they ask, "Where are you from?" I tell them the Philippines. And then they ask me if I'm poor! I'm from the Philippines so I must be poor. That really hurts. I'm a certified teacher in the Philippines, yet here I'm not allowed to teach [her teaching credential was not recognized]. I operated a beauty parlor in the Philippines, but here I have no certificate and so can't get a job. They won't consider my training because it comes from the Third World.

The experiences of Sabrine are very different. Owing to the sheer numbers of Filipinos in Southern California, she is not expected to be the "representative" of all things Philippine. Moreover, the constant interactions among Filipinos and non-Filipinos ensure a greater degree of understanding. This does not mean, however, that Sabrine has not encountered stereotypical remarks or other condescending attitudes. The difference, though, is that Sabrine is able to tap into other social networks and support groups. Unlike Maria, who is relatively isolated in her experiences, Sabrine has joined numerous social groups and associations. Sabrine is also able to "blend" into the larger community, and not always be perceived as an outsider or the "other."

As these brief vignettes illustrate, the migrant experience is fundamentally different depending on the geographic context. The extensive Philippine communities of places like Los Angeles and San Diego provide mechanisms to facilitate adjustment to the new environment. In smaller, rural locations, this mechanism is largely missing. As a result, issues of discrimination may be magnified; problems of isolation and vulnerability may increase precipitously. Our understandings of migrant experiences, as such, must be sensitive to the myriad contexts of communities in which Filipinos reside.[29]

The Forgotten Immigrants

Filipinos and Filipino Americans have been described as a "forgotten" population.[30] They have also been described as being "invisible,"[31] a statement composed of two parts. On one hand, the "invisibility" refers to the lack of a definitive presence on the landscape. Unlike the prominent Chinatowns, Little Tokyos, or Little Saigons, there are no comparable Little Manilas or Filipino Towns. Historically, of course, some cities or sections therein have assumed these titles. Delano, a farming town in central California, was known as "Filipino Town." Los Angeles, likewise, has been proclaimed "Manilatown"; the only *identifiable* marker to this designation, however, is a sign on the Hollywood freeway. On the other hand, the "invisibility" of Filipinos refers to the fact that Filipinos are largely missing in most accounts of U.S. history and in contemporary scholarship, excluded from numerous positions of power, and misrepresented (or not represented) in mainstream media, comprising a "silent minority" frequently lumped together with Chinese, Japanese, Korean, Indian, Vietnamese, and Cambodian peoples under the rubric Asian or Asian American.[32]

Scholars suggest that the invisibility of Filipino communities and, consequently, readily identifiable cultural landscapes, is related in part to the transitory nature of early Philippine settlements. Moreover, as most Filipino immigrants are relatively fluent in English, there has not been a need to spatially cluster as a form of social cohesion.[33] In turn, this lack of an explicit ethnic enclave development may have contributed to the relative invisibility of Filipinos and Filipino Americans in other venues (e.g., scholarship, the media).

Migrants from the Philippines have, however, long been concerned with questions of ethnic identity. This is most pronounced in the existence of community organizations. Fred Cordova relates a joke that says whenever two Filipinos get together, they form a club. Moreover, when those two Filipinos join with a third, the three Filipinos will organize themselves into a Filipino community. The proliferation of "voluntary organizations" and "communities" is often used to portray Philippine communities as divided and fractured. This is not the case, however. Cordova explains that the "Filipino Community" is a peculiarly Filipino phenomenon, a practice to promote and protect the interests of Filipinos and to cultivate unity and cooperation among Filipinos.[34] Community organizations, therefore, serve as social spaces that promote group solidarity and cohesiveness. As Yen Espiritu finds, "these organizations—through their activities—more often than not build linkages rather than erecting divisions within the Filipino American community."[35]

The participation of Filipinos in voluntary organizations and associations has a long history. Since their arrival in the United States in the early 1900s, regional loyalties and provincial ties have shaped Filipinos' choice of residence, their network of friends, and their patterns of organization.[36] As explained by Jonathan Okamura, in Hawaii Filipino plantation workers could receive familial aid and support by joining a *saranay* or mutual aid association. These "clubs" were organized by workers from the same hometown in the Philippines ("townmates") or from the wider Filipino plantation community to provide various social and security benefits for their members.[37] Social organizations continue to reflect regional source ties (Fig. 12.3).

With respect to recent post-1965 immigrants, the proliferation of hometown and regional associations has been widely reported.[38] Indeed, to bring some order to this proliferation, in 1971, to indicate just one example, the Council of Philippine American Organizations of San Diego County (COPAO) was founded to serve as an umbrella organization for all the local social, political, and professional organizations. By the late 1990s, there were an estimated 150 to 175 Filipino American community organizations in San Diego County.

Community organizations continue to serve as means to combat racism, discrimination, and to promote civil rights issues. Filipino American styles of politicking, often centered on community organizations, are principally geared toward creating and maintaining spaces where Filipinos can actively engage each other in the pursuit of shared interests in local political representation, in the protection of their civil rights, and in the improvement of their well-being.[39] These community organizations are historically rooted in the social and political conditions of Filipino immigration to and settlement in the United States; they are born of exclusionary conditions and the necessity for self-reliance and the impetus to develop community associations as alternative spaces; Filipino Americans have resorted to using the spaces of the community centers, churches, parks, and recreation centers as spaces to organize themselves and to build networks of mutual support outside traditional or mainstream political venues.[40] The physical spaces of Filipino communities may not always be readily visible, but their social spaces clearly are constructed through these activities. Consequently, the observation that visible ethnic enclaves are not prevalent does not mean that Filipinos are not actively pursuing the traditional objectives of enclave economies or politics. Rather, the material manifestations of these enclaves tend to be more ephemeral, located in churches, community centers, or backyard picnics.

Organizations are also important as conduits for Philippine culture. Identity questions are especially germane for second- and third-generation Filipino Americans. As Espiritu writes, these multiple-subject positions remind us that identities are not fixed or singular, but overlapping and simultaneous. Filipino immigrant children live with paradoxes: they feel strong symbolic loyalty to the Philippines, but they know very little about it and have little contact with their parents and other adults who might educate them about it. They feel pressured to become like Americans, but their experiences

Figure 12.3.   Regional Hometown Associations are a focal point for many Filipinos in the United States. Source: Author.

as racialized subjects leave them with an uneasy relationship with both Filipino and U.S. culture.[41] It is through various associations that younger generations of Filipinos and Filipino Americans are able to retain a sense of identity and heritage.

Lastly, it should be noted that hometown and other voluntary associations established and maintained by Filipino immigrants no longer function primarily as adaptive mechanisms for immigrants. Rather, other functions, such as the donations of monetary and other charitable contributions to places in the Philippines, have assumed greater importance.[42] This highlights the observation that a strong diasporic sense of identity has emerged, one that transcends the spaces of both the Philippines and the United States.

The Pan-Nationalism of the Philippine Diaspora

Although the United States remains the principal destination of Philippine emigrants, there are other substantial migratory systems. In the 1960s, for example, liberalized immigration policies in Australia, Canada, and New Zealand opened additional migration opportunities. Even so, Philippine immigration to these countries may yet exhibit a connection with the United States. Many of the Filipino immigrants to Canada, for example, arrived *after* a period of stay in the United States. In this case, Filipinos were able to move to the United States for either employment-training programs or higher education; their visas were for temporary stay only. Rather than returning to the Philippines, a certain number of these temporary migrants elected to move to Canada.

Overall emigration from the Philippines, however, increased greatly in size and scope during the 1970s as a result of the Philippine government's sponsorship of overseas employment. Currently, between four and five million Filipinos now live and work in over 190 countries and territories as annually more than 800,000 Filipinos are deployed as "overseas contract workers" (OCWs). Most of these workers are employed on either six-month or two-year contracts.[43] Unlike the migratory systems linking the Philippines with the United States or Canada, most labor-importing countries (e.g., Saudi Arabia, Singapore, and Japan) have imposed strict policies to prevent the formation of "permanent" communities. As a result, the migration of Filipino OCWs is of a transient nature. This does, though, impart an important component of the overall Philippine diaspora.

A prevalent metaphor of the Philippine diaspora, both within the United States and beyond, is one that we may refer to as *tahanang Pilipino*, or "Pilipino home." As is evident in the numerous social clubs and organizations, and their manifestation on Internet web-sites, Filipinos use cyberspace to construct ethnic identities. Diaspora communities are separated in "real space" from their homelands, but through computer technology are able to re-create a notion of home on the web. By way of explanation, consider the German-based Philippine web-site *Asiana*. This site is subtitled *Tahanang Pilipino*. This phrase, as indicated above, does not refer simply to a physical structure, but rather to the totality of Philippine culture, nationalism, and identity. The name is therefore symbolic of the Philippine diaspora, and of the understanding and sentiment that even though individual "family" members may reside in different countries, they will remain "under one roof."[44]

The significance of a "home" metaphor constitutes not a dichotomous hybrid identity, but instead a pan-identity—a deliberate attempt to maintain a more global presence rather than a dualistic identity between a specific diaspora local community and the homeland. The web site of *LakBayan: The Filipino Diaspora*, consequently, is "dedicated to the more than 4.5 M Filipinos living overseas."[45] The goals of *Filipinos in Kansas City* attest to the notions of a *tahanang Pilipino*: to promote understanding between the Filipino American community and the native, majority, and other ethnic cultures in greater Kansas City; to aid in perpetuating the Filipino culture for future generations of Filipino Americans; and to promote *Filipino community spirit regardless of geographic boundaries* (italics added).[46]

Philippine associations, therefore, located in both the United States and beyond, in general tend to foster a notion of a *pan*-national as opposed to a *trans*-national identity. *Trans-* refers to "crossing" as in crossing nations; *pan-*, however, is more appropriate in that it "encompasses" and "unites" communities. The concept of *tahanang Pilipino* recognizes that there are a shared history and geography among all Philippine *pan*-migrants, whether they reside in Los Angeles, Cleveland, Singapore, or Frankfurt.[47] In her study of Philippine communities in San Diego, Espiritu finds that while significant segments of foreign-born Filipinos regularly engage in transnational activities such as sending remittances or communicating with family members in the Philippines, most Filipino migrants do not live in transnational "circuits" but instead are settling permanently in the United States. She explains that their "lived reality"—their job, their church, their children's school, their social life—is primarily local. Significant, though, is that many Filipinos, even if they are unable to literally participate in transnational activities, continue to do so at the symbolic level—at the level of imagination, shared memory, and "inventions of tradition."[48]

The common use of *mabuhay* on diaspora web sites and in the promotion literature of social clubs also testifies to the construction of a pan-national Philippine identity. This word translates as "May you have life," and is often defined as being equivalent to the English word *greeting* or *welcome*. However, within Philippine culture *mabuhay* is more than a simple greeting, for it captures the concept of being alive, and of a collective enjoyment. *Mabuhay* thus speaks to a communal spirit, even among communities physically separated. Thus, when the web site *Filipinos in Kansas City* opens with the phrase "Mabuhay and welcome to the Filipino-American community in Kansas City," the phrase is not redundant (i.e., welcome and welcome), but instead serves to invite one into the larger Philippine community, the *tahanang Pilipino*.[49]

Filipino expatriates are not the only ones forwarding a diasporic pan-identity. Since the early 1970s the Philippine government has been actively fostering a sense of belonging of the overseas Filipino communities. In 1973, for example, under the presidential regime of Ferdinand Marcos, the Philippine government and travel/tourist industry initiated the politically and economically motivated *Balik-Bayan* (homecoming) program. Antonio Pido identifies three reasons for the implementation of this governmental sponsorship. First, the program served as a form of propaganda, to show Filipino expatriates that martial law was beneficial to the Philippines. Second, these government policies served to minimize the "brain drain" from the Philippines and promoted the use and directionality of the skills and talents of overseas Filipinos to help economic growth. Third, the program helped to increase tourism.[50] Components implemented in the *Balik-Bayan* program included discounts on hotels, restaurants, shops, and travel, as well as special immigration visa requirements.[51]

Conclusion

Despite being the second largest Asian group in the United States, Filipinos remain relatively invisible from mainstream society. This is not to suggest, however, that ethnic Filipinos have not contributed to the nation-building process of the United States. Indeed, Filipinos have labored for centuries in the United States, working in fields and fish canneries, hospitals and universities.

Ethnic Filipinos are widely distributed across the United States. Significant concentrations reflect historical and geographic trends of immigration, processes that span over three hundred years. These patterns are further related to both institutional and structural changes occurring in the United States.

Life within Filipino communities is varied. As the narratives of Maria and Sabrine reveal, the context of community is very important in the day-to-day activities of ethnic Filipinos. The stories of Maria and Sabrine, although unique, are played out many times over across the changing ethnic map of the United States and other destinations. Their experiences are shaped by a multitude of factors and are contingent upon local contexts, personal circumstances, particular histories and geographies. While they are frequently assigned identities through racialized stereotyping, they retain space to redefine and reassert their own positive identities.

The broader Philippine diaspora reflects also the malleability of ethnic and national identity. Members of the Philippine diaspora are actively constructing a pan-national Philippine identity. Filipinos living in Vancouver, for example, forge a sense of community, of home, with Filipinos living in Frankfurt, Singapore, and many other locations around the world. Emergent Philippine diasporic identities are limited not to a single origin-destination linkage, and the subsequent construction of hybrid identities, but rather are oriented to the development of a pan-Philippine national identity, of members all resident "under one roof," living within the *tahanang Pilipino*. And this geography of the diasporic Philippine community is certainly not invisible. It is very prevalent in the geographical imaginations of Filipinos worldwide.

Notes

1. Lorrain Crouchett, *Filipinos in California* (El Cerrito, CA: Downey Place Publishing, 1982).

2. Fred Cordova, *Filipinos: Forgotten Asian Americans, A Pictorial Essay, 1763–1963* (Dubuque, IA: Kendall/Hunt Publishing, 1983), 9.

3. Pauline Agbayani-Siewert and Linda Revilla, "Filipino Americans," in *Asian Americans: Contemporary Trends and Issues*, ed. Pyong Gap Min (Thousand Oaks, CA: Sage Publications, 1995), 136.

4. Quoted in Cordova, *Filipinos: Forgotten Asian Americans*, 14.

5. James A. Tyner and Olaf Kuhlke, "Pan-National Identities: Representations of the Philippine Diaspora on the World Wide Web," *Asia Pacific Viewpoint* 41 (2000): 231–252.

6. Luis V. Teodoro, *Out of This Struggle: The Filipinos in Hawaii* (Honolulu: University of Hawaii Press, 1981), 18.

7. Teodoro, *Out of This Struggle: The Filipinos in Hawaii*; Robert Anderson, with R. Coller and R. F. Pestano, *Filipinos in Rural Hawaii* (Honolulu: University of Hawaii Press, 1984).

8. Agbayani-Siewert and Revilla, "Filipino Americans," 139.

9. Bill O. Hing, *Making and Remaking Asian America through Immigration Policy, 1850–1990* (Stanford, CA: Stanford University Press, 1993), 62.

10. Tyner and Kuhlke, "Pan-National Identities," 235.

11. Yen L. Espiritu, "Filipino Settlements in the United States," in *Filipino American Lives*, ed. Yen L. Espiritu (Philadelphia: Temple University Press, 1995), 17.

12. Fred Arnold, Urmil Minocha, and James T. Fawcett, "The Changing Face of Asian Immigration to the United States," in *Pacific Bridges: The New Immigration from Asia and the Pacific Islands*, ed. James T. Fawcett and Benjamin V. Cariño (Staten Island, NY: Center for Migration Studies, 1987), Table 6.1.

13. Antonio J. A. Pido, *The Pilipinos in America: Macro/Micro Dimensions of Immigration and Integration* (New York: Center for Migration Studies, 1986), 86; Rick Bonus, *Locating Filipino Americans: Ethnicity and the Cultural Politics of Space* (Philadelphia: Temple University Press, 2000), 42.

14. James A. Tyner, "The Global Context of Gendered Labor Migration from the Philippines to the United States," *American Behavioral Scientist* 42 (1999): 671–689.

15. Benjamin V. Cariño, "The Philippines and Southeast Asia: Historical Roots and Contemporary Linkages," in *Pacific Bridges: The New Immigration from Asia and the Pacific Islands*, ed. James T. Fawcett and Benjamin V. Cariño (Staten Island, NY: Center for Migration Studies, 1987), 307–308.

16. Paul Ong and Tania Azores, "The Migration and Incorporation of Filipino Nurses," in *The New Asian Immigration in Los Angeles and Global Restructuring*, ed. Paul Ong, Edna Bonacich, and Lucie Cheng (Philadelphia: Temple University Press, 1994).

17. Paul Ong and John M. Lui, "U.S. Immigration Policies and Asian Migration," in *The New Asian Immigration in Los Angeles and Global Restructuring*, ed. Paul Ong, Edna Bonacich, and Lucie Cheng (Philadelphia: Temple University Press, 1994), 61.

18. Pido, *Pilipinos in America*, 71.

19. Agbayani-Siewert and Revilla, "Filipino Americans," 145.

20. Robert N. Anderson, *Filipinos in Rural Hawaii* (Honolulu: University of Hawaii Press, 1984).

21. Quoted in Cordova, *Filipinos: Forgotten Asian Americans*, 51.

22. Agbayani-Siewert and Revilla, "Filipino Americans," 145.

23. James P. Allen and Eugene James Turner, *We the People: An Atlas of America's Ethnic Diversity* (New York: Macmillan, 1988), 185.

24. Bonus, *Locating Filipino Americans*, 49.

25. Bonus, *Locating Filipino Americans*, 49.

26. Bonus, *Locating Filipino Americans*, 55.

27. This section is based, in part, on my earlier work. See James A. Tyner, "Geographics of Identity: The Migrant Experiences of Filipinas in Northeast Ohio," *Asia Pacific Viewpoint* 43 (2002): 311–326.

28. Jonathan Y. Okamura, *Imagining the Filipino American Diaspora: Transnational Relations, Identities, and Communities* (New York: Garland Publishing, 1998), 52.

29. Interested readers can consult Espiritu, *Filipino American Lives*, and Cordova, *Filipinos: Forgotten Asian Americans* for additional narratives.

30. Cordova, *Filipinos: Forgotten Asian Americans*.

31. Bonus, *Locating Filipino Americans*, 1.

32. Bonus, *Locating Filipino Americans*, 1.

33. Agbayani-Siewert and Revilla, "Filipino Americans," 145.

34. Cordova, *Filipinos: Forgotten Asian Americans*, 175.

35. Yen Le Espiritu, *Home Bound: Filipino American Lives across Cultures, Communities, and Countries* (Berkeley: University of California Press, 2003), 123.

36. Espiritu, *Home Bound*, 105.

37. Okamura, *Imagining the Filipino Diaspora*, 70.

38. Espiritu, *Home Bound*, 105.

39. Bonus, *Locating Filipino Americans*, 93–94.

40. Bonus, *Locating Filipino Americans*, 100–102.

41. Espiritu, *Home Bound*, 204.

42. Okamura, *Imagining the Filipino Diaspora*, 71.

43. Beginning in 1974 the Philippine state has facilitated the recruitment and deployment of contract-based overseas employment. Dominant markets for Philippine international labor migrants are concentrated in the oil-rich states of the Middle East (e.g., Saudi Arabia, Bahrain, Qatar, United Arab Emirates) and the newly industrializing countries and territories of Asia (e.g., Singapore, Japan, Taiwan, and Hong Kong). For further discussion, see James A. Tyner, *Made in the Philippines: Gendered Discourses and the Making of Migrants* (London: Routledge, 2004), and James A. Tyner, "The Philippines: The Dilemma of Philippine International Labor Migration," in *Migration and Immigration: A Global View*, ed. Maura I. Toro-Morn and Marixsa Alicea (Westport, CT: Greenwood Press, 2004), 161–175.

44. Tyner and Kuhlke, "Pan-National Identities," 247.

45. *LakBayan: The Filipino Diaspora*, <pubweb.acns.nwu.ed/~flip/immig.html>.

46. <www.geocities.com/Tokyo/Towers/3131>.

47. Tyner and Kuhlke, "Pan-National Identities," 248.

48. Espiritu, *Home Bound*, 213–214.

49. Tyner and Kuhlke, "Pan-National Identities," 248.

50. Pido, *Pilipinos in America*, 114.

51. Tyner and Kuhlke, "Pan-National Identities," 239.

CHAPTER 13

Asian Indians and the Construction of Community and Identity

Emily Skop

As of 2000, Asian Indians[1] are the third largest Asian ethnic group in the United States. Indians in the United States are one small slice of the very large Indian diaspora that numbers approximately 20 million individuals and includes countries such as Great Britain, Canada, Australia, Fiji, Mauritius, Guyana, Trinidad, Suriname, Malaysia, South Africa, and Sri Lanka. This substantial movement of Indians out of their homeland began with the subjugation and incorporation of India as a colony of the British Empire in the mid-1800s. As indentured workers on plantations and railroads, Indian communities emerged in far-flung parts of the empire and remained after their period of servitude ended. Some also left India and established themselves as petty traders and shopkeepers. In the post–World War II period, and especially since the 1960s, the dispersal of Indian labor and professionals has become a nearly worldwide phenomenon. This dispersal is not only from India, but from former colonial possessions where discrimination by newly independent governments in countries such as Uganda, Zimbabwe, and Fiji, to name a few, have pushed ethnic Indians to migrate to Great Britain, Canada, Australia, and of course the United States, where they constitute a rapidly growing ethnic group.

Context of Entry

While Indians have been immigrating to the United States since the late 1800s, it is only in the last forty years, since the enactment of the family and occupation preference–based 1965 U.S. immigration legislation, that any significant flow materialized (Fig. 13.1). By 2000, nearly 1.7 million individuals checked the "Asian Indian" category of the race question, according to the U.S. Census.[2] More than 65 percent of these individuals arrived as immigrants between 1980 and 2000, while the balance is largely second-generation Indians born after their parents settled permanently in the United States.

Why are there so many immigrants from India in the United States today? The answer is threefold, and relates to shifting global dynamics associated with Dual Market Theory and recent U.S. immigration policies. First, the rise of high-tech industries in the United States and the function of science and technology as sources of growth

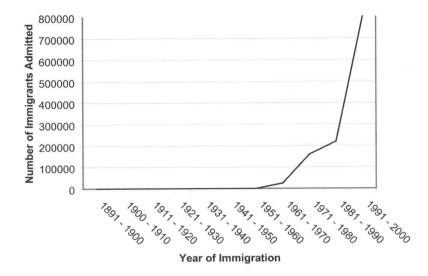

Figure 13.1.   Indian Immigration to the United States, 1890–2000.
Source: U.S. Immigration and Naturalization Service, 2002 Statistical
Yearbook (Washington: U.S. Government Printing Office, 2003).

and productivity have generated a demand for highly skilled laborers, creative and risk-taking entrepreneurs, and capital-rich investors. Immigrants from India are well prepared for, and fit into, the employment needs of the globalizing U.S. economy because the large majority arrive with high levels of education, professional training, entrepreneur skills, and/or financial resources needed in the burgeoning knowledge-based economy.[3] The prestigious Indian Institutes of Technology (IIT) and the Indian Institutes of Science (IIS) educate a significant number of engineers and scientists who are then recruited by major U.S. multinational corporations.[4] Indeed, the United States has been the recipient of important Indian human capital that benefits the national economy. Some famous Indians in the United States include Sabeer Bhatia, co-founder of Hotmail, Vinod Khosla, co-founder of Sun Microsystems, Fareed Zakaria, author and editor of *Newsweek International*, Deepak Chopra, personality development author, and Dinesh D'Souza, author and conservative political commentator.

At the same time, some immigrants from India use the popular channel of family reunification to qualify for admission and legal permanent residence in the United States. Since the mid-1960s, immediate relatives of recent arrivals, including spouses, sons and daughters, parents, and brothers and sisters, often take advantage of family sponsorship to enter the United States. In 2001, for instance, nearly 43 percent of Indian immigrants entered the United States via the family reunification program.[5] These immigrants are typically more heterogeneous in their socioeconomic and occupational characteristics than those newcomers who arrive from India via the occupational preference program. As a result, they find more limited opportunities than their highly skilled relatives and primarily turn to lower-status jobs in service industries.

Most recently, the U.S. government, responding to the needs of multinational corporations, set higher occupational visa limits in the 1990 Immigration and Nationality Act. As a result, highly skilled Indian immigration to the United States dramatically accelerated during the 1990s. The 1990 legislation tripled the number of permanent residency visas granted on the basis of occupational skills. Additionally, the H-1B non-immigrant visa program included in the 1990 measure significantly increased the number of temporary foreign workers permitted to enter the United States.

The H-1B visa program was designed for temporary workers employed in "specialty occupations" that require highly specialized knowledge and at least a bachelor's degree or its equivalent. The annual cap and length of stay for H-1B visas has been subject to change—the American Competitiveness and Workforce Improvement Act of 1998 (ACWIA) raised the cap from 65,000 to 115,000 workers a year and allowed H-1B visa holders to stay in the United States for a maximum of six years. Subsequent legislation raised the annual limit of H-1B visa petitions to 195,000, permitted H-1B visa holders to bring families, and encouraged temporary migrants to adjust their legal status to permanent residents during their six-year maximum visa period. As a result, some estimates indicate that more than 50 percent of H-1B visa holders have become permanent residents.

According to INS data, India is the leading contributor of H-1B workers since the enactment of legislation in 1990. For instance, nearly 43 percent of H-1B visa petitions between October 1999 and February 2000 were granted to persons born in India, which far exceeds China, the next leading country (with less than 10 percent of the petitions). While the recent economic downturn and security concerns related to the terrorist attacks of September 11, 2001, have intensified debates on immigration in general, and the H-1B visa program in particular, the flow of migrants from India has yet to decline in any significant manner.

Settlement Patterns

Observers have noted the ways in which ethnic groups tend to seek out others like themselves and live in close spatial proximity to other co-ethnics. Unlike other ethnic groups, however, Indians (both foreign- and native-born) are more evenly distributed at numerous geographical scales. Employment opportunities play a more important role than ethnic enclaves in determining settlement patterns. In other words, Indian immigrants generally tend to settle wherever their skills are in demand, as opposed to many other immigrants who settle in places where their relatives and friends have already established communities.

At the national scale, Indians possess a relatively even spatial distribution (Map 13.1). With approximately 25 percent of the national total, the largest single proportion of Indians (both foreign- and native-born) resides in New York and New Jersey. These two states absorbed a large number of Indian immigrant medical professionals in the late 1960s and early 1970s, resulting in a high concentration of Indian immigrants and their U.S.-born children. The New York metropolitan area, including Northern

New Jersey, continues to be a primary magnet for settlement, as it provides a variety of opportunities for Indians employed in health, educational, and service occupations.

A considerable number of both foreign-born and native-born Indians also live in urbanized areas of California, Illinois, Texas, Florida, and Washington D.C. (Map 13.1). With the expansion of the information technology economy, new locations have emerged as the latest destinations for Indian professionals. The Southwest has experienced the most intense growth, and California led all states in 1990 and 2000, where the population now numbers more than 350,000. U.S. Immigration and Naturalization Service data on immigrants' state of intended residence for 1991–2003 indicates that significant numbers of Indian immigrants continue to move to the southwestern corner of the country. For Indian immigrants, over 30 percent reported that they intended to stay in California, suggesting that California will soon replace New York and New Jersey as the principal region for new settlement. Unlike most other Asian ethnic groups, many mid-sized metropolitan places are home to a substantial number of Indians (Map 13.1). These mid-sized urban regions offer economic opportunities to professionals such as doctors, engineers, and university educators, as well as business-oriented activity such as hotel and motel ownership.

At the geographical scales of the county and metropolitan region, the settlement pattern of Indians is decidedly heterolocal in nature. Increasingly, both foreign- and native-born Indians move to suburban areas just as those activities that formerly concentrated in central cities relocate to suburbia. By virtue of their generally high levels of

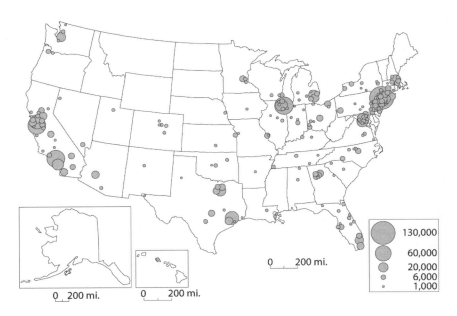

Map 13.1.   Geographical Distribution of Indians by County, 2000.
Source: 2000 Census of Population and Housing: Summary Tape File 4
(Washington: U.S. Government Printing Office, 2002).

human capital, both foreign-born and native-born Indians are financially capable of residing in suburban areas near their sources of employment. In fact, almost four in five residents of Indian descent now call the suburbs home, making Indians more likely to be suburbanites than any other ethnic group, including non-Hispanic whites.

Because of the heterolocal nature of Indian settlement, commercial hubs are not a distinctive feature of the Indian landscape. Indeed, the "Little India" commercial hubs are more common in older eastern cities. The most notable are New York City's Jackson Heights and Flushing neighborhoods; Edison, New Jersey; and Chicago's Devon Avenue. As commercial enclaves, these "Little Indias" provide cultural commodities such as food, clothing, jewelry, media, and a wide variety of ethnic services. Like other ethnic commercial enclaves, they conjure up the smells and sounds of "home." The following is a description by an immigrant walking down Chicago's Devon Avenue:

> For a few moments, I forgot that I was in Chicago. The sight of richly embroidered saris in the windows, the sound of Hindi film music blaring from the video shops, and the smell of spices frying in ghee in the restaurants magically transported me back home; I felt I was in one of New Delhi's busiest bazaars.[6]

Unlike traditional ethnic enclaves (like those operated by Cuban and Chinese immigrants, for example) where the spatial concentration of immigrants ensures access to community networks for both social and economic support, few organized networks exist in Indian commercial centers. The primary function of "Little India" business clusters, then, is to serve the immediate, specialized consumption needs of the group.

Socioeconomic Characteristics

Indians are striking in terms of their social and economic resources (Table 13.1). The majority possess a bachelor's degree or higher, and by virtue of their high educational level, most Indians hold good jobs and earn high incomes. As a group, Indians earned substantially higher household incomes than non-Hispanic white Americans and had the second-highest incomes among all Asian ethnic groups. Indians are more highly represented in professional occupations than any other ethnic group. Indeed, almost 60 percent of Indian workers are engaged in managerial, professional, or related occupations. Both males and females generally have high levels of participation in the labor force.

The majority of individuals also speak English well or very well. Given that many Indian immigrants attended schools where English was a required course—a remnant of British colonialism and its educational system, this is hardly surprising. English has also been adopted as an official language in India, primarily as a result of the post-independence Indian government's attempt to construct some linguistic cohesion in the face of enormous linguistic diversity. Thus many immigrants arrive with fluency in English, and this is critical to transferring their level of human capital. This fact results in a significant advantage when compared to other more traditional labor immigrants who lack English-speaking abilities when they arrive in the United States.

Table 13.1.   Indian Socioeconomic Characteristics

	Male	Female	Total for Indians	U.S.
Percent with Bachelor's Degree or Higher	69.66%	57.11%	63.89%	24.41%
Percent Labor Force Participation	79.11%	54.01%	67.47%	63.92%
Percent Professional, Managerial, or Related Occupation	63.49%	53.69%	59.952%	33.65%
Median Household Income	—	—	$63,669	$41,994
Percent Who Speak English Well or Very Well	—	—	73.31%	—

Source: *2000 Census of Population and Housing: Summary Tape File 4* (Washington: U.S. Government Printing Office, 2002).

This group (along with other Asian-origin ethnic groups) has commonly been characterized as a "model minority." Highlighted is the fact that, upon arrival, most Indian immigrants quickly assume an economic position comparable to that of the middle class in the United States. The popular press and academia refer to their "successful" assimilation and indicate that this success results from the immigrants' ambition and solid work ethic. Yet some evidence indicates that Indian workers do not always receive economic rewards comparable to their education and that despite high household incomes, the group encounters structural barriers and discrimination in the labor market.[7] In other words, Indian immigrants attain middle-class status, yet many are underemployed and overworked. There are also signs of the "glass ceiling" effect—characterized by mixed earnings, undefined career status, lack of promotion, and varied attrition of both foreign- and native-born Indian employees.[8]

Some critics also contend that the "model minority" terminology serves the majority population and rewards certain behaviors and attitudes, while unfairly using Indians as the standard which all minority groups should emulate. As Siva Vaidhyanathan suggests in an article published in *The Chronicle of Higher Education*:

> The costs of being a model minority include a capitulation to the ideology of white superiority, trepidation about forging alliances across class, ethnic, or religious boundaries, and a willingness to be used as a silent symbol in the rollback of social-justice initiatives like welfare and affirmative action.[9]

By emphasizing the importance of cultural traits and values in their "successful" adjustment, the positive stereotype of Indians in effect blames other minority populations for their own failure. Concurrently, the idea of the "model minority" ignores the very important influence of U.S. policy in immigrant selectivity and economic incorporation. As highly educated, state-selected immigrants, the "successful" assimilation of many Indian newcomers should not be unexpected.

At the same time, Indian women are largely left out of the "model-minority" construct. Their stories are typically cast in shadow by the success of their professional husbands. As Anannya Bhattacharjee suggests, "Her labor is rationalized on the grounds that she is her husband's helpmate; indeed, her labor becomes an extension of her household duties."[10]

Yet the majority of Indian women (both foreign- and native-born) work outside the home; as Table 13.1 indicates, 54 percent participate in the labor force and nearly 54 percent of those women work in professional occupations. Despite the many responsibilities associated with working outside the home, many Indian women are cast in traditional roles and encouraged (or forced) to become the torchbearers of family and culture as well.[11] Indeed, they become emblematic of what constitutes authentic "Indian-ness." What is this authentic "Indian-ness"? Sayantani and Shamita Dasgupta describe it as "the icon of the perfect Indian woman, preserving culture in the form of religion, language, dress, food, and childrearing, which upholds community integrity." As cultural custodians, Indian women become the primary transmitters of religious and cultural traditions within the household and in local associations. Thus, their socioeconomic achievements are likely to be less celebrated than perhaps their successes as mothers and community preservationists.

Indian taxicab drivers, small-business owners, and vendors expose another inadequacy of the "model minority" concept. Especially since the mid-1980s, the Indian community has become more socioeconomically and occupationally heterogeneous, largely as a result of the arrival of more lower- and lower-middle-class immigrants. This represents an important divide in the community. Despite some connection to other Indians through blood or marriage, these immigrants do not necessarily possess the same occupational and educational skills as the previous waves of Indian immigrants and their children. As a result, they find more limited opportunities than their relatives and turn to lower-status jobs. Many working-class Indians suffer a distancing from more economically successful cohorts. A documentary by Vivek Bald, *Taxi Meters and Plexiglass Partitions*, uncovers the classism that divides lower-class individuals from the middle- and upper-class Indian population.[12]

The legendary motel owners and operators form another distinct socioeconomic subgroup in the Indian community. These individuals, mostly immigrants who arrived in the 1960s and 1970s, came at a time when the U.S. motel industry was experiencing a lull. As Govind Bhakta explains, the new arrivals immediately began to take control of dilapidated, undervalued properties and converted them into moneymaking ventures.[13] By investing money and employing family members to ensure minimal labor costs, the hospitality industry soon proved to be a relatively stable business, with the added benefit of providing accommodation and jobs for the entire family. Having started off owning small properties, forward-minded individuals soon looked toward expansion. As a result, Indians (both foreign- and native-born) own as much as 60 percent of mid-sized motels and hotel properties in the United States.

Why has this impact on the American hospitality industry been called the "Patel motel" phenomenon? Nearly one-third of lodging facilities owned by Indians are owned by somebody named Patel; thus, the name has become so ingrained in the hotel industry that many people believe Patel is an Indian word meaning "hotel." In fact, as

Chhavi Dublish explains, the name Patel evolved from ancient India, where record keepers were appointed to keep track of crops planted on a parcel of land, or a *pat*.[14] Many Patels were literally born to sell under the Indian caste system that was designed to allow people to work according to their so-called natural tendencies.[15] Over generations, many Patels left their native Indian state of Gujarat to work as indentured servants in British colonies in Africa. After indentured labor was banned, many Patels stayed in Africa until political factors forced many to emigrate again, with several families making their way to the United States. Today, the results of this emigration and business specialization are clear: a significant number of savvy Indian entrepreneurs have crafted a formula for success in the hotel/motel industry.[16]

Community Case Study:
Maintaining Ethnic Identity

The Indian community in metropolitan Phoenix[17] provides an interesting case to explore the question of how individuals living in far-flung suburban or heterolocal neighborhoods negotiate their ethnic identity. The Indian population in metropolitan Phoenix has grown by more than 450 percent since 1980 (from a population of less than 2,000 to a population of more than 13,000—the vast majority of whom are foreign-born). At the same time, more than four in five residents of Indian descent in metropolitan Phoenix now call the suburbs home, making Indians more likely to be suburbanites than any other ethnic group, including non-Hispanic whites.

Indians in Phoenix utilize a variety of strategies in their attempts to (re)create and maintain a sense of cultural cohesion and solidarity. One strategy involves the building of permanent spaces as enduring sites for the demonstration and cultivation of Indian ethnic heritage. Another strategy makes use of temporary spaces as a more transitory way to bring families together to celebrate their cultural and religious traditions. Both strategies greatly affect community formation. Most significantly, the absence of a recognizable, visible ethnic community reinforces social fragmentation already apparent in the community before arrival in the United States, thus making any attempt at some sort of "Indian-ness" more difficult, if not impossible.

RESIDENTIAL PATTERNS

While the character of certain ethnic neighborhoods is quite prominent and based on the visible style and exterior decoration of housing, skin color, speech, and surnames of residents, no neighborhoods are easily "identifiable" as Indian in metropolitan Phoenix (Map 13.2). Despite being one of the larger ethnic groups in Phoenix, a "Little India" is not expressed in the landscape in part because of a heterolocal settlement pattern. The spatial dispersion of Indians is very pronounced because of three reasons. First, the vast majority of Indians live in the suburbs and only 10 percent live in Phoenix's central city. Second, the suburban population is relatively scattered, with the majority of

Indians residing in the newer suburbs of North Phoenix and the East Valley, an area that includes Chandler, Tempe, Mesa, Gilbert, and Ahwatukee. Third, no major residential concentrations have emerged despite the enormous growth in the Indian population over the last several years.

Both the North Phoenix and East Valley clusterings can be characterized as typical, newer suburbs, with relatively expensive housing. Single-family dwellings are neatly laid out on carefully plotted parcels of land in these residential zones. These neighborhoods exhibit the common characteristics of affluent suburban communities: higher-quality schools, lower crime rates, bigger and newer houses, and generally more agreeable surroundings. The communities include a relatively even distribution of housing, jobs, and retail sales, thus indicating a broad revenue base to pay for services to residents. These are also some of the more prestigious neighborhoods in metropolitan Phoenix where per capita incomes and property values are higher in comparison to other areas. Dramatically increasing housing prices reflect the intense desirability of these areas as well. On average, median resale housing prices in Scottsdale, Tempe, and Chandler grew by some 40 percent between 1994 and 1999.[18]

These same neighborhoods surround several high-tech industries, including Intel, Motorola, Allied Signal, and Honeywell, among others (Map 13.2). The sprinkling of these companies in the suburbs in many ways influences the residential distribution of Indians in Phoenix because the majority of Indians are employed in the professional occupations such as engineers, systems analysts, programmers, and scientists. In addition, large manufacturing companies, especially in aerospace and semiconductors, are generally located in North Phoenix and the southeast portions of the urban region—especially in Chandler and Mesa.

Interestingly, the area with the highest concentration of Indians is characterized by low-cost, high-density housing, consisting entirely of apartment complexes. Located directly to the east of Arizona State University, this area accommodates Indian students, who reside in this neighborhood due to its accessibility to the university. According to the university's admissions department, Arizona State has an average population of nearly 500 Indian students per year. Through time this area has become a popular residential choice for Indian students looking for low-rent apartments. They have come to numerically dominate one apartment complex and renamed it *Pariv Bhavan*—or India Palace.

Though the pattern of Indian settlement appears to be relatively scattered, some community leaders indicate a certain amount of regionalism that physically divides the community. They claim that though the process has been unintentional, northern Indians tend to have settled in North Phoenix, while Indians from Southern India concentrate more in the East Valley. A principal for the Telugu Association (a group organized by immigrants who speak Telugu—which is the native language of the southern Indian state, Andhra Pradesh) describes this patterning as the "North-South divide." He said during an interview, "Eighty percent of our Telugu Association membership comes from Chandler, Tempe . . . and I go, wow, this is really weird. So, I looked through our mailing list. 85226 (in Chandler) is our number one zip code in our mailing list." While the evidence is limited, this spatial patterning makes sense given the history of Indian immigration in the area and the development of Phoenix's suburbs in the past thirty years.

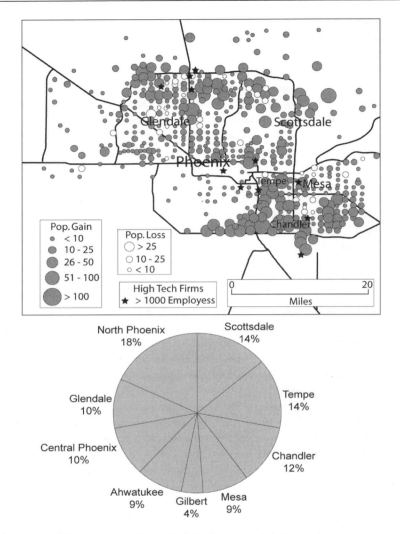

Map 13.2.   *Geographical Distribution of Indians in Metropolitan Phoenix, 2000. Source:* 2000 Census of Population and Housing: Summary Tape File 4 *(Washington: U.S. Government Printing Office, 2002).*

THE PATTERNING OF ETHNIC FACILITIES

An inventory of the Qwest telephone company directory reveals that ethnic shopping areas, places of worship, and sites of social activity are also spatially scattered.[19] More than thirty Indian grocery stores, specialty shops, and restaurants, three principal religious centers, and a cultural center exist in metro Phoenix. No focal point of activity is evident, though facilities are denser in the East Valley where there is a higher population of Indians. These businesses serve populations from all over the city. The India

Bazaar in Tempe, for example, attracts customers from such faraway places as Glendale and Queen Creek. Until recently, Pasand was the only restaurant in the Valley to serve "authentic" South Indian food, and its patrons include not only those from Tempe, but other Indians in Phoenix who come from southern portions of India.

Interestingly, many Indian businesses locate within a mile of high-tech companies like Intel and Motorola. India International Foods, India Fashions, Inc., and Kohinoor Sweets and Snacks are found in the same shopping center, which is directly across the street from a high-tech facility. Shopkeepers and restaurant owners claim that they draw in more customers by virtue of their close proximity to employment locations. The manager of Cuisine of India, located in Tempe, describes how the majority of his customers come from the Motorola plant located one mile to the east of the restaurant. He notices a significant number of single Indian men from Motorola who show up at the restaurant for most of their meals. The owner of the Indo-Pak grocery store in Chandler also uses his nearness to high-tech industries to attract Indian customers. He even offers a 10 percent discount to Intel employees.

Sites of Indian cultural and religious activities are spatially dispersed throughout the Valley. The Indo-American Cultural and Religious Center is situated in the middle of a largely Hispanic residential neighborhood, and is out-of-the-way for most Indians living in Phoenix, though the almost universal access to automobiles easily brings people together from dispersed locations. The same is true for the principal Indian religious centers, including the Hindu Temple of Arizona, the Bhaktivedanta Center (a Hindu temple), the Guru Nanak Dwara Ashram (a Sikh temple), and the Islamic Cultural Center (a mosque). No focal point of activity exists, though facilities are denser in the East Valley and North Phoenix, where greater numbers of Indians reside.

ETHNIC COMMUNITY WITHOUT SPATIAL PROPINQUITY

Although a vibrant ethnic community exists despite a heterolocal residential pattern, Indians have found a variety of ways to bring co-ethnics together and to keep their culture alive through the use of various permanent and transitory spaces.

Permanent Community Spaces

In Phoenix, the Indo-American Cultural and Religious Center is the Indian space that stands out among all others. This easily recognizable, warehouse-like structure serves as an important landmark and meeting hall for the Indian community living in the metropolitan area, and is a setting in which past and present place connections are reinforced. Within the meeting hall are sizeable areas for holding large festivals, along with a more intimate room for smaller get-togethers. One leader who directed the construction of the center describes a key reason for creating a permanent site dedicated to the collective place memory of Indian immigrants in Phoenix: "Immigrants first are busy with work and their own community activities. But then eventually there comes a time when we want to get back to our roots . . . to share our experiences and feelings. We needed a space where we can all get together."

The most popular event at the center is the annual festival that takes place every February. A leader in the community describes why he thinks it is important for festivals like this one to take place: "We first-generation immigrants bring with us many different traditions and religious faiths—we are Hindus, Muslims, Sikhs, and other faiths. We need to get together and share."

The Hindu Temple of Arizona is another important permanent site for the demonstration and cultivation of a broad Indian ethnic heritage.[20] Despite the fact that many Indians worship in private, Hinduism has become a centralizing and "public" feature in many newly established immigrant communities.[21] The Phoenix temple is now located in a former church in South Scottsdale, previously occupied by the Church of God. Nothing distinctive or particularly "Indian" sets apart this block-like building from the surrounding landscape with the exception of a temporary banner hung over the sign of the previous church.

Leaders are renovating the interior of the building to accommodate their notion of an all-encompassing Hinduism. For instance, the altar cobbles together numerous deities of Hinduism to produce a sort of "generic shrine," as one principal labeled it. The arrangement doesn't call upon any particular style; instead the altar brings together many deities celebrated differently by various subgroups of Indians across India. The religious display is based more on local knowledge and local Phoenix ethnic politics than on creating an "authentic" presentation of Hinduism as it is found in India. Leaders have made strategic decisions as to which aspects of the religion to single out, resulting in a highly subjective and rather generic conception of Hinduism. Divisions have been minimized in order to remake an identity upon which all will hopefully agree.

Though one of the aforementioned community sites focuses on culture while the other concentrates on religion, together they craft a conception that is remarkably similar: to fashion permanent spaces that call attention to the togetherness and collectivity of Indians living in Phoenix. Unfortunately, the "Indian-ness" presented by these community spaces has taken on a character that is significantly different from how many foreign- and native-born individuals conceive of themselves as "Indian." Planners have chosen to present certain images and notions of India, and to modify the past to create a pan-ethnic conception of Indian ethnic identity. This practice has in turn failed to capture the sentiments of many individual Indians, and has served to alienate some in the community, while at the same time contributing to a general confusion in coming to an understanding of "Indian-ness." Unfortunately, these collective permanent sites possess limited appeal with most Indian families living in Phoenix. Only a very select population from the community utilizes either space, and membership in the organizing associations has been modest, despite the enormous overall expansion of the Indian population in Phoenix.

Transitory Places of Community Interaction

Most Indians in Phoenix belong to tightly organized, parochial associations structured around the various regional and linguistic subgroups found on the Indian subcontinent (India has more than 1 billion residents separated into 25 states, speaking 15 official languages). Though socializing is made more difficult because of the heterolocal settlement pattern, many of the smaller Indian ethnic organizations successfully use weekend get-togethers in transitory spaces to (re)construct a sense of community. These "transitory" spaces include area schools, movie theaters, and public parks. In this "place-making" strategy, Indians (both the foreign-born immigrants and their native-born children) invoke and transform traditionally ordinary spaces into social and communal spaces that they temporarily call their own. Unlike permanent sites of ethnic maintenance that endure as visibly identifiable and generic "Indian" spaces, transitory sites are nearly always inconspicuous in the urban landscape. They exist as "Indian" places only briefly, to be returned to their customary purpose once events conclude.

For example, the Maharashtra Mandal gathering, Ganeshotsav (Ganesh festival), takes place annually in late August. Traced back to India, the festival focuses entirely on the Hindu god Ganesh.[22] Traditionally, the event required community members to pay tribute to Ganesh with visits to the local temple, followed by a period of meditation and contemplation. Ganeshotsav also provided the occasion to cook special foods, and to revel in dancing and music. In its Phoenix manifestation, Ganeshotsav is an all-day celebration at a local high school, and includes an afternoon banquet lunch followed by religious services. The central event of the day includes a roll call of all members to present gifts to Ganesh. From the eldest participant to the youngest, each individual recommits himself to the deity with the presentation of a special food offering (prepared days before by female association members). During the local rendering, Ganeshotsav serves not so much as a religious event but as a time of homecoming and remembrance for Indians with roots in the state of Maharashtra in west-central India. The celebration is tightly focused on members of the local Maharashtra Mandal rather than on the entire Indian community living in metropolitan Phoenix. It is a relatively small affair, with just over three hundred participants, most of whom claim Maharashtra as their regional homeland. Members temporarily transform the otherwise sterile school cafeteria with brightly colored decorations, a statue of Ganesh, and numerous tables loaded with food delicacies from Maharashtra. Neighbors and friends from all over metropolitan Phoenix meet and renew friendships. The festival becomes a site for both celebration and considerable socializing and catching up on community affairs.

Nearly every Saturday morning, Indians from different regions in India also transform a local cinema and watch movies imported from their home states. The theater, located in a typical suburban strip mall, usually caters to nearby non-Indian residents where $1.50 gets customers into older-release movies. Once a week, however, both foreign-born immigrants and their native-born children come to the theater to catch the latest releases in their native and regional language. The movies are a nostalgic link to their home regions and promote the solidarity of fellow language speakers through regionally specific cultural images.

Most local regional-linguistic associations also organize yearly picnics to bring together their widely scattered members. Many utilize the Deepavali holiday, an important Hindu festival, as a pretext to gather members for a picnic. During various times in the year, picnic tables at various local parks become the center of celebration for members of different Indian parochial associations in Phoenix. Picnickers drive from all over the metropolitan area to gather with compatriots, speak in their native tongue, and encourage their children to play with other children from their home states in

India. The picnics rarely include a religious element or entertainment program. Unlike other group affairs, which often include performances of indigenous song and dance, or a staged production by association members of a popular drama or religious ritual, the picnics adhere to more unceremonious and secular activities to foster a casual and relaxed sense of togetherness for immigrants and their children.

Besides the frequent gatherings that occur in schools, movie theaters, and local area parks, Indians can be found playing cricket or field hockey at assorted sports fields around the Valley, congregating in suburban homes for weekly devotional meetings, or celebrating the many Indian national and religious holidays in the conference rooms of Arizona State University or local hotels. These gatherings remain largely invisible to anyone except the participants themselves and leave no vivid imprints on the landscape. Instead, transitory spaces exist in a state of flux because the participants inhabit multiple social fields for brief periods, never setting their roots down for more than a short time. During social encounters, conventional sites become the target of place transformation, and individuals (re)create remarkable visions and feelings of "home."

IMPLICATIONS OF INVISIBILITY AT THE LOCAL SCALE

While some may assume that ethnic communities must be visibly manifest in order for individuals to be involved in a meaningful way, Indians in Metropolitan Phoenix demonstrate that it is possible to (re)create a sense of ethnicity despite living in dispersed suburban neighborhoods. The strategies employed by ethnic Indian organizations and the actions of individuals demonstrate the multiple ways in which "Indian-ness" has been (re)created, both materially and symbolically, within the local community. Despite geographical dispersal, the dozen local Indian associations form transitory spaces where they valorize parochial traditions and heritage. They generally aim to promote their own version of "Indian-ness" and attempt to improve socialization by (re)constructing a sense of togetherness among their members. Gujaratis hang out together, individuals with roots in Maharashtra give priority to other Maharashtrians, and Tamils, too, construct exclusive social spaces. In this way, they circumvent the nation- (India) and pan-ethnic- (Indian American) building politics of permanent spaces, like the Indo-American Cultural and Religious Center and the Hindu Temple of Arizona. While informal and formal networks have increased among associations, more introverted and parochial attachments prevail as the primary means by which individuals construct identities. Ultimately, small disparate groups and transitory spaces predominate in Phoenix as the community is continually defined and redefined by its socio-spatial fragmentation.

The Role of Transnationalism

In the contemporary context of globalization, especially with the advent of new technologies of transport, information, and communication, increasing numbers of Indians (both foreign- and native-born) become engaged in transnational activities. The High Level Committee on Indian Diaspora established in 2002, under the chairmanship of Dr. L. M. Singhvi, M.P., employs this concept of diaspora in a generic sense for "communities of migrants living or settled permanently in other countries, aware of its origins and identity and maintaining varying degrees of linkages with the mother country."[23] These linkages include hundreds of Indian Internet websites, thousands of airplane trips, millions of phone calls and email exchanges, and billions of remittance dollars between the two countries to reinforce ties between Indians abroad and their home communities.

REMITTANCES

Many Indian immigrants in the United States have immense interest in family economic advancement and the development of their communities of origin. In 2001, for instance, more than 10 billion U.S. dollars were sent to India from immigrants living in the United States.[24] Most often, immigrants send remittances to the families back home to buy land and other properties. They also contribute their remittances for the development of charities, hospitals, and educational centers in their home communities.

At other times, immigrants (as well as their children) invest their savings (accumulated overseas from professional salaries, business enterprises, and other profitable investments) as Non-Resident Indians (NRIs). These monies go to establishing industries and factories, buying land and transport companies, and investing in Indian banks.[25] NRIs are emerging as a new transnational business class which is attempting to carve out a role for itself, both in India and around the globe.

INDIA.COM

With the help of the Internet, web and news groups, and regular communication through e-mail, both foreign- and native-born Indians in the United States create virtual spaces of interaction with their home communities. Paul Adams and Rina Ghose discovered that the Internet has compressed both space and time between India and the United States in a magnitude never anticipated.[26] They found that Indians maintain websites for the purposes of cultural preservation and the maintenance of origin-country identities: these include local community association sites, national organization sites, religious sites, and sites for purchasing cultural commodities like clothing, jewelry, food items, music recordings, videos, DVDs, and books. Sites created in India also bridge the gap between the United States and India and include online versions of Indian newspapers, business sites, cultural sites, and sites supporting the search for marriage partners.

This last type of website, where marriage negotiation takes place (whether through personal ads, brokers, or parental mediators), is one of the more unique transnational uses of the Internet. Increasing colloquial evidence indicates that matrimonial sites are often used by families arranging marriages, in both India and the United States (matchmaking is an unquestioned responsibility of the traditional Indian family).[27] The sites contain incredible amounts of information relating to caste, religion, ethnicity, education, and employment, which are all considered essential by matchmaking families. When compared to early periods where marriage took place within the local context, the process has now gone global, reaching out to include the various Indian diasporic communities in Singapore, Kenya, Hong Kong, the U.K., Canada, and the United States. Marriage has truly become transnational with websites like <www.suitablematch.com>, <www.matrimonialonline.com>, and more region-specific websites like <www.tamilmatrimony.com> and <www.punjabimarriage.com>.

ZEE TELEVISION NETWORK

The expansion of satellite and cable networks has witnessed the spread of channels targeting the overseas Indian population. Zee Television Network is India's largest media and entertainment company and is very popular among Indians seeking to stay connected with popular culture in India.[28] The company began Hindi-language U.S. programming in 1998 and includes more than twenty channels of satellite programming like Zee TV—the entertainment channel, Zee Cinema—the cinema channel, Zee News—the 24-hour news channel, and Zee Music—the music channel.

Zee Television Network produces the largest volume of Hindi-language programming in the world, with more than 30,000 hours of original programming in its library. Zee TV reaches an estimated 250 million viewers in over 120 countries in regions across the globe. Yet Zee TV, with its reliance on Hindi-language broadcasting, and focus on "Indian" themes and characters, fails to captivate the imaginations of many living in the United States, primarily because of its nationalistic focus. The history of the Indian subcontinent's complex social relations underscores how subgroup differences and the lack of a national identity may make Zee Television Network less appealing to those foreign-born and native-born Indians in the United States. Many of these Indians identify more closely with regional identities in India. Interestingly, Zee Television Network has begun to recognize these parochialisms and is now test-marketing new satellite channels associated with various states in India (with programs spoken in the native language of that state), like Alpha Marathi, Alpha Bangla, and Alpha Punjabi. In response, the newer Sun Network offers similar satellite programming in a handful of southern Indian languages.

Conclusion

As part of a much larger and historical global scale diaspora, the U.S. Indian population has dramatically expanded over the past three decades to become the third largest Asian ethnic group in the country. Indians stand apart from most other ethnic groups in two major respects. First, geographical distribution is more dispersed at both national and metropolitan scales. Second, unlike many non-Western immigrants to the

United States, contemporary Asian Indian immigration includes highly educated and skilled labor migrants with English-language skills, all of which provides significant human capital that proves beneficial to the economic adjustment process. These characteristics often lead observers to label the group a "model minority" even though there is much evidence that this term disguises important socioeconomic variation within the Indian community.

As the Phoenix case demonstrates, many Indians retain their home identities because it is what they know and with what they are most familiar. Many foreign-born and native-born Indians also employ multiple transnational strategies to connect with their respective homes on a continual basis. Yet the reality is that with longer residence in the United States, their customs and traditions will take on a character much different from what they left behind.

How do the U.S.-born children and grandchildren of Indian immigrants forge their identities? The evidence for this process is somewhat limited because the constant influx of young migrants ensures a largely Indian-born population. Even so, the second generation is becoming an increasingly important segment of the Indian community. In 2000, nearly 33 percent of Indians were born in the United States. As these children come of age, the negotiation of Indian and American cultural values serves as a constant source of disagreement between generations.[29]

Second-generation Indians are faced with their parents' traditions and cultural heritage while simultaneously being confronted with "American" values. Indeed, American-born Confused Desi (ABCD) is a polarizing concept in the Indian community. First-generation immigrants use the ponderous and overused ABCD acronym to perpetuate the sense that American-born Indians are confused about who they are and where they belong. But few first-generation parents are willing to acknowledge their own role in this confusion. Often parents forcefully familiarize their children with a feigned "Indian-ness" through religion, art, language, ritual, and practice based on outdated modes of culture and standards which they themselves grew up with in India many years ago.

At the same time children are continuously exposed to "American" values and customs. Hurtling back and forth between distinct cultural worlds constitutes their lived reality. The bombardment of supposedly binary opposites encourages bewilderment among second-generation children. Hence, as Archana Pathak explains, "The Indian youth of America are highly traditional in a way that their Indian counterparts in India are not. Thus, Indian youth are both typical Americans and antique Indians at the same time."[30] Indian youth often intimate a feeling of exclusion from "American" culture, yet they express that they do not belong to an "Indian" world either. The result is a powerful sense of marginality.

Notes

This chapter is a compilation of materials gathered and written for my dissertation (Emily H. Skop, *The Saffron Suburbs: Asian Indian Immigrant Community Formation in Metropolitan*

Phoenix [Tempe: Arizona State University, 2002]). I would like to thank Alex Oberle and Brandon Vogt, both Ph.D. students in the Department of Geography at Arizona State University, Paul Peters, Ph.D. student in the Department of Sociology at UT-Austin, and Claire E. Altman, an undergraduate in the Urban Studies Program at UT-Austin, for helping me compile and create updated maps and statistical tables in this chapter.

1. From this point forward, I will utilize the label *Indian* to refer to those immigrants arriving in the United States from India. This is the most precise term and represents the way that most individual immigrants from India (and their children) identify themselves. It is a conscious step away from the "Asian Indian" categorization created by the U.S. Census Bureau—a largely political term created after much maneuvering on the part of the 1980 Census Advisory Committee for Asian/Pacific Americans. See Manoranjan Dutta, "Asian Indian Americans: Search for an Economic Profile," in *From India to America: A Brief History of Immigration, Problems of Discrimination, Admission, and Assimilation*, ed. S. Chandrasekhar (La Jolla, CA: Population Review Publications, 1982), 76–86.

2. These persons identified themselves as "Asian Indian alone" on the race question in the 2000 Census of Population.

3. Anna Lee Saxenian, *Silicon Valley's New Immigrant Entrepreneurs* (San Francisco: Public Policy Institute of California, 1999).

4. Joel Kotkin, *The New Geography: How the Digital Revolution Is Reshaping the American Landscape* (New York: Random House, 2002); and Kavita Pandit, "The Restructuring of Skilled Migrant Streams: The Dual Circuits of Indian Information Technology Workers in the United States" (paper presented at the annual meeting of the Association of American Geographers, Los Angeles, March 2002).

5. Ramah McKay, "Family Reunification," *Migration Information Source*, <www.migration information.org/USfocus/display.cfm?id=122> (3 October 2004).

6. Padma Rangaswamy, *Namasté America: Indian Immigrants in an American Metropolis* (University Park: Pennsylvania State University Press, 2000), iii.

7. Pyong Gap Min, "Major Issues Relating to Asian American Experiences" in *Asian Americans: Contemporary Trends and Issues*, ed. Pyong Gap Min (Thousand Oaks, CA: Sage Publications, 1995), 38–57; and Neil Gotanda, "Re-Producing the Model Minority Stereotype: Judge Joyce Karlin's Sentencing Colloquy in People v. Soon Ja Du," in *Reviewing Asian America: Locating Diversity*, ed. Wendy L. Ng et al. (Pullman: Washington State University Press, 1995), 87–106.

8. Marilyn Fernandez, "Asian Indian Americans in the Bay Area and the Glass Ceiling," *Sociological Perspectives* 41, no. 1 (March 1998): 119–149.

9. Siva Vaidhyanathan, "Inside a 'Model Minority': The Complicated Identity of South Asians," *Chronicle of Higher Education*, 23 June 2000, 1–7.

10. Anannya Bhattacharjee, "The Habit of Ex-Nomination: Nation, Woman, and the Indian Immigrant Bourgeoisie," *Public Culture* 5, no. 1 (March 1992): 19–44.

11. Sayantani Dasgupta and Shamita das Dasgupta, "Women in Exile: Gender Relations in the Asian Indian Community in the U.S.," in *Contours of the Heart: South Asians Map North America*, ed. Sunaina Maira and Rajini Srikanth (New York: The Asian American Writers' Workshop, 1996), 381–400; Radha S. Hegde, "Swinging the Trapeze: The Negotiation of Identity among Asian Indian Immigrant Women in the United States," in *Communication and Identity across Cultures*, ed. Dolores V. Tanno and Alberto Gonzalez (Thousand Oaks, CA: Sage Publications, 1998), 34–55; and Prema Kurien, "Gendered Ethnicity: Creating a Hindu Indian Identity in the United States," *American Behavioral Scientist* 42, no. 4 (December 1999): 648–670.

12. Vivek Bald, "Taxi Meters and Plexiglass Partitions," In *Contours of the Heart: South Asians*

Map North America, ed. Sunaina Maira and Rajini Srikanth (New York: The Asian American Writers' Workshop, 1996), 66–73.

13. Govind Bhakta, *Patels: A Gujurati Community History in the United States* (Los Angeles: UCLA Asian American Studies Center Press, 2003).

14. Chhavi Dublish, "America's Patel Motels," *BBC News*, <news.bbc.co.uk/go/pr/fr/ /2/hi/south_asia/3177054.stm> (20 September 2004).

15. Dublish, "America's Patel Motels."

16. Even as these individuals have been highly successful, they have faced some flagrant discrimination, especially in far-flung towns. After 9/11, especially, there was a certain increase in racial bias as some American motel owners began to display signs of "American-owned motel" in their windows. Jeremy Meyer, "'American Owned' Motels Cater to Growing Anti-Immigrant Sentiment," *Colorado Springs Gazette*, 9 November 2002.

17. During the following discussion, I will use the terms Phoenix, Metropolitan Phoenix, and the Valley interchangeably in referring to the Phoenix metropolitan area.

18. Catherine Reagor, "Home Sales Still Booming, Prices Rising," *The Arizona Republic*, 4 March 2001.

19. USWest, *The Yellow Pages* (Englewood, CO: US West, 2002).

20. There are other "permanent" religious sites that draw Indian followers, including the Guru Nanak Dwara Ashram (a Sikh temple) and the Islamic Cultural Center (an Islamic mosque). In this research, I have chosen to focus only on the Hindu site as a potential space for the (re) creation of an "Indian" ethnic identity. This is largely due to the fact that a majority of the Indians I spoke with in Phoenix are followers of Hinduism.

21. For a discussion of religion in the Indian community, see Harold Coward, "Hinduism in Canada," in *The South Asian Religious Diaspora in Britain, Canada, and the United States*, ed. Harold Coward, John R. Hinnells, and Raymond Williams (Albany: State University of New York Press, 2000), 151–172. Also see Stephen R. Warner and Judith G. Wittner, eds., *Gatherings in Diaspora: Religious Communities and the New Immigration* (Philadelphia: Temple University Press, 1998).

22. Ganesh is the elephant-headed deity, son of Shiva and Parvati and renowned for his benevolence in granting wishes and offering protection. See Kim Knott, "Hinduism in Britain," in *The South Asian Religious Diaspora in Britain, Canada, and the United States*, ed. Harold Coward, John R. Hinnells and Raymond Williams (Albany: State University of New York Press, 2000), 89–108.

23. High Level Committee on Indian Diaspora, *Executive Summary: The Report of the High Level Committee on Indian Diaspora* (New Delhi: Ministry of External Affairs, 2002).

24. Dilip Ratha, *Workers' Remittances: An Important and Stable Source of External Development Finance* (New York: Global Development Finance, World Bank, 2003).

25. Johanna Lessinger, "Investing or Going Home? A Transnational Strategy among Indian Immigrants in the United States," in *Towards a Transnational Perspective on Migration: Race, Class, Ethnicity, and Nationalism Reconsidered*, ed. Nina Glick Schiller, Linda Basch, and Cristina Blanc-Szanton (New York: New York Academy of Sciences, 1992), 53–80.

26. Much of the information for this section is taken from Paul Adams and Rina Ghose, "India.com: The Construction of a Space Between," *Progress in Human Geography* 27, no. 4 (August 2003): 414–437. Also see Emily Skop and Paul Adams, "Gender Roles and Asian Indian Appropriation of the Internet" (under review).

27. A single matrimonial site studied by Paul Adams and Rina Ghose (2003) had over 88,000 members!

28. The information for this section is taken from the company's website: <www.zeetelevision.com/> (20 September 2004).

29. To read more about the struggles of second-generation Indians, see Priya Agarwal, *Passage from India: Post-1965 Indian Immigrants and Their Children: Conflicts, Concerns, and Solutions* (Palos Verdes, CA: Yuvati Publications, 1991); Sunita S. Mukhi, *Doing the Desi Thing: Performing Indianness in New York City* (New York: Garland Publications, 2000); and Vijay Prashad, *The Karma of Brown Folk* (Minneapolis: University of Minnesota Press, 2000).

30. Archana Pathak, *To Be Indian (Hyphen) American: Communicating Diaspora, Identity, and Home* (Norman: University of Oklahoma, 1998), 71.

CHAPTER 14

Conflict Migrants from Mainland Southeast Asia

Christopher A. Airriess

A significant proportion of the post-1965 Asian immigrant stream to the United States is comprised of Mainland Southeast Asians from the countries of Viet Nam, Cambodia (Khmer Republic), and Laos. Of the 11,898,828 Asian Americans in 2000, approximately 1,814,301 or 15 percent listed their "race" as being connected to these three Mainland Southeast Asian countries. The largest of the three groups are Vietnamese at 1,223,736 (67.4%), followed by Cambodian at 206,052 (11.3%), Lowland Lao at 198,203 (10.9%), and Hmong or Highland Lao at 186,310 (10.2%).

Considering these four groups as a single category of Mainland Southeast Asians is partially justified by a number of characteristics. First, all three countries were established as French colonial possessions between the 1860s and 1890s under the single colonial government of the Union of Indochina. Second, Buddhism is the dominant religion, particularly in Cambodia and in Lowland Laos. In Viet Nam, Buddhism is mixed with Confucianism, and the country has a small Roman Catholic minority. Hmong are primarily Animists, with some converting to Protestantism during the early 1900s. Third, and most important, these four groups are for the most part "conflict migrants" who emigrated because of the U.S. government's failed Cold War regional strategy against Communism during the 1960s and 1970s. Presenting the United States with a moral obligation to provide safety for those who felt persecuted under newly installed Communist governments, most political refugees entered under special immigrant status that comprised the largest refugee resettlement program in U.S. history. We should not assume, however, that these four groups possess mutual affinities because, after all, the regional label of Mainland Southeast Asia is a convenient Western geographical construction of imagined regional homogeneity with which these four groups do not necessarily identify.

The Context of Conflict and Creating Refugees

After Japan's World War II defeat, France reclaimed Viet Nam as a colonial possession, but was challenged by both Nationalists and Communists in a protracted conflict in the north. The French were defeated by the Communist Vietminh, and Viet Nam was subsequently separated into two halves by the 1954 Geneva Agreement. In response, over one million northerners, many of whom were Roman Catholic, streamed into South Viet Nam to create a large pool of anti-Communists to bolster the pro-Western and capitalist government in the south. After sending military and political advisors in the late 1950s, the U.S. government deployed approximately 200,000 military personnel in 1965 to engage the Vietcong, the southern wing of the northern Vietminh. Despite huge foreign aid programs to win the hearts and minds of the Vietnamese peasantry, the relocation of five million refugees to regions of government control, massive bombing campaigns, as well as the deployment of more U.S. troops, the Vietcong were able to eventually control half the villages in the south. With an increasingly autocratic South Vietnamese government, plus waning political support for the war at home, a ceasefire was signed with North Viet Nam in 1973. After withdrawing all U.S. troops that same year, the capital of Sai Gon fell to Communist troops in April 1975, and Viet Nam became unified under a Communist government.[1]

Because of the fear of political and religious persecution, "first wave" refugees largely included those connected to the U.S. presence during the war, who were primarily urban and educated, and refugee Roman Catholic farmers and fishermen. These 125,000 "high risk" individuals were airlifted during the fall of Sai Gon, or evacuated by boat and rescued offshore by both military and civilian vessels. The more voluminous "second wave" refugee movement between 1977 and 1979 escaped in overcrowded boats in an effort to make safe landfall in the first asylum countries of Thailand, Malaysia, Indonesia, and the Philippines where the United Nations established refugee transit camps.[2] Numbering approximately 300,000 refugees and largely comprised of ethnic-Chinese Vietnamese, these "boat people" experienced boat sinkings, rape, and robbery at the hands of pirates. It is estimated that 40,000 to 150,000 refugees died at sea. In part because of the high mortality rate of refugees, the "third wave" refugee movement commenced in 1979 as part of the United Nations–sponsored Orderly Departure Program in which 125,000 individuals departed on commercial or special flights.[3] Today, the United States is home to 1,223,736 people of Vietnamese ancestry, but other countries such as France (300,000), Australia (174,200), Canada (151,410), and Germany (83,526) also host substantial numbers of Vietnamese conflict migrants and their post-migration offspring.

The impact of the Viet Nam War on Cambodia and Laos was just as tragic. Indirectly administered during the French colonial period, both possessions were granted independence in 1953. Remaining neutral throughout the Viet Nam War under a monarchical government, Cambodia was drawn into the war when the North Vietnamese Army established supply bases along the Cambodia–South Viet Nam border and allied itself with the pro-Communist Khmer Rouge guerillas. After having helped to install the Lon Nol government in 1970, the U.S. government began a covert bombing campaign against North Vietnamese supply bases. This "carpet" bombing escalated during 1971–1973 and produced approximately one million internal refugees. The same year that the United States left Viet Nam, the Khmer Rouge came to power and embarked on its reign of terror by emptying cities, murdering the elite, and collectivizing agriculture. These draconian policies led to the infamous "killing fields" in which

Cambodia's population of eight million was reduced by 25 percent.[4] In 1979 Viet Nam overthrew the Khmer Rouge government, but continued military conflict until the mid-1980s forced 250,000 refugees to seek refuge in United Nations' camps in neighboring Thailand.[5] In 1989, Viet Nam withdrew from Cambodia, a UN cease-fire was arranged in 1991, and an independent government was established in 1992.

Because of two very different culture groups, the situation in Laos is more complex than Cambodia's. Accounting for approximately 50 percent of the national population, the politically dominant and more urban lowland Lao or *Lao Loum* have traditionally inhabited the Mekong River lowlands. The other half of the national population is comprised of approximately sixty highland tribal groups referred to as highland Lao or *Lao Theung* inhabiting small clan-based villages and practicing shifting cultivation. One of the largest highland ethnic groups is the Hmong who were forced to migrate from southern China in the early 1800s, and comprised 10 percent of the national population in 1970. The Hmong were the most negatively impacted highland group during the Viet Nam War and its immediate aftermath. Allied with the returning French and royal Lao government against the pro-Communist Pathet Lao following World War II, the Hmong were later enlisted by the CIA in a secret war against the Communist Pathet Lao. By 1969, some 40,000 Hmong guerillas were also used to disrupt the North Vietnamese military supply lines leading south along the Ho Chi Minh Trail that straddled the Viet Nam–Laos border. The reward for the Hmong was the U.S. government promise that victory would mean an autonomous highland kingdom, or if defeated, a new place to live.[6] After the U.S. withdrawal in 1975, the Pathet Lao government forced many into reeducation camps, confiscated land, and engaged in genocidal chemical warfare against the Hmong. By 1985, some 350,000 Hmong and lowland Lao fled their country, many by foot to United Nations refugee camps across the Mekong River in Thailand.[7]

Crossing the Pacific

Between 1975 and 2002, approximately 1,670,019 Mainland Southeast Asian refugees, asylees, and immigrants arrived in the United States as their country of final residence. The volume of refugees and immigrants has changed through both space and time based on government policies on both sides of the Pacific (Fig. 14.1). The refugee "first wave" in 1975 consisted almost exclusively of refugees from Viet Nam and Laos. After a lull in migration in 1976, the "second wave" of refugees between 1977 and 1979 was characterized by an explosion of migration of Vietnamese from South China Sea camps, and Laotian, Hmong, and Cambodians from camps in Thailand. The less voluminous, but still considerable refugee "third wave" between 1979 and 1983 was marked by the implementation of the United Nations Orderly Departure Program as well as the U.S. 1980 Refugee Act which substantially raised the refugee admittance ceiling.

From the mid-1980s onwards, migration flow comprising the "fourth wave" becomes more complex. In nine of the sixteen years between 1986 and 2002, Vietnamese immigrants, rather than refugees, comprised the majority of entrants. The increased proportion of immigrants that sustained this steady flow never fell below

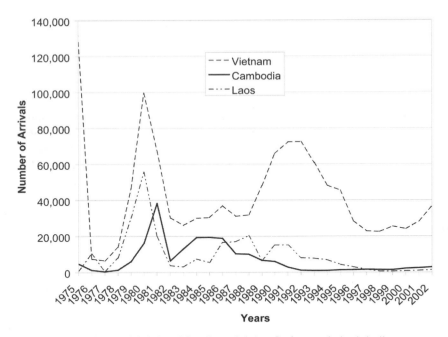

Figure 14.1.   Mainland Southeast Asian Refugee Arrivals in the United States, 1975–2002. Source: Max Niedzwieki and T. C. Duong, "Southeast Asian Statistical Profile" (Southeast Asian Resource Action Center, 2004) <www.searac.org/seastprofilemay04.pdf> (13 March 2004).

22,000 individuals per year because of three primary factors. First, the majority of the flow was family members who entered on family reunification visas. Second, the Vietnamese government began releasing detainees from "indoctrination camps," and this, coupled with the liberalization of the centrally planned economy in 1989, allowed former detainees and their families to emigrate. Third, this immigration stream included *Amerasians* who are the discriminated offspring of wartime American and Vietnamese sexual unions. Following the implementation of the 1988 Amerasian Homecoming Act, over 75,000 Amerasians and their family members were admitted with immigrant status, but were entitled to refugee services and benefits.

From 1987 onward, Cambodian refugee flows never accounted for more than 50 percent of the migration pool, and from 1995 to 2002, immigrants comprised 100 percent of that pool. The 1986–1991 increase of those originating from Laos was primarily Hmong. They entered the United States almost exclusively under refugee status until 1998 when all flows slowed to a trickle. Nevertheless, in 2003 some 15,000 Hmong remained at a single location in Thailand waiting for resettlement in the United States.

U.S. Resettlement Patterns

The resettlement geography of the four groups is characterized by complex and multiple patterns based upon resettlement policies, the activities of humanitarian organizations, the role of social and family networks, and the economic opportunities that some regions or locations provide migrants. The policy of the U.S. government toward the "first wave" refugees was to disperse them as widely as possible so that the social infrastructure of certain cities and counties would not be overburdened. This policy was based on the philosophy that geographical dispersal would quicken the assimilation process.[8] The dispersal process was enhanced by the government's use of a number of voluntary agencies or *Volags* representing particular ethnic, religious, and secular interests; they were responsible for recruiting sponsors for refugees and providing a variety of programs to assist in socioeconomic adjustment. Local *Volags* were very aggressive because first wave refugees were placed in 813 different zip codes in all fifty states.[9] There was, however, an urban bias because *Volags* were largely urban-based.

The dispersal policy began to break down, however, as some 45 percent of "first wave" refugees in the early 1980s had secondarily migrated to a different state than the state in which they first settled.[10] Geographical concentration increased with "second wave" and "third wave" refugees and immigrants because, as relatives and friends, "first wave" refugees were able to function as sponsors; by the early 1980s, for example, approximately two-thirds of arrivals had relatives or friends already living in the United States.[11] Often these secondary movers migrated to locations where relatives and friends live, but also to states or urban places with dynamic and healthy economies which not coincidentally possess better state-supported financial and medical services.

While the spatial distribution for each group is essentially different, three commonalities are observable. First, California and a different combination of a handful of other states account for the lion's share of each group's spatial concentration. Second, the California concentration remains dominant today, but has declined in its share of the national total through secondary migration, particularly to smaller urban centers in states that in 1990 possessed lower percentage shares of each group. Third, some urban regions or counties exhibit a significant spatial overlap of different combinations of each group.

VIETNAMESE

The spatial distribution of ethnic Vietnamese is the most regionally even of all ethnic groups, although with some quite notable concentrations (Map 14.1). Concentration in some states and regions is in part tied to the location of four reception centers for the 1975 "first wave" refugees at Camp Pendleton in Southern California, Fort Chafee, Arkansas, Eglin Air Force Base in the Florida Panhandle, and Fort Indiantown Gap, Pennsylvania.

With 443,110 ethnic Vietnamese, California accounts for 36 percent of the national population with three counties hosting 70 percent of the state total and an

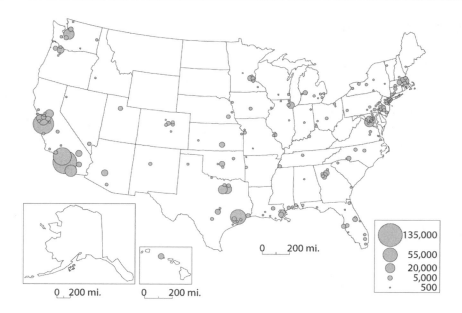

Map 14.1.   Population Distribution by Counties with More Than
500 Vietnamese. Source: U.S. Census, American Fact Finder, Summary
File 2 (SF2).

amazing 25 percent of the national ethnic Vietnamese population. The greatest concentration is in Orange County, which accounts for 30 percent of the state total and 11 percent of the national total. The other two counties are Los Angeles and Santa Clara, the latter being centered on the city of San Jose in the San Francisco Bay area. While the national percentage of ethnic Vietnamese in California declined between 1990 (45%) and 2000 (36%), selected urban places or regions have witnessed dramatic growth between 1990 and 2000. The more suburban Orange and Santa Clara counties grew by 87 percent and 78 percent respectively. Conversely, the more urban Los Angeles and San Francisco counties experienced only 23 percent and 8 percent growth respectively during the decadal period.

With 69,634 or 10.8 percent of the national total, Texas ranks second in the number of ethnic Vietnamese. Much like California, concentrations are in the two largest urban regions; Harris County centered on Houston, and Dallas and Tarrant counties centered on Dallas and Fort Worth respectively, account for 57 percent of the state's ethnic Vietnamese population. Although the state's national percentage remained the same between 1990 and 2000, and the percentage of the state's ethnic Vietnamese residing in these two urban regions declined from 71 percent in 1990 to 57 percent in 2000, their respective populations during the decadal period have grown dramatically; in Houston by 76 percent and in Dallas–Fort Worth by 117 percent.

Other regional concentrations of ethnic Vietnamese, albeit of secondary importance, deserve attention. With 32,764 ethnic Vietnamese, and the almost doubling of the population between 1990 and 2000, the largest single East Coast concentration of ethnic Vietnamese is the greater Washington, D.C., region comprising suburban Montgomery County, Maryland, and Fairfax County, Virginia. This concentration is associated with proximity to the Fort Indiantown Gap, Pennsylvania, reception center as well as the strong U.S. military presence. Another concentration is the Gulf South urban coastal archipelago of Pensacola, Mobile, Biloxi, Gulfport, New Orleans, and Baton Rouge; the 43,201 ethnic Vietnamese is a 15 percent increase over the 1990 population. This original concentration is in part explained by the close proximity to two of the "first wave" reception centers, strong military presence, and opportunities to engage in the commercial shrimp industry. Subsequent growth is not a result of increased economic opportunities, but secondary migration and immigrant influxes to join family and friends. The same is true for the Oklahoma City and Wichita, Kansas, concentrations; Oklahoma City's population of 9,525 and Wichita's population of 7,154 increased between 1990 and 2000 by 45 percent and 49 percent respectively.

CAMBODIANS

The settlement patterns of Cambodians are very much bi-coastal with California and the East Coast states of Massachusetts, Rhode Island, and Pennsylvania comprising 49.1 percent of the national population. California is home to 69,523 individuals, or 33 percent of the national total, down from its 46.2 percentage share in 1990. Los Angeles County accounts for 40 percent of the state total, with the majority of the county population living in the multiethnic and working-class municipality of Long Beach, popularly referred to as the "Cambodian Capital of the United States." With 19,536 individuals or 9.4 percent of the national total, Massachusetts is the second leading state, with the majority residing in the two Boston area counties of Essex and Middlesex. Boston was originally designated as the location of one of twelve national urban "Cambodian Cluster Resettlement Projects." Many refugees initially settled in Boston, but with escalating real estate prices, they soon migrated to smaller industrial urban places in surrounding counties such as Lowell, Lynn, and Revere where employment was available in industrial plants.[12] As a result of subsequent secondary migration of friends and relatives, the ethnic Cambodian population in the city of Lowell, for example, increased by 40 percent, from 6,296 to 9,766 between 1990 and 2000.

LAO

Like Vietnamese, ethnic Lao are also spatially dispersed. With 27.6 percent of the national population, but dramatically down from 39.3 percent in 1990, California, plus the states of Texas and Minnesota with 5 percent each, are the only states with greater than 5 percent of the national ethnic Lao population. There are numerous states, however, with small but significant and growing Lao populations that comprise between 1 and 2 percent or more of the national population. Murfreesboro, Tennessee, a small city just south of Nashville, witnessed the growth of its Lao population from

844 in 1990 to 1,675 in 2000. A less congested urban environment plus employment opportunities attract Lao to smaller communities. In New Iberia, Louisiana, for example, federal funds that provided training in pipe-fitting and welding related to the state's petroleum industry attracted the first early 1980s cohort of Lao families who then spread word of these job opportunities through ethnic networks. As a result, this type of employment became a male ethnic specialization, and by the mid-1990s the Lao community numbered between two and three thousand and was large enough to support a Buddhist temple.[13]

HMONG

The smallest of the four groups, and exhibiting the highest degree of spatial concentration, approximately 74 percent of the national Hmong population resides in the three states of California, Minnesota, and Wisconsin (Map 14.2). In 1990, this three-state share of the national total was slightly higher at 84 percent. Generally, the Hmong exhibit the settlement characteristics of residing in small and medium-sized urban places as a purposeful strategy by clan leaders to preserve Hmong culture.[14] Between 1990 and 2000, California's share of the national total declined from 49.0 percent to 34.7 percent while in Minnesota and Wisconsin these shares increased from 17.8 percent to 22.2 percent and 17.3 to 18.0 percent respectively. In California, 92 percent of

Map 14.2.   Population Distribution by Counties with More Than 100 Hmong.
Source: U.S. Census, American Fact Finder, Summary File 2 (SF2).

the state's total Hmong population is found in an archipelago of the Central Valley counties of Sacramento, San Joaquin, Merced, and Fresno. Settlement in these primarily medium and small-sized urban places is largely a result of secondary migration in that refugees were first placed in larger California metropolitan regions, but clan leaders concerned with the interdependent erosion of clan authority and women's traditional roles prompted movement to the agricultural-based cities in the Central Valley.

The arrival of large numbers of Hmong in Minnesota and Wisconsin is largely the result of very active religious organizations, primarily the Lutheran Church. In Minnesota, 92 percent of the state's Hmong population is concentrated in Hennepin and Ramsey counties that comprise metropolitan Minneapolis–St. Paul. Despite an increase of population from 16,155 to 38,131 between 1990 and 2000, the Twin Cities share of the state total slightly decreased from 96 percent. Much like California, the distribution of Hmong in Wisconsin is primarily among a handful of smaller urbanized counties centered on the cities of La Crosse, Stevens Point, Eau Claire, Wausau, Oshkosh, and Green Bay. The only exception is highly urbanized Milwaukee County which accounts for 23.3 percent of the state's Hmong population. There is a movement, however, among some more urban Hmong to migrate to some southern states where the cost of living in smaller urban centers is lower and access to agricultural land to promote food self-sufficiency is less expensive; North Carolina's Hmong population, for example, increased from 760 in 1990 to 7,093 in 2000 with 62 percent of this total residing in the two rural Piedmont counties of Burke and Catawaba.

URBAN SETTLEMENT PATTERNS

The urban residential patterns of the four ethnic groups exhibit a diverse array of forms embedded within urban agglomerations. These include poorer and traditional downtown and near-downtown mixed-ethnic enclaves, transitional residential and commercial zones of the mid-city, and more affluent and spacious suburban locations. Downtown settlement patterns are exemplified by ethnic Vietnamese in the low-income and transient population Tenderloin District of San Francisco. In the four census tracts that comprise the Tenderloin, ethnic Vietnamese and a handful of ethnic Lao comprise 18 percent of the total population that is primarily ethnic Asian (Fig. 14.2).

Near-downtown settlement patterns are exemplified by ethnic Vietnamese in Chicago and Hmong in Fresno, California. In Chicago, resettlement agencies placed Vietnamese refugees in low-rent apartment buildings in the near northside Uptown neighborhoods that cover five census tracts. In 1990, ethnic Vietnamese numbered 1,726, but increased to 2,101 in 2000, despite low employment opportunities, substandard housing, and crime problems. In 2000, ethnic Vietnamese comprised only 7.7 percent of the total population in the five census tracts, but 41 percent of all ethnic Asians. Located on or near Argyle Street in Uptown are numerous ethnic Vietnamese associations as well as commercial establishments that in 1990 accounted for approximately 80 percent of ethnic Vietnamese businesses in the entire Chicago region.[15] Another near-downtown settlement pattern example is the Hmong in Fresno, California, where a handful of enclaves have evolved. The majority of Hmong live in subsidized Section 8

Figure 14.2.   Lao and Vietnamese commercial establishments in San Francisco's downtown Tenderloin District. Source: Author.

apartments on the edge of downtown, but over time have migrated to similar Section 8 housing on Fresno's suburban edge. Each enclave has grocery stores selling goods critical to maintaining food traditions.[16]

An example of a more suburban residential and dispersed pattern is found in Orange County, California, particularly in the cities of Santa Ana, Garden Grove, and Westminister. Located adjacent to the refugee reception center of Camp Pendleton, Vietnamese refugees were attracted to Orange County because of an affordable housing stock as well as good employment opportunities in the electronics and aerospace industries. Incorporated in 1957, Westminister is a quintessential suburban municipality embedded within the larger Los Angeles urban region. As an example of an "ethnoburb,"[17] ethnic Vietnamese comprise 30.7 percent of Westminister's total population of 88,207 with whites accounting for 45.7 percent and Hispanics, primarily Mexican Americans, 21.4 percent. While not comprising the majority of residents, ethnic Vietnamese have transformed the suburban landscape into the most recognizable Vietnamese American city in the United States in part because of the thriving commercial district centered on Bolsa Avenue.

Community Study: Bolsa Avenue and the Contested Future of the Vietnamese Commercial Capital of the United States

Bolsa Avenue is the social and certainly the commercial center for ethnic Vietnamese in the municipality of Westminister and beyond. Once lined by aging strip malls, auto repair businesses, and mobile home parks surrounded by strawberry, lemon, and orange groves in the early 1970s, the avenue has been transformed through "ethnic reterritorialization"[18] into an ethnic Vietnamese commercial center. The emergence of this commercial district is in part linked to a handful of ethnic Chinese Vietnamese real estate developers who as "immigrant entrepreneurs"[19] utilized overseas Chinese capital to attract other co-ethnics to establish businesses here; some 40 percent of business owners in the early 1990s were ethnic Chinese Vietnamese[20] as were the largest mall owners. Covering four city blocks, some 2,000 commercial establishments cater to co-ethnic customers with products that are not available elsewhere (Fig. 14.3). "Little Saigon" provides a place where ethnic Vietnamese of different genders, ages, and experiences feel a sense of place, both past and present. Thus, Bolsa Avenue is not only commercial space, but an example of "ethnic sociocommerscapes"[21] because shopping is mixed with social interaction in a built environment where their culture is the norm.[22]

"Little Saigon," however, is unable to prosper based solely upon co-ethnic patrons in Westminster and must geographically enlarge its customer base. Indeed it has evolved into a business, cultural, and social center for approximately 70 percent of Vietnamese and other ethnic Asians that reside in auto-oriented Southern California, and ethnic Vietnamese throughout the United States recognize its importance at the national scale.[23] Indeed, "Little Saigon" receives up to 1,000,000 "visitors" per year. There has emerged, however, conflicts within the ethnic community when attempting to reach out to a needed non-ethnic customer base. As part of this goal to promote Little Saigon as a tourist destination for non-Vietnamese to experience Vietnamese culture, developers and the city council developed architectural design guidelines that allow only Asian and French Colonial architectural styles.[24] A hotel, a cultural center, a French Quarter with sidewalk cafes and Asian-style lamps along sidewalks have been proposed by developers

Figure 14.3.   Built in 1987, and supporting some three hundred different retail stores, the Asian Garden Mall is the largest along Bolsa Avenue. Source: Author.

to entice tourists from nearby Disneyland and Knotts Berry Farm.[25] Of course it is the handful of developers of ethnic Chinese Vietnamese background who stand to financially gain by "commodifying culture" through the creation of an "ethnic theme park" along Bolsa Avenue. We have a situation, then, in which a segment of the ethnic population are themselves constructing landscapes of "Otherness" for commercial gain. Some segments of the population, however, want to see "Little Saigon" remain as an ethnic enclave and not be transformed into a tourist-oriented "Chinatown" where the architecture "looks too Chinese" and where only old people live.[26] It appears that the antagonisms between ethnic Vietnamese and ethnic Chinese Vietnamese who dominated the urban economy of Viet Nam since the colonial period have resurfaced in a new and unpredictable way, and in a new locational context.

The second example of an ethnic Vietnamese suburban settlement pattern comes from the four Virginia and Maryland counties of greater Washington, D.C. In a classic heterolocal settlement pattern,[27] ethnic Vietnamese are scattered across many census tracts or municipalities embedded within a larger urban region and do not demographically dominate a single census tract (Map 14.3). In fact, of the 39,015 ethnic Vietnamese who resided in the greater metropolitan region in 2000, approximately 95

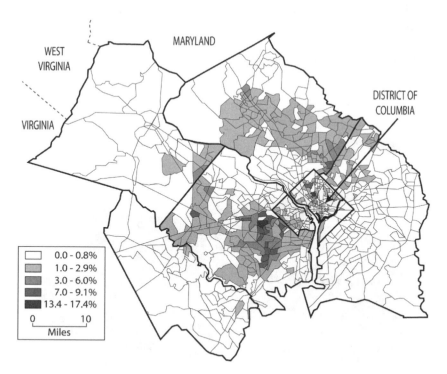

Map 14.3.   Distribution of Ethnic Vietnamese by Census Tract in the Greater Washington, D.C., Urban Region. Source: U.S. Census Bureau, American Fact Finder, Summary File 2 (SF2).

percent resided in the four suburban counties where ethnic Vietnamese comprised no greater than 9 percent of the total population of any census tracts, and the majority of census tracts were characterized by fewer than one percent ethnic Vietnamese. First- and second-order ethnic Vietnamese commercial complexes, in the form of strip malls and plazas, are concentrated along particular transport corridors to serve automobile-based suburban ethnic shoppers dispersed throughout the suburban frontier. Possessing a similar function as along Bolsa Avenue in Westminster, these commercial complexes attract ethnic Vietnamese from throughout the East Coast as well, and are examples of Vietnamese American "place making" connected to shopping and entertainment.[28]

Socioeconomic Adaptation

A snapshot of the adaptation of the four ethnic groups is afforded through an examination of simple quantitative and mutually reinforcing socioeconomic indicators (Table 14.1). One of the most basic quantitative measures of socioeconomic adaptation is median family income. Substantial income differences exist between the four ethnic groups with Vietnamese median family income approaching that of the total U.S. population. This relatively high income level is in part explained by the middle and upper classes that comprised much of the 1975 "first wave" refugees, although most experienced downward economic mobility upon arrival because of the inability to obtain work that matched their premigration skills. While Lao have experienced economic adaptation levels almost mirroring ethnic Vietnamese, and both Cambodian and

Table 14.1.   Social and Economic Indicators of Mainland Southeast Asian Groups Compared to the Total U.S. Population, 2000

	U.S.	Vietnamese	Cambodian	Lao	Hmong
Median Family Income $	50,046 (35,225)	46,929 (29,800)	35,434 (18,800)	42,838 (23,000)	32,224 (14,300)
% below Poverty Level	12.4	16	29.3	19.1	37.6
% Homeownership	66.2	52.8	43.2	51.5	38.5
% in Management, Professional & Related Occupations	33.6	27	17.8	13.6	17.1
% 25 Years or Older with Bachelor's Degree or Higher	24.4	19.5	9.1	7.6	7.4
Average Household Size	2.59	3.67	4.39	4.21	6.13
% Historically Linguistically Isolated	4.1	45	31.8	31.8	35.1
% Foreign-Born	12	76	65	68	55

Source: Max Niedzwieki and T. C. Duong, *Southeast Asian Statistical Profile* (Southeast Asian Resource Action Center, 2004). <www.searac.org/seastprofilemay04.pdf> (13 March 2004).

Hmong median family income levels have improved, levels of poverty for these two lat-ter groups remain more than double and triple the U.S. level, respectively. Having been primarily poor and rural in their origin countries, they arrived in the United States with little experience associated with trade and commerce. Indeed, like some other Ameri-cans, many Cambodians and Hmong have forfeited low-wage employment because public assistance affords access to expensive medical coverage. Levels of home owner-ship are positively correlated to median income and poverty levels with the majority of Vietnamese and Lao owning their own homes.

Also related to median family income are the interdependent variables of occupa-tional status and educational attainment. Again Vietnamese occupational status and educational attainment approach levels of the U.S. population, while the other groups on balance exhibit relatively low levels. Again, the origin of many Vietnamese was more urban-oriented, while the three other groups were of rural origin and brought with them much lower levels of education.

Variables associated with ethnic households provide a critical and multidimen-sional view of socioeconomic adaptation. Households are larger than the U.S. average, because (1) higher fertility levels characterize many immigrants from rural back-grounds, and (2) the extended family is of greater importance in many Asian cultures. An extended family, particularly one that has age and gender diversity, is viewed as a "cooperative economic unit" so that each adult family member possesses a particular economic role with reference to wages and self-employment income to best maximize scarce economic resources.[29] These two observations plus higher levels of poverty explain the 6.13 average members in Hmong households. The link between levels of median income, poverty, and household size is also positively related to households that are linguistically isolated. The high level of linguistically isolated Vietnamese house-holds is explained in part by a continued flow of non–English speaking immigrants from Viet Nam, as indicated in the high levels of foreign-born.

ADAPTATION, GENDER, AND IDENTITY

Ethnic Mainland Southeast Asian households, like many recent first-generation immi-grant households, are based on a family ideology of patriarchy.[30] This asymmetrical dynamic is hypothetically challenged as male and female roles change in the process of "modernization" associated with new economic conditions in the United States. Unlike in Mainland Southeast Asia, the economic contribution of men in the United States declined because low-paying and unstable employment opportunities do not allow them to function as the primary household breadwinner. This situation affords oppor-tunities for women to work outside domestic space and gain greater economic power, and in turn transform gender relationships. In addition, women are more likely to be members of female-centered economic-exchange networks, thus diversifying their "activity space" to acquire the social capital needed to access economic resources. This shift in gender relationships favoring females, however, is not sufficient enough to sig-nificantly alter family and gender relations, and the change that materializes is within the boundaries of traditional gender relationships.[31] For example, in Vietnamese culture, the establishment of a small business is often a wife's responsibility in the family division of labor. If a husband loses his job, the small business functions as family economic security.[32] As an extension of domestic space, the wife, along with another female relative working in the store, is also able to provide childcare at work.

Similarly, higher educational attainment for daughters is embedded within traditional family and gender roles. Educational success of daughters from the father's perspective is important because they are able to contribute to the income of their future families, make suitable wives, and confer status to their birth families. Mothers possess a similar ideology, but also view their daughter's educational attainment in support of her husband and family as a "feminine virtue."[33] Indeed, when compared to male offspring, females are expected to uphold cultural traditions and values,[34] which generally means gravitating more toward domestic space.

Another aspect of arrested gender equality in the "modernizing" environment of the United States comes from California's Silicon Valley centered on San Jose. During good economic times, some 50,000 ethnic Vietnamese are employed in the electronics industry, some of whom are independent female homeworkers who perform the lower value and manual assembly tasks of placement and soldering various components on circuit boards. Several hundred assembly houses and three hundred subcontractors arrange for parts to be delivered to homes where females assemble the boards within a few days. Although they hold regular daytime jobs, females must engage in this "putting out" piece-rate work because of the high rents or home mortgages. Although paid by the piece, the hourly wage equivalent is often below minimum wage with no overtime pay or health insurance, and home workers are subject to toxic chemical fluxes during the assembly process. This "sweatshop" home work is an example of a patriarchal-based and socially constructed "gendered division of labor" whereby females become part of the low-wage, docile, and flexible workforce that, not coincidentally, is characteristic of the female assembly worker in Viet Nam.[35]

For first-generation Hmong men who arrived in the United States as adults, adaptation has been especially difficult. Possessing superior decision-making power in their patriarchal clans, they experience their adjustment to life in the United States as a loss of power because their role as breadwinners, leaders, and protectors of the family has significantly diminished. The erosion of men's status is in part explained by the greater ability of older Hmong women to learn English, which in turn affords increased income-earning opportunities.[36] Further erosion of male authority has taken place as significant numbers of Hmong have converted to various forms of Protestantism that disapprove of the traditional practices of bride price, arranged marriages, bride kidnapping, and females marrying at puberty.[37] Nevertheless, gender inequality among the Hmong remains high as twice as many males (8.0%) as females (3.8%) over 25 years of age possessed bachelor's degrees in 2000.

ADAPTATION, AGE, AND IDENTITY

As with any new immigrant groups, the intergenerational differences in adaptation that develop between parents and offspring are substantial. First, adult refugees experience a serious loss of self-esteem as a result of a high dependence on public assistance, absence of employment opportunities, lack of English-language skills, and breakdown of the extended family structure. Second, as "conflict migrants," many adults who arrive as refugees experience mental health problems associated with being wrenched from their homelands.[38] This is particularly true for the Cambodian and Hmong who experienced horrific brutality in the process of being violently displaced from their villages, forced migration on foot, and years of refugee camp life. These experiences create a very strong attachment to their homelands as past and lost places that today can be retrieved only through memory and an attempt to materially reproduce past landscapes and place in the destination country.[39]

Expressions of this deep psychological attachment to past place materialize themselves in many forms. Among the Hmong, self-sufficiency and thus independence is central to their identity, in part because of their semi-nomadic agrarian life in the mountains of Laos.[40] A quote from an elderly Hmong male captures this modern dilemma: "Even though it [Laos] is a poor country I could take care of myself there. Here you work day to day and year to year and you worry too much about your job and you are hurt and you're scared. . . . Everything is money here. Over there even if you don't have a job, there is still a lot of land and you can grow potatoes and corn and rice and raise chickens and you are free yourself."[41] This observation in part explains Hmong geographical distributions in smaller urban centers where agricultural space is available. Such economic activity allows for a form of resistance against the process of assimilation into mainstream society by "reunifying kin in a common social space."[42] In New Orleans, the extensive vegetable plots cultivated exclusively by the Vietnamese elderly is viewed as "hortitherapeutic" activity whereby past environments or "reminiscent place" associated with an orderly world of commitment is re-created as part of their geographical experience.[43] Another expression of attachment to past place comes from Cambodian adults in Lowell, Massachusetts. Held on the banks of the Merrimack River, the annual Southeast Asian Water Festival is modeled on centuries-old water festivals along the Mekong River in Cambodia. Replete with Buddhist monks blessing the river water, the launching of colorful dragon boats, and traditional music and dance performances, the scene reminds one adult of the Mekong River as a "source of life."[44]

A somewhat different attachment to home among first-generation Vietnamese is expressed in the nexus between identity and politics. A visit to any sizeable Vietnamese community reveals former South Vietnamese flags atop flagpoles. In 2003, the governments of some thirteen cities across the country, plus the state of Louisiana, recognized the South Vietnamese flag as the official flag of these ethnic communities (Fig. 14.4). Informally referring to the "heritage and freedom flag," older Vietnamese simultaneously perceive this newly recognized flag as one that symbolically represents the nostalgic and lost place of former South Viet Nam and the space of "free Viet Nam" in which all diasporic *Viet Kieu* or Overseas Vietnamese live.

The 1.5 generation and especially the second generation young often experience an ambiguous "in between" identity as the forces of assimilation into mainstream culture and parental pressure to retain traditional cultural values act simultaneously. While this ambiguous position relative to traditional and mainstream culture is strongest among children and adolescents, young adults, in the process of ethnic reidentification,

Figure 14.4.   Dovetailed with an educational award ceremony for ethnic Vietnamese high school students in New Orleans is a celebration of the Louisiana legislature's official recognition of the South Vietnamese flag as the flag of the state's ethnic Vietnamese community. Multiple flags dot the stage with a handful of former uniformed military officers in attendance. Source: Author.

begin to contest the forces of assimilation by forming a strong ethnic identity or by creating new "hybrid" identities for themselves.[45] In a study of ethnic Vietnamese university students in San Diego, 83 percent identified with the label of "Vietnamese" and "Vietnamese American" rather than the "American" label because "American" is associated with being "White." Those that chose the "Vietnamese American" label indicated that race was not the only identity marker, but knowledge of both cultures as well. Likewise, 87 percent and 51 percent of the second and 1.5 generation, respectively, called the United States their "home." Approximately 42 percent of second-generation students did not speak Vietnamese well, but did watch ethnic videos and listen to Vietnamese-language programs.[46]

Growing up in the multiethnic and inner-city environment of Oakland, California, low-income Cambodian youth provide a different perspective of ethnic identity and assimilation. Although proud of their ethnic heritage, it is of a symbolic nature because traditions do not assist in their adaptation to the pervasive drug- and violence-prone environment of their neighborhoods. As a result, ethnic identity formation, that consists of "multiple layers" and which often is expressed in different spaces, reflects their process of adaptation. First, Khmer youth adopt the language, music, and dress of the dominant African American youth culture. Second, because of their marginal economic status, some youth band together in gangs that are co-ethnic and spatially based in an attempt to control territorial turf. Lastly, mainstream classification of Southeast Asians as "Asian" has promoted a pan-Asian identity among Khmer youth. In addition, government-sponsored programs such as the Asian Youth Center and the Asian Youth

Conference, plus discrimination against youth who look "Asian," promote the formation of a pan-ethnic identity.[47]

Music provides an interesting avenue to explore the process of ethnic re-identification or the formation of "hybrid" culture among the second generation. A popular ethnic Vietnamese musician in Southern California, for example, claims that as a child he listened only to American music, but in the process of ethnic re-identification appreciated only Vietnamese music as a teenager when "he learned to appreciate the lyrics."[48] A popular Khmer hip-hop musician in Long Beach, California, provides an example of cultural hybridity, transnationality, and second-generation adaptation. Supported by traditional flutes and drums in addition to modern electric instruments, the lyrics are a blend of Khmer and colloquial English. The subject matter addresses the senseless and random violence associated with both the Khmer Rouge regime and gang activity in Long Beach.[49]

Transnationalism

Among the "conflict migrants," the establishment of transnational spaces has been limited because of unfriendly political conditions in Viet Nam and Laos. Nevertheless, particular forms of unpredictable transnational engagement have materialized and changed through time with the simultaneous transformation of political and economic conditions in the source countries as well as the perceptions of the diasporic populations toward their homeland. Viet Nam remained a dictatorial Communist regime until 1986 when *doi moi* or economic liberalization policies were implemented to better engage the country with global capitalism. Also of critical importance was the re-establishment of diplomatic relations in 1995 between Hanoi and Washington which opened up trade opportunities. Following Viet Nam's lead, the socialist government of Laos in 1986 also embarked on a policy of economic reforms that encouraged private investment. Much like *Viet Kieu*, however, both Lowland Lao and Hmong still possess a deep-seated mistrust of these reformed Communist governments.

ECONOMIC TRANSNATIONALISM

The basic form of transnational economic engagement is remittances, but many Vietnamese Americans during the early diaspora years refused to remit for fear of propping up a regime they viewed as illegal. Nevertheless *Viet Kieu* sent remittances that by the mid-1980s reached $100 million per year which greatly lessened the economic hardship of relatives. By 2003, however, remittances from *Viet Kieu* reached $3 billion with American *Viet Kieu* accounting for approximately half that total. In fact, *Viet Kieu* remittances exceeded the value of foreign investments in the commercial capital of Sai Gon. Nevertheless, as first-generation refugees pass away and their second-generation offspring possess less of a commitment to relatives in Viet Nam, remittances will decline. Similarly, as Viet Nam's economy has prospered under *doi moi* and relatives are able to afford basic necessities, remittances will also decline. Younger *Viet Kieu* also travel to Viet Nam for reasons connected to business and the establishment of various non-governmental organizations to improve socioeconomic conditions.[50]

CULTURAL TRANSNATIONALISM

While minor in relation to the total *Viet Kieu* population, cultural tourism is increasing through time especially after 1995. The 1.5 generation visit as part of the process of ethnic re-identification because while their parents have told them much about the homeland, it remains only a symbolic rather than a real place.[51] Their experiences in Viet Nam express a common "in-betweenness" feature of transnational identities in that they are not accepted culturally in the United States, their country of citizenship, nor in Viet Nam because their authenticity of Vietnameseness is challenged in their imagined homeland. The most popular travel period is during the family-centered *Tet* or the Lunar New Year season when *Viet Kieu* "tourists" often bring gifts for family and friends, but inadvertently express superiority over recipients with this visual display of wealth that simultaneously functions as a critique of anti-consumer Communism. This power relationship has changed since the late 1990s as material conditions in Viet Nam have improved as a result of *doi moi* market reforms.[52]

The Hmong provide an unpredictable, and thus very interesting form of cultural transnationalism. Because of the perceived "Americanization" of Hmong women in the United States, some Hmong men have looked to southern China, the mythical and ancestral home of the Hmong people, to procure a "traditional" wife. The many subsequent encounters of Hmong male tourists with the so-called authentic Miao (in China Hmong are referred to as Miao) has unintentionally rekindled the desire for their cultural "origins." A by-product of these transnational encounters that promote ethnic re-identification are videos of nostalgic and romanticized images of Miao cultural and rural landscapes marketed by some twenty U.S.-based Hmong video companies for mail-order sale or for sale at the many Hmong New Year Festivals in California, Minnesota, and Wisconsin. In turn, their Miao entrepreneurial counterparts in China have begun exporting to the United States intricately stitched and highly prestigious ethnic clothing that possesses great social value because of its spatial connection to the "authentic" homeland. U.S. Hmong have also imported Miao folk culture entertainers for important ethnic festivals, who as cultural resources represent "the very past incarnate." Because Miao are ethnic cousins of the Hmong, the process of cultural transnationalism is also an example of pan-ethnic formation.[53]

Conclusion

As refugees, Mainland Southeast Asians migrated to the United States in response to failed Cold War strategies. The original policy of settlement dispersal to promote assimilation initially promoted a more diffuse distribution, but secondary migration because of family reunification resulted in a especially high geographical concentration in particular states and urban regions, particularly in California. Ethnic Hmong and

Khmer exhibit the highest degree of spatial concentration while the more affluent ethnic Vietnamese and Lao the least. Urban settlement patterns represent a diverse array of forms, from poorer downtown or near-downtown apartment complexes to more affluent single-family residences in distant suburban locations. By virtue of their larger numbers, only ethnic Vietnamese concentrations support substantial commercial districts.

As refugees from primarily rural backgrounds, economic adaptation has been a challenge, despite the strides made relative to the mainstream population. Ethnic Vietnamese have encountered the greatest economic progress while ethnic Hmong and Cambodians have experienced high rates of poverty and public assistance dependency relative to the mainstream population. Socioeconomic adaptation has brought about changed gender roles favoring females because adult males seem less adaptable to a new socioeconomic environment. While females have gained greater economic power, it has been within the boundaries of modified traditional culture; domestic space remains important to female identity. The older cohort remains psychologically tied to their homeland in a variety of ways. While the refugee experiences of parents impact their children, the "in between" second generation have forged new ethnic identities that include ethnic re-identification and "hybridity" based upon the cultural environment in which they are embedded as well as their imagined homeland. While tempered by political conditions in the source countries, transnational engagement is greatest among ethnic Vietnamese in both its economic and cultural forms. Whether it be socioeconomic adaptation, ethnic identity formation, or transnational behavior, the hyphenated ethnic experiences of the second generation have been significantly different than their first-generation and refugee parents.

Notes

1. Jeremy Hein, *From Vietnam, Laos and Cambodia: The Refugee Experience in the United States* (New York: Twayne, 1995), 11–15.

2. For an engaging account of the "boat people" experience, see Bruce Grant, *The Boat People: An "Age" of Investigation* (New York: Penguin, 1979).

3. Hein, *From Vietnam, Laos and Cambodia*, 37.

4. M. A. Martin, *Cambodia: A Shattered Society* (Berkeley: University of California Press, 1994).

5. Hein, *From Vietnam, Laos and Cambodia*.

6. Hein, *From Vietnam, Laos and Cambodia*.

7. Jane Hamilton-Merritt, *Tragic Mountains: The Hmong, the Americans and the Secret Wars for Laos, 1942–1992* (Bloomington: Indiana University Press, 1993).

8. Jacqueline Desbarats, "Indochinese Resettlement in the United States," *Annals of the Association of American Geographers* 75 (1985): 522–538.

9. Rubén G. Rumbaut, "A Legacy of War: Refugees from Vietnam, Laos and Cambodia," in *Origins and Destinies: Immigration, Race, and Ethnicity in America*, ed. Silvia Pedraza and Rubén G. Rubaut (Belmont, CA: Wadsworth, 1996), 322.

10. Rumbaut, "A Legacy of War," 322–323.

11. Rumbaut, "A Legacy of War," 322.

12. Nancy J. Smith-Hefner, *Khmer American: Identity and Moral Education in a Diasporic Community* (Berkeley: University of California Press, 1999), 9–10.

13. Carl L. Bankston III and Min Zhou, "De Facto Congregationalism and Socioeconomic Mobility in Laotian and Vietnamese Immigrant Communities: A Study of Religious Institutions and Economic Change," *Review of Religious Research* 41, no. 4 (2000): 453–470.

14. Ines M. Miyares, "Changing Perceptions of Space and Place as Measures of Hmong Acculturation," *Professional Geographer* 49, no. 2 (1997): 214–224.

15. Mark Pfeifer and Edward L. Jackiewicz, "Refugee Resettlement, Family Reunion, and Ethnic Identity: Evolving Patterns of Vietnamese Residence in Two American Metropolitan Areas," *The North American Geographer* 2, no. 2 (2000): 9–32.

16. Ines M. Miyares, "To Be Hmong in America: Settlement Patterns and Early Adaptation of Hmong Refugees in the United States," in *Human Geography in North America: New Perspectives and Trends in Research*, ed. Klaus Frantz, Innsbrucker Geographische Studien 26 (Innsbruck, 1996), 97–113.

17. Wei Li, "Los Angeles' Chinese Ethnoburb: From Ethnic Service Center to Global Economy Outpost," *Urban Geography* 19, no. 6 (1998): 502–528.

18. Anastasia Loukaitou-Sideris, "Regeneration of Urban Commercial Strips: Ethnicity and Space in Three Los Angeles Neighborhoods," *Journal of Architectural and Planning Research* 19, no. 4 (2002): 334–350.

19. Ivan Light, "Immigrant Place Entrepreneurs in Los Angeles 1970–99," *International Journal of Urban and Regional Research* 26, no. 2 (2002): 215–228.

20. Stephen J. Gold, "Chinese-Vietnamese Entrepreneurs in California," in *The New Asian Immigration in Los Angeles and Global Restructuring*, ed. P. Ong, E. Bonacich, and L. Cheng (Philadelphia: Temple University Press, 1994), 196–226.

21. Elizabeth Chacko, "Ethiopian Ethos and the Making of Ethnic Places in the Washington Metropolitan Area," *Journal of Cultural Geography* 20, no. 2 (2003): 21–42.

22. Colette M. McLaughlin and Paul Jesilow, "Conveying a Sense of Community along Bolsa Avenue: Little Saigon as a Model of Ethnic Commercial Belts," *International Migration* 36, no. 1 (1998): 49–65.

23. McLaughlin and Jesilow, "Conveying a Sense of Community."

24. Loukaitou-Sideris, "Regeneration of Urban Commercial Strips."

25. Bert Eljera, "Big Plans for Little Saigon," <www.asianweek.com/051796/LittleSaigon.html> (21 July 2004).

26. Daniel C. Tsang, "Little Irvine? Little Saigon Sees a Mainstream Future," <www.ocweekly.com/ink/02/37/news-tasang.php> (21 July 2004).

27. Wilbur Zelinsky and Barrett A. Lee, "Heterolocalism: An Alternative Model of the Sociospatial Behavior of Immigrant Ethnic Communities," *International Journal of Population Geography* 4, no. 4 (1998): 281–298.

28. Joseph S. Wood, "Vietnamese American Place Making in Northern Virginia," *Geographical Review* 87, no. 1 (1997): 58–72.

29. Nazli Kibria, "Household Structure and Family Ideologies: The Dynamics of Immigrant Economic Adaptation among Vietnamese Refugees," *Social Problems* 41, no. 1 (1994): 81–96.

30. Kibria, "Household Structure and Family Ideologies."

31. Nazli Kibria, "Power, Patriarchy, and Gender Conflict in the Vietnamese Immigrant Community," *Gender and Society* 4, no. 1 (1990): 9–24.

32. Stephen J. Gold, *Refugee Communities: A Comparative Field Study* (Newbury Park, CA: Sage, 1992).

33. Min Zhou and Carl L. Bankston III, "Family Pressure and the Educational Experience of the Daughters of Vietnamese Refugees," *International Migration* 39, no. 4 (2001): 133–151.

34. Yen Le Espiritu and Thom Tran, "Viet Nam, Nuoc Toi (Vietnam, My Country): Vietnamese Americans and Transnationalism," in *The Changing Face of Home: The Transnational Lives of the Second Generation*, ed. Peggy Levitt and Mary C. Waters (New York: Russell Sage, 2002), 367–398.

35. Angie Ngoc Tran, "Transnational Assembly Work: Vietnamese American Electronic and Vietnamese Garment Workers," *Amerasia Journal* 29, no. 1 (2003): 4–28.

36. Kou Yang, "Hmong Men's Adaptation to Life in the United States," *Hmong Studies Journal* 1, no. 2 (1997): 1–22.

37. Sucheng Chan, *Hmong Means Free: Life in Laos and America* (Philadelphia: Temple University Press, 1994).

38. Rubén Rumbaut, "Mental Health and Refugee Experience: A Comparative Study of Southeast Asian Refugees," in *Southeast Asian Mental Health*, ed. T. C. Owan (Washington: U.S. Department of Health and Human Services, 1985), 433–486.

39. Christopher A. Airriess, "Creating Vietnamese Landscapes and Place in New Orleans," in *Geographical Identities of Ethnic America: Race, Place, and Space*, ed. Kate A. Berry and Martha L. Henderson (Reno: University of Nevada Press, 2002), 228–254.

40. Jo Ann Koltyk, *New Pioneers in the Heartland: Hmong Life in Wisconsin* (Boston: Allyn and Bacon, 1998).

41. Hein, *From Vietnam, Laos and Cambodia*, 140.

42. Elizabeth Sheehan, "GREENS: Hmong Gardens, Farms and Land Ownership in America: Constructing Environment and Identity in the Carolinas," *Lao Studies Review* 2, no date, <home.vicnet.net.au/~lao/laostudy/garden.htm> (14 June 2004).

43. Airriess, "Creating Vietnamese Landscapes."

44. Sara Rimer, "The Sound of Home: An 8,690-Mile Echo," *New York Times*, 23 August 2002, F1.

45. Hung C. Thai, "Splitting Things in Half Is So White," *Amerasia Journal* 25, no. 1 (1999): 53–88.

46. Espiritu and Tran, "Viet Nam, Nuoc Toi."

47. Russell Jeung, "Southeast Asians in the House: Multiple Layers of Identity," in *Contemporary Asian American Communities: Intersections and Divergences*, ed. Linda Trinh Vo and Rick Bonus (Philadelphia: Temple University Press, 2002), 60–74.

48. Kieu Linh Caroline Valverde, "Making Vietnamese Music Transnational: Sounds of Home, Resistance and Change," *Amerasia Journal* 29, no. 1 (2003): 29–50.

49. Chris Richard, "Cambodian Rap," BBC The World, 16 January 2004, <www.mujestic.com/bbc11604> (17 June 2004).

50. Le Anh Tu Packard, "Asian American Economic Engagement: Vietnam Case Study," in *Across the Pacific: Asian Americans and Globalization*, ed. Evelyn Hu-DeHart (Philadelphia: Temple University Press, 1999), 79–108.

51. Espiritu and Tran, "Viet Nam, Nuoc Toi."

52. Ashley Carruthers, "The Accumulation of National Belonging in Transnational Fields: Ways of Being at Home in Vietnam," *Identities: Global Studies in Culture and Power* 9 (2002): 423–444.

53. Louisa Schein, "Forged Transnationality and Oppositional Cosmopolitanism," in *Cultural Compass: Ethnographic Explorations of Asian America*, ed. Martin F. Manalansan IV (Philadelphia: Temple University Press, 2000), 199–215.

CHAPTER 15

Immigrants from the Muslim World: Lebanese and Iranians

Elizabeth Chacko

In the wave of immigration numerically dominated by Latin Americans and Asians, a small but substantial number of immigrants from the Muslim countries of Southwest Asia have increased the complexity of America's ethnic geography. While immigrants from Southwest Asia originate from a variety of countries, the two countries that have contributed the most are Lebanon and Iran. Although comparable in numbers, the geographies of Lebanese (440,279) and Iranian (338,266) ancestry groups in the United States differ significantly. Both groups have very different migration histories in both space and time, are characterized by dissimilar settlement patterns at both the national and local geographical scales, and have experienced different social and economic adjustments to the larger destination country culture and economy.

A chapter concerning ethnic groups whose origins lie in the Middle East is important for two interdependent reasons. While newly established ethnic groups in America are often perceived as the "Other," the nature of "otherness" is heightened because of their Islamic faith. Second, their status as Americans is questioned because of the perceived role of Islam in the September 11, 2001, World Trade Towers terrorist tragedy.

Migration Experiences

Reasons explaining the emigration of Lebanese and Iranians are complex, but generally involve a combination of push factors related to economic and political hardship coupled with pull factors associated with prospects of a better economic future in the United States. Mediating the ebb and flow of people from these two countries to the United States were changing immigration policies and laws. Relative to the population of some 3 million in Lebanon, this sending country has one of the largest diasporas in the world. Over 10 million claiming Lebanese ancestry have scattered around the world with significant concentrations in the United States, Canada, Brazil, and other countries in South America, Australia, and countries comprising the former French colonial possessions in West Africa. The volume and spatial extent of the Iranian diaspora are less developed; with 68 million people in Iran, there are only 3–4 million that comprise the Iranian diaspora. Major concentrations of Iranian ancestry population are in the United States, Canada, Great Britain, and various Middle East countries.

LEBANESE

The first trickle of Arabic-speaking settlers in the United States arrived on the East Coast in the late 1870s. These early immigrants were mostly single men who hailed from Mount Lebanon, a Christian stronghold in Greater Syria, then a part of the Ottoman Empire.[1] Outmigration was spurred by population pressure, excessive taxation, and political turmoil in the declining years of the Ottoman Empire. The prospect of steady work and greater economic opportunities drew the Lebanese to the United States, although avoiding conscription in the Ottoman Army and escaping increasing discrimination were also motivating factors for these predominantly Christian immigrants.[2]

Lebanese immigration continued apace into the first decades of the twentieth century. Compelled by famine during World War I and the continued lack of opportunity in their home region, approximately 5,000 Lebanese migrated annually to the United States between 1900 and 1910. The number peaked at 9,000 immigrants during the 1913–1914 period.[3] As these immigrants put down roots and prospered, they encouraged family members from the home country to join them in the United States through chain migration. However, highly restrictive quota systems after World War I practically cut off emigration from all Arab regions, including Lebanon.

A second wave of immigration from the region took place after the liberalization of U.S. immigration laws in 1965 caused an upsurge of immigrants. Post-1965 immigration from Lebanon was also spurred by major social and political turmoil. The Lebanese Civil War, which began in the mid-1970s and continued until 1990, coupled with invasions by Israel of the Shi'a region of Bekaa in southern Lebanon in 1978 and 1982, further triggered waves of emigration. A third of Lebanon's population is believed to have emigrated between the years 1975 and 1991.[4]

While many immigrants came directly from Lebanon to the United States, thousands of people of Lebanese origin also arrived by way of Africa, Canada, and Europe. Unlike earlier movements, the post-1970s period witnessed the increasing immigration of Lebanese Muslims, many of them belonging to the Shi'a sect, a minority worldwide, but the dominant Muslim faction in Lebanon.[5] Lebanese Muslims are believed to constitute the largest population of any ethnic Arab Muslim group in the United States today.[6]

IRANIANS

Iranians in the United States are a relatively more recent immigrant group than the Lebanese. The Islamic Revolution of 1978–1979 in Iran is considered a watershed that differentiates two categories of immigrants with different attributes. Before the revolution, between 1950 and 1977, the annual number of Iranian immigrants to the United States averaged only 1,500 persons. Along with immigrants, some 17,000 non-immigrants, including students and visitors, entered the United States each year during this period.[7] In the late 1970s, Iran was the primary source of foreign students at American universities. Many Iranians acquiring degrees and professional training in scientific and technological disciplines would help meet the needs of their country's rapidly modernizing economy.[8] However, in the aftermath of the Islamic Revolution, the majority of Iranian students who had originally intended to return to their home country stayed in the United States.

The post-1979 wave of Iranian immigrants consisted largely of conflict migrants in the form of political refugees, exiles, and asylees who fled their homeland to escape the consequences of the Islamic Revolution. Disproportionately represented in this group were ethnic and religious minorities such as Jews, Armenians, Zoroastrians, and Baha'is who feared that they would be marginalized and persecuted by the new fundamentalist government of the Islamic Republic of Iran.[9] Many were supporters of the deposed Shah, Reza Pahlavi. Ironically, these new immigrants faced considerable antagonism in the United States during and in the wake of the so-called Iranian hostage crisis of 1980–1981 during which 52 Americans were held hostage for over one year in the capital of Teheran. American hostility was unfortunately directed toward Iranian immigrants, who became scapegoats for the actions of the captors.[10] Since the Revolution, migrants from Iran have arrived as families rather than individuals. Over a quarter of Iranian immigrants admitted to the United States between 1965 and 1994 were refugees and asylees.[11]

Demography and Settlement Patterns

LEBANESE

Persons of Lebanese heritage form the largest Arab ancestry group in the United States, accounting for 37 percent of the Arab total. Syrians and Egyptians are a distant second at 12 percent each. The number of people of Lebanese ancestry (first and second reported ancestries) in the United States increased from 394,180 in 1990 to 440,279 in 2000. Although this is an increase of about 12 percent, their share of the total Arab ancestry population in the country during the same period fell by 9 percent.[12] This relative downward shift reflects the greater proportional increase of other smaller Arab ancestry groups such as Yemeni, Jordanians, Palestinians, and Moroccans whose populations increased at least 50 percent between the two censuses. Data from the Immigration and Naturalization Services (INS) indicate that approximately 41,500 immigrants who were born in Lebanon entered the United States between 1981 and 1990, with 43,500 more arriving between 1991 and 2000.[13]

The spatial distribution of the Lebanese community in the United States reflects the settlement patterns of a mixture of recent immigrants and descendants of compatriots who entered the country as early as the last decades of the nineteenth century. Approximately 52 percent of the Lebanese ancestry population live in just six states: Michigan, California, Massachusetts, New York, Florida, and Ohio (Map 15.1). Their

Map 15.1.   *Population Distribution by Counties with More Than 500 Lebanese.*
Source: 2000 U.S. Census, American Fact Finder, Summary File 4 (SF4).

spatial distribution is, however, relatively dispersed. The states of Michigan and California account for a quarter of the ancestry group, each having well over 50,000 self-identified Lebanese.

Like other immigrant groups, Lebanese appear to gravitate toward metropolitan areas. In 2000, approximately 10 percent of Lebanese Americans (44,000) lived in metropolitan Detroit, making it the largest cluster of people of Lebanese descent. Among the other urban areas with substantial Lebanese populations are the cities of Los Angeles (19,788), Chicago (6,822), and Houston (6,668), which together account for an additional 8 percent.

IRANIANS

There are 338,266 persons who declare "Iranian" as their primary or secondary ancestry. This figure is contested by Iranian associations that argue that the population is at least twice this number.[14] From 1981 to 1990, approximately 155,000 Iranian immigrants entered the United States, but the number declined to 113,000 between 1991 and 2000. Additionally, between 1991 and 2000, some 71,000 Iranians entered as refugees. The Iranian community in the United States includes people of diverse ethnicities, who speak a variety of languages and dialects and adhere to different religions and religious denominations. Iranian immigrants include Muslims, Jews, Baha'is, Zoroastrians, Kurds, and the Christian Armenians and Assyrians.[15]

Unlike the more dispersed settlement distribution characteristic of Lebanese, Iranians exhibit a far more concentrated settlement pattern (Map 15.2). California accounts for 47 percent of Iranians in the United States. Trailing far behind are New York and Texas with 7 percent each, and Virginia and Maryland, each with approximately 4 percent of the Iranian American population. Together, these five states account for almost 70 percent of all Iranians in the United States. Iranian immigrants tend to settle in large metropolitan regions such as Los Angeles, the San Francisco Bay region, Washington, D.C., and New York. The Los Angeles Consolidated Metropolitan Statistical Area (CMSA) alone accounts for 22 percent of the national ethnic Iranian population. Of the 28,651 Iranians who live in Virginia, Maryland, and the District of Columbia, 23,213 live in the Washington Primary Metropolitan Statistical Area (PMSA), making it the second largest urban cluster of the group in the United States, accounting for a remarkable 81 percent of the Iranian population in the region.

About 48 percent of the Iranian population in California live in Los Angeles County (Map 15.2). Los Angeles's position as the city most favored for settlement by Iranian immigrants has earned the community the nicknames of "Irangeles" and "Tehrangeles."[16] Within Los Angeles, Iranians form concentrations in the upscale city of Beverly Hills, in other affluent neighborhoods of the Westside such as Brentwood and Westwood, and in the San Fernando Valley. However, subpopulations such as Iranian Jews tend to concentrate with co-religionists in traditional Jewish neighborhoods

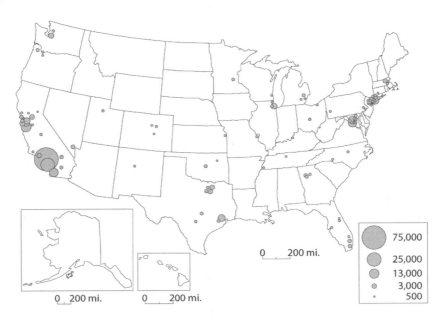

Map 15.2.   Population Distribution by Counties with More Than 500 Iranians.
Source: 2000 U.S. Census, American Fact Finder, Summary File 4 (SF4).

along Fairfax Avenue and in the western San Fernando Valley, while Armenians of Iranian origin are concentrated in the Glendale area.[17]

Socioeconomic and Cultural Characteristics

LEBANESE

The earliest Lebanese immigrants were largely male, uneducated, and poor. A history of commercial trading as a form of "cultural capital" drew many of these pioneers to peddling. They traveled from door to door with suitcases of "notions" (needles, thread, lace, etc.), linens, and other small commodities.[18] The more successful among these traveling salesmen settled in towns and cities, where they used their entrepreneurial skills to establish general stores. While a large number of those who entered through this process of chain migration became merchants or started businesses, many also became employed as unskilled and semi-skilled workers in the industrial cities of the Northeast and Midwest.[19]

Unlike those who came before, the post-1965 cohorts included large numbers of highly educated and affluent immigrants, among them lawyers, engineers, doctors, professors, and teachers. These professionals joined the third- and fourth-generation Lebanese who had worked their way from blue-collar to white-collar occupations. But people without college degrees and recognized professional skills are also well represented among later immigrants. Many of them are self-employed as traders and businessmen. However, as the United States continues its economic transition to a post-industrial country, there has been a concomitant decrease in the availability of well-paying jobs for semi-skilled and skilled workers. As a result, many uneducated and unskilled Lebanese immigrants joined the ranks of workers in low-end service occupations. Even in the industrial sector, this group tends to work in the more dangerous and poorly paid areas.[20]

Nearly 90 percent of Lebanese Americans have a high school diploma, while 41 percent have a bachelor's degree and 17 percent have a graduate degree (Table 15.1). The group's annual median household income of approximately $53,000 is over $10,000 higher than the national average, while only 6 percent of families live below the poverty level. As a whole, their educational qualifications have led to approximately 46 percent of ethnic Lebanese over 25 years old being in management and professional occupations. Sales and office jobs at 29 percent are also well represented, while 11 percent are in the service sector (Table 15.1).

IRANIANS

Iranian immigrants in the United States are often seen as wealthy professionals or entrepreneurs,[21] and there is some truth to this observation. The first wave of post-1970 Iranian immigrants was drawn from an educated, skilled, and affluent elite who entered

Table 15.1. Social and Economic Characteristics of Lebanese and Iranians in the United States, 2000

Variable	Lebanese American	Iranian American	United States
Total Population (2000)	440,279	338,266	282,421,906
Born in the United States	76%	31%	88%
Median Age	33.7 years	36 years	35.4 years
Average Family Size	3.29	3.38	3.14
Educational Attainment (Population 25 years & older)			
High school diploma	89%	90%	80%
Bachelor's degree or higher	41%	57%	24%
Master's degree or higher	17%	28%	9%
Economic Status			
Median household income (1999)	$52,575	$58,912	$41,994
% families below poverty level	6%	8%	9%
% in labor force (persons 16 years & over)	68%	65%	64%
Occupational Structure (Population 16 years & over)			
Management, professional, etc.	46%	53%	34%
Service occupations	11%	10%	15%
Sales & office occupations	29%	28%	27%
Construction, extraction, & maintenance	6%	4%	9%
Production, transportation	8%	6%	15%
Language spoken at home (Population 5 years and over)			
Speak only English	68%	20%	82%
Speak English less than "very well"	9%	29%	8%
Housing			
Own home	69%	59%	66%
Median value of home	$159,000	$268,100	$119,600

Source: U.S. Census Bureau, Census 2000 Summary File 4 (SF4).

well-paid professions or possessed the financial resources to establish thriving businesses. The affluence of the community is reflected in a median household income of about $59,000 in 1999, a figure almost a third greater than the national average. Approximately 8 percent of Iranian Americans had incomes that placed them below the poverty level (Table 15.1).

Iranian Americans are among the most highly educated ethnic groups in the United States. More than half of the community 25 years and older possess bachelor's degrees, and approximately 28 percent hold advanced and professional degrees (Table 15.1). With their American academic and professional degrees and fluency in English, Iranians have found it easier to obtain white-collar jobs than do many other immigrant groups. More than half are in highly lucrative professional and managerial occupations such as engineering, accounting, and medicine; 28 percent are in well-paid technical, sales, and administrative positions; while about 10 percent are in the service industry (Table 15.1). Iranian Americans who have achieved a high level of visibility in their chosen fields include the fashion designer Bijan, known for his exclusive men's apparel and perfumes; Pierre Omidyar, the founder and CEO of eBay; and Vartan Gregorian, who was president of Brown University, an Ivy League school.

Iranian immigrants possess entrepreneurial skills and have a higher rate of self-employment in the United States than do many other groups.[22] In particular, sub-groups like Armenians and Jews, who had a tradition of trading in Iran, used their experience and expertise as "cultural capital" to start their own businesses in the United States. They established restaurants, fast-food franchises, and were also involved in the trading of manufactured goods.[23] For example, many of the wholesale and retail clothing stores in Santee Alley in the garment district of Downtown Los Angeles are owned by Iranian immigrants.

Community Study: Dearborn, Michigan, an Arab American Capital

The city of Dearborn, Michigan, has a special quality that distinguishes it from other urban regions in the United States. Located in suburban Detroit and with almost 100,000 residents, Dearborn has the most highly concentrated population of Arab Americans in the United States. Persons of Arab extraction account for nearly 30 percent of the population of Dearborn. Arab Americans are found primarily in the eastern part of the city, where their concentrations are over 45 percent in many census tracts (Map 15.3). Dearborn's unique ethnic and religious composition has left an undeniably Arab and Muslim stamp on its socioeconomic and cultural landscapes.

SETTLEMENT HISTORY

Arab immigrants joined internal migrants from Michigan, the American South, and immigrants from Southern and Eastern Europe as autoworkers at the new Ford automobile plant in Dearborn in the early 1900s. Soon, a large blue-collar community locally known as the Southend developed adjacent to the Ford River Rouge plant in the southeastern part of the city.[24]

Beginning in the 1960s, substantial population shifts took place as the European population began to move out of Southend, while growing numbers of Lebanese, Yemeni, and Palestinian immigrants replaced them. By the late 1960s, Southend was majority Arab. Civil war in Lebanon during the 1970s promoted continued Lebanese immigration into Dearborn, while large-scale Palestinian immigration was triggered by the creation of the state of Israel in 1948, the Arab-Israeli war of 1967, and widespread economic stagnation that accompanied the subsequent occupation of their West Bank and Gaza homelands. Yemeni migration to the area gathered strength in the 1970s. Initially, most Yemeni in Dearborn were single male guest workers who sent remittances back to their home country and hoped to return there themselves after working for a period of time in the United States.[25]

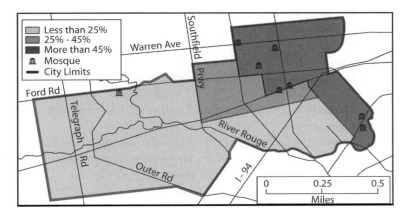

Map 15.3.   The city of Dearborn, Michigan, known for its concentration of Arab Americans.

In the mid-1980s, families began replacing single males among Yemeni immigrants to Dearborn. After the 1991 Gulf War and the unsuccessful Shi'a rebellion against Saddam Hussein, an increased flow of Iraqis, most of them refugees, joined the Dearborn Arab community.[26] Today, nearly 12 percent of the city's population is foreign-born non-U.S. citizens, evidence of continued international migration into the city.

Southend has always served as an important reception area or "port of entry" for Arab immigrants to the larger Detroit area.[27] As immigrants prospered, many left the Southend neighborhood for more affluent suburbs, while many recent Lebanese and Palestinian immigrants moved to wealthier neighborhoods in East Dearborn, to the north of the original Southend enclave. Given the outmigration of Arab immigrants from Dearborn, the prevailing strong Middle Eastern presence is dependent on the continued influx of new Arab immigrants. Of all the Arab nationalities, Lebanese are the longest settled and comprise the majority of the Arab population.[28] However, it is the waves of Palestinian immigrants who arrived in large numbers since the 1970s who are credited with changing the character of Arab Dearborn from primarily Christian to Muslim, and from working class to professional.[29]

ARAB ETHNIC PLACE IN DEARBORN

Both the Southend and East Dearborn neighborhoods exhibit qualities of typical ethnic enclaves, forming geographical and cultural niches with identifiable Arab and, often, Islamic features. A plethora of ethnic religious and secular institutions, businesses, and services in Dearborn provide for the specific needs of its Arab population, while also catering to the larger non-Arab community via largely Arab-owned businesses such as gas stations and convenience stores.[30]

Southend is hemmed in by railroad tracks, a freeway, and the factories of the Ford plant. The Arab presence here is particularly strong and palpable along its main commercial strip on Dix Avenue. Numerous ethnic businesses and institutions with signs and advertisements in Arabic, a preponderance of men on the street, *hejab*[31] worn by women, and the widespread use of Arabic in public and semi-public spaces, all bear witness to the Arab and Muslim essence of the neighborhood. Arab businesses also are clustered in the newer ethnic enclave in East Dearborn, centered at the intersection of Warren and Shaefer avenues.

Arab establishments in Dearborn such as restaurants and stores offer locales where co-ethnics can dine, buy goods, and also meet and mingle with each other. In both neighborhoods, food-related ethnic businesses are among the most common elements of the Middle Eastern cultural landscape. They include groceries that stock ingredients and products used in Middle Eastern cuisine, *halal*[32] butchers, restaurants and cafes, as well as fruit and vegetable stands (Fig. 15.1). Although these ethnic places have an overall Middle Eastern flavor, the specialties of different ethnic/nationality groups are well represented. The clientele of the ubiquitous coffee shops are often drawn to establishments owned by fellow nationals; Lebanese, Palestinians, Yemeni, and Iraqis congregate in discrete cafes.[33] Pastry shops selling the traditional phyllo-based and other Middle Eastern-style sweets as well as French baked goods are overwhelmingly owned by Lebanese.[34]

Among a profusion of ethnic institutions in Dearborn, those that are religious in nature predominate. Built in 1938, the Moslem Mosque on Dix Avenue with its

Figure 15.1. Lebanese-owned businesses. The cedar tree on the store canopy is the national symbol of Lebanon. Source: Bruce Harkness, City of Dearborn.

Figure 15.2.   Opened in summer 2005, Dearborn's newest mosque is located on Ford Road near the Muslim American Youth Academy. It can accommodate 1,000 worshippers during a single prayer service. Source: Bruce Harkness, City of Dearborn.

minarets and golden dome topped with the crescent moon symbol of Islam is a long-standing and clearly ethnic institution that provides a strong religious anchor to the Southend community. East Dearborn also has a large mosque, built on Joy Road in the 1960s. The growing Muslim community has necessitated the expansion of existing mosques and the building of new religious centers particularly over the last decade. In the summer of 2005, a new mosque in the form of the Islamic Center of America opened, said to be one of the largest mosques in the country (Fig. 15.2). Today, there are seven mosques in Dearborn, all with religious as well as social functions.

The Arab community in Dearborn also is knitted together by ethnic media and secular ethnic institutions such as business associations and charitable foundations. The *Arab American News* is published in Dearborn, and 30,000 copies of this newspaper are distributed daily to communities in Michigan, Indiana, Ohio, and Illinois.[35] The Arab American Chamber of Commerce, which is based in Dearborn, assists entrepreneurs and businesses in the Arab community and is also active in helping formulate new trade and investment agreements with overseas Arabs.[36] Other institutions promoting pan-ethnic solidarity are the newly constructed Arab-American Museum and the Dearborn Arab International Festival.

The rising prominence and influence of the Muslim Arab community in Dearborn have had an impact on the more secular arenas such as the city's public schools, super-markets, and hospitals. In the early 1990s, the school district banned pork from its lunches in response to pressure from Muslim parents. In 2001, at the request of the

Arab community and in recognition of the growing numbers of Muslims among the student body, many of Dearborn's 28 public schools began serving *halal* meat at meals.[37] Kroger supermarkets in Dearborn now sell *halal* chicken, while a local hospital has a special chef to prepare Middle Eastern food according to Islamic law, and offers Arabic translations of menu items.[38]

Although the growing Middle Eastern population in Dearborn has entrenched its Arab and Muslim presence in sociocultural and educational spheres, it is not as active in local government and politics. However, organizations such as the Arab American Political Action Committee endeavor to raise political awareness and engagement within the local community.[39] Especially since the terrorist attacks of September 11, 2001, the city's large foreign-born Arab Muslim population has attracted considerable scrutiny. Hezbollah, a well-known Lebanese political group headquartered in Beirut and identified as a foreign terrorist organization by the U.S. government, allegedly has local members in the Detroit area,[40] while connections are claimed between local Arabs and the al-Qaeda terrorist group.[41]

Identity, Ethnic Institutions, and Attachments

Race, ethnicity, nativity, class, religion, and gender play critical roles in identity formation, retention, and change in an increasingly multicultural environment in the United States. Identities are usually transformed with greater longevity in the host country and complicated by issues such as prevailing stereotypes in the country of settlement, shifts in prosperity of the immigrant group, as well as increased ethnic pride and the intensity of transnational linkages.

LEBANESE

Although ethnically Arab, Lebanese Americans are not a homogeneous group. There are entrenched divides between Christians and Muslims, as well as schisms within these religious groups. Lebanese Christians traditionally belonged to various branches of the Eastern Orthodox Church, or the Maronite or Melkite sects, which are now affiliated with the Roman Catholic Church. As the Lebanese Christian community grew in strength, each denomination built its own churches, engaged clergy trained in their theological traditions, and even had their own newspapers.[42]

Due in part to their longevity in the country, being perceived as White and having a greater tendency to marry outside the community, Lebanese Christians as a group have to a large extent joined mainstream society.[43] Third- and fourth-generation Lebanese also tend not to retain their Arabic-language skills as is reflected in the fact that 68 percent of persons of Lebanese ancestry speak only English at home according to the 2000 U.S. Census. Lebanese Christians tend to identify with "Lebanese American/ Lebanese" rather than "Arab," because they associate the latter with a Muslim identity. Newer immigrants are likely to select "Lebanese" as an identifier, while the preferred nomenclature among third- and fourth-generation immigrants is "Lebanese American." Despite joining mainstream society, Lebanese Christians maintain facets of their ethnic identity through their churches, ethnic associations, and social gatherings and cuisine.

As a more recently formed ethnic community, Lebanese Muslims have retained many of their ethnic characteristics when compared to their Christian counterparts. They are more likely on average to speak Arabic, dress according to Islamic code, and tend to interact less with persons outside the ethnic group. Most follow the Shi'a faith, although there are also a sizable number of Druze[44] among Lebanese Muslims. The feeling that they are a community under siege due to their religion and ethnic background has caused many Lebanese Muslims to express greater pan-ethnic solidarity with fellow Islamic Arabs in recent years.[45] When compared to Lebanese Christians, then, Lebanese Muslims are more likely to be perceived as the "Other" by the majority population.

The type of ethnic institutions and organizations in which immigrants are involved often reflects the degree of their acculturation and religious affiliation. Educated and acculturated Lebanese are often involved in national pan-Arab organizations engaged in activities that promote mainstreaming and a better understanding of the group by other Americans. Such organizations include the Association of Arab-American University Graduates, the Arab American Association, and the Arab American Anti-Discrimination League. More-acculturated Lebanese Muslims are likely to be members of national organizations such as the Islamic Society of North America, the Council on American-Islamic Relations, and the American Muslim Council. Recent immigrants may, however, restrict associations outside the family to the local community and ethnic institutions such as the local mosque.[46]

IRANIANS

Most Iranians claim a non-Arab ethnicity, separating their country's culture and identity from that of neighboring Middle Eastern states. Many Iranians who entered the country as students in the 1970s and later became permanent residents and citizens are highly secularized, particularly the Muslims and the Baha'is.[47] A high level of English proficiency even before arriving in the United States, a tendency to live and work in predominantly White middle to upper-class heterolocal neighborhoods, and the absence of true residential and commercial ethnic enclaves among this group has aided in rapid acculturation.[48]

The bulk of Iranians in the United States are foreign-born, although their proportion in the year 2000 (68%) is nearly 10 percent lower than the 77 percent reported in 1990. The weakness of Iranian currency relative to the American dollar, the need to go to a third country to receive a visa to enter the United States, and the post–September 11 vigilance against possible terrorists from Muslim countries have all made travel to and from Iran more difficult.

Iranians preserve their identities through religious and secular celebrations and ethnic media. Iranian periodicals, television and radio programs in Farsi, and films with Iranian themes often produced by directors in exile also knit the community together.[49]

Iranian academic, cultural, and business groups abound. For example, the Society for Iranian Studies is housed at Columbia University, while Ohio State University is home for the American Institute of Iranian Studies.[50] UCLA has the Iran Education and Research Group and offers an undergraduate major in Iranian Studies. Iranian computer scientists in Northern California have formed a networking group called "SiliconIran," which also strives to disseminate news and information to co-ethnics in Iran using electronic media.[51]

There has been a resurgence of interest in Persian literature, music, and the arts among second-generation Iranian Americans. This process of ethnic re-identification is promoted through organizations such as the National Iranian American Council (NIAC), which seeks to empower Iranian Americans through involvement in political discourse by self-identification as Iranian in the U.S. Census and demographic surveys, participation in local and national electoral processes, and running for public office.[52] While ethnic pride appears to be on the rise, it is tempered by hybridization and a tendency among immigrants to categorize themselves as "Persian" rather than "Iranian," thereby distancing themselves from the negativity associated with the latter term. This self-identification ethnic label switch is a clear response to the power and ability of external forces to define ethnicity.

Transnational Dynamics

LEBANESE

Lebanese Americans whose ancestors arrived in the early twentieth century are usually integrated into American society, and their links with the ancestral homelands are largely cultural in nature. Among the descendants of this group are well-known Americans in the arts (the poet-artist Khalil Gibran), academics (Edward Said), journalism (Helen Thomas), entertainment (comedian Danny Thomas and singer Paul Anka), sports (NFL quarterback Doug Flutie and race car driver Bobby Rahal), and politics (Donna Shalala, Health and Human Services Secretary under President Bill Clinton, Spencer Abraham, Energy Secretary under President George W. Bush), and Ralph Nader.

Immigrants who left Lebanon in the 1970s found it difficult to return to their homeland due to protracted civil war and the occupation of Lebanese lands by Syria and Israel, but they are now returning to forge business alliances and revitalize family ties, thereby also contributing to the country's tourist trade. For example, in the month following Israel's withdrawal from southern Lebanon in May 2000, after approximately eighteen years of military occupation, more than 3,000 Lebanese Americans applied for travel visas to Lebanon from southeastern Michigan alone.[53]

A plethora of Lebanese American clubs, societies, and foundations can be found in American cities with relatively large Lebanese-ancestry populations. While the specific objectives of these ethnic organizations vary, their overarching goal is usually to promote the interests of the Lebanese American community and help in the development of Lebanon. The American Lebanese Chamber of Commerce, created in 1994 to promote business relationships between Lebanon and the United States, is an example of such an organization.[54] Lebanon is a leading global recipient of remittances by migrants. Although the compilation and reporting of data from Lebanese banking systems are still in their infancy, the money is often critical for the migrants' family members and also for country development through investments. These remittances come largely from workers in the oil-rich countries of the Middle East.[55] However, newer immigrants to the United States also contribute to the flow of remittances to Lebanon. Lebanese Americans have been active in promoting better economic, political, and sociocultural relationships between the United States and Lebanon.

IRANIANS

Political tensions between Iran and the United States, and the closing of the American embassy in Iran have complicated travel between the two countries. Commercial relations between Iran and the United States also are constrained due to U.S. trade sanctions against the country. Despite these limitations, Iranians in America have found ways to communicate with and support their compatriots in the home country.

The media in Iran are highly censored and reflect only the views of the ruling political party. However, Iranian Americans regularly disseminate independent news and other broadcasts to Iran via satellite and the Internet in an effort to keep their co-ethnics informed about events in the home country and the rest of the world. As a form of "deterritorialized" political identity, Iranian dissidents in exile who support the resistance movement against the ruling Islamic theocracy use the Internet and other channels to call for democracy in Iran, champion secular values, and advocate a more moderate form of Islam. Iranian Americans are working toward reinstalling a U.S. embassy in Iran and re-establishing free travel between the two countries.[56]

Iranian Americans clearly demonstrated their concern for and solidarity with their countrymen in the aftermath of the 6.6 magnitude earthquake that killed approximately 35,000 people in Bam in southern Iran in December 2003. Various Iranian American groups raised over $1 million for relief efforts in Iran using telethons and other kinds of fund-raising strategies. Additionally, memorial services in the United States for the deceased where poems, scriptures, and elegies were read as well as calls to all Iranians were beamed to Iran via satellite.[57]

Conclusion

Lebanese and Iranians arrived in the United States as both economic and political immigrants. Over a century of immigration has led to the Lebanese being the largest Arab ancestry group in the United States, while the population of Iranian Americans has burgeoned only during the last three decades. As immigration from these Middle Eastern countries continued throughout the decade of the 1990s, Lebanese American and Iranian American communities struggled to find their place and identity in the United States through an amalgam of ethnic pride and Americanization.[58]

Highly concentrated in a few states and a handful of large urban centers, the largest clusters of both Lebanese and Iranians reflect the initial foci of settlement of the major wave of immigrants. Both groups are better educated, have higher incomes and better housing, and are more likely to be employed in high-status occupations than the average American.

However, newer immigrants, particularly those of the Islamic faith, continue to face unique challenges in adjusting to mainstream American society,[59] while American-born children of this group forge their own hybrid cultural identities that incorporate Islamic and American mores.[60] Negative media attention and recent immigration legislation targeting males from predominantly Islamic countries have caused feelings of alienation among Middle Eastern immigrants, drawing them into pan-ethnic coalitions built around the need to obtain fair treatment and parity with other ethnic groups.[61] Social and political organizations such as the NIAC and the Council of Lebanese American Organizations urge compatriots to participate in the American political process and civic activities, with a view to invalidate negative stereotypes and influence domestic and foreign policies.[62]

Notes

1. Alixa Naff, *The Arab Americans* (New York: Chelsea House, 1983).

2. Albert Hourani and Nadim Shehada, eds., *The Lebanese in the World: A Century of Immigration* (London: I. B. Tauris, 1992); and Linda Walbridge, "Lebanese Christians and Lebanese Muslims," in *American Immigrant Cultures: Builders of a Nation,* ed. D. Levinson and M. Ember (New York: Simon and Schuster, 1997), 578–588.

3. Walbridge, "Lebanese Christians and Lebanese Muslims," 578–588.

4. Patrick Belton, "In the Way of the Prophet: Ideologies and Institutions in Dearborn, Michigan, America's Muslim Capital," *The Next American City* 3 (2003): 15–18.

5. Sally Howell and Andrew Shryock, "Cracking Down on Diaspora: Arab Detroit and America's 'War on Terror,'" *Anthropological Quarterly* 76, no. 3 (2003): 443–462.

6. Walbridge, "Lebanese Christians and Lebanese Muslims," 578–588.

7. Mary Gillis, "Iranian Americans," in *The Gale Encyclopedia of Multicultural America*, ed. R. J. Vecoli (New York: International Thompson Publishing, 1995), 1:719–730.

8. Mehdi Bozorgmehr and Georges Sabagh, "High Status Immigrants: A Statistical Profile of Iranians in the United States," *Iranian Studies* 21 (1988): 5–36.

9. Ali Modarres, "Settlement Patterns of Iranians in the United States," *Iranian Studies* 31 (1998): 31–49.

10. Ron Kelley and Jonathan Friedlander, eds., *Irangeles: Iranians in Los Angeles* (Berkeley: University of California Press, 1993).

11. Mehdi Bozorgmehr, "Iranians," in *Refugees in America in the 1990s: A Reference Handbook*, ed. D. Haines (Westport, CT: Greenwood Press, 1996), 213–231.

12. U.S. Census 2000, *The Arab Population: 2000. Census 2000 Brief,* U.S. Department of Commerce, Economics and Statistics Administration, 2003.

13. U.S. Department of Commerce, 2003, *Statistical Abstract of the United States: The National Data Book.*

14. Ali Mostahari, "Factsheet on the Iranian-American Community," *Iranian Studies Group*

Research Series, 2004, <web.mit.edu/isg/PUBLICATIONS/factsheet_feb_04.pdf> (18 July 2004).

15. Bozorgmehr, "Iranians," 1996.

16. Kelly and Friedlander, *Irangeles*.

17. Pyong Gap Min and Mehdi Bozorgmehr, "Immigrant Enterpreneurship and Business Patterns: A Comparison of Koreans and Iranians in Los Angeles," *International Migration Review* 34, no. 3 (2000): 707–738.

18. Naff, *Arab Americans*.

19. Karen Rignall, "Building the Infrastructure of Arab American Identity in Detroit," in *Arab Detroit: From Margin to Mainstream*, ed. N. Abraham and A. Shryock (Detroit: Wayne State University Press, 2000), 49–59.

20. Rignall, "Arab American Identity."

21. Kelly and Friedlander, *Irangeles*.

22. Mehdi Bozorgmehr, Claudia Der-Martirosian, and Georges Sabagh, "Middle Easterners: A New Kind of Immigrant," in *Ethnic Los Angeles*, ed. R. Waldinger and M. Bozorgmehr (New York: Russell Sage Foundation, 1996), 345–378.

23. Claudia Der-Martirosian, "Economic Embeddedness and Social Capital of Immigrants: Iranians in Los Angeles," Ph.D. diss., University of California, Los Angeles, 1996.

24. Sameer Abraham, Nabeel Abraham, and Barbara Aswad, "The Southend: An Arab Muslim Working-Class Community," in *Arabs in the New World: Studies on Arab-American Communities*, ed. S. Abraham and N. Abraham (Detroit: Wayne State University Press, 1983), 163–181.

25. Belton, "Way of the Prophet."

26. Belton, "Way of the Prophet."

27. Abraham, Abraham, and Aswad, "The Southend."

28. Barbara Aswad, "The Southeast Dearborn Arab Community Struggles for Survival against Urban Renewal," in *Arabic Speaking Communities in U.S. Cities*, ed. B. Aswad (New York: Center for Migration Studies of New York, Inc., 1980), 53–83.

29. Belton, "Way of the Prophet."

30. Howell and Shryock, "War on Terror."

31. *Hejab:* traditional head covering worn by Muslim women.

32. *Halal:* an Arabic word meaning "lawful" or "permitted." *Halal* meat is prepared according to Islamic strictures, much like kosher food.

33. Laurel Wigle, "An Arab Muslim Community in Michigan," in *Arabic Speaking Communities in U.S. Cities*, ed. B. Aswad (New York: Center for Migration Studies of New York, Inc., 1980), 155–167.

34. William G. Lockwood and Yvonne R. Lockwood, "Continuity and Adaptation in Arab American Foodways," in *Arab Detroit: From Margin to Mainstream*, ed. N. Abraham, and A. Shryock (Detroit: Wayne State University Press, 2000), 515–549.

35. Duncan Moon, *N.P.R. Special Report: Muslims in America*, part 3, "Middle East Heritage in America's Heartland" (Washington: National Public Radio), 5 November 2001.

36. Howell and Shryock, "War on Terror."

37. Lisa M. Collins, "Michigan Muslims Want Halal Food," *Associated Press*, 24 February 2001.

38. George Hunter, "Muslim Mosques Expand: Large Centers Needed for Growing Population," *Detroit News,* 21 March 2001.

39. Belton, "Way of the Prophet."

40. Daniel Pipes, "The Hezbollah in America: An Alarming Network," *National Review* 28 (August 2000): 33–35.

41. BBC News, "Al-Qaeda Suspect Held in Detroit," 20 July 2002.

42. Michael W. Suleiman, "Introduction: The Arab Immigrant Experience," in *Arabs in America: Building a New Future* (Philadelphia: Temple University Press, 1999), 1–21.

43. Walbridge, "Lebanese Christians and Lebanese Muslims," 578–588.

44. The Druzes are a religious sect who trace their origins to an eleventh-century Islamic reform movement.

45. Walbridge, "Lebanese Christians and Lebanese Muslims," 578–588.

46. Howell and Shryock, "War on Terror"; Walbridge, "Lebanese Christians and Lebanese Muslims," 578–588.

47. Kelly and Friedlander, *Irangeles*.

48. Min and Bozorgmehr, "Immgirant Entrepreneurship"; Bozorgmehr, "Iranians."

49. Kelly and Friedlander, *Irangeles*; Hamid Naficy, *The Making of Exile Cultures: Iranian Television in Los Angeles* (Minneapolis: University of Minnesota Press, 1993).

50. Gillis, "Iranian Americans," 719–730.

51. Mary Anne Ostrom, "Iranian Americans Branch Out in Valley: Tech Leaders Form Networking Group," *Mercury News*, 25 July 2002.

52. NIAC (National Iranian American Council), *Annual Report: Transforming a Community: Promoting Iranian American Civic Participation,* <www.niacouncil.org/Files/annual_report.pdf> (25 July 2004).

53. "Thousands of Lebanese-Americans Seek Visas after Israel Withdrawal," Associated Press State & Local Wire, 2 June 2000.

54. "Heading to Lebanon, Dearborn Mayor Hopes to Strengthen Ties," Associated Press State & Local Wire, 22 September 2003.

55. Dilip Ratha, "Workers' Remittances: An Important and Stable Source of External Development Finance," in *Global Development Finance: Striving for Stability in Development Finance* (Washington: World Bank, 2003).

56. NIAC, *Annual Report*, 2004; Laura Wides, " US Iranians Shocked, Overjoyed at Nobel Peace Prize Selection," *Associated Press State & Local Wire*, 11 October 2003.

57. Daisy Nguyen, "Iranian-Americans Mourn Deaths of Thousands of Quake Victims," Associated Press State & Local Wire, 5 January 2004.

58. Marilynn Rashid, "What's Not in a Name," in *Arab Detroit: From Margin to Mainstream*, ed. N. Abraham and A. Shryock (Detroit: Wayne State University Press, 2000), 471–479.

59. Mona Faragallah, Walter Schumm, and Farrell Webb, "Acculturation of Arab-American Immigrants: An Exploratory Study," *Journal of Comparative Family Studies* 28, no. 3 (1997): 182–203.

60. Gary David and Kenneth Ayouby, "Being Arab and Becoming Americanized: Forms of Mediated Assimilation in Metropolitan Detroit," in *Muslim Minorities in the West*, ed. Y. Y Haddad and J. I. Smith (Walnut Creek, CA: AltaMira Press, 2002), 125–142.

61. Agha Saeed, "Muslim-American Politics: Developments, Debates and Directions," in *Muslims in the United States*, ed. P. Strumm and D. Tarantolo (Washington: Woodrow Wilson International Center for Scholars, 2003), 39–44.

62. NIAC, *Annual Report*, 2004; Mohamed Nimer, "Social and Political Institutions of American Muslims: Liberty and Civic Responsibility," in *Muslims in the United States*, ed. P. Strumm and D. Tarantolo (Washington: Woodrow Wilson International Center for Scholars, 2003), 45–61.

CHAPTER 16

New Urban Ethnic Landscapes

Brian J. Godfrey

> The cultural landscape is fashioned from a natural landscape by a culture group. Culture is the agent, the natural area is the medium, the cultural landscape the result.
>
> Carl Sauer, "Morphology of Landscape," 1925[1]

> Though much of the "new" cultural geography remains wedded to the idea of landscape, the approach adopted here emphasizes the plurality of cultures and the multiplicity of landscapes with which those cultures are associated.
>
> Peter Jackson, *Maps of Meaning*, 1989[2]

Ethnic identities have long incubated in the ghettos, barrios, and Chinatowns of urban America. In such districts newcomers of diverse origins have shaped ethnic identities within North American cultural frameworks and social hierarchies. U.S. categories such as "Latino" or "Asian" may have little relevance before migration in immigrant source regions, but on arrival such terms greatly influence group settlement and acculturation. Modern technologies of communication and entertainment only strengthen the roles of urban districts as cultural seedbeds of ethnicity. Television, film, and news media rely on urban landscape images—too often stereotypes—to depict ethnic groups, while advances in transportation, telecommunication, and money transfer encourage transnational linkages. In short, ethnic representations continue to emerge, now as in the past, largely in urban America.

This chapter interprets contemporary urban ethnic landscapes through a historical-geographical lens on migration and settlement, cultural politics, and community change. Case studies are drawn from three cities of varying sizes, locations, and ethnic compositions. The small city of Poughkeepsie, New York, once an important commercial and industrial hub in the Mid-Hudson Valley, has begun to reverse decades of economic decline with the unexpected arrival of a growing Mexican American population.[3] San Francisco, California, famous as a cosmopolitan and livable city with stunning views, has experienced widespread gentrification and soaring real-estate prices, which increasingly threaten ethnic groups with displacement.[4] New York City, long the country's premiere immigrant port of entry, has witnessed a post-industrial economic restructuring with an emphasis on corporate financial sectors, modifying the skyline and reshaping cultural geographies of ethnic districts.[5] Before considering these empirical examples, a brief literature review highlights continuity and change in the geographical treatment of ethnic landscapes.

Cultural Geography and Urban Ethnic Landscapes

The study of cultural landscapes has long been a leading paradigm in American academic geography. As the field's early engagement with environmental determinism faced mounting criticism, geographer Carl O. Sauer at the University of California proposed a focus on the cultural landscape in the 1920s.[6] Thus began an enduring approach, associated with the seminal work of Sauer and intellectual descendants of the "Berkeley School," which provided the conceptual compass for countless twentieth-century cultural geographers. Although early landscape studies may have focused on rural and relatively traditional societies, cultural geographers influenced by Sauer have studied a wide variety of topics and settings. In time, concepts called attention to the interwoven physical and social fabrics of urban landscapes. J. B. Jackson and his disciples examined the "vernacular landscape" in urban as well as in rural settings.[7] Similarly, Donald Meinig, Pierce Lewis, and others interpreted "ordinary landscapes" with an emphasis on contemporary urban and suburban cases.[8]

As geographers grappled with issues of social diversity, the urban landscape became an important site for theoretical innovation in the late twentieth century. A wave of younger scholars proclaimed a "new cultural geography," based on poststructural and postmodern interpretations of culture as a complex phenomenon loaded with overt and latent meanings, sometimes revealed and at times obscured by landscapes. Rather than focusing so intently on visible material cultures, this approach emphasized landscape's symbolic dimensions, multiple meanings, and social relations expressed in politics, modern media, and the arts. A rising tide of multiculturalism encouraged geographical studies of nationalism, class, gender, sexuality, race, and ethnicity. Despite continuing theoretical controversies, the concept of landscape remained alive and well in geographical scholarship, albeit in significantly revised form.[9]

This reinvigorated landscape tradition serves to highlight the changing ethnic geographies of U.S. cities since the watershed U.S. immigration changes of the 1960s. The urban landscape—the association of built forms and human patterns—serves as our "text" to "read" ethnicity in terms of social change in American urban places. Our focus retains the time-honored emphasis on material culture—the buildings, architectural adaptations, and evolving streetscapes—but also incorporates issues of social space, cultural politics, resistance, and empowerment characteristic of the new cultural geography. Such conceptions of urban landscapes have particular relevance for ethnic communities, which emerge not merely in abstract spaces, but more concretely in specific places. This chapter analyzes ethnic change in terms of three emblematic types of urban landscape defined by ethnicity:

1. *incipient urban landscapes of ethnic arrival:* the influx of a new ethnic group begins to alter an urban district's demographic profile and cultural landscape, reflected visibly in the establishment of ethnically identified businesses, streetscapes, and social spaces.
2. *consolidated urban landscapes of ethnic enclaves:* as an ethnic group dominates a district demographically, the urban cultural landscape comes to include new and enduring community institutions, landmarks, and monuments to foster a coherent sense of place.
3. *defensive urban landscapes of ethnic contention:* in districts undergoing urban revitalization and gentrification, established ethnic groups often resist displacement by means of diverse political strategies and defensive cultural landscape elements.

This typology assumes particular temporal periods, making it something of a community snapshot in time. Specific ethnic communities may historically pass through two or all three of these landscape types, but this does not imply an irrevocable progression or a unilinear "stage" model. Nor does it suggest that these types of ethnic landscape are all-encompassing. Even if this typology is not exhaustive, however, it does highlight what are arguably the most archetypical ethnic landscapes of urban America.

Incipient Urban Landscapes of Ethnic Arrival

Ethnic districts form initially through in-migration by groups defined by the dominant culture as distinctive in national, racial, regional, or religious terms. The diverse factors affecting migration vary from case to case, but successfully established immigrants typically attract more of their co-ethnics in time. The geographical specificity expressed in ethnic settlement concentrations often stems from "chain migration" in which communications among social networks of friends and families provide information and personal contacts in faraway places. Whatever the causes of outmigration from the sending region, localized constraints and opportunities in the receiving region ultimately shape U.S. ethnic landscapes. New ethnic districts emerge in part because of the presence of employment, housing, and service opportunities. Immigrants of modest means seek out cheap housing—usually in residential hotels or shared rental apartments—and a street life ensues as they frequent local establishments. Prosperous immigrants have more residential choice and often resettle in relatively affluent suburban neighborhoods. Although geographers have documented "ethnoburbs," which are multiethnic suburbs with immigrant businesses, ethnic landscapes generally emerge among struggling immigrants in working-class central cities. Many struggling U.S. urban centers, both mid-sized and large, have been repopulated and economically revitalized by recent waves of immigration, as in inner-city Poughkeepsie.

LATINO REVITALIZATION OF MAIN STREET, POUGHKEEPSIE, NEW YORK

Until recent years Latin Americans have not been highly visible in most small cities of upstate New York. Although migrant farmworkers from Mexico and Central America have toiled intermittently in the Hudson Valley's agricultural fields for decades, this rural population did not establish a significant presence in cities. Beginning in the 1980s another immigration current gave a new ethnic sense of place to central Poughkeepsie. The U.S. Census counted 3,117 resident Hispanics (10.5%) among the city's 29,871 residents in 2000—probably a significant undercount, given undocumented residents. Census data indicate that the Hispanic population of Poughkeepsie tripled since 1990.[10] Informed observers estimate that 20 to 25 percent of the city's population is now Latino, at least twice the official count of the 2000 census.

The origins of this Mexican American community can be traced to pioneer immigrants, who discovered the availability of local work and spread the news back home in the state of Oaxaca during the 1980s. Even minimum-wage jobs proved attractive, since an hour of U.S. work typically paid more than an entire day's labor in southern Mexico.[11] From modest beginnings, Mexicans now work in a broad range of jobs, including stores, restaurants, house painting, construction, landscaping, and fast-food establishments. While initial immigrants were predominantly male, a notable recent influx of women, children, and other relatives has balanced the sex ratio somewhat to provide a more stable family life. Mexican American children increasingly attend city schools, where they now constitute the largest group in many lower-grade classes. Since 1998 the *Liga Independiente de Fútbol Asociado* has encouraged young Latinos to play on soccer teams with linkages to communities in southern Mexico, as in other cities.[12]

Mexican immigrants first gained visibility with the 1991 opening of El Bracero Restaurant on Main Street. The owner, Honorio "Pie" Rodriguez, hailed from La Cienega, a Oaxacan village of some 3,000 residents. Probably a quarter of La Cienega's adult men worked in the Poughkeepsie area by the 1990s. Mounting migration from the Oaxacan villages of La Cienega, San Augustín Yatareni, and Zaachila provided compelling ethnographic evidence, in the words of geographers Alison Mountz and Richard Wright, that new conceptions "of space and time enabled the creation of this single transnational 'locale.'"[13] Oaxaca and upstate New York, once distant, overcame geographic barriers to create an increasingly diverse transnational community; immigrants now arrive from such Mexican cities as Puebla and Veracruz, in addition to Oaxaca, and small numbers are from Central America as well. Among those Hispanics officially counted by the 2000 U.S. Census, over half (51%) declared a Mexican origin, and one-quarter (26%) said they were Puerto Rican.[14] This curiously high proportion of Puerto Ricans probably reflects the undercount of Mexican-origin Latinos. Since there is no visible Puerto Rican presence in Poughkeepsie, interviews suggest that many undocumented Mexican immigrants declared "Puerto Rican" status to suggest legal residence when questioned by a governmental agency. Certainly Poughkeepsie's emerging Latino community appears to be overwhelmingly Mexican in origin.

The Mexican presence stands out most vividly in the city's impoverished central area, surrounding a deteriorated and still-partly-burned-out stretch of Main Street. This area long suffered from high vacancy rates among both storefronts and apartments. Latino men now can be seen along Main Street at all hours, often walking in groups; bicycles provide a common mode of transportation for commuting to and from jobs in outlying suburbs. Women, children, and families also are beginning to make their appearance, especially during the daytime hours, in this emerging ethnic social space. The median household income here was only $15,758 in 2000—the lowest in Poughkeepsie—as opposed to $29,389 for the entire city and $53,086 in Dutchess County. The population of Hispanics or Latinos in this core census tract officially accounted for 30 percent of the total in 2000.[15] Undoubtedly it is much higher now.

The incipient Latino landscape is most visible in commercial streetscapes, rather than in housescapes. The explanation lies in the newness of the Latino immigration, the low-income and renter status of most immigrants, and the city's lack of a previous Hispanic presence. Typically Latin American or Mexican morphological and cultural elements present in the Southwest such as historic street grids and plazas, brightly painted houses, and lots surrounded by fences or walls do not exist in Northeastern cities like Poughkeepsie.[16] Latino men often rent apartments with others in the inexpensive units along central Main Street, while those with families prefer renting houses

Figure 16.1.   Mexican businesses on Main Street, Poughkeepsie, illustrate the influx of immigrant entrepreneurs in an economically struggling downtown of upstate New York. Source: Author.

in surrounding working-class districts. Poughkeepsie apartment buildings and houses thus show little Latino influence in façade color or religious shrines, unlike parts of the U.S. Southwest. As Ines Miyares has noted for New York City, however, Latino streetscapes show abundant cultural landscape signatures in inner-city Poughkeepsie.[17]

An aspiring Latino entrepreneurial class has begun to revitalize Main Street, which declined for decades as the result of suburban retail flight. Since the founding of the Bracero Restaurant in 1991, approximately 25 other Spanish-language businesses emerged by September 2004, including nine restaurants, eight variety stores advertising money transfers to Latin America, three grocery stores, two *panaderias* or bakeries, two delicatessens, and a hair salon. Emblazoned with signs mixing Spanish and English, these businesses initially tend to be modest undertakings in appearance and size (Fig. 16.1). The signage is amateurish at first, but becomes more professional as operations grow. Established Latino businesses adopt visible Mexican or southwestern motifs in the windows, awnings, and façades. Most notable are the Mexican colors and flag, national symbols such as the saguero cactus and the indigenous past, and references to places and festivals. With the exception of a few of the more successful restaurants, the clientele of these Main Street businesses remain overwhelmingly Spanish-speaking, and Anglos do not provide a significant customer base. Given central-city Poughkeepsie's continuing working-class status, the emerging Mexican American business sector does not suggest gentrification, at least not yet, but the emerging Hispanic ethnic landscape provides renewed commercial activity in what for decades had been a deteriorated and largely boarded up central-city zone of transition.

This Latino immigration remained unnoticed by many residents until a hit-and-run car accident on April 10, 1998, left Jaime Gil Tenorio dead on a downtown expressway. Police investigation revealed him to be a 32-year-old undocumented migrant, who worked in landscaping to support a wife and four children in Oaxaca. With the aid of local churches and newspapers, some 2,500 local donors raised $22,583 for the Tenorio family. After the accident, the *Poughkeepsie Journal* reported that local residents "have grown curious and friendly" about the growing Mexican American population in their midst.[18]

Consolidated Urban Landscapes of Ethnic Enclaves

The urban cultural landscape reflects the degree to which an ethnic group becomes dominant in demographic, political, and economic terms. As a group passes a threshold of dominance, processes of neighborhood change and group succession typically accelerate and become more visible. If and when a district becomes the ethnic enclave of a dominant group, the urban landscape registers a full-fledged cultural imprint accordingly. Businesses typically cater to a diverse array of ethnic needs that include not only grocery stores, restaurants, and basic services, but also such higher-order businesses as doctors, insurance, and legal services. Signage in a foreign language or dialect illustrates this more comprehensive and complex ethnic transition, as do local street life and social space. Local institutions of church and state may offer bilingual services and ceremonies in native languages. Community art and architectural adaptation tend to reflect ethnic themes. Entrepreneurs often project certain regional or national images to attract business from local residents, visitors, and even tourists. Community monuments, historical landmarks, names of streets and public spaces, and other ethnic symbols suggest enhanced group status and political importance. In short, the urban ethnic landscape becomes a source of ethnic identity and collective memory.

CHINATOWN: FROM GHETTO TO ETHNOBURB

Long isolated as cultural outsiders in exotic "Chinatowns," the Chinese have constituted one of the country's most distinctive and segregated ethnic groups. San Francisco boasts the most famous Chinatown of America, where a major tourist attraction also constitutes a densely populated ethnic enclave that is more than 90 percent Chinese in origin (Map 16.1). This ethnic district dates from the mid-1800s California Gold Rush, when Cantonese peasants from southern China, mainly male—suffering from the ravages of civil strife, population pressure, and overfarming—came to *gum shan*, or the "golden mountain" of America. While most of the Chinese initially went to the

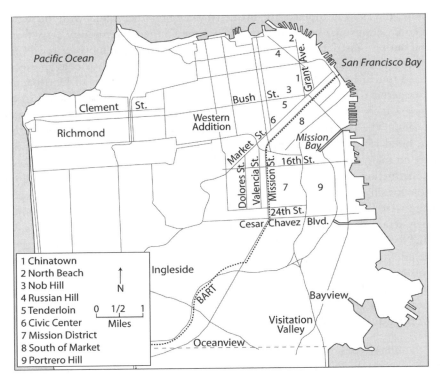

Map 16.1.   Chinatown, Western Districts, and the Latino Mission District of San Francisco.

goldfields, San Francisco remained the primary supply and service center. In 1851, some 3,000 Chinese could already be found in the city.[19] Rising popular resentment against the Chinese, fed by resentful white workers, soon intensified Chinese urbanization in the West. Passage of the Chinese Exclusion Act in 1882 and anti-miscegenation laws created a "bachelor society." By 1890, San Francisco had 25,833 Chinese residents, overwhelmingly male, representing almost 9 percent of the city's population.[20]

For a century San Francisco's Chinese were confined to a downtown district located along Dupont Street (later Grant Avenue). Speaking little English, restricted in housing, and fearful of attacks by outsiders, the Chinese had good reason to congregate. Chinatown became an insular ethnic enclave in which men outnumbered women by about 20 to 1 by the 1880s.[21] This gender imbalance encouraged the proliferation of vice operations catering to single men that featured such illicit activities as prostitution, gambling, and opium dens. Not surprisingly, Chinatown developed a reputation for licentiousness and moral depravity. The Chinese could not live outside of Chinatown, and whites regarded the area as dangerous and dirty. Ethnic associations, based upon surname, region of origin, and linguistic dialect, helped organize life in Chinatown; the more important organizations joined forces in the politically powerful Chinese Benevolent Association, popularly known as the Six Companies. Like so much else here, the Six Companies did not originate in the region of South China, but grew out of the American experience of urban segregation.[22]

After the 1906 earthquake and fire destroyed Chinatown, along with the rest of the city's core, serious plans proposed to relocate the Chinese community away from the central business district. Yet Chinatown proved too lucrative to move. Shrewd Chinese merchants saw the opportunity to redevelop the infamous vice district as an exotic but sanitized tourist haven. Unlike the situation in other Chinatowns of North America, where external white boosters often played more dominant roles, San Francisco's ethnic Chinese largely financed, directed, and marketed the reconstruction of Chinatown after 1906. The Chinese merchant community, with help from the Chinese government, hired white architects and contractors to rebuild Chinatown with pagoda-like towers on many commercial buildings to give an "oriental" look (Fig. 16.2). Residential construction emphasized three to four-story tenements, consisting of small rooms suitable for single immigrant men; overwhelmingly these units had inadequate plumbing and were substandard by city codes. Besides the continued crowding, rebuilt Chinatown retained the same basic boundaries, except for an expansion along Grant Avenue to Bush Street, where a steady tourist trade developed.[23] Grant Avenue became the ethnic main street, lined with Chinese restaurants, specialty shops, grocery stores, and other businesses. Paradoxically, the architecture and signage assumed an increasingly "oriental" look while the city's Chinese population—faced with a prohibition on further immigration due to the Chinese Exclusion Act—decreased to less than 10,000 by World War I.[24] As architectural historians have noted:

> Whereas the pre-fire Chinatown had been built largely of prefabricated wooden buildings of no architectural pretension or style, the post-fire "city within a city" was reconstructed of lasting materials such as brick. The district was also imprinted architecturally with Oriental stage-set trappings

Table 16.1. Population by Race and Hispanic Origin in New York City, Poughkeepsie, and San Francisco

City and District	Total Population 2000	Percent White		Percent Black		Percent Asian		Percent Hispanic Origin	
		1990	2000	1990	2000	1990	2000	1990	2000
New York City	8,008,278	52.5	44.7	28.7	26.4	7.0	9.8	24.4	27.0
Loisaida/ Alphabet City/ East Village	25,629	35.1	39.9	19.8	17.3	5.7	9.3	62.0	54.5
Harlem	107,109	1.5	2.0	87.6	77.3	0.4	0.9	10.1	16.8
Poughkeepsie, New York	29,871	65.4	53.4	31.5	35.8	1.5	1.3	3.8	10.5
Central Main St.	1,963	57.9	40.9	36.6	36.4	1.3	—	9.7	27.4
San Francisco	776,733	53.6	49.7	10.9	7.8	29.1	30.9	13.9	14.1
Chinatown	4,703	3.7	2.9	0.7	—	93.1	92.6	0.4	—
Inner Mission District	35,911	46.6	47.3	4.5	1.8	13.2	10.5	62.3	60.9

Sources: U.S. Census, American Factfinder, 1990 Summary Tape File 1 (STF 1), 100 Percent Data; U.S. Census, American Factfinder, 2000 Summary File 2 (SF 2), 100 Percent Data.

Note: Percentages do not total 100 because not all racial categories are included here. In addition, because Latino or Hispanic origin is not considered a race, it overlaps other categories. Dashes indicate populations below the threshold necessary for inclusion.

designed to lure tourists up from the downtown shopping area to a world-famous Oriental bazaar. The scheme worked.[25]

With its own distinctive customs and institutions, outsiders perceived Chinatown as a foreign district immune from outside authority. Architecture along the commercial streets assumed a "classic" Chinese design with brightly colored façades, ornamental dragons, pagoda roofs with curved eaves, painted balconies, windbells and flowered lanterns, brilliant neon signage. As in other western cities, the "exotic" urban landscape of San Francisco's Chinatown cannot be understood solely in terms of immigrant cultural adaptation, but also reflects the social construction of racialized images as shaped by ethnic constraints and commercial opportunities.[26] It is important to mention, however, that Chinatown entrepreneurs have themselves constructed these landscapes of "otherness" to commodify the exotic culture of Chinatown for commercial gain.

The Chinese moved into new districts of San Francisco after World War II through a relaxation of residential segregation and immigration constraints. The repeal of the Chinese Exclusion Act in 1943, and extension of the War Brides Act of 1945 to Chinese in 1947, finally permitted an end to the "bachelor society." As the lure of the suburbs produced vacancies in the city's older neighborhoods, Chinese Americans expanded beyond Chinatown into adjacent districts downtown and affluent neighborhoods of western San Francisco. With the passage of liberalized immigration laws implemented in 1965, which abolished the previous system of national quotas, San Francisco's Asian communities grew rapidly to constitute 22 percent of the city's population in 1980, 29 percent in 1990, and 31 percent in 2000 (Table 16.1).

The presence of a large Chinese population has attracted Asian financial capital to San Francisco. Hong Kong–based banks have proliferated in the financial district, and

Figure 16.2. Chinatown's symbolic entrance is the "Dragon Gate" at Grant and Bush streets. A gift of the Taiwan government, after completion in 1970 the Dragon Gate became a prominent landmark and tourist attraction. Source: Author.

overseas Chinese investors have found a culturally familiar environment in San Francisco. The influx of Asian investment contrasts sharply with the continuing poverty and crowding in Chinatown, where recent immigrants from southern China, Hong Kong, and Southeast Asia face inflated housing prices because of the bidding war for downtown property. Chinatown's core census tracts remain more than 90 percent Chinese, an unusual degree of ethnic concentration in the city, with population densities between 120 and 180 people an acre, or between 77,000 and 115,000 people per square mile—one of the highest urban densities in the country.[27] Chinatown still faces the paradox of widespread urban poverty while also serving as a major tourist attraction.

Affluent and acculturated Chinese Americans have moved to outlying areas of the city or to suburban locations (Map 16.1). The movement into areas adjacent to Chinatown has generated controversy, as North Beach, Russian and Nob Hills, and the Tenderloin have become largely Chinese American. The affluent western district of Richmond features Clement Street, where a secondary Chinatown emerged with scores of restaurants and other businesses. The housing morphology of the Richmond District, a mixture of single-family houses and multi-unit buildings (flats and apartments), appeals to Chinese extended families, who settle in close proximity or even under one roof. In addition, several transit lines run from the Richmond District directly to Chinatown downtown. This transportation connection has been important to maintain family ties, access to ethnic foods and other products, and social institutions.

Chinese Americans now move into neighborhoods along the city's BART (Bay Area Rapid Transit) southern corridor—such as Visitation Valley, Bayview, Oceanview, and Ingleside—which have evolved from satellites of Chinatown to more autonomous "suburbs" within the city (Map 16.1). In fact, Chinatown is no longer a necessary gateway for recent immigrants. Social service agencies are now more likely to send a poor immigrant to the Bayview or Tenderloin districts than to crowded Chinatown. Those Chinese who arrive with ample financial resources do not need the "gateway" community services and may move directly into homeownership in affluent western San Francisco or the suburbs. For example, Chinese American ethnoburbs have emerged with relatively high levels of education and income in "Silicon Valley" of the South Bay. According to geographer Wei Li: "Ethnoburbs are altering demographic composition, business practices and social relations in suburbia. They challenge the dominant view that assimilation is inevitable and the best solution for minorities."[28]

HARLEM AS THE BLACK GHETTO

Speculative overbuilding of the housing stock helped transform New York City's Harlem from a well-to-do white streetcar suburb of the late nineteenth century, served by elevated trains and the IRT subway lines to Lower Manhattan, into a crowded black ghetto by the early twentieth century (Map 16.2). A decisive turning point came during the economic depression of 1904–1905, when a building boom screeched to a halt and left an abundance of high-rent apartments and foreclosed mortgages. Philip A. Payton, an enterprising black real-estate agent, persuaded the white owners of property on West 134th Street to rent their vacant apartments to African Americans, whose numbers were increasingly due to migration from the U.S. South. Payton promised white landlords top rents and efficient management for "colored tenements." His Afro-American Realty Company facilitated the movement of blacks from the downtown slums of San Juan Hill and the Tenderloin to Harlem uptown. Despite some efforts of white residents and property owners to stop the growing influx, the district became predominantly African American by the 1920s.[29]

The Harlem Renaissance signaled a creative efflorescence by black artists, poets, and musicians during the 1920s. The emergence of the "New Negro" and a black bourgeoisie made Harlem a symbol of previously unimagined success, luxury, and cultural mystique. Harlem's fame grew with the success of the Cotton Club, Connie's Inn, and other uptown nightclubs where whites went "slumming" to enjoy black bands, singers,

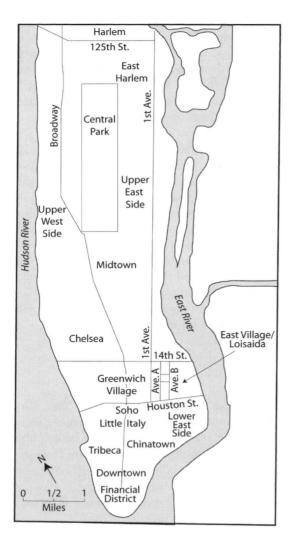

Map 16.2.   Selected Districts of Manhattan.

and dance shows. Black churches also joined the movement to Harlem during the 1920s. The exclusive St. Philip's Protestant Episcopal Church, long reputed to be the wealthiest black congregation in Harlem, sold its downtown property and bought large real-estate holdings on 135th Street, where it rented apartments to blacks. The Abyssinian Baptist Church under the Reverend Adam Clayton Powell Sr. also purchased property during the 1920s. Through the ups and downs of this district, the African American churches have remained pillars of the Harlem community.

As the Roaring Twenties gave way to the 1929 Depression, Harlem's glamour dissipated amid widespread unemployment, growing poverty, racial discrimination, housing deterioration, and declining living conditions. The district's public health situation was considered the worst in the city by the early 1930s. Living conditions declined as landlords cut back on building maintenance. To meet rents, many African Americans subdivided apartments, and the increased crowding paradoxically created a "slum boom" for property owners.[30] Although World War II brought greater employment opportunities for Harlem residents, overcrowding and physical deterioration of the neighborhood continued unabated. After the war, housing disinvestment and abandonment in Harlem steadily worsened, creating what historian Gilbert Osofsky called "the enduring ghetto."[31]

During the 1980s, after a half-century of steady decline, Harlem began to experience an unexpected economic upswing as affordable housing in Manhattan grew scarce. The financial-services boom and widespread gentrification downtown led to the beginnings of Harlem housing renovation.[32] Initially the prospects for gentrification seemed remote, and increasingly so when the district suffered a downturn during the stock-market decline of the late 1980s. Yet by the mid-1990s Harlem real estate was hot again. Rents and real-estate prices have continued to spiral steadily upward; restored townhouses in Harlem now sell for $1 million or more. The Historic District of Striver's Row, which was renovated as an elegant residential district, saw the sale of a townhouse for $1.7 million in 2003—an unheard-of amount at that point.[33]

Although some wealthy in-movers have been white, Harlem has become a place for many affluent African Americans, often not originally from Harlem or even New York City, to resettle as part of an ideology of "racial return and revival." These newcomers sometimes encounter unanticipated local differences of class, however, which can feed internal tensions within Harlem's African American community.[34] As *New York Magazine* put it in 1997, when the economic revitalization was under way in earnest: "Aided by an infusion of public money and new interest from national retailers, a cadre of young activists are pushing the capital of Black America toward another renaissance—and in the process, are struggling bitterly with Harlem's old guard."[35]

Harlem's ethnic main street lies along the commercial thoroughfare and transportation hub of 125th Street (Map 16.2). This corridor is home to world-famous cultural institutions and historical landmarks, including the Studio Museum, the Apollo Theater, the National Black Theater, the Cotton Club, and the Theresa Hotel (Fig. 16.3). The 125th Street Business Improvement District, formally created in 1993, has sponsored streetscape improvement projects and attempted with mixed success to resolve merchant complaints against street vendors on the sidewalks. In recent years, investments by national firms have made 125th Street a major shopping district for local residents and visitors. The "Harlem USA" retail complex is home to the Disney Store, Odeon Cineplex, Jazz Club, the Gap, and Pathmark. Other new businesses include Magic Johnson's Magic Theater Complex, Starbucks, fast-food outlets, and Blockbuster. Although widespread fears of displacement have surfaced in the community, the general focus of retail franchises on African American populations appears to be in harmony with the racial identity of Harlem.

The influence and real-estate holdings of powerful black institutions such as the Abyssinian Baptist Church and the Schomberg Center for Research in Black Culture have become part of Harlem's cultural identity and inhibit drastic racial change. The Abyssinian Baptist Church in particular has been a major force in community politics, social services, and housing redevelopment. Other symbols of Black Pride and African

Figure 16.3. A view of the famous Apollo Theater on 125th Street, Harlem, during renovation in October 2003. The high-rise in the background is the Adam Clayton Powell Jr. State Office Building, built in the 1970s as part of an urban renewal program that was only partially achieved, given community protests. Source: Author.

American culture include Malcolm X Park, Adam Clayton Powell Boulevard, and the Harlem State Office Building. The radical politics of Marcus Garvey's "back to Africa" movement in the 1920s, followed by the large-scale race riots of 1935, 1943, and 1964, have created a historical memory of civil-rights activism in Harlem. Although contemporary Harlem has become more affluent and socially diverse, it remains doubtful that the predominantly black population will lose its demographic, cultural, and political hold on this consolidated ethnic enclave in the near future.

Defensive Urban Landscapes of Ethnic Contention

As ethnic districts witness socioeconomic change through economic revitalization, urban renewal, or gentrification, established residents, who are fearful of displacement, often assume defensive stances toward an influx of newcomers. This phenomenon occurs most notably in neighborhoods undergoing processes of what human ecologists have called "invasion and succession" leading to racial transition, rather than in deteriorating areas undergoing "abandonment and replacement" in which displacement is not an important factor.[36] Defensive urban landscapes often experience social polarization, political organizing, community art and murals, and interethnic tensions. Sometimes youth gang activity in the form of graffiti, street presence, and a forbidding reputation serves to protect a "defended neighborhood" from displacement.[37] Ethnic solidarity may be heightened by such social conflict, as community tensions rise and various strategies of resistance take shape, as we see in the two ethnic Latino case studies.

SAN FRANCISCO'S MISSION DISTRICT: COMMUNITY MURAL ART IN A CONTESTED BARRIO

In San Francisco's Mission District, a distinctive Latino community has asserted its ethnic presence through activist politics, commercial streetscapes, cultural activities, and community art (Map 16.1). This Latino neighborhood, or *barrio,* has long defied predictions of its demise through community organizing.[38] Latinos began entering the Mission during the 1930s, when apartment rents here were among the city's cheapest. Many Latinos previously lived near the South-of-Market waterfront, where they worked on the docks or in warehouses, food-processing companies, and light industry. Much like previous European immigrant groups, Latin Americans followed the city's street pattern from this gritty area into the Mission District. With the continued influx of Latin American immigrants and the suburbanization of acculturated ethnic groups—especially the Irish and the Italians—the Mission District core became a Latino *barrio* by the 1960s. Along with the ethnic influx, however, came growing problems of neighborhood disinvestment, housing deterioration, linguistic barriers, and poverty.[39]

Because the Mission District's Latino population dwells largely in multi-apartment rental buildings, the ethnic presence is more evident in commercial streetscapes and community art than in housescapes. Outlying business districts on Valencia and 16th streets are multiethnic, trendy and popular with young professionals, and exhibit strong signs of gentrification. The heavily Latino Inner Mission (Table 16.1) features the ethnic banner streets of Mission Street (between 16th Street and César Chavez Boulevard) and lower 24th Street (between Valencia and Portrero streets). These commercial strips mix Latino restaurants, grocery and specialty shops, travel agencies advertising money transfers, and Latin music stores. Street vendors often clog the sidewalks selling their wares in both Spanish and English. These commercial streetscapes are remarkable in the wide variety of regional and national origins evident in the businesses. Restaurants advertise Mexican, Nicaraguan, Salvadoran, Guatemalan, Vietnamese, Chinese, New Age vegetarian, and other cuisines. Grocery and other specialty stores also mirror this multinational, heavily Latin American diversity. In fact, the Mission District's Latino population is unusually diverse: Mexican Americans constitute approximately 40 percent, while a plurality originate from El Salvador, Nicaragua, Guatemala, and other countries. Yet over time a Latino community has formed a broad pan-Hispanic cohesion. Ethnic identification also results from social and linguistic ties, cultural commonalities, and community festivals.[40]

Recent Latin American immigrants typically dwell in cheap residential hotels or crowd into apartments with friends and relatives. They toil in low-paid service jobs in restaurants, office cleaning, and domestic services. Informal employment in painting, construction, landscape gardening, and other household tasks is also common, despite frequent labor abuses in such casual work. The most vulnerable workers are the male day laborers, mostly undocumented Mexicans and Central Americans, who gather at known locations and bid for jobs on a project basis. Large groups of men assemble daily along César Chavez Boulevard, waiting for job bids from passing motorists, much to the chagrin of local residents who often summon the police.

Community art is an important sign of Latino ethnicity. Approximately 100 public murals have been painted since the early 1970s in a revival of the tradition of the great Mexican muralists—Rivera, Orozco, and Siqueiros—to announce the ethnicity of the *barrio*. Local cultural centers, inspired by the Chicano political movement, have sought to define the Mission District as Latino cultural space. Professional murals adorn many buildings, such as the Women's Building on 16th Street, while street art by amateurs has also proved immensely popular. For example, the murals lining Balmy Alley, started by the Mujeres Muralistas collective in the 1970s, have become a major tourist attraction in the Mission District. These and other local muralists have given rise to what is sometimes called the "Mission School," which combines classic Mexican styles with a range of postmodern sensibilities.[41]

Poster art also has been a controversial form of cultural politics. The San Francisco Print Collective, an activist group formed in 1999, has created polemical political posters satirizing the trendiness of the "ethnic" Mission or taking aim at local politicians, landlords, and developers. As fears of displacement intensified during the 1990s "dot-com" boom, anger at luxury housing development, rising rents, evictions of long-term residents, and loss of non-profit space led to an explosion of neighborhood activism. Demonstrations by the Mission Anti-Displacement Coalition, a coalition of community organizations, have made local headlines and highlighted the presence of an activist community committed to neighborhood preservation at all costs.

NEW YORK CITY'S LOISAIDA/EAST VILLAGE: COMMUNITY GARDENS AND THE PUERTO RICAN COMMUNITY

New York's Lower East Side (LES) is another neighborhood in which a defensive urban ethnicity has confronted urban renewal, gentrification, and displacement (Map 16.2). Like the Mission District, the LES was a working-class neighborhood of European immigrants that steadily declined in socioeconomic status by the mid-twentieth century. The district became one of the city's prime destinations for Puerto Rican immigrants after World War II, just as it developed a forbidding reputation as a drug-ridden slum. By the 1960s Puerto Ricans called the northeastern LES—roughly between Houston and 14th streets, from Avenue A to the East River—Loisaida, a "Spanglish" adaptation of the district's name. Although Loisaida never rivaled El Barrio of East Harlem as a Puerto Rican neighborhood, the Latino population reached 18,031 or 45 percent of the total in Loisaida (east of Avenue B) in 1970. After a decade of housing abandonment, arson, and demolition that decreased the Loisaida's population considerably, the number of Latinos fell in absolute terms to 16,492 but rose to 68 percent of Loisaida's total in 1980.[42]

Puerto Ricans could not retain hold over this area, in part because their migrations were more dispersed in spatial and historical terms than the previous Eastern European immigrants. The Puerto Ricans also faced drastic urban service reductions and landlord disinvestment in the city's fiscal squeeze of the 1970s, without the political weight to counter subsequent urban renewal.[43] The Latino population of Loisaida east of Avenue B fell to 15,677 or 62 percent in 1990, and to 13,969 or 54.5 percent in 2000. The Lillian Wald and Jacob Riis Public Houses—massive public housing projects, once mainly white, working-class families and now overwhelmingly Puerto Rican—became Loisaida's main Latino bastion in the face of massive displacement from adjacent private housing.[44] In the broader Manhattan LES Community District—including the entire East Village, Chinatown, and Little Italy—the Latino population fell from 32.3 percent in 1990 to 26.9 percent in 2000.[45]

As artists and countercultural elements trickled into this area of transition during the 1960s, it began to be called Alphabet City or the East Village—labels to many residents of gentrifiers, whites, and outsiders.[46] The proliferation of such nicknames in itself illustrates a century-long tradition of land conflict and social activism in what is widely considered the city's politically most organized district.[47] As the area gradually overcame its image as a dangerous neighborhood of drug-dealing and poverty to become a chic area for the young, hip, and the professional classes, real-estate interests and governmental agencies battled working-class and minority residents for control. Once developers determined they could profit from neighborhood redevelopment, they promoted the arts as a strategy to draw more affluent residents. In fact, Christopher Mele asserts that the main reason for reinvestment lay in the "symbolic representation of the East Village as an alluring arts district." Artists of the late 1970s and early 1980s created a "rebellious art genre" that appealed to wealthy patrons and developers, leading to a steady gentrification and displacement of original residents.[48] East Village artists, such as the late Keith Harin, have inadvertently popularized the area and sparked a local real-estate bonanza. On the other hand, the local history of activism inspired street demonstrations, protests, and the harrowing "police riots" in 1988 and 1991 to evict squatters from Tompkins Square Park.[49]

As the city reduced such basic neighborhood services as police patrols, garbage pickup, and street cleaning during the 1970s, many buildings were abandoned by landlords and burned by arsonists hired to collect insurance money. By some estimates, more than 3,400 housing units were demolished and at least 70 percent of the population displaced.[50] In the resulting "bombed-out war zone," neighborhood residents began squatter vegetable and flower gardens in the overgrown empty lots strewn with trash. The community garden movement can be traced to the Liz Christy Garden, started in 1973 by a group of women activists, who pressured the city government to grant permission to garden. That group later formed the Green Guerillas, which now provides support for community gardens throughout New York City. This movement gained financial and temporary legal status when in 1976 the Department of Housing Preservation and Development recognized gardens as an appropriate "interim use" for city-owned vacant lots. This designation of the gardens as temporary became a source of conflict by the 1990s, when a booming real-estate market encouraged the city to sell the vacant lots to private developers. While the city claims it needs land to develop new housing, community activists argue that the gardens provide valuable open space in a dense urban neighborhood. The struggle has escalated to pitched battles in some cases, such as in the emotional showdown between protesters and police at the bulldozing of Esperanza Garden in February 2000.[51]

By the mid-1980s some 75 community gardens existed in Loisaida,[52] most of which still can be found twenty years later. The gardens, tended by a variety of ethnic and social groups, range from the carefully manicured to the chaotic and overgrown. The garden spaces are used for a variety of social purposes, including picnics, parties, outdoor performances, sitting and talking. Weekends are most active as most gardens post "Open to Public" hours on Saturday and Sunday, or "whenever gardeners are present." Such public visiting hours are required at least twice a week for gardens leased on city-owned land and supported by the Operation Green Thumb program, which provides gardening supplies and program assistance. While the gardens are locked and fenced when not in use, the public is permitted to enter during open hours as long as people stay on the paths and do not pick flowers or vegetables. The gardens are locked at night and when no gardeners are present for reasons of security and to keep out vandals, the homeless, and drug users. Some of the older and better-maintained gardens have been designated official New York City Parkland, thus achieving permanent status.

About half of the Loisaida gardens reflect Latino ethnicity, primarily serving Puerto Ricans. Their gardens are typically small 15-by-50-foot lots, which often display the Puerto Rican flag and murals on the bordering walls with colorful pictures and messages in Spanish. The better-organized gardens are tended primarily by women, who often watch children while gardening. Gardens dominated by Latino men can be distinguished by a *casita* or "little house" on the lot, which harkens back to the mountains of Puerto Rico (Fig. 16.4). While some vegetables may be cultivated, along with the inevitable chickens and roosters, these *casitas* serve mainly as male gathering places to drink beer, play cards or dominos, socialize, relax, and even sleep. As Karen Schmelzkopf notes:

*Figure 16.4.   A Puerto Rican casita in the East Village,
New York, symbolically re-creates a tie to the ethnic
homeland as part of the community garden movement
and anti-displacement neighborhood politics.
Source: Author.*

Men of the casita-based gardens articulate their own personal benefits. The casita is a place where they can relax, where they can re-create a lifestyle similar to that of Puerto Rico, and where they do not have to answer to anyone else. Some of these men have no place else to go. They have become estranged from their families, and in the casitas they at least are able to remain a part of the community.[53]

In both the Mission District and Loisaida, a defensive community stance favoring preservation has employed the built environment and public space to make political statements. The creation of livable and aesthetically attractive areas, however, paradoxically encourages gentrification. The ultimate success of public art and community gardens as forms of resistance rooted in the urban landscape remains to be seen.

Conclusion

The evolution of urban landscapes of ethnicity is inextricably bound to a broad range of social, political, economic, and cultural developments. To "read" the urban landscape requires that we analyze the "text" in terms of the dynamic interaction between society and space. The interlocking human and physical factors, analyzed together, help explain the diversity of ethnic landscapes. A knowledgeable observer is able to discern ethnic flux through landscape clues—ranging from blatant to subtle and even hidden signs—suggesting dynamic processes of in-migration, resettlement, adaptation, and social relations.

Poughkeepsie's Main Street illustrates the emergence of an *incipient urban landscape of ethnic arrival.* The low-income, largely renter status of immigrants here largely inhibits the emergence of Latin American housescapes, but the commercial streetscapes proclaim the unmistakable signs of ethnic flux. Poughkeepsie's immigrant entrepreneurs have developed businesses in run-down areas as the ethnic populations grow. The case study shows how commercial streetscapes often are the first areas to proclaim the arrival of new groups.

Consolidated urban landscapes of ethnic enclaves feature a wide array of businesses, churches, social spaces, cultural centers, and architectural adaptations of ethnicity. In San Francisco's Chinatown, landmarks such as the Dragon Gate, and the many Chinese restaurants and stores catering to both local residents and tourists, suggest a thriving business district. In Harlem, the renovation of the Apollo Theater and the vibrant neighborhood churches provide evidence of community pride, even as the main thoroughfare of 125th Street has witnessed the proliferation of national business chains targeting a niche-market of African Americans.

Defensive urban landscapes of ethnic contention illustrate the social struggles of neighborhoods facing urban renewal, gentrification, or displacement. In both the Mission District and Loisaida, a sense of Latino territoriality has arisen that is defensive in its cultural landscape and assertive in its political activities. Anti-displacement initiatives in both districts have fueled larger political coalitions and resulted in significant manifestations in the cultural landscape, expressed in community art and community gardens. Such political activism draws meaning and sustenance from the urban landscape, but ethnic preservation efforts have also made low-income areas more attractive and in this sense contributed to gentrification.

These examples suggest widespread issues of community change and neighborhood succession in the United States. Accurate interpretation of urban landscapes requires an analysis of how built forms, commercial functions, social spaces, and ethnic symbols acquire meaning over time. Ethnic districts associate migrant histories, urban forms, and public spaces to create a geographical sense of place. Group identities emerge out of these interactions among people, built environments, and historical memories. Through historical-geographical analysis of urban ethnic landscapes, we may ponder the fate of particular communities as sites for social mobility or struggles for community preservation in urban America.

Notes

1. Carl Sauer, "The Morphology of Landscape," in *Land and Life: A Selection of the Writings of Carl Ortwin Sauer,* ed. John Leighly (Berkeley and Los Angeles: University of California Press, 1963), 315–350 (originally published in 1925).

2. Peter Jackson, *Maps of Meaning: An Introduction to Cultural Geography* (London: Unwin Hyman, 1989), 1.

3. Harvey K. Flad, "A Time of Readjustment: Urban Renewal in Poughkeepsie, 1955–1975," *Dutchess County Historical Society Year Book* 72 (1987): 152–180.

4. Brian J. Godfrey, *Neighborhoods in Transition: The Making of San Francisco's Ethnic and Nonconformist Communities* (Berkeley and Los Angeles: University of California Press, 1988), 131–171; and "Urban Development and Redevelopment in San Francisco," *Geographical Review* 87, no. 3 (July 1997): 310–333.

5. Janet Abu-Lughod, *New York, Chicago, and Los Angeles: America's Global Cities* (Minneapolis: University of Minnesota Press, 1999), 269–320; Brian J. Godfrey, "Restructuring and Decentralization in a World City," *Geographical Review* 85, no. 4 (October 1995): 436–457.

6. Sauer, "Morphology of Landscape," 315–350.

7. J. B. Jackson, "The Order of Landscape: Reason and Religion in Newtonian America," in *The Interpretation of Ordinary Landscapes: Geographical Essays,* ed. D. W. Meinig (Oxford, London, and New York: Oxford University Press, 1979), 153–163.

8. Pierce Lewis, "Axioms for Reading the Landscape," in *The Interpretation of Ordinary Landscapes,* 11–32.

9. James Duncan, "The Superorganic in American Cultural Geography," *Annals of the Association of American Geographers* 83 (1980): 181–198; Marie Price and Martin Lewis, "Reinventing Cultural Geography," *Annals of the Association of American Geographers* 83 (1993): 1–17.

10. U.S. Census, American Factfinder, *1990 Summary Tape File 1 (STF 1)—100 Percent Data*; and U.S. Census, American Factfinder, *2000 Summary File 2 (SF 2)—100 Percent Data,* <factfinder.census.gov/home> (25 August 2004).

11. Mary Beth Pfeiffer, "From Poverty to the Green Valley," *Poughkeepsie Journal,* 16 July 1998, 1–10 (E).

12. Marie Price and Courtney Whitworth, "Soccer and Latino Cultural Space: Metropolitan Washington Fútbol Leagues," in *Hispanic Spaces, Latino Places,* ed. Daniel Arreola (Austin: University of Texas Press, 2004), 167–186.

13. Alison Mountz and Richard A. Wright, "Daily Life in the Transnational Migrant Community of San Agustín, Oaxaca, and Poughkeepsie, New York," *Diaspora* 6 (1996): 403–428.

14. U.S. Census, American Factfinder, *Census 2000 Summary File 4* <factfinder.census.gov/home> (25 August 2004).

15. U.S. Census, American Factfinder, *Census 2000 Summary File 4* <factfinder.census.gov/home> (25 August 2004).

16. Daniel D. Arreola, "Mexican American Housescapes," *Geographical Review* 78, no. 3 (July 1998): 229–315.

17. Ines M. Miyares, "Changing Latinization of New York City," in *Hispanic Spaces, Latino Places,* 146–148.

18. Joseph Berger, "Detective's Kindness Helps Awaken a City; After a Death, Poughkeepsie Notices Its 3,000 Mexicans and Their Roots," *New York Times,* 7 January 1999, 1 (B).

19. Willard T. Chow, *The Re-emergence of an Inner City: The Pivot of Chinese Settlement in the East Bay Region of the San Francisco Bay Area* (San Francisco: R and E Research Associates, 1977), 20.

20. Victor G. Nee and Brett de Bary Nee, *Longtime Californ': A Documentary Study of an American Chinatown* (New York: Pantheon Books, 1972), 30–57; U.S. Census Bureau, *Thirteenth Census of the United States, 1910. Statistics for California* (Washington: Government Printing Office, 1914), 593.

21. U.S. Census Bureau, *Thirteenth Census of the United States*, 593.

22. Nee and Nee, *Longtime Californ'*, xxii; Chow, *Re-emergence of an Inner City*, 67–68.

23. Connie Young Yu, "A History of San Francisco Chinatown Housing," *Amerasia Journal* 8 (Spring/Summer 1981): 95–100.

24. U.S. Census Bureau, *Thirteenth Census of the United States*, 593.

25. Sally B. Woodbridge and John M. Woodbridge, *Architecture San Francisco: The Guide* (San Francisco: American Institute of Architects, 1982), 37.

26. Don Mitchell, *Cultural Geography: A Critical Introduction* (Malden, MA: Blackwell, 2000), 104–109.

27. Nee and Nee, *Longtime Californ'*, xxii.

28. Wei Li, "UConn researcher examines multi-racial neighborhoods in Silicon Valley," University of Connecticut, 3/29/00, <www.news.uconn.edu/2000/mar2000/rel00040.htm> (19 August 2004).

29. Gilbert Osofsky, *Harlem: The Making of a Ghetto* (New York: Harper and Row, 1964), 92–123.

30. Osofsky, *Harlem,* 141–145.

31. Osofky, *Harlem,* 189–202.

32. Neil Smith, *The New Urban Frontier: Gentrification and the Revanchist City* (London and New York: Routledge, 1996), 140–164.

33. Motoko Rich, "For Harlem Homebuyers, Prices Head North," *New York Times,* 20 November 2003 <query.nytimes.com/gst/fullpage.html?> (21 November 2003).

34. Monique Taylor, *Harlem: Between Heaven and Hell* (Minneapolis: University of Minnesota Press, 2002), 1–205.

35. Craig Horowitz, "The Battle for the Soul of Harlem," *New York Magazine*, 27 January 1997, 22–31.

36. Ernest W. Burgess, "The Growth of the City: An Introduction to a Research Project," in *The City,* ed. Robert E. Park, Ernest W. Burgess, and Roderick D. McKenzie (Chicago: University of Chicago Press, 1925, reprinted in 1967), 54–56; James E. Vance, *This Scene of Man: The Role and Structure of the City in the Geography of Western Civilization* (New York: Harper and Row, 1977), 369; Godfrey, *Neighborhoods in Transition,* 37–39.

37. Gerald D. Suttles, *The Social Construction of Communities* (Chicago: University of Chicago Press, 1972), 21–43.

38. Manuel Castells, *The City and the Grassroots: A Cross-Cultural Theory of Urban Social Movements* (Berkeley and Los Angeles: University of California Press, 1983), 99–137.

39. Godfrey, *Neighborhoods in Transition,* 148–164; and "Barrio under Siege: Latino Sense of Place in San Francisco," in *Hispanic Spaces, Latino Places*, 217–232.

40. Godfrey, *Neighborhoods in Transition*, 156; and Godfrey, "Barrio under Siege," 95.

41. Timothy Drescher, "Street Subversion: The Political Geography of Murals and Graffiti," in *Reclaiming San Francisco: History, Politics, Culture,* ed. James Brook, Chris Carlsson, and Nancy J. Peters (San Francisco: City Lights Books, 1998), 231–245.

42. Christopher Mele, "Neighborhood 'Burn-Out': Puerto Ricans at the End of the Queue," in *From Urban Village to East Village*, ed. Janet Abu-Lughod (Cambridge, MA: Blackwell Publishers, 1994), 130–136; Christopher Mele, *Selling the Lower East Side: Culture, Real Estate, and Resistance in New York City* (Minneapolis: University of Minnesota Press, 2000), 194–197.

43. Mele, "Neighborhood 'Burn-Out,'" 130–131.

44. Mele, "Neighborhood 'Burn-Out,'" 130–136; and Mele, *Selling the Lower East Side*, 194–197.

45. New York City Department of City Planning, "Manhattan Community District 3 Profile," <home.nyc.gov/html/dcp/html/lucds/cdstext.html> (1 September 2004).

46. Karen Schmelzkopf, "Urban Gardens as Contested Space," *Geographical Review* 85, no. 3 (July 1995): 366.

47. Diana R. Gordon, "A Resident's View of Conflict on Tompkins Square Park," in *From Urban Village to East Village*, 228.

48. Mele, *Selling the Lower East Side*, 223–228.

49. Janet Abu-Lughod, "The Battle for Tompkins Square Park," in *From Urban Village to East Village*, 235; and Neil Smith, *The New Urban Frontier: Gentrification and the Revanchist City* (London and New York: Routledge, 1996), 4–12.

50. Schmelzkopf, "Urban Gardens as Contested Space," 365–367.

51. Karen Schmelzkopf, "Incommensurability, Land Use, and the Right to Space: Community Gardens in New York City," *Urban Geography* 23, no. 4 (2002): 323–343.

52. Schmelzkopf, "Urban Gardens as Contested Space," 367–369.

53. Schmelzkopf, "Urban Gardens as Contested Space," 374.

CHAPTER 17

Immigrants at Work

Michael Reibel

"In America, the Streets Are Paved with Gold"

This is the folklore that has brought immigrants to the United States for centuries. As native-born Americans know all too well, and as immigrants are reminded the moment they arrive on these shores, the stories are not even figuratively true. The United States is a remarkably open and accessible society that offers potentially great opportunities. But our economy requires enormous effort combined with lots of luck in order to succeed, and it is far less forgiving to the economically unsuccessful than are most developed countries. Many immigrant workers are highly skilled and do very well in the United States. But a far greater number are poor, lack education, and have few prospects upon arrival other than low-paid, often difficult and dangerous work. While some of these less-skilled immigrants will eventually succeed economically, often as small entrepreneurs, the majority will work just as hard and, for lack of capital, never break free of jobs with long hours, poor working conditions, and no benefits.

Potential migrants to the United States are generally aware of this good news and bad news with respect to work and its rewards here, and they make decisions as best they can with the specific information they can gather. Immigrants often make the difficult and emotionally costly decision to leave their home countries for reasons of civil and military conflict, various forms of persecution, and environmental disasters. But the primary reason for most international migration is economic opportunity. Even those who leave for other reasons, such as refugees, must normally be economically active in their destination country. For these reasons, the economic fate of immigrants to the United States and the economic impact of immigrants on receiving communities are of utmost importance to understanding ethnic communities in the United States.

This chapter begins with a discussion of the immigration process as a type of investment in which immigrants are drawn by higher wages relative to their home countries, economically valuable learning opportunities, and the chance to prosper over the long term. We then discover the socioeconomic diversity of immigrants to the United States. The next section deals with the job-seeking and entrepreneurial practices among immigrants, and the common patterns of employment concentration for immigrants that result from these practices. This is followed by a look at immigrants and informal or "off-the-books" labor, and the final section deals with U.S. immigration issues and policies from the point of view of labor markets.

The Economic Logic of Migration

What are the economic opportunities for immigrants to the United States? In the world's largest national economy, which is also among the richest and most open, the potential opportunities are vast and varied. Technically skilled immigrants such as doctors and software developers sometimes come close to experiencing the golden streets of legend. Yet many others come knowing that they are likely destined to work hard, in often dangerous and low-paid jobs like the meat-packing industry or the so-called sweat-shop garment factories in Los Angeles and New York. Some knowingly sell themselves into indentured servitude, like temporary slavery, in order to pay the cost of entering the United States.

How are we to make sense of this type of personal choice? Understanding migration, and many other social realities, requires looking at two scales at once: examining the big-picture trends in terms of causes and effects, while also explaining how the big picture is made up of the actions of many different individuals possessing different motives. A consistent theme of this chapter, therefore, is that there is no typical immigrant worker, indeed no typical immigrant at all as far as economic opportunity and economic impacts are concerned.

Migration, especially international migration, is costly. Moreover, the actual out-of-pocket costs for transportation and shipping are small compared to the psychic (emotional) costs. Psychic costs are the difficulty and pain of leaving behind friends, loved ones, and a familiar environment, and having to adapt in a strange land. When we think about how painful international migration is, we are confronted with a conundrum: if the cost is so high, the benefits must be even higher. But this does not seem to conform to the conventional wisdom that immigrants primarily do poorly paid, difficult, unpleasant, and often dangerous jobs. What were immigrants who are working in such jobs thinking? Did they miscalculate? Did they make an economic mistake by coming to the United States?

There are several reasons why even low-paid immigrant workers may be smart to migrate to the United States, given their other options. For one thing, there are far more jobs in the United States, and more different kinds of jobs in more sectors of the economy than in their less developed countries of origin. Workers from such countries can reasonably conclude that they will enjoy more (hence better) employment options from the moment of their arrival in the United States than they had at home. But the real potential benefit may materialize over time, as some of the more fortunate immigrant workers with skills or access to start-up capital climb occupational and entrepreneurial ladders. Several studies show higher income growth for immigrants to the United States than for native-born workers with similar backgrounds and qualifications. Recent immigrants earn less, but after ten to fifteen years in the United States, immigrants tend to earn slightly more than their native-born peers.[1] One possible explanation for this is that immigrants as a group are more enterprising and motivated on average than the native-born because they have already been sorted out by virtue of succeeding in the difficult migration process itself.

Over a period of years in this country, immigration to the United States creates varying levels of opportunity for immigrants to pursue secondary and higher education, English-language training, technical training programs, and to learn the details of business operations in various jobs and sectors that would not be open to them in their less developed origin countries. We take for granted nowadays that education is, in effect, an investment of one's time with the expectation of a positive economic return in the future. But formal education and training is only one type of investment in so-called human capital, which also includes building social networks for employment and business as well as the knowledge gained from experience on the job. All these enhanced opportunities for investment in human capital help explain immigrants' migration decisions that often do not pay off for a number of years.[2]

Perhaps most important, especially for those immigrants who face little but hardship in their own working lives, the long-run returns of migration to the United States extend further to include benefits for their children. Many immigrants have willingly and knowingly endured hardships that would not pay off directly in their lifetimes so that their children might prosper. The willingness of immigrants to make sacrifices for their children is a powerful example of the strength of families and the desire to contribute to posterity.

A final consideration is what might be called *wage arbitrage*. Arbitrage is a way of taking advantage of price differences in different markets, often in different places. In this case, the key gaps are the wage differences and differences in the cost of living that persist between sending and receiving countries. An immigrant to the United States from a low-wage, low-cost country who can save even a few dollars can make that money work much harder by bringing it back home or sending it back to the home country in the form of remittances.[3] Many immigrants to the United States have saved enough from low-wage jobs to return to their home countries and become entrepreneurs, thus stimulating growth and helping to reduce the wage gap they took advantage of in the first place. The desire to maximize savings and remittances leads many low-wage immigrants to live as cheaply as possible, which in the high-cost cities that often serve as immigrant portals, often translates into severe overcrowding in housing.[4]

Multiple Labor Markets

Labor markets are the supply-and-demand conditions for various types of work that exist in a region. As such, they are inherently geographical. A region's labor supply depends on both the number of people in the region willing to work and the skills those people possess. Labor demand depends on the number and type of existing jobs in the region, as well as economic growth that results in employment opportunities. Ideally, the number of available workers and their skills will exactly match the available jobs, but this never actually happens. There are always mismatches in labor markets that result in varying degrees of unemployment or underemployment.

Immigrant labor markets, which operate within and alongside regional labor markets as a whole, are somewhat more complex. Immigrants are subject to the same fundamental supply-and-demand conditions that confront native-born workers, but immigrants also have additional advantages and disadvantages. The disadvantages often include geographical isolation, non-native English-language skills, a lack of locally acceptable educational credentials, and a lack of cultural familiarity with American workplace practices such as the details of expectations for customer service. The main advantages many immigrants enjoy are immigrant and co-ethnic employment networks, that is, networks of persons belonging to the immigrants' respective ethnic groups. These social networks lead to successive word-of-mouth hiring of friends and related individuals, typically in smaller businesses in which a particular immigrant group has a foothold locally. These businesses might, but need not, be owned or operated by co-ethnic entrepreneurs who are themselves part of the extended immigrant social network from which they hire. Often, the members of these networks come not only from the same home country, but also from the same village or local area.

Immigrant labor markets are thus shaped simultaneously by a number of variables, all of which change over time: the skills (including language skills) of immigrants, the labor demand for immigrants' particular skill mix, opportunities for (particularly co-ethnic) small business enterprise, and competition from other immigrants and immigrant groups and the native-born. In this section we examine the types of work and particular industries in which immigrants are concentrated. This is followed by offering explanations for those patterns of typical immigrant work that normally involve worker skills, capital formation, and social networks. Finally, we will note changes in these patterns and their causes over time.

THE FOREIGN-BORN LABOR FORCE

According to the Census Bureau, approximately 14 percent of the civilian labor force in the United States is foreign-born. The labor force is defined as all persons of working age either working or actively seeking jobs. The country-of-origin composition (breakdown) of the foreign-born labor force is very similar to the overall country-of-origin composition for all immigrants, whether within or outside the labor force. This is not surprising, since nearly all immigrants of working age must work. The labor force participation rate, which is the percentage of working-age people who are in the labor force, is similar for immigrants and the native-born, except that the rate for immigrant men is slightly higher than for native-born men, while the rate for immigrant women is slightly lower than for native-born women.[5]

The Census Bureau further classifies workers by occupation and industry. Foreign-born workers can be found in every occupation and industry, but they tend to concentrate in particular sectors to a greater or lesser degree when compared to native-born workers (Table 17.1). Foreign-born workers are much less likely than the native-born

Table 17.1. Occupations of Employed Native- and Foreign-Born Workers in the United States, Age 16 Years or Older

Occupation	% Foreign-Born	% Native-Born
Executive, administrative, & managerial	9.9	15.3
Professional	13.5	15.9
Technical	2.9	3.3
Sales	9.8	12.4
Clerical & support	8.9	14.5
Services	18.9	12.7
Precision production, craft, & repair	12.8	10.8
Operators, fabricators, & laborers	18.9	12.8
Farming, forestry, & fishing	4.4	2.2

Source: Adapted from Abraham Mosisa, "The Role of Foreign-Born Workers in the U.S. Economy," *Monthly Labor Review* 125, no. 5 (2002): 3–14.

to work as managers and professionals, or in technical, sales, or administrative positions. By contrast, the foreign-born are twice as likely as the native-born to work in farming, forestry, and fishing, and half again as likely to work on the shop floor in factories, as drivers and laborers, and in service occupations.

The industrial breakdown of immigrants overall more closely resembles that for the native-born than does immigrants' occupational breakdown. The main difference is that there are proportionally fewer immigrants in industries with a high percentage of white-collar jobs, such as professional services, finance, insurance and real estate, and proportionally more in industries where the jobs involve mostly manual labor in manufacturing, construction, and repair services.[6]

The most important realities of immigrant labor, however, are the ones that do not appear in overall national-level breakdowns. The immigrant work experience is very different for different national origin immigrant groups. For example, 55 percent of immigrants from Mexico and Central America work in blue-collar jobs such as manufacturing, farming, fishing and forestry, construction, or craft and repair positions, while only 35 percent of the foreign-born overall and 24 percent of the native-born do. This example suggests that in some important ways, the labor market differences between groups of immigrants are greater than the differences between immigrants and the native-born overall. Local observation reveals much more dramatic concentrations involving specific groups. In Los Angeles, for instance, Vietnamese immigrants operate nearly all the nail salons offering manicures, while doughnut shop franchises are disproportionately likely to be operated by Cambodian immigrants.

THE SKILLS GAP

What accounts for the wide differences in the labor market experiences of various national origin immigrant groups? The single most important variable is education. To a much greater extent than ever before, today's immigrants occupy the extremes of educational attainment. In other words, they tend more strongly than native-born workers either to have less than a high school education or to be a college graduate or hold a post-graduate degree. Compared to the native-born population, few immigrants are in the middle ground of high school/some college (Fig. 17.1).[7]

Logically, the U.S. labor market is attracting immigrants at the extremes of education and skill attainment because these people have the most to economically gain by migrating to the United States. This does not necessarily mean that most of the available jobs in the United States require skill sets that are concentrated at these extremes. For example, it is possible that Mexican high school graduates with two semesters of college could be just as successful competing for work in their respective employment niche in the United States, but they have more to lose by leaving their home country behind than do the poorest and least educated Mexicans. As a result, Mexicans with mid-range educational attainment by U.S. standards are less likely to migrate to the

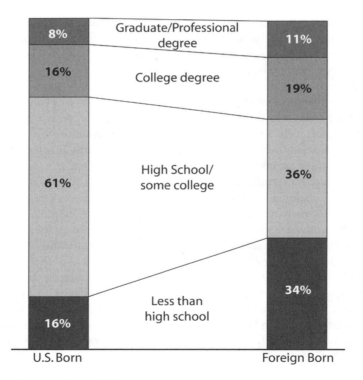

Figure 17.1.   2002 Educational Levels of U.S.-Born Americans and Foreign-Born Americans Who Arrived in or after 1900, Percent of People Ages 25 or Older. Source: Reproduced with permission from Phillip Martin and Elizabeth Midgely, "Immigration: Shaping and Re-Shaping America," Population Bulletin 58, no. 2 (2003): 24.

United States. Lower-skilled immigrants, on the other hand, are typically more vulnerable economically to home conditions of rapid population increase and large-scale economic restructuring, which puts them at a higher risk for long-term unemployment unless they migrate.

At the lower end of the immigrant skill and educational attainment spectrum, therefore, the incentive to migrate is clearly shaped first by what migration scholars call push factors, that is, unfavorable conditions at home that push the migrant out into the wider world.[8] Meanwhile, highly skilled immigrants from less developed countries often have excellent opportunities at home by the standards of their own countries, but recognize better opportunities in developed countries such as the United States. In other words, the movement of lower-skilled immigrants is explained by Neo-Classical Theory while higher-skilled international movement is best conceptualized as part of Dual Market Theory.

As a result of these differences, international migration of low-skilled persons entails very different labor market consequences for both the origin and destination countries than does the international migration of highly skilled persons. Low-skill international migration is a kind of safety valve that reduces economic (and consequently political) pressure on the origin country, with less certain consequences for the destination. High-skill international migration, by contrast, is a benefit to technical and professional employers in developed countries such as the United States, and often a painful loss of much needed expertise for less developed origin countries. These less-developed-country governments often invest heavily in the education of their most talented citizens, only to lose many of them to higher-wage-country economies in a globalizing labor market. This type of international migration is often accompanied by what is sometimes referred to as "brain drain."

Enclaves, Ethnic Economies, and Immigrants

As we have seen, immigrant labor markets, like labor markets generally, are largely determined by the education and skills that potential workers bring to that market. But immigrants have special conditions that shape and direct their job search and career strategies, conditions that nearly all immigrants share and which do not apply to native-born workers. To varying degrees, immigrants lack some of the credentials (such as valid professional licenses) and cultural skills (often including language skills) that are necessary for success in many occupations. In the mainstream economy, this tends to steer many immigrants away from professional, financial, corporate and business-service jobs, as well as many less well paid clerical jobs, and toward manual labor, services, and retail sales.

But immigrants often have an alternative to the mainstream economy in the form of an *ethnic economy*, composed of fellow immigrants from their place of origin and U.S.-born co-ethnics. Ethnic economies are geographically specific in that they exist where a sizeable number of ethnic group members work together, own and operate businesses that are associated with the group, and cooperate economically. Such places, known as *ethnic enclaves*, are typically, but not always, places where relatively high concentrations of an ethnic group's members reside. In the Koreatown neighborhood of

Los Angeles, for example, Koreans are a minority (albeit a significant minority) of the population, but they almost completely dominate local business and real estate.

ETHNIC ENCLAVES AS ECONOMIC SPACES

Most ethnic enclaves evolve and persist because they help reduce the difficulty and pain of living as a member of a non-dominant ethnic group. The fundamental explanation for ethnic enclaves is that there is strength in numbers because group members benefit personally and economically from the strong social networks they share within their enclaves. These benefits are many and mutually reinforcing. For example, immigrants and native-born co-ethnics share not just a (typically non-English) language but a business and economic culture that is rooted in that language, and in the traditions of the home country and region.[9] To the extent that ethnic enclave economies specialize in variations of products and services that originate with the group, the cultural benefits extend to the area of marketing know-how.

A Chinese restaurant in a U.S. Chinese enclave provides an example. The inner workings of the restaurant operation (the kitchen, business operations, etc.) are culturally Chinese—not just Chinese, but Fujianese, Shanghainese, or culturally rooted in some other Chinese region. That means the language, the cuisine, and the people nearly all trace their origins to that particular region. Not only will such a restaurant provide a relatively soft landing in the form of jobs for recent immigrants from the region, but the familiar and comfortable social environment and regionally authentic food make it a center for other immigrants and co-ethnics with ties to the region to gather, exchange news, and help each other find jobs and housing. The restaurant thus helps to reproduce the geographical cohesion and the internal social cohesion of the enclave.

Ethnic enclave specialization in production is not limited to the groups' own cultural specialty products and services, however. Some very large ethnic enclaves are often centers of mass-market production in industries such as clothing, furniture, and electronics assembly, in which owners (but not always the rank-and-file employees) are typically members of the enclave's dominant ethnic group. The particular industries that thrive in ethnic enclaves have certain characteristics in common.[10] They tend to be vertically disintegrated, meaning individual enterprises are small and specialized in a narrow range of the production process. They pass the partially finished product on to a separate enterprise when their task is finished. As a result, they require little start-up capital, but substantial cooperation with suppliers and clients who are typically members of the same ethnic production complex. These industries tend also to be relatively low-tech and labor-intensive, with fast production runs—all characteristics that make them suitable for a strong network of entrepreneurs with more energy and determination than capital or world-class technical abilities.

The classic example of an ethnic enclave industry and one that has been characteristic of many large ethnic enclaves for more than one hundred years is the garment industry. Because it is so well suited to ethnic enclave economies, the garment industry has expanded in recent years in immigrant-rich Los Angeles and New York, even as it has declined in otherwise booming states like the Carolinas and Alabama. Unfortunately, the sector of the garment industry that is dominated by immigrant entrepreneurs also provides many good examples of the extreme exploitation of relatively powerless immigrant workers. Some garment-factory owners and some owners in other immigrant industries routinely ignore health, safety, and compensation laws. A few are directly or indirectly involved with immigrant smuggling, since smuggled immigrants can be paid little or nothing and are in no position to complain about working conditions.

Other industries that thrive in ethnic enclave economies include furniture making, electronics assembly, and some types of food processing. Specialized retail and wholesale operations also emerge in ethnic enclave economies. One example is the several Japanese American–owned nursery and garden supply operations in the Japanese enclave of Sawtelle in West Los Angeles. These businesses were founded decades ago by entrepreneurs who started out working as gardeners, and they are still operated by family members even though the traditionally Japanese American craft of gardening in Southern California is now largely dominated by Latinos.

Even outsiders who are not members of the dominant group respond to, and benefit from, the existence of ethnic enclaves. As consumers seeking authentic Shanghainese food, for example, customers are likely to focus their search on the largest enclave associated with that group. As business people seeking partners or subcontractors, they are also likely to search in enclaves that are known to specialize in a particular sector such as garment finishing. Ethnic enclaves thus possess a competitive advantage as locations for many types of businesses because they enjoy economies of scale in addition to spatial agglomeration. This means they are large, distinctive, and efficient economic spaces with recognized specialty products and services—some, but not all, of which build on the special culture of the immigrant ethnic group in question. Ethnic enclaves tend to lose their identity a few decades after significant immigration of co-ethnics ends as the second- and third-generation offspring relocate to more affluent suburbs. In many of these enclaves, the basic infrastructure of ethnic economies comprised of older, low-tech industrial spaces and specialized retail storefronts remains intact and is inherited by a new ethnic group that settles in that part of the city.

A number of studies have examined the operation of ethnic social networks in immigrant labor markets. Researchers have found that insider referrals are more important in job seeking for immigrants (especially recent immigrants) than they are for the native-born,[11] and that certain immigrant groups (notably Koreans) tend to cluster together in relatively few industries.[12] One study of Israeli immigrants in Los Angeles illustrates the complex identity issues common in ethnic networks. The Israeli immigrants cooperated economically with American-born Jews (their co-ethnics, although not necessarily with a similar family migration history), but more strongly with each other. Cooperation was strongest of all among Persian-origin Israeli immigrants and those who grew up on the same kibbutz, a type of communal farm still fairly common in Israel.[13]

This last observation is a good example of the hierarchy of identities which is a recurring issue in ethnic and immigrant life. At both extremes on the spectrum from persecution to acceptance, the specifics of identity fade. These ethnicities within ethnicities fade amidst acceptance because ethnic identification in general matters less, so the fine details of identity are gradually forgotten, and they fade amidst persecution because no one cares about such distinctions when the larger group—all Jews or all

Chinese—are threatened. Ethnic enclaves are places in between; places where there are many recent immigrants among the population, so that ethnic identity and consciousness of local origins remain strong, but where during normal times the community is isolated enough from outside pressure to have the luxury of caring about the specific-origin geography and subgroup characteristics of co-ethnics. In such places, the fine details of identity become a natural basis for the operation of social and economic networks. In the sort of exchange that is often repeated in real-life enclave situations, the young Vito Corleone in the *Godfather II* attempts to curry favor with a neighborhood big shot, appealing to him in a Southern Italian dialect that they are *quasi paisan*, meaning "almost from the same country," because the man is from Calabria and Corleone is from Sicily, neighboring Italian provinces separated by a two-mile stretch of water.

The operation of ethnic enclave economies also calls into question the relative importance for immigrants of (1) human capital, the training and know-how described earlier, and (2) social capital, which is the size, quality, and usefulness of an immigrant's personal contacts. One study found that immigrants who rely on social capital tend to stay in each job longer, while immigrants who are hired because of their human capital change jobs more often.[14] Such job mobility is associated with better economic prospects because given a choice workers typically leave only for a better job. Low-skill immigrants who must rely on social capital thus tend to have slower earnings growth over the long term than skilled immigrants, the implication being that it's better to have skills than friends. This will be true, however, only in labor markets where immigrants are free to offer their skills to employers who will pay them accordingly. Another study found that enforcement of the Immigration Reform and Control Act of 1986 (IRCA) profoundly impaired hiring and job-holding conditions for undocumented immigrants, making human capital relatively less important than social capital in finding jobs, and causing wages to decline.[15]

ETHNIC ECONOMIES, IMMIGRANT SELF-EMPLOYMENT, AND ENTREPRENEURSHIP

At this point we must further distinguish between ethnic enclaves and ethnic economies. Although ethnic entrepreneurs are at the heart of ethnic enclave economies, many operate outside the spaces of the enclave identified with their ethnic group while still relying on ethnic business networks for their operations. Whether or not these ethnic entrepreneurs are immigrants themselves, and whether or not they operate within the geographical or market confines of an ethnic consumer economy or client base, they are important to our story because many of them hire immigrants.

Who are ethnic entrepreneurs? They are, of course, very diverse, but as always we can look for spatial patterns. We might expect immigrants who become entrepreneurs to be better educated, but one study of Canadian immigrants showed that low-skill immigrants are more likely to be self-employed than those with higher skill levels.[16] A different set of characteristics for the self-employed is revealed by an analysis of Los Angeles which shows immigrant self-employment concentration is directly proportional to the prosperity of the immigrants' neighborhoods, and inversely proportional to concentrations of manufacturing near where immigrants live (Map 17.1). We can thus conclude that self-employed immigrants are highly spatially concentrated and separated from industrial immigrant workers, and that they are generally more prosperous than foreign-born employees. These findings for Los Angeles, with its very large immigrant population and large enclaves, are consistent with a study showing depressed wages for self-employed immigrants (relative to immigrant employees) in relatively small ethnic enclave economies, while the self-employed immigrant tends to do slightly better than immigrant employees in larger enclaves.[17]

Because immigrant-owned businesses are often small, not all of them hire employees. We have seen, however, that larger ethnic enclave enterprises are an important draw for immigrants seeking work, so it is an important question to what degree ethnic entrepreneurs who do hire workers hire immigrants. There is considerable variation in the degree to which immigrant and/or ethnic entrepreneurs hire co-ethnics, and these differences appear to be due to the degree of spatial concentration of such jobs within ethnic enclaves.[18] In other words, ethnic entrepreneurs whose operations are located within their respective ethnic enclaves are more likely to hire co-ethnic immigrants. Another study compared the hiring practices of immigrant Mexican employers to those of U.S.-born ethnic Mexican (Chicano) employers in ethnic Mexican enclaves in the American Southwest, and found the immigrant employers are more dependent on (other) immigrants for both employees and customers than are the Chicano employers.[19]

We can conclude that although ethnic economies vary significantly between metropolitan regions, they have a life cycle of about two generations, and important distinctions based on absolute and perhaps relative size. Immigrant entrepreneurship and ethnic economies generally depend on the strength of their connections to ethnic enclaves, tending to dissolve into the general economy of the region as that particular ethnic group's tenure in an enclave declines over time.

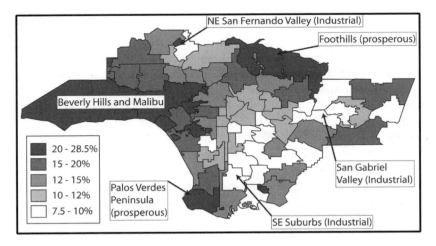

Map 17.1. *Percent Foreign-Born Who Are Self-Employed, Los Angeles County, 2000. Source: 5% U.S. Census PUMS, Courtesy IPUMS, University of Minnesota.*

Immigrant Informal Labor Markets

Perhaps the most difficult aspect of understanding the working lives of immigrants is the lack of accurate information about informal labor markets. Informal labor markets consist of work by employees or the self-employed in the informal economy, that is, economic activities that are legal but unregulated. In other words, informal labor activities are not illegal in and of themselves, but are illegal because they are unreported and thus beyond the supervision of the authorities with respect to labor, safety, environmental and community standards, and most especially, taxation.[20] Cash wages are the norm in informal labor markets and income is unreported by employee and employer alike. Consequently neither income nor payroll taxes are withheld.

We must distinguish at the outset between work done by undocumented immigrants and the informal economy. There is considerable overlap between the two, and historically undocumented workers were concentrated in the informal sector. But many native-born workers and documented immigrants also work in the informal economy in restaurants and bars, as performers and domestic employees, and in many other service occupations. Conversely, since the IRCA went into effect, undocumented immigrants are increasingly forced to work in the regulated economy using fraudulent identification credentials—a practice that shifts risk, and much of the cost of operating above board, from employers to the immigrants themselves.[21] Some observers have concluded that the way immigration enforcement is targeted and carried out functions more as a means of keeping labor docile and regulating wages than really trying to deport all undocumented immigrants and punish their employers.[22]

In fact, much of the economics behind informal labor markets is based on shifting costs. By evading income taxes, entrepreneurs who rely on informal labor are able to offer lower prices to their customers and clients while remaining profitable. By evading payroll taxes, employers in the informal sector can cut labor costs without cutting wages, or even while offering slightly higher wages than predominate in the equivalent formal sector. In practice, cost shifting between employers and employees in informal markets is even more complicated because bonds of mutual obligation typically complicate labor relationships. When both sides must conceal the details of compensation from the authorities, a reciprocal relationship develops in which favors are exchanged, but ultimately almost always in ways that primarily benefit the employer.[23]

Immigrants are well represented in the informal sector partly because immigrant and ethnic networks are ideal for the type of word-of-mouth referrals and hiring required by informal operations,[24] and partly because they are a concentrated, cheap, and flexible labor force available for labor-intensive, low-wage unregulated manufacturing. Consequently, immigrants are typically drawn into the informal sector in two broad industrial categories. The first is the aforementioned type of fringe manufacturing, notably the unregulated assembly operations sometimes called sweatshops. Businesses in the second group, which capitalize on informal referrals and hiring, are able to operate off the books because they have no fixed or formal business address. This category includes domestic work, construction, farm labor, and a variety of self-employed service providers, such as peddlers, day laborers, gypsy (unlicensed) cab drivers, family daycare, and backyard mechanics (Fig. 17.2). The final type of informal work is based

Figure 17.2.   An informal labor market where day laborers are waiting to be hired, Azusa, California. Source: Author.

on manufacturing homework (typically paid by the piece) and combines unregulated manufacturing with an informal, unfixed (home) setting.

Issues and Policies in Immigrant Labor Markets

International migration is an important social and political issue for receiving countries, and one that has evolved over time. During the colonial and early national history of the United States, Canada, Australia, and other major international migrant destinations, immigration was vital to the new societies' economic growth. The most pressing economic problem in these colonial and post-colonial societies was growth in order to achieve economies of scale because small, remote, dependent offshoots of European economies were inefficient until they could grow large enough to produce for broad self-sufficiency, generate exports, and attract substantial capital investment from abroad. In this earlier period, economic growth was fueled by population growth, and population growth was hard to stimulate because of the high cost of transportation and the high risks and limited returns facing migrants. In such a climate of persistent labor shortages, which, among other things, gave rise to the slave trade in the Western Hemisphere, it is not surprising that immigration was not highly regulated for most of North American history and, with the notorious exception of the Chinese Exclusion Act of 1882, was not systematically restricted until the 1920s.

To a great degree, national governments have always viewed immigration from a cost-benefit standpoint, and continue to do so. Indeed, rather than being determined mostly by racial or cultural bias, U.S. immigration policy has been driven primarily by the perceived economic consequences of immigration, notably its effect on labor markets. This is not to say that Americans are or have ever been of one mind with respect to immigration. While a broad pro-growth consensus existed during the early years of the republic, it was never unanimous with respect to the details of immigration policy. Particularly since the emergence of a significant urban working class in U.S. cities in the 1840s, there has been tension over immigration between native-born working-class Americans who feared competition from immigrants would drive down wages, and the class of employers who hoped for precisely this outcome. For example, the deep and visceral hatred against the successive waves of Irish immigration that began in the 1840s was only incidentally colored by religious bigotry or, strange as it seems today, racism.[25] We must recognize, rather, that it was primarily rooted in fierce economic competition between immigrant and native workers.

To this day, these competing interests fuel U.S. policy debate on immigration. Business wishes for more (hence cheaper) labor, and workers and labor groups are concerned about damaging competition. The situation has grown more complicated in recent years due to increased capital mobility. Employers do not need immigrants to reduce labor costs if they can move jobs offshore, and organized labor in the United States has begun to respond with their own more global strategy of promoting better working conditions and higher wages around the world. But many key economic sectors, including the service and construction sectors toward which many immigrants gravitate, are locationally sticky because these jobs are not easy to outsource. When jobs are not easily moved, local labor market competition between the native-born and immigrants remains an issue.

The key question, therefore, is whether immigration at various levels can be linked to unemployment and/or declining wages for U.S.-born workers, or alternatively, whether U.S.-born workers tend to leave areas of high immigration to avoid damaging competition in metropolitan labor markets. The results are mixed because there are indications that high immigration at the metropolitan level is positively related to lower wages for native-born workers,[26] although this depressing effect on wages may, perhaps ironically, be concentrated among native-born ethnic minorities (chiefly Asians and Hispanics).[27] But research on the impact of H1-B temporary visa holders on high-tech salaries showed no evidence of negative wage effects for native-born workers in the sector.[28]

With respect to the economic displacement of native-born workers, again the results are mixed. The impact seems to be opposite depending on the skill level of the native-born workers in question. Blue-collar workers have been found to leave metropolitan areas experiencing heavy immigration, but this is offset by the attraction of native-born professionals who appear to benefit from high levels of immigration locally.[29] A later study determined that the net loss of native-born workers from high-immigration cities is in fact spurious. In other words, it is not caused by immigration, but rather both high immigration and the departure of less skilled native-born workers from metropolitan areas are caused by economic restructuring, particularly in the largest cities which also function as immigrant gateways.[30]

This latter finding raises an important chicken-or-egg question: do restructuring economies attract immigrants, or do large pools of immigrant labor create opportunities for economic restructuring in advanced economies? There is evidence that manufacturers in developed countries have taken advantage of large local concentrations of immigrants to profit by substituting labor for capital, in other words, changing their operations to save money on expensive equipment by hiring more low-wage labor.[31] In low-wage services as well, there have been sweeping changes in the labor situation involving massive wage reductions that have coincided with a shift from native-born to primarily immigrant workers.

In the U.S. urban sanitation industry, the work of janitors in commercial buildings shifted from direct employment to subcontractor firms en masse during the 1980s. In Los Angeles during this period, wages for janitors fell by about 50 percent and the workforce switched from overwhelmingly native-born white and African American to overwhelmingly immigrant, chiefly Central American. Not surprisingly, working conditions also deteriorated. In response, immigrant cleaning workers in many cities organized under the Justice for Janitors campaign of the Service Employees International Union, a drive that culminated in a massive strike in 2000 that began in Los Angeles and spread to a number of other cities across the country. The strike was successful, leading to significant wage increases and better oversight of working conditions. In 2005, Justice for Janitors was chosen by almost five thousand Houston janitors, nearly all Latina/o immigrants, to represent them—one of the largest successful unionization campaigns in a southern state in decades.

We can conclude that economic restructuring is a predictable reaction by employers to the pressures and opportunities of a changing global economy.[32] That is, the world is changing in ways that often give employers opportunities to cut labor costs and pursue greater flexibility in labor relations, whether or not there is significant immigration locally. The only thing that can prevent the deterioration of workers' status as a result of such changes, whether or not those workers are immigrants, is labor organizations that can bargain with employers from a position of strength. The truth is that there would almost certainly be both economic restructuring and resistance to restructuring in a world without international migration, but immigration has intensified the changes. The geography of immigration has helped shape the landscape of restructuring by presenting local opportunities as well as local obstacles to employers' attempts to minimize costs at the expense of their employees.

MACROECONOMIC COSTS AND BENEFITS

Aside from these essentially microeconomic questions of wage levels and displacement in the labor market experiences of individuals, there are macroeconomic considerations rooted in labor markets upon which immigration also has an impact. One of the issues immigration opponents constantly argue is that immigrants are a net loss to society in terms of their consumption of public services. Immigrants, the argument goes, often work in the informal economy, hence pay no taxes. According to this viewpoint, even those immigrants who do pay taxes earn low wages; thus their large families and health care needs lead them to take more than they contribute to society when it comes to public revenues and expenditures.

In fact it appears that immigrants as a group are now taxed at similar levels to their economic peers among the native-born. This is due largely to the convergence, mentioned above, between the native-born and immigrants with respect to their rates of participation in the informal economy. More of the native-born workforce is concentrated in the informal sector, while immigrants, especially undocumented immigrants, find it increasingly necessary to work in regulated jobs, even if they must use fraudulent documentation to do so.

The widespread use of fraudulent documentation in the wake of post-IRCA enforcement raises another important point, this time on the benefit side. Not surprisingly, social security, Medicare, and other benefit programs are relatively lax when verifying the identity of contributors to their funds (i.e., employees from whose payrolls these special taxes are deducted). These same agencies are much more vigilant in uncovering fraud when a claim is filed for benefits. Because they fear federal prosecution for fraud, undocumented immigrants rarely file for benefits under these very programs to which they often contributed for decades. The large and growing numbers of undocumented immigrants who work using fraudulent documentation are thus a "bargain" for the national economy because they pay their fair share, but in many cases they never collect the benefits to which they would ordinarily be entitled. Needless to say, this is no bargain for immigrant workers.

Because most immigrants are of working age, immigration lowers the dependency ratio (the ratio of non–working age people to the total population) and relieves pressure on retirement programs like Medicare and social security. Most developed nations like the United States have experienced long-term decline in the birth rates of their native-born population since the mid-1960s, and a consequent rise in dependency ratios as their populations age. Because public pension systems like social security depend on current payroll taxes to support the pensions of retired persons, a high dependency ratio due to aging populations squeezes revenues and threatens the pension systems with bankruptcy. This has been a growing concern not just in the United States, but in Europe, Japan, and South Korea as well.[33] The immigration of young working-age people helps to restore the dependency ratio to a healthier balance. The countries whose public pension systems are in the most trouble—Germany and Japan—are, not coincidentally, those with restrictive immigration policies.

In the private sector as well, the native-born benefit from immigration in the form of lower consumer costs for many goods and services. Food, for example, has never been cheaper relative to incomes, largely because of immigrant farm labor. Inexpensive, often immigrant-provided services such as child care, gardening, and housecleaning have shifted the mathematics of household budgets and domestic labor, freeing up native-born wage and salary earners to work more. Given such levels of economic interdependence between immigrants and the native-born, one can assert that simple macroeconomic arguments about the contributions and social costs of immigrants miss the mark entirely. The question is not whether immigrants contribute as much in property taxes to support schools as they cost to educate. The more important fact is that the entire economy is healthier, more flexible, and more innovative because of the strong immigrant presence.

Conclusion

We have seen that immigrants as a group come to the United States primarily for economic reasons and that most participate in the labor market, either as workers or employers. There is a huge economic gap between the large minority of highly educated or well-off immigrants, who are often from relatively privileged backgrounds in less developed countries, and the majority of immigrants who have little education and other forms of human capital when they arrive in the United States. Both classes of immigrants tend to work very hard, and many succeed according to the standards of their class. Moreover, different-origin-region groups of immigrants have different typical success strategies for coping with a lack of skills and capital. Needless to say, we must resist the urge to overgeneralize, as immigrants from each group are found pursuing almost every conceivable work strategy for success. Long-term success for poorer immigrants from Latin America often means learning a trade as a skilled craftsman and, in many cases, becoming self-employed or a small employer working in that craft. Poorer immigrants from Asia often rely on immigrant social networks and extended family networks for loans or equity partners in order to become small retailers or service providers. More privileged or higher skilled immigrants from all regions often work as professionals, notably in science and technology, or as members of the business class in real estate and finance or larger-scale manufacturing and service firms.

Particularly in the case of some poorer immigrants, coming to the United States makes economic sense, but only indirectly. These immigrants never experience a net benefit from immigration while they live in the United States because few are able to achieve the economic and material goals that comprise the American Dream. Rather, immigrants sometimes benefit from migration to the United States by saving money and returning to their homelands with a significant store of accumulated wealth. Alternatively, they may never benefit personally at all, but their hard work does benefit their children in the United States through greater economic opportunity, or their extended families in their homelands via remittances. As a result, the quest among many poorly paid immigrants to live cheaply while they are in the United States so that they can maximize savings, remittances, or investments in their children's futures can seriously aggravate conditions of poverty and overcrowded housing. This is especially true in the high-cost metropolitan regions that typically serve as immigrant gateways.

We have seen that the economic life of immigrants is often shaped by ethnic neighborhoods and regional ethnic economies. These ethnic neighborhoods and ethnic economies, which are linked but distinct from one another, serve as a bridge between many immigrants and mainstream U.S. social and ethnic life. Ethnic neighborhoods and ethnic economies, on the other hand, evolve amidst local conditions of high immigration and gradually decline (or are displaced by new immigrant groups) as the waves of heavy immigration from the founding region of origin recede into the past.

Informal labor markets in some economic sectors and in some regions are dominated by immigrants, and particularly undocumented immigrants. On the other hand, there has been considerable convergence between native-born and immigrant workers with respect to participation in the formal versus the informal labor force. While more native-born Americans are working off the books, more immigrants are being granted citizenship or resident alien status and working legally in the formal economy. Meanwhile, undocumented immigrants are increasingly forced to use fraudulent credentials to work legitimate jobs, thereby shifting risk from employers to themselves and paying for unemployment, retirement, and other worker programs from which they will never derive any benefits.

Immigrants and native-born workers appear to compete for some jobs, especially low-skilled manufacturing jobs, construction, and other manual labor. In other economic sectors, such as education and health care, immigrants do not compete directly with native-born workers to any great extent, and immigration actually helps native-born workers in these sectors by creating more demand for their services. Moreover, direct competition for jobs between immigrants and the native-born is hard to measure in a climate of rapid and pervasive economic restructuring and outsourcing. In some industries, such as sanitation, large pools of immigrant labor create opportunities for employers to drastically lower labor costs at workers' expense, but subsequently these same immigrant workers organize, agitate, and successfully restore decent working conditions—perhaps to the point where native-born workers will return to the industry. In other economic sectors, such as manufacturing assembly, employers don't bother replacing native-born workers with immigrants but rather simply export many of the jobs. It's doubtful whether immigration affects native-born workers negatively over the long term in such situations.

In terms of immigrants' impact on social costs and benefits, convergence between immigrants and native-born workers in terms of work in the formal versus the informal economy has led to convergence in terms of taxation as well. Strong immigration also reduces the dependency ratio, taking pressure off revenue-funded entitlement programs like social security. Some (certainly not all) of employers' cost savings from using low-cost immigrant labor are passed on to consumers, and consumers benefit directly from these lower labor costs when they are themselves the employers of landscape workers, nannies, and house cleaners. On the other hand, locally heavy immigration can place burdens on local services, notably public schools.

As is the case with job competition, the broader question of whether immigration costs or benefits society at large is impossible to prove conclusively with statistics. Common sense tells us, however, that immigration helps economic growth by providing skilled professionals and infusions of entrepreneurial capital, by lowering costs for many goods and services, by helping to correct the age imbalance in our population, and by introducing useful ideas and practices native to other economic regions. Moreover, immigration is culturally consistent with the distinct American economic philosophy of openness, innovation, diversity, and flexibility. Culturally, immigration has made the United States a more diverse and culturally richer society. Finally, immigration is part of our tradition, both as a nation and (with few exceptions) as individuals and families.

Notes

1. Barry Chiswick, "The Effect of Americanization on the Earnings of Foreign-Born Men," *Journal of Political Economy* 86, no. 5 (1978): 897–921.

2. Gary Becker, "Investment in Human Capital: A Theoretical Analysis," *Journal of Political Economy* 70, no. 5 (1962): 9–49.

3. Manuel Orozco, "The Remittance Marketplace: Prices, Policy and Financial Institutions," in *Pew Hispanic Center Reports* (Los Angeles: Pew Hispanic Center, 2002).

4. Carlos Vargas-Ramos, "Housing Emergency and Overcrowding: Latinos in New York City," in *Centro Policy Brief*, Centro de Estudios Puertoriquenos (New York: Hunter College, CUNY, 2003).

5. Abraham Mosisa, "The Role of Foreign-Born Workers in the U.S. Economy," *Monthly Labor Review* 125, no. 5 (2002): 3–14.

6. Elizabeth Grieco, "What Kind of Work Do Immigrants Do?" *Immigration Facts* no. 3, (Washington: Migration Policy Institute, 2004).

7. Phillip Martin and Elizabeth Midgely, "Immigration: Shaping and Re-Shaping America," *Population Bulletin* 58, no. 2 (Washington: Population Reference Bureau, 2003).

8. CSIS Staff, "A Student's Guide to Globalization: Migration Push Factors," Center for Strategic and International Studies (CSIS), <www.globalization101.org/issue/migration/3a.asp> (4 September 2004).

9. Kenneth Wilson and Alejandro Portes, "Immigrant Enclaves: An Analysis of the Labor Market Experiences of Cubans in Miami," *American Journal of Sociology* 86, no. 3 (1980): 295–319.

10. Allen Scott, *Metropolis* (Berkeley: University of California Press, 1988).

11. James Elliot, "Referral Hiring and Ethnically Homogeneous Jobs: How Prevalent Is the Connection and for Whom?" *Social Science Research* 30, no. 3 (2001): 401–425.

12. Mark Ellis and Richard Wright, "The Industrial Division of Labor among Immigrants and Internal Migrants to the Los Angeles Economy," *International Migration Review* 33, no. 1 (1999): 26–54.

13. Steven Gold, "Patterns of Economic Cooperation among Israeli Immigrants in Los Angeles," *International Migration Review* 28, no. 1 (1994): 114–135.

14. Michael Aguilera, "The Impact of the Worker: How Social Capital and Human Capital Influence the Job Tenure of Formerly Undocumented Mexican Immigrants," *Sociological Inquiry* 73, no. 1 (2003): 52–83.

15. Julie Phillips and Douglas Massey, "The New Labor Market: Immigrants and Wages after IRCA," *Demography* 36, no. 2 (1999): 233–246.

16. Fernando Mata and Ravi Pendakur, "Immigration, Labor Force Integration and the Pursuit of Self-Employment," *International Migration Review* 33, no. 1 (1999): 378–402.

17. David Spener and Frank Bean, "Self-Employment Concentration and Earnings among Mexican Immigrants in the U.S.," *Social Forces* 77, no. 3 (1999): 1021–1047.

18. Suzanne Model, "Ethnic Economy and Industry in Mid Twentieth Century Gotham," *Social Problems* 44, no. 4 (1997): 445–463.

19. Niles Hansen and Gilberto Cardenas, "Immigrant and Native Ethnic Enterprises in Mexican-American Neighborhoods: Differing Perceptions of Immigrant Mexican Workers," *International Migration Review* 22, no. 2 (1988): 226–242.

20. Manuel Castells and Alejandro Portes, "World Underneath: The Origins, Dynamics and Effects of the Informal Economy," in *The Informal Economy: Studies in Advanced and Less*

Developed Countries, ed. Alejandro Portes, Manuel Castells, and Lauren Benton (Baltimore: Johns Hopkins University Press, 1989), 11–40.

21. Julie Phillips and Douglas Massey, "The New Labor Market: Immigrants and Wages after IRCA," *Demography* 36, no. 2 (1999): 233–246.

22. Joseph Nevins, *Operation Gatekeeper: The Rise of the "Illegal Alien" and the Remaking of the U.S.-Mexico Boundary* (New York: Routledge, 2002).

23. Doreen Mattingly, "The Home and the World: Domestic Service and International Networks of Caring Labor," *Annals of the Association of American Geographers* 91, no. 2 (2001): 370–386.

24. Saskia Sassen, "Informalization in Advanced Market Economies," *Issues in Development Discussion Paper* no. 20 (Geneva: International Labor Office, 1997).

25. Noel Ignatiev, *How the Irish Became White* (New York: Routledge, 1996).

26. George Borjas, "The Labor Demand Curve *Is* Downward Sloping: Reexamining the Impact of Immigration on the Labor Market," *Quarterly Journal of Economics* 118, no. 4 (2003): 1335–1374.

27. Leslie McCall, "Sources of Racial Wage Inequality in Metropolitan Labor Markets: Racial, Ethnic, and Gender Differences," *American Sociological Review* 66, no. 4 (2001): 520–541.

28. B. Lindsay Lowell, "Skilled Temporary and Permanent Immigrants in the United States," *Population Research and Policy Review* 20, no. 1 (2001): 33–58.

29. Robert Walker, Mark Ellis, and Richard Barff, "Linked Migration Systems—Immigration and Internal Labor Flows in the United States," *Economic Geography* 68, no. 3 (1992): 234–248.

30. Richard Wright, Mark Ellis, and Michael Reibel, "The Linkage between Immigration and Internal Migration in Large Metropolitan Areas in the United States," *Economic Geography* 73, no. 2 (1997): 234–254.

31. Saskia Sassen, *The Mobility of Labor and Capital: A Study in International Investment and Labor Flow* (London: Cambridge, 1988).

32. Edward Soja, "Los Angeles, 1965–1992: From Crisis-Generated Restructuring to Restructuring-Generated Crisis," in *The City: Los Angeles and Urban Theory at the End of the Twentieth Century,* ed. Allen Scott and Edward Soja (Los Angeles: University of California Press, 1996), 426–462.

33. Population Division, UN Department of Economic and Social Affairs, *Replacement Level Fertility: Is It a Solution to Declining and Ageing Populations?* (New York: United Nations, 2000).

CHAPTER 18

Ethnic Festivals, Cultural Tourism, and Pan-Ethnicity

Michael Hawkins

This chapter addresses the performance of ethnicity on the urban landscape in the form of ethnic festivals and parades, particularly in the context of the post-1965 West Indian immigrant communities of New York as they adapt and reinvent themselves in twenty-first-century America. In the context of globalization and increasing mobility of populations, immigration is often seen as a counterpoint to the expansion of global tourism, and this chapter also focuses on the consumption of ethnicity as a product by the tourism industry. In order to gain a sense of the ethnic experience that festivals offer, the reader should imagine him- or herself as a tourist in an unfamiliar American city who gazes upon the following scene.

Visitors enter the festival grounds and are immediately enveloped by the sights, sounds, smells, and tastes of faraway places. The pungent odors of Vietnamese fish sauce and spicy South Asian curries mingle with the aromas of sauerkraut and grilled Polish sausage. Filipino or Mexican empanadas and Jamaican jerked chicken compete with crawfish gumbo and Swedish meatballs for the visitors' attention. The pulsing Afro-Caribbean sounds of soca, reggae, and cumbia are juxtaposed with the lilt of Irish fiddles and intertwined voices singing African American spirituals. The intricate movements of elaborately costumed Cambodian court dancers contrast with brawny men in kilts tossing large rocks and Texas–Czech polka dancing. Visitors admire Hmong embroidery and the bright patterns of handwoven Maya textiles from Guatemala interspersed with stalls selling "Kiss me I'm Italian" T-shirts and lederhosen. Native Americans from both the United States and Chiapas, Mexico man tables strewn with political posters and pamphlets seeking redress for injustices past and present next to a representative of the Northern Irish Aid Committee (NORAID) urging visitors to support political prisoners.[1]

Festivals, Boundaries, and Place

This composite snapshot of a multiethnic festival is repeated many times over in virtually every major city in North America and many smaller communities as well. The festival grounds provide public space for the performance of ethnic identity and have been designated as ethnic space for the duration of the festival. Settings for ethnic festivals can vary in geographical scale from large public parks, convention centers, and fairgrounds to church basements and school cafeterias. The sights, sounds, smells, and tastes the visitors experience impart what geographers call a "sense of place" to this public space. It is human experience that transforms the rather abstract concept of space into a place.[2] The festival organizers in this case have consciously created a multiethnic sense of place by displaying a diverse array of ethnic markers—dance, music, food, and crafts—which signify that this place is special, or outside the mainstream of the dominant national culture. The connection between identity and place becomes even more concrete and territorial when individual ethnic groups stage festivals in the context of their own urban ethnic neighborhoods, rural ethnic islands, or large regional entities in North America called ethnic homelands.

Performances of ethnic identity delineate physical space, whether it be the temporary "festival space" of a large urban park or the territorial boundaries of an ethnic neighborhood. Festivals are also a highly visible public means of reinforcing, reviving, and even inventing ethnic identity by drawing cultural boundaries between "Us" and the "Other."[3] Although "Kiss me I'm Italian" T-shirts on sale at our hypothetical festival may seem to be contrived and blatantly commercial markers of ethnic difference compared to traditional handmade Guatemalan textiles, the contrast illustrates the range and fluidity of cultural behaviors used to represent ethnic identities. T-shirts are no less symbolic of contemporary Italian American and other older, mostly European group identity than the presumably authentic handicrafts of more recent immigrant groups. Descendants of European immigrants that arrived in the late nineteenth and early twentieth centuries tend to express their ethnic identities sporadically and individually as a form of "symbolic ethnicity" rather than living the culture of the homeland, or now moribund ethnic neighborhood, as taken for granted everyday practice.[4] Attending and participating in festivals is as likely to be a leisure activity as an expression of symbolic identity for these older immigrant groups.

PERFORMANCE OF IDENTITY

New immigrant groups, such as those arriving after the 1965 Immigration Reform Act, are far more likely to maintain direct connections with their homelands and cling to cultural practices of the old country in everyday life rather than utilize them as an occasional symbolic gesture. For example, South Asians serving food to the public at ethnic festivals are only replicating a practice they continue at home, whereas European Americans may consume their ethnic foods only at festivals, or perhaps on special occasions at home. For recent immigrants with an "in between" or "transnational identity," festivals function to increase the visibility of these often unfamiliar groups to outsiders as well as reinforce a sense of group identity. Another frequent expression of transnationality on display at ethnic festivals can be found in the political activities evident in the introductory paragraphs. The Irish American soliciting donations for NORAID addresses his message mainly toward fellow ethnics and appeals to a latent and symbolic sense of transnational identity common in older immigrant groups. It is an attempt to transform nostalgia for the "Old Sod" into support for a political cause that most Irish Americans only vaguely understand. The Native Americans from Chiapas, however, direct their appeal toward festival attendees from outside their own group in order to gain visibility and support from a wider public. Visibility provided by participating in ethnic and folk festivals is especially important to new immigrant groups who lack the political connections and public recognition achieved by previous immigrants. Furthermore, their cultural traditions are considered more exotic and often more desirable than those of more familiar immigrant groups.

ETHNICITY AND CONSUMPTION

Markers of ethnicity on display at festivals function in symbolic and transnational ways to reinforce group solidarity and differentiate one group from another, but they are also products to be consumed by the public. Ethnicity is a marketable commodity or product, and festivals provide a marketplace where ethnicity is packaged, sold, and consumed by insiders and outsiders alike. Listening to world or ethnic music, dining at ethnic restaurants, visiting heritage sites, and attending an ethnic or folk festival are examples of "commodification of culture" (Fig. 18.1). Ethnic foods, of course, are quite literally

Figure 18.1.   Ethnic foods are a popular commodity on display at festivals. This typical Jamaican menu offers a taste of home for West Indians and a taste of the exotic for tourists.
Source: Staceyjoy Elkin.

consumed at festivals, but cultural commodities of all kinds have become increasingly important as consumption patterns in the United States and other post-industrial countries have moved from standardized mass-produced goods to goods and services tailored to specific lifestyles and tastes. In the last three decades the United States has also moved from an assimilationist to a multicultural view of immigrant groups, and consumers increasingly embrace cultural goods that not only evoke re-identification with their own ethnicity, but display their interest in the culture of others as well. Ethnic products, especially those of indigenous or non-Western groups, have become more sought after in post-industrial countries as culture on a global scale is perceived as becoming more homogeneous and "westernized" because of rapid advances in mass media, transnational corporate marketing, and communications technology. Difference sells and the more exotic the cultural product the better. As one observer noted, "In an age that celebrates diversity and multiculturalism, it has become almost a civic duty to have an ethnicity as well as to appreciate that of others."[5]

Ethnic Festivals and Cultural Tourism

Culture and commerce are especially intertwined in the emerging sector of the travel and tourism industry called "cultural tourism." The tourism industry plays a major role in the commodification of culture worldwide as tourists seek out ethnic difference from the most remote corners of the globe to urban areas and small towns closer to home. Tourism is one of the world's most important economic activities, and cultural tourism is among the most rapidly growing segments of the industry.[6]

The impacts of tourism extend beyond the commercial aspect of ethnic festivals. The fact that tourists show an interest in ethnic culture may serve as an impetus toward the revitalization of ethnic identity, or ethnic re-identification. In response to the economic lure of tourism and the desire for increased visibility to outsiders, previously marginalized groups may reconstruct their identities, often by merging with other groups under a common "pan-ethnic" identity. Pan-ethnic identities require a common interest, often political or economic, and a system of cultural symbols that are selected or invented to serve as a "cultural umbrella" for the varied groups united under a pan-ethnic label.[7] Pan-ethnicities are sometimes so fluid and tenuous that festivals may become the primary symbol of common identity. Transnational links may also stimulate tourism as members of diasporic communities often view festivals as an opportunity to reconnect with their ethnic roots and with family and friends who have immigrated.

TOURISM AND ETHNIC IDENTITY

The field of cultural tourism is as diverse and fluid as are the meanings and implications of the word *culture* itself. In the past, culture with a capital "C," or high culture, was viewed as the exclusive property of the Eurocentric elite and demarcated class boundaries. In a more democratized form, concert music and theater festivals, art exhibitions, and museums are certainly still components of cultural tourism. As the Industrial Revolution progressed in Europe and North America in the late nineteenth century, mass or popular culture arose as counterpoint to high culture. America's elite feared that as rural folk culture receded before the onslaught of urbanization and the first great wave of immigration from Europe, "traditional" American values would be corrupted by foreign ideas and beliefs like socialism and Catholicism. An idealized version of national identity arose in the form of material remnants, reminders, and reconstructions of the past. Henry Ford's Greenfield Village, John D. Rockefeller's Colonial Williamsburg, and plantation tours in the South have remained popular "historical tourism" destinations since the 1930s and until recently emphasized Anglo-American history and culture while excluding the contributions of Native Americans, immigrants, and African Americans.

In the 1960s and 1970s, previously marginalized ethnic groups demanded that their histories be portrayed as well. The rise of the Civil Rights Movement, the American Indian Movement (AIM), and the Hispanic Raza Unida Party in the United States coincided with the Immigration Reform Act in 1965 and expanded the scope of cultural tourism to include groups beyond the American mainstream. African Americans, inspired by Alex Haley's fictionalized book *Roots* and television version of his family's sojourn from Africa as slaves to North America and eventual freedom, joined Irish Americans in pilgrimages to their respective ancestral homelands in a type of cultural tourism called "roots tourism." By the late 1970s historic sites and living history exhibits like Williamsburg were offering predominately white tourists interpretations of the past that included portrayals of enslaved African Americans. Historical tourism has become "heritage tourism," which implies that each group inherits and celebrates its own version of the past. History purports to be a set of unalterable facts, whereas heritage, like ethnic identity, is malleable and fluid. Heritage tourism is more about interpretation than authenticity.

With the passage of the Ethnic Heritage Act in 1974, multiculturalism and the celebration of ethnicity received official government sanction and funding, and ethnic festivals became an increasingly popular form of heritage tourism. Older, established ethnic festivals staged mostly in the interest of community or neighborhood solidarity have turned outward, adapting themselves toward a wider audience. Festivals in both small towns and urban areas are vigorously promoted by state and local tourist agencies and supported by corporate sponsors, local businesses, and non-profit "grass roots" organizations. New festivals and new markers of ethnicity are being invented and revised. Ethnicity as a public performance, like culture itself, is not static, but constantly changing.

TOURISM AND CULTURAL CAPITAL

An often quoted survey by the Travel Industry Association of America reported that in 2000 two-thirds of adult American tourists (92.7 million) included a cultural event in their itinerary, and that 20 percent of those travelers attended a heritage or ethnic festival. Moreover, these tourists are demographically older, more affluent, and better educated than average.[8] Cultural tourism therefore represents a significant source of income in a world in which cities and regions compete for increasingly mobile intellectual and economic resources. Ethnic diversity not only represents economic capital in the form of tourist dollars, but also enhances the unique place image of a city or region, providing a form of "cultural capital." For example, the official Chicago–Cook County government website meant to promote the region to potential businesses, residents, and tourists cites the fact that the area "has one of the country's most ethnically diverse populations with more than 100 represented" as the first item under its "quality of life" category.[9] While quality of life through ethnic diversity may seem to be an elusive and intangible form of cultural capital, it is made tangible by the wide array of ethnic festivals Chicago offers.

Other Midwestern cities lacking Chicago's long-held reputation for ethnic diversity have sought to broaden their touristic appeal and to project a more cosmopolitan image than is usually associated with the region. Milwaukee, for example, long known as the "most German city in America," is now christened by its boosters as "the city of festivals."[10] In addition to the long-established Festa Italiana, Polish Fest, German Fest, and Irish Fest, the city's Henry Maier Festival Park now hosts the Asian Moon Festival, a Native American festival called Indian Summer, the African World Festival, the Arab World Fest, and somewhat surprisingly, the Cajun Fest.

TOURISM AND THE (RE)CONSTRUCTION OF ETHNICITY

Much of the early scholarly literature on tourism emphasized the negative impact of the industry on local culture and identity.[11] A more balanced view has emerged since the 1980s, and one of the most cited case studies concerns the Cajun cultural revival in South Louisiana and the role of festivals and tourism in encouraging ethnic re-identification. Cajuns are the descendants of French-speaking exiles from Acadia in Nova Scotia who found refuge in Louisiana over two hundred years ago. By the 1960s the Cajun French dialect, long the primary marker of ethnic difference, was in decline, and Cajun culture had lost much of its distinctive character. Not only had Cajun identity become largely symbolic, but young people especially made an effort to distance themselves from their heritage. A number of factors in the mid-1970s sparked a revival of interest among Cajuns in their own culture including the commodification of their culture through tourism and the growth of national and local festivals showcasing Cajun music and food. The national resurgence of interest in regional folkways and the acclaimed performance of old-time Cajun fiddler Dewey Balfa at the Newport Folk Festival in 1964 brought Cajun culture to national attention, and Balfa's tours of France and Canada in the 1970s initiated a growing stream of foreign Francophone tourists from France, Belgium, and Canada, who in a form of reverse roots tourism sought to reestablish transnational links with their kin in Louisiana.[12]

State and local governments, small businesses, individual entrepreneurs, and local organizations in South Louisiana saw an opportunity to both capitalize on and promote their own culture. The number of festivals specifically showcasing Cajun dance, music, and food in the region now officially called Acadiana grew from 36 in 1977 to 240 in 1998.[13] Cajuns responded to the commodification of their culture as a touristic and mass consumer product with a renewed appreciation of their own heritage. The Louisiana Office of Culture, Recreation and Tourism now vigorously promotes cultural tourism in the United States and abroad, and in 1999 sponsored a year-long celebration of the 300th anniversary of the state called FrancoFête. Attracting French-speaking tourists was, of course, the primary goal of FrancoFête, but it also strengthened transnational connections between Louisiana and the country of origin, and simultaneously extended the umbrella of pan-ethnicity to include Louisianians of Afro-French and white Creole heritage, Francophone Louisiana Indians, and the French Caribbean.

West Indian Carnival: A Moveable Feast

The West Indian Carnival in New York City is an example of an urban ethnic festival in which ethnic boundaries are spatially and symbolically negotiated, and ethnic identities have been invented and redefined. The carnival is actually a cluster of events taking place in Brooklyn before Labor Day and culminating in New York's largest parade, attracting over three million spectators and participants, and thus exceeding attendance figures for the better-known St. Patrick's Day Parade. The *Lonely Planet* and *Frommer's* guidebooks for New York City describe the Brooklyn Carnival respectively as the biggest event and "best" parade in the city.[14] Despite a history of friction between public authorities and parade organizers and participants which parallels its origins in Trinidad, the West Indian Carnival is now embraced and promoted by state and city officials. Nevertheless, the sheer size of the festival, the anti-authoritarian nature of carnival celebrations in general, and the fact that the event reflects social tensions within the city and among various ethnic groups, cause public officials to exercise as much control as possible.

The term *West Indian* is commonly used to refer to the inhabitants of the English-speaking Caribbean including the "big" islands of Jamaica and Trinidad, the string of small islands composing the Lesser Antilles, Guyana on the South American mainland, and the Caribbean coast of Central America from Panama to Belize. West Indians in the context of the Caribbean identify themselves first as Jamaican, Trinidadian, or St. Lucian, for example. As a result, an attempt sponsored by the British government to unite the islands as the West Indies Federation from 1958 to 1962 foundered on inter-island rivalry, especially between the larger islands of Jamaica and Trinidad. As immigrants from the British Caribbean began to arrive in New York in the early twentieth century, they began to identify themselves to outsiders as West Indian, thus assuming a wider pan-ethnic identity. The process of forming a larger collective identity accelerated as the second wave of migration after 1965 swelled the numbers of West Indians in the city. This pan-ethnic identity served to distinguish people from the Anglophone Caribbean from the city's much larger African-American community, to reinforce ethnic boundaries between themselves and immigrants from the Hispanic Caribbean, and to increase their visibility and political power.

As a marker of ethnic identity the celebration of carnival itself embodies many strands of diffusion, migration, and cultural synthesis. Pre-Lenten festivals marked by a period of suspension of the normal rules of behavior in society before Ash Wednesday initiates the somber fasting of Lent were once common throughout Europe until the Protestant Reformation. Carnival celebrations, however, survived and flourished in Catholic Europe where they were characterized by elaborate costume balls or masquerades staged by the wealthy, and spontaneous and often rowdy street processions conducted by the lower classes. The upper classes were openly mocked and satirized in the course of these unruly street processions, and in response civil authorities sometimes felt compelled to crack down on the proceedings. Carnival diffused to the Spanish, French, and Portuguese colonies in the New World, and continues to be celebrated, most famously in the form of Mardi Gras in Louisiana and *carnaval* in Brazil. In New Orleans and Rio de Janeiro the carnival season has taken on meaning far beyond that of a prelude to Lent and is now closely linked to the place image and identity of the two cities; needless to say, carnival has also become the premier tourist event of the year in both cities.

ORIGINS OF THE WEST INDIAN CARNIVAL

Although the celebration of carnival is now arguably the most important pan-ethnic marker of identity for the large and diverse West Indian diaspora communities in the United States, Canada, and Britain, the festival is indigenous to only one major island in the English-speaking Caribbean—Trinidad. The island is truly the "melting pot" of the Caribbean, and the celebration of carnival served as an arena where ethnic and class identities were defined and negotiated. Carnival in Trinidad evolved in much the same way as Mardi Gras in New Orleans in that both were essentially a fusion of French Catholic and African traditions and were regarded by British and American authorities as unruly and perhaps subversive public displays. Trinidad was a sparsely settled backwater of the Spanish empire until a large influx of French planters, free people of color, and slaves arrived in the late eighteenth century at the invitation of the Spanish crown. Like the American purchase of Louisiana in 1803, when Trinidad became a British possession in 1797, the new rulers inherited a colony with a largely French-speaking Creole and African population. British officials, merchants, planters, slaves, and freedmen arrived with British rule, and after the abolition of slavery in 1838, Hindu and Muslim indentured workers from South Asia were added to the existing mix. As the most Catholic of important British possessions in the Caribbean, carnival celebrations in Trinidad continued under the disapproving eyes of colonial officials, and a synthesis of African and European traditions emerged as distinctly Trinidadian cultural forms which later became the basis of the West Indian Carnival in New York. Trinidadian Carnival, like its counterpart in New York, emerged as a multivocal expression of evolving ethnic and class identities, as well as a highly visible forum where public discontent with the dominant culture could be articulated.

The elaborate masked balls and open houses held by the wealthy French Creole elite during carnival did not unduly concern the authorities, but the first British governor quickly imposed strict limitations on the celebration of carnival by free people of color and slaves. In accordance with the generally more restrictive slave codes imposed in all Anglo-American colonies, the use of drums was forbidden because of the possibility that they might be used by rebellious slaves as a form of communication. Slaves were allowed to dance during carnival season only at designated times and places. Free people of color were subjected to a curfew and were required to obtain a special permit to hold balls after 8:00 PM. Attempts to regulate carnival, especially as it was celebrated by the lower classes, continued after the full emancipation of slaves in 1838. In 1849 an ordinance was passed restricting carnival to two days and prohibiting blacks from wearing masks. Beginning in 1868, censorship was imposed on the lyrics of carnival songs that officials considered to be obscene or inflammatory. The kaiso and lavway song forms were predecessors to the calypsos that are so closely identified with both the Trinidadian and New York carnivals, and were, like the calypso, by their very nature often lewd and anti-authoritarian.[15]

CARNIVAL AND TRINIDADIAN IDENTITY

British officials continued to impose regulations, curfews, and censorship right up to the end of the colonial era in 1962. These attempts at social control met with resistance, especially from the growing working-class population in the capital, Port of Spain, and serious clashes between revelers and police occurred in 1858, 1881, and 1883. Even as the celebration of carnival was co-opted or "improved" by the urban middle class in the late nineteenth and early twentieth centuries, the festival still served as an outlet for protest against colonial political and social policies. Clubs, called social unions, based on ethnicity, class, immigrant groups, or profession served the same purpose as krewes in New Orleans, that is, to institutionalize carnival and make it respectable. Social unions in Trinidad, however, encompassed a much broader cross section of society than the largely Anglo-American krewes of New Orleans. They organized the "fancy" masquerade, or mas' band, competitions where social union members dressed in elaborate costumes paraded through the main streets of Port of Spain during carnival accompanied by a lead singer called a chantwell. The chantwells carried on the tradition of social commentary by composing and performing topical songs written especially for the carnival season processions.

By the early 1900s, calypsos, as they were now called, had assumed an importance beyond that of a mere accompaniment to the mas' band parades. Calypsonians dueled with each other under tents sponsored by the social unions and attended by audiences that cut across class, color, and language boundaries. Early calypsos were sung in French patois, in part to circumvent the British censors. In the 1920s and 1930s as audiences grew more diverse, and English-language education became available to the working classes, English Creole lyrics began to supplant French patois as the lingua franca of carnival. This shift toward a creolized form of Trinidadian English mirrored the emergence of a distinctly Trinidadian identity—a synthesis, like carnival, of French Creole, Caribbean English, and, to a lesser extent, East Indian elements—and made the festival more accessible to foreign tourists who in the 1930s became a noticeable presence at the calypso tents and mas' band processions. In spite of the language shift in lyrics, calypsonians continued to defy the censors. For example, the following verses by calypsonian Atilla question the competence of a local colonial magistrate:

Kenneth Vincent Brown,
You always doing something that's wrong;
West Indian papers all freely state
That you are no good as a magistrate,
For you always cause dissatisfaction
With your rotten jurisdiction.[16]

This excerpt from a calypso by Lord Protector, on the other hand, amounts to a sweeping indictment of British colonialism:

We are ruled with the iron hand.
Britain boasts of democracy, brotherly love, and fraternity,
But British colonists have been ruled in perpetual misery.[17]

Not all calypso lyrics were so blatantly anti-authoritarian. Calypsonians commented on current events ranging from local scandals to the invasion of Ethiopia by Mussolini, gender relations, and changing economic and social conditions as Trinidad became an important petroleum-producing and refining center in the early twentieth century.

REVIVAL OF AFRO-CREOLE ROOTS

The third element of Trinidadian carnival transferred to New York and other centers of the West Indian diaspora, the steel drum or "pan," emerged somewhat later than mas' band processions and the calypso. However, it is rooted in the older traditions of rural laborers who migrated to Port of Spain as the island's economy shifted from plantation agriculture to a growing industrial base. These marginalized and often unemployed workers were largely of African descent and were crowded into hastily built quarters called barrack yards. Physically and socially isolated from the more respectable mas' band and calypso forms of carnival celebrations, this new urban proletariat reintroduced older African-derived customs to the back streets of Port of Spain. The tradition of torchlight processions accompanied by drumming called *camboulay*, originally meant to control the annual burning of the cane fields (*cannes brulées* in French), evolved into a pre-dawn carnival celebration that revived many of the rowdier aspects of the festival.[18] *J'ouvert*, meaning "break of day," as these processions were called, revived many of the Africanized traditions of carnival that had been suppressed in order to make the festival more palatable to the authorities and the middle class. The colonial government reissued its ban on drums, hoping to curb *J'ouvert* and keep the inhabitants of the barrack yards in their place. Revelers responded by forming "tamboo bamboo" bands that substituted varying lengths and widths of bamboo for drums to produce percussive sounds of various tones. The lengths of bamboo also proved useful when bands from rival barrack yards met in the back streets and alleys to reenact the *calinda*—an African-derived form of stick fighting also forbidden by law.

By the 1930s pots, garbage can lids, brake drums, and biscuit tins had been added to the repertoire of the tamboo bamboo bands, and the raucous clank of metal on metal began to replace bamboo in these illegal, early morning processions. *J'ouvert* reached its final stage as an expression of the "re-Africanization" of carnival by the Trinidadian lower classes in the adaptation of discarded oil drums as musical instruments just before World War II. The concave head of the oil drum was carefully hammered and dented to produce a variety of pitches, and the drum itself could be cut to various lengths to produce different octaves. Unlike most other percussion instruments, this tuning allows the steel drum bands, or pans as they are called, to play a full range of melody and harmony parts and thus to play popular calypso tunes to accompany the fancy masquerade processions. In spite of the official ban imposed on outdoor carnival celebrations in 1942 because of the war, the new steel drum bands defiantly took to the streets and clashed with the police in the lower-class neighborhood of Lavantille. At first, middle-class Trinidadians remained aloof from the illegal and "rude" celebrations of *J'ouvert*. After the war, as steel bands proliferated, aided by the thousands of discarded oil drums left by the U.S. military, the unique sound and range of musical possibilities provided by steel drum bands were realized. Full acceptance of the steel band and *J'ouvert* as an essential element of both carnival and an emerging Trinidadian national identity was signaled by a 1951 government-supported London tour by the Trinidad All Stars Percussion Orchestra.

CARNIVAL AS COMMODITY

Celebration of carnival helped forge a sense of national identity by providing a common symbol for Trinidad's disparate class and ethnic groups. However, by the 1950s, calypso and steel band music had been commodified and diffused well beyond the island by the international recording industry. When markers of ethnic identity become cultural products, their symbolic meaning is altered. For example, the well-known calypso "Rum and Coca Cola" was first sung by Lord Invader at the 1943 carnival as a social commentary on the changes wrought by the presence of large numbers of American servicemen stationed at two large bases in Trinidad during World War II. The lyrics complain that Trinidadian women preferred to go out with free-spending soldiers and sailors rather than their own countrymen, but the text can also be read as a reaction to the growing influence of American economic power and cultural hegemony.

> They bought rum and Coca Cola, way down Point Cumana;
> Both mother and daughter working for the Yankee dollar.[19]

Ironically, the song was picked up by American servicemen who had largely replaced prewar tourists at the calypso tents and was sold by an enterprising USO entertainer to Decca Records as his own composition.[20] The Andrews Sisters, the most popular female swing group at the time, recorded "Rum and Coca Cola" for Decca in 1945, and it shot to the top of the charts.

In the Trinidadian context, calypso music and steel bands were intimately linked with carnival and symbolized national identity and resistance to authority. For Americans who were exposed to these forms through the lens of popular culture, they brought to mind images of a generic tropical paradise inhabited by simple, carefree, and "sensual" people. The postwar boom in up-market Caribbean tourism and the continuing popularity of calypso throughout the 1950s and early 1960s, especially as performed by Jamaican-American Harry Belafonte in a highly polished style for American audiences, ensured that elements of Trinidadian carnival plucked from their original context were a fixture in every posh tourist resort in the English-speaking Caribbean from Jamaica to Barbados. Although some Trinidadians resented this appropriation of their own markers of identity by the tourism industry and mass popular culture, in the eyes of many Americans calypso, steel bands, and elements of the fancy masquerade had acquired a wider, pan-ethnic meaning.[21]

All of We Is One

It is Labor Day in Brooklyn, New York. Between 2 and 3 million people line Eastern Parkway, the wide boulevard that bisects the mixed West Indian, Haitian, and Hassidic Jewish neighborhood of Crown Heights (Map 18.1). The crowd is so packed along the two-mile parade route that it spills over into the side streets resembling a huge open-air market lined with stalls where jerked chicken and pork sizzle on grills and the pungent smell of roti and curried goat permeates the air. People of all ages and colors, but predominantly of African descent, dance and shout their approval behind metal barriers to the cacophony of sound emanating from the parkway. Tractors drawing floats decorated with banners, flags, corporate logos, and scantily clad gyrating dancers, or more modestly dressed West Indian beauty queens, alternate with bands of masqueraders on foot dressed in elaborate sequined and plumed costumes accompanied by steel bands playing the latest "road march" calypso from Trinidad (Fig. 18.2). They are followed by more numerous processions of groups sporting T-shirts emblazoned with their national colors, waving their national flags, and accompanied by sound trucks blasting Jamaican reggae and dance hall music, Haitian konpa, or Trinidadian soca music. Interspersed throughout the parade are individuals dressed as "ole mas" stock characters—"jab jab" the devil, "moko jumbie" stilt walkers, and "bad behaviour" sailor—all drawn directly from the traditional Afro-Creole carnival in Trinidad (Fig. 18.3).

This portrayal of the West Indian Carnival Labor Day Parade echoes the vignette of an urban multiethnic festival presented at the beginning of the chapter, but there are a number of important differences. First, the multiethnic festival is a composite that is replicated in many cities and towns across the country, whereas the West Indian parade takes place in a specific geographical and temporal context. The transferal of carnival to New York required a number of adaptations just as the disparate traditions of carnival were adapted to the Trinidadian context. Second, multiethnic festivals are institutionalized in that they are usually conceived and coordinated by a single entity, whether it be a governmental agency or a nonprofit institution. The West Indian parade, on the other hand, originated as an organic or grassroots festival, which implies that relations with the authorities and other ethnic groups, as they were in Trinidad, are in a constant state of negotiation and sometimes confrontation. Third, although both festivals include a diverse array of ethnic groups, the New York carnival draws together a num-

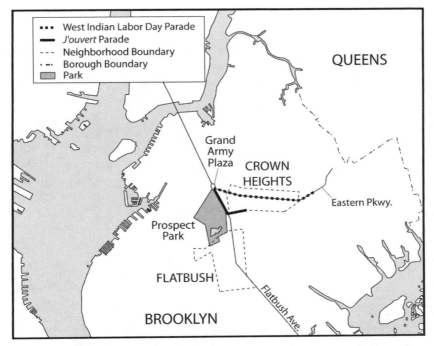

*Map 18.1.   The Labor Day West Indian Parade Route
in Brooklyn, New York.*

ber of different groups under an overarching pan-ethnic identity. The core markers of Trinidadian identity that we have examined in some depth have remained central to the parade, but in the ongoing process of identity formation others have been added. Finally, multiethnic festivals are designed to appeal primarily to cultural tourists from mainstream society who seek out experiences of the exotic "Other" as a form of cultural capital. Although the Brooklyn Carnival has since the 1990s increasingly attracted tourists from outside the pan-ethnic group, it has traditionally been a destination for members of the transnational West Indian diaspora.

HISTORICAL CONTEXT

The first wave of West Indian immigration to New York occurred in the early 1900s. Settlement was spatially concentrated in Harlem, and included both working-class and well-educated middle-class immigrants. By 1925 there were approximately 35,000 "foreign-born Negroes" in Harlem most of whom were from the British Caribbean.[22] West Indians participated fully in the Harlem Renaissance. Jamaican poet Claude Mackay and pan-Africanist Marcus Garvey rubbed shoulders with W. E. B. Dubois, Langston Hughes, and other African American luminaries of the period. Nevertheless, West Indians were uncomfortable with the racial order in America with its overt prejudice

Figure 18.2. These "fancy" masquerade costumes are fabricated in traditional Trinidadian style in mas' camps scattered throughout storefronts and warehouses in Brooklyn. Source: Staceyjoy Elkin.

Figure 18.3.   Stilt walkers, or moko jumbies, are Trinidadian carnival characters descended from West African prototypes and transferred to Brooklyn. Source: Staceyjoy Elkin.

and "one drop rule" (any degree of African descent) of racial discrimination. They also felt a certain amount of underlying prejudice from African Americans and took refuge in their own social clubs organized primarily by island of origin.

In the 1920s the first indoor costume balls were held by Trinidadians in Harlem, many of them organized by social clubs. The respectable pre-Lenten costume balls held in rented ballrooms paralleled the activities of the middle-class social unions in Trinidad. New York had become a center for the West Indian recording industry by the 1910s, and calypsonians traveled regularly back and forth from Trinidad for recording sessions, in part to avoid colonial government censors in Trinidad. At an early date Caribbean music and musicians established transnational links which continue to today. Calypso competitions were held in Harlem ballrooms in imitation of the calypso tent competitions in Port of Spain. The first informal street processions began in the 1930s, and in 1947 a permit was obtained by a Trinidadian woman, Jessie Wardell, to hold a street parade on Lennox Avenue in Harlem. An important adaptation was made at this juncture in the context of New York winters; carnival was rescheduled to Labor Day instead of the traditional pre-Lenten moveable date in late February or March. More formalized and elaborate mas' bands were organized for the Lennox Avenue parade; and following the public acceptance of steel bands in Trinidad, this third ingredient of carnival and marker of Trinidadian culture was introduced to New York in the 1950s.[23]

Although other West Indians had by the 1960s joined in carnival celebrations in Harlem, participating in mas' bands and steel bands—calypso had already been widely adopted as a form of popular culture throughout the Caribbean and beyond—carnival in New York was still an essentially Trinidadian affair. In 1965 changes in the flow of migration at the global, national, and regional scales combined to transform carnival in New York into an event that transcended its status as a local ethnic festival, albeit with strong transnational ties. Legislation passed in 1924 had slowed immigration from the Caribbean to no more than a steady trickle, but with the 1965 Immigration Reform Act global immigration patterns changed radically and the flow from the West Indies soared. Partially because of ties with the existing West Indian community, their primary destination was New York. Eighty percent of the 300,000 West Indian immigrants who lived in New York in 1980 arrived after 1965.[24] Although Harlem continued to receive a share of these new arrivals, many of them settled in other parts of the city as middle-class whites migrated to the suburbs. Carnival followed the demographic trend to the new locational context of Brooklyn.

New York now supports the largest West Indian city in the world. According to the 2000 census, in Brooklyn alone 11.5 percent (310,416) of the population is of West Indian descent. All of the English-speaking islands and mainland areas of the Caribbean Basin as well as Haitians are represented in the West Indian population, but Jamaicans (27%), Haitians (23.5%), Trinidadians (14.7%), and Guyanese (12%) form the largest groups in that order. The large number of foreign-born in the borough, 37.8 percent of the population, insures that there are strong transnational links. Brooklyn's population is extremely diverse with many different ethnic groups, including large numbers of African Americans, interspersed throughout the borough, but the most recognizable West Indian and Haitian neighborhoods are concentrated in Flatbush and Crown Heights (Map 18.1). Men playing dominos, Caribbean-style shops and restaurants, music blaring from the many record stores that line streets like Nostrand Avenue or Fulton Avenue evoke a sense of place that any West Indian would recognize as reminiscent of home.

CONFRONTATION AND NEGOTIATION

The term *bacchanal* is used in both Trinidad and New York as a synonym for the more unruly aspects of carnival. We have seen that in Trinidad the celebration of carnival was often the occasion for confrontations between revelers and the authorities or between rival groups. There are conflicting reports of incidents that occurred at carnival time in Harlem before its change of venue to Brooklyn. A "brawl" at the carnival parade was reported in 1961 by the *New York Amsterdam News*.[25] Another source reports that "hoodlums," presumably African Americans, pelted masqueraders with rocks and bottles in 1964, and as a result the city withdrew permission to parade on Lennox Avenue.[26] What is certain is that in the wake of the Watts Riot of 1964 in Los Angeles, Harlem erupted into violence reflecting the climate of racial tension in the country as a whole. The police suspended the right to free assembly, and the 1965 carnival parade was cancelled.

Small informal block parties were held in Brooklyn in the late 1960s, but in view of the suspicion between the police and blacks in general, an organization was needed to act as an intermediary between the authorities and carnival revelers. Rufus Gorin, a Trinidadian costume maker who had been active in organizing the Harlem parades, formed the United West Indian Day Development Association and obtained a permit from the city to hold a small parade in Brooklyn in 1967. Fifty thousand people showed up. The name of the organization indicates a conscious sense of pan-ethnic identity developing among West Indians in New York, perhaps as a way of differentiating themselves from African Americans in light of the ongoing tension between blacks and the authorities. In 1971 another Trinidadian, Carlos Lezama, petitioned for a permit to parade on the Olmstead-designed Eastern Parkway through Crown Heights. He changed the name of the organization to the West Indian American Day Carnival Association (WIADCA). Again the use of the term "West Indian American" indicates a desire to legitimize the organization in the eyes of the dominant culture. In spite of reports of disturbances and occasional muggings, attendance at the parade mushroomed during the 1970s. By 1977 police estimated the size of the crowd at 500,000 to 700,000, and the police contingent in full riot gear detailed to patrol the route exceeded 1,500.[27] Many of the spectators resented the presence of so many police in battle array, especially in a city that was strapped for cash and cutting back on social services. In the late 1970s there were literally hundreds of scuffles and minor confrontations between police and spectators. Calypsonian Mighty Sparrow commented in his song "One More Jam Mr Police Officer":

> People want to jump up,
> People want to wail;
> We come here to mash up,
> We not in jail.[28]

In 1980 the authorities imposed a number of regulations on the carnival celebrations in a manner that many considered to be reminiscent of the British colonial authorities. The parade would end promptly at 6:00 PM rather than 11:00 PM. Afterwards the parkway would be cleared by a mounted police force. Large sound systems were banned from the nearby streets, mas' bands were required to hire marshals to prevent spectators from "jumping up," that is, from crossing the barrier to dance with the participants, and vendors were required to register with the WIADCA.[29] The WIADCA was widely criticized for acquiescing to police regulations, even though the size of the crowd in 2004 was estimated at 3.5 million and there have been few serious incidents in the last five years.

PAN-ETHNICITY

The Brooklyn West Indian Carnival is still recognizably Trinidadian in form, and the WIADCA's leadership which exercises loose control over the proceedings remains predominantly Trinidadian. The parade and constellation of events that surround it have diversified to an extent that would be unthinkable in Trinidad. There are mas' bands, floats, and sound trucks sponsored by island nations with no past tradition of carnival whatsoever. Events surrounding the parade include Jamaican beauty queen contests, reggae, dub, and dance hall concerts. Barbadian spooge bands compete with Martiniquais zouk groups, Caribbean East Indian chutney soca, and Haitian konpa bands for attention.

The most striking and recent addition to this pan-ethnic umbrella is the inclusion of Haitians and small numbers of immigrants from Martinique and Guadeloupe. One of the criteria for constructing a pan-ethnic identity is a symbol of common identity. If West Indian refers to the English-speaking Caribbean, then how do Haitians fit into the group? The answer lies in the roots of the festival itself as Trinidad and Haiti share a common carnival heritage. This is a heritage that was fluid and malleable enough for Trinidadians to make it serve as a national symbol in their struggle against British colonialism and then to adapt it to embrace Anglophone West Indians in New York. Haitians too can look to a partly imagined past and find a commonality with Trinidadian and, by extension, West Indian carnival. Trinidadian French Creoles lost their language, but they still had carnival as a symbol of their identity. Haitians in New York will eventually lose their Creole French, but they will help to reinvent carnival to fit their need for a new symbol of identity.

In 1999, an example of reinventing part of the heritage of carnival as a reaction to pan-ethnicity finally caught the attention of the media and is now the only carnival event to be televised—*camboulay* or *J'ouvert*. Carnival had become so diverse and the amplified sound so overwhelming that the once arresting sound of the steel bands was drowned out. Throughout the 1980s the number of steel bands in the parade rapidly dwindled. Many of the traditional ole mas' characters were also disappearing from the procession. Some Trinidadians felt that they were losing part of their own identity in the cause of constructing a new pan-ethnicity.[30] They reached into their past to revive the Afro-Creole custom of *J'ouvert* which originally spawned the steel band in Trinidad.

Sometime in the early 1990s a few steel drum players gathered in the pre-dawn hours to march down Flatbush Avenue on Monday morning before the parade. They attracted the attention of passersby who spontaneously joined in. These impromptu processions were repeated with more steel bands and were soon augmented by costumed characters of the ole' mas tradition. These characters from the earliest incarnation of carnival dress as goblins and devils, throw mud on each other and bystanders, and act out slapstick and often bawdy satires for the onlookers. *J'ouvert* now attracts over 200,000 spectators and revives an older pan-African sense of identity.[31]

Conclusion

Tourism and migration are parallel forms of mobility that intersect in the performance of identity through ethnic festivals. The hypothetical multicultural festival we glimpsed at the beginning of the chapter showcasing an array of ethnic identities was intentionally performed as a commodity for tourist consumption. The markers of ethnic identity were displayed as if on a stage for tourists to gaze upon. These symbols of difference are intended to make us step outside the boundaries of mainstream twenty-first-century American life and sample a taste of the exotic "Other."

The festival series staged by the city of Milwaukee serves to bolster the identity or place image of the city as a diverse, tolerant, and sophisticated outpost of civilization in the heartland. The product being offered here is not ethnic identity but the city itself. The type of mobility in question is the mobility of economic and intellectual capital. In order to compete, Milwaukee must achieve distinctiveness in the global market and offers up a menu of old and new ethnic identities on display. The city has even gone to the lengths of staging a festival for an ethnic group it essentially lacks—the Cajun Fest. There were exactly 138 people who claimed Cajun ancestry in the Milwaukee metropolitan area in 2000.

South Louisiana, on the other hand, is an example of a region that stumbled on the economic value of its symbolic capital in the form of ethnic distinctiveness as if by accident after fifty years of assimilationist policy. The state did its utmost to erase markers of Cajun ethnicity until it was realized that outsiders, especially those who shared a similar heritage, were eager to consume "Cajunness" as a commodity. The state responded by repealing legislation that hindered the use of French in 1968, finally establishing a state tourism office in 1977, and launching a series of vigorous promotional campaigns. The realization that Cajun identity was a valuable touristic commodity led to two beneficial results: Cajun ethnic reidentification and reestablishment of transnational ties after nearly three hundred years.

Of the festivals we have discussed in this chapter the West Indian Carnival stands out as the only traditional seasonal festival. First, it demonstrates the use of ethnic and racial markers as well as space as instruments of defiance in the struggle against colonialism in the Caribbean. While continuing to function as a source of ethnic identity in post-colonial Trinidad, the carnival tradition became popularized throughout the English-speaking Caribbean as a tourist commodity. Much like the colonial period, however, the use of public space to assert ethnic identity, and thus the periodic construction of "spaces of difference," in New York was contested by the dominant authorities. Although carnival diffused to New York as a marker of Trinidadian identity, the post-1965 immigration of West Indians resulted in a transformed carnival becoming pan-ethnic in nature. In response to a perceived loss of ethnic identity, ethnic Trinidadians reinvented older Afro-Caribbean carnival traditions. Such a response is an expression of fluid or flexible ethnic identity formation in the changing post-1965 global context.

Notes

1. Data for this composite sketch were gathered from a number of ethnic festival websites and the author's fieldwork. For examples, see Lowell Folk Festival, "Schedule," *Lowell Folk Festival 2004*, <www.lowellfolkfestival.org/schedules.htm> (15 August 2004); and Ethnic Enrichment Commission of Kansas City, Missouri, "Ethnic Enrichment Festival," <www.eeckc.org/events/festival.html> (15 August 2004).

2. Yi-Fu Tuan, *Space and Place: The Perspective of Experience* (Minneapolis: University of Minnesota Press, 1977).

3. Frederik Barth, "Introduction," in *Ethnic Groups and Boundaries: The Social Organization of Culture Difference*, ed. Frederik Barth (London: George Allen and Unwin, 1969), 1–15.

4. Herbert J. Gans, "Symbolic Ethnicity: The Future of Ethnic Groups in America," *Ethnic and Racial Studies* 2, no. 3 (January 1979): 1–20.

5. Robert Wood, "Tourist Ethnicity: A Brief Itinerary," *Ethnic and Racial Studies* 21, no. 2 (1998): 230.

6. Melanie K. Smith, *Issues in Cultural Tourism Studies* (London: Routledge, 2003).

7. Laurie Kay Summers, "Inventing Latinismo: The Creation of Hispanic Panethnicity in the United States," *Journal of American Folklore* 104, no. 411 (1991): 35.

8. Americans for the Arts, "Issues," <www.americansforthearts.org/issues/otherinterests/other_article.asp?id=350> (7 December 2004).

9. Sydney Salvadori, "Quality of Life." *Living in Cook County*, 2001, <www.chicago-cook.org/b2k/living/index.html> (7 December 2004).

10. See, for example, About, Inc., "Milwaukee City of Festivals," *About Milwaukee, Wisconsin*, 2005, <milwaukee.about.com/b/a /087923.htm> (13 February 2005); and Key Milwaukee, "Welcome to Milwaukee," *Key Milwaukee Magazine*, 2005, <www.keymilwaukee.com/about.html> (13 February 2005).

11. Malcolm Crick, "Representations of International Tourism in the Social Sciences: Sun, Sex, Sights, Savings, and Servility," *Annual Review of Anthropology* 18 (1989): 307–344.

12. Marjorie Esman, "Tourism as Ethnic Preservation: The Cajuns of Louisiana," *Annals of Tourism Research* 11 (1984): 451–467.

13. Carl L. Bankston III and Jacques Henry, "Spectacles of Ethnicity: Festivals and the Commodification of Ethnic Culture among Louisiana Cajuns," *Sociological Spectrum* 20 (2000): 377–400.

14. Frommer's, "Frommer's Favorite Experiences," *Frommer's New York City 2004*, <www.frommers.com/destinations/newyorkcity/0021026218.html> (21 October 2004); and Lonely Planet, "New York City," *Lonely Planet World Guide*, <www.lonelyplanet.com/destinations/north_america/new_york_city/facts.htm#event> (21 October 2004).

15. Donald R. Hill, *Calypso Calaloo: Early Carnival Music in Trinidad* (Gainesville: University Press of Florida, 1993), 194–195.

16. Atilla, quoted in Hill, *Calypso Calaloo*, 194.

17. Lord Protector, quoted in Peter Manuel, Kenneth Bilby, and Michael Largey, *Caribbean Currents: Caribbean Music from Rumba to Reggae* (Philadelphia: Temple University Press, 1995), 189.

18. Manuel, Bilby, and Largey, *Caribbean Currents*, 186.

19. Manuel, Bilby, and Largey, *Caribbean Currents*, 191.

20. Hill, *Calypso Calaloo*, 235.

21. Manuel, Bilby, and Largey, *Caribbean Currents*, 191.

22. W. A. Domino, "The Tropics in New York," *The Survey Graphic Harlem Number, 1925*, (27 February 2005).

23. Rachel Buff, *Immigration and the Political Economy of Home: West Indian Brooklyn and American Indian Minneapolis, 1945–1992* (Berkeley: University of California Press, 2001); Donald R. Hill, "A History of West Indian Carnival in New York City to 1978," *New York Folklore* 20, nos.1–2 (1994); and Remco van Capelleveen, "The Caribbeanization of New York City: West Indian Carnival in Brooklyn," in *Feasts and Celebrations*, ed. Ramon Gutierrez and Genevieve Fabre (Albuquerque: University of New Mexico Press, 1995), 159–172.

24. Van Capelleveen, "Caribbeanization of New York," 160.

25. Buff, *Immigration*, 102.

26. Hill, "A History of West Indian Carnival," 49.

27. Hill, "A History of West Indian Carnival," 63–64.

28. Buff, *Immigration*, 106.

29. Buff, *Immigration*, 105–106.

30. Ray Allen, "J'Ouvert! Steel Pan and Ole Mas' Traditions in Brooklyn Carnival," City Lore 1999, <www.citylore.org/pdf/jouvert.pdf> (25 February 2005).

31. Buff, *Immigration*, 112–113.

Index

About the Contributors

Christopher A. Airriess is professor of geography at Ball State University. His research interests include the development, ethnic, cultural, and landscape geographies of Southeast Asia and China. Much of his work in ethnic geography has focused on Vietnamese Americans in New Orleans, Louisiana, where he is currently examining the various impacts of Hurricane Katrina on a single Vietnamese American community. In addition to book chapters in *Landscapes of Ethnic Economies*, *Geographical Identities of Ethnic America*, and *Ethnicity in Contemporary America*, his most recent journal articles appear in *Journal of Historical Geography*, *Geoforum*, and *Journal of Transport Geography*.

Daniel D. Arreola is professor in the School of Geographical Sciences, and affiliate faculty with the Department of Transborder Chicana/o and Latina/o Studies at Arizona State University. He has published numerous journal articles and book chapters on topics relating to the cultural geography of the Mexican American borderlands. He is a coauthor of *The Mexican Border Cities: Landscape Anatomy and Place Personality*, author of *Tejano South Texas: A Mexican American Cultural Province*, and editor and author of *Hispanic Spaces, Latino Places: Community and Cultural Diversity in Contemporary America*. Arreola serves on the editorial boards of several leading geography journals, an international cross-cultural architecture journal, and is a contributing editor to the Hispanic Division of the Library of Congress.

Kate A. Berry is associate professor of geography at the University of Nevada, Reno. Her research interests address the policy and cultural issues associated with water management, tribal governance, Latino landscapes, and the geographic and historic dimensions of ethnic and racial identities. Dr. Berry has worked in the American West, Hawai'i, and Latin America. In addition to being coeditor of *Geographical Identities of Ethnic America*, she has recently published book chapters in the three-volume series *History of Water*, as well as *Hispanic Spaces, Latino Places: Community and Cultural Diversity in Contemporary America* and *Geography in America at the Dawn of the 21st Century*.

Thomas D. Boswell is professor of geography at the University of Miami and has research and teaching interests in world population problems, migration, ethnicity, housing segregation and discrimination, and poverty. In addition to numerous journal articles, his most recent coauthored or edited books are *Facts about Immigration and Asking "Six Big Questions" for Florida and Miami-Dade County*, *Puerto Rico Atlas*, and *Caribbean Islands*. He is currently working on research addressing immigration from the West Indies to the United States.

Elizabeth Chacko is associate professor of geography and international affairs at The George Washington University in Washington, D.C. An immigrant herself, her teaching and research interests include the formation and transformation of racial, national and ethnic identities among immigrants, and the creation of urban ethnic spaces by immigrant communities. Much of her work in ethnic geography has focused on Ethiopian communities in Washington, D.C., and Los Angeles. Her most recent research articles appear in *The Journal of Feminist Geography*, *Singapore Journal of Tropical Geography*, and *The Geographical Review*.

Brian J. Godfrey is professor of geography at Vassar College. His scholarship focuses on comparative urbanization, community and neighborhood change, and the historical geography of cities in the Americas. He has carried out field research in the United States, Brazil, Chile, and Mexico. His most recent journal articles appear in *Geographical Review* and *Urban Geography*. In addition to numerous book chapters, his books include *Neighborhoods in Transition: The Making of San Francisco's Ethnic and Nonconformist Communities*, *Rainforest Cities: Urbanization, Development, and Globalization of the Brazilian Amazon*, and *Cidades da Floresta*.

Zoltán Grossman is a member of the faculty in geography and Native American & World Indigenous Peoples Studies at The Evergreen State College in Olympia, Washington. In addition to book chapters in *Forging Radical Alliances across Difference* and *In the Way of Development: Indigenous Peoples, Civil Society, and the Environment*, his most recent journal articles appear in *Agricultural History*, *Cultural Survival Quarterly*, and *American Indian Culture and Research Journal*. He has been active in indigenous solidarity movements for more than twenty-five years.

Michael Hawkins is assistant professor of geography at Ball State University where he teaches classes in cultural geography, Latin America and the Caribbean, and travel and tourism. His most recent publications includes a journal article in *The Southeastern Geographer*, a book chapter in *Plantation Society and Race Relations*, as well as a textbook chapter on folk and popular cultures in *Human Geography*. His present research work addresses issues of cultural representation in Jamaican tourism and ethnicity and memory in Kosovo.

Terry-Ann Jones is assistant professor of sociology at Fairfield University. Her recently completed dissertation, "Comparative Diasporas: Jamaicans in South Florida and Toronto," compares Jamaican immigrants in the two metropolitan areas, examining the racial and ethnic setting and labor markets of the two areas, and the immigration policies of the two countries. Her areas of research and teaching interest are in international migration, particularly movement between the Caribbean and North America. She is currently working on an edited book on comparative migration.

Wei Li is associate professor in geography and Asian Pacific American Studies at Arizona State University. Her research foci are urban ethnicity and ethnic geography, immigration and integration, and financial sector and minority community development. She is the editor of *From Urban Enclave to Ethnic Suburb: New Asian Communities in Pacific Rim Countries*, and her journal articles have appeared in *Annals of Association of American Geographers, Environment and Planning A, Geographical Review, Urban Studies, Urban Geography, Social Science Research*, and *Journal of Asian American Studies*.

Ines M. Miyares is professor of geography at Hunter College-CUNY and teaches undergraduate and graduate courses in the geography of Latin America, population geography, and international migration and ethnicity. She coordinates an annual ethnic geography in Hawaii field course, and has led several Peru Study Abroad programs during summers. In addition to numerous book chapters, her most recent journal articles appear in *Geographical Review, Journal of Latin American Geographers, Gender, Place and Culture*, and *Global Networks*. Her current research interests focus on the changing geographies of Latinos in the United States, New York City's ethnic communities, and ethnic geographies of Hawaii. Additionally she serves as the executive director of the Conference of Latin Americanist Geographers.

L. HoMana Pawiki is of Hopi and Navajo ancestry and currently studies part-time in the master's program in Rural Geography and Planning at Northern Arizona University. She worked for fourteen years at local, regional, and national U.S. Census Bureau offices and is currently employed by the U.S. Department of Veterans Affairs in developing and administering outreach programs to American Indian and Alaska Native veterans.

Marie Price is associate professor of geography and international affairs at The George Washington University. She is coauthor of two textbooks—*Diversity amid Globalization: World Regions, Environment and Development*, now in its third edition, and *Globalization and Diversity: Geography of a Changing World*. Her recent articles have appeared in *Urban Geography, Geographical Review*, and the *International Journal of Urban and Regional Research*. Her forthcoming coedited book is *Migrants to the Metropolis: The Rise of Immigrant Gateway Cities*. Her current research focuses on Latin American immigration and global urban immigrant destinations.

Michael Reibel is associate professor of geography at California State Polytechnic University, Pomona. He is an urban geographer with expertise in small area demography, ethnic geography, and processes of neighborhood economic and demographic change. His current research is on developing statistics to measure neighborhood ethnic transitions, and on techniques for the areal interpolation of spatially aggregated data. His recent research has been published in the *American Journal of Public Health*, *Environment and Planning A*, and *Geographical Analysis*. He is currently guest-editing a special issue of *Urban Geography* on new measures of segregation and neighborhood change.

Dana G. Reimer is both assistant to the chair and adjunct lecturer in geography at Hunter College-CUNY. While her interests are focused on both population and medical geography, she continues to examine the impact of a changing economy on female Korean immigrants in New York City.

Emily Skop is assistant professor of geography in the Department of Geography and the Environment at The University of Texas at Austin. Her interests include international migration, the social and spatial constructions of racial/ethnic/gender identities, and inequality in the contexts of the United States and Latin America. Dr. Skop combines a variety of qualitative and quantitative techniques, directing her interests to multiple migrant groups, and endeavoring to work in collaborative, interdisciplinary settings. She has published findings in *International Migration Review*, *Geographical Review*, *Population, Space, and Place*, *Professional Geographer*, and *Yearbook of the Association of Pacific Coast Geographers*.

James A. Tyner is associate professor of geography at Kent State University. His interests include population, social, and ethnic geography, with a regional focus on Southeast Asia. He is the author of six books and numerous articles and book chapters. His most recent books include *The Geography of Malcolm X: Black Radicalism and the Remaking of American Space* and *Oriental Bodies: Discourse and Discipline in U.S. Immigration Policy, 1875–1942*.

Milton Vickerman is associate professor of sociology at the University of Virginia. His main areas of research are race, immigration, and processes of minority adaptation to American society. Most recently, he has written about immigration and assimilation for the *Virginia Journal of Social Policy and the Law*. He has also written extensively on West Indian immigrants in *Crosscurrents: West Indian Immigrants and Race* and other publications. Additionally, he has conducted extensive research on patterns of social mobility among African Americans and is completing a manuscript on contradictions surrounding their assimilation and that of immigrant blacks into American society.

Bobby M. Wilson is professor of geography at the University of Alabama. He is author of *America's Johannesburg: Industrialization and Racial Transformation in Birmingham* and *Race and Place: The Civil Rights and Neighborhood Movement in Birmingham*. His most recent journal articles appear in *The Annals of the Association of American Geographers*, *The Professional Geographer*, and *Southeastern Geographer*. His current research examines blacks in the consumer society from a political economic perspective.